The Specification Book For U.S. Cars 1930–1969

(INCLUDES CANADIAN AUTOMOBILES)

G. Marshall Naul, *Editor*
R. Perry Zavitz

ISBN: 0-87938-068-3

Library of Congress Number: 80-11999

Book and cover printed and bound in the United States of America.

1 2 3 4 5 6 7 8 9 10

Library of Congress Cataloging in Publication Data

Naul, G Marshall, 1919-
The specification book for U. S. cars, 1930-1969.

1. Automobiles--United States--History. 2. Automobiles--Specifications--United States. I. Zavitz, R. Perry. II. Title.
TL23.N39 629.2'222'0973 80-11999
ISBN 0-87938-068-3

CONTENTS

INTRODUCTION

The compilation of data in this book serves as a reference for a forty-year period, 1930-1969. If one agrees that the U.S. automotive industry began in 1900, it constitutes just half of the 'era of the automobile.' This book is an extension of the previous publication, The Specification Book for U.S. Cars 1920-1929, and together the two volumes cover seventy-five percent of the time that automobiles have been produced in the U.S.

The years since 1930 have had a profound effect not only on automobiles but also on the automobile industry. The Great Depression in 1930 and its subsequent economic effects brought to an end what is now recognized as the Classic Era. During the 1940's for a period of nearly four years no cars were produced while the industry produced war materiel. The resulting demand for new cars following the end of World War II was greater than the U.S. industry alone could supply, leading to the importing of cars from Europe, and the importation of automobiles has continued to grow. The 1950's and 1960's saw the development and marketing of auto engines of greater and greater power output. These years might be called the Great V-8 Age. With diminishing supplies of petroleum, such an age is unlikely to return.

This book is an attempt to gather together basic technical information for makes and models of U.S. and Canadian cars produced between 1930 and 1969. A claim to have covered all makes and models would be rash, for there are always those obscure makes which elude even the most careful researcher. It will be apparent to the reader that despite the considerable research required for a volume of this sort, some information was not available. It is also probable that not all readers will agree with the information which was chosen for inclusion, but in a matter of judgement of this kind, the final choice must rest with the authors.

There are several valid reasons for including Canadian-built automobiles in this book. The automobile industry in the U.S. is virtually inseparable from that in Canada as the corporations involved have common roots. Many Canadian-built models differed considerably from their U.S. counterparts, yet the Canadian industry has been long neglected by automotive historians living south of the border. For Canadian-built cars, only those models which differed significantly from their U.S.-built counterparts are listed, and no imported cars are given.

The assembling of this type of information would have been a practical impossibility without the support of a number of individuals whose specialized knowledge of this area have been invaluable. As it is impossible to list the contributors in order of importance, it is logical to place them in alphabetical order: Ted Dahlman, San Francisco; Keith Marvin, Troy, New York; George Risley, Detroit, Michigan; Fred Roe, Holliston, Massachusetts; and Lois Watson, Reference Librarian, The Craven Foundation, Toronto, Canada.

Manufacturers who helped in the puzzles of carburetors were: Carter Carburetor Division, ACF Industries; and Holley Carburetor Division, Colt Industries.

The various engines available as options for a particular make and year are given at the end of that year's group. The engines are numbered (1), (2), (3), etc. These numbers are the cross-references to the particular model to which they applied. After each model designation will be found one or more numbers in () which numbers correspond with optional engines for that model. In many cases more than one engine was available for a particular model and several numbers will be found in ().

EXPLANATION OF TABLES

The automobiles included in this book qualify under the following definition for a passenger car:

> A motor vehicle which is intended to transport passengers only, on a casual basis and is licensable as an automobile.

This definition excludes motorcycles, pickups and trucks, buses, taxis, and off-road types. Specifically excluded also are kit cars and one-off privately-built cars not intended for production. Quasi-buses such as the International Travelall and the Plymouth, Dodge, Chevrolet and Ford counterparts have not been listed. Utility vehicles also ignored include Ford Bronco and Jeep and International Scout.

The appendix is an alphabetical listing of reported cars for which either sufficient information is unavailable or which are unverified reportings of passenger car makes.

The automobiles in the U.S. and Canadian sections are in alphabetical order with the name of the make or brand at the heading. This is followed by the name and address of the manufacturer. Only the most important names and addresses are given, and these should not be assumed to give the complete corporate history of each manufacturer. The dates of first and last model years for the make follow the address. In cases where the last model year is unknown, it is indicated by a dash, as in: 1957-. Where the make is still in production it is shown by a plus, as in: 1957+.

Specifications are listed in columns. In order from left to right these are:

YEAR: Model year, in all cases, and not necessarily the calendar year in which a particular car was built.

MODEL: This includes the sales or popular designation and, in many cases, the technical or engineering designation as well. Occasionally, no model designation was used. In some cases an asterisk will be found to be part of the model name; otherwise asterisks refer to footnotes.

ENGINE: The six columns under this title are:

CYLS: The number and configuration of the cylinders. V indicates V-type engine, and F indicates flat, opposed cylinders. Otherwise, its understood engine is an in-line type.

BORE: Cylinder diameter in inches, shown to a maximum of four significant figures rather than in fractions.

STROKE: Piston stroke, inches, shown to a maximum of four significant figures.

DISPL: Total piston displacement, cubic inches, given to a maximum of four significant figures.

HP @ RPM: Horsepower at revolutions per minute.

C.R.: Compression ratio, the ratio of cylinder volume above piston at bottom dead-center to that at top dead-center. In the 1930's many manufacturers offered optional high-compression heads, but most without designated engine horse-power.

VLV: Type of valving:
DOHC = Double overhead valves with twin overhead camshafts.
F = F-head or inlet-over-exhaust valves.
L = L-head or side valves.
OH = Overhead valves.
OHC = Overhead camshaft and valves.
S = Sleeve valves.
H = Horizontal valves.

CARBURETOR: Under this heading is listed:

MFR: The carburetor manufacturers' abbreviations:
A = Autolite
B = Ball & Ball
C = Carter (including later Ball & Ball)
CG = Chandler-Grove
D = Detroit
F = Ford
H = Holley
J = Johnson
Ju = Juhasz
M = Marvel
O = 'Own,' or car manufacturer's own make.
R = Rochester
S = Stromberg
Sc = Schebler
So = Solex
T = Tillotson
W = Weber
Z = Zenith

MODEL: The model shown is for a typical carburetor and not necessarily used in each car so listed. It is not generally known that many running changes have been made, specifically with carburetors, and as many as six different carburetors may have been used in a given model of automobile. It is impractical to list each so the model shown can be considered to be typical only. Furthermore, in those cases where multiple carburetors were used, only one such model is given.

VEN: Indicates the number of venturis or 'barrels.' In cases where multiple carburetors were used, the number of carburetors is shown first, followed by the number of venturis in each carburetor. For example, 3x2 indicates three 2-barrel carburetors. F.I. indicates fuel injection.

WHEELBASE: Shown in inches. Where two or more lengths were available, the most common is given first with other(s) separated by /. In cases where fractional dimensions were used by the manufacturer, the wheelbase is listed to the nearest 0.1 inch, in lieu of the more cumbersome fraction.

TIRES: Given in conventional sizes, with optional size(s) separated by /.

BODY: Designates the body type for which the weight and price applied. The passenger rating is given first, as in 6p for six passengers, followed by the letter(s) indicating the particular type of body:

b = brougham (two-door sedan or coach)
c = coupe, two-door
cc = club coupe
ch = chassis only
cs = club sedan (close-coupled)
cv = convertible
ht = hardtop
l = limousine
p = phaeton (folding top, non-permanent windows)
r = roadster, two-door
s = sedan, four-door
sc = sports coupe, two-door
sw = station wagon

The number which follows the above letter(s) indicates the nominal number of doors. For example, 6pcv2 designates a six-passenger, two-door convertible, or convertible coupe. In all cases, c (for coupe), r (for roadster) and s (for sedan) implies the number of doors: two doors for roadster and coupe, and four doors for sedan.

WEIGHT: Normally the shipping weight, in pounds, for the car and body type shown.

PRICE: F.O.B. or retail price for the body type given. It should be realized that this is not an absolute price and can vary considerably, and frequently does, from reference to reference. Therefore the price should be considered indicative only.

SPECIFICATIONS FOR AMERICAN CARS
1930-1969

YEAR	MODEL	ENGINE CYLS	BORE	STROKE	DISPL	HP@RPM	C.R.	VLV

AIR-CAR — — Curtiss-Wright Corp., Wood Ridge, N.J., 1959

YEAR	MODEL	CYLS	BORE	STROKE	DISPL	HP@RPM	C.R.	VLV
		4				85		
	This possibly cannot be classed as an automobile, as it was a ground-effect vehicle.							
Successor to the above prototype was to have two four-cylinder engines.								

AIROMOBILE (LEWIS AIROMOBILE) — — Lewis American Airways Co., New York, N.Y., 1937

YEAR	MODEL	CYLS	BORE	STROKE	DISPL	HP@RPM	C.R.	VLV
1937		F4	3.438	3.50	129.9	57@3700	6.5	OH
	Engine was air-cooled with flat, opposed cylinders.							

AIRWAY — — T. P. Hall Engineering Corp., San Diego, Cal., 1949-50

YEAR	MODEL	CYLS	BORE	STROKE	DISPL	HP@RPM	C.R.	VLV
1949						10.6		
	Engine was an air-cooled Onan.							

ALLSTATE — — Sears, Roebuck Co., Chicago, Ill., 1952-53

YEAR	MODEL	CYLS	BORE	STROKE	DISPL	HP@RPM	C.R.	VLV
1952	Basic, 4	4	3.125	4.375	134.2	68@4000	7.0	L
	Standard, 4	4	3.125	4.375	134.2	68@4000	7.0	L
	DeLuxe, 4	4	3.125	4.375	134.2	68@4000	7.0	L
	Basic, 6	6	3.125	3.50	161.1	80@3800	7.0	L
	DeLuxe, 6	6	3.125	3.50	161.1	80@3800	7.0	L
1953	Standard, 4	4	3.125	4.375	134.2	68@4000	7.0	L
	DeLuxe, 4	4	3.125	4.375	134.2	68@4000	7.0	L
	DeLuxe, 6	6	3.125	3.50	161.1	80@3800	7.0	L
	The Allstate was essentially the Henry J with but very minor modifications.							

AMERICAN AUSTIN — — American Austin Car Co., Inc., Butler, Pa., 1930-35

YEAR	MODEL	CYLS	BORE	STROKE	DISPL	HP@RPM	C.R.	VLV
1930	A	4	2.20	3.00	45.7	12@3000		L
1931	A	4	2.20	3.00	45.7	13@3200		L
1932	2-75	4	2.20	3.00	45.7	13@3200		L
1933	2-75	4	2.20	3.00	45.7	13@3200		I
1934	3-35	4	2.20	3.00	45.7	13@3200		L
1935	4-75	4	2.20	3.00	45.7	13@3200		L
	The manufacturer claimed no yearly model changes.							

AMERICAN MATHIS — — Durant Motors Co., Lansing, Mich.; American Mathis, Inc., Lansing, Mich., 1931

YEAR	MODEL	CYLS	BORE	STROKE	DISPL	HP@RPM	C.R.	VLV
1931		4	2.75	3.25	77.0	31@3200		L
	Although exhibited at several auto shows, it is probable that only prototypes of this car were ever							
built, based on the French Mathis. Plans were made for Durant to build theseunder license.								

AMERICAN MOTORS — — American Motors Corp., Detroit, Mich., 1954+ (Continuation of NASH)

YEAR	MODEL	CYLS	BORE	STROKE	DISPL	HP@RPM	C.R.	VLV
1955	Rambler Deluxe (1)	6	3.125	4.25	195.6	90@2800	7.30	L

MFR	CARBURETOR MODEL	VEN	WHEEL-BASE	TIRES	BODY	WEIGHT	PRICE
S	1A	1	126	5.50 x 16	5 ps2	2200	550
					2 pc	775	750
C	820SB	1	100	5.90 x 15	5 ps2	2300	1395
C	820SB	1	100	5.90 x 15	5 ps2	2300	1486
C	820SB	1	100	5.90 x 15	5 ps2	2300	1539
C	833SB	1	100	5.90 x 15	5 ps2	2325	1594
C	833SB	1	100	5.90 x 15	5 ps2	2325	1693
C	820SB	1	100	5.90 x 15	5 ps2	2405	1528
C	820SB	1	100	5.90 x 15	5 ps2	2405	1589
C	833SB	1	100	5.90 x 15	5 ps2	2455	1785
T		1	75	3.75 x 18	2 pc	1130	465
T		1	75	3.75 x 18	2 pc	1130	395
T		1	75	3.75 x 18	2 pc	1130	395
T		1	75	3.75 x 18	2 pc	1130	275
T		1	75	3.75 x 18	2 pc	1130	295
T		1	75	3.75 x 18	2 pc	1150	295
T			96	4.00 x 18	2 pc	1500	455
C	YF-2014S	1	108/100	6.40 x 15	6 ps	2567	1695

YEAR	MODEL	ENGINE						
		CYLS	BORE	STROKE	DISPL	HP@RPM	C.R.	VLV
	Rambler Super (1)	6	3.125	4.25	195.6	90@2800	7.30	L
	Rambler Custom (1)	6	3.125	4.25	195.6	90@2800	7.30	L
	Statesman Super (2)	6	3.125	4.25	195.6	100@3800	7.45	L
	Statesman Custom (2)	6	3.125	4.25	195.6	100@3800	7.45	L
	Ambassador Super (3)	6	3.50	4.375	252.6	130@3700	7.60	OH
	Ambassador Custom (3)	6	3.50	4.375	252.6	130@3700	7.60	OH
	Ambassador Super	V8	3.938	3.50	320.0	208@4200	7.80	OH
	Ambassador Custom	V8	3.938	3.50	320.0	208@4200	7.80	OH
	Optional engines:							
	(1)	6	3.125	4.25	195.6	100@3800	7.45	L
	(2)	6	3.50	4.375	252.6	140@4000		OH
	(3)	6	3.125	4.25	195.6	110@4000		L
1956	Rambler Deluxe	6	3.125	4.25	195.6	120@4200	7.47	OH
	Rambler Super	6	3.125	4.25	195.6	120@4200	7.47	OH
	Rambler Custom	6	3.125	4.25	195.6	120@4200	7.47	OH
	Statesman Super	6	3.125	4.25	195.6	120@4200	7.47	OH
	Ambassador Super (1)	6	3.50	4.375	252.6	135@3200	7.60	OH
	Ambassador Super	V8	4.00	3.50	326.7	220@4800	9.55	OH
	Ambassador Custom	V8	4.00	3.50	326.7	220@4800	9.55	OH
	Optional engine:							
	(1)	6	3.50	4.375	252.6	145@4000		OH
1957	Rambler Deluxe (1)	6	3.125	4.25	195.6	125@4200	8.25	OH
	Rambler Super (1)	6	3.125	4.25	195.6	125@4200	8.25	OH
	Rambler Custom (1)	6	3.125	4.25	195.6	125@4200	8.25	OH
	Rambler Super	V8	3.50	3.25	250.1	190@4900	8.0	OH
	Rambler Custom	V8	3.50	3.25	250.1	190@4900	8.0	OH
	Ambassador Super	V8	4.00	3.25	326.7	255@4700	9.0	OH
	Ambassador Custom	V8	4.00	3.25	326.7	255@4700	9.0	OH
	Optional engine:							
	(1)	6	3.125	4.25	195.6	135@4500		OH
1958	Rambler Amer. Deluxe (1)	6	3.125	4.25	195.6	90@3800	8.00	L
	Rambler Amer. Super (1)	6	3.125	4.25	195.6	90@3800	8.00	L
	Rambler Deluxe	6	3.125	4.25	195.6	127@4200	8.70	OH
	Rambler Super	6	3.125	4.25	195.6	127@4200	8.70	OH
	Rambler Custom	6	3.125	4.25	195.6	127@4200	8.70	OH
	Rebel Deluxe	V8	3.50	3.25	250.1	215@4900	8.70	OH
	Rebel Super	V8	3.50	3.25	250.1	215@4900	8.70	OH
	Rebel Custom	V8	3.50	3.25	250.1	215@4900	8.70	OH
	Ambassador Super	V8	4.00	3.25	326.7	270@4700	9.70	OH
	Ambassador Custom	V8	4.00	3.25	326.7	270@4700	9.70	OH
	Optional engine: (1)	6	3.125	4.25	195.6	138@4500		OH

MFR	CARBURETOR MODEL	VEN	WHEEL-BASE	TIRES	BODY	WEIGHT	PRICE
C	YF-2014S	1	108/100	6.40 x 15	6 ps	2570	1798
C	YF-2014S	1	108/100	6.40 x 15	6 ps	2606	1989
C	WCD-2061S	1	114.2	6.70 x 15	6 ps	3134	2215
C	WCD-2061S	1	114.2	6.70 x 15	6 ps	3204	2385
C	YH-895S	1	124.2	7.10 x 15	6 ps	3538	2480
C	YH-895S	1	124.2	7.10 x 15	6 ps	3576	2675
C	2231S	2	124.2	7.10 x 15	6 ps	3795	2775
C	2231S	2	124.2	7.10 x 15	6 ps	3827	2965
C	AS-2349S	1	108	6.40 x 15	6 ps	2891	1829
C	AS-2349S	1	108	6.40 x 15	6 ps	2906	1939
C	AS-2349S	1	108	6.40 x 15	6 ps	2929	2059
C	AS-2349S	1	114.2	6.70 x 15	6 ps	3199	2345
C	YH-895S	1	121.2	7.10 x 15	6 ps	3555	2644
C	WGD-2231S	2	121.2	7.60 x 15	6 ps	3748	2956
C	WGD-2231S	2	121.2	7.60 x 16	6 ps	3846	3195
C							
C	AS-2580S	1	108	6.40 x 15	6 ps	2911	1757
C	AS-2580S	1	108	6.40 x 15	6 ps	2914	1890
C	AS-2580S	1	108	6.40 x 15	6 ps	2938	1974
C	WGD-2352SA	2	108	6.70 x 15	6 ps	3223	2011
C	WGD-2352SA	2	108	6.70 x 15	6 ps	3259	2095
C	WCFB-2593SA	4	121.2	8.00 x 14	6 ps	3639	2520
C	WCFB-2593SA	4	121.2	8.00 x 14	6 ps	3701	2697
C	YF-2014S	1	100	5.90 x 15	5 ps2	2463	1789
C	YF-2014S	1	100	5.90 x 15	5 ps2	2475	1874
C	YF-2014S	1	108	6.40 x 15	6 ps	2947	2047
C	YF-2014S	1	108	6.40 x 15	6 ps	2960	2212
C	YF-2014S	1	108	6.40 x 15	6 ps	2968	2327
H	4150C	4	108	7.50 x 14	6 ps	3287	2177
H	4150C	4	108	7.50 x 14	6 ps	3300	2342
H	4150C	4	108	7.50 x 14	6 ps	3313	2457
H	4150C	4	117	8.00 x 14	6 ps	3456	2587
H	4150C	4	117	8.00 x 14	6 ps	3462	2732
		2					

YEAR	MODEL	ENGINE						
		CYLS	BORE	STROKE	DISPL	HP@RPM	C.R.	VLV
1959	Rambler Amer. Deluxe (1)	6	3.125	4.25	195.6	90@3800	8.0	L
	Rambler Amer. Super (1)	6	3.125	4.25	195.6	90@3800	8.0	L
	Rambler Six Deluxe	6	3.125	4.25	195.6	127@4200	8.7	OH
	Rambler Six Super	6	3.125	4.25	195.6	127@4200	8.7	OH
	Rambler Six Custom	6	3.125	4.25	195.6	127@4200	8.7	OH
	Rebel V8 Deluxe	V8	3.50	3.25	250.1	215@4900	8.7	OH
	Rebel V8 Super	V8	3.50	3.25	250.1	215@4900	8.7	OH
	Rebel V8 Custom	V8	3.50	3.25	250.1	215@4900	8.7	OH
	Ambassador Super	V8	4.00	3.25	326.7	270@4700	9.7	OH
	Ambassador Custom	V8	4.00	3.25	326.7	270@4700	9.7	OH
	Optional engine: (1)	6	3.125	4.25	195.6	138@4500		OH
1960	Rambler Amer. Deluxe (1)	6	3.125	4.25	195.6	90@3800	8.0	L
	Rambler Amer. Super (1)	6	3.125	4.25	195.6	90@3800	8.0	L
	Rambler Amer. Custom	6	3.125	4.25	195.6	90@3800	8.0	L
	Rambler Deluxe (2)	6	3.125	4.25	195.6	127@4200	8.7	OH
	Rambler Super (2)	6	3.125	4.25	195.6	127@4200	8.7	OH
	Rambler Custom (2)	6	3.125	4.25	195.6	127@4200	8.7	OH
	Rebel V8 Deluxe (3)	V8	3.50	3.25	250.1	200@4900	8.7	OH
	Rebel V8 Super (3)	V8	3.50	3.25	250.1	200@4900	8.7	OH
	Rebel V8 Custom (3)	V8	3.50	3.25	250.1	200@4900	8.7	OH
	Ambassador Deluxe (4)	V8	4.00	3.25	326.7	250@4700	8.7	OH
	Ambassador Super (4)	V8	4.00	3.25	326.7	250@4700	8.7	OH
	Ambassador Custom (4)	V8	4.00	3.25	326.7	250@4700	8.7	OH
	Optional engines:							
	(1)	6	3.125	4.25	195.6	125@4200	8.7	OH
	(2)	6	3.125	4.25	195.6	138@4800		OH
	(3)	V8	3.50	3.25	250.1	215@4900		OH
	(4)	V8	4.00	3.25	326.7	270@4700		OH
1961	Rambler Amer. Deluxe (1)	6	3.125	4.25	195.6	90@3800	8.0	L
	Rambler Amer. Super (1)	6	3.125	4.25	195.6	90@3800	8.0	L
	Rambler Amer. Custom	6	3.125	4.25	195.6	125@4200	8.7	OH
	Rambler Amer. Custom 400	6	3.125	4.25	195.6	125@4200	8.7	OH
	Rambler Classic 6 Deluxe (2)	6	3.125	4.25	195.6	127@4200	8.7	OH
	Rambler Classic 6 Super (2)	6	3.125	4.25	195.6	127@4200	8.7	OH
	Rambler Classic 6 Custom (2)	6	3.125	4.25	195.6	127@4200	8.7	OH
	Rambler Classic 6 Custom 400 (2)	6	3.125	4.25	195.6	127@4200	8.7	OH
	Rambler Classic Deluxe (3)	V8	3.50	3.25	250.1	200@4900	8.7	OH

MFR	CARBURETOR MODEL	VEN	WHEEL-BASE	TIRES	BODY	WEIGHT	PRICE
C	YF - 2014S	1	100	5.90 x 15/	5 ps 2	2476	1835
				/6.40 x 15			
C	YF - 2014S	1	100	5.90/6.40 x 15	5 ps 2	2492	1920
H	1904 - FC	1	108		6 ps	2934	2098
H	1904 - FC	1	108	6.40 x 15	6 ps	2951	2268
H	1904 - FC	1	108	6.40 x 15	6 ps	2956	2383
H	4150C	4	108	7.50 x 14	6 ps	3283	2228
H	4150C	4	108	7.50 x 14	6 ps	3287	2398
H	4150C	4	108	7.50 x 14	6 ps	3295	2513
H	4150C	4	117	8.00 x 14	6 ps	3428	2587
H	4150C	4	117	8.00 x 14	6 ps	3437	2732
C	YF - 2014S	1	100	5.90 x 15/	6 ps	2474	1844
				6.40 x 15			
C	YF - 2014S	1	100	5.90 x 15/	6 ps	2490	1929
				6.40 x 15			
C	YF - 2014S	1	100	5.90 x 15/	6 ps	2551	2059
				6.40 x 15			
H	1904 - FC	1	108	6.40 x 15	6 ps	2912	2098
H	1904 - FC	1	108	6.40 x 15	6 ps	2930	2268
H	1904 - FC	1	108	6.40 x 15	6 ps	2929	2383
H	2040	2	108	7.50 x 14	6 ps	3252	2217
H	2040	2	108	7.50 x 14	6 ps	3270	2387
H	2040	2	108	7.50 x 14	6 ps	3278	2505
H	2040	2	117	8.00 x 14	6 ps	3384	2395
H	2040	2	117	8.00 x 14	6 ps	3395	2587
H	2040	2	117	8.00 x 14	6 ps	3408	2732
		1					
C	YF - 2014S	1	100	6.00 x 15	6 ps	2523	1896
C	YF - 2014S	1	100	6.00 x 15	6 ps	2530	1981
H	1908 - FC	1	100	6.00 x 15	6 ps	2588	2111
H	1908 - FC	1	100	6.00 x 15	6 ps	2606	2201
H	1908 - FC	1	108	6.50 x 15	6 ps	2905	2100
H	1908 - FC	1	108	6.50 x 15	6 ps	2923	2270
H	1908 - FC	1	108	6.50 x 15	6 ps	2863	2415
H	1908 - FC	1	108	6.50 x 15	6 ps	2873	2565
H	2040	2	108	7.50 x 14	6 ps	3237	2229

YEAR	MODEL	ENGINE						
		CYLS	BORE	STROKE	DISPL	HP@RPM	C.R.	VLV
	Rambler Classic Super (3)	V8	3.50	3.25	250.1	200@4900	8.7	OH
	Rambler Classic Custom (3)	V8	3.50	3.25	250.1	200@4900	8.7	OH
	Rambler Classic Custom (3)	V8	3.50	3.25	250.1	200@4900	8.7	OH
	Rambler Ambassador Deluxe (4)	V8	4.00	3.25	326.7	250@4700	8.7	OH
	Rambler Ambassador Super (4)	V8	4.00	3.25	326.7	250@4700	8.7	OH
	Rambler Ambassador Custom (4)	V8	4.00	3.25	326.7	250@4700	8.7	OH
	Rambler Ambassador Cust. 400 (4)	V8	4.00	3.25	326.7	250@4700	8.7	OH
	Optional engines:							
	(1)	6	3.125	4.25	195.6	125@4200	8.7	OH
	(2)	6	3.125	4.25	195.6	138		OH
	(3)	V8	3.50	3.25	250.1	215		OH
	(4)	V8	4.00	3.25	326.7	270		OH
1962	Rambler Amer. Deluxe (1)	6	3.125	4.25	195.6	90@3800	8.0	L
	Rambler Amer. Custom (1)	6	3.125	4.25	195.6	90@3800	8.0	L
	Rambler Amer. 400 (1)	6	3.125	4.25	195.6	90@3800	8.0	L
	Rambler Classic Deluxe (2)	6	3.125	4.25	195.6	127@4200	8.7	OH
	Rambler Classic Custom (2)	6	3.125	4.25	195.6	127@4200	8.7	OH
	Rambler Classic 400 (4)	6	3.125	4.25	195.6	138@4500	8.7	OH
	Rambler Ambassador Deluxe (3)	V8	4.00	3.25	326.7	250@4700	8.7	OH
	Rambler Ambassador Custom (3)	V8	4.00	3.25	326.7	250@4700	8.7	OH
	Rambler Ambassador 500 (3)	V8	4.00	3.25	326.7	250@4700	8.7	OH
	Optional engines:							
	(1)	6	3.125	4.25	195.6	125@4200	8.7	OH
	(2)	6	3.125	4.25	195.6	138@4500	8.7	OH
	(3)	V8	4.00	3.25	326.7	270@4700	9.7	OH
	(4)	6	3.125	4.25	195.6	127@4200	8.7	OH
1963	Rambler Amer. 220 (1, 2)	6	3.125	4.25	195.6	90@3800	8.0	L
	Rambler Amer. 330 (1, 2)	6	3.125	4.25	195.6	90@3800	8.0	OH
	Rambler Amer. 440 (2)	6	3.125	4.25	195.6	125@4200	8.7	OH
	Rambler Amer. 440H	6	3.125	4.25	195.6	138@4500	8.7	OH
	Rambler Classic 550 (2, 3)	6	3.125	4.25	195.6	126@4200	8.7	OH
	Rambler Classic 660 (2, 3)	6	3.125	4.25	195.6	126@4200	8.7	OH
	Rambler Classic 770 (2, 3)	6	3.125	4.25	195.6	126@4200	8.7	OH
	Rambler Ambassador 800 (3)	V8	4.00	3.25	326.7	250@4700	8.7	OH
	Rambler Ambassador 880 (3)	V8	4.00	3.25	326.7	250@4700	8.7	OH
	Rambler Ambassador 990 (3)	V8	4.00	3.25	326.7	250@4700	8.7	OH
	Optional engines:							
	(1)	6	3.125	4.25	195.6	125@4200	8.7	OH
	(2)	6	3.125	4.25	195.6	138@4200	8.7	OH
	(3)	V8	4.00	3.25	326.7	270@4700	9.7	OH
1964	Rambler Amer. 220	6	3.125	4.25	195.6	90@3800	8.0	L

MFR	CARBURETOR MODEL	VEN	WHEEL-BASE	TIRES	BODY	WEIGHT	PRICE
H	2040	2	108	7.50 x 14	6 ps	3255	2399
H	2040	2	108	7.50 x 14	6 ps	3262	2514
H	2040	2	108	7.50 x 14	6 ps	3283	2664
H	2040	2	117	8.00 x 14	6 ps	3343	2397
H	2040	2	117	8.00 x 14	6 ps	3361	2539
H	2040	2	117	8.00 x 14	6 ps	3380	2684
H	2040	2	117	8.00 x 14	6 ps	3387	2814
H	1908 - FC	1					
C	3206	1	100	6.00 x 15	6 ps	2500	1895
C	3206	1	100	6.00 x 15	6 ps	2512	1958
C	3206	1	100	6.00 x 15	6 ps	2585	2089
H	1908 - FC	1	108	6.50 x 15	6 ps	2888	2050
H	1908 - FC	1	108	6.50 x 15	6 ps	2898	2200
H	1908 - FC	1	108	6.50 x 15	6 ps	2853	2349
H	2300	2	108	7.50 x 14	6 ps	3249	2336
H	2300	2	108	7.50 x 14	6 ps	3259	2464
H	2300	2	108	7.50 x 14	6 ps	3283	2605
H	1908 - FC	1					
H	1908 - FC	1					
H	4150	4					
H	1908 - FC	1					
C	RBS - 3487S	1	100	6.00 x 15	6 ps	2485	1895
C	RBS - 3487S	1	100	6.00 x 15	6 ps	2500	1958
H	1909 - 2555	1	100	6.00 x 15	6 ps	2575	2089
C	WCD - 3434S	2	100	6.00 x 15	4 pht 2	2567	2281
H	1909 - 2387-1	1	112	6.50 x 14	4 pht 2	2729	2105
H	1909 - 2387-1	1	112	6.50 x 14	4 pht 2	2740	2245
H	1909 - 2387-1	1	112	6.50 x 14	4 pht 2	2686	2349
H	2300 - 2442	2	112	7.50 x 14	4 pht 2	3140	2391
H	2300 - 2442	2	112	7.50 x 14	4 pht 2	3145	2519
H	2300 - 2442	2	112	7.50 x 14	4 pht 2	3158	2660
H	1909 - 2555	1					
O	WCD - 3434S	2					
H	4150 - 1957-1	4					
C	RBS - 3708S	1	106	6.00 x 14	6 ps	2527	1964

YEAR	MODEL	ENGINE						
		CYLS	BORE	STROKE	DISPL	HP@RPM	C.R.	VLV
	Rambler Amer. 330	6	3.125	4.25	195.6	90@3800	8.0	L
	Rambler Amer. 440	6	3.125	4.25	195.6	125@4200	8.7	OH
	Rambler Amer. 440H	6	3.125	4.25	195.6	138@4600	8.7	OH
	Rambler Classic 550 (1)	6	3.125	4.25	195.6	127@4200	8.7	OH
	Rambler Classic 660 (1)	6	3.125	4.25	195.6	127@4200	8.7	OH
	Rambler Classic 770 (1)	6	3.125	4.25	195.6	127@4200	8.7	OH
	Rambler Ambassador 990 (2)	V8	4.00	3.25	326.7	250@4700	8.7	OH
	Rambler Ambassador 990H	V8	4.00	3.25	326.7	270@4700	9.7	OH
	Optional engines:							
	(1)	6	3.125	4.25	195.6	138@4600	8.7	OH
	(1)	V8	3.75	3.25	287.2	198@4700	8.7	OH
	(2)	V8	4.00	3.25	326.7	270@4700	9.7	OH
1965	American 220	6	3.125	4.25	195.6	90@3800	8.0	L
	American 330	6	3.125	4.25	195.6	90@3800	8.0	L
	American 440 (1)	6	3.125	4.25	195.6	125@4200	8.7	OH
	American 440H (1)	6	3.125	4.25	195.6	125@4200	8.7	OH
	Classic 550	6	3.75	3.00	198.8	128@4400	8.5	OH
	Classic 660 (3)	6	3.75	3.50	231.9	145@4300	8.5	OH
	Classic 770 (3)	6	3.75	3.50	231.9	145@4300	8.5	OH
	Classic 550 (2)	V8	3.75	3.25	287.2	198@4700	8.7	OH
	Classic 660 (2)	V8	3.75	3.25	287.2	198@4700	8.7	OH
	Classic 770 (2)	V8	3.75	3.25	287.2	198@4700	8.7	OH
	Ambassador 880	6	3.75	3.50	231.9	155@4400	8.5	OH
	Ambassador 990	6	3.75	3.50	231.9	155@4400	8.5	OH
	Ambassador 880	V8	3.75	3.25	287.2	198@4700	8.7	OH
	Ambassador 990	V8	3.75	3.25	287.2	198@4700	8.7	OH
	Ambassador 900H	6	3.75	3.50	231.9	155@4400	8.5	OH
	Ambassador 990H	V8	3.75	3.25	287.2	198@4700	8.7	OH
	Marlin	6	3.75	3.50	231.9	145@4300	8.5	OH
	Marlin	V8	3.75	3.25	287.2	198@4700	8.7	OH
	Optional engines:							
	(1)	6	3.75	3.50	231.9	145@4300	8.5	OH
	(2)	V8	4.00	3.25	326.7	270@4700	9.7	OH
	(3)	6	3.75	3.50	231.9	155@4400	8.5	OH
1966	American 220 (1, 4)	6	3.75	3.00	198.8	128@4400	8.5	OH
	American 440 (1, 4)	6	3.75	3.00	198.8	128@4400	8.5	OH
	American Rogue (1, 4)	6	3.75	3.00	198.8	128@4400	8.5	OH
	Classic 550 (4)	6	3.75	3.50	231.9	145@4300	8.5	OH
	Classic 770 (4)	6	3.75	3.50	231.9	145@4300	8.5	OH

MFR	CARBURETOR MODEL	VEN	WHEEL-BASE	TIRES	BODY	WEIGHT	PRICE
C	RBS - 3708S	1	106	6.00 x 14	6 ps	2526	2057
H	1909 - 2555-2	1	106	6.00 x 14	6 ps	2572	2150
C	WCD - 3706S	2	106	6.00 x 14	5pht2	2617	2292
C	RBS - 2727S	1	112	6.50 x 14	6 ps	2755	2116
C	RBS - 2727S	1	112	6.50 x 14	6 ps	2758	2256
C	RBS - 2727S	1	112	6.50 x 14	6 ps	2763	2360
H	2300 - 2442-1	2	112	7.50 x 14	6 ps	3204	2671
H	4150 - 1957-1	4	112	7.50 x 14	5pht2	3255	2906
C	WCD - 3706S	2					
H							
C	WCD - 3706S	2					
C	RBS - 3708S	1	106	6.45 x 14	6 ps	2518	1997
C	RBS - 3708S	1	106	6.45 x 14	6 ps	2522	2088
H	1909 - 2555-3	1	106	6.45 x 14	6 ps	2580	2179
H	1909 - 2555-3	1	106	6.45 x 14	4pht2	2622	2282
C	RBS - 3766S	1	112	6.95 x 14	6pht2	2827	2150
C	WDC - 3882	2	112	6.95 x 14	6pht2	2882	2287
C	WDC - 3882	2	112	6.95 x 14	6pht2	2895	2389
H	2209 - 2699	2	112	7.35 x 14	6pht2	3147	2272
H	2209 - 2699	2	112	7.35 x 14	6pht2	3149	2390
H	2209 - 2699	2	112	7.35 x 14	6pht2	3162	2492
C	WCD - 3888S	2	116	7.35 x 14	6pht2	3000	2519
C	WCD - 3888S	2	116	7.35 x 14	6pht2	3031	2608
H	2209 - 2699	2	116	7.75 x 14	6pht2	3240	2610
H	2209 - 2699	2	116	7.75 x 14	6pht2	3271	2699
C	WCD - 3888S	2	116	7.35 x 14	6pht2	3078	2785
H	2209 - 2699	2	116	7.75 x 14	6pht2	3318	2876
C	WDC - 3888S	2	112	7.35 x 14	6pht2	3100	2841
H	2209 - 2699	2	112	7.35 x 14	6pht2	3367	2931
C	WDC - 3888S	2					
H	4150 - 3044	4					
C	WCD - 3888S	2					
H	1931 - 3251	1	106	6.45 x 14	6 ps	2574	2086
H	1931 - 3251	1	106	6.45 x 14	6 ps	2582	2203
H	1931 - 3251	1	106	6.45 x 14	5pht2	2630	2370
H	1931 - 3253	1	112	6.95 x 14/	6 ps	2885	2238
				7.35 x 14			
H	1931 - 3253	1	112	6.95 x 14/	6 ps	2905	2337
				7.35 x 14			

YEAR	MODEL	ENGINE						
		CYLS	BORE	STROKE	DISPL	HP@RPM	C.R.	VLV
	Classic Rebel (4)	6	3.75	3.50	231.9	145@4300	8.5	OH
	Classic 550 (2, 3)	V8	3.75	3.25	287.2	198@4700	8.7	OH
	Classic 770 (2, 3)	V8	3.75	3.25	287.2	198@4700	8.7	OH
	Classic Rebel (3)	V8	3.75	3.25	287.2	198@4700	8.7	OH
	Marlin (4)	6	3.75	3.50	231.9	145@4300	8.5	OH
	Marlin	V8	3.75	3.25	287.2	198@4700	8.7	OH
	Ambassador 880	6	3.75	3.50	231.9	155@4400	8.5	OH
	Ambassador 990	6	3.75	3.50	231.9	155@4400	8.5	OH
	Ambassador DPL	6	3.75	3.50	231.9	155@4400	8.5	OH
	Ambassador 880 (2)	V8	3.75	3.25	287.2	198@4700	8.7	OH
	Ambassador 990 (2)	V8	3.75	3.25	287.2	198@4700	8.7	OH
	Ambassador DPL (2)	V8	3.75	3.25	287.2	198@4700	8.7	OH
	Optional engines:							
	(1)	6	3.75	3.50	231.9	145@4300		OH
	(1)	V8	3.75	3.25	287.2	200		OH
	(1)	V8	3.75	3.25	287.2	225		OH
	(2)	V8	4.00	3.25	326.7	250@4700	8.7	OH
	(3)	V8	4.00	3.25	326.7	270@4700	9.7	OH
	(4)	6	3.75	3.50	231.9	155@4400	8.5	OH
1967	American 220 (1, 2, 3, 5)	6	3.75	3.00	198.8	128@4400	8.5	OH
	American 440 (1, 2, 3, 5)	6	3.75	3.00	198.8	128@4400	8.5	OH
	American Rogue (1, 2, 3, 5)	6	3.75	3.00	198.8	128@4400	8.5	OH
	Rebel 550 (2, 5)	6	3.75	3.50	231.9	145@4300	8.5	OH
	Rebel 770 (2, 5)	6	3.75	3.50	231.9	145@4300	8.5	OH
	Rebel SST (2, 5)	6	3.75	3.50	231.9	145@4300	8.5	OH
	Rebel 550 (3, 4, 5)	V8	3.75	3.28	289.8	200@4600	9.0	OH
	Rebel 770 (3, 4, 5)	V8	3.75	3.28	289.8	200@4600	9.0	OH
	Rebel SST (3, 4, 5)	V8	3.75	3.28	289.8	200@4600	9.0	OH
	Marlin (2, 5)	6	3.75	3.50	231.9	145@4300	8.5	OH
	Marlin (3, 4, 5)	V8	3.75	3.28	289.8	200@4600	9.0	OH
	Ambassador 880 (2, 5)	6	3.75	3.50	231.9	155@4400	8.5	OH

MFR	CARBURETOR MODEL	VEN	WHEEL-BASE	TIRES	BODY	WEIGHT	PRICE
H	1931 - 3253	1	112	7.35 x 14	5pht2	2950	2523
H	2209 - 3305	2	112	7.35 x 14	6 ps	3166	2344
H	2209 - 3305	2	112	7.35 x 14	6 ps	3186	2244
H	2209 - 3305	2	112	7.35 x 14	5pht2	3231	2629
H	1931 - 3253	1	112	7.35 x 14	6pht2	3050	2601
H	2209 - 3305	2	112	7.35 x 14	6pht2	3331	2707
C	WCD - 3888S	2	116	7.35 x 14	6 ps	3006	2455
C	WCD - 3888S	2	116	7.35 x 14	6 ps	3034	2574
C	WCD - 3888S	2	116	7.35 x 14	5pht2	3090	2756
H	2209 - 3305	2	116	7.75 x 14	6 ps	3260	2559
H	2209 - 3305	2	116	7.75 x 14	6 ps	3288	2678
H	2209 - 3305	2	116	7.75 x 14	6pht2	3344	2860
H	1931 - 3253	1					
H	4160 - 3201	4					
C	WCD - 3888S	2					
H	1931C - 3705	1	106	6.45 x 15/	6 ps	2621	1945
				6.95 x 14			
H	1931C - 3705	1	106	6.45 x 15/	6 ps	2613	2083
				6.95 x 14			
H	1931C - 3705	1	106	6.45 x 15	6pht2	2663	2266
H	1931C - 3253	1	114	7.35 x 14/	6 ps	3055	2319
				7.75 x 14			
H	1931C - 3253	1	114	7.35 x 14/	6 ps	3053	2418
				7.75 x 14			
H	1931C - 3253	1	114	7.35 x 14/	6pht2	3109	2604
				7.75 x 14			
H	2209 - 3308-1	2	114	7.35 x 14/	6 ps	3246	2425
				7.75 x 14			
H	2209 - 3308-1	2	114	7.35 x 14/	6 ps	3244	2524
				7.75 x 14			
H	2209 - 3308-1	2	114	7.35 x 14/	6pht2	3300	2710
				7.75 x 14			
H	1931C - 3253	1	118	7.35 x 14	6pht2	3174	2859
H	2209 - 3308-1	2	118	7.75 x 14	6pht2	3342	2963
H	1931C - 3253	1	118	7.35 x 14/	6 ps	3111	2553
				7.75 x 14			

YEAR	MODEL	ENGINE						
		CYLS	BORE	STROKE	DISPL	HP@RPM	C.R.	VLV
	Ambassador 990 (2, 5)	6	3.75	3.50	231.9	155@4400	8.5	OH
	Ambassador DPL (2, 5)	6	3.75	3.50	231.9	155@4400	8.5	OH
	Ambassador 880 (4, 5)	V8	3.75	3.28	289.8	200@4600	9.0	OH
	Ambassador 990 (4, 5)	V8	3.75	3.28	289.8	200@4600	9.0	OH
	Ambassador DPL (4, 5)	V8	3.50	3.28	289.8	200@4600	9.0	OH
	Optional engines:							
	(1)	6	3.75	3.50	231.9	145@4300	8.5	OH
	(2)	6	3.75	3.50	231.9	155@4400	8.5	OH
	(2)	V8	3.75	3.28	289.8	200@4600	9.0	OH
	(3)	V8	3.75	3.28	289.8	225@4700	10.0	OH
	(4)	V8	4.08	3.28	343.1	235@4400	9.0	OH
	(5)	V8	4.08	3.28	343.1	280@4800	10.2	OH
1968	American (1, 4, 6, 7)	6	3.75	3.00	198.8	128@4400	8.5	OH
	American 440 (1, 4, 6, 7)	6	3.75	3.00	198.8	128@4400	8.5	OH
	American Rogue (3, 4)	6	3.75	3.50	231.9	145@4300	8.5	OH
	Javelin	6	3.75	3.50	231.9	145@4300	8.5	OH
	Javelin SST	6	3.75	3.50	231.9	145@4300	8.5	OH
	Javelin	V8	3.75	3.28	289.8	200@4600	9.0	OH
	Javelin SST (3, 4, 6, 7)	V8	3.75	3.28	289.8	200@4600	9.0	OH
	AMX (6, 7)	V8	3.75	3.28	289.8	225@4700	10.0	OH
	Rebel 550 (2, 3)	6	3.75	3.50	231.9	145@4300	8.5	OH
	Rebel 770 (2, 3)	6	3.75	3.50	231.9	145@4300	8.5	OH
	Rebel 550 (5, 6, 7)	V8	3.75	3.28	289.8	290		OH
	Rebel 770 (5)	V8	3.75	3.28	289.8	290		OH
	Rebel SST (5)	V8	3.75	3.28	289.8	290		OH
	Ambassador	6	3.75	3.50	231.9	145@4300	8.5	OH
	Ambassador DPL (2, 3)	6	3.75	3.50	231.9	145@4300	8.5	OH
	Ambassador	V8	3.75	3.28	289.8	200@4600	9.0	OH
	Ambassador DPL (5, 6, 7)	V8	3.75	3.28	289.8	200@4600	9.0	OH
	Ambassador SST (5, 6, 7)	V8	3.75	3.28	289.8	200@4600	9.0	OH
	Optional engines: (1)	6	3.75	3.50	231.9	145@4300	8.5	OH
	(2)	6	3.75	3.50	231.9	155@4400	8.5	OH
	(3)	V8	3.75	3.28	289.8	200@4600	9.0	OH
	(4)	V8	3.75	3.28	289.8	225@4700	10.0	OH
	(5)	V8	4.08	3.28	343.0	235@4400	9.0	OH
	(6)	V8	4.08	3.28	343.0	280@4800	10.2	OH

MFR	CARBURETOR MODEL	VEN	WHEEL-BASE	TIRES	BODY	WEIGHT	PRICE
H	1931C-3253	1	118	7.35 x 14/	6 ps	3156	2671
				7.75 x 14			
H	1931C-3253	1	118	7.35 x 14	6 pht2	3226	2854
H	1931C-3308-1	2	118	7.75 x 14	6 ps	3279	2657
H	1931C-3308-1	2	118	7.75 x 14	6 ps	3324	2776
H	1931C-3308-1	2	118	7.75 x 14	6 pht2	3396	2958
H	1931C-3253	1					
H	1931C-3253	1					
H	1931C-3308-L	2					
H							
H							
H							
H	1931-3966A	1	106	6.45 x 14	6 ps	2638	2024
H	1931-3966A	1	106	6.45 x 14/	6 ps	2643	2166
				6.95 x 14			
H	1931-3968A	1	106	6.45 x 14	6 pht2	2678	2244
H	1931-3968A	1	109	6.95 x 14	6 pht2	2826	2482
H	1931-3968A	1	109	7.35 x 14	6 pht2	2836	2587
O	8HM2	2	109	7.35 x 14	6 pht2	3089	2587
O	8HM2	2	109	7.35 x 14	6 pht2	3099	2692
O	8HM2	2	97	E70 x 14	4 pht2	3097	3245
H	1931-3968A	1	114	7.35 x 14/	6 ps	3062	2443
				7.75 x 14			
H	1931-3968A	1	114	7.35 x 14/	6 ps	3074	2542
				7.75 x 14			
C	AFB-4467S	4	114	7.35/7.75x14	6 ps	3277	2549
C	AFB-4467S	4	114	7.35 x 14/	6 ps	3289	2648
				7.75 x 14			
C	AFB-4467S	4	114	7.35 x 14	6 pht2	3348	2775
H	1931-3968A	1	118	7.35 x 14	6 ps	3193	2820
H	1931-3968A	1	118	7.35 x 14	6 ps	3265	2920
O	8HM2	2	118	7.75 x 14	6 ps	3385	2926
O	8HM2	2	118	7.75 x 14	6 ps	3457	3026
O	8HM2	2	118	7.75 x 14	6 ps	3476	3151
H	1931-3968A	1					
H	1931-3968A	1					

YEAR	MODEL	ENGINE CYLS	BORE	STROKE	DISPL	HP@RPM	C.R.	VLV
	(7)	V8	4.17	3.57	390.0	315@4600	10.2	OH
1969	Rambler (1)	6	3.75	3.00	198.8	128@4400	8.5	OH
	Rambler 440 (1)	6	3.75	3.00	198.8	128@4400	8.5	OH
	Rambler Rogue (1)	6	3.75	3.50	231.9	145@4300	8.5	OH
	Javelin (2)	6	3.75	3.50	231.9	145@4300	8.5	OH
	Javelin SSJ (2)	6	3.75	3.50	231.9	145@4300	8.5	OH
	Javelin (2, 3)	V8	3.75	3.28	289.8	200@4600	9.0	OH
	Javelin SST (2, 3)	V8	3.75	3.28	289.8	200@4600	9.0	OH
	AMX (2, 3)	V8	3.75	3.28	289.8	225@4700	10.0	OH
	Rebel (4)	6	3.75	3.50	231.9	145@4300	8.5	OH
	Rebel SSJ (4)	6	3.75	3.50	231.9	145@4300	8.5	OH
	Rebel	V8	3.75	3.28	289.8	200@4600	9.0	OH
	Rebel SST	V8	3.75	3.28	289.8	200@4600	9.0	OH
	Ambassador (3, 5)	6	3.75	3.50	231.9	155@4400	8.5	OH
	Ambassador DPL (3, 5)	6	3.75	3.50	231.9	155@4400	8.5	OH
	Ambassador (3, 5)	V8	3.75	3.28	289.8	200@4600	9.0	OH
	Ambassador DPL	V8	3.75	3.28	289.8	200@4600	9.0	OH
	Optional engines:							
	(1)	V8	3.75	3.28	289.8	200@4600	9.0	OH
	(1)	V8	3.75	3.28	289.8	225@4700	10.0	OH
	(2)	V8	4.08	3.28	343.1	280@4800	10.2	OH
	(3)	V8	4.17	3.57	390.0	315@4600	10.2	OH
	(4)	6	3.75	3.50	231.9	155@4400	8.5	OH
	(5)	V8	3.75	3.50	309.2	235@4400	9.0	OH
	(5)	V8	4.08	3.28	343.1	280@4800	10.2	OH

APOLLO — — International Motor Cars, Inc., 1962-63, Oakland, Cal.; Apollo International Corp., Pasadena, Cal., 1963-64

YEAR	MODEL	CYLS	BORE	STROKE	DISPL	HP@RPM	C.R.	VLV
1962	GT	V8	3.50	2.80	215.5	190	9.0	OH
1963	GT	V8	3.50	2.80	215.5	200@5000	11.0	OH
1964		V8	3.75	3.40	300.4	250	11.0	OH
	Presumably became Vetta Ventura.							

ARGONAUT — — Argonaut Motor Machine Co., Cleveland, Ohio, 1959-63

YEAR	MODEL	CYLS	BORE	STROKE	DISPL	HP@RPM	C.R.	VLV
1959	Steed	V12				1020		

MFR	CARBURETOR MODEL	VEN	WHEEL-BASE	TIRES	BODY	WEIGHT	PRICE
C	RBS - 4633S	1	106	6.45 x 14	6 ps	2667	2076
C	RBS - 4633S	1	106	6.45 x 14/	6 ps	2679	2218
				6.95 x 14			
C	RBS - 4631S	1	106	6.45 x 14	6pht2	2717	2296
C	RBS - 4631S	1	109	6.95 x 14	6pht2	2810	2512
C	RBS - 4631S	1	109	6.95 x 14	6pht2	2826	2633
C	WCD - 4667S	2	109	7.35 x 14	6pht2	3093	2613
C	WCD - 4667S	2	109	7.35 x 14	6pht2	3103	2738
C	AFB - 4660S	4	97	E70 x 14	4pht2	3094	3297
C	RBS - 4631 S	1	114	7.35 x 14/	6 ps	3089	2484
				7.75 x 14			
C	RBS - 4631S	1	114	7.35 x 14/	6 ps	3074	2584
				7.75 x 14			
C	AFB - 4660S	4	114	7.35 x 14/	6 ps	3277	2582
				7.75 x 14			
C	AFB - 4660S	4	114	7.35 x 14/	6 ps	3289	2682
				7.75 x 14			
C	WCD - 4667S	2	122	7.75 x 14	6 ps	3276	2914
C	WCD - 4667S	2	122	7.75 x 14/	6 ps	3320	3165
				8.25 x 14			
C	WCD - 4667S	2	122	7.75 x 14	6 ps	3550	3270
C	WCD - 4667S	2	122	7.75 x 14/	6 ps	3516	3605
				8.25 x 14			
C	WCD - 4667S	2					
C	AFB - 4660S	4					
C	AFB - 4662S	4					
C	AFB - 4665S	4					
C	WCD - 4667S	2					
C	AFB - 4663S	4					
C	AFB - 4662S	4					
			97		2 pc		6597
			97		2 pc		6597
		4	97		2 pc		7965
			126.5				25,150

YEAR	MODEL	CYLS	BORE	STROKE	DISPL	HP@RPM	C.R.	VLV
	Limousine	V12				1020		

Also known as Smoke. At least one chassis was built but construction of complete automobile has not been proven.

ARNOLT — — S. H. Arnolt, Inc., Chicago, Ill., 1953-63

YEAR	MODEL	CYLS	BORE	STROKE	DISPL	HP@RPM	C.R.	VLV
1953-54	MG	4	2.62	3.54	76.3	54@5400	7.1	OH
1954-63	Bristol	6	2.59	3.77	120.2	130@5500	9.0	OH

The above two models were powered by MG and Bristol engines, respectively. This make is commonly referred to as Arnolt-Bristol. Bertone bodies were assembled to chassis in Warsaw, Ind.

ARROWHEAD — — (Manufacturer and location unknown) ca 1936

YEAR	MODEL	CYLS	BORE	STROKE	DISPL	HP@RPM	C.R.	VLV
1936		V8						

This car was a teardrop-shaped three-wheeler with front-wheel drive and was designed in 1936 by W. Everitt Miller. It was used for publicity purposes by manufacturers of Arrowhead Spring Drinking Water. It was not intended for sale.

ASARDO — — American Special Automotive Research & Design Organization, North Bergen, N.J., 1959

YEAR	MODEL	CYLS	BORE	STROKE	DISPL	HP@RPM	C.R.	VLV
1959	Typo 1500, AR-S	4	3.08	2.97	88.5	136@6800	11.5	DOHC

This car used a modified Alfa Romeo engine.

ASCOT — — Glasspar Co., Santa Ana, Cal., 1955

YEAR	MODEL	CYLS	BORE	STROKE	DISPL	HP@RPM	C.R.	VLV
1955		6	3.00	4.375	185.6	101@4000	7.5	L

Based on Studebaker engine, although optional engines were available.

ASTRA — — Jay Everett, Los Angeles, Cal., 1955

YEAR	MODEL	CYLS	BORE	STROKE	DISPL	HP@RPM	C.R.	VLV
1955		V8						OH

Used a modified Oldsmobile engine.

AUBURN — — Auburn Automobile Co., Auburn, Ind., 1900-36

YEAR	MODEL	CYLS	BORE	STROKE	DISPL	HP@RPM	C.R.	VLV
1930	6 - 85	6	2.875	4.75	185.0	70@3400	5.5	L
	8 - 95	8	2.875	4.75	246.7	100@3700	5.24	L
	125	8	3.25	4.50	298.6	125@3600	5.25	L
1931	8 - 98	8	3.00	4.75	286.6	98@3400	5.26	L
	8 - 98A	8	3.00	4.75	286.6	98@3400	5.26	L
1932	8 - 100 Standard	8	3.00	4.75	286.6	98@3400	5.26	L
	8 - 100 A Custom	8	3.00	4.75	286.6	98@3400	5.26	L
	12 - 160 Standard	V12	3.125	4.25	391.0	160@3400	5.50	H
	12 - 160A Custom	V12	3.125	4.25	391.0	160@3400	5.50	H
1933	8 - 101	8	3.00	4.75	286.6	100@3400	5.26	L
	8 - 105	8	3.00	4.75	286.6	100@3400	5.26	L
	12 - 161 Standard	V12	3.125	4.25	391.0	160@3500	5.75	H

MFR	CARBURETOR MODEL	VEN	WHEEL-BASE	TIRES	BODY	WEIGHT	PRICE
			154				36,000
			94	5.50 x 15	4 pcv		3145
So		3x1	96	5.50 x 16	2 pr	1396	
			125		3 pc		
W		2x2	88	5.90 x 15	2 pc	1500	5875
C	2108S	1	94		2 pr	1770	
			102		2 pc		
Sc	TX - 5		120	5.50 x 18	5 ps	3300	1095
Sc	UX - 51		125	6.00 x 18	5 ps	3590	1295
Sc	SX - 418		129	6.50 x 18	5 ps	3995	1595
Sc	EE - 22		127	5.50 x 17	5 ps	3700	995
Sc	EE - 22		127	5.50 x 17	5 ps	3750	1195
Sc	URO - 2		127/136	6.00 x 17	5 ps	3725	775
Sc	URO - 2		127/136	6.00 x 17	5 ps	3815	905
S	EX - 2	2	133	6.00 x 17	5 ps	4515	1075
S	EX - 2	2	133	6.00 x 17	5 ps	4615	1205
S	URO - 2		127	5.50 x 17	5 ps	3678	845
S	EX - 32		127	6.00 x 17	5 ps	3955	1095
S	EX - 2	2	133	6.00 x 17	5 ps	4465	1245

YEAR	MODEL	ENGINE						
		CYLS	BORE	STROKE	DISPL	HP@RPM	C.R.	VLV
	12 - 161A Custom	V12	3.125	4.25	391.0	160@3500	5.75	H
	12 - 165	V12	3.125	4.25	391.0	160@3500	5.75	H
1934	6 - 52X Standard	6	3.062	4.75	209.9	85@3500	6.20	L
	6 - 52Y Custom	6	3.062	4.75	209.9	85@3500	6.20	L
	8 - 50 Standard	8	3.062	4.75	279.9	100@3400	5.30	L
	8 - 50 Custom	8	3.062	4.75	279.9	100@3400	5.30	L
	12 - 165	V12	3.125	4.25	391.0	160@3400	5.75	H
1935	6 - 53 Custom 6	6	3.062	4.75	209.9	85@3500	6.20	L
	6 - 53 Salon 6	6	3.062	4.75	209.9	85@3500	6.20	L
	851 Custom 8	8	3.062	4.75	279.9	115@3600	6.20	L
	851 Salon 8	8	3.062	4.75	279.9	115@3600	6.20	L
	851SC (Super-charged)	8	3.062	4.75	279.9	150@4000	6.20	L
1936	654	6	3.062	4.75	209.9	85@3500	6.20	L
	852	8	3.062	4.75	279.9	115@3600	6.20	L
	852SC (Super-charged)	8	3.062	4.75	279.9	150@4000	6.20	L

AUBURN — — Auburn-Cord-Duesenberg Co., Tulsa, Okla., 1968+

YEAR	MODEL	CYLS	BORE	STROKE	DISPL	HP@RPM	C.R.	VLV
1968+	866	V8	4.36	3.59	428.8	360@4600		OH
	A replicar based on the 1935 Auburn Speedster. Uses optional Ford Thunderbird engine.							

AUTO CUB — — Randall Products, Hampton, N.H., 1956

YEAR	MODEL	CYLS	BORE	STROKE	DISPL	HP@RPM	C.R.	VLV
1956		1				1.6		

AVANTI II — — Avanti Motor Corp., South Bend, Ind., 1966+

YEAR	MODEL	CYLS	BORE	STROKE	DISPL	HP@RPM	C.R.	VLV
1966-67		V8	4.00	3.25	326.7	300@5000	10.5	OH
1968		V8	4.00	3.25	326.7	300@5000	10.25	OH
1969		V8	4.00	3.25	326.7	300@5000	10.25	OH
Late 1969		V8	4.00	3.48	349.8	300@4800		OH
	Engine was by Chevrolet.							

MFR	CARBURETOR MODEL	VEN	WHEEL-BASE	TIRES	BODY	WEIGHT	PRICE
S	EX - 2	2	133	6.00 x 17	5 ps	4552	1395
S	EX - 2	2	133	6.00 x 17	5 ps	4870	1635
C	288S	1	119	5.50 x 17	5 ps	3263	745
C	288S	1	119	5.50 x 17	5 ps		845
S	EE - 1	2	126	6.25 x 16	5 ps	3668	995
S	EE - 1	2	126	6.25 x 16	5 ps	3775	1125
S	EX - 2	2x1	133	6.00 x 17	5 ps	4710	1445
S	EE - 1		120	5.50 x 17/	5 ps	3388	952
				6.25 x 16			
S	EE - 1		120	5.50 x 17/	5 ps	3533	982
				6.25 x 17			
S	EE - 1		127	6.50 x 16	5 ps	3679	1188
S	EE - 1		127	6.50 x 16	5 ps	3835	1268
S	EX - 22		127	7.00 x 16	5 ps	3729	1545
S	EX - 22		120	6.00 x 17	5 ps	3279	795
S	EE - 1		127	6.50 x 16	5 ps	3850	1095
S	EE - 1		127	6.50 x 16	5 ps	3915	1545
		4	127	H70 x 15	2 pr	3100	8450
					1 pr	115	170
		4	109	7.75 x 15	4pht2	3181	6041
		4	109		4pht2	3217	7200
R		4	109	F70 x 15	4pht2	3350	7145
		4	109		4pht2		

YEAR	MODEL	ENGINE CYLS	BORE	STROKE	DISPL	HP@RPM	C.R.	VLV

BANNER BOY BUCKBOARD – – Banner Welder, Inc., Milwaukee, Wis., 1958

YEAR	MODEL	CYLS	BORE	STROKE	DISPL	HP@RPM	C.R.	VLV
1958		1				2.75		
	Engine was by Briggs & Stratton.							

BANTAM (AMERICAN BANTAM) – – American Bantam Car Co., Butler, Pa., 1938-41

YEAR	MODEL	CYLS	BORE	STROKE	DISPL	HP@RPM	C.R.	VLV
1938		4	2.20	3.00	45.6	19@4000	7.0	L
1939	60	4	2.20	3.00	45.6	20@4000	7.0	L
1940	65	4	2.20	3.125	50.1	22@3800	8.2	L
1941	65	4	2.26	3.125	50.1	22@3800	8.2	L

BASSON'S STAR – – Basson's Industries, Bronx, N.Y., 1956

YEAR	MODEL	CYLS	BORE	STROKE	DISPL	HP@RPM	C.R.	VLV
1956		1				10		

BEARCAT – – American Buckboard Corp., Los Angeles, Cal., 1956-

YEAR	MODEL	CYLS	BORE	STROKE	DISPL	HP@RPM	C.R.	VLV
1956		2						
	Used chain drive to a fifth wheel.							

BEECHCRAFT – – Beech Aircraft Co., Wichita, Kans., 1946

YEAR	MODEL	CYLS	BORE	STROKE	DISPL	HP@RPM	C.R.	VLV
1946	Plainsman	4						
	This was a gas-electric car using an aircraft engine.							

BLACKHAWK – – Stutz Motor Car Co. of America, Indianapolis, Ind., 1929-30

YEAR	MODEL	CYLS	BORE	STROKE	DISPL	HP@RPM	C.R.	VLV
1930	L6	6	3.375	4.50	241.5	85@3200	5.0	OH
	L6 (Weymann)	6	3.375	4.50	241.5	85@3200	5.0	OH
	L8	8	3.00	3.75	212.1	90@3200	5.5	OH
	L8 (Weymann)	8	3.00	3.75	212.1	90@3200	5.5	OH
	Weymann indicates special fabric-covered bodies, thus the reduced weight, at extra cost.							

B.M.C. SPORTS – – British Motor Co., San Francisco, Cal., 1952

YEAR	MODEL	CYLS	BORE	STROKE	DISPL	HP@RPM	C.R.	VLV
1952		4	2.875	3.52	91.4	48@4500	7.0	OH
	This car used British Singer engine.							

B.M.W. – – Boulevard Machine Works, Los Angeles, Cal., ca 1949-ca 1970

YEAR	MODEL	CYLS	BORE	STROKE	DISPL	HP@RPM	C.R.	VLV
1966	Electrics only.							

BOBBI-KAR – – Bobbi Motor Car Corp., San Diego, Cal., 1945-46; Dixie Motor Car Corp., Birmingham, Ala., 1947

YEAR	MODEL	CYLS	BORE	STROKE	DISPL	HP@RPM	C.R.	VLV
1945-47		4	2.625	3.00	64.9	25@4000	6.1	L
	Bobbi-Kar was the forerunner of the Keller. Engine was in the rear.							

MFR	CARBURETOR MODEL	VEN	WHEEL-BASE	TIRES	BODY	WEIGHT	PRICE
			62		1 pr		400
T	M10BX	1	75	5.00 x 15	2 pc	1250	469
T	M10BX	1	75	5.00 x 15	2 pc	1240	399
Z	61A5	1	75	4.00 x 15	2 pc	1261	399
Z	61A5	1	75	4.00 x 15	2 pc	1261	399
							999
			70		2 pr		ca1000
					5 ps		5000
Z	105DS	1	127.5	6.00 x 19	5 ps	4520	2395
Z	105DS	1	127.5	6.00 x 19	5 ps	3890	2595
Z	105DS	1	127.5	6.00 x 19	5 ps	4185	2395
Z	105DS	1	127.5	6.00 x 19	5 ps	3890	2595
			92	4.50 x 12	2pcv	600	400-500

YEAR	MODEL	ENGINE CYLS	BORE	STROKE	DISPL	HP@RPM	C.R.	VLV

BOCAR — — Bocar Mfg. Co., Denver, Colo., 1958-ca 1960

YEAR	MODEL	CYLS	BORE	STROKE	DISPL	HP@RPM	C.R.	VLV
1958-59		V8	3.875	3.00	283.0	312		OH

Price was less engine. Various high-performance engines were available.

BOLIDE — — Bolide Motor Car Corp., Huntington, N.Y., 1969-

YEAR	MODEL	CYLS	BORE	STROKE	DISPL	HP@RPM	C.R.	VLV
1969	Can - Am 2	V8	4.00	3.50	351.9			OH

This had a Ford engine.

BREMAC — — Bremac Motor Car Corp., Sidney, Ohio, 1932

YEAR	MODEL	CYLS	BORE	STROKE	DISPL	HP@RPM	C.R.	VLV
1932		8				80		L

The Bremac was designed to be a rear-engine type, although this project may have never progressed beyond the blueprint stage.

BRIGGS — — Briggs Mfg. Co., Detroit, Mich., 1933-34

YEAR	MODEL	CYLS	BORE	STROKE	DISPL	HP@RPM	C.R.	VLV
1934		V8			165	80@4700		L

This was an experimental car designed by John Tjaarda, and was not intended for production. Exterior design was adopted for 1936 Lincoln Zephyr.

BUCKBOARD — — Automotive Associates Co., White Plains, N.Y., 1956

YEAR	MODEL	CYLS	BORE	STROKE	DISPL	HP@RPM	C.R.	VLV
1956						43@6200		

This car used an Aeriel motorcycle engine.

BUICK — — Buick Motor Car Co., Div. General Motors, Flint, Mich., 1903+

YEAR	MODEL	CYLS	BORE	STROKE	DISPL	HP@RPM	C.R.	VLV
1930	40	6	3.438	4.625	257.5	80@2800	4.5	OH
	50	6	3.75	5.00	331.4	98@2800	5.3	OH
	60	6	3.75	5.00	331.4	98@2800	5.3	OH
1931	8 - 50	8	2.875	4.25	220.7	77@3200	4.75	OH
	8 - 60	8	3.062	4.625	272.6	90@3000	4.63	OH
	8 - 80	8	3.312	4.625	344.8	104@2800	4.5	OH
	8 - 90	8	3.312	4.625	344.8	104@2800	4.5	OH
1932	50	8	2.938	4.25	230.4	78@3200	4.65	OH
	60	8	3.062	4.625	272.6	90@3000	4.63	OH
	80	8	3.312	5.00	344.8	104@2900	4.4	OH
	90	8	3.312	5.00	344.8	104@2900	4.4	OH
1933	50	8	2.938	4.25	230.4	86@3200	5.25	OH
	60	8	3.062	4.625	272.6	97@3200	5.25	OH
	80	8	3.312	5.00	344.8	113@3200	4.8	OH
	90	8	3.312	5.00	344.8	113@3200	4.8	OH
1934	50	8	2.969	4.25	253.3	88@3200	5.25	OH
	60	8	3.094	4.625	278.1	100@3200	5.25	OH

MFR	CARBURETOR MODEL	VEN	WHEEL-BASE	TIRES	BODY	WEIGHT	PRICE
	F. I		90		2 pc	2290	4416+
			105				3500
			146	7.50 x 15	5 ps	2600	
			125				
			94				
M	T3		118	5.50 x 19	5 ps	3881	1330
M	T4		124	6.50 x 19	5 ps	4443	1540
M	T4		130	7.00 x 19	5 pb	4540	1760
M	T3		114	5.25 x 18	5 ps	3265	1095
M	TD2S		118	5.50 x 19	5 ps	3795	1355
M	TD3		124	6.50 x 19	5 ps	4255	1565
M	TD3		132	6.50 x 19	5 ps	4360	1785
M			114	5.50 x 18	5 ps	3450	995
M	TD2S		118	6.00 x 18	5 ps	3980	1310
M	TD3		126	7.00 x 18	5 ps	4450	1570
M	TD3		134	7.00 x 18	5 ps	4565	1805
M	ED1S	2	119	6.00 x 17	5 ps	3705	1045
M	ED2S	2	127	6.50 x 17	5 ps	4115	1310
M	ED3	2	130	7.00 x 17	5 ps	4505	1570
M	ED3	2	138	7.00 x 17	5 ps	4595	1805
M	ED1S	2	119	7.00 x 16	5 ps	3852	1230
M	ED2S	2	128	7.50 x 16	5 ps	4303	1425

YEAR	MODEL	ENGINE						
		CYLS	BORE	STROKE	DISPL	HP@RPM	C.R.	VLV
	90	8	3.312	5.00	344.8	116@3200	4.95	OH
	40	8	3.094	3.875	233.0	93@3200	5.45	OH
1935	40	8	3.094	3.875	233.0	93@3200	5.45	OH
	50	8	2.969	4.25	235.2	88@3200	5.25	OH
	60	8	3.094	4.625	278.1	100@3200	5.25	OH
	90	8	3.312	5.00	344.8	116@3200	4.95	OH
1936	Special, 40	8	3.094	3.875	233.0	93@3200	5.65	OH
	Century, 60	8	3.438	4.312	320.2	120@3200	5.45	OH
	Roadmaster, 80	8	3.438	4.312	320.2	120@3200	5.45	OH
	Limited, 90	8	3.438	4.312	320.2	120@3200	5.45	OH
1937	Special, 40	8	3.094	4.125	248.0	100@3200	5.70	OH
	Century, 60	8	3.438	4.312	320.2	130@3400	5.90	OH
	Roadmaster, 80	8	3.438	4.312	320.2	130@3400	5.90	OH
	Limited, 90	8	3.438	4.312	320.2	130@3400	5.90	OH
1938	Special, 40	8	3.094	4.125	248.0	107@3400	6.15	OH
	Century, 60	8	3.438	4.312	320.2	141@3600	6.35	OH
	Roadmaster, 80	8	3.438	4.312	320.2	141@3600	6.35	OH
	Limited, 90	8	3.438	4.312	320.2	141@3600	6.35	OH
1939	Special, 40	8	3.094	4.125	248.0	107@3400	6.10	OH
	Century, 60	8	3.438	4.312	320.2	141@3600	6.25	OH
	Roadmaster, 80	8	3.438	4.312	320.2	141@3600	6.25	OH
	Limited, 90	8	3.438	4.312	320.2	141@3600	6.25	OH
1940	Special, 40	8	3.094	4.125	248.0	107@3400	6.10	OH
	Super, 50	8	3.094	4.125	248.0	107@3400	6.10	OH
	Century, 60	8	3.438	4.312	320.2	141@3600	6.25	OH
	Roadmaster, 70	8	3.438	4.312	320.2	141@3600	6.25	OH
	Limited, 80	8	3.438	4.312	320.2	141@3600	6.25	OH
	Limited, 90	8	3.438	4.312	320.2	141@3600	6.25	OH
1941	Special, 40	8	3.094	4.125	248.0	115@3500	6.50	OH
	Special, 40A	8	3.094	4.125	248.0	115@3500	6.50	OH
	Super, 50	8	3.094	4.125	248.0	125@3800	7.00	OH
	Century, 60	8	3.438	4.312	320.2	165@3800	7.00	OH
	Roadmaster, 70	8	3.438	4.312	320.2	165@3800	7.00	OH
	Limited, 90	8	3.438	4.312	320.2	165@3800	7.00	OH
1942	Special, 40A	8	3.094	4.125	248.0	110@3400	6.00	OH
	Special, 40B	8	3.094	4.125	248.0	110@3400	6.00	OH
	Super, 50	8	3.094	4.125	248.0	118@3600	6.30	OH
	Century, 60	8	3.438	4.312	320.2	165@3800	6.70	OH
	Roadmaster, 70	8	3.438	4.312	320.2	165@3800	6.70	OH
	Limited, 90	8	3.438	4.312	320.2	165@3800	6.70	OH
1946	Special, 40	8	3.094	4.125	248.0	110@3600	6.30	OH

MFR	CARBURETOR MODEL	VEN	WHEEL-BASE	TIRES	BODY	WEIGHT	PRICE
M	ED3	2	136	7.50 x 16	5 ps	4691	1945
M	ED1		117	6.25 x 16	5 ps	3155	895
S	EE1		117	6.25 x 16	5 ps	3180	895
M	ED1S		119	7.00 x 16	5 ps	3822	1190
M	ED2S		128	7.50 x 16	5 ps	4273	1425
M	ED3		136	7.50 x 16	5 ps	4661	1945
S	EE1		118	6.50 x 16	5 ps	3360	885
S	EE22		122	7.00 x 15	5 ps	3780	1095
S	EE22		131	7.00 x 16	5 ps	4228	1255
S	EE22		138	7.50 x 16	5 ps	4517	1695
S	AA1		122	6.50 x 16	5 ps	3510	950
S	AA2		126	7.00 x 15	5 ps	3750	1162
S	AA2		131	7.00 x 16	5 ps	4159	1418
S	AA2		138	7.50 x 16	5 ps	4469	1966
C	WDO-419S	2	122	6.50 x 16	5 ps	3535	1022
S	AAV-26	2	126	7.00 x 15	5 ps	3785	1272
S	AAV-26	2	133	7.00 x 16	6 ps	4245	1645
S	AAV-26	2	140	7.50 x 16	6 ps	4580	2176
S	AAV-16	2	120	6.50 x 16	5 ps	3417	955
S	AAV-26	2	126	7.00 x 15	5 ps	3707	1205
S	AAV-26	2	133	7.00 x 16	6 ps	4262	1543
S	AAV-26	2	140	7.00 x 16	6 ps	4568	2074
S	AAV-16	2	121	6.50 x 16	5 ps	3605	955
S	AAV-16	2	121	6.50 x 16	5 ps	3760	1109
S	AAV-26	2	126	7.00 x 15	5 ps	3935	1211
S	AAV-26	2	126	7.00 x 16	6 ps	4045	1359
S	AAV-26	2	133	7.50 x 16	6 ps	4380	1553
S	AAV-26	2	140	7.50 x 16	6 ps	4590	1942
S	AAV-16	2	121	6.50 x 16	6 ps	3730	1052
S	AAV-16	2	118	6.50 x 15	6 ps	3670	1021
S	AAV-16	2	121	6.50 x 15	6 ps	3770	1185
S	AAV-16	2	126	7.00 x 15	6 ps	4025	1288
S	AAV-16	2	126	7.00 x 15	6 ps	4010	1364
S	AAV-16	2	139	7.50 x 16	6 ps	4575	2155
S	AAV-16	2	118	6.50 x 15	6 ps	3650	1080
S	AAV-16	2	121	6.50 x 16	6 ps	3760	1120
C	WCD-528SF		124	6.50 x 16	6 ps	3890	1280
C	WCD-533SF		126	7.00 x 15	6 ps	4065	1350
C	WCD-533SF		129	7.00 x 15	6 ps	4150	1465
C	WCD-533SF		139	7.50 x 15	6 ps	4665	2245
S	AAV-16	2	121	6.50 x 16	6 ps	3720	1580

YEAR	MODEL	ENGINE						
		CYLS	BORE	STROKE	DISPL	HP@RPM	C.R.	VLV
	Super, 50	8	3.094	4.125	248.0	110@3600	6.30	OH
	Roadmaster, 70	8	3.438	4.312	320.2	144@3600	6.60	OH
1947	Special, 40	8	3.094	4.125	248.0	110@3500	6.30	OH
	Super, 50	8	3.094	4.125	248.0	110@3600	6.30	OH
	Roadmaster, 70	8	3.438	4.312	320.2	144@3600	6.60	OH
1948	Special, 40	8	3.094	4.125	248.1	110@3600	6.30	OH
	Super, 50	8	3.094	4.125	248.1	110@3600	6.30	OH
	Roadmaster, 70	8	3.438	4.312	320.2	144@3600	6.60	OH
1949	Special, 40	8	3.094	4.125	248.1	110@3600	6.30	OH
	Super, 50	8	3.094	4.125	248.1	115@3600	6.60	OH
	Roadmaster, 70	8	3.438	4.312	320.2	150@3600	6.90	OH
1950	Special, 40	8	3.094	4.125	248.1	115@3600	6.60	OH
	Super, 50	8	3.188	4.125	263.3	124@3600	6.90	OH
	Roadmaster, 70	8	3.438	4.312	320.2	152@3600	7.20	OH
1951	Special, 40	V8	3.188	4.125	263.3	120@3600	6.60	OH
	Super, 50	V8	3.188	4.125	263.3	124@3600	6.90	OH
	Roadmaster, 70	V8	3.438	4.312	320.2	152@3600	7.20	OH
1952	Special, 40	V8	3.188	4.125	263.3	120@3600	6.60	OH
	Special Deluxe, 40	V8	3.188	4.125	263.3	120@3600	6.60	OH
	Super, 50	V8	3.188	4.125	263.3	124@3600	6.90	OH
	Roadmaster, 70	V8	3.438	4.312	320.2	170@3800	7.50	OH
1953	Special, 40	V8	3.188	4.125	263.3	125@3800	7.00	OH
	Super, 50	V8	4.00	3.20	321.7	164@4000	8.00	OH
	Super, 50 Riviera	V8	4.00	3.20	321.7	164@4000	8.00	OH
	Roadmaster, 70	V8	4.00	3.20	321.7	188@4000	8.50	OH
	Roadmaster, 70, Riviera	V8	4.00	3.20	321.7	188@4000	8.50	OH
	Skylark	V8	4.00	3.20	321.7	188@4000	8.50	OH
1954	Special, 40	V8	3.625	3.20	264.2	143@4200	7.20	OH
	Super, 50	V8	4.00	3.20	321.7	177@4100	8.00	OH
	Century, 60	V8	4.00	3.20	321.7	195@4100	8.00	OH
	Roadmaster, 70	V8	4.00	3.20	321.7	200@4100	8.50	OH
	Skylark, 100	V8	4.00	3.20	321.7	200@4100	8.50	OH
1955	Special, 40	V8	3.625	3.20	264.2	188@4400	8.40	OH
	Century, 60	V8	4.00	3.20	321.7	236@4600	9.00	OH
	Super, 50	V8	4.00	3.20	321.7	236@4600	9.00	OH
	Roadmaster, 70	V8	4.00	3.20	321.7	236@4600	9.00	OH
1956	Special, 40	V8	4.00	3.20	321.7	220@4400	8.90	OH
	Century, 60, Riviera	V8	4.00	3.20	321.7	255@4400	9.50	OH
	Super, 50	V8	4.00	3.20	321.7	255@4400	9.50	OH
	Roadmaster, 70	V8	4.00	3.20	321.7	255@4400	9.50	OH

MFR	CARBURETOR MODEL	VEN	WHEEL-BASE	TIRES	BODY	WEIGHT	PRICE
S	AAV-16	2	124	6.50 x 16	6 ps	3935	1822
S	AAV-26	2	129	7.00 x 15	6 ps	4165	2110
S	AAV-16	2	121	6.50 x 16	6 ps	3720	1673
S	AAV-16	2	129	6.50 x 16	6 ps	4190	2232
S	AAV-26	2	129	7.00 x 15	6 ps	4190	2232
S	AAV-267	2	121	6.50 x 16	6 ps	3705	1809
S	AAV-16	2	124	6.50 x 16	6 ps	3855	2087
S	AAV-267	2	129	7.00 x 15	6 ps	4160	2418
S	AAV-167	2	121	6.50 x 16	6 ps	3695	1809
S	AAV-167	2	121	7.60 x 15	6 ps	3835	2087
S	AAV-267	2	126	8.20 x 15	6 ps	4205	2662
S	AAVB-267	2	121.5	7.60 x 15	6 ps	3715	1780
S	AAVB-267	2	121.5	7.60 x 15	6 ps	3870	2058
S	AAVB-267	2	126.2	8.00 x 15	6 ps	4220	2543
C	WCD-725S	2	121.5	7.60 x 15	6 ps	3605	1810
C	WCD-725S	2	121.5	7.60 x 15	6 ps	3755	1989
C	WCD-726S	2	126.2	8.00 x 15	6 ps	4240	2568
S	AAUVB-267	2	121.5	7.60 x 15	6 ps	3650	2209
S	AAUVB-267	2	121.5	7.60 x 15	6 ps	3665	2255
S	AAUVB-267	2	121.5/	7.60 x 15	6 ps	3825	2563
			125.5				
S	AAUVB-267	2	126.5	8.00 x 15	6 ps	4235	3306
S	AAUVB-267	2	121.5	7.60 x 15	6 ps	3710	2255
S	AAVB-26	2	121.5	7.60 x 15	6pht2	3845	2611
S	AAVB-26	2	125.5	7.60 x 15	6pht2	3905	2696
C	WCFB-996S	4	121.5	8.00 x 15	6 ps	4125	3358
C	WCFB-996S	4	125.5	8.00 x 15	6 ps	4100	3254
C	WCFB-996S	4	121.5	8.00 x 15	6pcv	4315	5000
S	AAVB-267	2	122	7.60 x 15	6 ps	3735	2265
S	AAVB-267	2	127	7.60 x 15	6 ps	4105	2711
S	AUVB-267	4	122	7.60 x 15	6 ps	3805	2520
S	AUVB-267	4	127	8.00 x 15	6 ps	4250	3269
S	AUVB-267	4	122	7.60 x 15	6pcv	4260	4483
S	AAVB-267	2	122	7.10 x 15	6 ps	3745	2291
R	4G	4	122	7.60 x 15	6 ps	3825	2548
R	4G	4	127	7.60 x 15	6 ps	4140	2876
R	4G	4	127	8.00 x 15	6 ps	4300	3349
C	WGD	2	122	7.10 x 15	6 ps	3790	2416
C	WCFB	4	122	7.60 x 15	6pht4	4000	3041
C	WCFB	4	127	7.60 x 15	6 ps	4200	3250
C	WCFB	4	127	8.00 x 15	6 ps	4280	3503

YEAR	MODEL	ENGINE						
		CYLS	BORE	STROKE	DISPL	HP@RPM	C.R.	VLV
1957	Special, 40	V8	4.125	3.40	363.5	250@4400	9.50	OH
	Century, 60	V8	4.125	3.40	363.5	300@4600	10.0	OH
	Super, 50, Riviera	V8	4.125	3.40	363.5	300@4600	10.0	OH
	Roadmaster, 70, Riviera	V8	4.125	3.40	363.5	300@4600	10.0	OH
	Roadmaster, 75, Riviera	V8	4.125	3.40	363.5	300@4600	10.0	OH
1958	Special, 40	V8	4.125	3.40	363.5	250@4400	9.50	OH
	Century, 60	V8	4.125	3.40	363.5	300@4600	10.00	OH
	Super, 50, Riviera	V8	4.125	3.40	363.5	300@4600	10.00	OH
	Roadmaster, 75, Riviera	V8	4.125	3.40	363.5	300@4600	10.00	OH
1959	LaSabre, 4400	V8	4.125	3.40	363.5	250@4400	10.50	OH
	Invicta, 4600	V8	4.188	3.64	401.0	325@4400	10.50	OH
	Electra, 4700	V8	4.188	3.64	401.0	325@4400	10.50	OH
	Electra 225, Riviera 4800	V8	4.188	3.64	401.1	325@4400	10.50	OH
1960	LeSabre, 4400 (1)	V8	4.125	3.40	363.5	250@4000	10.25	OH
	Invicta, 4600	V8	4.188	3.64	401.0	325@4400	10.25	OH
	Electra, 4700	V8	4.188	3.64	401.0	325@4400	10.25	OH
	Electra, 4800	V8	4.188	3.64	401.0	325@4400	10.25	OH
	Optional engine:							
	(1)	V8	4.125	3.40	363.5	235@4400	9.00	OH
1961	Special Standard, 4000	V8	3.50	2.797	215.3	155@4600	8.80	OH
	Special Deluxe, 4100, 4300	V8	3.50	2.797	215.3	155@4600	8.80	OH
	LeSabre, 4400 (1)	V8	4.125	3.406	364.1	250@4400	10.25	OH
	Invicta, 4600	V8	4.188	3.641	401.2	325@4400	10.25	OH
	Electra, 4700	V8	4.188	3.641	401.2	325@4400	10.25	OH
	Electra 225 Riviera, 4800	V8	4.188	3.641	401.2	325@4400	10.25	OH
	Optional engine:							
	(1)	V8	4.125	3.406	364.1	235@4400	9.00	OH
1962	Special Standard, 4000 (1)	V6	3.625	3.203	198.3	135@4600	8.80	OH
	Special Deluxe, 4100 (1)	V8	3.50	2.797	215.3	155@4600	9.00	OH
	Special Skylark, 4300	V8	3.50	2.797	215.3	190@4800	11.0	OH
	LeSabre, 4400 (2)	V8	4.188	3.641	401.2	280@4400	10.25	OH
	Invicta, 4600 (2)	V8	4.188	3.641	401.2	325@4400	10.25	OH
	Electra 225, 4800 (3)	V8	4.188	3.641	401.2	325@4400	10.25	OH
	Optional engines:							
	(1)	V8	3.50	2.797	215.3	190@4800	11.0	OH
	(2)	V8	4.188	3.641	401.2	265@4400	9.00	OH
	(3)	V8	4.188	3.641	401.2	325@4400	10.25	OH
1963	Special Standard, 4000 (1)	V6	3.625	3.203	198.3	135@4600	8.8	OH
	Special Deluxe, 4100 (1)	V6	3.625	3.203	198.3	135@4600	8.8	OH
	Special Deluxe, 4100	V8	3.50	2.797	215.3	155@4600	9.0	OH

MFR	CARBURETOR MODEL	VEN	WHEEL-BASE	TIRES	BODY	WEIGHT	PRICE
C	WGD	2	122	7.10 x 15	6 ps	4012	2660
C	AFB	4	122	7.60 x 15	6 ps	4137	3234
C	AFB-2507	4	127.5	7.60 x 15	6pht4	4356	3681
C	AFB-2507	4	127.5	8.00 x 15	6pht4	4469	4053
C	AFB-2507	4	127.5	8.00 x 15	6 ps	4539	4483
C	WGD	2	122	7.10 x 15/	6 ps	4115	2700
				7.60 x 15			
C	AFB-2507	4	122	7.60 x 15	6 ps	4241	3316
C	AFB-2507	4	127.5	7.60 x 15	6pht4	4500	3789
C	AFB-2507	4	127.5	8.00 x 15	6pht4	4668	4667
S			123	7.60 x 15	6 ps	4229	2804
R	7010070	4	123	7.60 x 15	6 ps	4331	3357
R	7010070	4	126.3	8.00 x 15	6 ps	4557	3856
R	7010070	4	126.3	8.00 x 15	6 ps	4632	4300
C	WGD-3089	2	123	7.60 x 15	6 ps	4219	2870
R	7010070	4	123	7.60 x 15	6 ps	4324	3357
R	7010070	4	126.3	8.00 x 15	6 ps	4544	3856
R	7010071	4	126.3	8.00 x 15	6 ps	4653	4300
R		2	112	6.50 x 13	6 ps	2610	2384
R		2	112	6.50 x 13	6 ps	2632	2519
R	7019040	4	123	7.60 x 15	6 ps	4102	3107
R	4GC	4	123	7.60 x 15	6pht4	4179	3515
R	4GC	4	126	8.00 x 15	6 ps	4298	3825
R	4GC	4	126	8.00 x 15	6 ps	4417	4350
R	2GC	2	112	6.50 x 13	6 ps	2666	2358
R	2GC	2	112	6.50 x 13	6 ps	2648	2593
R	4GC	4	112	6.50 x 13	6pht2	2707	2787
R	2GC	2	123	7.60 x 15	6 ps	4104	3227
R	4GC	4	123	7.60 x 15	6pht4	4159	3667
R	4GC	4	126	8.00 x 15	6 ps	4304	4051
R	4GC	4					
R	2GC	2					
R	4GC	4					
R	2GC	2	112.1	6.50 x 13	6 ps	2696	2363
R	2GC	2	112.1	6.50 x 13	6 ps	2735	2521
R	4GC	4	112.1	6.50 x 13	6 ps	2684	2592

YEAR	MODEL	ENGINE						
		CYLS	BORE	STROKE	DISPL	HP@RPM	C.R.	VLV
	Special Skylark, 4300	V8	3.50	2.797	215.3	200@5000	11.0	OH
	LeSabre, 4400 (2)	V8	4.188	3.641	401.2	280@4400	10.25	OH
	Invicta, 4600	V8	4.188	3.641	401.2	325@4400	10.25	OH
	Wildcat, 4600	V8	4.188	3.641	401.2	325@4400	10.25	OH
	Electra 225, 4800	V8	4.188	3.641	401.2	325@4400	10.25	OH
	Riviera, 4700	V8	4.188	3.641	401.2	325@4400	10.25	OH
	Optional engines:							
	(1)	V8	3.50	2.797	215.3	200@5000	11.1	OH
	(2)	V8	4.188	3.641	401.2	265@4400	9.0	OH
1964	Special, 4000 (1)	V6	3.75	3.406	225.7	155@4400	9.0	OH
	Special Deluxe, 4100 (1)	V6	3.75	3.406	225.7	155@4400	9.0	OH
	Skylark, 4200, 4300 (1)	V6	3.75	3.406	225.7	155@4400	9.0	OH
	LeSabre, 4400 (1)	V8	3.75	3.406	300.9	210@4600	9.0	OH
	Wildcat, 4600 (2)	V8	4.188	3.641	401.2	325@4400	10.25	OH
	Electra 225, 4800 (2)	V8	4.188	3.641	401.2	325@4400	10.25	OH
	Riviera, 4700 (2)	V8	4.312	3.641	425.5	340@4400	10.25	OH
	Optional engines:							
	(1)	V8	3.75	3.406	300.9	250@4800	11.0	OH
	(2)	V8	4.312	3.641	425.5	360@4400	10.25	OH
1965	Special (1, 3, 4)	V6	3.75	3.406	225.7	155@4400	9.0	OH
	Special Deluxe (1, 3, 4)	V6	3.75	3.406	225.7	155@4400	9.0	OH
	Skylark (1, 3, 4)	V6	3.75	3.406	225.7	155@4400	9.0	OH
	LeSabre (4)	V8	3.75	3.406	300.9	210@4600	9.0	OH
	LeSabre Custom (4)	V8	3.75	3.406	300.9	210@4600	9.0	OH
	Wildcat (2)	V8	4.188	3.641	401.2	325@4400	10.25	OH
	Wildcat Deluxe (2)	V8	4.188	3.641	401.2	325@4400	10.25	OH
	Wildcat Custom (2)	V8	4.188	3.641	401.2	325@4400	10.25	OH
	Electra (2)	V8	4.188	3.641	401.2	325@4400	10.25	OH
	Electra Custom (2)	V8	4.188	3.641	401.2	325@4400	10.25	OH
	Riviera (2)	V8	4.188	3.641	401.2	325@4400	10.25	OH
	Optional engines:							
	(1)	V6	3.75	3.406	225.7	210@4600	9.0	OH
	(2)	V8	4.312	3.641	425.5	360@4400	10.25	OH
	(3)	V8	3.75	3.406	300.9	210@4600	9.0	OH
	(4)	V8	3.75	3.406	300.9	250@4800	10.25	OH
1966	Special Standard, 43300	V6	3.75	3.406	225.7	160@4200	9.0	OH

MFR	CARBURETOR MODEL	VEN	WHEEL-BASE	TIRES	BODY	WEIGHT	PRICE
R	4GC	4	112.1	6.50 x 13	6 psc2	2757	2857
R	2GC	2	123	7.60 x 15	6 ps	3970	3004
C	AFB	4	123	7.60 x 15	6psw4	4397	3969
C	AFB	4	123	7.60 x 15	6pht4	4222	3871
C	AFB	4	126	7.60 x 15	6 ps	4241	4051
C	AFB	4	117	7.10 x 15	6pht2	3998	4333
R	4GC	4					
C	AFB	4					
R	BC	1	115	6.50 x 14	6 ps	3000	2397
R	BC	1	115	6.50 x 14	6 ps	3018	2490
R	BC	1	115	6.50 x 14	6 ps	3078	2740
R	2GC	2	123	7.10 x 15/	6 ps	3693	2980
				7.60 x 15			
C	AFB	4	123	7.60 x 15	6 ps	4021	3164
C	AFB	4	126	8.00 x 15	6 ps	4212	4059
C	AFB-3635	4	117	7.10 x 15	6 psc	3951	4385
R	4GC	4					
C	AFB-3635	4					
R	BC	1	115	6.95 x 14/	6 ps	3010	2345
				7.35 x 14			
R	BC	1	115	6.95 x 14/	6 ps	3016	2436
				7.35 x 14			
R	BC	1	115	6.95 x 14	6 ps	3086	2611
R	7025046	2	123	8.15 x 15	6 ps	3788	2888
R	7025046	2	123	8.15 x 15	6 ps	3777	2962
C	AFB-3921	4	126	8.45 x 15	6 ps	4058	3117
C	AFB-3921	4	126	8.45 x 15	6 ps	4046	3218
C	AFB-3921	4	126	8.45 x 15	6pht4	4160	3552
C	AFB-3921	4	126	8.75 x 15	6 ps	4261	3989
C	AFB-3921	4	126	8.75 x 15	6 ps	4292	4168
C	AFB-3921	4	117	8.45 x 15	6 psc	4036	4318
C	AFB	4					
C	AFB	2x4					
R	7025046	2					
C	AFB	4					
R	2GC	2	115	6.95 x 14/	6 ps	3046	2401
				7.35 x 14/			
				7.75 x 14			

YEAR	MODEL	ENGINE						
		CYLS	BORE	STROKE	DISPL	HP@RPM	C.R.	VLV
	Special Deluxe, 43500	V6	3.75	3.406	225.7	160@4200	9.0	OH
	Skylark, 44300	V6	3.75	3.406	225.7	160@4200	9.0	OH
	Special Standard, 43400	V8	3.75	3.406	300.5	210@4600	9.0	OH
	Special Deluxe, 43600	V8	3.75	3.406	300.5	210@4600	9.0	OH
	Skylark, 44400	V8	3.75	3.406	300.5	210@4600	9.0	OH
	Skylark Gran Sport, 44600	V8	4.188	3.64	401.0	325@4400	10.25	OH
	Sport Wagon, 44200	V8	3.75	3.85	340.2	220@4000	9.0	OH
	Sport Wagon Custom, 44400	V8	3.75	3.85	340.2	220@4000	9.0	OH
	LeSabre, 45200 (1)	V8	3.75	3.85	340.2	220@4000	9.0	OH
	LeSabre Custom, 45400 (1)	V8	3.75	3.85	340.2	220@4000	9.0	OH
	Wildcat, 46400 (1)	V8	4.188	3.64	401.0	325@4400	10.25	OH
	Wildcat Custom, 46600 (1)	V8	4.188	3.64	401.0	325@4400	10.25	OH
	Electra 225, 48200 (1)	V8	4.188	3.64	401.0	325@4400	10.25	OH
	Electra 225 Custom, 48400 (1)	V8	4.188	3.64	401.0	325@4400	10.25	OH
	Riviera	V8	4.312	3.64	425.3	340@4400	10.25	OH
	Optional engine:							
	(1)	V8	4.312	3.64	425.3	340@4400	10.25	OH
1967	Special Standard, 43300 (1)	V6	3.75	3.406	225.3	160@4200	9.0	OH
	Special Deluxe, 43500 (1)	V6	3.75	3.406	225.3	160@4200	9.0	OH
	Skylark, 44300 (1)	V6	3.75	3.406	225.3	160@4200	9.0	OH
	Special, Standard, 43400 (1)	V8	3.75	3.406	300.9	210@4600	9.0	OH
	Special Deluxe, 43600 (1)	V8	3.75	3.406	300.9	210@4600	9.0	OH
	Skylark, 44400 (1)	V8	3.75	3.406	300.9	210@4600	9.0	OH
	Skylark Gran Sport , 44600	V8	4.04	3.90	400.0	340@5000	10.25	OH
	Skylark Gran Sport, (1)	V8	3.75	3.85	340.2	220@4000	9.0	OH
	Sport Wagon Custom, 44400	V8	3.75	3.85	340.2	220@4000	9.0	OH
	LeSabre, 45200 (2)	V8	3.75	3.85	340.2	220@4000	9.0	OH
	LeSabre Custom, 45400 (2)	V8	3.75	3.85	340.2	220@4000	9.0	OH
	Wildcat, 46400	V8	4.188	3.90	429.7	360@5000	10.25	OH
	Wildcat Custom, 46600	V8	4.188	3.90	429.7	360@5000	10.25	OH
	Electra 225, 48200	V8	4.188	3.90	429.7	360@5000	10.25	OH
	Electra 225 Custom, 48400	V8	4.188	3.90	429.7	360@5000	10.25	OH

MFR	CARBURETOR MODEL	VEN	WHEEL-BASE	TIRES	BODY	WEIGHT	PRICE
R	2GC	2	115	6.95 x 14 /	6 ps	3045	2485
				7.35 x 14 /			
				7.75 x 14			
R	2GC	2	115	6.95 x 14 /	6pht2	3069	2687
				7.35 x 14			
R	2GC	2	115	6.95 x 14 /	6 ps	3148	2471
				7.35 x 14 /			
				7.75 x 14			
R	2GC	2	115	6.95 x 14 /	6 ps	3156	2555
				7.35 x 14 /			
				7.75 x 14			
R	2GC	2	115	6.95 x 14 /	6pht2	3152	2757
				7.35 x 14			
C	AFB	4	115	6.95 x 14 /	6pht2	3019	3428
				7.35 x 14			
C	AFB-4055	4	120	8.24 x 14	6psw4	3713	3025
C	AFB-4055	4	120	8.24 x 14	6psw4	3720	3155
C	AFB-4055	4	123	8.15 x 15	6 ps	3796	2942
C	AFB-4055	4	123	8.15 x 15	6 ps	3788	3035
C	AFB-4054	4	126	8.45 x 15	6 ps	4340	3211
C	AFB-4054	4	126	8.45 x 15	6pht4	4176	3606
C	AFB-4054	4	126	8.45 x 15	6 ps	4255	4022
C	AFB-4054	4	126	8.45 x 15	6 ps	4292	4201
R	4MC	4	119	8.45 x 15	6pht2	4180	4424
R	4MC	4					
R	2GC	2	115	7.75 x 14	6 ps	3077	2462
R	2GC	2	115	7.75 x 14	6 ps	3142	2545
R	2GC	2	115	7.75 x 14	6 pc	3137	2665
R	2GC	2	115	7.75 x 14	6 ps	3196	2532
R	2GC	2	115	7.75 x 14	6 ps	3205	2615
R	2GC	2	115	7.75 x 14	6 ps	3324	2767
R	4MV	4	115	7.75 x 14	6pht2	3500	3019
R	2GC	2	115	7.75 x 14	6pht2	3283	2845
R	2GC	2	120	8.25 x 14	6psw4	3772	3202
R	2GC	2	123	8.45 x 15	6 ps	3847	3002
R	2GC	2	123	8.45 x 15	6 ps	3855	3096
R	4MV	4	123	8.45 x 15	6 ps	4008	3277
R	4MV	4	123	8.45 x 15	6pht4	4119	3652
R	4MV	4	126	8.85 x 15	6 ps	4246	4054
R	4MV	4	126	8.85 x 15	6 ps	4312	4270

YEAR	MODEL	ENGINE						
		CYLS	BORE	STROKE	DISPL	HP@RPM	C.R.	VLV
	Riviera	V8	4.188	3.90	429.7	360@5000	10.25	OH
	Optional engines:							
	(1)	V8	3.75	3.85	340.2	260@4000	10.25	OH
	(2)	V8	4.188	3.90	429.7	360@5000	10.25	OH
1968	Special Deluxe, 43300	V6	3.875	3.53	249.8	155@4200	8.5	OH
	Skylark, 43500	V6	3.875	3.53	249.8	155@4200	8.5	OH
	Special Deluxe, 43400 (1)	V8	3.80	3.85	349.3	230@4400	9.0	OH
	Skylark, 43500	V8	3.80	3.85	349.3	230@4400	9.0	OH
	Skylark Custom, 44400 (1)	V8	3.80	3.85	349.3	230@4400	9.0	OH
	Gran Sport 350	V8	3.80	3.85	349.3	230@4400	9.0	OH
	Gran Sport 400	V8	4.04	3.90	400.0	340@5000	10.25	OH
	Sport Wagon, 44400 (1, 2)	V8	3.80	3.85	349.3	230@4400	9.0	OH
	LaSabre, 45200 (1)	V8	3.80	3.85	349.3	230@4400	9.0	OH
	LeSabre Custom (1)	V8	3.80	3.85	349.3	230@4400	9.0	OH
	Wildcat, 46400	V8	4.188	3.90	429.7	360@5000	10.25	OH
	Wildcat Custom, 46600	V8	4.188	3.90	429.7	360@5000	10.25	OH
	Electra 225, 48200	V8	4.188	3.90	429.7	360@5000	10.25	OH
	Electra 225 Custom, 48400	V8	4.188	3.90	429.7	360@5000	10.25	OH
	Riviera	V8	4.188	3.90	429.7	360@5000	10.25	OH
	Optional engines:							
	(1)	V8	3.80	3.85	349.3	280@4600	10.25	OH
	(2)	V8	4.04	3.90	400.0	340@5000	10.25	OH
1969	Special Deluxe	V6	3.875	3.53	249.8	155@4200	8.5	OH
	Skylark	V6	3.875	3.53	249.8	155@4200	8.5	OH
	Special Deluxe (2)	V8	3.80	3.85	349.3	230@4400	8.5	OH
	Skylark	V8	3.80	3.85	349.3	230@4400	8.5	OH
	Skylark Custom	V8	3.80	3.85	349.3	230@4400	8.5	OH
	California, GS (1)	V8	3.80	3.85	349.3	280@4600	10.25	OH
	GS-350 (1)	V8	3.80	3.85	349.3	280@4600	10.25	OH
	GS-400	V8	4.04	3.90	400.0	340@5000	10.25	OH
	Sportwagon (1)	V8	3.80	3.85	349.3	230@4400	8.5	OH
	LeSabre (2)	V8	3.80	3.85	349.3	230@4400	8.5	OH
	LeSabre Custom	V8	3.80	3.85	349.3	230@4400	8.5	OH
	Wildcat	V8	4.188	3.90	429.7	360@5000	10.25	OH
	Wildcat Custom	V8	4.188	3.90	429.7	360@5000	10.25	OH
	Electra 225	V8	4.188	3.90	429.7	360@5000	10.25	OH
	Electra 225 Custom	V8	4.188	3.90	429.7	360@5000	10.25	OH
	Riviera	V8	4.188	3.90	429.7	360@5000	10.25	OH

MFR	CARBURETOR MODEL	VEN	WHEEL-BASE	TIRES	BODY	WEIGHT	PRICE
R	4MV	4	119	8.45 x 15	6pht2	4189	4469
R	7026046	2					
R	4MV	4					
R	MV	1	116/112	7.75 x 14	6 ps	3217	2564
R	MV	1	116/112	7.75 x 14	6 ps	3282	2666
R	2GV	2	116/112/	7.75 x 14/	6 ps		2669
			121	8.25 x 14			
R	2GV	2	116/112	7.75 x 14	6 ps	3435	2771
R	2GV	2	116/112	7.75 x 14	6 ps	3377	2924
R	2GV	2	112	7.75 x 14	6pht2	3375	2926
R	4MV	4	112	7.75 x 14	6pht2	3514	3127
R	2GV	2	121	8.25 x 14/	6psw4	3975	3341
				8.55 x 14			
R	2GV	2	123	8.45 x 15	6 ps	3946	3141
R	2GV	2	123	8.45 x 15	6 ps	3950	3235
R	4MV	4	126	8.45 x 15	6 ps	4076	3416
R	4MV	4	126	8.45 x 15	6pht4	4162	3791
R	4MV	4	126	8.85 x 15	6 ps	4253	4200
R	4MV	4	126	8.85 x 15	6 ps	4304	4415
R	4MV	4	119	8.45 x 15	6pht2	4222	4615
R	4MV	4					
R	4MV	4					
R	MV	1	116/112	7.75 x 14	6 ps	3182	2613
R	MV	1	116/112	7.75 x 14	6 ps	3209	2715
R	2GV	2	116/112/	7.75 x 14/	6 ps		2724
			121	8.55 x 14			
R	2GV	2	116/112	7.75 x 14	6 ps		2826
R	2GV	2	116/112	7.75 x 14	6 ps	3397	2978
R	4MV	4	112	7.75 x 14	6 psc		
R	4MV	4	112	7.75 x 14	6pht2	3406	2980
			112	7.75 x 14	6pht2	3549	3181
R	2GV	2	121	8.55 x 14	6psw4	4106	3465
R	2GV	2	123.2	8.55 x 15	6 ps	3966	3216
R	2GV	2	123.2	8.55 x 15	6 ps	3941	3310
R	4MV	4	123.2	8.55 x 15	6 ps	4102	3491
R	4MV	4	123.2	8.55 x 15	6pht2	4134	3817
R	4MV	4	119	8.55 x 15	6 ps	4238	4302
R	4MV	4	119	8.55 x 15	6 ps	4281	4517
R	4MV	4	119	8.55 x 15	6 psc	4199	4701

YEAR	MODEL	ENGINE						
		CYLS	BORE	STROKE	DISPL	HP@RPM	C.R.	VLV
	Optional engines:							
	(1)	V8	3.80	3.85	349.3	280@4600	10.25	OH
	(2)	V8	4.04	3.90	400.0	340@5000	10.25	OH

MFR	CARBURETOR MODEL	VEN	WHEEL-BASE	TIRES	BODY	WEIGHT	PRICE
R	4MV	4					

YEAR	MODEL	ENGINE						
		CYLS	BORE	STROKE	DISPL	HP@RPM	C.R.	VLV

CADILLAC – – Cadillac Motor Car Division, General Motors Corp., Detroit, Mich., 1903+

YEAR	MODEL	CYLS	BORE	STROKE	DISPL	HP@RPM	C.R.	VLV
1930	353	V8	3.375	4.938	353.0	95@3000	5.15	L
	452	V16	3.00	4.00	452.4	150@3200	5.5	OH
1931	355	V8	3.375	4.938	353.0	95@3000	5.35	L
	370	V12	3.125	4.00	368.0	134@3400	5.27	OH
	452	V16	3.00	4.00	452.4	165@3400	5.11	OH
1932	355B	V8	3.375	4.938	353.0	115@3000	5.38	L
	370B	V12	3.125	4.00	368.0	135@3400	5.3	OH
	452B	V16	3.00	4.00	452.4	165@3500	5.35	OH
1933	355C	V8	3.375	4.938	353.0	115@3000	5.4	L
	370C	V12	3.125	4.00	368.0	135@3400	5.6	OH
	452C	V16	3.00	4.00	452.4	165@3400	5.7	OH
1934	355D	V8	3.375	4.938	353.0	130@3400	6.25	L
	370D	V12	3.125	4.00	368.0	150@3600	6.25	OH
	452D	V16	3.00	4.00	452.4	180@3800	6.25	OH
1935	355D	V8	3.375	4.938	353.0	130@3400	6.25	L
	370D	V12	3.125	4.00	368.0	150@3600	6.00	OH
	452D	V16	3.00	4.00	452.4	185@3800	6.00	OH
1936	60	V8	3.375	4.50	322.2	125@3400	6.25	L
	70	V8	3.50	4.50	346.0	135@3400	6.25	L
	75	V8	3.50	4.50	346.0	135@3400	6.25	L
	80	V12	3.125	4.00	368.0	150@3600	6.00	OH
	85	V12	3.125	4.00	368.0	150@3600	6.00	OH
	90	V16	3.00	4.00	452.4	185@3800	6.00	OH
1937	37 - 60	V8	3.50	4.50	346.4	135@3400	6.25	L
	37 - 60	V8	3.50	4.50	346.4	135@3400	6.25	L
	37 - 70	V8	3.50	4.50	346.4	135@3400	6.25	L
	37 - 75	V8	3.50	4.50	346.4	135@3400	6.25	L
	37 - 85	V12	3.125	4.00	368.0	150@3600	6.00	OH
	37 - 90	V16	3.00	4.00	452.4	185@3800	6.00	OH
1938	38 - 60	V8	3.50	4.50	346.4	135@3400	6.25	L
	38 - 60S	V8	3.50	4.50	346.4	135@3400	6.25	L
	38 - 65	V8	3.50	4.50	346.4	135@3400	6.25	L
	38 - 75, Fleetwood	V8	3.50	4.50	346.4	135@3400	6.25	L
	38 - 90	V16	3.25	3.25	431.4	175@3600	6.75	L
1939	39 - 61	V8	3.50	4.50	364.4	135@3400	6.25	L
	39 - 60S, Special	V8	3.50	4.50	364.4	135@3400	6.25	L
	39 - 75, Fleetwood	V8	3.50	4.50	364.4	140@3400	6.70	L

MFR	CARBURETOR MODEL	VEN	WHEEL-BASE	TIRES	BODY	WEIGHT	PRICE
O			140	7.00 x 19	5 ps	5055	3695
O			148	7.00 x 19	5 ps	5835	5950
O			134	6.50 x 19	5 ps	4660	2795
O			140	7.00 x 19	5 ps	5230	3895
O			148	7.00 x 19	5 ps	5850	5950
O		1	134/140	7.00 x 17	5 ps	4885	2895
D	51	2 x 1	134/140	7.50 x 17	5 ps	5175	3595
D	51	2 x 1	143/149	7.50 x 18	5 ps	5625	4595
O		1	134/140	7.00 x 17	5 ps	5000	2895
D	51	2 x 1	134/140	7.50 x 17	5 ps	5335	3595
D	51	2 x 1	143/149	7.50 x 17	5 ps	6070	6250
D	X8244	1	128/136/	7.00 x 17	5 ps	4715	2625
			146				
D	51	2 x 1	146	7.50 x 17	5 ps	5735	4195
D	51	2 x 1	154	7.50 x 17	7 ps	6190	7100
O			128/136/	7.00 x 17	5 ps	4715	2445
			146				
D	51	2 x 1	146	7.50 x 17	5 ps	5735	3995
D	51	2 x 1	154	7.50 x 17	5 ps	6085	7000
S	EE25		121	7.00 x 16	5 ps	4010	1695
S	EE25		131	7.50 x 16	5 ps	4670	2445
S	EE25		138	7.50 x 16	5 ps	4805	2645
D	51	2 x 1	131	7.50 x 16	5 ps	4945	3145
D	51	2 x 1	138	7.50 x 16	5 ps	5115	3345
D	51	2 x 1	154	7.50 x 17	7 ps	6085	7450
S	AA25		124	7.00 x 16	5 ps	3845	1790
S	AA25		131	7.00 x 16	5 ps	4385	2190
S	AA25		131	7.50 x 16	5 ps	4420	2695
S	AA25		138	7.50 x 16	5 ps	4745	2915
D	51	2 x 1	138	7.50 x 16	5 ps	5050	3635
D	51	2 x 1	154	7.50 x 17	5 ps	6085	7595
S	AAV25		124	7.00 x 16	5 ps	3940	1780
S	AAV25		127	7.00 x 16	5 ps	4170	2090
S	AAV25		132	7.50 x 16	5 ps	4540	2290
S	AAV25		141	7.50 x 16	5 ps	4865	3080
C	WDO-407S	2 x 2	141	7.50 x 16	5 ps	5105	5140
S	AAV26	2	126	7.00 x 16	5 ps	3770	1680
S	AAV26	2	127	7.00 x 16	5 ps	4110	2090
S	AAV26	2	141	7.50 x 16	5 ps	4785	2995

YEAR	MODEL	ENGINE						
		CYLS	BORE	STROKE	DISPL	HP@RPM	C.R.	VLV
	39 - 90	V16	3.25	3.25	431.4	185@3600	6.75	L
1940	40 - 60S, Special	V8	3.50	4.50	364.4	135@3400	6.25	L
	40 - 62	V8	3.50	4.50	364.4	135@3400	6.25	L
	40 - 72, Fleetwood	V8	3.50	4.50	364.4	140@3400	6.70	L
	40 - 75, Fleetwood	V8	3.50	4.50	364.4	140@3400	6.70	L
	40 - 90	V16	3.25	3.25	431.4	185@3600	6.75	L
1941	41 - 61	V8	3.50	4.50	346.4	150@3400	7.25	L
	41 - 62	V8	3.50	4.50	346.4	150@3400	7.25	L
	41 - 63	V8	3.50	4.50	346.4	150@3400	7.25	L
	41 - 60S, Special	V8	3.50	4.50	346.4	150@3400	7.25	L
	41 - 67	V8	3.50	4.50	346.4	150@3400	7.25	L
	41 - 75, Fleetwood	V8	3.50	4.50	346.4	150@3400	7.25	L
1942	42 - 60S	V8	3.50	4.50	346.4	150@3400	7.25	L
	42 - 61	V8	3.50	4.50	346.4	150@3400	7.25	L
	42 - 62	V8	3.50	4.50	346.4	150@3400	7.25	L
	42 - 63	V8	3.50	4.50	346.4	150@3400	7.25	L
	42 - 67	V8	3.50	4.50	346.4	150@3400	7.25	L
	42 - 75, Fleetwood	V8	3.50	4.50	346.4	150@3400	7.25	L
1946	61	V8	3.50	4.50	346.4	150@3600	7.25	L
	62	V8	3.50	4.50	346.4	150@3600	7.25	L
	60S, Special	V8	3.50	4.50	346.4	150@3600	7.25	L
	75, Fleetwood	V8	3.50	4.50	346.4	150@3600	7.25	L
1947	61	V8	3.50	4.50	346.4	150@3600	7.25	L
	62	V8	3.50	4.50	346.4	150@3600	7.25	L
	60S, Special	V8	3.50	4.50	346.4	150@3600	7.25	L
	75, Fleetwood	V8	3.50	4.50	346.4	150@3600	7.25	L
1948	61	V8	3.50	4.50	346.4	150@3600	7.25	L
	62	V8	3.50	4.50	346.4	150@3600	7.25	L
	60S, Special	V8	3.50	4.50	346.4	150@3600	7.25	L
	75, Fleetwood	V8	3.50	4.50	346.4	150@3600	7.25	L
1949	61	V8	3.812	3.625	331.1	160@3800	7.50	OH
	62	V8	3.812	3.625	331.1	160@3800	7.50	OH
	60S, Special	V8	3.812	3.625	331.1	160@3800	7.50	OH
	75, Fleetwood	V8	3.812	3.625	331.1	160@3800	7.50	OH
1950	61	V8	3.812	3.625	331.1	160@3800	7.50	OH
	62	V8	3.812	3.625	331.1	160@3800	7.50	OH
	60S, Special	V8	3.812	3.625	331.1	160@3800	7.50	OH
	75S, Fleetwood	V8	3.812	3.625	331.1	160@3800	7.50	OH
1951	61	V8	3.812	3.625	331.1	160@3800	7.50	OH
	62	V8	3.812	3.625	331.1	160@3800	7.50	OH
	60, Special	V8	3.812	3.625	331.1	160@3800	7.50	OH

MFR	CARBURETOR MODEL	VEN	WHEEL-BASE	TIRES	BODY	WEIGHT	PRICE
C	WDO-407S	2 x 2	141	7.50 x 16	5 ps	5190	5140
S	AAV26	2	127	7.00 x 16	5 ps	4070	2090
S	AAV26	2	129	7.00 x 16	5 ps	4030	1745
S	AAV26	2	138	7.50 x 16	5 ps	4670	2670
S	AAV26	2	141	7.50 x 16	5 ps	4900	2995
C	WDO-407/408	2 x 2	141	7.50 x 16	5 ps	5190	5140
S	AAV26	2	126	7.00 x 15	5 ps	4065	1445
S	AAV26	2	126	7.00 x 15	5 ps	4030	1495
S	AAV26	2	126	7.00 x 15	5 ps	4140	1695
S	AAV26	2	126	7.00 x 15	5 ps	4230	2195
S	AAV26	2	139	7.50 x 16	5 ps	4555	2595
S	AAV26	2	141	7.50 x 16	5 ps	4900	2995
S	AAV26	2	133	7.00 x 15	5 ps	4310	2265
S	AAV26	2	126	7.00 x 15	5 ps	4115	1530
S	AAV26	2	129	7.00 x 15	5 ps	4185	1630
S	AAV26	2	126	7.00 x 15	5 ps	4115	1745
S	AAV26	2	139	7.50 x 16	5 ps	4605	2700
S	AAV26	2	136	7.50 x 16	5 ps	4750	3080
S	AAV26	2	126	7.00 x 15	5 ps	4145	1947
S	AAV26	2	129	7.00 x 15	5 ps	4251	2254
S	AAV26	2	133	7.00 x 15	5 ps	4348	2993
S	AAV26	2	136.2	7.50 x 16	5 ps	4848	4193
S	AAV26	2	126	7.00 x 15	5 ps	4138	2324
S	AAV26	2	129	7.00 x 15	5 ps	4201	2523
S	AAV26	2	133	7.00 x 15	5 ps	4351	3195
S	AAV26	2	136	7.50 x 16	5 ps	4836	4471
S	AAV26	2	126	8.20 x 15	5 ps	4145	2833
S	AAV26	2	126	8.20 x 15	5 ps	4180	2996
S	AAV26	2	133	8.20 x 15	5 ps	4370	3820
S	AAV26	2	136.2	7.50 x 16	5 ps	4865	4779
C	WCD-682S	2	126	8.20 x 15	5 ps	3910	2893
C	WCD-682S	2	126	8.20 x 15	5 ps	3951	3050
C	WCD-682S	2	133	8.20 x 15	5 ps	4124	3828
C	WCD-682S	2	136	7.50 x 16	5 ps	4580	4750
C	WCD-742S	2	122	8.00 x 15	5 ps	3822	2865
C	WCD-742S	2	126	8.00 x 15	5 ps	4012	3234
C	WCD-742S	2	130	8.00 x 15	5 ps	4136	3797
C	WCD-742S	2	146.5	8.20 x 15	7 ps	4555	4737
C	WCD-845S	2	122	7.60 x 15	5 ps	3839	2940
C	WCD-845S	2	126	8.00 x 15	5 ps	4062	3528
C	WCD-845S	2	130	8.00 x 15	5 ps	4234	4142

YEAR	MODEL	ENGINE						
		CYLS	BORE	STROKE	DISPL	HP@RPM	C.R.	VLV
	75, Fleetwood	V8	3.812	3.625	331.1	160@3800	7.50	OH
1952	62	V8	3.812	3.625	331.1	190@4000	7.50	OH
	60, Special	V8	3.812	3.625	331.1	190@4000	7.50	OH
	75, Fleetwood	V8	3.812	3.625	331.1	190@4000	7.50	OH
1953	60, Special	V8	3.812	3.625	331.1	210@4150	8.25	OH
	62	V8	3.812	3.625	331.1	210@4150	8.25	OH
	75, Fleetwood	V8	3.812	3.625	331.1	210@4150	8.25	OH
1954	60, Special	V8	3.812	3.625	331.1	230@4400	8.25	OH
	62	V8	3.812	3.625	331.1	230@4400	8.25	OH
	75, Fleetwood	V8	3.812	3.625	331.1	230@4400	8.25	OH
	Eldorado	V8	3.812	3.625	331.1	230@4400	8.25	OH
1955	60, Special	V8	3.812	3.625	331.1	250@4600	9.10	OH
	62	V8	3.812	3.625	331.1	250@4600	9.10	OH
	75, Fleetwood	V8	3.812	3.625	331.1	250@4600	9.10	OH
	Eldorado	V8	3.812	3.625	331.1	270@4600	9.10	OH
1956	62	V8	4.00	3.625	364.4	285@4600	9.75	OH
	60, Special	V8	4.00	3.625	363.4	285@4600	9.75	OH
	75, Fleetwood	V8	4.00	3.625	363.4	285@4600	9.75	OH
	Eldorado	V8	4.00	3.625	363.4	305@4700	9.75	OH
1957	62	V8	4.00	3.625	364.4	300@4800	10.0	OH
	60, Special	V8	4.00	3.625	364.4	300@4800	10.0	OH
	75, Fleetwood	V8	4.00	3.625	364.4	300@4800	10.0	OH
	Eldorado Brougham	V8	4.00	3.625	364.4	300@4800	10.0	OH
	Eldorado (1)	V8	4.00	3.625	364.4	300@4800	10.0	OH
	Optional engine:							
	(1)	V8	4.00	3.625	364.4	325@4800	10.0	OH
1958	62	V8	4.00	3.625	364.4	310@4800	10.25	OH
	60, Special	V8	4.00	3.625	364.4	310@4800	10.25	OH
	75, Fleetwood	V8	4.00	3.625	364.4	310@4800	10.25	OH
	Eldorado	V8	4.00	3.625	364.4	310@4800	10.25	OH
	Eldorado Brougham	V8	4.00	3.625	364.4	310@4800	10.25	OH
1959	62	V8	4.00	3.875	389.6	325@4800	10.50	OH
	60, Special	V8	4.00	3.875	389.6	325@4800	10.50	OH
	75, Fleetwood	V8	4.00	3.875	389.6	325@4800	10.50	OH
	De Ville	V8	4.00	3.875	389.6	325@4800	10.50	OH
	Eldorado	V8	4.00	3.875	389.6	345@4800		OH
	Eldorado Brougham	V8	4.00	3.875	389.6	325@4800	10.50	OH
1960	62	V8	4.00	3.875	389.6	325@4800	10.50	OH
	De Ville	V8	4.00	3.875	389.6	325@4800	10.50	OH

MFR	CARBURETOR MODEL	VEN	WHEEL-BASE	TIRES	BODY	WEIGHT	PRICE
C	WCD-845S	2	146.8	8.20 x 15	5 ps	4621	5200
C	WFCB-896S	4	126	8.00 x 15	5 ps	4140	3684
C	WFCB-896S	4	130	8.00 x 15	5 ps	4255	4323
C	WFCB-896S	4	146.8	8.20 x 15	5 ps	4698	5428
C	WCFB-2005S	4	130	8.00 x 15	5 ps	4415	4305
C	WCFB-2005S	4	126	8.00 x 15	5 ps	4225	3666
C	WCFB-2005S	4	147	8.20 x 15	8 ps	4830	5408
C	WCFB-2109S	4	133	8.20 x 15	5 ps	4500	4683
C	WCFB-2109S	4	129	8.20 x 15	5 ps	4370	3933
C	WCFB-2109S	4	149.8	8.20 x 15	8 ps	5055	5875
C	WCFB-2109S	4	129	8.20 x 15	6pcv2	4809	6286
C	WCFB-2185S	4	133	8.00 x 15	5 ps	4540	4728
C	WCFB-2185S	4	129	8.00 x 15	5 ps	4370	3977
C	WCFB-2185S	4	149.8	8.20 x 15	8 ps	5020	6187
R	7007240+	2 x 4	129	8.20 x 15	6pcv2	4809	6286
	7007241						
C	WCFB-2333S	4	129	8.00 x 15	6 ps	4370	4241
C	WCFB-2333S	4	133	8.00 x 15	6 ps	4540	4992
C	WCFB-2333S	4	149.8	8.20 x 15	8 ps	5015	6558
C	2371S +	2 x 4	129	8.20 x 15	6pht4	4665	6556
	2372S						
C	2479S	4	129.5	8.20 x 15	6pht4	4595	4781
C	2479S	4	133	8.20 x 15	6pht4	4755	5614
C	2479S	4	149.8	8.20 x 15	6pht4	5340	7440
C	2479S	4	129.5	8.20 x 15	6pht4		13,074
C	2479S	4	129.5	8.20 x 15	6pht2	4810	7286
		2 x 4					
C	AFB-2896	4	129.5	8.00 x 15	6pht4	4675	4891
C	AFB-2896	4	133	8.00 x 14	6pht4	4930	6232
C	AFB-2896	4	149.8	8.20 x 15	6 ps	5360	8460
C	AFB-2896	4	129.5	8.20 x 15	6pht2	4910	7500
C	AFB-2896	4	126	8.40 x 15	6pht4	5315	13,074
C	2814S	4	130	8.00 x 15	6 ps	4770	5080
C	2814S	4	130	8.00 x 15	6 ps	4890	6233
C	2814S	4	149.8	8.20 x 15	9 ps	5490	9533
C	2814S	4	130	8.20 x 15	6pht4	4825	5498
		3 x 2	130	8.20 x 15	6pht2		7401
C	2814S	4	130	8.40 x 15	6pht4		13,075
C	2814S	4	130	8.00 x 15	6 ps	4775	5080
C	2814S	4	130	8.00 x 15	6pht4	4815	5498

YEAR	MODEL	ENGINE						
		CYLS	BORE	STROKE	DISPL	HP@RPM	C.R.	VLV
	Eldorado	V8	4.00	3.875	389.6	345@4800	10.50	OH
	Eldorado Brougham	V8	4.00	3.875	389.6	325@4800	10.50	OH
	60, Special	V8	4.00	3.875	389.6	325@4800	10.50	OH
	75, Fleetwood	V8	4.00	3.875	389.6	325@4800	10.50	OH
1961	62	V8	4.00	3.875	389.6	325@4800	10.50	OH
	60, Special	V8	4.00	3.875	389.6	325@4800	10.50	OH
	75, Fleetwood	V8	4.00	3.875	389.6	325@4800	10.50	OH
	Eldorado	V8	4.00	3.875	389.6	325@4800	10.50	OH
	De Ville	V8	4.00	3.875	389.6	325@4800	10.50	OH
1962	62	V8	4.00	3.875	389.6	325@4800	10.50	OH
	60, Special	V8	4.00	3.875	389.6	325@4800	10.50	OH
	75, Fleetwood	V8	4.00	3.875	389.6	325@4800	10.50	OH
	De Ville	V8	4.00	3.875	389.6	325@4800	10.50	OH
	Eldorado	V8	4.00	3.875	389.6	325@4800	10.50	OH
1963	62	V8	4.00	3.875	389.6	325@4800	10.50	OH
	60, Special	V8	4.00	3.875	389.6	325@4800	10.50	OH
	75, Fleetwood	V8	4.00	3.875	389.6	325@4800	10.50	OH
	De Ville	V8	4.00	3.875	389.6	325@4800	10.50	OH
	Eldorado	V8	4.00	3.875	389.6	325@4800	10.50	OH
1964	62	V8	4.125	4.00	427.6	340@4600	10.50	OH
	60, Special	V8	4.125	4.00	427.6	340@4600	10.50	OH
	75, Fleetwood	V8	4.125	4.00	427.6	340@4600	10.50	OH
	De Ville	V8	4.125	4.00	427.6	340@4600	10.50	OH
	Eldorado	V8	4.125	4.00	427.6	340@4600	10.50	OH
1965	Calais	V8	4.125	4.00	427.6	340@4600	10.50	OH
	De Ville	V8	4.125	4.00	427.6	340@4600	10.50	OH
	Eldorado	V8	4.125	4.00	427.6	340@4600	10.50	OH
	60, Special, Fleetwood	V8	4.125	4.00	427.6	340@4600	10.50	OH
	75, Fleetwood	V8	4.125	4.00	427.6	340@4600	10.50	OH
1966	Calais	V8	4.125	4.00	427.6	340@4600	10.50	OH
	De Ville	V8	4.125	4.00	427.6	340@4600	10.50	OH
	Eldorado	V8	4.125	4.00	427.6	340@4600	10.50	OH
	Fleetwood, Brougham	V8	4.125	4.00	427.6	340@4600	10.50	OH
	60, Special	V8	4.125	4.00	427.6	340@4600	10.50	OH
	75, Fleetwood	V8	4.125	4.00	427.6	340@4600	10.50	OH
1967	Calais	V8	4.125	4.00	427.6	340@4600	10.50	OH
	De Ville	V8	4.125	4.00	427.6	340@4600	10.50	OH
	Fleetwood Eldorado	V8	4.125	4.00	427.6	340@4600	10.50	OH
	60, Special	V8	4.125	4.00	427.6	340@4600	10.50	OH
	Fleetwood Brougham	V8	4.125	4.00	427.6	340@4600	10.50	OH
	75, Fleetwood	V8	4.125	4.00	427.6	340@4600	10.50	OH

MFR	CARBURETOR MODEL	VEN	WHEEL-BASE	TIRES	BODY	WEIGHT	PRICE
C		3 x 2	130	8.20 x 15	6pht2		7401
C	2814S	4	130	8.20 x 15	6pht4		13,075
C	2814S	4	130	8.00 x 15	6 ps	4880	6233
C	2814S	4	149.8	8.20 x 15	6 ps	5475	9533
R	701930	4	129.5	8.00 x 15	6 ps	4680	5080
R	701930	4	129.5	8.00 x 15	6 ps	4770	6233
R	701930	4	149.8	8.20 x 15	6 ps	5390	9533
R	701930	4	129.5	8.20 x 15	6pcv2	5950	6477
R	701930	4	129.5	8.00 x 15	6pht4	4710	5498
R	701930	4	129.5	8.00 x 15	6 ps	4640	5213
R	701930	4	129.5	8.00 x 15	6 ps	4710	6366
R	701930	4	149.8	8.20 x 15	9 ps	5325	9722
R	701930	4	129.5	8.00 x 15	6 ps	4660	5631
R	701930	4	129.5	8.00 x 15	6pcv2	4620	6610
C	3840	4	129.5	8.00 x 15	6 ps	4610	5214
C	3840	4	129.5	8.00 x 15	6 ps	4690	6366
C	3840	4	149.8	8.20 x 15	9 ps	5240	9724
C	3840	4	129.5	8.00 x 15	6 ps	4650	5633
C	3840	4	129.5	8.00 x 15	6pcv2	4640	6608
C	AFB-3655S	4	129.5	8.00 x 15	6 ps	4575	5236
C	AFB-3655S	4	129.5	8.00 x 15	6 ps	4680	6388
C	AFB-3655S	4	149.8	8.20 x 15	9 ps	5215	9746
C	AFB-3655S	4	129.5	8.00 x 15	6 ps	4600	5655
C	AFB-3655S	4	129.5	8.00 x 15	6pcv2	4605	6630
C	AFB-3903S	4	129.5	8.00 x 15	6 ps	4490	5247
C	AFB-3903S	4	129.5	8.00 x 15	6 ps	4555	5666
C	AFB-3903S	4	129.5	9.00 x 15	6 ps	4670	6479
C	AFB-3903S	4	129.5	8.00 x 15	6 ps	4690	6366
C	AFB-3903S	4	149.8	8.20 x 15	9 ps	5190	9553
R	7026030	4	129.5	9.00 x 15	6 ps	4460	5171
R	7026030	4	129.5	9.00 x 15	6 ps	4535	5581
R	7026030	4	129.5	9.00 x 15	6pcv2	4500	6631
R	7026030	4	133	9.00 x 15	6 ps	4665	6695
R	7026030	4	133	9.00 x 15	6 ps	4615	6378
R	7026030	4	149.8	8.20 x 15	9 ps	5320	10,312
R	7027230	4	129.5	9.00 x 15	6 ps	4499	4865
R	7027230	4	129.5	9.00 x 15	6 ps	4536	5255
R	7027230	4	120	9.00 x 15	6 ps	4500	5875
R	7027230	4	133	9.00 x 15	6 ps	4685	6423
R	7027230	4	133	9.00 x 15	6 ps	4735	6739
R	7027230	4	149.8	8.20 x 15	9 ps	5335	10,360

YEAR	MODEL	ENGINE						
		CYLS	BORE	STROKE	DISPL	HP@RPM	C.R.	VLV
1968	Calais	V8	4.30	4.06	472.0	375@4400	10.50	OH
	De Ville	V8	4.30	4.06	472.0	375@4400	10.50	OH
	Fleetwood Eldorado	V8	4.30	4.06	472.0	375@4400	10.50	OH
	60, Special	V8	4.30	4.06	472.0	375@4400	10.50	OH
	Fleetwood Brougham	V8	4.30	4.06	472.0	375@4400	10.50	OH
	75, Fleetwood	V8	4.30	4.06	472.0	375@4400	10.50	OH
1969	Calais	V8	4.30	4.06	472.0	375@4400	10.50	OH
	De Ville	V8	4.30	4.06	472.0	375@4400	10.50	OH
	Fleetwood Eldorado	V8	4.30	4.06	472.0	375@4400	10.50	OH
	60, Special Fleetwood	V8	4.30	4.06	472.0	375@4400	10.50	OH
	Fleetwood Brougham	V8	4.30	4.06	472.0	375@4400	10.50	OH
	75, Fleetwood	V8	4.30	4.06	472.0	375@4400	10.50	OH

CHADWICK — — Chadwick Engineering Works, Pottstown, Pa., 1960

YEAR	MODEL	CYLS	BORE	STROKE	DISPL	HP@RPM	C.R.	VLV
1960	300	1	2.83	2.875	18.1	13		OH
	The Chadwick used a BMW motorcycle engine. This is the second Chadwick built in Pottstown, the first was in 1907-16.							

CHARLES TOWN-ABOUT — — Stinson Aircraft Tool & Engineering Co., San Diego, Cal., 1958-59

YEAR	MODEL	CYLS	BORE	STROKE	DISPL	HP@RPM	C.R.	VLV
1958	Battery-powered electric					two motors		
	This electric was built on Karmann-Ghia chassis.					@ 3.2		

CHECKER — — Checker Motors Corp., Kalamazoo, Mich., 1960+

YEAR	MODEL	CYLS	BORE	STROKE	DISPL	HP@RPM	C.R.	VLV
1960	Superba	6	3.312	4.375	226.0	80@3100	7.3	L
	Optional engine:	6	3.312	4.375	226.0	122@4000	8.0	OH
1961	Superba	6	3.312	4.375	226.0	80@3100	7.3	L
	Marathon	6	3.312	4.375	226.0	80@3100	7.3	L
	Optional engine for both lines:	6	3.312	4.375	226.0	122@4000	8.0	OH
1962	Superba	6	3.312	4.375	226.0	80@3100	7.3	L
	Marathon	6	3.312	4.375	226.0	80@3100	7.3	L
	Optional engine for both lines:	6	3.312	4.375	226.0	122@4000	8.0	OH
1963	Superba	6	3.312	4.375	226.0	80@3100	7.3	L
	Marathon	6	3.312	4.375	226.0	80@3100	7.3	L
	Optional engine for both lines:	6	3.312	4.375	226.0	141@4400	8.0	OH
1964	Marathon	6	3.312	4.375	226.0	80@3100	7.3	L
	Optional engine:	6	3.312	4.375	226.0	141@4400	8.0	OH
1965	Marathon	6	3.875	3.25	230.0	140@4000	8.5	OH

MFR	CARBURETOR MODEL	VEN	WHEEL-BASE	TIRES	BODY	WEIGHT	PRICE
R	7028230	4	129.5	9.00 x 15	6pht4	4640	5491
R	7028230	4	129.5	9.00 x 15	6 ps	4680	5785
R	7028230	4	120	9.00 x 15	5pht2	4590	6277
R	7028230	4	133	9.00 x 15	6 ps	4795	6583
R	7028230	4	133	9.00 x 15	6pht4	4805	6899
R	7028230	4	149.8	9.00 x 15	9 ps	5300	10,629
R	7028230	4	129.5	9.00 x 15	6pht4	4577	5642
R	7028230	4	129.5	9.00 x 15	6 ps	4635	5936
R	7028230	4	120	9.00 x15	5pht2	4537	6693
R	7028230	4	133	9.00 x 15	6 ps	4711	6761
R	7028230	4	133	9.00 x 15	6 ps	4770	7110
R	7028230	4	149.8	9.00 x 15	9 ps	5430	10,841
			58	4.80 x 10			
			94.5	5.60 x 15	4pht2	1875	
			120	6.70 x 15	6 ps	3410	2542
C	AS-2858S	1	120	6.70 x 15	6 ps	3320	2542
C	AS-2858S	1	120	6.70 x 15	6 ps	3345	2650
Z	O-12469	1	120	6.70 x 15/	6 ps	3320	2642
				7.10 x 15			
Z	O-12469	1	120	6.70 x 15/	6 ps	3345	2793
				7.10 x 15			
Z	O-12469	1	120	6.70 x 15/	6 ps	3485	2642
				7.10 x 15			
Z	O-12469	1	120	6.70 x 15/	6 ps	3485	2793
				7.10 x 15			
C	3933	1	120	6.70 x 15/	6 ps	3625	2814
				7.10 x 15			
R	7023096	2					
C	3933	1	120	7.10 x 15	6 ps	3360	2874

YEAR	MODEL	ENGINE						
		CYLS	BORE	STROKE	DISPL	HP@RPM	C.R.	VLV
	Optional engine:	V8	3.875	3.00	283.0	195@4800	9.25	OH
1966	Marathon	6	3.875	3.25	230.0	140@4400	8.25	OH
	Optional engine:	V8	3.875	3.00	283.0	195@4600	9.25	OH
1967	Marathon	6	3.875	3.25	230.0	140@4000	8.25	OH
	Optional engine:	V8	3.875	3.00	283.0	195@4400	9.25	OH
1968	Marathon	V8	3.875	3.25	283.0	200@4600	9.0	OH
	Optional engines:	V8	4.001	3.25	326.9	235@4800	9.0	OH
		6	3.875	3.25	230.0	140@4400	8.5	OH
1969	Marathon	V8	4.001	3.25	326.9	235@4800	9.0	OH
	Optional engines:	6	3.875	3.53	249.8	155@4200	8.5	OH
		6	3.875	3.25	230.0	141@4200	8.5	OH
CHEVROLET — — General Motors Corp., Detroit, Mich., 1911+								
1930	Universal, AD	6	3.312	3.75	194.0	50@2600	5.02	OH
1931	Independence, AE	6	3.312	3.75	194.0	50@2600	5.02	OH
1932	Confederate, BA	6	3.312	3.75	194.0	60@3000	5.2	OH
	Deluxe, BA	6	3.312	3.75	194.0	60@3000	5.2	OH
1933	Standard, CC	6	3.312	3.50	181.0	60@3000	5.2	OH
	Eagle, CA	6	3.312	3.75	194.0	65@2800	5.2	OH
1934	Standard, DC	6	3.312	3.50	181.0	60@3000	5.2	OH
	Master, DA	6	3.312	4.00	206.8	80@3300	5.45	OH
1935	Standard, EC	6	3.312	4.00	206.8	74@3200	5.45	OH
	Master, ED	6	3.312	4.00	206.8	80@3300	5.45	OH
	Master, EA	6	3.312	4.00	206.8	80@3300	5.45	OH
1936	Standard, FC	6	3.312	4.00	206.8	79@3200	6.0	OH
	Master, FD	6	3.312	4.00	206.8	79@3200	6.0	OH
	Master, FA	6	3.312	4.00	206.8	79@3200	6.0	OH
1937	Master, GB	6	3.50	3.75	216.5	85@3200	6.25	OH
	Master, Deluxe, GA	6	3.50	3.75	216.5	85@3200	6.25	OH
1938	Master, HB	6	3.50	3.75	216.5	85@3200	6.25	OH
	Master Deluxe, HA	6	3.50	3.75	216.5	85@3200	6.25	OH
1939	Master, JB	6	3.50	3.75	216.5	85@3200	6.25	OH
	Master Deluxe, JA	6	3.50	3.75	216.5	85@3200	6.25	OH
1940	Master, KB	6	3.50	3.75	216.5	85@3400	6.25	OH
	Master Deluxe, KH	6	3.50	3.75	216.5	85@3400	6.25	OH
	Special Deluxe, KA	6	3.50	3.75	216.5	85@3400	6.25	OH
1941	Master Deluxe, AG	6	3.50	3.75	216.5	90@3300	6.5	OH
	Special Deluxe, AH	6	3.50	3.75	216.5	90@3300	6.5	OH
1942	Stylemaster, BG	6	3.50	3.75	216.5	90@3300	6.5	OH
	Fleetmaster, BH	6	3.50	3.75	216.5	90@3300	6.5	OH
	Fleetline, BH	6	3.50	3.75	216.5	90@3300	6.5	OH

MFR	CARBURETOR MODEL	VEN	WHEEL-BASE	TIRES	BODY	WEIGHT	PRICE
R	7024100	1					
R	7023000	1	120	8.15 x 15	6 ps	3360	2874
R	7024100	2					
R		1	120	8.15 x 15	6 ps	3400	2874
R	7024186	2					
			120	8.15 x 15	6 ps	3390	3221
R		4					
R		4	120	8.15 x 15	6 ps		3290
R	7029017	1					
R	7029017	1					
C	150S	1	107	4.75 x 19	5 ps		675
C	150S	1	109	4.75 x 19	5 ps		635
C	150S	1	109	5.25 x 18	5 ps	2750	590
C	150S	1	109	5.25 x 18	5 ps	2850	630
C	W1	1	107	5.25 x 17	5 pc	2425	455
C	W1	1	110	5.25 x 18	5 ps	2830	565
C	W1	1	107	5.25 x 17	5 ps	2665	495
C	W1	1	112	5.50 x 17	5 ps	3080	640
C	284S	1	107	5.25 x 17	5 ps	2625	485
C	284S	1	113	5.50 x 17	5 ps	3055	640
C	284S	1	113	5.50 x 17	5 ps	3085	660
C	319S	1	109	5.25 x 17	5 ps	2775	575
C	319S	1	113	5.50 x 17	5 ps	3060	640
C	319S	1	113	5.50 x 17	5 ps	3110	660
C	W1	1	112.2	6.00 x 16	5 ps	2845	698
C	W1	1	112.2	6.00 x 16	5 ps	2935	770
C	W1	1	112.2	6.00 x 16	5 ps	2840	730
C	W1	1	112.2	6.00 x 16	5 ps	2915	796
C	W1-420S	1	112.2	6.00 x 16	5 ps	2805	689
C	W1-420S	1	112.2	6.00 x 16	5 ps	2875	745
C	W1-420S	1	113	6.00 x 16	5 ps	2930	740
C	W1-420S	1	113	6.00 x 16	5 ps	2965	725
C	W1-420S	1	113	6.00 x 16	5 ps	3010	802
C	W1-483S	1	116	6.00 x 16	5 ps	3090	795
C	W1-483S	1	116	6.00 x 16	5 ps	3125	851
C	W1-483S	1	116	6.00 x 16	5 ps	3110	840
C	W1-483S	1	116	6.00 x 16	5 ps	3145	895
C	W1-483S	1	116	6.00 x 16	5 ps	3105	880

YEAR	MODEL	ENGINE						
		CYLS	BORE	STROKE	DISPL	HP@RPM	C.R.	VLV
1946	Stylemaster	6	3.50	3.75	216.5	90@3300	6.5	OH
	Fleetmaster	6	3.50	3.75	216.5	90@3300	6.5	OH
	Fleetline	6	3.50	3.75	216.5	90@3300	6.5	OH
1947	Stylemaster	6	3.50	3.75	216.5	90@3300	6.5	OH
	Fleetmaster	6	3.50	3.75	216.5	90@3300	6.5	OH
	Fleetline	6	3.50	3.75	216.5	90@3300	6.5	OH
1948	Stylemaster, FJ	6	3.50	3.75	216.5	90@3300	6.5	OH
	Fleetmaster, FK	6	3.50	3.75	216.5	90@3300	6.5	OH
	Fleetline	6	3.50	3.75	216.5	90@3300	6.5	OH
1949	Special Styleline, GJ	6	3.50	3.75	216.5	90@3300	6.6	OH
	Deluxe Styleline, GK	6	3.50	3.75	216.5	90@3300	6.6	OH
	Fleetline Special, GJ	6	3.50	3.75	216.5	90@3300	6.6	OH
	Fleetline Special, GK	6	3.50	3.75	216.5	90@3300	6.6	OH
1950	Styleline Special, HJ	6	3.50	3.75	216.5	92@3400	6.6	OH
	Fleetline Special, HJ	6	3.50	3.75	216.5	92@3400	6.6	OH
	Styleline Deluxe, HK	6	3.50	3.75	216.5	92@3400	6.6	OH
	Fleetline Deluxe, HK	6	3.50	3.75	216.5	92@3400	6.6	OH
1951	Styleline Special, JJ	6	3.50	3.75	216.5	92@3400	6.6	OH
	Fleetline Special, JJ	6	3.50	3.75	216.5	92@3400	6.6	OH
	Styleline Deluxe, JK	6	3.50	3.75	216.5	92@3400	6.6	OH
	Fleetline Deluxe, JK	6	3.50	3.75	216.5	92@3400	6.6	OH
1952	Styleline Special, KJ	6	3.50	3.75	216.5	92@3400	6.6	OH
	Styleline Deluxe, KK	6	3.50	3.75	216.5	92@3400	6.6	OH
	Fleetline Deluxe, KK	6	3.50	3.75	216.5	92@3400	6.6	OH
1953	Special, 150	6	3.562	3.938	235.5	108@3600	7.1	OH
	Deluxe, 210	6	3.562	3.938	235.5	108@3600	7.1	OH
	Bel Air, 240	6	3.562	3.938	235.5	108@3600	7.1	OH
	Corvette, 290	6	3.562	3.938	235.5	150@4200	8.0	OH
1954	Special, 150	6	3.562	3.938	235.5	115@3700	7.5	OH
	Deluxe, 210	6	3.562	3.938	235.5	115@3700	7.5	OH
	Bel Air, 240	6	3.562	3.938	235.5	115@3700	7.5	OH
	Corvette, 290	6	3.562	3.938	235.5	150@4200	8.0	OH
1955	Special, 150	6	3.562	3.938	235.5	123@3800	7.5	OH
	210	6	3.562	3.938	235.5	123@3800	7.5	OH
	Bel Air	6	3.562	3.938	235.5	123@3800	7.5	OH
	Corvette, 2934	6	3.562	3.938	235.5	155@4200	8.0	OH
	Special, 150 (1)	V8	3.75	3.00	265.1	162@4400	8.0	OH
	210 (1)	V8	3.75	3.00	265.1	162@4400	8.0	OH
	Bel Air (1)	V8	3.75	3.00	265.1	162@4400	8.0	OH

MFR	CARBURETOR MODEL	VEN	WHEEL-BASE	TIRES	BODY	WEIGHT	PRICE
C	W1-574S	1	116	6.00 x 16	5 ps	3145	1072
C	W1-574S	1	116	6.00 x 16	5 ps	3165	1194
C	W1-574S	1	116	6.00 x 16	5 ps	3140	1165
C	W1-574S	1	116	6.00 x 16	5 ps	3075	1219
C	W1-574S	1	116	6.00 x 16	5 ps	3125	1286
C	W1-574S	1	116	6.00 x 16	5 ps	3125	1313
C	W1-574S	1	116	6.00 x 16	5 ps	3075	1219
C	W1-574S	1	116	6.00 x 16	5 ps	3125	1286
C	W1-574S	1	116	6.00 x 16	6 ps	3150	1492
C	W1-684S	1	115	6.70 x 15	6 ps	3090	1460
C	W1-684S	1	115	6.70 x 15	6 ps	3125	1539
C	W1-684S	1	115	6.70 x 15	6 ps	3095	1460
C	W1-684S	1	115	6.70 x 15	6 ps	3135	1539
R	7002050	1	115	6.70 x 15	6 ps	3120	1450
R	7002050	1	115	6.70 x 15	6 ps	3115	1450
R	7002050	1	115	6.70 x 15	6 ps	3150	1529
R	7002050	1	115	6.70 x 15	6 ps	3145	1529
R	7003152	1	115	6.70 x 15	6 ps	3130	1594
R	7003152	1	115	6.70 x 15	6 ps	3130	1594
R	7003152	1	115	6.70 x 15	6 ps	3140	1680
R	7003152	1	115	6.70 x 15	6 ps	3155	1680
R	7004447	1	115	6.70 x 15	6 ps	3115	1670
R	7004447	1	115	6.70 x 15	6 ps	3145	1761
R	7004447	1	115	6.70 x 15	6 ps2	3110	1707
R	7004915	1	115	6.70 x 15	6 ps	3215	1670
R	7004915	1	115	6.70 x 15	6 ps	3250	1761
R	7004915	1	115	6.70 x 15/	6 ps	3275	1874
				7.10 x 15			
			102	6.70 x 15	2pcv2	2705	3513
R	7005921	1	115	6.70 x 15	6 ps	3210	1680
R	7005921	1	115	6.70 x 15	6 ps	3230	1771
R	7005921	1	115	6.70 x 15/	6 ps	3255	1884
				7.10 x 15			
R	3706989	1	102	6.70 x 15	2pcv2	2705	3523
R	7007181	1	115	6.70 x 15	6 ps	3165	1728
R	7007181	1	115	6.70 x 15	6 ps	3180	1819
R	7007181	1	115	6.70 x 15	6 ps	3200	1932
C	3706989	3 x 1	102	6.70 x 15	2pcr	2650	2799
R	7008005	2	115	6.70 x 15	6 ps	3135	1827
R	7008005	2	115	6.70 x 15	6 ps	3150	1918
R	7008005	2	115	6.70 x 15	6 ps	3170	2031

YEAR	MODEL	ENGINE						
		CYLS	BORE	STROKE	DISPL	HP@RPM	C.R.	VLV
	Corvette, 2934	V8	3.75	3.00	265.1	195@5000	8.0	OH
	Optional engine:							
	(1)	V8	3.75	3.00	265.1	185@4600		OH
1956	150	6	3.562	3.938	235.5	140@4200	8.0	OH
	210	6	3.562	3.938	235.5	140@4200	8.0	OH
	Bel Air	6	3.562	3.938	235.5	140@4200	8.0	OH
	150 (1)	V8	3.75	3.00	265.1	162@4400	8.0	OH
	210 (1)	V8	3.75	3.00	265.1	162@4400	8.0	OH
	Bel Air (1)	V8	3.75	3.00	265.1	162@4400	8.0	OH
	Corvette, 2934	V8	3.75	3.00	265.1	225@5200	9.25	OH
	Optional engine:							
	(1)	V8	3.75	3.00	265.1	205@4600	9.25	OH
1957	150	6	3.567	3.938	235.5	140@4200	8.0	OH
	210	6	3.567	3.938	235.5	140@4200	8.0	OH
	Bel Air	6	3.567	3.938	235.5	140@4200	8.0	OH
	150 (1)	V8	3.75	3.00	265.1	162@4400	8.0	OH
	210 (1)	V8	3.75	3.00	265.1	162@4400	8.0	OH
	Bel Air (1)	V8	3.75	3.00	265.1	162@4400	8.0	OH
	Corvette, 2934 (2)	V8	3.875	3.00	283.0	220@4800	9.5	OH
	Optional engines:							
	(1)	V8	3.75	3.00	265.1	220@4800	9.5	OH
	(1)	V8	3.75	3.00	265.1	185@4600	8.5	OH
	(2)	V8	3.875	3.00	283.0	283@6200	10.5	OH
1958	Delray, 1100	6	3.562	3.938	235.5	145@4200	8.25	OH
	Biscayne, 1500	6	3.562	3.938	235.5	145@4200	8.25	OH
	Bel Air, 1700	6	3.562	3.938	235.5	145@4200	8.25	OH
	Delray, 1200 (1)	V8	3.875	3.00	283.0	185@4600	8.0	OH
	Biscayne, 1600 (1)	V8	3.875	3.00	283.0	185@4600	8.0	OH
	Bel Air, 1800 (1)	V8	3.875	3.00	283.0	185@4600	8.0	OH
	Corvette, 867	V8	3.875	3.00	283.0	230@4800	9.5	OH
	Optional engine:							
	(1)	V8	4.125	3.25	347.5	250@4400	9.5	OH
1959	Biscayne, 1100	6	3.5625	3.938	235.6	135@4000	8.25	OH
	Bel Air, 1500	6	3.5625	3.938	235.6	135@4000	8.25	OH
	Impala, 1700	6	3.5625	3.938	235.6	135@4000	8.25	OH
	Biscayne, 1200 (1)	V8	3.875	3.00	283.0	185@4600	8.5	OH
	Bel Air, 1600 (1)	V8	3.875	3.00	283.0	185@4600	8.5	OH

MFR	CARBURETOR MODEL	VEN	WHEEL-BASE	TIRES	BODY	WEIGHT	PRICE
R	7008005		102	6.70 x 15	2pcr2	2620	2934
		4					
R	7009255	1	115	6.70 x 15	6 ps	3206	1869
R	7009255	1	115	6.70 x 15	6 ps	3212	1955
R	7009255	1	115	6.70 x 15	6 ps	3231	2068
R	7008287	2	115	6.70 x 15	6 ps	3186	1968
R	7008287	2	115	6.70 x 15	6 ps	3192	2054
R	7008287	2	115	6.70 x 15	6 ps	3211	2167
C	WCFB-2419S	4	102	6.70 x 15	2pcv2	2764	3149
R	7009657	1	115	7.50 x 14	6 ps	3241	2048
R	7009657	1	115	7.50 x 14	6 ps	3275	2174
R	7009657	1	115	7.50 x 14	6 ps	3281	2290
R	7010647	2	115	7.50 x 14	6 ps	3232	2148
R	7010647	2	115	7.50 x 14	6 ps	3266	2274
R	7010647	2	115	7.50 x 14	6 ps	3272	2390
C	3744925	4	102	6.70 x 15	2pcv2	2730	3465
R		F.I.					
R	7012127	1	117.5	7.50 x 14	6 ps	3439	2155
R	7012127	1	117.5	7.50 x 14	6 ps	3447	2290
R	7012127	1	117.5	7.50 x 14/	6 ps	3467	2440
				8.00 x 14			
R	7012133	2	117.5	7.50 x 14	6 ps	3442	2262
R	7012133	2	117.5	7.50 x 14	6 ps	3450	2397
R	7012133	2	117.5	7.50 x 14/	6 ps	3470	2547
				8.00 x 14			
C		4	102	6.70 x 15	2pcv2	2793	3631
C	2656	4					
R	7013003	1	119	7.50 x 14	6 ps	3605	2301
R	7013003	1	119	7.50 x 14	6 ps	3600	2440
R	7013003	1	119	7.50 x 14/	6 ps	3625	2592
				8.00 x 14			
R	7013007	2	119	7.50 x 14	6 ps	3600	2419
R	7013007	2	119	7.50 x 14	6 ps	3615	2558

YEAR	MODEL	ENGINE						
		CYLS	BORE	STROKE	DISPL	HP@RPM	C.R.	VLV
	Impala, 1800 (1)	V8	3.875	3.00	283.0	185@4600	8.5	OH
	Corvette, 867	V8	3.875	3.00	283.0	230@4800	9.5	OH
	Optional engine:							
	(1)	V8	4.125	3.25	347.5	250@4400	9.5	OH
1960	Corvair Standard, 500 (1)	F6	3.375	2.60	139.6	80@4400	8.0	OH
	Corvair Deluxe, 700 (1)	F6	3.375	2.60	139.6	80@4400	8.0	OH
	Corvair Monza, 900 (1)	F6	3.375	2.60	139.6	80@4400	8.0	OH
	Biscayne Fleetmaster, 1300	6	3.562	3.938	235.6	135@4000	8.25	OH
	Biscayne, 1100	6	3.562	3.938	235.6	135@4000	8.25	OH
	Bel Air, 1500	6	3.562	3.938	235.6	135@4000	8.25	OH
	Impala, 1700	6	3.562	3.938	235.6	135@4000	8.25	OH
	Biscayne Fleetmaster, 1400 (2, 3)	V8	3.875	3.00	283.0	170@4200	8.5	OH
	Biscayne, 1200 (2, 3)	V8	3.875	3.00	283.0	170@4200	8.5	OH
	Bel Air, 1600 (2, 3)	V8	3.875	3.00	283.0	170@4200	8.5	OH
	Impala, 1800 (2, 3)	V8	3.875	3.00	283.0	170@4200	8.5	OH
	Corvette, 800 (2)	V8	3.875	3.00	283.0	230@4800	9.5	OH
	Optional engines:							
	(1)	F6	3.375	2.60	139.6	95@4800	9.5	OH
	(2)	V8	4.125	3.25	347.5	250@4400	9.5	OH
	(3)	V8	3.875	3.00	283.0	230@4800	9.5	OH
1961	Corvair, 500 (1)	F6	3.438	2.609	144.8	80@4400	8.0	OH
	Corvair, 700 (1)	F6	3.438	2.609	144.8	80@4400	8.0	OH
	Corvair Monza 900	F6	3.438	2.609	144.8	80@4400	8.0	OH
	Corvair Greenbrier 95 (1)	F6	3.438	2.609	144.8	80@4400	8.0	OH
	Biscayne Fleetmaster, 1300	6	3.562	3.938	235.5	135@4000	8.25	OH
	Biscayne, 1100	6	3.562	3.938	235.5	135@4000	8.25	OH
	Bel Air, 1500	6	3.562	3.938	235.5	135@4000	8.25	OH
	Impala, 1700	6	3.562	3.938	235.5	135@4000	8.25	OH
	Biscayne Fleetmaster, 1400 (2)	V8	3.875	3.00	283.0	170@4200	8.5	OH
	Biscayne, 1200 (2)	V8	3.875	3.00	283.0	170@4200	8.5	OH
	Bel Air, 1600 (2)	V8	3.875	3.00	283.0	170@4200	8.5	OH
	Impala, 1800 (2)	V8	3.875	3.00	283.0	170@4200	8.5	OH
	Corvette, 800 (2)	V8	3.875	3.00	283.0	230@4800	9.5	OH
	Optional engines:							
	(1)	F6	3.438	2.60	144.8	98@4600		OH

MFR	CARBURETOR MODEL	VEN	WHEEL-BASE	TIRES	BODY	WEIGHT	PRICE
R	7013007	2	119	7.50 x 14 /	6 ps	3620	2710
				8.00 x 14			
C	2816	4	102	6.70 x 15	2pcv2	2840	3875
C	2816	4					
R	7015311	2 x 1	108	6.50 x 13	6 ps	2305	2038
R	7015311	2 x 1	108	6.50 x 13	6 ps	2315	2103
R	7015311	2 x 1	108	6.50 x 13	4pcc	2280	2238
R	7013003	1	119	7.50 x 14	6 ps	3545	2284
R	7013003	1	119	7.50 x 14	6 ps	3555	2316
R	7013003	1	119	7.50 x 14	6 ps	3565	2438
R	7013003	1	119	7.50 x 14	6 ps	3575	2590
R	7013007	2	119	7.50 x 14	6 ps	3560	2391
R	7013007	2	119	7.50 x 14	6 ps	3570	2423
R	7013007	2	119	7.50 x 14	6 ps	3580	2545
R	7013007	2	119	7.50 x 14	6 ps	3580	2697
C	3756676	4	102	6.70 x 15	2pcv2	2840	3872
R	7019101	2 x 1	108	6.50 x 13/	6 ps	2355	1974
				7.00 x 13			
R	7019101	2 x 1	108	6.50 x 13/	6 ps	2380	2039
				7.00 x 13			
R	7019101	2 x 1	108	6.50 x 13 /	6 ps	2420	2201
				7.00 x 13			
R	7019101	2 x 1	95	7.00 x 14	6psw6	2895	2651
R	7013003	1	119	7.50 x 14	6 ps	3495	2284
R	7013003	1	119	7.50 x 14	6 ps	3500	2316
R	7013003	1	119	7.50 x 14	6 ps	3515	2438
R	7013003	1	119	7.50 x 14/	6 ps	3530	2590
				8.00 x 14			
R	7019007	2	119	7.50 x 14	6 ps	3500	2391
R	7019007	2	119	7.50 x 14	6 ps	3505	2423
R	7019007	2	119	7.50 x 14	6 ps	3520	2545
R	7019007	2	119	7.50 x 14/	6 ps	3525	2697
				8.00 x 14			
C	3779178	4	102	6.70 x 15	2pcv2	2905	3934

YEAR	MODEL	ENGINE						
		CYLS	BORE	STROKE	DISPL	HP@RPM	C.R.	VLV
	(2)	V8	4.125	3.25	347.5	250@4400	9.5	OH
	(2)	V8	4.125	3.25	347.5	305@5200	9.5	OH
	(2)	V8	4.125	3.25	347.5	340@5800	11.25	OH
	(2)	V8	4.125	3.25	347.5	350@6000	11.25	OH
	(2)	V8	4.312	3.50	409.0	360@5800	11.25	OH
1962	Corvair, 500 (3)	F6	3.438	2.609	145.3	80@4400	8.0	OH
	Corvair, 700 (3)	F6	3.438	2.609	145.3	80@4400	8.0	OH
	Corvair Monza, 900 (3)	F6	3.438	2.609	145.3	80@4400	8.0	OH
	Corvair Greenbrier (3)	F6	3.438	2.609	145.3	80@4400	8.0	OH
	Spyder (3)	F6	3.438	2.609	145.3	80@4400	8.0	OH
	Chevy II, 100	4	3.875	3.25	153.3	90@4000	8.5	OH
	Chevy II, 300	4	3.875	3.25	153.3	90@4000	8.5	OH
	Chevy II, 100 (1, 5)	6	3.562	3.25	194.4	120@4400	8.5	OH
	Chevy II, 300 (1, 5)	6	3.562	3.25	194.4	120@4400	8.5	OH
	Nova, 400 (1, 5)	6	3.562	3.25	194.4	120@4400	8.5	OH
	Biscayne, 1100	6	3.562	3.938	235.5	135@4000	8.25	OH
	Bel Air, 1500	6	3.562	3.938	235.5	135@4000	8.25	OH
	Impala, 1700	6	3.562	3.938	235.5	135@4000	8.25	OH
	Biscayne, 1200 (1, 2, 4, 5)	V8	3.875	3.00	283.0	170@4200	8.5	OH
	Bel Air, 1600 (1, 2, 4, 5)	V8	3.875	3.00	283.0	170@4200	8.5	OH
	Impala, 1800 (1, 2, 4, 5)	V8	3.875	3.00	283.0	170@4200	8.5	OH
	Corvette, V-800 (5)	V8	4.00	3.25	326.7	250@4400	10.5	OH
	Optional engines:							
	(1)	V8	4.00	3.25	326.7	250@4400	10.5	OH
	(2)	V8	4.312	3.50	409.0	409@6000	11.0	OH
	(2)	V8	4.312	3.50	409.0	380@5800	11.0	OH
	(3)	F6	3.438	2.609	145.3	102@4400	9.0	OH
	(4)	V8	4.00	3.25	326.7	300@5000	10.5	OH
	(5)	V8	4.00	3.25	326.7	340@6000	11.25	OH
	(5)	V8	4.00	3.25	326.7	360@6000	11.25	OH
1963	Corvair, 500 (3)	F6	3.438	2.609	145.3	80@4400	8.0	OH
	Corvair, 700 (3)	F6	3.438	2.609	145.3	80@4400	8.0	OH
	Corvair Monza, 900 (3)	F6	3.438	2.609	145.3	80@4400	8.0	OH
	Corvair Greenbrier (3)	F6	3.438	2.609	145.3	80@4400	8.0	OH
	Chevy II, 100	4	3.875	3.25	153.3	90@4000	8.5	OH

MFR	CARBURETOR MODEL	VEN	WHEEL-BASE	TIRES	BODY	WEIGHT	PRICE
C		4					
C		4					
C		4					
R	7013973	3 x 2					
C		4					
R	7020101	2 x 1	108	7.00 x 13	6 ps	2350	1992
R	7020101	2 x 1	108	7.00 x 13	6 ps	2410	2111
R	7020101	2 x 1	108	7.00 x 13	6 ps	2455	2273
R	7020101	2 x 1	95	7.00 x 14	6psw2	3030	2655
R	7020101	2 x 1	108	7.00 x 13	6pht2		
R	7020103	1	110	6.00 x 13/	6 ps	2445	2041
				6.50 x 13			
R	7020103	1	110	6.00 x 13/	6 ps	2460	2122
				6.50 x 13			
R	7020105	1	110	6.00 x 13/	6 ps	2535	2101
				6.50 x 13			
R	7020105	1	110	6.00 x 13/	6 ps	2550	2182
				6.50 x 13			
R	7020105	1	110	6.50 x 13	6 ps	2575	2226
R	7013000	1	119	7.00 x 14	6 ps	3480	2378
R	7013000	1	119	7.50 x 14	6 ps	3480	2510
R	7013000	1	119	7.50 x 14	6 ps	3510	2662
R	7020007	2	119	7.00 x 14	6 ps	3475	2485
R	7020007	2	119	7.00 x 14	6 ps	3475	2617
R	7020007	2	119	7.00 x 14	6 ps	3505	2769
C	3788246	4	102	6.70 x 15	2pcv2	2925	4038
C							
C	3345	2 x 4					
R	7020101	2 x 1					
C	3310	4					
C		4					
R	7017360	F. I.					
R	7023101	2 x 1	108	6.50 x 13	6 ps	2330	1992
R	7023101	2 x 1	108	6.50 x 13	6 ps	2385	2110
R	7023101	2 x 1	108	6.50 x 13	6 ps	2450	2326
R	7023101	2 x 1	108	6.50 x 13	6psw2	2990	2655
C	3379	1	110	6.00 x 13/	6 ps	2455	2040
				6.50 x 13			

YEAR	MODEL	ENGINE						
		CYLS	BORE	STROKE	DISPL	HP@RPM	C.R.	VLV
	Chevy II, 300	4	3.875	3.25	153.3	90@4000	8.5	OH
	Chevy II, 100	6	3.562	3.25	194.4	120@4400	8.5	OH
	Chevy II, 300	6	3.562	3.25	194.4	120@4400	8.5	OH
	Nova, 400	6	3.562	3.25	194.4	120@4400	8.5	OH
	Biscayne, 1100	6	3.875	3.25	230.0	140@4400	9.25	OH
	Bel Air, 1500	6	3.875	3.25	230.0	140@4400	9.25	OH
	Impala, 1700	6	3.875	3.25	230.0	140@4400	9.25	OH
	Biscayne, 1200 (1, 2, 4)	V8	3.875	3.00	283.0	195@4800	9.25	OH
	Bel Air, 1600 (1, 2, 4)	V8	3.875	3.00	283.0	195@4800	9.25	OH
	Impala, 180C (1, 2, 4)	V8	3.875	3.00	283.0	195@4800	9.25	OH
	Corvette, 800 (5)	V8	4.00	3.25	326.7	250@4400	10.5	OH
	Optional engines: (1)	V8	4.00	3.25	326.7	250@4400	10.5	OH
	(1)	V8	4.312	3.50	409.0	380@5800	11.0	OH
	(1)	V8	4.312	3.50	409.0	400@5800	11.0	OH
	(1)	V8	4.312	3.50	409.0	425@6000	11.0	OH
	(2)	V8	4.00	3.25	326.7	300@5000	10.5	OH
	(3)	F6	3.438	2.609	145.3	84@4400	9.0	OH
	(3)	F6	3.438	2.609	145.3	102@4400	9.0	OH
	(3)	F6	3.438	2.609	145.3	150@4400	8.0	OH
	(4)	V8	4.00	3.25	326.7	340@6000	11.25	OH
	(5)	V8	4.00	3.25	326.7	360@6000	11.25	OH
1964	Corvair 500 (3)	F6	3.438	2.938	163.6	95@3600	8.25	OH
	Corvair 700 (3)	F6	3.438	2.938	163.6	95@3600	8.25	OH
	Corvair Monza 900 (3)	F6	3.438	2.938	163.6	95@3600	8.25	OH
	Monza Spyder	F6	3.438	2.938	163.6	150@4000	8.25	OH
	Corvair Greenbrier 95 (3)	F6	3.438	2.938	163.6	95@3600	8.25	OH
	Chevy II, 100	4	3.875	3.25	153.3	90@4000	8.5	OH
	Chevy II, 100 (1)	6	3.562	3.25	194.4	120@4400	8.5	OH
	Chevy II Nova, 400 (1)	6	3.562	3.25	194.4	120@4400	8.5	OH
	Chevy II Nova Super Sport	6	3.562	3.25	194.4	120@4400	8.5	OH
	Chevelle 300 (1)	6	3.562	3.25	194.4	120@4400	8.5	OH
	Chevelle Malibu	6	3.562	3.25	194.4	120@4400	8.5	OH
	Chevelle Malibu SS (1)	6	3.562	3.25	194.4	120@4400	8.5	OH

MFR	CARBURETOR MODEL	VEN	WHEEL-BASE	TIRES	BODY	WEIGHT	PRICE
C	3379	1	110	6.00 x 13/	6 ps	2470	2121
				6.50 x 13			
R	7023103	1	110	6.00 x 13/	6 ps	2545	2099
				6.50 x 13			
R	7023103	1	110	6.00 x 13/	6 ps	2560	2180
				6.50 x 13			
R	7023103	1	110	6.00 x 13/	6 ps	2590	2235
				6.50 x 13			
R	7023003	1	119	7.00 x 14	6 ps	3280	2376
R	7023003	1	119	7.00 x 14	6 ps	3280	2508
R	7023003	1	119	7.00 x 14/	6 ps	3310	2661
				7.50 x 14			
R	7023007	2	119	7.00 x 14	6 ps	3415	2483
R	7023007	2	119	7.00 x 14	6 ps	3415	2615
R	7023007	2	119	7.00 x 14/	6 ps	3435	2768
				7.50 x 14			
C	3461	4	98	6.70 x 15	2 pc	2859	4252
C	3826003	4					
R	7020023	4					
C	3783	4					
C	3361	2 x 4					
C	3269	4					
R	7023100	2 x 1					
R	7023102	2 x 1					
C	3817245	3					
C	3826004	4					
		F. I.					
R	7024023	2 x 1	108	6.50 x 13	5 pc	2365	2000
R	7024023	2 x 1	108	6.50 x 13	6 ps	2415	2119
R	7024023	2 x 1	108	6.50 x 13	6 ps	2470	2335
R			108	6.50 x 13	4pht2	2470	2599
R	7024023	2 x 1	95	6.50 x 13	6psw4	2990	2666
C	3379	1	110	6.00 x 13	6 ps	2495	2048
R	7023105	1	110	6.00 x 13	6 ps	2580	2108
R	7023105	1	110	6.50 x 13	6 ps	2595	2243
R	7023105	1	110	6.50 x 13	4pht2	2675	2433
R	7023105	1	115	6.50 x 14/	6 ps	2850	2268
				7.00 x 14			
R	7023105	1	115	6.50 x 14/	6 ps	2870	2349
				7.00 x 14			
R	7023105	1	115	6.50 x 14	4pht2	2875	2538

YEAR	MODEL	ENGINE						
		CYLS	BORE	STROKE	DISPL	HP@RPM	C.R.	VLV
	Chevelle 300 (4)	V8	3.875	3.00	283.0	195@4800	9.25	OH
	Chevelle Malibu (4)	V8	3.875	3.00	283.0	195@4800	9.25	OH
	Chevelle Malibu SS (4)	V8	3.875	3.00	283.0	195@4800	9.25	OH
	Biscayne, 1100	6	3.875	3.25	230.0	140@4400	8.5	OH
	Bel Air, 1500	6	3.875	3.25	230.0	140@4400	8.5	OH
	Impala, 1700	6	3.875	3.25	230.0	140@4400	8.5	OH
	Impala Super Sport, 1300	6	3.875	3.25	230.0	140@4400	8.5	OH
	Biscayne, 1200 (2)	V8	3.875	3.00	283.0	195@4800	9.25	OH
	Bel Air, 1600 (2)	V8	3.875	3.00	283.0	195@4800	9.25	OH
	Impala, 1800 (2)	V8	3.875	3.00	283.0	195@4800	9.25	OH
	Impala SS, 1400 (2)	V8	3.875	3.00	283.0	195@4800	9.25	OH
	Corvette, 800 (5)	V8	4.00	3.25	326.7	250@4400	10.5	OH
	Optional engines:							
	(1)	6	3.875	3.25	230.0	155@4400	8.5	OH
	(1)	V8	3.875	3.00	283.0	195@4800	9.25	OH
	(2)	V8	4.312	3.50	409.0	400@5800	11.0	OH
	(2)	V8	4.312	3.50	409.0	425@6000	11.0	OH
	(2)	V8	3.875	3.00	283.0	300@5000	10.5	OH
	(3)	F6	3.438	2.938	163.6	110@4400	9.25	OH
	(4)	V8	3.875	3.00	283.0	220@4800	9.25	OH
	(4)	V8	3.875	3.00	283.0	300@5000	10.5	OH
	(5)	V8	4.00	3.25	326.7	365@6200	11.0	OH
	(5)	V8	4.00	3.25	326.7	300@5000	10.5	OH
	(5)	V8	4.00	3.25	326.7	375@6200	11.0	OH
1965	Corvair, 500 (1)	F6	3.438	2.938	163.6	95@3600	8.25	OH
	Corvair Monza (1)	F6	3.438	2.938	163.6	95@3600	8.25	OH
	Corvair Corsa (2)	F6	3.438	2.938	163.6	140@5200	9.25	OH
	Corvair, 95	F6	3.438	2.938	163.6	95@3600	8.25	OH
	Chevy II, 100	4	3.875	3.25	153.3	90@4000	8.5	OH

MFR	CARBURETOR MODEL	VEN	WHEEL-BASE	TIRES	BODY	WEIGHT	PRICE
R	7024101	2	115	6.50/7.00 x 14	6 ps	2980	2376
R	7024101	2	115	6.50 x 14/	6 ps	2995	2457
				7.00 x 14			
R	7024101	2	115	6.50 x 14	4pht2	3000	2646
R	7023003	1	119	7.00 x 14/	6 ps	3300	2417
				8.00 x 14			
R	7023003	1	119	7.00 x 14/	6 ps	3305	2519
				8.00 x 14			
R	7023003	1	119	7.00 x 14/	6 ps	3340	2671
				7.50 x 14/			
				8.00 x 14			
R	7023003	1	119	7.00 x 14/	4pht2	3325	2839
				7.50 x 14			
R	7024101	2	119	7.00 x 14/	6 ps	3430	2524
				8.00 x 14			
R	7024101	2	119	7.00 x 14/	6 ps	3440	2626
				8.00 x 14			
R	7024101	2	119	7.00 x 14/	6 ps	3460	2779
				7.50 x 14/			
				8.00 x 14			
R	7024101	2	119	7.00 x 14/	4pht2	3450	2947
				7.50 x 14			
C	3846247	4	98	7.00 x 14/	2 pc	2960	4252
				7.50 x 14			
R	7023003	1					
R	7024101	2					
C	3827324	4					
C	3815403	2 x 4					
C	3846247	4					
R	7024024	2 x 1					
R	7024125	4					
R	7024125	4					
H	3849804	4					
C	3826004	4					
R	7017380	F. I.					
R	7025023	2 x 1	108	6.50 x 13	6 ps	2405	2096
R	7025023	2 x 1	108	6.50 x 13	6 ps	2465	2370
R	7025023	4 x 1	108	6.50 x 13	4psc2	2475	2465
R	7025023	2 x 1	95	6.50 x 13	6psw6	2990	2609
C	3379	1	110	6.50 x 14	6 ps	2520	2005

YEAR	MODEL	ENGINE						
		CYLS	BORE	STROKE	DISPL	HP@RPM	C.R.	VLV
	Chevy II, 100 (3)	6	3.562	3.25	194.4	120@4400	8.5	OH
	Chevy Nova (3)	6	3.562	3.25	194.4	120@4400	8.5	OH
	Chevy II Nova SS (3)	6	3.562	3.25	194.4	120@4400	8.5	OH
	Chevelle, 300 (3)	6	3.562	3.25	194.4	120@4400	8.5	OH
	Chevelle Deluxe, 300 (3)	6	3.562	3.25	194.4	120@4400	8.5	OH
	Chevelle Malibu (3)	6	3.562	3.25	194.4	120@4400	8.5	OH
	Chevelle Malibu SS (3)	6	3.562	3.25	194.4	120@4400	8.5	OH
	Chevelle, 300 (3)	V8	3.875	3.00	383.0	195@4800	9.25	OH
	Chevelle Deluxe, 300 (3)	V8	3.875	3.00	383.0	195@4800	9.25	OH
	Chevelle Malibu (3)	V8	3.875	3.00	383.0	195@4800	9.25	OH
	Chevelle Malibu SS (3)	V8	3.875	3.00	383.0	195@4800	9.25	OH
	Biscayne	6	3.875	3.25	230.0	140@4400	8.5	OH
	Bel Air	6	3.875	3.25	230.0	140@4400	8.5	OH
	Impala	6	3.875	3.25	230.0	140@4400	8.5	OH
	Impala SS	6	3.875	3.25	230.0	140@4400	8.5	OH
	Biscayne (3)	V8	3.875	3.00	283.0	195@4800	9.25	OH
	Bel Air (3)	V8	3.875	3.00	283.0	195@4800	9.25	OH
	Impala (3)	V8	3.875	3.00	283.0	195@4800	9.25	OH
	Impala SS (3)	V8	3.875	3.00	283.0	195@4800	9.25	OH
	Corvette (3, 4)	V8	4.00	3.25	326.7	250@4400	10.5	OH
	Optional engines:							
	(1)	F6	3.438	2.938	163.6	110@4400	9.25	OH
	(1)	F6	3.438	2.938	163.6	140@5200	9.25	OH
	(2)	F6	3.438	2.938	163.6	180@4000	9.25	OH
	(3)	V8	4.00	3.25	326.7	300@5000	10.5	OH
	(3)	V8	4.00	3.25	326.7	425@6400	11.0	OH
	(3)	V8	4.00	3.25	326.7	400@5800	11.0	OH
	(4)	V8	4.00	3.25	326.7	350@5000	11.0	OH

MFR	CARBURETOR MODEL	VEN	WHEEL-BASE	TIRES	BODY	WEIGHT	PRICE
R	7023105	1	110	6.50 x 14/	6 ps	2620	2070
				7.00 x 13			
R	7023105	1	110	6.50 x 14/	6 ps	2645	2195
				7.00 x 13			
R	7023105	1	110	6.95 x 14	4psc2	2690	2381
R	7023105	1	115	6.95 x 14/	6 ps	2900	2146
				7.35 x 14			
R	7023105	1	115	6.95 x 14/	6 ps	2910	2220
				7.35 x 14			
R	7023105	1	115	6.95 x 14/	6 ps	2945	2299
				7.35 x 14			
R	7023105	1	115	6.95 x 14	4psc2	2980	2484
R	7024101	2	115	6.95 x 14/	6 ps	3035	2251
				7.35 x 14			
R	7024101	2	115	6.95 x 14/	6 ps	3050	2326
				7.35 x 14			
R	7024101	2	115	6.95 x 14/	6 ps	3080	2405
				7.35 x 14			
R	7024101	2	115	6.95 x 14	4psc2	3115	2590
R	7025003	1	119		6 ps	3365	2367
R	7025003	1	119		6 ps	3380	2467
R	7025003	1	119		6 ps	3460	2617
R	7025003	1	119		4pht2	3435	2780
R	7024101	2	119	7.35 x 14/	6 ps	3515	2472
				8.25 x 14			
R	7024101	2	119	7.35 x 14/	6 ps	3530	2572
				8.25 X 14			
R	7024101	2	119	7.35 x 14/	6 ps	3595	2722
				7.75 x 14/			
				8.25 x 14			
R	7024101	2	119	7.35 x 14/	4pht2	3570	2886
				8.25 x 14			
C	3846247	4	98	7.35 x 14	2 pc	2975	4233
R	7025024	2 x 1					
R	7025023	4 x 1					
C	3856713						
C	3851761	4					
H	3869923	4					
C	3855581	4					
H	3863150	4					

YEAR	MODEL	ENGINE						
		CYLS	BORE	STROKE	DISPL	HP@RPM	C.R.	VLV
	(4)	V8	4.00	3.25	326.7	365@6200	11.0	OH
	(4)	V8	4.00	3.25	326.7	375@6200	11.0	OH
1966	Corvair 500 (5)	6	3.438	2.938	163.6	95@3600	8.25	OH
	Corvair Monza (5)	F6	3.438	2.938	163.6	95@3600	8.25	OH
	Corvair Corsa (6)	F6	3.438	2.938	163.6	140@3600	8.25	OH
	Chevy II, 100	F6	3.875	3.25	153.3	90@4000	8.5	OH
	Chevy II, 100 (1, 2, 7, 8)	6	3.562	3.25	194.3	120@4400	8.5	OH
	Chevy II Nova (1, 2, 7, 8)	6	3.562	3.25	194.3	120@4400	8.5	OH
	Chevy II Nova SS (1, 2, 7, 8)	6	3.562	3.25	194.3	120@4400	8.5	OH
	Chevelle 300 (1, 2, 7)	6	3.562	3.25	194.3	120@4400	8.5	OH
	Chevelle Deluxe 300 (1, 2, 7)	6	3.562	3.25	194.3	120@4400	8.5	OH
	Chevelle Malibu (1, 2, 7)	6	3.562	3.25	194.3	120@4400	8.5	OH
	Chevelle Malibu 300	V8	3.875	3.00	283.0	195@4800	9.25	OH
	Chevelle Deluxe 300 (3, 9)	V8	3.875	3.00	283.0	195@4800	9.25	OH
	Chevelle Malibu (3)	V8	3.875	3.00	283.0	195@4800	9.25	OH
	Chevelle SS	V8	3.875	3.00	283.0	195@4800	9.25	OH
	Biscayne	6	3.875	3.53	249.8	155@4200	8.5	OH
	Bel Air	6	3.875	3.53	249.8	155@4200	8.5	OH
	Impala	6	3.875	3.53	249.8	155@4200	8.5	OH
	Impala SS	6	3.875	3.53	249.8	155@4200	8.5	OH
	Biscayne (2, 3, 7, 10)	V8	3.875	3.00	283.0	195@4800	9.25	OH
	Bel Air (2, 3, 7, 10)	V8	3.875	3.00	283.0	195@4800	9.25	OH
	Impala (2, 3, 7, 10)	V8	3.875	3.00	283.0	195@4800	9.25	OH
	Impala SS (2, 3, 7, 10)	V8	3.875	3.00	283.0	195@4800	9.25	OH

MFR	CARBURETOR MODEL	VEN	WHEEL-BASE	TIRES	BODY	WEIGHT	PRICE
H	3849804	4					
R	7017380	F. I.					
R	7026023	2 x 1	108	7.00 x 14	6 ps	2445	2157
R	7026023	2 x 1	108	7.00 x 14	6 ps	2495	2424
R	7026023	4 x 1	108	7.00 x 14	4pht2	2485	2519
C	3895011	1	110	6.50 x 13	6 ps	2535	2065
R	7025105	1	110	6.50 x 13/	6 ps	2635	2127
				6.95 x 13			
R	7025105	1	110	6.50 x 13/	6 ps	2640	2245
				6.95 x 13			
R	7025105	1	110	6.50 x 13	4pht2	2740	2430
R	7025105	1	115	6.95 x 14	6 ps	2935	2202
R	7025105	1	115	6.95 x 14/	6 ps	2945	2276
				7.75 x 14			
R	7025105	1	115	6.95 x 14/	6 ps	2960	2352
				7.75 x 14			
R	7024101	2	115	6.95 x 14	6 ps	3080	2308
R	7024101	2	115	6.95 x 14/	6 ps	3095	2382
				7.75 x 14			
R	7024101	2	115	6.95 x 14/	6 ps	3110	2458
				7.75 x 14			
R	7024101	2	115	7.75 x 14	5psc2	3375	2776
C	3891593	1	119	7.75 x 14/	6 ps	3375	2431
				7.35 x 14/			
				8.55 x 14			
C	3891593	1	119	7.75 x 14/	6 ps	3390	2531
				7.35 x 14/			
				8.55 x 14			
C	3891593	1	119	7.75 x 14/	6 ps	3435	2685
				7.35 x 14/			
				8.55 x 14			
C	3891593	1	119	7.75 x 14	4pht2	3460	2842
R	7024101	2	119	7.75 x 14/	6 ps	3510	2537
				8.55 x 14			
R	7024101	2	119	7.75 x 14/	6 ps	3525	2636
				8.55 x 14			
R	7024101	2	119	7.75 x 14/	6 ps	3565	2783
				8.55 x 14			
R	7024101	2	119	7.75 x 14	5pht2	3585	2941

YEAR	MODEL	ENGINE						
		CYLS	BORE	STROKE	DISPL	HP@RPM	C.R.	VLV
	Caprice (2, 3, 7, 10)	V8	3.875	3.00	283.0	195@4800	9.25	OH
	Corvette (4, 10)	V8	4.00	3.25	326.7	300@5000	10.25	OH
	Optional engines:							
	(1)	6	3.875	3.25	230.0	140@4400	8.5	OH
	(2)	V8	4.00	3.25	236.7	275@4800	10.25	OH
	(2)	V8	3.875	3.00	283.0	195@4300	9.25	OH
	(3)	V8	4.09	3.76	396.0	325@4800	10.25	OH
	(4)	V8	4.25	3.76	427.0	390@5200	10.25	OH
	(5)	F6	3.438	2.938	163.6	110@4400	9.25	OH
	(5)	F6	3.438	2.938	163.6	140@5200	9.25	OH
	(6)	F6	3.438	2.938	163.6	180@4000	8.25	OH
	(7)	V8	3.875	3.00	283.0	220@4800	9.25	OH
	(8)	V8	4.00	3.25	326.7	350@5800	11.0	OH
	(9)	V8	4.09	3.76	396.0	360@5200	10.25	OH
	(9)	V8	4.09	3.76	396.0	375@5600	11.0	OH
	(10)	V8	4.25	3.76	427.0	425@5600	11.0	OH
1967	Corvair 500 (1)	F6	3.438	2.938	163.6	95@3600	8.25	OH
	Corvair Monza (1)	F6	3.438	2.938	163.6	95@3600	8.25	OH
	Chevy II 100	4	3.875	3.25	153.3	90@4000	8.5	OH
	Chevy II 100 (2, 3)	6	3.50	3.25	187.6	120@4000	8.5	OH
	Chevy Nova (2, 3)	6	3.50	3.25	187.6	120@4000	8.5	OH
	Chevy Nova SS (2, 3)	6	3.50	3.25	187.6	120@4000	8.5	OH
	Chevelle 300 (2)	6	3.875	3.25	230.0	140@4400	8.5	OH
	Chevelle Deluxe 300 (2)	6	3.875	3.25	230.0	140@4400	8.5	OH
	Chevelle Malibu (2)	6	3.875	3.25	230.0	140@4400	8.5	OH
	Chevelle Concors (2)	6	3.875	3.25	230.0	140@4400	8.5	OH
	Chevelle 300 (3, 4, 7)	V8	3.875	3.00	283.0	195@4800	9.25	OH
	Chevelle Deluxe 300 (3, 4, 7)	V8	3.875	3.00	283.0	195@4800	9.25	OH
	Chevelle Malibu (3, 4, 7)	V8	3.875	3.00	283.0	195@4800	9.25	OH
	Chevelle Super Sport	V8	4.09	3.76	395.2	325@4800	10.25	OH
	Chevelle Concors (3, 4)	V8	3.875	3.00	283.0	195@4800	9.25	OH
	Camaro	6	3.875	3.25	230.0	140@4400	8.5	OH
	Camaro (3, 5)	V8	4.00	3.25	326.7	210@4600	8.75	OH

MFR	CARBURETOR MODEL	VEN	WHEEL-BASE	TIRES	BODY	WEIGHT	PRICE
R	7024101	2	119	7.75 x 14/	6pht4	3675	3063
				8.55 x 14			
H	3884505	4	98	7.75 x 14	2 pc	2985	4295
R	7026023	2 x 1					
R	7026023	4 x 1					
C							
R	7025127	4					
H	3877413	4					
H	3866067	4					
H	3893229	4					
H	3865067	4					
R	7026023	2 x 1	108	7.00 x 13	6 ps	2470	2194
R	7026023	2 x 1	108	7.00 x 13	6 ps	2515	2464
C	3905971	1	110	6.95 x 14	6 ps	2560	2120
R	7025105	1	110	6.95 x 14	6 ps	2650	2182
R	7025105	1	110	6.95 x 14	6 ps	2660	2298
R	7025105	1	110	6.95 x 14	4pht2	2690	2487
R	7027003	1	115	7.35 x 14/	6 ps	2955	2250
				7.75 x 14			
R	7027003	1	115	7.35 x 14/	6 ps	2980	2324
				7.75 x 14			
R	7027003	1	115	7.35 x 14/	6 ps	3000	2400
				7.75 x 14			
R	7027003	1	115	7.75 x 14	6psw4	3270	2827
R	7027101	2	115	7.35 x 14/	6 ps	3090	2356
				7.75 x 14			
R	7027101	2	115	7.35 x 14/	6 ps	3110	2430
				7.75 x 14			
R	7027101	2	115	7.35 x 14/	6 ps	3130	2506
				7.75 x 14			
R	7027201	4	115	F70 x 14	4pht2	3415	2825
R	7027101	2	115	7.75 x 14	6psw4	3405	2933
R	7027003	1	108	7.35 x 14	4pht2	2770	2466
R	7027101	2	108	7.35 x 14	4pht2	2920	2572

YEAR	MODEL	ENGINE CYLS	BORE	STROKE	DISPL	HP@RPM	C.R.	VLV
	Biscayne	6	3.875	3.53	249.8	155@4200	8.5	OH
	Bel Air	6	3.875	3.53	249.8	155@4200	8.5	OH
	Impala	6	3.875	3.53	249.8	155@4200	8.5	OH
	Impala Super Sport	6	3.875	3.53	249.8	155@4200	8.5	OH
	Biscayne (3)	V8	3.875	3.00	283.0	195@4800	9.25	OH
	Bel Air (3)	V8	3.875	3.00	283.0	195@4800	9.25	OH
	Impala (3)	V8	3.875	3.00	283.0	195@4800	9.25	OH
	Impala Super Sport (3)	V8	3.875	3.00	283.0	195@4800	9.25	OH
	Caprice (3)	V8	3.875	3.00	283.0	195@4800	9.25	OH
	Corvette (6)	V8	4.00	3.25	326.7	300@5000	10.0	OH
	Optional engines:							
	(1)	F6	3.438	2.938	163.6	110@4400	9.25	OH
	(2)	6	3.875	3.53	249.8	155@4200	8.5	OH
	(3)	V8	4.00	3.25	326.7	275@4800	10.0	OH
	(4)	V8	4.00	3.25	326.7	325@5600	11.0	OH
	(5)	V8	4.00	3.48	350.0	295@4800	10.25	OH
	(6)	V8	4.00	3.25	326.7	350@5800	11.0	OH
	(7)	V8	4.09	3.76	395.2	350@5200	10.25	OH
1968	Corvair 500 (1)	F6	3.438	2.938	163.6	95@3600	8.25	OH
	Corvair Monza (1)	F6	3.438	2.938	163.6	95@3600	8.25	OH
	Chevy II Nova	4	3.875	3.25	153.3	90@4000	8.5	OH
	Chevy II Nova (7)	6	3.875	3.25	230.0	140@4400	8.5	OH
	Chevelle 300 (2)	6	3.875	3.25	230.0	140@4400	8.5	OH
	Chevelle Deluxe 300 (2)	6	3.875	3.25	230.0	140@4400	8.5	OH
	Chevelle Malibu (2)	6	3.875	3.25	230.0	140@4400	8.5	OH
	Chevelle Concors (2)	6	3.875	3.25	230.0	140@4400	8.5	OH
	Chevelle 300 (3, 4, 5)	V8	3.875	3.25	306.6	200@4600	9.0	OH
	Chevelle Deluxe 300 (3, 4, 5)	V8	3.875	3.25	306.6	200@4600	9.0	OH

MFR	CARBURETOR MODEL	VEN	WHEEL-BASE	TIRES	BODY	WEIGHT	PRICE
R	7026027	1	119	8.25 x 14/	6 ps	3395	2484
				8.55 x 14			
R	7026027	1	119	8.25 x 14/	6 ps	3410	2584
				8.55 x 14			
R	7026027	1	119	8.25 x 14/	6 ps	3455	2723
				8.55 x 14			
R	7026027	1	119	F70 x 14	4pht2	3500	2898
R	7027101		119	8.25 x 14/	6 ps	3525	2589
				8.55 x 14			
R	7027101		119	8.25 x 14/	6 ps	3535	2689
				8.55 x 14			
R	7027101		119	8.25 x 14/	6 ps	3575	2828
				8.55 x 14			
R	7027101		119	8.25 x 14	4pht2	3615	3003
R	7027101		119	8.25 x 14/	6pht4	3710	3130
				8.55 x 14			
R	3096631	4	98	7.75 x 14	2pht2	3000	4353
R	7026027	1					
R	7027201	4					
R	7028005	2 x 1	108	7.00 x 13	6 ps	2477	2243
R	7028005	2 x 1	108	7.00 x 13	4psc2	2506	2507
R	7028009	1	111	7.35 x 14	6 ps	2773	2252
R	7028017	1	111	7.35 x 14	6 ps	2877	2314
R	7028017	1	116/112	7.35 x 14/	4pc2	2988	2341
				7.75 x 14			
R	7028017	1	116/112	7.35 x 14/	6 ps	3071	2445
				7.75 x 14			
R	7028017	1	116/112	7.35 x 14/	6 ps	3090	2534
				7.75 x 14			
R	7028017	1	116	7.75 x 14	6psw4	3426	2978
R	7028101	2	116/112	7.35 x 14/	4pc2	3124	2447
				7.75 x 14			
R	7028101	2	116/112	7.35 x 14/	6 ps	3207	2550
				7.75 x 14			

YEAR	MODEL	ENGINE						
		CYLS	BORE	STROKE	DISPL	HP@RPM	C.R.	VLV
	Chevelle Malibu (3, 4, 5)	V8	3.875	3.25	306.6	200@4600	9.0	OH
	Chevelle Concors (3, 4, 5)	V8	3.875	3.25	306.6	200@4600	9.0	OH
	Chevelle SS 396 (9)	V8	4.09	3.76	396.0	325@4000	10.25	OH
	Camaro (2)	6	3.875	3.25	230.0	140@4400	8.5	OH
	Camaro (4,7,8)	V8	4.00	3.25	326.7	210@4000	8.75	OH
	Biscayne	6	3.875	3.53	249.8	155@4200	8.5	OH
	Bel Air	6	3.875	3.53	249.8	155@4200	8.5	OH
	Impala	6	3.875	3.53	249.8	155@4200	8.5	OH
	Biscayne (3, 4, 8, 10)	V8	3.875	3.25	306.6	200@4600	10.0	OH
	Bel Air (3, 4, 8, 10)	V8	3.875	3.25	306.6	200@4600	10.0	OH
	Impala (3, 4, 8, 10)	V8	3.875	3.25	306.6	200@4600	10.0	OH
	Caprice (3, 4, 8, 10)	V8	3.875	3.25	306.6	200@4600	10.0	OH
	Corvette (6)	V8	4.00	3.25	326.7	300@5000	10.25	OH
	Optional engines:							
	(1)	F6	3.438	2.938	163.6	110@4400	9.25	OH
	(1)	F6	3.438	2.938	163.6	140@5200	9.25	OH
	(2)	6	3.875	3.53	249.8	155@4200	8.5	OH
	(3)	V8	4.00	3.25	326.7	250@4800	8.75	OH
	(4)	V8	4.00	3.25	326.7	275@4800	10.0	OH
	(5)	V8	4.00	3.25	326.7	325@5600	11.0	OH
	(6)	V8	4.00	3.25	326.7	350@5800	11.0	OH
	(7)	V8	4.00	3.48	349.8	295@4800	10.25	OH
	(8)	V8	4.09	3.76	396.0	325@4800	10.25	OH
	(9)	V8	4.09	3.76	396.0	350@5200	10.25	OH
	(10)	V8	4.25	3.76	426.7	385@5200	10.25	OH
	(11)	V8	4.25	3.76	426.7	390@5400	10.25	OH
	(11)	V8	4.25	3.76	426.7	400@5400	10.25	OH
	(11)	V8	4.25	3.76	426.7	435@5800	11.0	OH
1969	Corvair 500 (1)	F6	3.438	2.938	163.6	95@3600	8.25	OH
	Corvair Monza (1)	F6	3.438	2.938	163.6	95@3600	8.25	OH
	Chevy II Nova	4	3.875	3.25	153.3	90@4000	8.5	OH
	Chevy II Nova (2, 3)	6	3.875	3.25	230.0	140@4400	8.5	OH
	Chevelle Deluxe 300 (2)	6	3.875	3.25	230.0	140@4400	8.5	OH
	Chevelle Malibu (2)	6	3.875	3.25	230.0	140@4400	8.5	OH

MFR	CARBURETOR MODEL	VEN	WHEEL-BASE	TIRES	BODY	WEIGHT	PRICE
R	7028101	2	116/112	7.35 x 14/	6 ps	3223	2629
				7.75 x 14			
R	7028101	2	116	7.75 x 14	6psw4	3561	3083
R	7028211	4	116/112	F70 x 14	4pht2	3475	2899
R	7028017	1	108	7.35 x 14	4pht2	2855	2588
R	7028101	2	108	7.35 x 14	4pht2	2985	2694
R	7028017	1	119	8.25 x 14/	6 ps	3464	2623
				8.55 x 14			
R	7028017	1	119	8.25 x 14/	6 ps	3466	2723
				8.55 x 14			
R	7028017	1	119	8.25 x 14	6 ps	3513	2846
R	7028101	2	119	8.25 x 14/	6 ps	3581	2728
				8.55 x 14			
R	7028101	2	119	8.25 x 14/	6 ps	3582	2828
				8.55 x 14			
R	7028101	2	119	8.25 x 14/	6 ps	3623	2951
				8.55 x 14			
R	7028101	2	119	8.25 x 14/	6pht4	3754	3271
				8.55 x 14			
R	7028207	4	98	F70 x 15	2pht2	3055	4663
R	7028005	2 x 1	108	7.00 x 13	4psc2	2515	2258
R	7028005	2 x 1	108	7.00 x 13	4psc2	2545	2522
R	7029008	1	111	7.35 x 14	6 ps	2810	2267
R	7029017	1	111	7.35 x 14	6 ps	2920	2345
R	7029017	1	116/112	7.35 x 14	6 ps	3100	2488
R	7029017	1	116/112	7.75 x 14	6 ps	3130	2567

YEAR	MODEL	ENGINE						
		CYLS	BORE	STROKE	DISPL	HP@RPM	C.R.	VLV
	Chevelle Deluxe 300 (3)	V8	3.875	3.25	306.6	200@4600	9.0	OH
	Chevelle Malibu (3, 5, 6)	V8	3.875	3.25	306.6	200@4600	9.0	OH
	Camaro	6	3.875	3.25	230.0	140@4400	8.5	OH
	Camaro (3, 5)	V8	4.00	3.25	326.7	210@4600	9.0	OH
	Biscayne	6	3.875	3.53	249.8	155@4200	8.5	OH
	Bel Air	6	3.875	3.53	249.8	155@4200	8.5	OH
	Impala	6	3.875	3.53	249.8	155@4200	8.5	OH
	Biscayne (3, 4, 7, 8)	V8	4.00	3.25	326.7	235@4800	9.0	OH
	Bel Air (3, 4, 7, 8)	V8	4.00	3.25	326.7	235@4800	9.0	OH
	Impala (3, 4, 7, 8)	V8	4.00	3.25	326.7	235@4800	9.0	OH
	Caprice (3, 4, 7, 8)	V8	4.00	3.25	326.7	235@4800	9.0	OH
	Corvette (8, 9)	V8	4.00	3.48	349.8	300@4800	10.25	OH
	Optional engines:							
	(1)	F6	3.438	2.938	163.6	110@4400	9.25	OH
	(1)	F6	3.438	2.938	163.6	140@5200	9.25	OH
	(2)	V8	3.875	3.25	306.6	200@4600	9.0	OH
	(3)	V8	4.00	3.48	349.8	255@4800	9.0	OH
	(4)	V8	4.09	3.76	396.0	265@4800	9.0	OH
	(5)	V8	4.09	3.76	396.0	325@4800	10.25	OH
	(6)	V8	4.09	3.76	396.0	350@5200	10.25	OH
	(7)	V8	4.25	3.76	427.0	335@4800	10.25	OH
	(8)	V8	4.25	3.76	427.0	390@4800	10.25	OH
	(9)	V8	4.25	3.76	427.0	400@5400	10.25	OH
	(9)	V8	4.25	3.76	427.0	435@5800	11.00	OH

CHICAGOAN — — Triplex Industries, Ltd., Blue Island, Ill., 1952-54

YEAR	MODEL	CYLS	BORE	STROKE	DISPL	HP@RPM	C.R.	VLV
1952-54		6	3.125	3.50	161.1	90@4400	7.6	F
	Engine used was by Willys.							

CHRYSLER — — Chrysler Corp., Detroit, Mich., 1925+

YEAR	MODEL	CYLS	BORE	STROKE	DISPL	HP@RPM	C.R.	VLV
1930	Six, CJ (1)	6	3.125	4.25	195.6	62@3200	5.2	L
	66, C-66	6	3.125	4.75	218.6	68@3000	5.1	L
	70, V-70	6	3.125	4.75	218.6	75@3200	5.1	L
	70, V*-70 (2)	6	3.375	5.00	268.9	93@3200	5.0	L
	77, W-77 (2)	6	3.375	5.00	268.9	93@3200	5.0	L
	Imperial, L* (3)	6	3.625	5.00	309.6	100@3000	4.75	L
	Optional engines:							
	(1)	6	3.125	4.25	195.6	70@3200	6.2	L
	(2)	6	3.375	5.00	268.9	102@3200	5.8	L
	(3)	6	3.625	5.00	309.6	112@3000	6.0	L

MFR	CARBURETOR MODEL	VEN	WHEEL-BASE	TIRES	BODY	WEIGHT	PRICE
			116/112	7.35 x 14/	6 ps	3230	2577
				7.75 x 14			
			116/112	7.75 x 14	6 ps	3265	2667
R	7029017	1	108	7.35 x 14	4pht2	3040	2638
			108	F70 x 14	4pht2	3050	2727
R	7029017	1	119	8.25 x 14	6 ps	3590	2687
R	7029017	1	119	8.25 x 14	6 ps	3590	2787
R	7029017	1	119	8.25 x 14	6 ps	3640	2911
R	7029127	2	119	8.25 x 14	6 ps	2735	2793
R	7029127	2	119	8.25 x 14	6 ps	3725	2893
R	7029127	2	119	8.25 x 14	6 ps	3760	3016
R	7029127	2	119	8.25 x 14	6pht4	3895	3346
R	7029203	4	98	F70 x 15	2pht2	3140	4781
C	YS-924S	1			2 pc		
C		1	109	5.00 x 19	5 ps	2455	835
S	U-2	1	112.8	5.50 x 18	5 ps	2930	1095
S	BXV-2		116.6	5.50 x 18	5 ps	3590	1445
S	BXV-2		116.6	5.50 x 18	5 ps	3590	1450
S	BXV-2		124.6	6.00 x 18	5 ps	3750	1495
S			136	7.00 x 18	5 ps	4335	3075

YEAR	MODEL	ENGINE						
		CYLS	BORE	STROKE	DISPL	HP@RPM	C.R.	VLV
1931	Six, CM	6	3.25	4.375	217.9	78@3400	5.35	L
	Eight, CD	8	3.00	4.25	240.3	80@3400	5.2	L
	Imperial Eight, CG	8	3.50	5.00	384.8	125@3200	5.2	L
	Later models:							
	Eight, CD	8	3.125	4.25	260.8	88@3400	5.3	L
	Deluxe Eight, CD*	8	3.25	4.25	282.1	100@3400	5.2	L
1932	Six, CI	6	3.25	4.50	224.0	82@3400	5.35	L
	Eight, CP	8	3.25	4.50	297.8	100@3400	5.2	L
	Imperial Eight, CH	8	3.50	5.00	384.8	125@3200	5.2	L
	Imperial Custom Eight, CL	8	3.50	5.00	384.8	125@3200	5.2	L
1933	Six, CO (1)	6	3.25	4.50	224.0	83@3400	5.35	L
	Royal Eight, CT (2)	8	3.25	4.125	273.8	90@3400	5.4	L
	Imperial Eight, CQ (3)	8	3.25	4.50	298.7	108@3400	6.2	L
	Custom Imperial, CL* (4)	8	3.50	5.00	384.8	135@3200	5.8	L
	Optional engines:							
	(1)	6	3.25	4.50	224.0	89@3400	6.2	L
	(2)	8	3.25	4.125	273.8	98@3400	6.2	L
	(3)	8	3.25	4.50	298.7	100@3400	5.2	L
	(4)	8	3.50	5.00	384.8	125@3200	5.2	L
1934	Six, CA (1)	6	3.375	4.50	241.6	93@3400	5.4	L
	Six, CB (1)	6	3.375	4.50	241.6	93@3400	5.4	L
	Airflow Eight, CU	8	3.25	4.50	298.7	122@3400	6.5	L
	Airflow Imperial, CV	8	3.25	4.875	323.5	130@3400	6.5	L
	Airflow Custom Imperial, CX	8	3.25	4.875	323.5	130@3400	6.5	L
	Airflow Custom Imperial, CW	8	3.50	5.00	384.8	150@3200	6.5	L
	Optional engine:							
	(1)	6	3.375	4.50	241.6	100@3400	6.2	L
1935	Airstream Six, C-6 (1)	6	3.375	4.50	241.5	93@3400	6.0	L
	Airstream Eight, CZ (2)	8	3.25	4.125	273.8	105@3400	6.2	L
	Airflow Eight, C-1 (3)	8	3.25	4.875	323.5	115@3400	6.2	L
	Airflow Imperial, C-2 (4)	8	3.25	4.875	323.5	130@3400	6.5	L
	Airflow Custom Imperial, C-3 (4)	8	3.25	4.875	323.5	130@3400	6.5	L
	Airflow Custom Imperial, CW*	8	3.50	5.00	384.8	150@3200	6.5	L
	Optional engines:							
	(1)	6	3.375	4.50	241.5	100@3400	6.5	L
	(2)	8	3.25	4.125	273.8	110@3400	7.0	L
	(3)	8	3.25	4.875	323.5	120@3400	6.5	L
	(4)	8	3.25	4.875	323.5	138@3400	7.45	L
1936	Airstream Six, C-7 (1)	6	3.375	4.50	241.5	93@3400	6.0	L
	Airstream Eight, C-8 (2)	8	3.25	4.125	273.8	105@3400	6.2	L
	Airflow Eight, C-9 (3)	8	3.25	4.875	323.5	115@3400	6.2	L

MFR	CARBURETOR MODEL	VEN	WHEEL-BASE	TIRES	BODY	WEIGHT	PRICE
S	UR-2		116.4	5.25 x 19	5 ps	2815	895
S	BXV-2		124	5.50 x 18	5 ps	3365	1525
S	DD-3		145	7.00 x 18	5 ps	4705	2745
			124	5.50 x 18			
S	DXC-3		124	6.50 x 17	5 ps	3640	1565
C	6A1		116.4	5.50 x 18	5 ps	3135	895
S	DXR-3		125	6.50 x 17	5 ps	3885	1475
S	DD-3		135	7.00 x 18	5 ps	4645	1945
S	DD-3		146	7.50 x 17	5 ps	5150	2895
S	EX-32	1	116.5	5.50 x 17	5 ps	3143	785
S	EX-32	1	119.5	6.00 x 17	5 ps	3483	925
S	EX-32	1	126	6.50 x 17	5 ps	3864	1295
S	EE-3	2	146	7.50 x 17	7 ps	5240	2995
B		1	117	6.50 x 16	5 ps	3123	820
B		1	121	6.50 x 16	5 ps		900
S	EX-32	1	122.8	7.00 x 16	6 ps	3760	1345
S	EE-22	1	128	7.50 x 16	6 ps	3974	1625
S	EE-22	1	137.5	7.50 x 16	6 ps	4154	2245
S	EE-3	2	146.5	7.50 x 17	8 ps	5780	5000
C	E6F2	1	118	6.25 x 16	5 ps	3013	830
S	EX-32	1	121	6.50 x 16	5 ps	3213	975
S	EX-32	2	123	7.00 x 16	6 ps	3828	1245
S	EE-22	2	128	7.50 x 16	6 ps	3998	1485
S	EE-22	2	137.5	7.50 x 16	6 ps	4208	2245
S	EE-3	2	146.5	7.50 x 17	8 ps	5785	5000
C	E6G1 (BB)	1	118	6.25 x 16	5 ps	3137	875
S	EXV-3	1	121/133	6.50 x 16	5 ps	3345	1045
S	EXV-3	1	123	7.00 x 16	6 ps	4102	1345

YEAR	MODEL	ENGINE						
		CYLS	BORE	STROKE	DISPL	HP@RPM	C.R.	VLV
	Airflow Imperial, C-10 (4)	8	3.25	4.875	323.5	130@3400	6.5	L
	Airflow Custom Imperial, C-11 (4)	8	3.25	4.875	323.5	130@3400	6.5	L
	Optional engines:							
	(1)	6	3.375	4.50	241.5	100@3400	6.2	L
	(2)	8	3.25	4.125	273.8	110@3400	7.0	L
	(3)	8	3.25	4.875	323.5	120@3400	6.5	L
	(4)	8	3.25	4.875	323.5	138@3400	7.45	L
1937	Royal Six, C-16 (1)	6	3.375	4.25	228.1	93@3600	6.5	L
	Airflow Eight, C-17 (2)	8	3.25	4.875	323.5	130@3400	6.5	L
	Imperial, C-14 (3)	8	3.25	4.125	273.8	110@3600	6.7	L
	Custom Imperial, C-15 (2)	8	3.25	4.875	323.5	130@3400	6.5	L
	Optional engines:							
	(1)	6	3.375	4.25	228.1	100@3600	7.0	L
	(2)	8	3.25	4.875	323.5	138@3400	7.45	L
	(3)	8	3.25	4.125	273.8	115@3600	7.4	L
1938	Royal Six, C-18 (1)	6	3.375	4.50	241.5	95@3600	6.2	L
	New York Special, C-19* (2)	8	3.25	4.50	298.6	110@3400	6.2	L
	Imperial, C-19 (2)	8	3.25	4.50	298.6	110@3400	6.2	L
	Custom Imperial, C-20 (3)	8	3.25	4.875	323.5	130@3400	6.5	L
	Optional engines:							
	(1)	6	3.375	4.50	241.5	102@3600	7.0	L
	(2)	8	3.25	4.50	298.6	122@3400	7.4	L
	(3)	8	3.25	4.875	323.5	138@3400	7.45	L
1939	Royal Six, C-22 (1)	6	3.375	4.50	241.5	100@3600	6.5	L
	Royal Windsor, C-22 (1)	6	3.375	4.50	241.5	100@3600	6.5	L
	Saratoga, C-23 (2)	8	3.25	4.875	323.5	130@3400	6.8	L
	New Yorker, C-23 (2)	8	3.25	4.875	323.5	130@3400	6.8	L
	Imperial, C-23 (2)	8	3.25	4.875	323.5	130@3400	6.8	L
	Custom Imperial, C-24 (2)	8	3.25	4.875	323.5	132@3400	6.8	L
	Optional engines:							
	(1)	6	3.375	4.50	241.5	107@3600	7.0	L
	(2)	8	3.25	4.875	323.5	138@3400	7.45	L
1940	Royal Six, C-25S (1)	6	3.375	4.50	241.5	108@3600	6.5	L
	Windsor, C-25W (1)	6	3.375	4.50	241.5	108@3600	6.5	L
	Traveler, C-26K (2)	8	3.25	4.875	323.5	135@3400	6.8	L
	New Yorker, C-26N (2)	8	3.25	4.875	323.5	135@3400	6.8	L
	Saratoga, C-26S (2)	8	3.25	4.875	323.5	135@3400	6.8	L
	Crown Imperial, C-27 (2)	8	3.25	4.875	323.5	137@3400	6.8	L

MFR	CARBURETOR MODEL	VEN	WHEEL-BASE	TIRES	BODY	WEIGHT	PRICE
S	EE-22	2	128	7.50 x 16	6 ps	4175	1475
S	EE-22	2	137	7.50 x 16	6 ps		2475
S	E6K1-4 (BB)	1	116/133	6.25 x 16	5 ps	3134	920
S	EE-22	2	128	7.50 x 16	6 ps	4300	1610
S	AAOV-1	2	121	6.50 x 16	5 ps	3564	1100
S	AAOV-1	2	140	7.50 x 16	5 ps	4522	2060
C	E6M1	1	119/138	6.25 x 16	5 ps	3180	1010
S	AAV-2	2	125	6.50 x 16	5 ps	3600	1370
S	AAV-2	2	125	6.50 x 16	5 ps	3565	1198
S	AAV-2	2	144	7.50 x 16	5 ps	4495	2295
C	E6N1-3	1	119/136	6.25 x 16/	5 ps	3265	1010
				6.50 x 16			
C	E6N1	1	119	6.25 x 16	5 ps	3275	1075
S	AAV-2	2	125	7.00 x 16	5 ps	3720	1443
S	AAV-2	2	125	7.00 x 16	5 ps	3695	1298
S	AAV-2	2	125	7.00 x 16	5 ps	3640	1198
S	AAV-2	2	144	7.50 x 16	5 ps	4590	2595
C	BB-E6S1	1	122.5/	6.25 x 16/	6 ps	3125	995
			139.5	6.50 x 16			
C	BB-E6S1	1	122.5/	6.25 x 16/	6 ps	3210	1025
			139.5	6.50 x 16			
S	AAV-2	2	128.5	6.50 x 16	6 ps	3590	1180
S	AAV-2	2	128.5	7.00 x 15	6 ps	3635	1260
S	AAV-2	2	128.5	7.00 x 15	6 ps	3790	1375
S	AAV-2	2	145.5	7.50 x 16	6 ps	4340	2245

YEAR	MODEL	ENGINE						
		CYLS	BORE	STROKE	DISPL	HP@RPM	C.R.	VLV
	Optional engines:							
	(1)	6	3.375	4.50	241.5	112@3600	7.0	L
	(2)	8	3.25	4.875	323.5	143@3400	7.45	L
1941	Royal, C-28S (1)	6	3.375	4.50	241.5	112@3600	6.8	L
	Windsor, C-28W (1)	6	3.375	4.50	241.5	112@3600	6.8	L
	Saratoga, C-30K (2)	8	3.25	4.875	323.5	140@3400	6.8	L
	New Yorker, C-30N (2)	8	3.25	4.875	323.5	140@3400	6.8	L
	Crown Imperial, C-34S	8	3.25	4.875	323.5	140@3400	6.8	L
	Optional engines:							
	(1)	6	3.375	4.50	241.5	115@3600	7.2	L
	(2)	8	3.25	4.875	323.5	140@3400	6.8	L
1942	Royal, C-34S	6	3.438	4.50	250.8	120@3800	6.6	L
	Windsor, C-34W	6	3.438	4.50	250.8	120@3800	6.6	L
	Saratoga, C-36K	8	3.25	4.875	323.5	140@3600	6.8	L
	New Yorker, C-36N	8	3.25	4.875	323.5	140@3600	6.8	L
	Crown Imperial, C-37	8	3.25	4.875	323.5	140@3600	6.8	L
1946	Royal, C-38S	6	3.438	4.50	250.8	114@3600	6.6	L
	Windsor, C-38W	6	3.438	4.50	250.8	114@3600	6.6	L
	Town & Country, C-38W	6	3.438	4.50	250.8	114@3600	6.6	L
	Saratoga, C-39K	8	3.25	4.875	323.5	135@3400	6.8	L
	New Yorker, C-39N	8	3.25	4.875	323.5	135@3400	6.8	L
	Town & Country, C-39N	8	3.25	4.875	323.5	135@3400	6.8	L
	Crown Imperial, C-40	8	3.25	4.875	323.5	135@3400	6.8	L
1947	Royal, C38S	6	3.438	4.50	250.6	114@3600	6.6	L
	Windsor, C38W	6	3.438	4.50	250.6	114@3600	6.6	L
	Town & Country, C38W	6	3.438	4.50	250.6	114@3600	6.6	L
	Saratoga, C39K	8	3.25	4.875	323.5	135@3400	7.25	L
	New Yorker, C39N	8	3.25	4.875	323.5	135@3400	7.25	L
	Town & Country, C39N	8	3.25	4.875	323.5	135@3400	7.25	L
	Crown Imperial, C40	8	3.25	4.875	323.5	135@3400	7.25	L
1948	Royal, C38S	6	3.438	4.50	250.6	114@3600	6.6	L
	Windsor, C38W	6	3.438	4.50	250.6	114@3600	6.6	L

MFR	CARBURETOR MODEL	VEN	WHEEL-BASE	TIRES	BODY	WEIGHT	PRICE
C	BB-E6W1	1	121.5/	6.25 x 16/	6 ps	3300	1091
			139.5	6.50 x 16			
C	BB-E6W1	1	121.5/	6.25 x 16/	6 ps	3300	1165
			139.5	6.50 x 16			
S	AAV-2	2	127.5	7.00 x 15	6 ps	3755	1320
S	AAV-2	2	127.5	7.00 x 15	6 ps	3775	1389
S	AAV-2	2	145.5	7.50 x 15	6 ps	4435	2595
C	EE-1	1	121.5/	6.25 x 16/	6 ps	3476	1177
			139.5	6.50 x 16			
C	EE-1	1	121.5/	6.25 x 16/	6 ps	3496	1255
			139.5	6.50 x 16			
S	AAV-2	2	127.5	7.00 x 15	6 ps	3833	1405
S	AAV-2	2	127.5	7.00 x 15	6 ps	3873	1475
S	AAV-2	2	145.5	7.50 x 15	6 ps	4565	2815
C	BB-EX1	1	121.5/	6.50 x 15	6 ps	3523	1561
			139.5				
C	BB-EX1	1	121.5	6.50 x 15	6 ps	3528	1611
C	BB-EX1	1	121.5	6.50 x 15	6 ps	3917	2366
S	AAV-2	2	127.5	7.00 x 15	6 ps	3972	1863
S	AAV-2	2	127.5	7.00 x 15	6 ps	3987	1963
S	AAV-2	2	127.5	7.00 x 15	6 ps	4300	2718
S	AAV-2	2	145.5	7.50 x 15	8 ps	4814	3875
C	BB-EX1	1	121.5/	6.50 x 15	6 ps	3523	1661
			139.5				
C	BB-EX1	1	121.5/	6.50 x 15	6 ps	3528	1711
			139.5				
C	BB-EX1	1	121.5	6.50 x 15	6 ps	3955	2713
S	AAV-2	2	127.5	7.00 x 15	6 ps	3972	1973
S	AAV-2	2	127.5	7.00 x 15	6 pcv	3987	2073
S	AAV-2	2	127.5	7.00 x 15	6 pcv	4332	2998
S	AAV-2	2	145.5	7.50 x 15	8 ps	4865	4205
C	BB-EX1	1	121.5/	7.60 x 15	6 ps	3523	1955
			139.5				
C	BB-EX1	1	121.5/	7.60 x 15	6 ps	3528	2021
			139.5				

YEAR	MODEL	ENGINE						
		CYLS	BORE	STROKE	DISPL	HP@RPM	C.R.	VLV
	Town & Country, C38W	6	3.438	4.50	250.6	114@3600	6.6	L
	Saratoga, C39K	8	3.25	4.875	323.5	135@3400	7.25	L
	New Yorker, C39N	8	3.25	4.875	323.5	135@3400	7.25	L
	Town & Country, C39N	8	3.25	4.875	323.5	135@3400	7.25	L
	Crown Imperial, C40	8	3.25	4.875	323.5	135@3400	7.25	L
1949	Royal, C-45-1	6	3.438	4.50	250.6	116@3600	7.0	L
	Windsor, C-45-2	6	3.438	4.50	250.6	116@3600	7.0	L
	Saratoga, C-46-1	8	3.25	4.875	323.5	135@3200	7.25	L
	New Yorker, C46-2	8	3.25	4.875	323.5	135@3200	7.25	L
	Town & Country, C46-2	8	3.25	4.875	323.5	135@3200	7.25	L
	Imperial, C46-2	8	3.25	4.875	323.5	135@3200	7.25	L
	Crown Imperial, C47	8	3.25	4.875	323.5	135@3200	7.25	L
1950	Royal, C48-1	6	3.438	4.50	250.6	116@3600	7.0	L
	Windsor, C48-2	6	3.438	4.50	250.6	116@3600	7.0	L
	Saratoga, C49-1	8	3.25	4.875	323.5	135@3200	7.25	L
	New Yorker, C49-2	8	3.25	4.875	323.5	135@3200	7.25	L
	Town & Country, C49-2	8	3.25	4.875	323.5	135@3200	7.25	L
	Imperial, C49N	8	3.25	4.875	323.5	135@3200	7.25	L
	Crown Imperial, C50	8	3.25	4.875	323.5	135@3200	7.25	L
1951	Windsor, C51-1	6	3.438	4.50	250.6	116@3600	7.0	L
	Windsor Deluxe, C51-2	6	3.438	4.50	250.6	116@3600	7.0	L
	Saratoga, C55	V8	3.812	3.625	331.1	180@4000	7.5	OH
	New Yorker, C52	V8	3.812	3.625	331.1	180@4000	7.5	OH
	Imperial, C54	V8	3.812	3.625	331.1	180@4000	7.5	OH
	Crown Imperial, C53	V8	3.812	3.625	331.1	180@4000	7.5	OH
1952	Windsor, C51-1	6	3.438	4.75	264.5	119@3600	7.0	L
	Windsor Deluxe, C51-2	6	3.438	4.75	264.5	119@3600	7.0	L
	Saratoga, C55	V8	3.812	3.625	331.1	180@4000	7.5	OH
	New Yorker, C52	V8	3.812	3.625	331.1	180@4000	7.5	OH
	Imperial, C54	V8	3.812	3.625	331.1	180@4000	7.5	OH
	Crown Imperial, C53	V8	3.812	3.625	331.1	180@4000	7.5	OH

MFR	CARBURETOR MODEL	VEN	WHEEL-BASE	TIRES	BODY	WEIGHT	PRICE
C	BB-E7A1	1	121.5	7.60 x 15	6 ps	3955	2860
S			127.5	8.20 x 15	6 ps	3972	2291
S			127.5	8.20 x 15	6 ps	3987	2411
S			127.5	8.20 x 15	6 pcv	4332	3395
S			145.5	8.90 x 15	8 ps	4865	4662
C	BB-E7L1-2		125.5/	7.60 x 15/	6 ps	3550	2154
			139.5	8.20 x 15			
C	BB-E7L1-2		125.5/	7.60 x 15/	6 ps	3681	2329
			139.5	8.20 x 15			
C	BB-E7J1-2		131.5	8.20 x 15	6 ps	4103	2610
C	BB-E7J1-2		131.5	8.20 x 15	6 ps	4113	2726
C	BB-E7J1-2		131.5	8.20 x 15	6 pcv	4630	3970
C	BB-E7J1-2		131.5	8.20 x 15	6 ps	4300	4665
C	BB-E7J1-2		145.5	8.90 x 15	8 ps	5250	5229
C	BB-EX3	1	125.5/	7.60 x 15/	6 ps	3610	2134
			139.5	8.20 x 15			
C	BB-EX3	1	125.5/	7.60 x 15/	6 ps	3765	2329
			139.5	8.20 x 15			
C	BB-E7J4	1	131.5	8.20 x 15	6 ps	4170	2642
C	BB-E7J4	1	131.5	8.20 x 15	6 ps	4190	2758
C	BB-E7J4	1	131.5	8.20 x 15	6 pht2	4670	4003
C	BB-E7J4	1	131.5	8.20 x 15	6 ps	4245	3055
C	BB-E7J4	1	145.5	8.90 x 15	8 ps	5235	5229
C	E9A1	1	125.5/	7.60 x 15/	6 ps	3627	2410
			139.5	8.20 x 15			
C	E9A1	1	125.5/	7.60 x 15/	6 ps	3775	2628
			139.5	8.20 x 15			
C	WCD-830S	2	125.5	8.00 x 15/	6 ps	4018	3041
				8.20 x 15			
C	WCD-830S	2	131.5	8.20 x 15	6 ps	4260	3403
C	WCD-830S	2	131.5	8.20 x 15	6 ps	4350	3699
C	WCD-830S	2	145.5	8.90 x 15	8 ps	5360	6623
C	E9C1	1	125.5/	7.60 x 15/	6 ps	3640	2518
			139.5	8.20 x 15			
C	E9C1	1	125.5	7.60 x 15	6 ps	3775	2747
C	WCD-884S	2	125.5/	8.00 x 15/	6 ps	4010	3240
			139.5	8.20 x 15			
C	WCD-884S	2	131.5	8.20 x 15	6 ps	4205	3555
C	WCD-884S	2	131.5	8.20 x 15	6 ps	4315	3864
C	WCD-884S	2	145.5	8.90 x 15	8 ps	5395	6922

YEAR	MODEL	ENGINE						
		CYLS	BORE	STROKE	DISPL	HP@RPM	C.R.	VLV
1953	Windsor, C60 - 1	6	3.438	4.75	264.5	119@3600	7.0	L
	Windsor Deluxe, C60 - 2	6	3.438	4.75	264.5	119@3600	7.0	L
	New Yorker, C56 - 1	V8	3.812	3.625	331.1	180@4000	7.5	OH
	New Yorker Deluxe, C56 - 2	V8	3.812	3.625	331.1	180@4000	7.5	OH
	Custom Imperial, C58	V8	3.812	3.625	331.1	180@4000	7.5	OH
	Crown Imperial, C59	V8	3.812	3.625	331.1	180@4000	7.5	OH
1954	Windsor Deluxe, C62	6	3.438	4.75	264.5	119@3600	7.0	L
	New Yorker, C63 - 1	V8	3.812	3.625	331.1	195@4400	7.5	OH
	New Yorker Deluxe, C63 - 2	V8	3.812	3.625	331.1	235@4400	7.5	OH
	Custom Imperial, C64	V8	3.812	3.625	331.1	235@4400	7.5	OH
	Crown Imperial, C66	V8	3.812	3.625	331.1	235@4400	7.5	OH
1955	Windsor Deluxe, C-67	V8	3.625	3.625	299.3	188@4400	8.0	OH
	New Yorker Deluxe, C-68	V8	3.812	3.625	331.1	250@4600	8.5	OH
	300, C300	V8	3.812	3.625	331.1	300@5200		OH
1956	Windsor, C-71	V8	3.812	3.625	331.1	225@4400	8.5	OH
	New Yorker, C-72	V8	3.938	3.625	353.1	280@4600	9.0	OH
	300B, C72 - 300	V8	3.938	3.625	353.1	340@5200	9.1	OH
1957	Windsor, C75-1	V8	3.938	3.625	353.1	285@4600	9.25	OH
	Saratoga, C75-2	V8	3.938	3.625	353.1	295@4600	9.25	OH
	New Yorker, C76	V8	4.00	3.90	392.1	325@4600	9.25	OH
	300, C76 (1)	V8	4.00	3.90	392.1	375@5200	9.25	OH
	Optional engine:							
	(1)	V8	4.00	3.90	392.1	390@5400	10.0	OH
1958	Windsor, LC1-L	V8	3.938	3.625	353.1	290@4600	10.0	OH
	Saratoga, LC2 - M	V8	3.938	3.625	353.1	310@4600	10.0	OH
	New Yorker, LC-3 - H	V8	4.00	3.90	392.1	345@4600	10.0	OH
	300D, LC3 -S (1)	V8	4.00	3.90	392.1	380@5200	10.0	OH
	Optional engine:							
	(1)	V8	4.00	3.90	392.1	390@5400	10.0	OH
1959	Windsor, MC1 - L	V8	4.03	3.75	382.7	305@4600	10.0	OH
	Saratoga, MC2 - M	V8	4.03	3.75	382.7	325@4600	10.0	OH
	New Yorker, MC3 - H	V8	4.188	3.75	413.2	350@4600	10.1	OH
	300E, MC3 - H	V8	4.188	3.75	413.2	380@5000	10.1	OH

MFR	CARBURETOR MODEL	VEN	WHEEL-BASE	TIRES	BODY	WEIGHT	PRICE
C	E9C1	1	125.5/	7.60 x 15/	6 ps	3660	2492
			139.5	8.20 x 15			
C	E9C1	1	125.5	7.60 x 15	6 ps	3775	2721
C	WCD-935S	2	125.5/	8.00 x 15/	6 ps	4005	3185
			139.5	8.20 x 15			
C	WCD-935S	2	125.5	8.00 x 15	6 ps	4025	3328
C	WCD-935S	2	131.5/	8.20 x 15	6 ps	4205	4260
			133.5				
C	WCD-992S	2	145.5	8.90 x 15	8 ps	5235	6922
C	E9B1	1	125.5/	7.60 x 15/	6 ps	3655	2562
			139.5	8.20 x 15			
C	BBD-919S	2	125.5/	8.00 x 15/	6 ps	3970	3229
			139.5	8.20 x 15			
C	WCFB-2041S	4	125.5	8.00 x 15	6 ps	4065	3433
C	WCFB-2041S	4	133.5/	8.20 x 15	6 ps	4355	4260
			131.5				
C	WCFB-2041S	4	145.5	8.90 x 15	8 ps	5220	6922
C	BBD-2190S	2	126	7.60 x 15	6 ps	3925	2660
C	WCFB-2126S	4	126	8.00 x 15	6 ps	4160	3494
C		2 x 4	126	8.00 x 15	6pht2	4110	4005
C	BBD-2312S	2	126	7.60 x 15	6 ps	3900	2870
C	WCFB-2314S	4	126	8.00 x 15	6 ps	4110	3779
C		2 x 4	126	8.00 x 15	6 pht2	4145	4419
C	BBD-2527S	2	126	8.50 x 14	6 ps	3995	3088
C	WCFB-2589S	4	126	8.50 x 14	6 ps	4165	3718
C	WCFB-2590S	4	126	9.00 x 14	6 ps	4315	4173
C	WCFB-2534S	2 x 4	126	9.00 x 14	6 pht2	4325	4929
C		2 x 4					
C	BBD-2733S	2	122	8.00 x 14/	6 ps	3895	3129
				8.50 x 14			
C	AFB-2650S	4	126	8.50 x 14	6 ps	4120	3818
C	AFB-2651S	4	126	9.00 x 14	6 ps	4195	4295
C	WCFB-2741S	2 x 4	126	9.00 x 14	6 pht2	4305	5173
C	BBD-2872S	2	122	8.00 x 14	6 ps	3800	3204
C	AFB-2797S	4	126	8.50 x 14	6 ps	4010	3966
		4	126	9.00 x 14	6 ps	4120	4424
C	AFB-2798S	2 x 4	126	9.00 x 14	6 pht2	4290	5319

YEAR	MODEL	ENGINE						
		CYLS	BORE	STROKE	DISPL	HP@RPM	C.R.	VLV
1960	Windsor, PC1 - L	V8	4.03	3.75	382.7	305@4600	10.0	OH
	Saratoga, PC2 - M	V8	4.03	3.75	382.7	325@4600	10.0	OH
	New Yorker, PC3 - H	V8	4.188	3.75	413.2	350@4600	10.0	OH
	300F, PC3 - H	V8	4.188	3.75	413.2	380@5000	10.0	OH
1961	Windsor, RC2 - M	V8	4.25	3.375	383.0	305@4800	10.0	OH
	Newport, RC1 - L	V8	4.125	3.375	360.8	265@4400	9.0	OH
	New Yorker, RC3 - H	V8	4.188	3.75	413.3	350@4600	10.1	OH
	300G, RC4 - P	V8	4.188	3.75	413.3	375@5000	10.1	OH
1962	Newport, SC1 - L	V8	4.125	3.375	361.8	265@4400	9.0	OH
	300, SC2 - M (1)	V8	4.25	3.375	383.0	305@4600	10.0	OH
	New Yorker, SC3 - H	V8	4.188	3.75	413.3	340@4600	10.1	OH
	300H, SC2 - M	V8	4.188	3.75	413.3	380@5200	10.1	OH
	Optional engine:							
	(1)	V8	4.188	3.75	413.3	340@4600	10.1	OH
1963	Newport, TC1 - L	V8	4.125	3.375	360.8	265@4400	9.0	OH
	300, TC2M - 300 (1)	V8	4.25	3.375	383.0	305@4600	10.0	OH
	New Yorker, TC3 - H	V8	4.188	3.75	413.8	340@4600	10.0	OH
	300J, TC2-M300	V8	4.188	3.75	413.8	390@4800	10.0	OH
	Optional engine:							
	(1)	V8	4.188	3.75	413.2	360@4800	10.1	OH
1964	Newport, VC1 - L	V8	4.125	3.375	360.8	265@4400	9.0	OH
	300, VC2-M-300 (1)	V8	4.25	3.375	383.0	305@4600	10.0	OH
	New Yorker, VC3 - H	V8	4.188	3.75	413.8	340@4600	10.0	OH
	300K, VC2-M-300 (2)	V8	4.188	3.75	413.8	360@4800	10.1	OH
	Optional engines: (1)	V8	4.188	3.75	413.2	360@4800	10.0	OH
	(2)	V8	4.188	3.75	413.2	390@4800	9.6	OH
1965	Newport, AC1 - L (1)	V8	4.25	3.375	383.0	270@4400	9.2	OH
	300, AC2 - M (2)	V8	4.25	3.375	383.0	315@4400	10.0	OH
	New Yorker, AC3 - H (2)	V8	4.188	3.75	413.8	340@4600	10.1	OH
	300L, AC2 - P	V8	4.188	3.75	413.8	360@4800	10.1	OH
	Optional engines:							
	(1)	V8	4.25	3.375	383.0	315@4400	10.0	OH
	(2)	V8	4.188	3.75	413.2	360@4800	10.1	OH
1966	Newport, BC1 - L (1, 2)	V8	4.25	3.375	383.0	270@4400	9.2	OH

MFR	CARBURETOR MODEL	VEN	WHEEL-BASE	TIRES	BODY	WEIGHT	PRICE
C	BBD-2924S	2	122	8.00 x 14/	6 ps	3815	3194
				8.50 x 14			
C	AFB-2927S	4	126	8.50 x 14	6 ps	4010	3929
C	AFB-2903S	4	126	9.00 x 14	6 ps	4145	4409
C	AFB-2903S	2 x 4	126	9.00 x 14	6 pht2	4270	5411
C	BBD-2923SA	2	122	8.00 x 14	6 ps	3730	3220
S	WWC3-188	2	122	8.00 x 14	6 ps	3710	2964
C	AFB-3108S	4	126	8.50 x 14	6 ps	4055	4125
C	AFB-2903S	2 x 4	126	8.00 x 15	4 pht2	4260	5413
S	WWC3-201A	2	122	8.00 x 14/	6 ps	3690	2964
				8.50 x 14			
C	BBD-3244S	2	122	8.00 x 14	6 pht4	3760	3400
C	AFB-3251S	4	126	8.50 x 14	6 ps	3925	4125
C	AFB-3258S	2 x 4	122	7.60 x 15	4 pht2	4010	5090
C	AFB-3251S	4					
S	WWC-3-221	2	122	8.00 x 14/	6 ps	3770	2964
				8.50 x 14			
C	BBD-3476S	2	122	7.60 x 15/	6 pht4	3815	3400
				8.00 x 14			
C	AFB-3256S	4	122	8.50 x 14/	6 ps	3910	3981
				9.00 x 14			
C	AFB-3505S	2 x 4	122	7.60 x 15	5 pht2	4000	5184
C	AFB-3478S	2 x 4					
S	WWC-3-244	2	122	8.00 x 14	6 ps	3805	2901
C	BBD-3685S	2	122	8.00 x 14	6 pht4	3865	3521
C	AFB-3615S	4	122	8.50 x 14/	6 ps	4015	3994
				9.00 x 14			
C	AFB-3614S	4	122	8.00 x 14	5 pht4	3965	4056
C	AFB-3614S	4					
C	AFB-3505SA	2 x 4					
C	BBD-3849S	2	124/121	8.55 x 14	6 ps	4045	2968
C	AFB-3855S	4	124/121	8.55 x 14	6 pht4	4150	3575
C	AFB-3858S	4	124	8.55 x 14/	6 ps	4265	4042
				9.00 x 14			
C	AFB-3860S	4	124	8.55 x 14	5 pht2	4245	4090
C	AFB-3855S	4					
C	AFB-3859S	4					
C	BBD-4125S	2	124	8.55 x 14	6 ps	3875	3052

YEAR	MODEL	ENGINE						
		CYLS	BORE	STROKE	DISPL	HP@RPM	C.R.	VLV
	300, BC2 - M (2)	V8	4.25	3.375	383.0	325@4800	10.0	OH
	New Yorker, BC3 - H (2)	V8	4.326	3.75	440.9	350@4400	10.1	OH
	Optional engines:							
	(1)	V8	4.25	3.375	383.0	325@4800	10.0	OH
	(2)	V8	4.326	3.75	440.9	365@4600	10.1	OH
1967	Newport, CC1 - E (1, 2)	V8	4.25	3.375	383.0	270@4400	9.2	OH
	Newport Custom, CC1 - L (1, 2)	V8	4.25	3.375	383.0	270@4400	9.2	OH
	300, CC2 - M (2)	V8	4.326	3.75	440.7	350@4400	10.1	OH
	New Yorker, CC3-H (2)	V8	4.326	3.75	440.7	350@4400	10.1	OH
	Optional engines:							
	(1)	V8	4.25	3.375	383.0	325@4800	10.0	OH
	(2)	V8	4.326	3.75	440.7	375@4600	10.1	OH
1968	Newport, CE (1, 2)	V8	4.25	3.375	383.0	290@4400	9.2	OH
	Newport Custom, CL (1, 2)	V8	4.25	3.375	383.0	290@4400	9.2	OH
	300, CM (2)	V8	4.326	3.75	440.7	350@4400	10.1	OH
	New Yorker, CH (2)	V8	4.326	3.75	440.7	350@4400	10.1	OH
	Optional engines:							
	(1)	V8	4.25	3.375	383.0	330@5000	10.0	OH
	(2)	V8	4.312	3.75	438.2	375@4600	10.1	OH
1969	Newport, CE (1, 2)	V8	4.25	3.375	383.0	290@4400	9.2	OH
	Newport Custom, CL (1, 2)	V8	4.25	3.375	383.0	290@4400	9.2	OH
	300, CM (2)	V8	4.326	3.75	440.7	350@4400	10.1	OH
	New Yorker, CM (2)	V8	4.326	3.75	440.7	350@4400	10.1	OH
	Town & Country, CP (3)	V8	4.25	3.375	383.0	290@4400	9.2	OH
	Optional engines:							
	(1)	V8	4.25	3.375	383.0	330@5000	10.0	OH
	(2)	V8	4.326	3.75	440.7	375@4600	10.1	OH
	(3)	V8	4.326	3.75	440.7	350@4600		OH

CLIPPER — — Packard Motor Car Co., Detroit, Mich., 1954-56

YEAR	MODEL	CYLS	BORE	STROKE	DISPL	HP@RPM	C.R.	VLV
1954	Special, 5400	8	3.50	3.75	288.6	150@4000	7.7	L
	Deluxe, 5401	8	3.50	4.25	327.1	165@3600	8.0	L
	Super, 5411	8	3.50	4.25	327.1	165@3600	8.0	L
1955	Deluxe, 5540	V8	3.812	3.50	319.6	225@4600	8.5	OH
	Super, 5540	V8	3.812	3.50	319.6	225@4600	8.5	OH
	Custom, 5560	V8	4.00	3.50	351.9	245@4600	8.5	OH
1956	Deluxe, 5640	V8	4.00	3.50	351.9	240@4600	9.5	OH
	Super, 5640	V8	4.00	3.50	351.9	240@4600	9.5	OH

MFR	CARBURETOR MODEL	VEN	WHEEL-BASE	TIRES	BODY	WEIGHT	PRICE
C	AFB-4130S	4	124	8.55 x 14	6 pht4	4000	3659
C	AFB-4131S	4	124	8.55 x 14	6 ps	4110	4101
C	AFB-4132S	4					
C	AFB-4136S	4					
C	BBD-4296S	2	124/122	8.25 x 14/	6 ps	3880	3159
				8.85 x 14			
C	BBD-4296S	2	124	8.55 x 14	6 ps	3915	3347
H	R-3667A	4	124	8.55 x 14	6 pht4	4035	4012
H	R-3667A	4	124	8.55 x 14	6 ps	4080	4208
C	BBD-4422S	2	124/122	8.55 x 14/	6 ps	3850	3306
				8.85 x 14			
C	BBD-4422S	2	124	8.55 x 14	6 ps	3855	3493
H	R-3918A	4	124	8.55 x 14	6 pht4	4015	4086
H	R-3918A	4	124	8.55 x 14	6 ps	4055	4367
C	BBD-4613S	2	124	8.85 x 14/	6 ps	4001	3414
				8.55 x 14			
C	BBD-4613S	2	124	8.55 x 14	6 ps	4016	3580
H	R-4166A	4	124	8.55 x 14	6 pht4	4150	4183
H	R-4166A	4	124	8.55 x 14	6 ps	4185	4487
C	BBD-4613S	2	122	8.85 x 14	6 psw4	4425	4583
C	WGD-986S	2	122	7.60 x 15	6 ps	3650	2594
C	WGD-2102S	2	122	7.60 x 15	6 ps	3660	2695
C	WGD-2102S	2	122	7.60 x 15	6 ps	3695	2815
C	WCFB-2232S	4	122	7.60 x 15	6 ps	3680	2586
C	WCFB-2232S	4	122	7.60 x 15	6 ps	3670	2686
R	4GC	4	122	7.60 x 15	6 ps	3885	2926
R		2	122	7.60 x 15	6 ps	3745	2731
R		2	122	7.60 x 15	6 ps	3800	2866

YEAR	MODEL	ENGINE CYLS	BORE	STROKE	DISPL	HP@RPM	C.R.	VLV
	Custom, 5660	V8	4.00	3.50	351.9	275@4600	9.5	OH

Note: Aside from the above years during which the Clipper was considered a separate make, distinct from the parent Packard, Clipper was a model of Packard.

COBRA (AC COBRA) — — Shelby-American, Inc., Venice, Cal., 1963-67

YEAR	MODEL	CYLS	BORE	STROKE	DISPL	HP@RPM	C.R.	VLV
1963	AC Cobra	V8	3.80	2.875	260.8	260@5800	9.2	OH
1964	289	V8	4.00	2.875	288.5	271@6000	11.6	OH
1965	289	V8	4.00	2.875	288.5	271@6000	11.6	OH
1966	427	V8	4.125	3.98	426.7	425@6000	10.0	OH

COLT — — Colt Motors Corp., Boston, Mass., 1958

YEAR	MODEL	CYLS	BORE	STROKE	DISPL	HP@RPM	C.R.	VLV
1958		1	3.00	3.25	23.0			
	Engine was an air-cooled Wisconsin.							

COMET — — General Developing Co., Ridgewood, L.I., N.Y., 1947-48

YEAR	MODEL	CYLS	BORE	STROKE	DISPL	HP@RPM	C.R.	VLV
1947-48		2				4.5		

The Comet was a three-wheeler with a tubular frame and bicycle wheels.

CONTINENTAL — — Continental Automobile Co. (subsidiary of Continental Motors Corp.), Detroit, Mich., 1933-34

YEAR	MODEL	CYLS	BORE	STROKE	DISPL	HP@RPM	C.R.	VLV
1933	Beacon, C400	4	3.375	4.00	143.1	40@2800	5.05	L
	Flyer, C600	6	3.00	4.00	169.6	65@3500	5.20	L
	Ace, 80	6	3.375	4.00	214.7	85@3600	5.35	L
1934	Beacon, 41	4	3.375	4.00	143.1	38@3600	5.05	L

CORD — — Auburn Automobile Co., Auburn, Ind., 1930-33; 1936-37

YEAR	MODEL	CYLS	BORE	STROKE	DISPL	HP@RPM	C.R.	VLV
1930	L-29	8	3.25	4.50	298.6	125@3600	5.25	L
1931	L-29	8	3.25	4.50	298.6	125@3600	5.25	L
1932	L-29	8	3.25	4.50	298.6	125@3600	5.25	L
1933	L-29	8	3.25	4.50	298.6	125@3600	5.25	L
1936	810	V8	3.50	3.75	288.6	125@3500	6.5	L
1937	812	V8	3.50	3.75	288.6	125@3500	6.5	L
	812SC (Supercharged)	V8	3.50	3.75	288.6	175@4200	6.32	L

CORD 8/10 — — Cord Automobile Co.; S.A.M.C.O., Inc., Tulsa Okla., 1967-69

YEAR	MODEL	CYLS	BORE	STROKE	DISPL	HP@RPM	C.R.	VLV
1967	Sportsman	F6	3.438	2.938	163.6	140@5200	9.25	OH
	Optional engine:	F6	3.438	2.938	163.6	180@4000	8.25	OH
	Above were Chevrolet Corvair engines.							
1969	Royale	V8	4.00	3.00	301.6	210@4600	9.0	OH
	1969 engine was by Ford.							

MFR	CARBURETOR MODEL	VEN	WHEEL-BASE	TIRES	BODY	WEIGHT	PRICE
R		4	122	7.60 x 15	6 ps	3860	3069
		4	90	6.50/6.70 x 15	2 pr	2020	5995
F		4	90	7.35 x 15	2 pr	2170	5995
H		4	108	7.75 x 15	2 pr	2550	
F		2 x 4	90	8.15 x 15	2 pr	2450	
			77		2 pr	700	995
				2.5 x 26	3 pr	175	500
M	AC	1	101.5	5.25 x 17	5 ps	2145	395
M	B	1	107	5.25 x 17	5 ps	2245	535
M	B	1	114	5.50 x 17	5 ps	3070	765
M	AC	1	101.5	5.25 x 17	5 ps	2145	495
Sc	SX-411	2	137.5	7.00 x 18	5 ps	4530	3095
Sc	SX-411	2	137.5	7.00 x 18	5 ps	4630	2395
Sc	SX-411	2	137.5	7.00 x 18	5 ps	4560	2395
Sc	SX-411	2	137.5	7.00 x 18	5 ps	4560	2395
S	EE-15		125	6.50 x 16	5 ps	3500	1995
S	EE-15		125	6.50 x 16	5 ps	3715	2445
S	AA-25		125	6.50 x 16	5 ps	3765	2860
R	7025023	2 x 1	100	7.00 x 13	2 pcv2	2100	4000
C	3856713	2					
A		2	109		2 pcv2	2960	7325

YEAR	MODEL	ENGINE						
		CYLS	BORE	STROKE	DISPL	HP@RPM	C.R.	VLV
CROSLEY — — Crosley Motors, Inc., Cincinnati, Oh., 1939-52								
1939	2A	2	3.00	2.75	38.9	12@4200		L
1940	2A	2	3.00	2.75	38.9	12@4200	5.5	L
1941	CB41	2	3.00	2.50	35.3	12@4000	5.6	L
1942	CB42	2	3.00	2.50	35.3	12@4000	5.6	L
1946	CC-46	4	2.50	2.25	44.2	28@5200	7.5	OH
1947	CC-47	4	2.50	2.25	44.2	26.5@5400	7.5	OH
1948	CC	4	2.50	2.25	44.2	26.5@5400	7.5	OH
1949	CD	4	2.50	2.25	44.2	26.5@5400	7.8	OH
	VC	4	2.50	2.25	44.2	26.5@5400	7.8	OH
1950	CD	4	2.50	2.25	44.2	26.5@5400	7.8	OH
	Super CD	4	2.50	2.25	44.2	26.5@5400	7.8	OH
	VC	4	2.50	2.25	44.2	26.5@5400	7.8	OH
	Super VC	4	2.50	2.25	44.2	26.5@5400	7.8	OH
1951	CD	4	2.50	2.25	44.2	26.5@5400	7.8	OH
	Super CD	4	2.50	2.25	44.2	26.5@5400	7.8	OH
	VC	4	2.50	2.25	44.2	26.5@5400	7.8	OH
	Super VC	4	2.50	2.25	44.2	26.5@5400	7.8	OH
1952	CD	4	2.50	2.25	44.2	26.5@5400	7.8	OH
	Super CD	4	2.50	2.25	44.2	26.5@5400	7.8	OH
	VC	4	2.50	2.25	44.2	26.5@5400	7.8	OH
	Super VC	4	2.50	2.25	44.2	26.5@5400	7.8	OH
CUNNINGHAM — — James Cunningham Sons & Co., Rochester, N.Y., 1907-35								
1930	V-9	V8	3.75	5.00	441.8	110@2500	5.0	L
1931	V-9	V8	3.75	5.00	441.8	110@2500	5.0	L
1932	V-10	V8	3.875	5.00	471.7	140@2800	5.0	L
CUNNINGHAM — — B. S. Cunningham Co., West Palm Beach, Fla., 1951-55								
1953	Continental, C3	V8	3.812	3.625	331.1	220@4000	7.5	OH
1954	Continental, C3	V8	3.812	3.625	331.1	220@4000	7.5	OH
	Cunningham used Chrysler engines.							

CARBURETOR			WHEEL-	TIRES	BODY	WEIGHT	PRICE
MFR	MODEL	VEN	BASE				
T		1	80	4.25 x 12	4 pcv2	975	325
T	DY-1A	1	80	4.25 x 12	4 ps2	950	362
T	DY-1A	1	80	4.25 x 12	4 pcv2	975	390
T	DY-1A	1	80	4.25 x 12	4 ps2	1050	515
T	DY-9B	1	80	4.50 x 12			
T	DY-9B	1	80	4.50 x 12	4 ps2	1155	888
T	DY-9B	1	80	4.50 x 12	4 ps2	1115	943
T	DY-9C	1	80	4.50 x 12	4 ps2	1363	899
T	DY-9C	1	85	4.50 x 12	2 pr	1175	849
T	DY-9C	1	80	4.50 x 12	4 ps2	1363	882
T	DY-9C	1	80	4.50 x 12	4 ps2	1363	951
T	DY-9C	1	85	4.50 x 12	2 pr	1175	872
T	DY-9C	1	85	4.50 x 12	2 pr	1175	925
T	DY-9C	1	80	4.50 x 12	4 psw2	1403	1002
T	DY-9C	1	80	4.50 x 12	4 ps2	1363	1033
T	DY-9C	1	85	4.50 x 12	2 pr	1184	952
T	DY-9C	1	85	4.50 x 12	2 pr	1184	1029
C	WO-870S	1	80	4.50 x 12	4 psw2	1340	943
C	WO-870S	1	80	4.50 x 12	4 ps2	1363	1033
C	WO-870S	1	85	4.50 x 12	2 pr	1175	952
C	WO-870S	1	85	4.50 x 12	2 pr	1175	1029
S			134/142	7.00 x 20	6 pt	4800	8000
S			134/142	7.00 x 20	6 pt	4800	8000
S	UUR2	2	142	7.50 x 18	6 pt	4800	8000
			105	7.10 x 15	2 pc	3500	9000
			105		4 pht2	2800	10,000

YEAR	MODEL	ENGINE						
		CYLS	BORE	STROKE	DISPL	HP@RPM	C.R.	VLV

DARRIN — — Howard A. Darrin Automotive Design, Los Angeles, Cal., 1946; 1955-58

YEAR	MODEL	CYLS	BORE	STROKE	DISPL	HP@RPM	C.R.	VLV
1946		6			187.0	90		
1955		V8	3.812	3.625	331.1	270@4600	9.0	OH
1956		V8	4.00	3.625	364.4	307@4700	9.75	OH
1957		V8	4.00	3.625	364.4	325@4800	10.0	OH
1958		V8	4.00	3.625	364.4	310@4800	10.25	OH

The Darrin in the years 1955-58 used Cadillac engines in leftover Kaiser - Darrin chassis.

DART (MARTIN) — — Martin Motors, Inc., Washington, D.C., 1928-ca 1931

YEAR	MODEL	CYLS	BORE	STROKE	DISPL	HP@RPM	C.R.	VLV
1930-31		4	2.188	2.438	36.6			

This small car was supposed to sell for $200, but this seems to have been a fanciful price. Only prototypes were built.

DAVIS — — Davis Motor Co., Van Nuys, Cal., 1947-49

YEAR	MODEL	CYLS	BORE	STROKE	DISPL	HP@RPM	C.R.	VLV
1948	D-2	4	3.25	4.00	132.7	60@3200	L	

This three-wheeler used engines by Hercules or Continental. About seventeen were constructed.

DAYTONA — — Randall Products, Hampton, N.H., 1956

YEAR	MODEL	CYLS	BORE	STROKE	DISPL	HP@RPM	C.R.	VLV
1956		1				2		

Engine was by Briggs & Stratton.

DEBONNAIRE — — Replac Corp., Euclid, Oh., 1955

YEAR	MODEL	CYLS	BORE	STROKE	DISPL	HP@RPM	C.R.	VLV
1955								

DELCAR — — American Motors, Inc., Troy, N.Y., 1947-49

YEAR	MODEL	CYLS	BORE	STROKE	DISPL	HP@RPM	C.R.	VLV
1947-49		4				25		

This company made mostly delivery cars, but at least one station wagon.

DEL MAR — — Del Mar Motors, Inc., San Diego, Cal., 1949

YEAR	MODEL	CYLS	BORE	STROKE	DISPL	HP@RPM	C.R.	VLV
1949		4	3.438	4.375	162.5	63		L

DE SOTO — — Chrysler Corp., Detroit, Mich., 1928-60

YEAR	MODEL	CYLS	BORE	STROKE	DISPL	HP@RPM	C.R.	VLV
1930	Finer Six, CK	6	3.00	4.125	174.9	57@3400	5.2	L
	Eight, CF	8	2.875	4.00	207.7	70@3400	5.2	L
1931	Six, SA	6	3.25	4.125	205.3	67@3200	5.2	L
	Eight, CF	8	2.875	4.00	207.7	75@3400	5.4	L
1932	Six, SC, Custom	6	3.25	4.25	211.5	75@3400	5.4	L
	Six, SC, Standard	6	3.25	4.25	211.5	75@3400	5.4	L
	Eight, CF*	8	2.875	4.25	220.7	77@3400	5.4	L
1933	Six, SD, Custom	6	3.25	4.375	217.8	82@3400	6.0	L

CARBURETOR MFR	MODEL	VEN	WHEEL-BASE	TIRES	BODY	WEIGHT	PRICE
			115		5 pcv2	2400	1950
			100		2 pcv2		
			100		2 pcv2		
			100		2 pcv2	2450	
			100		2 pcv2		
			60		2 pc		
Z	28-AV-10	1	108	5.50 x 15	4 ps	1385	995
					2 pr	235	495
			114		2 pr		1800
			60		4 psw2		
S			104	6.40 x 12	2 pcv2		1170
			109	5.00 x 19	5 ps	2645	885
S	DX3		114	5.25 x 19	5 ps	2965	995
C	188SR		109.4	5.00 x 19	5 ps	2680	695
S	DX3		114	5.25 x 19	5 ps	3025	995
C	6B2		112.4	5.25 x 18	5 ps	3028	835
C	6B2		112.4	5.25 x 18	5 ps	2993	775
S	DX3		114.4	5.25 x 19	5 ps	3025	995
C	E6A3	1	114.4	7.00 x 15	5 ps	3150	795

YEAR	MODEL	ENGINE						
		CYLS	BORE	STROKE	DISPL	HP@RPM	C.R.	VLV
	Six, CD, Standard	6	3.25	4.375	217.8	82@3400	6.0	L
1934	Airflow, SE	6	3.375	4.50	241.5	100@3400	6.2	L
1935	Airstream, SF	6	3.375	4.50	241.5	93@3400	6.0	L
	Airflow, SG	6	3.375	4.50	241.5	100@3400	6.5	L
1936	Airstream, S1	6	3.375	4.50	241.5	93@3400	6.0	L
	Airstream, S1, Custom	6	3.375	4.50	241.5	93@3400	6.0	L
	Airflow, S2	6	3.375	4.50	241.5	100@3400	6.5	L
1937	Six, S3	6	3.375	4.25	228.1	93@3600	6.5	L
1938	Six, S5	6	3.375	4.25	228.1	93@3600	6.5	L
1939	De Luxe, S6	6	3.375	4.25	228.1	93@3600	6.5	L
	Custom, S6	6	3.375	4.25	228.1	93@3600	6.5	L
1940	DeLuxe, S7	6	3.375	4.25	228.1	105@3600	6.5	L
	Custom, S7	6	3.375	4.25	228.1	105@3600	6.5	L
1941	DeLuxe, S8	6	3.375	4.25	228.1	100@3600	6.5	L
	Custom, S8	6	3.375	4.25	228.1	105@3600	6.8	L
1942	DeLuxe, S10	6	3.438	4.25	236.7	115@3800	6.6	L
	Custom, S10	6	3.438	4.25	236.7	115@3800	6.6	L
1946 -	DeLuxe, S11	6	3.438	4.25	236.7	109@3600	6.6	L
1948	Custom, S11	6	3.438	4.25	236.7	109@3600	6.6	L
1949	DeLuxe, S13	6	3.438	4.25	236.7	112@3600	7.0	L
	Custom, S13	6	3.438	4.25	236.7	112@3600	7.0	L
1950	DeLuxe, S14	6	3.438	4.25	236.7	112@3600	7.0	L
	Custom, S14	6	3.438	4.25	236.7	112@3600	7.0	L
1951	DeLuxe, S15-1	6	3.438	4.50	250.6	116@3600	7.0	L
	Custom, S15-2	6	3.438	4.50	250.6	116@3600	7.0	L
1952	DeLuxe, S15-1	6	3.438	4.50	250.6	116@3600	7.0	L
	Custom, S15-2	6	3.438	4.50	250.6	116@3600	7.0	L
	Firedome, S17	V8	3.625	3.344	276.1	160@4000	7.1	OH

MFR	CARBURETOR MODEL	VEN	WHEEL-BASE	TIRES	BODY	WEIGHT	PRICE
C	E6A3	1	114.4	5.50 x 17	5 ps	3060	735
C	E6B1	1	115.5	6.50 x 16	6 ps	3378	995
C	E6F2	1	116	6.25 x 16	5 ps	2990	795
C	E6F2	1	115.5	6.50 x 16	6 ps	3390	1015
C	E6G1	1	118	6.25 x 16	5 ps	3111	810
C	E6G1	1	118/130	6.25 x 16	5 ps	3126	865
C	E6G1	1	115.5	6.50 x 16	6 ps	3490	1095
C	E6K4	1	116/133	6.00 x 16	5 ps	3123	870
C	E6M1	1	119/136	6.00 x 16	5 ps	3134	958
C	E6N1		119/136	6.00 x 16	5 ps	3174	970
C	E6N1		119/136	6.00 x 16	5 ps	3179	1023
C	E6N2		122.5/	6.00 x 16/	5 ps	3104	905
			139.5	6.50 x 16			
C	E6N2		122.5/	6.00 x 16/	5 ps	3104	945
			139.5	6.50 x 16			
B	E6N3		121.5/	6.25 x 16/	5 ps	3254	1035
			139.5	6.50 x 16			
B	E6N3		121.5/	6.25 x 16/	5 ps	3269	1085
			139.5	6.50 x 16			
C	EE-1		121.5/	6.25 x 15	5 ps	3330	1159
			139.5				
C	EE-1		121.5	6.25 x 15	5 ps	3315	1103
C	EX1	1	121.5	6.50 x 15	6 ps	3397	1426
C	EX1	1	121.5	6.50 x 15	6 ps	3433	1511
			125.5	7.60 x 15	6 ps	3520	2006
			125.5/	7.60 x 15/	6 ps	3645	2194
			139.5	8.20 x 16			
C	Ex-3	1	125.5/	7.60 x 15/	6 ps	3525	2006
			139.5	8.20 x 15			
C	Ex-3	1	125.5	7.60 x 15/	6 ps	3640	2194
				8.20 x 15			
C			125.5/	7.60 x 15/	6 ps	3570	2247
			139.5	8.20 x 15			
C			125.5/	7.60 x 15/	6 ps	3685	2458
			139.5	8.20 x 15			
B	E9C1	1	125.5/	7.60 x 15/	6 ps	3540	2353
			139.5	8.20 x 15			
B	E9C1	1	125.5/	7.60 x 15/	6 ps	3660	2572
			139.5	8.20 x 15			
C	WCD-884S	2	125.5/	7.60 x 15/	6 ps	3760	2760
			139.5	8.20 x 15			

YEAR	MODEL	ENGINE						
		CYLS	BORE	STROKE	DISPL	HP@RPM	C.R.	VLV
1953	Power Master, S18	6	3.428	4.50	250.6	116@3600	7.0	L
	Firedome, S16	V8	3.625	3.344	276.1	160@4400	7.1	OH
1954	Power Master, S20	6	3.438	4.50	250.6	116@3600	7.0	L
	Firedome, S19	V8	3.625	3.344	276.1	170@4400	7.5	OH
1955	Firedome, S22	V8	3.72	3.344	291.0	185@4400	7.5	OH
	Fireflite, S21	V8	3.72	3.344	291.0	200@4400	7.5	OH
1956	Firedome, S23	V8	3.72	3.80	330.4	230@4400	8.5	OH
	Fireflite, S24	V8	3.72	3.80	330.4	255@4400	8.5	OH
	Adventurer, S24	V8	3.78	3.80	341.1	320@5200	9.25	OH
1957	Firesweep, S27 (1)	V8	3.69	3.80	325.1	245@4400	8.5	OH
	Firedome, S25	V8	3.78	3.80	341.2	270@4600	9.25	OH
	Fireflite, S26	V8	3.78	3.80	341.2	295@4600	9.25	OH
	Adventurer, S26A	V8	3.80	3.80	344.8	345@5200	9.25	OH
	Optional engine:							
	(1)	V8	3.78	3.80	341.2	295@4600	9.25	OH
1958	Firesweep, LS1-L (1)	V8	4.062	3.375	350.0	280@4600	10.0	OH
	Firedome, LS2-M	V8	4.125	3.375	360.8	295@4600	10.0	OH
	Fireflite, LS3-H	V8	4.125	3.375	360.8	305@4600	10.0	OH
	Adventurer, LS3-S (2)	V8	4.125	3.375	360.8	345@5000	10.25	OH
	Optional engines:							
	(1)	V8	4.125	3.375	360.8	295@4600	10.0	OH
	(2)	V8	4.125	3.375	360.8	355@5000	10.25	OH
1959	Firesweep, MS1-L	V8	4.125	3.375	360.8	295@4600	10.0	OH
	Firedome, MS2-M	V8	4.25	3.375	393.0	305@4600	10.1	OH
	Fireflite, MS3-H	V8	4.25	3.375	383.0	325@4600	10.1	OH
	Adventurer, MS3-H	V8	4.25	3.375	383.0	350@5000	10.1	OH
1960	Fireflite, PS1-L	V8	4.125	3.375	360.8	295@4600	10.0	OH
	Adventurer, PS3-M	V8	4.25	3.375	383.0	305@4600	10.0	OH
1961	Adventurer, RS1-L	V8	4.125	3.375	360.8	265@4400	9.0	OH

DETROIT ELECTRIC — — Detroit Electric Car Co., Detroit, Mich., 1907-ca 1936

YEAR	MODEL	CYLS	BORE	STROKE	DISPL	HP@RPM	C.R.	VLV
1930	97							
	99							
1931	97							
	99							
1932	97							
	99							

MFR	CARBURETOR MODEL	VEN	WHEEL-BASE	TIRES	BODY	WEIGHT	PRICE
B	E9C1	1	125.5/	7.60 x 15/	6 ps	3535	2386
			139.5	8.20 x 15			
C	BBD-909S	2	125.5/	7.60 x 15/	6 ps	3720	2673
			139.5	8.20 x 15			
B	E9C1	1	125.5/	7.60 x 15/	6 ps	3570	2386
			139.5	8.20 x 15			
C	2067S	1	125.5/	7.60 x 15/	6 ps	3790	2673
			139.5	8.20 x 15			
C	BBD-2117S	2	126	7.60 x 15	6 ps	3810	2498
C	WCFB-2210S	4	126	7.60 x 15	6 ps	3935	2727
C	BBD-2312S	2	126	7.60 x 15	6 ps	3855	2673
C	BBD-2312S	2	126	7.60 x 15	6 ps	4005	3115
C	WCFB-2311S	4	126	7.60 x 15	6 pht2	3870	3728
S	WW-3-149	2	122	8.00 x 14	6 ps	3675	2777
C	BBD-2522S	2	126	8.50 x 14	6 ps	3955	2958
C	WCFB-2588S	2	126	8.50 x 14	6 ps	4025	3487
C			126	8.50 x 14	6 pht2	4040	3997
C	WCFB-2588S	2					
C	BBD-2637S	2	122	8.00 x 14	6 ps	3660	2819
C	BBD-2637S	2	126	8.50 x 14	6 ps	3965	3085
C	AFB-2642S	4	126	8.50 x 14	6 ps	3990	3583
C	AFB-2652S	2 x 4	126	8.50 x 14	6 pht2	4000	4071
C	BBD-26375	2					
		F.I.					
C	BBD-2870S	2	122	8.00 x 14	6 ps	3670	2904
C	BBD-2871S	2	126	8.50 x 14	6 ps	3840	3243
C	BBD-2794	2	126	8.50 x 14	6 ps	3920	3763
C	AFB-2794	2 x 4	126	8.50 x 14	6 pht2	3980	4427
C	BBD-2923S	2	122	8.00 x 14	6 ps	3865	3017
C	BBD-2923S	2	122	8.00 x 14	6 pht4	3895	3579
S	WWC-3-188	2	122	8.00 x 14	6 pht4	3820	3167
					4 ps2	3400	2800
					4 ps2	4175	4250
					4 ps2	3400	2800
					4 ps2	4175	4250
					4 pb	3400	2940
					5 ps2	4240	4250

YEAR	MODEL	ENGINE CYLS	BORE	STROKE	DISPL	HP@RPM	C.R.	VLV
1933	97							
	99							
1934	97							
	99							

These were all electrics, fitted to various chassis by others.

DE VAUX — — DeVaux-Hall Motors Corp., Grand Rapids, Mich., 1931-32

YEAR	MODEL	CYLS	BORE	STROKE	DISPL	HP@RPM	C.R.	VLV
1931	Six	6	3.375	4.00	214.7	65@3400		L
1932	6-75	6	3.375	4.00	214.7	70@3400	5.47	L

One author claims that the 1932 model was designated 6 - 80, and that there were Standard and Custom versions. Specification sheets do not agree with this. There also is confusion over the wheelbase for the 1932 model, given variously as 113, 114 and 115 inches. De Vaux was built in Canada as Frontenac, q.v. De Vaux was superseded by Continental.

DEVIN — — Devin Enterprises, El Monte, Cal., 1959

YEAR	MODEL	CYLS	BORE	STROKE	DISPL	HP@RPM	C.R.	VLV
1959	SS	V8	3.875	3.00	283.0	220@4800	9.5	OH

A Corvette engine was used. This car was assembled in Ireland.

DIEHLMOBILE — — H. L. Diehl Co., South Willington, Conn., 1962-64

YEAR	MODEL	CYLS	BORE	STROKE	DISPL	HP@RPM	C.R.	VLV
1962-64						4		

A Briggs & Stratton engine was used in this car.

DIE VALKYRIE — — Fiberfab Div., Velocidad, Inc. (location unknown), 1967-

YEAR	MODEL	CYLS	BORE	STROKE	DISPL	HP@RPM	C.R.	VLV
1967		V8				450		

An earlier car (1955) by the same rather pompous name was built on a Cadillac chassis by Imprex International Co., Cleveland, Ohio. There is no known connection between the two organizations.

DOBLE — — Doble Steam Motors Corp., Emeryville, Cal., 1914-31

YEAR	MODEL	CYLS	BORE	STROKE	DISPL	HP@RPM	C.R.	VLV
1930	E	2	2.625	4.50		65@1025		
		2	4.50	4.50				

This famed steamer had two high-pressure and two low-pressure cylinders. It is just possible that at at least one of these cars was assembled in the 1930 - 31 period.

DODGE — — Chrysler Corp., Detroit, Mich., 1914+

YEAR	MODEL	CYLS	BORE	STROKE	DISPL	HP@RPM	C.R.	VLV
1930	Six, DA	6	3.375	3.875	208.0	63@3000	5.2	L
	Senior Six, DB	6	3.375	4.50	241.5	78@3000	5.2	L
	New Six, DD	6	3.125	4.125	189.8	61@3400	5.2	L
	Eight, DC	8	2.875	4.25	220.7	75@3400	5.2	L
1931	New Six, DD	6	3.125	4.125	189.8	60@3400	5.2	L
	Six, DH	6	3.25	4.25	211.5	68@3200	5.2	L
	Eight, DC	8	2.875	4.25	220.7	75@3400	5.2	L

CARBURETOR MFR	MODEL	VEN	WHEEL-BASE	TIRES	BODY	WEIGHT	PRICE
			110		4 ps2	3400	2800
			112		4 ps2	4175	3750
			100		4 ps2	3400	2800
			112		4 ps2	4175	3750
T	J	1	113	5.00 x 19	5 ps	2725	695
T	J	1	113	5.00 x 19	5 ps	2785	685
			92	6.40 x 15	2 pr	2550	5950
						225	300
					2 pc		12,000
			142	6.20 x 30	ch	4250	6800
S			112	5.00 x 19	5 ps	2867	995
S			120	5.00 x 19	5 ps	3513	1595
C			109	5.00 x 19	5 ps	2668	865
S			114	5.50 x 18	5 ps	3043	1145
C			114	5.00 x 19	5 ps	2668	765
C	197S	1	114	5.00 x 19	5 ps	2820	845
S			114	5.50 x 18	5 ps	3043	1045

YEAR	MODEL	ENGINE						
		CYLS	BORE	STROKE	DISPL	HP@RPM	C.R.	VLV
	Eight, DG	8	3.00	4.25	240.3	84@3400	5.2	L
1932	Six, DD	6	3.125	4.125	189.8	60@3400		L
	New Six, DH	6	3.25	4.25	211.5	74@3400		L
	Eight, DC	8	2.875	4.25	220.7	75@3400		L
	New Eight, DG	8	3.00	4.25	240.3	84@3400		L
	New Eight, DK	8	3.25	4.25	282.1	90@3400	5.2	L
1933	Six, DP	6	3.125	4.375	201.3	75@3600	5.5	L
	Six (second series), DP	6	3.125	4.375	201.3	75@3600	5.5	L
	Eight, DO	8	3.25	4.25	282.1	92@3400	6.2	L
1934	New Standard, DRXX	6	3.25	4.375	217.8	87@3600	6.5	L
	Six, DR	6	3.25	4.375	217.8	87@3600	6.5	L
	Six, DS	6	3.25	4.375	217.8	87@3600	6.5	L
1935	New Value Line, DU	6	3.25	4.375	217.8	87@3600	6.5	L
1936	Beauty Winner Line, D2	6	3.25	4.375	217.8	87@3600	6.5	L
1937	Six, D5	6	3.25	4.375	217.8	87@3600	6.5	L
1938	Six, D8	6	3.25	4.375	217.8	87@3600	6.5	L
1939	Special Six, D11	6	3.25	4.375	217.8	87@3600	6.5	L
	DeLuxe Six, D11	6	3.25	4.375	217.8	87@3600	6.5	L
1940	Luxury Liner Special, D17	6	3.25	4.375	217.8	87@3600	6.5	L
	Luxury Liner DeLuxe, D14	6	3.25	4.375	217.8	87@3600	6.5	L
1941	Custom, D19C	6	3.25	4.375	217.8	91@3800	6.5	L
	DeLuxe, D19S	6	3.25	4.375	217.8	91@3800	6.5	L
1942	Custom, D22	6	3.25	4.625	230.2	105@3600	6.7	L
	DeLuxe, D22	6	3.25	4.625	230.2	105@3600	6.7	L
1946	Custom, D24	6	3.25	4.625	230.2	102@3800	6.7	L
	DeLuxe, D24	6	3.25	4.625	230.2	102@3800	6.7	L
1947	Custom, D24	6	3.25	4.625	230.2	102@3600	6.7	L
	DeLuxe, D24	6	3.25	4.625	230.2	102@3600	6.7	L
1948	Custom, D24	6	3.25	4.625	230.2	102@3600	6.7	L
	DeLuxe, D24	6	3.25	4.625	230.2	102@3600	6.7	L
1949	Wayfarer, D29	6	3.25	4.625	230.2	103@3600	7.0	L
	Meadowbrook, D30	6	3.25	4.625	230.2	103@3600	7.0	L

MFR	CARBURETOR MODEL	VEN	WHEEL-BASE	TIRES	BODY	WEIGHT	PRICE
S	DXC-3	1	118.5	5.50 x 18	5 ps	3043	1045
C			114	5.00 x 19	5 ps	2810	765
C			114.2	5.00 x 19	5 ps	2820	845
S			114	5.50 x 18	5 ps	3091	1080
S	DXC-3	1	118.2	5.50 x 18	5 ps	3174	1135
S	DXR-3	1	118	6.00 x 18	5 ps	3488	1145
S	EX-22	1	111.2	6.00 x 16	5 ps	2632	670
S	EX-22	1	115	6.00 x 16	5 ps	2661	675
C	E8A	2	122	6.50 x 17	5 ps	3580	1145
S	EX-22	1	117	6.25 x 16	5 ps	2940	745
S	EX-22	1	117	6.25 x 16	5 ps	2940	765
S	EX-22	1	121	6.25 x 16	5 pb	2905	845
S	EX-22	1	116/128		5 ps	2868	760
S	EXV-2	1	116.2/128	6.00 x 16	5 ps	2923	735
S	EXV-2	1	115/132	6.00 x 16/	5 ps	2982	820
				6.50 x 16			
S	EXV-2	1	115/132	6.00 x 15/	5 ps	2977	898
				6.50 x 16			
S	BXV-3	1	117	6.00 x 16	5 ps	2995	855
S	BXV-3	1	117/134	6.00 x 16/	5 ps	3045	905
				6.50 x 16			
S	BXV-3	1	119.5	6.00 x 16	5 ps	2997	855
S	BXV-3	1	119.5/	6.00 x 16/	5 ps	3028	905
			139.5	6.50 x 16			
S	BXV-3	1	119.5/	6.00 x 16/	6 ps	3194	965
			137.5	6.50 x 16			
S	BXV-3	1	119.5	6.00 x 16	6 ps	3149	954
S	BXV-3	1	119.5/	6.00 x 16/	6 ps	3206	1048
			137.5	6.50 x 16			
S	BXV-3	1	119.5	6.00 x 16	6 ps	3171	998
S	BXV-3	1	119.5/	6.00 x 16/	6 ps	3281	1389
			137.5	6.50 x 16			
S	BXV-3	1	119.5	6.00 x 16	6 ps	3256	1339
S	BXV-3	1	119.5/	6.00 x 16/	6 ps	3281	1507
			137.5	6.50 x 16			
S	BXV-3	1	119.5	6.00 x 16	6 ps	3256	1457
S	BXV-3	1	119.5/	7.10 x 15	6 ps	3256	1718
			137.5				
S	BXV-3	1	119.5	7.10 x 15	6 ps	3281	1787
S	BXVD-3-93A	1	115	6.70 x 15	6 ps2	3180	1756
S	BXVD-3-93A	1	123.5	7.10 x 15	6 ps	3355	1866

YEAR	MODEL	CYLS	BORE	STROKE	DISPL	HP@RPM	C.R.	VLV
		ENGINE						
	Coronet, D30	6	3.25	4.625	230.2	103@3600	7.0	L
1950	Wayfarer, D33	6	3.25	4.625	230.2	103@3600	7.0	L
	Coronet, D34	6	3.25	4.625	230.2	103@3600	7.0	L
	Meadowbrook, D34	6	3.25	4.625	230.2	103@3600	7.0	L
1951	Wayfarer, D41	6	3.25	4.625	230.2	103@3600	7.0	L
	Coronet, D42	6	3.25	4.625	230.2	103@3600	7.0	L
	Meadowbrook, D42	6	3.25	4.625	230.2	103@3600	7.0	L
1952	Wayfarer, D41	6	3.25	4.625	230.2	103@3600	7.0	L
	Coronet, D42	6	3.25	4.625	230.2	103@3600	7.0	L
	Meadowbrook, D42	6	3.25	4.625	230.2	103@3600	7.0	L
1953	Meadowbrook Special, D46	6	3.25	4.625	230.2	103@3600	7.0	L
	Meadowbrook, D46	6	3.25	4.625	230.2	103@3600	7.0	L
	Coronet, D46	6	3.25	4.625	230.2	103@3600	7.0	L
	Meadowbrook, D47	6	3.25	4.625	230.2	103@3600	7.0	L
	Coronet, D44	V8	3.438	3.25	241.3	140@4400	7.1	OH
	Coronet, D48	V8	3.438	3.25	241.3	140@4400	7.1	OH
1954	Meadowbrook, D51-1; D51-1A	6	3.25	4.625	230.2	110@3600	7.25	L
	Coronet, D51-2	6	3.25	4.625	230.2	110@3600	7.25	L
	Coronet, D52	6	3.25	4.625	230.2	110@3600	7.25	L
	Meadowbrook, D50 - 1; D50-1A	V8	3.312	3.25	241.3	140@4400	7.1	OH
	Coronet, D50-2	V8	3.312	3.25	241.3	150@4400	7.5	OH
	Coronet, D53-2	V8	3.312	3.25	241.3	150@4400	7.5	OH
	Royal, D50-3	V8	3.312	3.25	241.3	150@4400	7.5	OH
	Royal, D53-3	V8	3.312	3.25	241.3	150@4400	7.5	OH
1955	Coronet, D56-1	6	3.25	4.625	230.2	123@3600	7.4	L
	Coronet, D55-1	V8	3.625	3.256	268.8	175@4400	7.6	OH
	Royal, D55-2	V8	3.625	3.256	268.8	175@4400	7.6	OH
	Custom Royal, D55-3	V8	3.625	3.256	268.8	183@4400	7.6	OH
1956	Coronet, D62	6	3.25	4.625	230.2	131@3600	7.6	L
	Coronet, D63-1	V8	3.625	3.256	268.8	189@4400	8.0	OH
	Royal, D63-2	V8	3.625	3.80	313.7	218@4400	8.0	OH
	Custom Royal, D63-3	V8	3.625	3.80	313.7	218@4400	8.0	OH
1957	Coronet, D72	6	3.25	4.625	230.2	138@4000	8.0	L

MFR	CARBURETOR MODEL	VEN	WHEEL-BASE	TIRES	BODY	WEIGHT	PRICE
S	BXVD-3-93A	1	123.5/	7.10 x 15/	6 ps	3380	1945
			137.5	7.60 x 15/			
				8.20 x 15			
S	BXVD-3-93	1	115	6.70 x 15	6 ps2	3200	1756
S	BXVD-3-93	1	123.5/	7.10 x 15/	6 ps	3405	1945
			137.5	7.60 x 15/			
				8.20 x 15			
S	BXVD-3-93	1	123.5	7.10 x 15	6 ps	3395	1856
S	BXVD-3-93	1	115	6.70 x 15	6 ps2	3210	1954
S	BXVD-3-93	1	123.5/	7.10 x 15 /	6 ps	3415	2166
			137.5	7.60 x 15/			
				8.20 x 15			
S	BXVD-3-93	1	123.5	7.10 x 15	6 ps	3415	2077
S	BXVD-3-93	1	115				
S	BXVD-3-93	1	123.5/	7.10 x 15/	6 ps	3385	2274
			137.5	7.60 x 15/			
				8.20 x 15			
S	BXVD- 3-93	1	123.5	7.10 x 15	6 ps	3355	2182
C	D6H2	1	119	6.70 x 15	6 ps	3195	2025
C	D6H2	1	119	6.70 x 15	6 ps	3175	2025
C	D6H2	1	119	7.10 x 15	6 ps	3220	2136
C	D6H2	1	114	6.70 x 15	6 psw2	3190	2201
S	WW3-108	2	119	7.10 x 15	6 ps	3385	2245
S	WW3-108	2	114	7.10 x 15	6 pht2	3310	2386
C	D6U1	1	119	6.70 x 15	6 ps	3195	2025
C	D6U1	1	119	7.10 x 15	6 ps	3235	2136
C	D6U1	1	114	6.70 x 15	6 psw4	3430	2719
S	WW-3-108	2	119	7.10 x 15	6 ps	3390	2176
S	WW-3-108	2	119	7.10 x 15	6 ps	3405	2245
S	WW-3-108	2	114/119	7.10 x 15	6 pht4	3310	2380
S	WW-3-108	2	119	7.10 x 15	6 ps	3425	2373
S	WW-3-108	2	114	7.10 x 15	6 pht4	3355	2503
S	WW3-124	2	120	6.70 x 15	6 ps	3295	2093
S	WW3-131	2	120	7.10 x 15	6 ps	3395	2196
S	WW3-131	2	120	7.10 x 15	6 ps	3425	2310
S	WW3-131	2	120	7.10 x 15	6 ps	3485	2473
S	WW3-124	2	120	6.70 x 15	6 ps	3295	2229
S	WW3-135	2	120	7.10 x 15	6 ps	3435	2336
S	WW3-138	2	120	7.10 x 15	6 ps	3520	2584
S	WW3-138	2	120	7.60 x 15	6 ps	3475	2474
S	WW3-159	2	122	7.50 x 14	6 ps	3470	2451

YEAR	MODEL	ENGINE						
		CYLS	BORE	STROKE	DISPL	HP@RPM	C.R.	VLV
	Coronet, D66	V8	3.688	3.797	324.4	245@4400	8.5	OH
	Royal, D67-1	V8	3.688	3.797	324.4	245@4400	8.5	OH
	Royal Custom, D67-2	V8	3.688	3.797	324.4	260@4400		OH
	Station Wagon, D70	V8	3.688	3.797	324.4	245@4400	8.5	OH
	Station Wagon Custom, D71	V8	3.688	3.797	324.4	245@4400	8.5	OH
	Coronet, D501	V8	3.938	3.625	353.1	340@5200	10.0	OH
1958	Coronet, LD-1	6	3.25	4.625	230.2	138@4000	8.0	L
	Coronet, LD-2L (1)	V8	3.688	3.797	324.4	252@4400	9.0	OH
	Royal, LD-2M (1)	V8	3.688	3.797	324.4	265@4600	9.0	OH
	Custom Royal, LD-3 (1)	V8	4.062	3.388	350.0	295@4400	10.0	OH
	Regal Lancer (1)	V8	4.062	3.338	350.0	295@4400	10.0	OH
	Station Wagon, LD-3 (1)	V8	4.062	3.388	350.0	295@4400	10.0	OH
	Optional engine:							
	(1) D-500	V8	4.125	3.375	360.8	305@4600	10.0	OH
1959	Coronet, MD1-L	6	3.25	4.625	230.2	135@3600	8.0	L
	Coronet, MD2-L (1)	V8	3.953	3.31	325.2	255@4000	9.2	OH
	Royal, MD3-M (1)	V8	4.125	3.375	360.8	295@4600	10.1	OH
	Custom Royal, MD3-H (1)	V8	4.125	3.375	360.8	305@4600	10.1	OH
	Sierra, MD3-L	V8	4.125	3.375	360.8	295@4600	10.1	OH
	Custom Sierra, MD3-H (1)	V8	4.125	3.375	360.8	305@4600	10.1	OH
	Optional engines:							
	(1) D-500	V8	4.25	3.375	383.0	320@4600		OH
	(1) Super D-500	V8	4.25	3.375	383.0	345@5000		OH
1960	Dart Seneca, PD3-L	6	3.406	4.125	225.5	145@4000	8.5	OH
	Dart Pioneer, PD3-M	6	3.406	4.125	225.5	145@4000	8.5	OH
	Dart Phoenix, PD3-H	6	3.406	4.125	225.5	145@4000	8.5	OH
	Dart Seneca, PD4-L	V8	3.906	3.31	317.6	230@4400	9.0	OH
	Dart Pioneer, PD4-M (1)	V8	3.906	3.31	317.6	230@4400	9.0	OH
	Dart Phoenix, PD4-H (1, 2)	V8	3.906	3.31	317.6	255@4400	9.0	OH
	Matador, PD1-L (2)	V8	4.125	3.375	360.8	295@4600	10.0	OH
	Polara, PD2-H	V8	4.25	3.375	383.0	325@4600	10.0	OH
	Optional engines:							
	(1)	V8	4.125	3.375	360.8	295@4600	10.0	OH
	(2)	V8	4.25	3.375	383.0	325@4600	10.0	OH
	(2)	V8	4.25	3.375	383.0	330@4600		OH

MFR	CARBURETOR MODEL	VEN	WHEEL-BASE	TIRES	BODY	WEIGHT	PRICE
S	WW3-149	2	122	7.50 x 14/	6 ps	3620	2559
				8.00 x 14			
S	WW3-149	2	122	8.00 x 14	6 ps	3620	2712
C	WCFB-2532S	4	122	8.00 x 14	6 ps	3690	2881
S	WW3-149	2	122	8.00 x 14	6 psw4	3930	2946
S	WW3-149	2	122	8.00 x 14	6 psw4	3960	3087
			122	7.60 x 15	6 ps2	3885	3314
S	WW3-159	2	122	7.50 x 14	6 ps	3410	2530
S	WW3-163	2	122	7.50 x 14/	6 ps	3555	2637
				8.00 x 14			
C	WCFB-2660S	4	122	8.00 x 14	6 ps	3570	2797
C	AFB-2773S	4	122	8.00 x 14	6 ps	3640	3030
C	AFB-2773S	4	122	8.00 x 14	6 pht2		3245
C	AFB-2773S	4	122	8.00 x 14	6 psw4	3930	3035
C		4					
C	BBS-2567S	1	122	7.50 x 14	6 ps	3425	2587
S	WW3-164	2	122	7.50 x 14/	6 ps	3615	2707
				8.00 x 14			
C	BBD-2870S	2	122	8.00 x 14	6 ps	3640	2934
C	AFB-2773S	4	122	8.00 x 14	6 ps	3660	3145
C	BBD-2870S	2	122	8.00 x 14	6 psw4	3940	3103
C	AFB-2870S	4	122	8.00 x 14	6 psw4	3980	3318
		4					
		4					
C	BBS-2985S	1	118/122	7.50 x 14/	6 ps	3420	2330
				8.00 x 14			
C	BBS-2985S	1	118/122	7.50 x 14/	6 ps	3430	2459
				8.00 x 14			
C	BBS-2985S	1	118	7.50 x 14	6 ps	3420	2595
C	BBD-2921S	2	118/122	7.50 x 14/	6 ps	3600	2449
				8.00 x 14			
C	BBD-2921S	2	118/122	7.50/8.00 x14	6 ps	3610	2578
C	AFB-2948S	4	118	7.50 x 14	6 ps	3610	2715
S	WWC-3-188	2	122	8.00 x 14	6 ps	3725	2930
H	R-1971A	4	122	8.00 x 14	6 ps	3735	3141
S	WWC-3-188	2					
H	R-1971A	4					

YEAR	MODEL	ENGINE						
		CYLS	BORE	STROKE	DISPL	HP@RPM	C.R.	VLV
1961	Lancer 170, RW1-L (1)	6	3.40	3.125	170.2	101@4400	8.2	OH
	Lancer 770, RW1-H	6	3.40	3.125	170.2	101@4400	8.2	OH
	Dart Seneca, RD3-L	6	3.40	4.125	224.7	145@4000	8.2	OH
	Dart Pioneer, RD3-M	6	3.40	4.125	224.7	145@4000	8.2	OH
	Dart Phoenix, RD3-H	6	3.40	4.125	224.7	145@4000	8.2	OH
	Dart Seneca, RD4-L (2)	V8	3.91	3.31	318.2	230@4400	9.0	OH
	Dart Pioneer, RD4-M (2)	V8	3.91	3.31	318.2	230@4400	9.0	OH
	Dart Phoenix, RD4-H (2)	V8	3.91	3.31	318.2	230@4400	9.0	OH
	Dodge Polara, RD1-L (3)	V8	4.12	3.375	360.8	265@4400	9.0	OH
	Optional engines:							
	(1)	6	3.40	4.125	224.7	145@4000	8.2	OH
	(1)	6	3.40	4.125	224.7	195@5200	8.2	OH
	(2)	V8	4.25	3.375	383.0	320@4800	10.0	OH
	(2)	V8	4.125	3.375	360.8	305@4800	9.0	OH
	(2)	V8	4.25	3.375	383.0	340@5000	10.0	OH
	(2)	V8	4.25	3.375	383.0	330@5200	10.0	OH
	(2)	V8	4.188	3.75	413.2	350@4600	10.0	OH
	(2)	V8	4.188	3.75	413.2	375@5000	10.0	OH
	(3)	V8	4.25	3.375	383.0	325@4600	10.0	OH
	(3)	V8	4.25	3.375	383.0	330@4800	10.0	OH
	(3)	V8	4.25	3.375	383.0	340@5000	10.0	OH
1962	Dart, SD1-L	6	3.40	4.125	224.7	145@4000	8.2	OH
	Dart 330, SD1-M	6	3.40	4.125	224.7	145@4000	8.2	OH
	Dart 440, SD1-H	6	3.40	4.125	224.7	145@4000	8.2	OH
	Dart, SD2-L (1)	V8	3.91	3.312	318.2	230@4400	9.0	OH
	Dart 330, SD2-M (1)	V8	3.91	3.312	318.2	230@4400	9.0	OH
	Dart 440, SD2-H (1)	V8	3.91	3.312	318.2	230@4400	9.0	OH
	Polara 500, SD2-P	V8	4.125	3.375	360.8	305@4800	9.0	OH
	Lancer 170, SL1-L (2)	6	3.40	3.125	170.2	101@4400	8.2	OH
	Lancer 770, SL1-H (2)	6	3.40	3.125	170.2	101@4400	8.2	OH
	Lancer GT, SL1-P (2)	6	3.40	3.125	170.2	101@4400	8.2	OH
	Custom 880, SD3-L	V8	4.12	3.375	360.8	305@4800	9.0	OH
	Optional engines:							
	(1)	V8	4.125	3.375	360.8	305@4800	9.0	OH
	(2)	V8	3.40	4.125	224.7	145@4000	8.2	OH
1963	Dart 170, TL1-L (4)	6	3.40	3.125	170.2	101@4400	8.2	OH
	Dart 270, TL1-M (4)	6	3.40	3.125	170.2	101@4400	8.2	OH

MFR	CARBURETOR MODEL	VEN	WHEEL-BASE	TIRES	BODY	WEIGHT	PRICE
C	BBS-3093S	1	106.5	6.50 x 13	6 ps	2595	2043
C	BBS-3093S	1	106.5	6.50 x 13	6 ps	2605	2139
C	BBS-3098S	1	118/122	7.00 x 14/	6 ps	3335	2332
				8.00 x 14			
C	BBS-3098S	1	118/122	7.00 x 14/	6 ps	3335	2595
				8.00 x 14			
C	BBS-3098S	1	118	7.00 x 14	6 ps	3350	2597
S	WW-1543	2	118/122	7.50 x 14/	6 ps	3515	2451
				8.00 x 14			
S	WW-1543	2	118/122	7.50 x 14/	6 ps	3510	2580
				8.00 x 14			
S	WW-1543	2	118	7.50 x 14	6 ps	3535	2717
S	WWC-3-188	2	122	8.00 x 14	6 ps	3700	2968
C	BBS-3098S	1					
C	AFB-3083S	4					
C	AFB-2903S	4					
C	AFB-3105S	4					
C	AFB-3084S	2 x 4					
C	AFB-2970S	2 x 4					
C	AFB-3108S	4					
C	AFB-3084S	2 x 4					
C	AFB-3152S	4					
C	AFB-2903S	2 x 4					
C	AFB-3084S	4					
C	BBS-3231S	1	116	6.50 x 14	6 ps	3000	2297
C	BBS-3231S	1	116	6.50 x 14	6 ps	3000	2432
C	BBS-3231S	1	116	6.50 x 14	6 ps	3045	2584
C	BBD-3240S	2	116	7.00 x 14	6 ps	3170	2404
C	BBD-3240S	2	116	7.00 x 14	6 ps	3170	2540
C	BBD-3240S	2	116	7.00 x 14	6 ps	3205	2691
C	AFB-3252S	4	116	7.00 x 14	6 pht4	3360	2960
C	BBS-3229S	1	106.5	6.50 x 13	6 ps	2525	2011
C	BBS-3229S	1	106.5	6.50 x 13	6 ps	2540	2114
C	BBS-3229S	1	106.5	6.50 x 13	6 pht4	2560	2257
C	AFB-3252	4	122	8.00 x 14	6 ps	3655	2464
C	AFB-3252S	4					
C	BBS-3231S	1					
C	BBS-3462S	1	111/106	6.50 x 13	6 ps	2625	2041
C	BBS-3462S	1	111/106	6.50 x 13	6 ps	2635	2135

YEAR	MODEL	ENGINE						
		CYLS	BORE	STROKE	DISPL	HP@RPM	C.R.	VLV
	Dart GT, TL1-P (4)	6	3.40	3.125	170.2	101@4400	8.2	OH
	Dodge 330, TD1-L	6	3.40	4.125	224.7	145@4000	8.2	OH
	Dodge 440, TD1-M	6	3.40	4.125	224.7	145@4000	8.2	OH
	Polara, TD1-H	6	3.40	4.125	224.7	145@4000	8.2	OH
	Dodge 330, TD2-L (2, 3)	V8	3.91	3.31	318.0	230@4400	9.0	OH
	Dodge 440, TD2-M (2, 3)	V8	3.91	3.31	318.0	230@4400	9.0	OH
	Polara, TD2-H (2)	V8	3.91	3.31	318.0	230@4400	9.0	OH
	Polara 500, TD2-P (2)	V8	4.25	3.375	383.0	305@4600	10.0	OH
	Polara 880, TA3-E (1, 3)	V8	4.125	3.375	383.0	265@4400	9.0	OH
	Custom 880, TA3-L (1, 3)	V8	4.125	3.375	383.0	265@4400	9.0	OH
	Optional engines:							
	(1)	V8	4.188	3.75	413.2	360@4800		OH
	(2)	V8	4.25	3.375	383.0	415@5600	9.7	OH
	(3)	V8	4.25	3.375	383.0	305@4600	10.0	OH
	(4)	6	3.40	4.125	224.7	145@4000	8.2	OH
1964	Dart 170, VL1-L (1)	6	3.40	3.125	170.2	101@4400	8.5	OH
	Dart 270, VL1-H (1)	6	3.40	3.125	170.2	101@4400	8.5	OH
	Dart GT, VL1-P (1)	6	3.40	3.125	170.2	101@4400	8.5	OH
	Dodge 330, VD1-L	6	3.40	4.125	224.7	145@4000	8.4	OH
	Dodge 440, VD1-M	6	3.40	4.125	224.7	145@4000	8.4	OH
	Dodge Polara, VD1-H	6	3.40	4.125	224.7	145@4000	8.4	OH
	Dodge 330, VD2-L (2)	V8	3.91	3.312	318.2	230@4400	9.0	OH
	Dodge 440, VD2-M (2)	V8	3.91	3.312	318.2	230@4400	9.0	OH
	Dodge Polara, VD2-H (2)	V8	3.91	3.312	318.2	230@4400	9.0	OH
	Dodge 880, VA3-E (2)	V8	4.125	3.375	360.8	265@4400	9.0	OH
	Dodge Custom, 880, VA3-L (2)	V8	4.125	3.375	360.8	265@4400	9.0	OH
	Optional engines:							
	(1)	6	3.406	4.125	224.7	145@4000	8.4	OH
	(1)	V8	3.625	3.312	273.5	180		
	(1)	V8	3.625	3.312	273.5	235		
	(2)	V8	4.25	3.375	383.0	305@4600	10.0	OH
	(2)	V8	4.25	3.375	383.0	330@4600	10.0	OH
	(2)	V8	4.25	3.75	413.2	415@5600	11.0	OH
	(2)	V8	4.25	3.75	413.2	425@5600		OH
	(2)	V8	4.25	3.75	413.2	365@4800	10.3	OH
1965	Dart 170, AL1-L (1)	6	3.406	3.125	170.2	101@4400	8.5	OH
	Dart 270, AL1-H (1)	6	3.406	3.125	170.2	101@4400	8.5	OH
	Dart GT, AL1-P (1)	6	3.406	3.125	170.2	101@4400	8.5	OH

MFR	CARBURETOR MODEL	VEN	WHEEL-BASE	TIRES	BODY	WEIGHT	PRICE
C	BBS-3462S	1	119/116	7.00 x 14	6 pht2	2690	2289
H	R-2418A	1	119/116	7.00 x 14	6 ps	3070	2301
H	R-2418A	1	119/116	7.00 x 14	6 ps	3075	2438
H	R-2418A	1	119/116	7.00 x 14	6 ps	3105	2602
S	3-222A	2	119/116	7.00 x 14	6 ps	3245	2408
S	3-222A	2	119/116	7.00 x 14	6 ps	3250	2596
S	3-222A	2	119/116	7.00 x 14	6 ps	3275	2709
C	BBD-3475S	2	119/116	7.00 x 14	6 pht2	3375	2965
C	BBD-34763	2	122	8.00 x 14	6 ps	3800	2813
C	BBD-34763	2	122	8.00 x 14	6 ps	3815	2964
C	BBD-3476S	2					
H	R-2418A	1					
C	BBS-3675S	1	111/106	6.50 x 13	6 ps	2640	2053
C	BBS-3675S	1	111/106	6.50 x 13	6 ps	2645	2160
C	BBS-3675S	1	111	6.50 x 13	6 pht2	2670	2318
C	BBS-3679S	1	119/116	7.00 x 14/	6 ps	3145	2317
				7.50 x 14			
C	BBS-3679S	1	119	7.00 x 14	6 ps	3145	2454
C	BBS-3679S	1	119	7.00 x 14	6 ps	3170	2615
C	BBD-3682S	2	119/116	7.00 x 14/	6 ps	3325	2424
				7.50 x 14			
C	BBD-3682S	2	119/116	7.00 x 14/	6 ps	3330	2562
				7.50 x 14			
C	BBD-3682S	2	119	7.00 x 14	6 ps	3365	2722
S	WWC-3-244	2	122	8.00 x 14	6 ps	3795	2826
S	WWC-3-244	2	122	8.00 x 14	6 ps	3825	2977
C	BBS-3677S	1					
C	BBD-3684S	4					
C		2 x 4					
C		2 x 4					
C							
C	BBS-3833S	1	111/106	6.50 x 13	6 ps	2660	2112
C	BBS-3833S	1	111/106	6.50 x 13	6 ps	2670	2218
C	BBS-3833S	1	111/106	6.50 x 13	5 pht2	2715	2372

YEAR	MODEL	ENGINE						
		CYLS	BORE	STROKE	DISPL	HP@RPM	C.R.	VLV
	Coronet, AW1-L	6	3.406	4.125	224.7	145@4000	8.4	OH
	Coronet DeLuxe, AW1-L	6	3.406	4.125	224.7	145@4000	8.4	OH
	Coronet, AW1-H	6	3.406	4.125	224.7	145@4000	8.4	OH
	Coronet, AW2-L (2)	V8	3.625	3.312	273.5	180@4200	8.8	OH
	Coronet DeLuxe, (2)	V8	3.625	3.312	273.5	180@4200	8.8	OH
	Coronet 440, AW2-H (2)	V8	3.625	3.312	273.5	180@4200	8.8	OH
	Coronet 500, AW2-P (2)	V8	3.625	3.312	273.5	180@4200	8.8	OH
	Polara, AD2-L (3, 4)	V8	4.25	3.375	383.0	270@4400	9.2	OH
	Custom 880, AD2-H (3, 4)	V8	4.25	3.375	383.0	270@4400	9.2	OH
	Monaco, AD2-P (4)	V8	4.25	3.375	383.0	315@4400	10.0	OH
	Optional engines:							
	(1)	6	3.406	4.125	224.5	145@4000	8.4	OH
	(1)	V8	3.625	3.312	273.5	180@4200	8.8	OH
	(1)	V8	3.625	3.312	273.5	235@5200	10.5	OH
	(2)	V8	3.906	3.312	317.6	230@4400	9.0	OH
	(2)	V8	4.125	3.375	360.8	265@4400	9.0	OH
	(2)	V8	4.25	3.375	383.0	330@4600	10.0	OH
	(2)	V8	4.25	3.75	425.6	365@4800	10.3	OH
	(3)	V8	4.25	3.375	383.0	315@4400	10.0	OH
	(4)	V8	4.188	3.75	413.2	340@4600	10.1	OH
1966	Dart, BL1-L (1)	6	3.406	3.125	170.2	101@4400	8.5	OH
	Dart 270, BL1-H (1)	6	3.406	3.125	170.2	101@4400	8.5	OH
	Dart GT, BL1-P (1)	6	3.406	3.125	170.2	101@4400	8.5	OH
	Coronet, BW1-L	6	3.406	4.125	224.7	145@4000	8.4	OH
	Coronet DeLuxe, BW1-L	6	3.406	4.125	224.7	145@4000	8.4	OH
	Coronet 440, BW1-H	6	3.406	4.125	224.7	145@4000	8.4	OH
	Coronet 500, BW2-P	6	3.406	4.125	224.7	145@4000	8.4	OH
	Coronet BW2-L (2, 3)	V8	3.625	3.31	273.5	180@4200	8.8	OH
	Coronet DeLuxe, BW2-L (2, 3)	V8	3.625	3.31	273.5	180@4200	8.8	OH
	Coronet 440, BW2-H (2, 3)	V8	3.625	3.31	273.5	180@4200	8.8	OH

MFR	CARBURETOR MODEL	VEN	WHEEL-BASE	TIRES	BODY	WEIGHT	PRICE
C	BBS-3839S	1	117	7.35 x 14	6 ps	3095	2227
C	BBS-3839S	1	117	7.35 x 14/	6 ps	3140	2267
				7.75 x 14			
C	BBS-3839S	1	117	7.35 x 14/	6 ps	3125	2346
				7.75 x 14			
C	BBD-3843S	2	117	7.35 x 14/	6 ps	3195	2321
				7.75 x 14			
C	BBD-3843S	2	117	7.35 x 14/	6 ps	3210	2361
				7.75 x 14			
C	BBD-3843S	2	117	7.35 x 14/	6 ps	3230	2440
				7.75 x 14			
C	BBD-3843S	2	117	7.35 x 14	6 pht2	3255	2637
C	BBD-3849S	2	121	8.25 x 14/	6 ps	3847	2695
				8.55 x 14			
C	BBD-3849S	2	121	8.25 x 14/	6 ps	3915	2970
				8.55 x 14			
C	AFB-3855S	4	121	8.25 x 14	5 pht2	4000	3308
C	BBS-3839S	1					
C	BBD-3843S	2					
C	AFB-3853S	4					
C	BBD-3847S	2					
C	AFB-3859S	4					
C	AFB-3855S	4					
C	AFB-3858S	4					
C	BBS-4099S	1	111/106	6.50 x 13	6 ps	2695	2158
C	BBS-4099S	1	111/106	6.50 x 13/	6 ps	2680	2280
				7.00 x 13			
C	BBS-4099S	1	111	6.50 x 13/	5 pht2	2735	2417
				7.00 x 13			
H	R-3271A	1	117	6.95 x 14	6 ps	3077	2302
H	R-3271A	1	117	6.95 x 14	6 ps	3075	2341
H	R-3271A	1	117	6.95 x 14	6 ps	3070	2432
H	R-3271A	1	117	6.95 x 14	6 ps	3115	2586
C	BBD-4113S	2	117	7.35 x 14	6 ps	3245	2396
C	BBD-4113S	2	117	7.35 x 14/	6 ps	3240	2435
				8.25 x 14			
C	BBD-4113S	2	117	7.35 x 14/	6 ps	3220	2526
				8.25 x 14			

YEAR	MODEL	ENGINE						
		CYLS	BORE	STROKE	DISPL	HP@RPM	C.R.	VLV
	Coronet 500, BW2-P (2, 3)	V8	3.625	3.31	273.5	180@4200	8.8	OH
	Charger, BX2-P (3, 4)	V8	3.91	3.31	318.0	230@4400	9.0	OH
	Polara 318, BD2-L (5)	V8	3.91	3.31	318.0	230@4400	9.0	OH
	Polara, BD2-L (5)	V8	4.25	3.375	383.0	270@4400	9.2	OH
	Monaco, BD2-H (5)	V8	4.25	3.375	383.0	270@4400	9.2	OH
	Monaco 500, BD2-P-23 (5)	V8	4.25	3.375	383.0	325@4800	10.0	OH
	Optional engines:							
	(1)	6	3.406	4.125	224.7	145@4000	8.4	OH
	(1)	V8	3.625	3.312	273.5	180@4200	8.8	OH
	(1)	V8	3.625	3.312	273.5	235@5200	10.5	OH
	(2)	V8	4.125	3.375	360.8	265@4400	9.0	OH
	(3)	V8	4.25	3.75	425.6	425@5000	10.25	OH
	(4)	V8	4.25	3.375	383.0	325@4800	10.0	OH
	(5)	V8	4.312	3.75	440.0	350@4400	10.1	OH
1967	Dart, CL1-L (1)	6	3.40	3.125	170.2	115@4400	8.5	OH
	Dart 270, CL1-H (1)	6	3.40	3.125	170.2	115@4400	8.5	OH
	Dart GT, CL1-P (1)	6	3.40	3.125	170.2	115@4400	8.5	OH
	Coronet, CW1-E (2)	6	3.40	4.125	224.7	145@4000	8.4	OH
	Coronet DeLuxe, CW1-L (2)	6	3.40	4.125	224.7	145@4000	8.4	OH
	Coronet 440, CW1-H (2)	6	3.40	4.125	224.7	145@4000	8.4	OH
	Coronet 500, CW1-P (2)	6	3.40	4.125	224.7	145@4000	8.4	OH
	Coronet, CW2-E (3)	V8	3.625	3.31	273.5	180@4200	8.8	OH
	Coronet DeLuxe, CW2-L (3)	V8	3.625	3.31	273.5	180@4200	8.8	OH
	Coronet 440, CW2-H (3, 4, 5)	V8	3.625	3.31	273.5	180@4200	8.8	OH
	Coronet 500, CW2-P (3, 4, 5)	V8	3.625	3.31	273.5	180@4200	8.8	OH
	Coronet R/T, CW2-P (4, 5)	V8	3.625	3.31	273.5	180@4200	8.8	OH
	Charger, CW2-P (4, 5, 7)	V8	3.91	3.310	318.0	230@4400	9.2	OH
	Polara 318, CD2-L (7)	V8	4.25	3.375	383.6	270@4400	9.2	OH
	Polara, CD2-L	V8	4.25	3.375	383.6	270@4400	9.2	OH
	Polara 500, CD2-M (4, 6, 7)	V8	4.25	3.375	383.6	325@4800	10.0	OH

MFR	CARBURETOR MODEL	VEN	WHEEL-BASE	TIRES	BODY	WEIGHT	PRICE
C	BBD-4113S	2	117	7.35 x 14	6 ps	3280	2680
S	WW3-258	2	117	7.35 x 14	5 pht2	3499	3146
S	WW3-258	2	121	8.25 x 14/	6 ps	3765	2763
				8.55 x 14			
C	BBD-4125S	2	121	8.25 x 14/	6 ps	3820	2838
				8.55 x 14			
C	BBD-4125S	2	121	8.25 x 14/	6 ps	3890	3033
				8.55 x 14			
C	BBD-4125S	2	121	8.25 x 14	5 pht2	3895	3604
C	BBS-4286-S	1	111	6.50 x 13/	6 ps	2715	2224
				7.00 x 13			
C	BBS-4286-S	1	111	6.50 x 13/	6 ps	2720	2362
				7.00 x 13			
C	BBS-4286-S	1	111	6.50 x 13/	5 pht2	2735	2499
				7.00 x 13			
H	R-3279-1A	1	117	7.35 x 14	6 psw4	3465	2622
H	R-3279-1A	1	117	7.35 x 14/	6 ps	3080	2397
				7.75 x 14			
H	R-3279-1A	1	117	7.35 x 14/	6 ps	3070	2475
				7.75 x 14			
H	R-3279-1A	1	117	7.35 x 14	6 ps	3090	2645
C	BBD-4113-SA	2	117	8.25 x 14	6 psw4	3570	2716
C	BBD-4113-SA	2	117	7.35 x 14/	6 ps	3235	2491
				8.25 x 14			
C	BBD-4113-SA	2	117	7.35 x 14/	6 ps	3225	2569
				8.25 x 14			
C	BBD-4113-SA	2	117	7.35 x 14	6 ps	3260	2748
C	BBD-4113-SA	2	117	7.75 x 14	6 pht2	3475	3199
S	WW3-272	2	117	7.35 x 14	6 pht2	3475	3128
S	WW3-272	2	122	8.25 x 14	6 ps	3700	2843
S	WW3-272	2	122	8.25 x 14/	6 ps	3815	2918
				8.45 x 14			
C	BBD-4296-S	2	122	8.25 x 14	6 pht2	3825	3155

YEAR	MODEL	ENGINE						
		CYLS	BORE	STROKE	DISPL	HP@RPM	C.R.	VLV
	Monaco, CD2-H (4, 6, 7)	V8	4.25	3.375	383.6	270@4400	9.2	OH
	Monaco 500, CD2-P (4, 6, 7)	V8	4.25	3.375	383.6	270@4400	9.2	OH
	Optional engines:							
	(1)	6	3.40	4.125	255.0	145@4000	8.4	OH
	(1)	V8	3.625	3.31	273.5	235@5200	10.5	OH
	(2)	V8	3.91	3.31	318.0	230@4400	9.2	OH
	(3)	V8	4.25	3.375	383.6	270@4400	9.2	OH
	(4)	V8	4.25	3.375	383.6	325@4800	10.0	OH
	(5)	V8	4.25	3.375	383.6	425@5000	10.25	OH
	(6)	V8	4.32	3.75	440.0	350@4400	10.1	OH
	(7)	V8	4.32	3.75	440.0	375@4600	10.1	OH
1968	Dart, DL1-L (1)	6	3.40	3.125	170.2	115@4400	8.5	OH
	Dart 270, DL1-H (1, 2)	6	3.40	3.125	170.2	115@4400	8.5	OH
	Dart GT, DL1-P (1)	6	3.40	3.125	170.2	115@4400	8.5	OH
	Dart GTS, DW1-L (2, 3)	V8	4.04	3.31	339.7	275@5000	10.5	OH
	Coronet DeLuxe, DW1-L	6	3.40	4.125	224.7	145@4000	8.4	OH
	Coronet 440, DW1-H	6	3.40	4.125	224.7	145@4000	8.4	OH
	Coronet DeLuxe, DW2-L (2, 4, 5, 6)	V8	3.63	3.31	273.5	190@4400	9.0	OH
	Coronet Superbee, DW2-H	V8	4.25	3.38	383.0	335@5000	10.0	OH
	Coronet 440, DW2-H (2,4,5,6)	V8	3.63	3.31	273.5	190@4400	9.0	OH
	Coronet 500, DW2-P (4, 5)	V8	3.63	3.31	273.5	190@4400	9.0	OH
	Coronet R/T, DW2-S (6)	V8	3.63	3.31	273.5	190@4400	9.0	OH
	Charger, DX1-S	6	3.40	4.125	224.7	145@4000	8.4	OH
	Charger R/T, DX2-S (6)	V8	4.32	3.75	440.7	375@4600	10.1	OH
	Polara, DD2-L	V8	3.91	3.31	318.0	230@4400	8.4	OH
	Polara 500, DD2-M (4, 5, 7)	V8	3.91	3.31	318.0	230@4400	8.4	OH
	Monaco, DD2-H	V8	4.25	3.375	383.6	290@4400	9.2	OH
	Monaco 500, DD2-P (5, 7)	V8	4.25	3.375	383.6	290@4400	9.2	OH
	Optional engines:							
	(1)	6	3.40	4.125	224.7	145@4000	8.4	OH
	(2)	V8	3.91	3.31	318.0	230@4400	9.2	OH
	(3)	V8	4.25	3.375	383.6	300@4400	10.0	OH
	(4)	V8	4.25	3.375	383.6	290@4400	9.2	OH

MFR	CARBURETOR MODEL	VEN	WHEEL-BASE	TIRES	BODY	WEIGHT	PRICE
S	WW3-272	2	122	8.25 x 14/	6 ps	3850	3138
				8.45 x 14			
S	WW3-272	2	122	8.25 x 14	6 pht2	3850	3712
H	R-3279-1A	1					
S	WWS-272	2					
S	WWS-272	2					
C	BBD-4296-S	2					
C	AFB-4326-S	4					
C	BBS-4114-S	1	111	6.50 x 13	6 ps	2725	2360
C	BBS-4114-S	1	111	6.50 x 13	6 ps	2725	2499
C	BBS-4114-S	1	111	6.50 x 13/	6 pht2	2715	2637
				7.00 x 13			
C	AVS-4424-S	4	111	E70 x 14	6 pht2	3065	3189
H	R-3921-A	1	117	7.35/8.25 x 14	6 ps	3035	2525
H	R-3921-A	1	117	7.35 x 14/	6 ps	3035	2603
				8.25 x 14			
C	BBD-4416-S	2	117	7.35 x 14/	6 ps	3220	2619
				8.25 x 14			
C	BBD-4422-S	2	117	7.35 x 14	4 pc	3395	3027
C	BBD-4416-S	2	117	7.35 x 14/	6 ps	3220	2608
				8.25 x 14			
C	BBD-4416-S	2	117	7.35 x 14/	6 ps	3240	2911
				8.25 x 14			
C	BBD-4416-S	2	117	F70 x 14	5 pht2	3530	3378
H	R-3921-A	1	117	7.35 x 14	5 pht2	3100	
C	AVS-4428-S	4	117	F70 x 14	5 pht2	3575	3505
C	BBD-4420-S	2	122	8.25 x 14/	6 ps	3735	3004
				8.55 x 14			
C	BBD-4420-S	2	122	8.25 x 14	5 pht2	3740	3225
C	BBD-4422-S	2	122	8.25 x 14/	6 ps	3885	3293
				8.55 x 14			
C	BBD-4422-S	2	122	8.25 x 14	5 pht2	3885	3868
H	R-3921-A	1					
C	BBD-4420-S	2					
C	BBD-4422-S	2					

YEAR	MODEL	CYLS	BORE	STROKE	DISPL	HP@RPM	C.R.	VLV
		ENGINE						
	(5)	V8	4.25	3.375	383.6	330@5000	10.0	OH
	(6)	V8	4.25	3.75	425.6	425@5000	10.25	OH
	(7)	V8	4.32	3.75	440.7	375@4600	10.1	OH
1969	Dart Swinger (1)	6	3.40	3.125	170.2	115@4400	8.5	OH
	Dart (1)	6	3.40	3.125	170.2	115@4400	8.5	OH
	Dart Custom (1)	6	3.40	3.125	170.2	115@4400	8.5	OH
	Dart GT (1)	6	3.40	3.125	170.2	115@4400	8.5	OH
	Dart Swinger 340	V8	3.63	3.31	273.5	190@4400	9.0	OH
	Dart GTS (2)	V8	3.63	3.31	273.5	190@4400	9.0	OH
	Coronet DeLuxe	6	3.40	4.125	224.7	145@4000	8.4	OH
	Coronet 440	6	3.40	4.125	224.7	145@4000	8.4	OH
	Coronet DeLuxe (2)	V8	3.91	3.31	318.0	230@4400	9.2	OH
	Coronet 440 (2)	V8	3.91	3.31	318.0	230@4400	9.2	OH
	Coronet 500 (2, 3)	V8	3.91	3.31	318.0	230@4400	9.2	OH
	Coronet Superbee	V8	4.25	3.38	383.6	335@5000	10.0	OH
	Coronet R/T (3)	V8	3.91	3.31	318.0	230@4400	9.2	OH
	Charger	6	3.40	4.125	224.7	145@4000	8.4	OH
	Charger (2, 3)	V8	3.91	3.31	318.0	230@4400	9.2	OH
	Charger R/T (3)	V8	4.32	3.75	440.7	375@4000	10.1	OH
	Charger 500	V8	4.32	3.75	440.7	375@4000	10.1	OH
	Polara (2)	V8	3.91	3.31	318.0	230@4400	9.2	OH
	Polara 500 (2)	V8	3.91	3.31	318.0	230@4400	9.2	OH
	Monaco (2)	V8	4.25	3.375	383.6	290@4400	9.2	OH
	Optional engines:							
	(1)	V8	3.625	3.312	274.0	190@4400	9.0	OH
	(2)	V8	4.25	3.375	383.6	330@5200	10.0	OH
	(3)	V8	4.25	3.75	425.6	425@5000	10.25	OH

DTL — — Detroit Testing Laboratories, Detroit, Mich., 1960-

YEAR	MODEL	ENGINE
1960		Electric motors, two @ 1/3 hp.
	This may be same vehicle as Dow.	

DUAL-GHIA — — Dual Motors, Inc., Detroit, Mich., 1955-58; 1963

1955-57 Optional engines:

MFR	CARBURETOR MODEL	VEN	WHEEL-BASE	TIRES	BODY	WEIGHT	PRICE
C	AVS-4422-S	4					
C	BBS-4601-S	1	111	6.50 x 13	6 pht2	2721	2400
C	BBS-4601-S	1	111	6.50 x 13	6 ps	2736	2413
C	BBS-4601-S	1	111	6.50 x 13	6 ps	2736	2550
C	BBS-4601-S	1	111	6.50 x 13	6 pht2	2726	2672
C	4605	2	111	7.00 x 13	6 pht2	3095	2836
C	4605	2	111	7.00 x 13	5 pht2	3120	3226
H	R-4163-A	1	117	7.35 x 14/	6 ps	3018	2589
				8.25 x 14			
H	R-4163-A	1	117	7.35 x 14/	6 ps	3023	2670
				8.25 x 14			
C	BBD-4607-S	2	117	7.35 x 14/	6 ps	3196	2692
				8.25 x 14			
C	BBD-4607-S	2	117	7.35 x 14/	6 ps	3201	2773
				8.25 x 14			
C	BBD-4607-S	2	117	7.35 x 14/	6 ps	3241	2963
				8.25 x 14			
C	BBD-4615-S	2	117	7.75 x 14	5 pht2	3465	3076
C	BBD-4607-S	2	117	7.35 x 14	5 pht2	3495	3442
H	R-4163-A	1	117	7.35 x 14	5 pht2	3098	3020
C	BBD-4607-S	2	117	7.35 x 14	5 pht2	3256	3126
C	AVS-4617-S	4	117	F70 x 14	5 pht2	3641	3592
C	AVS-4617-S	4	117	F70 x 14	5 pht2	3225	3843
C	BBD-4607-S	2	122	8.25 x 15/	6 ps	3836	3095
				8.85 x 15			
C	BBD-4607-S	2	122	8.25 x 15	5 pht2	3746	3314
C	BBD-4613-S	2	122	8.25 x 15/	6 ps	3906	3452
				8.85 x 15			
			47		2 pr	447	800

YEAR	MODEL	ENGINE						
		CYLS	BORE	STROKE	DISPL	HP@RPM	C.R.	VLV
		V8	3.625	3.80	313.7	230@4400	8.5	OH
		V8	3.625	3.80	313.7	260@4800	9.5	OH
		V8	3.625	3.80	313.7	285@4800		OH
1958	375	V8	4.00	3.90	392.1	375@5500	9.25	OH
	400	V8	4.00	3.90	392.1	400@6000	9.25	OH
1963	L 6.4	V8	4.25	3.375	383.0	335@5200		OH
	Chassis were Chrysler as were the engines, with bodies from Italy.							

DUESENBERG — — Duesenberg, Inc., Indianapolis, Ind., 1920-37

YEAR	MODEL	CYLS	BORE	STROKE	DISPL	HP@RPM	C.R.	VLV
1930	J	8	3.75	4.75	420.0	265@4200	5.2	DOHC
1931	J	8	3.75	4.75	420.0	265@4200	5.2	DOHC
1932	J	8	3.75	4.75	420.0	265@4200	5.2	DOHC
	J (Supercharged)	8	3.75	4.75	420.0	320@4750	5.2	DOHC
1933	J	8	3.75	4.75	420.0	265@4200	5.2	DOHC
	J (Supercharged)	8	3.75	4.75	420.0	320@4750	5.2	DOHC
1934	J	8	3.75	4.75	420.0	265@4200	5.2	DOHC
	J (Supercharged)	8	3.75	4.75	420.0	320@4750	5.2	DOHC
1935	J	8	3.75	4.75	420.0	265@4200	5.2	DOHC
	J (Supercharged)	8	3.75	4.75	420.0	320@4750	5.2	DOHC
1936	J	8	3.75	4.75	420.0	265@4200	5.2	DOHC
	J (Supercharged)	8	3.75	4.75	420.0	320@4750	5.2	DOHC
1937	J	8	3.75	4.75	420.0	265@4200	5.2	DOHC
	J (Supercharged)	8	3.75	4.75	420.0	320@4750	5.2	DOHC

DUESENBERG — — Duesenberg Corp., Indianapolis, Ind., 1966

YEAR	MODEL	CYLS	BORE	STROKE	DISPL	HP@RPM	C.R.	VLV
1966		V8	4.325	3.75	427.0	425		OH
	This was the first Duesenberg revival, using a Ford engine.							

CARBURETOR			WHEEL-	TIRES	BODY	WEIGHT	PRICE
MFR	MODEL	VEN	BASE				
			115	6.70 x 15	4 pcv2		7646
		4					
		2 x 4					
			126	9.00 x 14	4 pc		15,000
			126	9.00 x 14	4 pht2		15,000
					4 pht2		15,000
Sc			142.5/	7.00 x 19	ch		8500
			153.5				
Sc			142.5/	7.00 x 19	ch		8500
			153.5				
Ju			142.5/	7.00 x 19	ch		9500
			153.5				
			142.5/	7.00 x 19	ch		11,750
			153.5				
			142.5/	7.00 x 19	ch		9500
			153.5				
			142.5/	7.00 x 19	ch		11,750
			153.5				
			142.5/	7.50 x 17/	ch		9500
			153.5	7.00 x 19			
S	UU-3	2	142.5/	7.50 x 17/	ch		11,750
			153.5	7.00 x 19			
S		2	142.5/	7.50 x 17/	ch		9500
			153.5	7.00 x 19			
			142.5/	7.50 x 17/	ch		11,750
			153.5	7.00 x 19			
			142.5/	7.50 x 17/	ch		9500
			153.5	7.00 x 19			
			142.5/	7.50 x 17/	ch		11,750
			153.5	7.00 x 19			
S	UUR-2	2	142.5/	7.50 x 17/			
			153.5	7.00 x 19			
S	UUR-2	2	142.5/	7.50 x 17/			
			153.5	7.00 x 19			
			137.5		6 ps	5700	approx. 19,500

YEAR	MODEL	CYLS	BORE	STROKE	DISPL	HP@RPM	C.R.	VLV
		ENGINE						

DU PONT – – DuPont Motors, Inc., Wilmington, Del., 1920-32

YEAR	MODEL	CYLS	BORE	STROKE	DISPL	HP@RPM	C.R.	VLV
1930	G	8	3.375	4.50	322.1	114@3200	5.3	L
1931	G	8	3.375	4.50	322.1	114@3200	5.3	L
	H	8	3.375	4.50	322.1	130@3200	5.3	L
1932	G	8	3.375	4.50	322.1	130@3200	5.3	L

It has been reported that only three of the model H cars were built, presumably in 1931.

DURANT – – Durant Motors, Inc., New York, N.Y., 1921-32

YEAR	MODEL	CYLS	BORE	STROKE	DISPL	HP@RPM	C.R.	VLV
1930	6-14	6	3.25	4.00	199.0	58@3100	5.3	L
	6-17	6	3.375	4.625	248.0	70@3000	5.06	L
1931	610	4	3.875	4.25	200.5			L
	612	6	3.25	4.00	199.0	71@3300	5.32	L
	614	6	3.25	4.00	199.0	71@3300	5.32	L
	619	6	3.25	4.00	199.0	71@3300	5.32	L
	407*	4	3.875	4.25	200.5			
1932	621	6	3.25	4.00	199.0	71@3300	5.32	L
	622	6	3.25	4.00	199.0	71@3300	5.32	L

* One reference claims this model was built only at Oakland, California plant.

DYMAXION – – Buckminster Fuller, Bridgeport, Conn., 1933-34

YEAR	MODEL	CYLS	BORE	STROKE	DISPL	HP@RPM	C.R.	VLV
1933-34		V8	3.062	3.75	221.0			L

Three examples of the Dymaxion were built of which one is extant. These were three-wheelers with a unique dual chassis. Ford engines were used.

CARBURETOR			WHEEL-	TIRES	BODY	WEIGHT	PRICE
MFR	MODEL	VEN	BASE				
Sc			141	7.00 x 20	5 ps	4550	4410
Sc			141	7.00 x 20	5 ps	4550	
Sc			146				
Sc			141	7.00 x 20	5 ps	4550	
S	U-2	1	112		5 ps	2780	845
S	U-2	1	115		5 ps	3165	1065
T	J	1	112		5 ps	2780	695
S	U-2	1	112	4.75 x 19	5 ps	2765	795
S	U-2	1	112	5.00 x 19	5 ps	2945	995
S	U-2	1	109	4.75 x 19	5 ps	2710	695
			109		5 ps	2750	645
T		1	112	5.25 x 18	5 ps	2820	600
T		1	116	5.25 x 18	5 ps		700
			144		6 ps2	1800	

YEAR	MODEL	ENGINE						
		CYLS	BORE	STROKE	DISPL	HP@RPM	C.R.	VLV

EDSEL — — Ford Motor Co., Detroit, Mich., 1958-60

YEAR	MODEL	CYLS	BORE	STROKE	DISPL	HP@RPM	C.R.	VLV
1958	Ranger	V8	4.05	3.50	360.7	303@4600	10.5	OH
	Pacer	V8	4.05	3.50	360.7	303@4600	10.5	OH
	Corsair	V8	4.20	3.70	410.0	345@4600	10.5	OH
	Citation	V8	4.20	3.70	410.0	345@4600	10.5	OH
1959	Ranger (1, 2)	V8	3.75	3.30	291.6	200@4400	8.8	OH
	Corsair (2)	V8	4.00	3.30	311.3	225@4400	8.9	OH
	Villager (1, 2)	V8	3.75	3.30	291.6	200@4400	8.8	OH
	Optional engines:							
	(1)	V8	4.00	3.30	311.3	225@4400	8.9	OH
	(1)	6	3.625	3.60	222.9	145@4400	8.4	OH
	(2)	V8	4.05	3.50	360.7	303@4600	9.6	OH
1960	Ranger	V8	3.75	3.30	291.6	185@4200	8.8	OH
	Villager	V8	3.75	3.30	291.6	185@4200	8.8	OH
	Optional engines for both:							
		V8	4.00	3.50	351.8	300@4600	9.6	OH
		6	3.625	3.60	222.9	145@4000	8.4	OH

EDWARDS — — Edwards Engineering Co., San Francisco, Cal., 1953-54

YEAR	MODEL	CYLS	BORE	STROKE	DISPL	HP@RPM	C.R.	VLV
1953-54	America	V8	3.812	3.50	317.5	205@4200	8.0	OH

The fewer than ten Edwards that were built and sold used three different engines. Above data is for those which used Lincoln engines.

ELCAR — — Elcar Motor Co., Elkhart, Ind., 1915-31

YEAR	MODEL	CYLS	BORE	STROKE	DISPL	HP@RPM	C.R.	VLV
1930-31	140	8	3.375	4.50	322.1	140@3300	5.25	L

ELECTRA KING — — B & Z Electric Car Co., Long Beach Cal., 1961-

YEAR	MODEL	CYLS	BORE	STROKE	DISPL	HP@RPM	C.R.	VLV
1961	Three-wheel					1		
	Four-wheel					1.5		

ELECTRICAR — — Boulevard Machine Works, North Hollywood, Cal., 1950-

YEAR	MODEL	CYLS	BORE	STROKE	DISPL	HP@RPM	C.R.	VLV
1950	Cutie, Jr.					4x0.17		
	Cutie					4x0.17		
	Boulevard					0.17		

These models were electric. Cutie, Jr., used four electric motors, and Cutie used two. Each of these were rated at 1/6 hp. See BMW.

MFR	CARBURETOR MODEL	VEN	WHEEL-BASE	TIRES	BODY	WEIGHT	PRICE
H			118/116	8.00 x 14	6 ps	3805	2592
H			118/116	8.00 x 14	6 ps	3826	2735
H			124	8.50 x 14	6 pht4	4235	3425
H			124	8.50 x 14	6 pht4	4230	3615
H			120	7.50 x 14	6 ps	3774	2684
H			120	8.00 x 14	6 ps	3696	2812
H			120	8.00 x 14	6 psw4	3842	2971
H	R-1929 AAS	2	120	7.50 x 14/ 8.00 x 14	6 ps	3700	2697
H	R-1929 AAS	2	120	8.00 x 14	6 psw4	4029	2989
H		4	107	8.20 x 15	2 pcv2	2800	4995
Sc	S-1 ¼		135	7.00 x 30	5 ps		2645
			68.5			990	
			64			1090	
					2 pr		
					1 pr		
					1 pr		

YEAR	MODEL	ENGINE CYLS	BORE	STROKE	DISPL	HP@RPM	C.R.	VLV

ELECTRIC SHOPPER – – Electric Shopper, Inc., Long Beach , Cal., 1956-62

YEAR	MODEL	CYLS	BORE	STROKE	DISPL	HP@RPM	C.R.	VLV
1956-62						1.5		
	This electric was available with metal or fiberglass body.							

EL MOROCCO – – Reuben Allender, Detroit, Mich., 1956-57

YEAR	MODEL	CYLS	BORE	STROKE	DISPL	HP@RPM	C.R.	VLV
1957		V8	3.875	3.00	283.0	220@4800	9.5	OH

ERSKINE – – Studebaker Corp., South Bend, Ind., 1927-30

YEAR	MODEL	CYLS	BORE	STROKE	DISPL	HP@RPM	C.R.	VLV
1930	53	6	3.25	4.125	205.7	70@3200	5.2	L

ESHELMAN – – Chester L. Eshelman Co., Baltimore, Md., ca 1955-ca 1960

YEAR	MODEL	CYLS	BORE	STROKE	DISPL	HP@RPM	C.R.	VLV
1955	Sportabout					8.4		
	This car used a Briggs & Stratton engine.							

ESSEX – – Hudson Motor Car Co., Detroit, Mich., 1918-32

YEAR	MODEL	CYLS	BORE	STROKE	DISPL	HP@RPM	C.R.	VLV
1930	Challenger	6	2.75	4.50	161.4	58@3600	5.8	L
1931	Challenger	6	2.875	4.50	175.3	60@3300	5.8	L
1932	Greater Super Six	6	2.938	4.75	193.1	70@3200	5.8	L
	Standard Super Six	6	2.938	4.75	193.1	70@3200	5.8	L
	Essex became Terraplane for 1933.							

ESTATE CARRIAGE – – Peter Stengel, Hollywood, Cal., ca 1960

YEAR	MODEL	CYLS	BORE	STROKE	DISPL	HP@RPM	C.R.	VLV
1960		V8	4.00	3.875	389.6	325@4800	10.5	OH
	A stock Cadillac engine was used.							

EXCALIBUR – – SS Automobiles, Inc., Milwaukee, Wis., 1964+

YEAR	MODEL	CYLS	BORE	STROKE	DISPL	HP@RPM	C.R.	VLV
1964	SS	V8	3.56	3.625	288.7	289@4000	9.0	OH
1966	SS	V8	4.00	3.25	326.7	300@5000	10.5	OH
1967	SS	V8	4.00	3.25	327.7	300@5000	10.5	OH
1968	SS	V8	4.00	3.25	326.7	300@5000	10.5	OH
1969	SS	V8	4.00	3.25	326.7	300@5000	10.5	OH

EXCALIBUR J – – Beassie Engineering Co., Milwaukee, Wis., 1952-53

YEAR	MODEL	CYLS	BORE	STROKE	DISPL	HP@RPM	C.R.	VLV
1953		6	3.125	3.50	199.7	100		F
		4	3.24	3.46	114.1	80		DOHC
	The six-cylinder engine was by Willys, while the four-cylinder one was by Alfa Romeo.							

CARBURETOR MFR	CARBURETOR MODEL	VEN	WHEEL-BASE	TIRES	BODY	WEIGHT	PRICE
			61				750
		4	115		5 pht2		
S	U2	1	114	5.25 x 19	5 ps	2950	985
					1 pr	675	
M	V3	1	113	5.00 x 19	5 ps	2805	825
M	VE3	1	113	5.00 x 19	5 ps	2750	695
M	VE3	1	113	5.25 x 18	5 ps	2980	775
M	VE3	1	113	5.25 x 18	5 ps	2870	735
			130		6 psw4		14,000
C		4	109	6.70 x 15	2 pr	2510	6000
H	3884505	4	109	7.00 x 15	2 pr	2558	
H	3906631	4	109		2 pr		
R	7828207	4	109	8.25 x 15	4 pp	2558	9850
R	7828207	4	109	8.25 x 15	4 pp	2540	10,200
			100		2 pr	1520	2500
			100		2 pr		

YEAR	MODEL	ENGINE CYLS	BORE	STROKE	DISPL	HP@RPM	C.R.	VLV

FAGEOL — — Twin Coach Co., Kent, Oh., 1948

YEAR	MODEL	CYLS	BORE	STROKE	DISPL	HP@RPM	C.R.	VLV
1948	Supersonic				404	275	10.1	OHC
	This presumed experimental car used liquid propane for fuel.							

FERGUS — — Fergus Motors, Inc., New York, N.Y., 1949

YEAR	MODEL	CYLS	BORE	STROKE	DISPL	HP@RPM	C.R.	VLV
1949		4	2.578	3.50	73.1	40@4300	7.25	OH
	Engine was same as used in British Austin A40. Fergus Motors had previous experience in manufacturing automobiles, by same name, back in 1915 - 22.							

FERRER — — Ferrer Motors, Inc., Miami, Fla., 1966+

YEAR	MODEL	CYLS	BORE	STROKE	DISPL	HP@RPM	C.R.	VLV
1966	GT	4	3.03	2.72	78.4	50		

FINA SPORT — — Fina Imported Motor Car Co., New York, N.Y., 1953-55

YEAR	MODEL	CYLS	BORE	STROKE	DISPL	HP@RPM	C.R.	VLV
1953		V8	3.812	3.623	330.9	210@4150	8.25	OH
	Cadillac engines were standard, with optional Lincoln or Chrysler engines.							

FITCH — — Sports & Utility Motors, Inc., White Plains, N.Y., 1949-51; 1966

YEAR	MODEL	CYLS	BORE	STROKE	DISPL	HP@RPM	C.R.	VLV
1949-51	Type B	V8	2.60	3.20	135.9			L
	Engine was Ford 60.							
1966	Phoenix	F6	3.44	2.94	164.0	170@5200	9.25	OH
	The Phoenix was a modified Chevrolet Corvair.							

FLINTRIDGE-DARRIN — — Flintridge Motor Mfg. Corp. of California, Los Angeles, Cal., 1957

YEAR	MODEL	CYLS	BORE	STROKE	DISPL	HP@RPM	C.R.	VLV
1957								
	This was a rebodied DKW and possibly used a DKW engine.							

FORD — — Ford Motor Co., Detroit, Mich., 1903+

YEAR	MODEL	CYLS	BORE	STROKE	DISPL	HP@RPM	C.R.	VLV
1930	A	4	3.875	4.25	205.5	40@2200	4.2	L
1931	A	4	3.875	4.25	205.5	40@2200	4.2	L
1932	B	4	3.875	4.25	205.5	50@2800	4.2	L
	V8	V8	3.062	3.75	221.0	65@3400		L
1933	46	4	3.875	4.25	205.5	50@2800	4.6	L
	40	V8	3.062	3.75	221.0	82@3900	5.5	L
1934	40	V8	3.062	3.75	221.0	90@3800	6.3	L
1935	48	V8	3.062	3.75	221.0	90@3800	6.3	L
1936	Standard, 68	V8	3.062	3.75	221.0	90@3800	6.3	L
	DeLuxe, 68	V8	3.062	3.75	221.0	90@3800	6.3	L
1937	Standard, 78	V8	3.062	3.75	221.0	85@3800	6.17	L
	DeLuxe, 78	V8	3.062	3.75	221.0	85@3800	6.17	L
	V8-60, 74	V8	2.60	3.20	135.9	60@3400	6.75	L

MFR	CARBURETOR MODEL	VEN	WHEEL-BASE	TIRES	BODY	WEIGHT	PRICE
			124			3250	
			94.5		2 pc	1400	3400
			115	6.50 x 15	2 pc	3700	9800
			95			1520	2950
W	36DCLD	2	95		2 pc	2150	8300
			92				3195
Z			103.5	4.50 x 21	5 ps	2488	640
Z			103.5	4.75 x 19	5 ps	2462	590
Z			106	5.25 x 18	5 ps	2388	540
Z			106.5	5.25 x 18	5 ps	2531	645
Z		1	112	5.50 x 17	5 ps	2465	510
D		1	112	5.50 x 17	5 ps	2590	560
S	EE-1	2	112	5.50 x 17	5 ps	2590	575
S	EE-1	2	112	6.00 x 16	5 ps	2760	575
S	EE-1	2	112	6.00 x 16	5 ps	2699	580
S	EE-1	2	112	6.00 x 16	5 ps	2746	625
CG	AA-1	2	112	6.00 x 16	5 ps	2666	696
CG	AA-1	2	112	6.00 x 16	5 ps	2671	734
S	EE-7/8	2	112	5.50 x 16	5 ps	2435	639

YEAR	MODEL	ENGINE						
		CYLS	BORE	STROKE	DISPL	HP@RPM	C.R.	VLV
1938	Standard, 81A	V8	3.062	3.75	221.0	85@3800	6.12	L
	DeLuxe, 81A	V8	3.062	3.75	221.0	85@3800	6.12	L
	V8-60, 82A	V8	2.60	3.20	135.9	60@3400	6.75	L
1939	Standard, 91A	V8	3.062	3.75	221.0	85@3800	6.15	L
	DeLuxe, 91A	V8	3.062	3.75	221.0	85@3800	6.15	L
	V8-60, 922A	V8	2.60	3.20	135.9	60@3400	6.6	L
1940	Standard, 01A	V8	3.062	3.75	221.0	85@3800	6.15	L
	DeLuxe, 01A	V8	3.062	3.75	221.0	85@3800	6.15	L
	V8-60, 02A	V8	2.60	3.20	135.9	60@3500	6.6	L
1941	Special, 1GA	6	3.30	4.40	225.8	90@3300	6.7	L
	DeLuxe, 1GA	6	3.30	4.40	225.8	90@3300	6.7	L
	Super DeLuxe, 1GA	6	3.30	4.40	225.8	90@3300	6.7	L
	Special, 11A	V8	3.062	3.75	221.0	85@3800	6.15	L
	DeLuxe, 11A	V8	3.062	3.75	221.0	85@3800	6.15	L
	Super DeLuxe, 11A	V8	3.062	3.75	221.0	85@3800	6.15	L
1942	Special, 2GA	6	3.30	4.40	225.8	90@3300	6.70	L
	DeLuxe, 2GA	6	3.30	4.40	225.8	90@3300	6.70	L
	Super DeLuxe, 2GA	6	3.30	4.40	225.8	90@3300	6.70	L
	DeLuxe, 21A	V8	3.062	3.75	221.0	90@3800	6.20	L
	Super DeLuxe, 21A	V8	3.062	3.75	221.0	90@3800	6.20	L
1946	6GA	6	3.30	4.40	225.8	90@3300	6.7	L
	69A	V8	3.188	3.75	239.4	100@3800	6.75	L
1947	DeLuxe, 7GA	6	3.30	4.40	225.8	90@3300	6.7	L
	Super DeLuxe, 7GA	6	3.30	4.40	225.8	90@3300	6.7	L
	DeLuxe, 79A	V8	3.188	3.75	239.4	100@3800	6.75	L
	Super DeLuxe, 79A	V8	3.188	3.75	239.4	100@3800	6.75	L
1948	DeLuxe, 87HA	6	3.30	4.40	225.8	90@3300	6.7	L
	Super DeLuxe, 87HA	6	3.30	4.40	225.8	90@3300	6.7	L
	DeLuxe, 89A	V8	3.188	3.75	239.4	100@3800	6.75	L
	Super DeLuxe, 89A	V8	3.188	3.75	239.4	100@3800	6.75	L
1949	DeLuxe, 98HA	6	3.30	4.40	225.8	95@3300	6.8	L
	Custom, 98HA	6	3.30	4.40	225.8	95@3300	6.8	L
	DeLuxe, 98BA	V8	3.188	3.75	239.4	100@3600	6.8	L
	Custom, 98BA	V8	3.188	3.75	239.4	100@3600	6.8	L
1950	DeLuxe, OHA	6	3.30	4.40	225.8	95@3300	6.8	L
	Custom, OHA	6	3.30	4.40	225.8	95@3300	6.8	L
	DeLuxe, OBA	V8	3.188	3.75	239.4	100@3600	6.8	L

MFR	CARBURETOR MODEL	VEN	WHEEL-BASE	TIRES	BODY	WEIGHT	PRICE
CG	AA-1	2	112	6.00 x 16	5 ps	2697	710
CG	AA-1	2	112	6.00 x 16	5 ps	2773	770
S	EE-7/8	2	112	5.50 x 16	5 ps	2481	685
CG	AA-1-120	2	112	6.00 x 16	5 ps	2850	727
CG	AA-1-120	2	112	6.00 x 16	5 ps	2898	788
CG	AA-7/8	2	112	5.50 x 16	5 ps	2623	686
CG	AA1	1	112	6.00 x 16	5 ps	2936	747
CG	AA1	1	112	6.00 x 16	5 ps	2927	762
CG	AA-7/8	1	112	5.50 x 16	5 ps	2669	660
H	847F	1	114	6.00 x 16	5 ps	3020	761
H	847F	1	114	6.00 x 16	5 ps	3100	797
H	847F	1	114	6.00 x 16	5 ps	3131	802
CG	AA1	1	114	6.00 x 16	5 ps	3033	777
CG	AA1	1	114	6.00 x 16	5 ps	3132	813
CG	AA1	1	114	6.00 x 16	5 ps	3110	818
H	847F	1	114	6.00 x 16	6 ps	3093	850
H	847F	1	114	6.00 x 16	6 ps	3141	875
H	847F	1	114	6.00 x 16	6 ps	3179	920
S	EE1	2	114	6.00 x 16	6 ps	3161	885
S	EE1	2	114	6.00 x 16	6 ps	3200	930
H	847F	1	114	6.00 x 16	5 ps		
H	94	2	114	6.00 x 16	5 ps	3240	
H	847F	1	114	6.00 x 16	5 ps	3213	1154
H	847F	1	114	6.00 x 16	5 ps	3233	1195
H	94	2	114	6.00 x 16	5 ps	3246	1204
H	94	2	114	6.00 x 16	5 ps	3266	1279
H	847F	1	114	6.00 x 16	5 ps	3213	1334
H	847F	1	114	6.00 x 16	5 ps	3233	1458
H	94	2	114	6.00 x 16	5 ps	3246	1412
H	94	2	114	6.00 x 16	5 ps	3266	1529
H		1	114	6.00 x 16	6 ps	2990	1472
H		1	114	6.00 x 16/	6 ps	2993	1558
				7.10 x 16			
H	AA-1	2	114	6.00 x 16	6 ps	3030	1546
H	AA-1	2	114	6.00 x 16/	6 ps	3033	1637
				7.10 x 16			
H	847FS	1	114	6.00 x 16	6 ps	3040	1471
H	847FS	1	114	6.00 x 16/	6 ps	3047	1558
				7.10 x 16			
H	AA-1	2	114	6.00 x 16	6 ps	3080	1545

YEAR	MODEL	ENGINE						
		CYLS	BORE	STROKE	DISPL	HP@RPM	C.R.	VLV
	Custom, OBA	V8	3.188	3.75	239.4	100@3600	6.8	L
1951	DeLuxe, 1HA	6	3.30	4.40	225.8	95@3300	6.8	L
	Custom, 1HA	6	3.30	4.40	225.8	95@3300	6.8	L
	DeLuxe, 1BA	V8	3.188	3.75	239.4	100@3600	6.8	L
	Custom, 1BA	V8	3.188	3.75	239.4	100@3600	6.8	L
1952	Mainline	6	3.56	3.60	215.3	101@3500	7.0	OH
	Customline	6	3.56	3.60	215.3	101@3500	7.0	OH
	Mainline	V8	3.188	3.75	239.4	110@3800	7.2	L
	Customline	V8	3.188	3.75	239.4	110@3800	7.2	L
	Crestline	V8	3.188	3.75	239.4	110@3800	7.2	L
1953	Mainline	6	3.56	3.60	215.3	101@3500	7.0	OH
	Customline	6	3.56	3.60	215.3	101@3500	7.0	OH
	Mainline	V8	3.188	3.75	239.4	110@3800	7.2	L
	Customline	V8	3.188	3.75	239.4	110@3800	7.2	L
	Crestline	V8	3.188	3.75	239.4	110@3800	7.2	L
1954	Mainline	6	3.625	3.60	222.9	115@3900	7.2	OH
	Customline	6	3.625	3.60	222.9	115@3900	7.2	OH
	Crestline	6	3.625	3.60	222.9	115@3900	7.2	OH
	Mainline	V8	3.50	3.10	239.4	130@3400	7.2	OH
	Customline	V8	3.50	3.10	239.4	130@3400	7.2	OH
	Crestline	V8	3.50	3.10	239.4	130@3400	7.2	OH
1955	Mainline	6	3.625	3.60	222.9	120@4000	7.5	OH
	Customline	6	3.625	3.60	222.9	120@4000	7.5	OH
	Fairlane	6	3.625	3.60	222.9	120@4000	7.5	OH
	Mainline	V8	3.625	3.60	272.5	162@4400	7.6	OH
	Customline	V8	3.625	3.60	272.5	162@4400	7.6	OH

MFR	CARBURETOR MODEL	VEN	WHEEL-BASE	TIRES	BODY	WEIGHT	PRICE
H	AA-1	2	114	6.00 x 16/	6 ps	3087	1637
				7.10 x 15			
H	847FS	1	114	6.00 x 16	6 ps	3089	1573
H	847FS	1	114	6.70 x 15	6 ps	3089	1666
O	8BA	2	114	6.00 x 16	6 ps	3114	1652
O	8BA	2	114	6.70 x 15	6 ps	3114	1750
H	847FS	1	115	7.10 x 15/	6 ps	3173	1678
				6.00 x 16			
H	847FS	1	115	6.70 x 15	6 ps	3173	1769
O	8BA	2	115	6.00 x 16	6 ps	3207	1754
O	8BA	2	115	7.10 x 15/	6 ps	3207	1845
				6.70 x 15			
O	8BA	2	115	6.70 x 15/	6 pht2	3274	2104
				7.10 x 15			
H	1904F	1	115	6.70 x 15/	6 ps	3115	1690
				7.10 x 15			
H	1904F	1	115	6.70 x 15	6 ps	3115	1783
H	2100	2	115	7.10 x 15/	6 ps	3181	1766
				6.70 x 15			
H	2100	2	115	6.70 x 15/	6 ps	3193	1858
				7.10 x 15			
H	2100	2	115	6.70 x 15/	6 pht2	3250	2120
				7.10 x 15			
H	1904F	1	115.5	6.70 x 15/	6 ps	3142	1701
				7.10 x 15			
H	1904F	1	115.5	6.70 x 15/	6 ps	3155	1793
				7.10 x 15			
H	1904F	1	115.5	6.70 x 15/	6 ps	3159	1898
				7.10 x 15			
H	AA-1	2	115.5	6.70 x 15/	6 ps	3263	1777
				7.10 x 15			
H	AA-1	2	115.5	6.70 x 15/	6 ps	3276	1870
				7.10 x 15			
H	AA-1	2	115.5	6.70 x 15/	6 ps	3280	1975
				7.10 x 15			
H		1	115.5	6.70 x 15	6 ps	3106	1753
H		1	115.5	6.70 x 15/	6 ps	3126	1845
				6.70 x 15			
H		1	115.5	6.70 x 15	6 ps	3134	1960
H		2	115.5	6.70 x 15	6 ps	3216	1853
H		2	115.5	6.70 x 15	6 ps	3236	1945

YEAR	MODEL	ENGINE						
		CYLS	BORE	STROKE	DISPL	HP@RPM	C.R.	VLV
	Fairlane	V8	3.625	3.60	272.5	162@4400	7.6	OH
	Thunderbird	V8	3.75	3.50	291.6	193@4400	8.1	OH
	Beginning 1955, station wagons were listed separately as Country Sedan, Country Squire, Ranch Wagon, etc. However, these had same specs as basic line, aside from using next-larger size tires.							
1956	Mainline	6	3.625	3.60	222.9	137@4200	8.0	OH
	Customline	6	3.62	3.60	222.9	137@4200	8.0	OH
	Fairlane	6	3.62	3.60	222.9	137@4200	8.0	OH
	Mainline	V8	3.62	3.30	272.5	173@4400	8.0	OH
	Customline	V8	3.62	3.30	272.5	173@4400	8.0	OH
	Fairlane	V8	3.75	3.30	291.6	200@4600	8.0	OH
	Thunderbird (1)	V8	3.75	3.30	291.6	202@4600	8.4	OH
	Optional engine:							
	(1)	V8	3.80	3.44	312.9	215@4600	8.4	OH
1957	Custom	6	3.62	3.60	222.9	144@4200	8.6	OH
	Custom 300	6	3.62	3.60	222.9	144@4200	8.6	OH
	Fairlane	6	3.62	3.60	222.9	144@4200	8.6	OH
	Fairlane 500	6	3.62	3.60	222.9	144@4200	8.6	OH
	Custom (1)	V8	3.62	3.30	272.5	190@4500	8.6	OH
	Custom 300 (1)	V8	3.62	3.30	272.5	190@4500	8.6	OH
	Fairlane (1)	V8	3.75	3.30	291.6	212@4200	9.1	OH
	Fairlane 500	V8	3.75	3.30	291.6	212@4200	9.1	OH
	Thunderbird (2)	V8	3.75	3.30	291.6	212@4500	9.1	OH
	Optional engines:							
	(1)	V8	3.80	3.44	312.0	245@4500	9.1	OH
	(2)	V8	3.80	3.44	312.0	270@4800	9.1	OH
1958	Custom 300	6	3.62	3.60	222.9	145@4200	8.6	OH
	Fairlane	6	3.62	3.60	222.9	145@4200	8.6	OH
	Fairlane 500	6	3.62	3.60	222.9	145@4200	8.6	OH
	Custom 300 (1)	V8	3.75	3.30	291.6	205@4500	9.1	OH
	Fairlane (1)	V8	3.75	3.30	291.6	205@4500	9.1	OH
	Fairlane 500 (1)	V8	4.00	3.30	331.8	265@4600	9.5	OH
	Thunderbird	V8	4.00	3.50	351.8	300@4600	10.2	OH
	Optional engine:							
	(1)	V8	4.00	3.50	351.8	300@4600	10.2	OH
1959	Custom 300	6	3.625	3.60	222.9	145@4000	8.4	OH
	Fairlane	6	3.625	3.60	222.9	145@4000	8.4	OH
	Fairlane 500	6	3.625	3.60	222.9	145@4000	8.4	OH

CARBURETOR MFR	MODEL	VEN	WHEEL-BASE	TIRES	BODY	WEIGHT	PRICE
H		2	115.5	6.70 x 15	6 ps	3268	2060
H		4	102	6.70 x 15	2 pcv2	2980	2944
O		1	115.5	6.70 x 15	6 ps	3127	1895
O		1	115.5	6.70 x 15	6 ps	3147	1985
O		1	115.5	6.70 x 15	6 ps	3147	2093
O		2	115.5	6.70 x 15	6 ps	3238	1995
O		2	115.5	6.70 x 15	6 ps	3258	2086
O		2	115.5	6.70 x 15	6 ps	3290	2194
O		4	102	6.70 x 15	2 pcv	3038	3151
H		1	116	7.50 x 14	6 ps	3193	2042
H		1	116	7.50 x 14	6 ps	3208	2157
H		1	118	7.50 x 14	6 ps	3315	2286
H		1	118	7.50 x 14	6 ps	3330	2333
O		2	116	7.50 x 14	6 ps	3315	2142
O		2	116	7.50 x 14	6 ps	3330	2257
O		2	118	7.50 x 14	6 ps	3437	2386
H		2	118	7.50 x 14/	6 ps	3452	2433
				8.00 x 14			
H		4	102	7.50 x 14	2 pcv	3145	3408
		2 x 4					
H			116	7.50 x 14	6 ps	3222	2119
H			118	7.50 x 14	6 ps	3371	2285
H			118	7.50 x 14	6 ps	3379	2438
			116	7.50 x 14	6 ps	3334	2256
			118	7.50 x 14	6 ps	3483	2409
H	R-1406A	2	118	7.50 x 14/	6 ps	3526	2562
				8.00 x 14			
			102	7.50 x 14	2 pht	3876	3631
H		1	118	7.50 x 14	6 ps	3385	2273
H		1	118	7.50 x 14	6 ps	3415	2411
H		1	118	7.50 x 14	6 ps	3417	2530

YEAR	MODEL	ENGINE						
		CYLS	BORE	STROKE	DISPL	HP@RPM	C.R.	VLV
	Galaxie	6	3.625	3.6	222.3	145@4000	8.4	OH
	Custom 300 (1, 2)	V8	3.75	3.30	291.6	200@4400	8.8	OH
	Fairlane (1, 2)	V8	3.75	3.30	291.6	200@4400	8.8	OH
	Fairlane 500 (1, 2)	V8	3.75	3.30	291.6	200@4400	8.8	OH
	Galaxie (1, 2)	V8	3.75	3.30	291.6	200@4400	8.8	OH
	Thunderbird (1)	V8	4.00	3.50	351.8	300@4600	9.6	OH
	Optional engines:							
	(1)	V8	4.30	3.70	383.4	350@4400	10.0	OH
	(2)	V8	4.00	3.30	331.8	225@4400	8.9	OH
1960	Falcon	6	3.50	2.50	144.3	90@4200	8.7	OH
	Custom 300	6	3.625	3.60	222.9	145@4000	8.4	OH
	Fairlane	6	3.625	3.60	222.9	145@4000	8.4	OH
	Fairlane 500	6	3.625	3.60	222.9	145@4000	8.4	OH
	Galaxie	6	3.625	3.60	222.9	145@4000	8.4	OH
	Custom 500 (2)	V8	3.75	3.30	291.6	185@4200	8.8	OH
	Fairlane (2)	V8	3.75	3.30	291.6	185@4200	8.8	OH
	Fairlane 500 (2)	V8	3.75	3.30	291.6	185@4200	8.8	OH
	Galaxie (2)	V8	3.75	3.30	291.6	185@4200	8.8	OH
	Thunderbird (1)	V8	4.00	3.50	351.8	300@4600	9.6	OH
	Optional engines:							
	(1)	V8	4.30	3.70	383.4	350@4600	10.1	OH
	(2)	V8	4.00	3.50	351.8	300@4600	9.6	OH
1961	Falcon (1)	6	3.50	2.50	144.3	85@4200	8.7	OH
	Fairlane	6	3.625	3.60	222.9	135@4000	8.4	OH
	Fairlane 500	6	3.62	3.60	222.9	135@4000	8.4	OH
	Galaxie	6	3.62	3.60	222.9	135@4000	8.4	OH
	Fairlane (2)	V8	3.75	3.30	291.6	175@4200	8.8	OH
	Fairlane 500 (2)	V8	3.75	3.30	291.6	175@4200	8.8	OH
	Galaxie (2)	V8	3.75	3.30	291.6	175@4200	8.8	OH
	Thunderbird	V8	4.05	3.78	389.6	300@4600	9.6	OH
	Optional engines:							

MFR	CARBURETOR MODEL	VEN	WHEEL-BASE	TIRES	BODY	WEIGHT	PRICE
H		1	118	7.50 x 14	6 ps	3405	2582
H		2	118	7.50 x 14	6 ps	3486	2391
H		2	118	7.50 x 14	6 ps	3516	2529
H		2	118	7.50 x 14	6 ps	3518	2648
H		2	118	7.50 x 14	6 ps	3506	2700
C	2853	4	113	8.00 x 14	5 pht2	3813	3696
H		1	109.5	6.00 x 13/	6 ps	2288	1974
				6.50 x 13			
H		1	119	7.50 x 14/	6 ps		2284
				8.00 x 14			
H		1	119	7.50 x 14/	6 ps	3606	2311
				8.00 x 14			
H		1	119	7.50 x 14/	6 ps	3610	2388
				8.00 x 14			
H		1	119	7.50 x 14/	6 ps	3634	2603
				8.00 x 14			
H		2	119	7.50 x 14/	6 ps		2391
				8.00 x 14			
H		2	119	7.50 x 14/	6 ps	3706	2424
				8.00 x 14			
H		2	119	7.50 x 14/	6 ps	3710	2501
				8.00 x 14			
H		2	119	7.50 x 14/	6 ps	3734	2716
				8.00 x 14			
H		4	113	8.00 x 14	4 pht2	3799	3755
		4					
H	1904	1	109.5	6.00 x 13/	6 ps	2289	1976
				6.50 x 13			
H		1	119	7.50 x 14	6 ps	3585	2317
H		1	119	7.50 x 14	6 ps	3593	2432
H		1	119	7.50 x 14	6 ps	3570	2592
O		2	119	7.50 x 14	6 ps	3683	2433
O		2	119	7.50 x 14	6 ps	3691	2548
O		2	119	7.50 x 14	6 ps	3668	2708
O		4	119	7.50 x 14	4 pht2	3958	4172

YEAR	MODEL	ENGINE						
		CYLS	BORE	STROKE	DISPL	HP@RPM	C.R.	VLV
	(1)	6	3.50	2.94	169.7	101@4400	8.7	OH
	(2)	V8	4.00	3.50	351.8	220@4400	8.9	OH
	(2)	V8	4.05	3.78	389.6	300@4600	9.6	OH
1962	Falcon Standard, 10 (3)	6	3.50	2.50	144.3	85@4200	8.7	OH
	Falcon DeLuxe Futura (3)	6	3.50	2.50	144.3	85@4200	8.7	OH
	Fairlane 30	6	3.50	2.938	170.0	101@4400	8.7	OH
	Fairlane 500, 40	6	3.50	2.938	170.0	101@4400	8.7	OH
	Galaxie, 50	6	3.625	3.610	223.0	138@4200	8.4	OH
	Galaxie 500, 60	6	3.625	3.610	223.0	138@4200	8.4	OH
	Fairlane 30 (4)	V8	3.50	2.875	221.5	145@4400	8.7	OH
	Fairlane 500, 40 (4)	V8	3.50	2.875	221.5	145@4000	8.7	OH
	Galaxie, 50 (2, 5)	V8	3.75	3.30	291.6	170@4200	8.8	OH
	Galaxie 500, 60 (2, 5)	VՑ	3.75	3.30	291.6	170@4200	8.8	OH
	Galaxie 500XL (2, 5)	V8	3.75	3.30	291.6	170@4200	8.8	OH
	Thunderbird, 70 (1)	V8	4.070	3.782	390.0	300@4600	9.6	OH
	Optional engines:							
	(1)	V8	4.05	3.784	390.0	340@5000	10.5	OH
	(2)	V8	3.75	3.30	291.6	170@4200	8.8	OH
	(2)	V8	4.00	3.50	351.9	220@4300	8.9	OH
	(2)	V8	4.05	3.784	390.0	375@6000	10.4	OH
	(2)	V8	4.05	3.784	390.0	401@6000	11.1	OH
	(3)	V8	3.50	2.938	170.0	101@4400	8.7	OH
	(4)	V8	3.80	2.875	260.8	164@4400	8.7	OH
	(5)	V8	4.125	3.782	406.0	385@5800	10.9	OH
1963	Falcon 06 (3)	6	3.50	2.50	144.3	85@4200	8.7	OH
	Falcon Futura, 10 (1, 3)	6	3.50	2.50	144.3	85@4200	8.7	OH
	Fairlane, 30 (2)	6	3.50	2.938	169.7	101@4400	8.7	OH
	Fairlane 500, 40 (2)	6	3.50	2.938	169.7	101@4400	8.7	OH
	Fairlane, 30 (3, 4)	6	3.50	2.875	166.1	145@4400	8.7	OH
	Fairlane 500, 40 (3, 4)	V8	3.50	2.875	221.5	145@4400	8.7	OH
	Ford 300, 50	6	3.625	3.60	222.9	138@4200	8.4	OH
	Galaxie, 50	6	3.625	3.60	222.9	138@4200	8.4	OH
	Galaxie 500, 60	6	3.625	3.60	222.9	138@4200	8.4	OH
	Ford 300, 50	V8	3.80	2.87	260.8	164@4400	8.7	OH
	Galaxie, 50	V8	3.80	2.87	260.8	164@4400	8.7	OH
	Galaxie 500, 60	V8	3.80	2.87	260.8	164@4400	8.7	OH
	Galaxie 500XL, 60	V8	3.80	2.87	260.8	164@4400	8.7	OH
	Thunderbird, 80 (5)	V8	4.05	3.78	389.6	300@4600	9.6	OH

MFR	CARBURETOR MODEL	VEN	WHEEL-BASE	TIRES	BODY	WEIGHT	PRICE
H	R1806A	2					
H	1909	1	109.5	6.00 x 13/	6 ps	2279	2047
				6.50 x 13			
H	1909	1	109.5	6.00 x 13/	6 ps	2285	2133
				6.50 x 13			
H	1909	1	115.5	6.50 x 13	6 ps	2769	2216
H	1909	1	115.5	6.50 x 13	6 ps	2786	2304
H			119	7.50 x 14	6 ps	3581	2507
H			119	7.50 x 14	6 ps	3594	2667
O			115.5	7.00 x 13	6 ps	2927	2319
O			115.5	7.00 x 13	6 ps	2944	2407
O			119	7.50 x 14	6 ps	3692	2616
O			119	7.50 x 14	6 ps	3705	2776
O			119	7.50 x 14	6 pht2	3672	
O		3 x 2	113	8.00 x 14	4 pht2	4132	4321
		3 x 2					
		3 x 2					
H							
O	C3DF-9510	1	109.5	6.00 x 13	6 ps	2337	2047
O	C3DF-9510	1	109.5	6.00 x 13/	6 ps	2345	2165
				6.50 x 13			
O	C3DF-9510A	1	115.5	6.50 x 13	6 ps	2864	2216
O	C30F-9510A	1	115.5	6.50 x 13	6 ps	2879	2304
O	C30F-9510C	2	115.5	7.00 x 14	6 ps	2996	2319
O	C30F-9510C	2	115.5	7.00 x 14	6 ps	3011	2407
O	C3AF-9510	1	119	7.50 x 14	6 ps	3630	2378
O	C3AF-9510	1	119	7.50 x 14	6 ps	3650	2509
O	C3AF-9510	1	119	7.50 x 14	6 ps	3670	2667
O	C3DF-9510	2	119	7.50 x 14	6 ps	3624	2487
O	C3DF-9510	2	119	7.50 x 14	6 ps	3644	2616
O	C3DF-9510	2	119	7.50 x 14	6 ps	3664	2776
O	C30F-9510	2	119	7.50 x 14	6 ps	3691	3333
O		4	119	7.50 x 14	4 pht2	4195	4445

YEAR	MODEL	ENGINE						
		CYLS	BORE	STROKE	DISPL	HP@RPM	C.R.	VLV
	Optional engines:							
	(1)	6	3.50	2.938	170.0	101@4400	8.7	OH
	(2)	6	3.68	3.13	199.7	116@4400	8.7	OH
	(3)	V8	3.80	2.875	260.0	164@4400	8.7	OH
	(4)	V8	4.00	2.875	289.0	271@6000	11.6	OH
	(5)	V8	4.047	3.782	390.0	340@5000	10.5	OH
1964	Falcon Standard (3, 7)	6	3.50	2.50	144.0	85@4200	8.4	OH
	Falcon Futura (3, 7)	6	3.50	2.50	144.0	85@4200	8.4	OH
	Falcon Sprint	V8	3.798	2.875	260.0	164@4400	8.4	OH
	Fairlane (1)	6	3.50	2.938	170.0	101@4400	8.4	OH
	Fairlane 500 (1)	6	3.50	2.938	170.0	101@4400	8.4	OH
	Fairlane (2, 3, 4, 5)	V8	3.798	2.875	260.0	164@4400	8.4	OH
	Fairlane 500 (2, 3, 4, 5)	V8	3.798	2.875	260.0	164@4400	8.4	OH
	Custom	6	3.625	3.297	223.0	138@4200	8.4	OH
	Custom 500	6	3.625	3.297	223.0	138@4200	8.4	OH
	Galaxie 500	6	3.625	3.297	223.0	138@4200	8.4	OH
	Custom (3, 5, 6)	V8	4.00	3.50	352.0	250@4400	8.9	OH
	Custom 500 (3, 5, 6)	V8	4.00	3.50	352.0	250@4400	8.9	OH
	Galaxie 500 (3, 5, 6)	V8	4.00	3.50	352.0	250@4400	8.9	OH
	Galaxie 500XL (3, 5, 6)	V8	4.00	3.50	352.0	250@4400	8.9	OH
	Thunderbird (3, 5, 6)	V8	4.047	3.782	390.0	300@4600	9.7	OH
	Optional engines:							
	(1)	6	3.688	3.125	200.2	116@4400	8.4	OH
	(2)	V8	4.00	2.875	289.0	271@6000	10.5	OH
	(3)	V8	4.00	3.50	351.9	250@4400	8.9	OH
	(4)	V8	4.00	2.875	289.0	195@4400	8.6	OH
	(4)	V8	4.047	3.781	389.1	300@4600	9.7	OH
	(4)	V8	4.234	3.797	427.7	410		OH
	(5)	V8	4.234	3.797	427.7	425@6000	11.1	OH
	(6)	V8	4.047	3.781	389.1	330@5000	10.1	OH
	(7)	6	3.50	2.93	170.0	101@4400	8.4	OH
1965	Falcon Standard	6	3.50	2.938	169.6	105@4400	9.1	OH
	Falcon Futura	6	3.688	3.125	200.2	120@4400	9.2	OH
	Fairlane	6	3.688	3.125	200.2	120@4400	9.2	OH

MFR	CARBURETOR MODEL	VEN	WHEEL-BASE	TIRES	BODY	WEIGHT	PRICE
O							
O	C30F-9510-E	2					
H		2 x 3					
O	C40F-9510-G	1	109.5	6.00 x 13	6 ps	2400	2058
O	C40F-9510-G	1	109.5	6.00/6.50 x 13	5 ps	2410	2176
O	C40F-9510-E	2	109.5	6.00 x 13/	5 pht2	2813	2436
				6.50 x 13			
O	C30F-9510-AK	1	115.5	6.50 x 13	6 ps	2828	2235
O	C30F-9510-AK	1	115.5	6.50 x 13	6 ps	2843	2317
O	C40F-9510-E	2	115.5	7.00 x 13	6 ps	2962	2335
O	C40F-9510-E	2	115.5	7.00 x 13	6 ps	2977	2417
O	C3AF-9510-BL	1	119	7.50 x 14	6 ps	3621	2415
O	C3AF-9510-BL	1	119	7.50 x 14	6 ps	3661	2518
O	C3AF-9510-BL	1	119	7.50 x 14	6 ps	3676	2678
O	C4AF-9510-N	2	119	7.50 x 14	6 ps	3617	2524
O	C4AF-9510-N	2	119	7.50 x 14	6 ps	3657	2627
O	C4AF-9510-N	2	119	7.50 x 14	6 ps	3672	2787
O	C4AF-9510-N	2	119	7.50 x 14	6 pht4	3722	3298
O	C4SF-9510-B	4	113.2	8.15 x 15	4 pht2	4431	4486
O	C30F-9510AJ	4					
O	C4AF-9510N	2					
O	C4AF-9510B	2					
O	C3AF-9510BU	4					
O	C3AF-9510BY	4					
O	C5DF-9510-E	1	109.5	6.00 x 13/	5 ps	2406	2038
				6.50 x 13/			
				6.45 x 14			
O	C5DF-9510-E	1	109.5	6.00 x 13/	5 ps	2413	2146
				6.50 x 13/			
				6.45 x 14			
O	C5ZF-9510-A	2	116/115.5	6.45 x 14/	6 ps	2858	2223
				7.35 x 14			

YEAR	MODEL	ENGINE						
		CYLS	BORE	STROKE	DISPL	HP@RPM	C.R.	VLV
	Fairlane 500	6	3.688	3.125	200.2	120@4400	9.2	OH
	Fairlane (1,2)	V8	4.00	2.875	289.0	200@4400	9.3	OH
	Fairlane 500 (1, 2)	V8	4.00	2.875	289.0	200@4400	9.3	OH
	Mustang	6	3.688	3.125	200.2	120@4400	9.2	OH
	Mustang (1, 2)	V8	4.00	2.875	289.0	200@4400	9.3	OH
	Custom	6	4.00	3.188	240.3	150@4000	9.2	OH
	Custom 500	6	4.00	3.188	240.3	150@4000	9.2	OH
	Galaxie 500	6	4.00	3.188	240.3	150@4000	9.2	OH
	Custom (5)	V8	4.00	2.875	289.0	200@4400	9.3	OH
	Custom 500 (3, 4, 5)	V8	4.00	2.875	289.0	200@4400	9.3	OH
	Galaxie 500 (3, 4, 5)	V8	4.00	2.875	289.0	200@4400	9.3	OH
	Galaxie 500XL (3, 4, 5)	V8	4.00	2.875	289.0	200@4400	9.3	OH
	Galaxie 500 LTD (3, 4, 5)	V8	4.00	2.875	289.0	200@4400	9.3	OH
	Thunderbird (4)	V8	4.047	3.781	389.1	300@4600	10.1	OH
	Optional engines:							
	(1)	V8	4.00	2.875	289.0	225@4800	10.0	OH
	(2)	V8	4.00	2.875	289.0	271@6000	10.5	OH
	(3)	V8	4.00	3.50	351.9	250@4400	9.3	OH
	(3)	V8	4.047	3.781	389.1	300@4600	10.1	OH
	(4)	V8	4.234	3.797	427.7	425@6000	11.1	OH
	(5)	V8	4.047	3.781	389.1	330@5000	10.1	OH
1966	Falcon Standard	6	3.50	2.938	169.6	105@4400	9.2	OH
	Falcon Futura	6	3.50	2.938	169.6	105@4400	9.2	OH
	Fairlane (1)	6	3.688	3.125	200.2	120@4400	9.2	OH
	Fairlane 500 (1)	6	3.688	3.125	200.2	120@4400	9.2	OH
	Fairlane 500XL (1)	6	3.688	3.125	200.2	120@4400	9.2	OH
	Fairlane (3)	V8	4.00	2.875	289.0	200@4400	9.3	OH
	Fairlane 500 (3)	V8	4.00	2.875	289.0	200@4400	9.3	OH
	Fairlane 500XL (3)	V8	4.00	2.875	289.0	200@4400	9.3	OH
	Fairlane 500GT	V8	4.048	3.781	389.2	315@4600	10.5	OH
	Mustang	6	3.688	3.125	200.2	120@4400	9.2	OH
	Mustang (3)	V8	4.00	2.875	289.0	200@4400	9.3	OH
	Custom (1)	6	4.00	3.188	240.3	150@4000	8.75	OH
	Custom 500 (1)	6	4.00	3.188	240.3	150@4000	8.75	OH
	Galaxie 500 (1)	6	4.00	3.188	240.3	150@4000	8.75	OH

MFR	CARBURETOR MODEL	VEN	WHEEL-BASE	TIRES	BODY	WEIGHT	PRICE
O	C5ZF-9510-A	2	116/	6.45 x 14/	6 ps	2863	2303
			115.5	7.35 x 14			
O	C5ZF-9510-A	2	116/	6.45 x 14/	6 ps	3050	2329
			115.5	7.35 x 14			
O	C5ZF-9510-A	2	116/	6.45 x 14/	6 ps	3055	2409
			115.5	7.35 x 14			
O	C50F-9510-E	1	108	6.50 x 13	5 pht2	2445	2321
O	C5ZF-9510-A	2	108	6.95 x 14	5 pht2	2720	2427
O	C5AF-9510-T	1	119	7.35 x 15	6 ps	3356	2366
O	C5AF-9510-T	1	119	7.35 x 15	6 ps	3386	2467
O	C5AF-9510-T	1	119	7.35 x 15	6 ps	3418	2623
O	C5AF-9510-A	2	119	7.35 x 15	6 ps	3400	2472
O	C5AF-9510-A	2	119	7.35 x 15	6 ps	3430	2573
O	C5AF-9510-A	2	119	7.35 x 15	6 ps	3462	2730
O	C5AF-9510-A	2	119	7.35 x 15	6 pht2	3497	3167
O	C5AF-9510-A	2	119	7.35 x 15	6 pht4	3578	3245
O	C4SF-9510-B	4	113.2	8.15 x 15	4 pht2	4470	4394
O	C5ZF-9510-C	4					
O	C40F-9510-AL	4					
O	C5AF-9510-E	4					
O	C5AF-9510-E	4					
O	C4AF-9510-BJ	4					
O	C5AF-9510-J	4					
O	C5DF-9510-L	1	110.9	6.50 x 13	6 ps	2559	2114
O	C5DF-9510-L	1	110.9	6.50 x 13	6 ps	2567	2237
O	C50F-9510-Y	1	116	6.95 x 14	6 ps	2792	2280
O	C50F-9510-Y	1	116	6.95 x 14	6 ps	2798	2357
O	C50F-9510-Y	1	116	6.95 x 14	5 pht2	2884	2543
O	C6AF-9510	2	116	6.95 x 14	6 ps	2961	2386
O	C6AF-9510	2	116	6.95 x 14	6 ps	2967	2463
O	C6AF-9510	2	116	6.95 x 14	5 pht2	3053	2649
O	C6MF-9510	2	116	6.95 x 14	5 pht2	3493	2843
O	C50F-9510-Y	1	108	6.95 x 14	4 pht2	2488	2416
O	C6DF-9510-A	2	108	6.95 x 14	4 pht2	2733	2522
O	C8AF-9510	1	119	7.35 x 15	6 ps	3433	2432
O	C8AF-9510	1	119	7.35 x 15/	6 ps	3444	2533
				7.75 x 15/			
				8.15 x 15			
O	C8AF-9510	1	119	7.35 x 15/	6 ps	3456	2677
				7.75 x 15/			

YEAR	MODEL	ENGINE						
		CYLS	BORE	STROKE	DISPL	HP@RPM	C.R.	VLV
	Custom (2)	V8	4.00	2.875	289.0	200@4400	9.3	OH
	Custom 500 (2)	V8	4.00	2.875	289.0	200@4400	9.3	OH
	Galaxie 500 (2)	V8	4.00	2.875	289.0	200@4400	9.3	OH
	Galaxie 500 (2) XL	V8	4.00	2.875	289.0	200@4400	9.3	OH
	Ford LTD (2)	V8	4.00	2.875	289.0	200@4400	9.3	OH
	Galaxie 500-71	V8	4.125	3.98	428.0	345@4600	10.5	OH
	Thunderbird (4)	V8	4.048	3.781	389.2	315@4600	10.5	OH
	Optional engines:							
	(1)	6	4.00	3.188	240.3	135@4000	8.75	OH
	(3)	V8	4.00	2.875	289.0	225@4800	10.1	OH
	(3)	V8	4.00	2.875	289.0	271@6000	10.5	OH
	(3)	V8	4.05	3.78	389.2	275@4400	9.5	OH
	(2)	V8	4.05	3.78	389.2	315@4600	10.5	OH
	(2)	V8	4.23	3.78	427.0	380@5400	10.5	OH
	(2)	V8	4.125	3.98	428.0	425@6000	11.1	OH
	(4)	V8	4.125	3.98	428.0	345@4600	10.5	OH
1967	Falcon Standard (1, 2)	6	3.50	2.94	169.6	105@4400	9.1	OH
	Falcon Futura (1, 2)	6	3.68	3.125	200.2	120@4400	9.2	OH
	Fairlane	6	3.68	3.125	200.2	120@4400	9.2	OH
	Fairlane 500	6	3.68	3.125	200.2	120@4400	9.2	OH
	Fairlane 500XL	6	3.68	3.125	200.2	120@4400	9.2	OH
	Fairlane	V8	4.00	2.875	289.0	200@4400	9.3	OH
	Fairlane 500 (4, 6)	V8	4.00	2.875	289.0	200@4400	9.3	OH
	Fairlane 500XL (4, 6)	V8	4.00	2.875	289.0	200@4400	9.3	OH
	Fairlane GT	V8	4.00	2.875	289.0	200@4400	9.3	OH
	Mustang (2)	6	3.68	3.125	200.2	120@4400	9.2	OH
	Mustang (2, 3, 6)	V8	4.00	3.875	289.0	200@4400	9.3	OH
	Custom	6	4.00	3.188	240.3	135@4000	9.2	OH
	Custom 500	6	4.00	3.188	240.3	135@4000	9.2	OH
	Galaxie 500	6	4.00	3.188	240.3	135@4000	9.2	OH
	Custom (4)	V8	4.00	2.875	289.0	200@4400	9.3	OH
	Custom 500 (4, 5, 7, 8, 9)	V8	4.00	2.875	289.0	200@4400	9.3	OH
	Galaxie 500 (4, 5, 6, 7, 8, 9)	V8	4.00	2.875	289.0	200@4400	9.3	OH

MFR	CARBURETOR MODEL	VEN	WHEEL-BASE	TIRES	BODY	WEIGHT	PRICE
				8.15 x 15			
O	C60F-9510-A	2	119	7.35 x 15	6 ps	3477	2539
O	C60F-9510-A	2	119	7.35 x 15	6 ps	3488	2638
O	C60F-9510-A	2	119	7.35 x 15/	6 ps	3500	2784
				7.75 x 15/			
				8.15 x 15			
O	C60F-9510-A	2	119	7.75 x 15/	5 pht2	3616	3231
				8.15 x 15			
O	C60F-9510-A	2	119	7.75 x 15	6 pht4	3649	3278
O	C4AF-9510	2 x 4	119	7.75 x 15/	5 pht2	3914	3621
				8.15 x 15			
O	C6SF-9510-C	4	113	8.15 x 15	4 pht2	4386	4426
O	C6AF-9510	1					
O	C6ZF-9510-A	4					
O	C60F-9510-C	4					
O		2					
O	C6AF-9510	4					
O		2 x 4					
O	C6AF-9510	4					
O	C6SF-9510-C	4					
O	C7DF-9510-S	1	111	6.95 x 14	6 ps	2598	2167
O	C7DF-9510-J	1	111	6.95 x 14/	6 ps	2631	2322
				7.35 x 14			
O	C60F-9510-AD	1	116	7.35 x 14	6 ps	2813	2339
O	C60F-9510-AD	1	116	7.35 x 14	6 ps	2833	2417
O	C60F-9510-AD	1	116	7.35 x 14	5 pht2	2890	2619
O	C7DF-9510-S	2	116	7.35 x 14	6 ps	2966	2445
O	C7DF-9510-S	2	116	7.35 x 14	6 ps	2986	2522
O	C7DF-9510-S	2	116	7.35 x 14	5 pht2	3043	2724
O	C7DF-9510-S	2	116	F70 x 14	5 pht2	3004	2839
O	C60F-9510-AD	1	108	6.95 x 14	4 pht2	2624	2461
O	C70F-9510-S	2	108	6.95 x 14	4 pht2	2803	2567
O	C6AF-9510	1	119	7.75 x 15	6 ps	3445	2496
O	C6AF-9510	1	119	7.75 x 15	6 ps	3459	2595
O	C6AF-9510	1	119	7.75 x 15/	6 ps	3464	2732
				8.15 x 15			
O	C7DF-9510-S	2	119	7.75 x 15	6 ps	3483	2602
O	C70F-9510-S	2	119	7.75 x 15	6 ps	3497	2701
O	C70F-9510-S	2	119	7.75 x 15/	6 ps	3502	2838
				8.15 x 15			

YEAR	MODEL	ENGINE						
		CYLS	BORE	STROKE	DISPL	HP@RPM	C.R.	VLV
	Ford XL (4, 5, 6, 7, 8, 9)	V8	4.00	2.875	289.0	200@4400	9.3	OH
	Ford LTD (4, 5, 6, 7, 8, 9)	V8	4.00	2.875	289.0	200@4400	9.3	OH
	Thunderbird (9)	V8	4.00	3.875	389.2	315@4600	10.5	OH
	Optional engines:							
	(1)	6	3.68	3.125	200.2	120@4400	9.2	OH
	(2)	V8	4.00	2.875	289.0	225@4800	9.3	OH
	(3)	V8	4.00	2.875	289.0	271@6000	10.0	OH
	(4)	V8	4.05	3.78	390.0	270@4400	9.5	OH
	(5)	V8	4.05	3.78	390.0	315@4600	10.5	OH
	(6)	V8	4.05	3.78	390.0	320@4800	10.5	OH
	(7)	V8	4.23	3.78	427.0	410@5600	11.1	OH
	(7)	V8	4.23	3.78	427.0	425@6000	11.1	OH
	(8)	V8	4.125	3.98	428.0	345@4600	10.5	OH
	(9)	V8	4.125	3.98	428.0	360@5400	10.5	OH
1968	Falcon Standard (1, 2, 3)	6	3.50	2.938	169.6	100@4000	8.7	OH
	Falcon Futura (2, 3)	6	3.688	3.125	200.2	115@3800	8.8	OH
	Fairlane (2)	6	3.688	3.125	200.2	115@3800	8.8	OH
	Fairlane 500	6	3.688	3.125	200.2	115@3800	8.8	OH
	Fairlane Torino	6	3.688	3.125	200.2	115@3800	8.8	OH
	Fairlane	V8	4.00	3.00	301.6	210@4600	9.0	OH
	Fairlane 500 (5, 8)	V8	4.00	3.00	301.6	210@4600	9.0	OH
	Fairlane Torino (5, 8)	V8	4.00	3.00	301.6	210@4600	9.0	OH
	Fairlane Torino GT (5, 8)	V8	4.00	3.00	301.6	210@4600	9.0	OH
	Mustang (2)	6	3.68	3.125	200.2	115@3800	8.8	OH
	Mustang (8)	V8	4.00	2.875	289.0	195@4600	8.7	OH
	Custom	6	4.00	3.188	240.3	150@4000	9.2	OH
	Custom 500	6	4.00	3.188	240.3	150@4000	9.2	OH
	Custom XL (4, 5, 6, 7, 8)	6	4.00	3.188	240.3	150@4000	9.2	OH
	Custom (4, 5, 6, 7, 8)	V8	4.00	3.00	301.6	210@4600	9.0	OH
	Custom 500 (4)	V8	4.00	3.00	301.6	210@4600	9.0	OH
	Galaxie 500	6	4.00	3.188	240.3	150@4000	9.2	OH

MFR	CARBURETOR MODEL	VEN	WHEEL-BASE	TIRES	BODY	WEIGHT	PRICE
O	C70F-9510-S	2	119	7.75/8.15 x 15	5 pht2	3574	3243
O	C70F-9510-S	2	119	8.15 x 15	6 ps	3562	3298
O	C7AF-9510-AD	4	115	8.15 x 15	4 pht2	4228	4603
A	C8DF-9510-C	1	111/113	6.95 x 14/ 7.75 x 14	6 ps	2714	2301
A	C8DF-9510-E	1	111/113	6.95 x 14/ 7.75 x 14	6 ps	2719	2456
A	C8DF-9510-E	1	116/113	7.35 x 14/ 7.75 x 14	6 ps	3083	2463
A	C8DF-9510-E	1	116/113	7.35 x 14/ 7.75 x 14	6 ps	2927	2543
A	C8DF-9510-E	1	116/113	7.35 x 14/ 7.75 x 14	6 ps	2965	2688
A	C8AE-9510-AF	2	116/113	7.35 x 14/ 7.75 x 14	6 ps	3122	2551
A	C8AE-9510-AF	2	116/113	7.35 x 14/ 7.75 x 14	6 ps	3131	2631
A	C8AE-9510-AF	2	116/113	7.35 x 14/ 7.75 x 14	6 ps	3185	2776
A	C8AE-9510-AF	2	116/113	7.35 x 14/ 7.75 x 14	6 pht2	3194	2772
A	C80F-9510-E	1	108	6.95 x 14	4 pht2	2635	2602
A	C8AF-9510-AF	2	108	6.95 x 14	4 pht2	2861	2707
A	C8AF-9510-V	1	119	7.75 x 15	6 ps	3516	2642
A	C8AF-9510-V	1	119	7.75 x 15	6 ps	3530	2741
A	C8AF-9510-V	1	119	7.75 x 15	6 pht2	3607	2985
A	C8AF-9510-AF	2	119	7.75 x 15	6 ps	3556	2749
A	C8AF-9510-AF	2	119	7.75 x 15	6 ps	3570	2842
A	C8AF-9510-V	1	119	7.75 x 15	6 ps	3547	2864

YEAR	MODEL	ENGINE						
		CYLS	BORE	STROKE	DISPL	HP@RPM	C.R.	VLV
	Galaxie 500 (4, 5, 6, 7, 8)	V8	4.00	3.00	301.6	210@4600	9.0	OH
	XL (4, 5, 6, 7, 8)	V8	4.00	3.00	301.6	210@4600	9.0	OH
	LTD (4, 5, 6, 7, 8)	V8	4.00	3.00	301.6	210@4600	9.0	OH
	Thunderbird (8)	V8	4.05	3.78	390.0	315@4800	10.5	OH
	Optional engines:							
	(1)	6	3.688	3.125	200.2	115@3800	8.8	OH
	(2)	V8	4.00	3.00	301.6	230@4800	10.0	OH
	(3)	V8	4.00	2.875	289.0	195@4600	8.7	OH
	(4)	V8	4.05	3.78	389.6	265@4400	9.5	OH
	(4)	V8	4.05	3.78	389.6	315@4600	10.5	OH
	(4)	V8	4.05	3.78	389.6	325@4800	10.5	OH
	(5)	V8	4.125	3.98	428.0	335@4800		OH
	(6)	V8	4.125	3.98	428.0	340@4600	10.5	OH
	(7)	V8	4.123	3.78	427.0	390@5600	10.9	OH
	(8)	V8	4.36	3.59	429.0	360@4600	10.5	OH
1969	Falcon (1)	6	3.50	2.94	169.6	100@4000	8.7	OH
	Falcon Futura (1)	6	3.68	3.125	200.2	115@3800	8.8	OH
	Fairlane	6	3.68	3.91	249.5	155@4000	8.5	OH
	Fairlane 500	6	3.68	3.91	249.5	155@4000	8.5	OH
	Torino	6	3.68	3.91	249.5	155@4000	8.5	OH
	Fairlane (2, 3)	V8	4.00	3.00	301.6	220@4600	9.5	OH
	Fairlane 500 (2, 3)	V8	4.00	3.00	301.6	220@4600	9.5	OH
	Torino (2, 3)	V8	4.00	3.00	301.6	220@4600	9.5	OH
	Torino GT (2, 3)	V8	4.00	3.00	301.6	220@4600	9.5	OH
	Cobra	V8	4.13	3.98	428.0	335@5200	10.6	OH
	Mustang	6	3.68	3.125	200.2	115@3800	8.8	OH
	Mustang Grande	6	3.68	3.125	200.2	115@3800	8.8	OH
	Mustang	V8	4.00	3.00	301.6	220@4600	9.5	OH
	Mustang Grande (3, 5)	V8	4.00	3.00	301.6	220@4600	9.5	OH
	Mustang Mach1 (5)	V8	4.00	3.50	351.8	250@4600	9.0	OH

CARBURETOR MFR	MODEL	VEN	WHEEL-BASE	TIRES	BODY	WEIGHT	PRICE
A	C8AF-9510-AF	2	119	7.75/8.15 x 15	6 ps	3587	2971
A	C8AF-9510-AF	2	119	7.75 x 15	6 pht2	3647	3092
A	C8AF-9510-AF	2	119	8.15 x 15	6 ps	3614	3135
A	C8AF-9510-B	4	117.2	8.15 x 15/ 8.45 x 15	6 pht4	4427	4924
A	C8DF-9510-C	1	111/113	6.95 x 14/ 7.75 x 14	6 ps	2735	2333
A	C80F-9510-E	1	111/113	6.95 x 14/ 7.75 x 14	6 ps	2748	2498
A	C90F-9510-B	1	116/113	7.35 x 14/ 7.75 x 14	6 ps	3012	2488
A	C90F-9510-B	1	116/113	7.35 x 14/ 7.75 x 14	6 ps	3029	2568
A	C90F-9510-B	1	116/113	7.35 x 14/ 7.75 x 14	6 ps	3075	2733
A	C8AF-9510-BD	2	116/113	7.35 x 14/ 7.75 x 14	6 ps	3119	2578
A	C8AF-9510-BD	2	116/113	7.35 x 14/ 7.75 x 14	6 ps	3136	2658
A	C8AF-9510-BD	2	116/113	7.35 x 14/ 7.75 x 14	6 ps	3182	2823
A	C8AF-9510-BD	2	116	7.35 x 14/ 7.75 x 14	6 pht2	3173	2865
A	C8AF-9510-B	4	116	7.35 x 14	6 pht2	3490	3206
A	C9DF-9510-B	1	108	C78 x 14	6 ps	2690	2635
A	C80F-9510-E	1	108	C78 x 14	4 pht2	2765	2866
A	C8AF-9510-BD	2	108	C78 x 14	4 pht2	2906	2740
A	C8AF-9510-BD	2	108	C78 x 14	4 pht2	2981	2971
A	C9ZF-9510-A	2	108	E70 x 14	4 pht2	3174	3122

YEAR	MODEL	ENGINE						
		CYLS	BORE	STROKE	DISPL	HP@RPM	C.R.	VLV
	Custom	6	4.00	3.18	240.3	150@4000	9.2	OH
	Custom 500	6	4.00	3.18	240.3	150@4000	9.2	OH
	Galaxie 500	6	4.00	3.18	240.3	150@4000	9.2	OH
	Galaxie XL	6	4.00	3.18	240.3	150@4000	9.2	OH
	Custom (6)	V8	4.00	3.00	301.6	220@4600	9.5	OH
	Custom 500 (6)	V8	4.00	3.00	301.6	220@4600	9.5	OH
	Galaxie 500 (6)	V8	4.00	3.00	301.6	220@4600	9.5	OH
	Galaxie XL (6)	V8	4.00	3.00	301.6	220@4600	9.5	OH
	Galaxie LTD (6)	V8	4.00	3.00	301.6	220@4600	9.5	OH
	Thunderbird	V8	4.36	3.59	429.0	360@4600	10.0	OH
	Optional engines:							
	(1)	V8	4.00	3.00	301.6	220@4600	9.5	OH
	(2)	V8	4.125	3.98	428.0	335		OH
	(3)	V8	4.00	3.50	351.8	250@4600	9.0	OH
	(4)	V8	4.00	3.50	351.8	290@4800	10.7	OH
	(4)	V8	4.05	3.78	389.6	265		OH
	(4)	V8	4.05	3.78	389.6	320@4400	10.5	OH
	(5)	V8	4.00	3.50	351.8	290@4800	10.7	OH
	(5)	V8	4.00	3.50	351.8	335@5200	10.6	OH
	(6)	V8	4.36	3.59	429.0	320@4400	10.5	OH
	(6)	V8	4.36	3.59	429.0	360@4600	10.0	OH

FRANKLIN – – H. H. Franklin Mfg. Co., Syracuse, N.Y., 1901-34

YEAR	MODEL	CYLS	BORE	STROKE	DISPL	HP@RPM	C.R.	VLV
1930	145	6	3.50	4.75	274.0	87@3000	5.3	OH
	147	6	3.50	4.75	274.0	87@3000	5.3	OH
	147 Custom*	6	3.50	4.75	274.0	87@3000	5.3	OH
	* Custom bodies by Durham, Locke, Holbrook, Dietrich.							
1931	15	6	3.50	4.75	274.0	100@3200	5.3	OH
	15 DeLuxe	6	3.50	4.75	274.0	100@3200	5.3	OH
1932	16	6	3.50	4.75	274.0	100@3200	5.3	OH
	17	V12	3.25	4.00	398.0	150@3100		OH
1933	16B	6	3.50	4.75	274.0	100@3100	5.12	OH
	17B	V12	3.25	4.00	398.0	150@3100	5.12	OH
	Olympic Six, 18	6	3.50	4.75	274.0	100@3100	5.12	OH

CARBURETOR			WHEEL-	TIRES	BODY	WEIGHT	PRICE
MFR	MODEL	VEN	BASE				
C	C8AF-9510-BF	1	121	7.75 x 15/	6 ps	3608	2691
				8.55 x 15			
C	C8AF-9510-BF	1	121	7.75 x 15/	6 ps	3620	2790
				8.55 x 15			
C	C8AF-9510-BF	1	121	7.75 x 15/	6 ps	3670	2914
				8.55 x 15			
C	C8AF-9510-BF	1	121	7.75 x 15	6 pht2	3785	3069
A	C8AF-9510-BD	2	121	7.75 x 15/	6 ps	3648	2796
				8.55 x 15			
A	C8AF-9510-BD	2	121	7.75 x 15/	6 ps	3660	2895
				8.55 x 15			
A	C8AF-9510-BD	2	121	7.75 x 15/	6 ps	3710	3019
				8.55 x 15			
A	C8AF-9510-BD	2	121	7.75 x 15	6 pht2	3825	3174
A	C8AF-9510-BD	2	121	7.75 x 15/	6 ps	3745	3110
				8.55 x 15			
A	C8SF-9510-H	4	114.7	8.25 x 15	6 ps	4458	5043
A	C8AF-9510-BD	2					
A	C9ZF-9510-A	2					
		4					
		2					
		4					
A	C8AF-9510-B	4					
		2					
A	C8SF-9510-H	4					
S	U3	1	125	6.50 x 19	5 ps	3930	2585
S	U3	1	132	6.50 x 19	5 ps	4060	2715
S	U3	1	132	6.50 x 19	5 ps		5100
S	U3	1	125	6.50 x 19	5 ps	3930	1795
S	U3	1	125	6.50 x 19	5 ps	4230	2395
S	UR02	1	132	6.50 x 19	5 ps	4420	2345
S	EE-2	2 x 1	144	7.50 x 17	5 ps	5600	3885
S	URO-2	1	132	6.50 x 19	5 ps	4420	1935
S	EE-2	2 x 1	144	7.50 x 17	5 ps	5630	2885
S	URO2	1	118	6.00 x 17	5 ps	3625	1385

YEAR	MODEL	ENGINE						
		CYLS	BORE	STROKE	DISPL	HP@RPM	C.R.	VLV
	18B	6	3.50	4.75	274.0	100@3100	5.12	OH
1934	17B	V12	3.25	4.00	398.0	150@3100	5.12	OH
	Olympic Six, 18C	6	3.50	4.75	274.0	100@3100	5.12	OH
	Airman, 19, 19B	6	3.50	4.75	274.0	100@3100	5.12	OH

FRAZER – – Kaiser-Frazer Corp., Willow Run, Mich., 1947-51

YEAR	MODEL	CYLS	BORE	STROKE	DISPL	HP@RPM	C.R.	VLV
1947	F-47	6	3.312	4.375	226.2	100@3600	7.3	L
	F-47, Manhattan	6	3.312	4.375	226.2	100@3600	7.3	L
1948	F485	6	3.312	4.375	226.2	100@3600	7.3	L
	F486, Manhattan	6	3.312	4.375	226.2	100@3600	7.3	L
1949	F495	6	3.312	4.375	226.2	112@3600	7.3	L
	F496, Manhattan	6	3.312	4.375	226.2	112@3600	7.3	L
1950	F505	6	3.312	4.375	226.2	112@3600	7.3	L
	F506, Manhattan	6	3.312	4.375	226.2	112@3600	7.3	L
1951	F515	6	3.312	4.375	226.2	112@3600	7.3	L
	F516, Manhattan	6	3.312	4.375	226.2	112@3600	7.3	L

FRICK – – Bill Frick Motors, Rockville Center, L.I., N.Y., 1955

YEAR	MODEL	CYLS	BORE	STROKE	DISPL	HP@RPM	C.R.	VLV
1955		V8	3.812	3.623	330.9	250@4000	9.1	OH

	CARBURETOR		WHEEL-	TIRES	BODY	WEIGHT	PRICE
MFR	MODEL	VEN	BASE				
S	URO2	1	118	6.00 x 17	5 ps	3625	1435
S	EE-2	2 x 1	144	7.50 x 17	5 ps	5630	2855
S	URO2	1	118	6.00 x 17	5 ps	3525	1435
S	URO2	1	132	7.00 x 17	5 ps	4500	2185
C	WA1-622S	1	123.5	6.50 x 15	6 ps	3340	2152
C	WA1-622S	1	123.5	6.50 x 15	6 ps	3375	2550
C	WA1	1	123.5	7.10 x 15	6 ps	3453	2374
C	WA1	1	123.5	7.10 x 15	6 ps		2846
C	WCD	2	123.5	7.10 x 15	6 ps	3386	2395
C	WCD	2	123.5	7.10 x 15	6 ps	3391	2595
C	WCD	2	123.5	7.10 x 15	6 ps	3386	2395
C	WCD	2	123.5	7.10 x 15	6 ps	3391	2595
C	WGD	2	123.5	7.10 x 15	6 ps	3456	2359
C	WGD	2	123.5	7.10 x 15	6 ps	3771	3075
			110			3000	

YEAR	MODEL	CYLS	BORE	STROKE	DISPL	HP@RPM	C.R.	VLV

GADABOUT — — Detroit Industrial Designers, Detroit, Mich., 1945

YEAR	MODEL	CYLS	BORE	STROKE	DISPL	HP@RPM	C.R.	VLV
1945								

GARDNER — — Gardner Motor Car Co., St. Louis, Mo., 1919-31

YEAR	MODEL	CYLS	BORE	STROKE	DISPL	HP@RPM	C.R.	VLV
1930	136	6	2.875	4.75	185.0	70@3500	5.05	L
	140	8	2.875	4.75	246.6	90@3300	5.15	L
	150	8	3.25	4.50	298.6	126@3300	5.20	L
	(Front-wheel-drive)*	6	3.375	4.625	248.0	80@3000		L
1931	136	6	2.875	4.75	185.0	70@3500		L
	148	8	2.875	4.75	246.6	90@3300		L
	158	8	3.25	4.50	298.6	126@3300		L

* GARDNER's front-wheel-drive model appears not to have been given a model number. At least one, a 5ps, was built.

GASLIGHT — — Gaslight Motors Corp., Detroit, Mich., 1960-ca 1961

YEAR	MODEL	CYLS	BORE	STROKE	DISPL	HP@RPM	C.R.	VLV
1960		1				4		

GAYLORD — — Gaylord Cars, Ltd., Chicago, Ill., 1955-56

YEAR	MODEL	CYLS	BORE	STROKE	DISPL	HP@RPM	C.R.	VLV
1955		V8	3.812	3.625	330.9	300@5200		OH
1956		V8	4.00	3.625	364.4	305@4700		OH

The 1955 engine was by Chrysler and 1956 from Cadillac.

GLASCAR — — Bob Tucker, Richmond, Ind., 1956

YEAR	MODEL	CYLS	BORE	STROKE	DISPL	HP@RPM	C.R.	VLV
1956		V8	3.875	3.438	324.3			OH

Prototype engine was from Oldsmobile, but production engine was to have been a Ford V8.

GLASSIC — — Glassic Industries, Inc., West Palm Beach, Fla., 1968+

YEAR	MODEL	CYLS	BORE	STROKE	DISPL	HP@RPM	C.R.	VLV
1968+		4	3.875	3.219	151.8	93@4400	8.1	OH

Modeled after the Ford Model A; uses an International Harvester engine.

GOFF — — Charles Goff, Texarkana, Tex., 1956

YEAR	MODEL	CYLS	BORE	STROKE	DISPL	HP@RPM	C.R.	VLV
1956		V8	3.00	3.75	221.0	85@3800		L

Engine was 1939 Ford; other engines optional.

GORDON — — H. Gordon Hansen, San Lorenzo, Cal., 1948

YEAR	MODEL	CYLS	BORE	STROKE	DISPL	HP@RPM	C.R.	VLV
1948	Diamond	V8	3.19	3.75	239.0	100@3800		L

Wheels were in diamond formation, thus the enormous wheel base was measured from frontmost to rearmost wheel.

MFR	CARBURETOR MODEL	VEN	WHEEL-BASE	TIRES	BODY	WEIGHT	PRICE
			80		2 pr	1100	
Sc	MV		122/135	5.50 x 19	5 ps	3330	1295
Sc	5X381		125/138	5.50 x 19	5 ps	3500	1695
Sc	5X356		130/142	6.50 x 18	5 ps	3890	1995
Sc			133	6.00 x 19	5 ps	c.3000	c.3000
Sc			122	5.50 x 19	5 ps	3330	1370
Sc			125	5.50 x 19	5 ps	3500	1845
Sc	SX-256		130	6.50 x 18	5 ps	3890	2170
			77		2 pr	640	1495
		2 x 4	100	7.10 x 15	2 pc	3985	10,000
			100	7.10 x 15	2 pc		17,500
			100		2 pc		
			102		2 pr	2420	5995
					5 pcv		1500
			156			3700	

YEAR	MODEL	ENGINE						
		CYLS	BORE	STROKE	DISPL	HP@RPM	C.R.	VLV
GRAHAM — — Graham-Paige Motors Corp., Detroit, Mich., 1927-41								
1930	Standard Six	6	3.125	4.50	207.1	66@3200	5.41	L
	Special Six	6	3.25	4.50	224.0	76@3400	5.49	L
	Standard Eight	8	3.25	4.50	298.6	100@3400	5.2	L
	Special Eight	8	3.25	4.50	298.6	100@3400	5.2	L
	Custom Eight	8	3.375	4.50	322.1	120@3200	5.41	L
1931	Standard Six	6	3.25	4.50	224.0	76@3400	5.49	L
	Special Six	6	3.25	4.50	224.0	76@3400	5.49	L
	Six, 621	6	3.50	5.00	288.6	97@3200		L
	Standard Eight	8	3.25	4.50	298.6	100@3400		L
	Special Eight	8	3.25	4.50	298.6	100@3400		L
	Custom Eight	8	3.375	4.50	322.1	120@3200		L
	Second Series:							
	Standard Six	6	3.25	4.50	224.0	76@3400		L
	Special Six	6	3.25	4.50	224.0	76@3400		L
	Prosperity Six	6	3.125	4.50	207.1	70@3200		L
	Special, 820	8	3.125	4.00	245.4	85@3400		L
	Custom Eight, 834	8	3.25	4.50	298.6	100@3400		L
1932	Prosperity Six	6	3.125	4.50	207.1	70@3200	5.4	L
	Standard Six	6	3.25	4.50	224.0	76@3400		L
	Special Six	6	3.25	4.50	224.0	76@3400		L
	Special Eight, 820	8	3.125	4.00	245.4	85@3400		L
	Special Eight, 822	8	3.25	4.50	298.6	100@3400		L
	New Custom Eight, 834	8	3.25	4.50	298.6	100@3400		L
	Second Series:							
	Six	6	3.125	4.50	207.1	70@3200	5.4	L
	Eight	8	3.125	4.00	245.4	90@3400		L
1933	Standard Six, 65	6	3.25	4.50	224.0	85@3400	6.5	L
	Standard Eight, 64	8	3.125	4.00	245.4	95@3400	6.5	L
	Custom Eight, 57A	8	3.125	4.00	245.4	95@3400	6.5	L
1934	Standard Six	6	3.25	4.50	224.0	85@3400	6.5	L
	Deluxe Six	6	3.25	4.50	224.0	85@3400	6.5	L
	Standard Eight	8	3.125	4.00	245.4	95@3400	6.7	L
	Custom Eight	8	3.25	4.00	265.4	135@4000	6.7	L
1935	Six	6	3.00	4.00	169.6	60@3500	5.8	L
	Special Six	6	3.25	4.50	224.0	85@3400	6.5	L
	Eight	8	3.125	4.00	245.4	95@3400	6.7	L
	Supercharged Eight, 75	8	3.25	4.00	265.4	140@4000	6.7	L
1936	Crusader, 6-80	6	3.00	4.00	169.6	70@3500	6.9	L
	Cavalier, 6-90	6	3.25	4.375	217.8	85@3300	6.7	L
	Supercharger, 6-110	6	3.25	4.375	217.8	112@4000	6.7	L

CARBURETOR			WHEEL-	TIRES	BODY	WEIGHT	PRICE
MFR	MODEL	VEN	BASE				
D	51	1	115	5.25 x 19	5 ps	3015	895
D	51	1	115	5.50 x 18	5 ps	3390	1225
D	51	1	122	6.00 x 18	5 ps	3795	1445
D	51	1	122	6.00 x 18	5 ps	3875	1595
J			127/137	6.50 x 19	5 ps	4300	2025
Sc			115	5.50 x 18	5 ps	3220	955
Sc			115	5.50 x 18	5 ps	3330	1035
J			121	6.00 x 19	5 ps	4130	1595
D			122/134	6.00 x 19	5 ps	3795	1445
D			122/134	6.00 x 19	5 ps	3875	1635
J			127/137	6.50 x 19	5 ps	4300	2025
D			115	5.50 x 18	5 ps	3265	955
D			115	6.00 x 17	5 ps	3330	1035
Sc			113	5.00 x 19	5 ps	3100	825
D			120	6.00 x 17	5 ps	3560	1245
D			134	6.50 x 18	5 ps	4100	1845
Sc	T		113	5.00 x 17/ 5.00 x 19	5 ps	3100	825
Sc			115	5.50 x 18	5 ps	3265	995
Sc			115	6.00 x 17	5 ps	3330	1035
D	51		120	6.00 x 17	5 ps	3560	1285
D	51		122	6.00 x 18	5 ps	3875	1635
D	51		134	6.50 x 18	5 ps	4100	1895
Sc			113	5.50 x 17	5 ps	3205	795
			123	6.00 x 17	5 ps	3665	1145
Sc	T		113	5.50 x 17	5 ps	3265	795
D	51		119	6.00 x 17	5 ps	3500	895
D	51		123	6.00 x 17	5 ps	3695	1095
S	EX-22		116	6.25 x 16	5 ps	3240	795
S	EX-22		116	6.25 x 16	5 ps		–
S	URO-2	1	123	6.50 x 16	5 ps	3460	895
D			123	7.00 x 16	5 ps	3670	1095
			111	5.25 x 17	5 ps	2655	635
S	EX-22		116	6.00 x 17	5 ps	3265	845
S	EXV-2		123	6.50 x 16	5 ps	3530	975
S	EX-22		123	7.00 x 16	5 ps	3640	1145
M	B2SU		111	6.00 x 16	5 ps	2680	665
M	B2		115	6.00 x 16	5 ps	2995	795
M	B3		115	6.25 x 16	5 ps	3070	895

YEAR	MODEL	ENGINE						
		CYLS	BORE	STROKE	DISPL	HP@RPM	C.R.	VLV
1937	Crusader, 85	6	3.00	4.00	169.6	70@3500	6.8	L
	Cavalier, 95	6	3.25	4.00	199.1	85@3300	6.7	L
	Supercharger, 116	6	3.25	4.00	199.1	106@4000	6.7	L
	Supercharger, 120	6	3.25	4.375	217.8	116@4000	6.7	L
1938	Standard Six, 96	6	3.25	4.375	217.8	90@3600	6.7	L
	Special Six, 96	6	3.25	4.375	217.8	90@3600	6.7	L
	Supercharger, 97	6	3.25	4.375	217.8	116@4000	6.7	L
	Custom Supercharger, 97	6	3.25	4.375	217.8	116@4000	6.7	L
1939	Special Six, 96	6	3.25	4.375	217.8	90@3600	6.7	L
	Custom Special Six, 96	6	3.25	4.375	217.8	90@3600	6.7	L
	Supercharger, 97	6	3.25	4.375	217.8	116@4000	6.7	L
	Custom Supercharger, 97	6	3.25	4.375	217.8	116@4000	6.7	L
1940	DeLuxe, 108	6	3.25	4.375	217.8	93@3800	6.65	L
	Custom Six, 108	6	3.25	4.375	217.8	93@3800	6.65	L
	DeLuxe Supercharger, 107	6	3.25	4.375	217.8	120@4000	6.65	L
	Custom Supercharger, 107	6	3.25	4.375	217.8	120@4000	6.65	L
	Hollywood Cus. Superchgr., 109	6	3.25	4.375	217.8	120@4000	6.65	L
1941	Hollywood Custom, 113	6	3.25	4.375	217.8	95@3800		L
	Hollywood Cus. Superchgr 109	6	3.25	4.375	217.8	124@4000		L

GREGORY — — Gregory Front-Drive Motor Cars, Kansas City, Mo., 1949; 1952

YEAR	MODEL	CYLS	BORE	STROKE	DISPL	HP@RPM	C.R.	VLV
1949		F4	3.188	3.75	119.8	40@3000		L
1952		F4	3.15	2.91	90.7	75@5200	8.2	OH

The earlier model used an air-cooled, flat opposed Continental engine, and the one in the later model was from Porsche. Both models used the unusual configuration of rear engine/front-wheel drive.

GRIFFITH — — Griffith Motor Car Co., Syosset, N.Y.; Plainview, N.Y., 1963-66

YEAR	MODEL	CYLS	BORE	STROKE	DISPL	HP@RPM	C.R.	VLV
1963-64	200	V8	4.00	2.875	289.0	195@4400	8.6	OH
	400	V8	4.00	2.875	289.0	271@6000	10.5	OH
	600							
1966		V8	3.625	3.312	273.5	235@5200		OH

The Griffith was based on the British TVR and used Ford engines in the 200 and 400 models, but a Plymouth engine for 1966.

MFR	CARBURETOR MODEL	VEN	WHEEL-BASE	TIRES	BODY	WEIGHT	PRICE
M	B2SU	1	111	5.25 x 17/	5 ps	2695	770
				6.00 x 16			
M	B2	1	116	6.00 x 16	5 ps	2960	905
M	B2	1	116	6.25 x 16	5 ps	3125	1050
M	B2	1	116	6.50 x 16	5 ps	3200	1160
M	C2		120	6.00 x 16	6 ps	3250	1025
M	C2		120	6.00 x 16	6 ps	3275	1075
M	C3		120	6.25 x 16	6 ps	3345	1198
M	C3		120	6.50 x 16	6 ps	3350	1320
M	C2		120	6.00 x 16	6 ps	3240	965
M	C2		120	6.00 x 16	6 ps	3255	1095
M	C3		120	6.25 x 16	6 ps	3295	1095
M	C3		120	6.25 x 16	6 ps	3325	1225
C	WAI-472S		120	6.00 x 16	5 ps	3195	1015
C	WAI-472S		120	6.00 x 16	5 ps	3320	1160
C	WAI-473S		120	6.25 x 16	5 ps	3250	1160
C	WAI-473S		120	6.25 x 16	5 ps	3370	1295
C	WAI-473S		120	6.25 x 16	5 ps	2965	1250
C	WDO-399S	2	115	6.00 x 16	5 ps	2860	895
C	WDO-399S	2	115	6.25 x 16	5 ps	2965	1045
			94	5.50 x 15	5 ps2	1900	1050
			94				
		2	85.5		2 pc	1450	4160
		4	85.5		2 pcv		4655
					2 pc		
C			94.5		2 pc	2540	6095

YEAR	MODEL	ENGINE						
		CYLS	BORE	STROKE	DISPL	HP@RPM	C.R.	VLV

HENNEY -- Henney Motor Car Co., Freeport, Ill., 1930-31

YEAR	MODEL	CYLS	BORE	STROKE	DISPL	HP@RPM	C.R.	VLV
1930-31		8	3.25	4.50	298.6	125@3600	5.25	L
	Henney built just four convertible sedans during 1930-31, using Lycoming engines.							

HENNEY -- Henney Motor Co., Div. National Union Electric Co., Bloomington, Ill., 1960-64

YEAR	MODEL	CYLS	BORE	STROKE	DISPL	HP@RPM	C.R.	VLV
1960-64	Kilowatt					7		
	This electric was based on a Renault Dauphine chassis and body.							

HENRY J -- Kaiser-Frazer Corp., Willow Run, Mich., 1951-54

YEAR	MODEL	CYLS	BORE	STROKE	DISPL	HP@RPM	C.R.	VLV
1951	513	4	3.125	4.375	134.2	68@4000	7.0	L
	514, DeLuxe	6	3.125	3.50	161.0	80@3800	7.0	L
1952	Vagabond, 513	4	3.125	4.375	134.2	68@4000	7.0	L
	Vagabond DeLuxe, 524	6	3.125	3.50	161.0	80@3800	7.0	L
	Corsair, 523	4	3.125	4.375	134.2	68@4000	7.0	L
	Corsair DeLuxe, 524	6	3.125	3.50	161.0	80@3800	7.0	L
1953	Corsair, 533	4	3.125	4.375	134.2	68@4000	7.0	L
	Corsair DeLuxe, 534	6	3.125	3.50	161.0	80@3800	7.0	L
1954	Corsair, K543	4	3.125	4.375	134.2	68@4000	7.0	L
	Corsair DeLuxe, K544	6	3.125	3.50	161.0	80@3800	7.0	L

HOPPENSTAND -- Hoppenstand Motors, Inc., Greenville, Pa., 1948-49

YEAR	MODEL	CYLS	BORE	STROKE	DISPL	HP@RPM	C.R.	VLV
1948-49		F2			21.4		8.5	
	Engine was an air-cooled, opposed type.							

HUDSON -- Hudson Motor Car Co., Detroit, Mich.; American Motors Corp., Kenosha, Wis., 1909-57

YEAR	MODEL	CYLS	BORE	STROKE	DISPL	HP@RPM	C.R.	VLV
1930	Great Eight, 119	8	2.75	4.50	213.8	80@3400	5.8	L
	Great Eight, 126	8	2.75	4.50	213.8	80@3400	5.8	L
1931	Great Eight, 119	8	2.875	4.50	233.7	87@3600	5.8	L
	Great Eight, 126	8	2.875	4.50	233.7	87@3600	5.8	L
1932	Standard	8	3.00	4.50	254.5	101@3600	5.8	L
	Sterling	8	3.00	4.50	254.5	101@3600	5.8	L
	Major	8	3.00	4.50	254.5	101@3600	5.8	L
1933	Super Six	6	2.938	4.75	193.1	73@3200	6.2	L
	Pacemaker Standard	8	3.00	4.50	254.5	101@3600	6.2	L
	Pacemaker Major	8	3.00	4.50	254.5	101@3600	6.2	L
1934	Major, LL	8	3.00	4.50	254.5	108@3800	5.8	L
	Major DeLuxe, LLU	8	3.00	4.50	254.5	108@3800	5.8	L
	Challenger, LTS	8	3.00	4.50	254.5	108@3800	5.8	L
1935	Big Six	6	3.00	5.00	212.1	93@3800	6.25	L
	Special Eight	8	3.00	4.50	254.5	113@3800	6.0	L
	DeLuxe Eight	8	3.00	4.50	254.5	113@3800	6.0	L

MFR	CARBURETOR MODEL	VEN	WHEEL-BASE	TIRES	BODY	WEIGHT	PRICE
			137.5	7.00 x 18	5 pcv4		5000
			89	5.50 x 15	5 ps	2135	
C	YF	1	100	5.90 x 15	5 ps2	2293	1363
C	YF	1	100	5.90 x 15	5 ps2	2341	1499
C	YF	1	100	5.90 x 15	5 ps2	2365	1407
C	YF	1	100	5.90 x 15	5 ps2	2385	1552
C	YF	1	100	5.90 x 15	5 ps2	2370	1517
C	YF	1	100	5.90 x 15	5 ps2	2405	2664
C	YF	1	100	5.90 x 15	5 ps2	2395	1399
C	YF	1	100	5.90 x 15	5 ps2	2445	1561
C	YF	1	100	5.90 x 15	5 ps2	2405	1404
C	YF	1	100	5.90 x 15	5 ps2	2455	1566
			90		2 pc	684	1000
M	XH-4		119	6.50 x 18	5 ps	3200	1150
M	XH-4		126	6.50 x 18	7 ps	3385	1650
M	XH-4		119	5.50 x 18	5 ps	3115	995
M	XH 4		126	5.50 x 18	7 ps	3230	1195
M	XH-4		119	6.00 x 17	5 ps	3285	1095
M	XH-4		126		5 ps	3415	1295
M	XH-4		132		5 ps	3590	1595
M		1	119	5.25 x 18	5 ps	3345	1045
M		1	119	6.00 x 17	5 ps	3345	1045
M		1	132	6.50 x 17	7 ps	3605	1350
C	282S		116	6.50 x 16	5 ps	2975	1000
C	282S		123	6.50 x 16	5 ps	3085	1070
C	282S		116	6.25 x 16	5 ps	2910	765
C	309S		116	6.00 x 16	5 ps	2780	770
C	310S		117	6.25 x 16	5 ps	2890	840
C	310S		117	6.25 x 16	5 ps	2945	935

YEAR	MODEL	ENGINE						
		CYLS	BORE	STROKE	DISPL	HP@RPM	C.R.	VLV
	Custom Eight	8	3.00	4.50	254.5	113@3800	6.0	L
1936	Six, Custom, 63	6	3.00	5.00	212.1	93@3800	6.25	L
	Eight, DeLuxe, 64, 66	8	3.00	4.50	254.4	113@3800	6.00	L
	Eight, Custom, 65, 67	8	3.00	4.50	254.4	113@3800	6.00	L
1937	Six, Custom, 73	6	3.00	5.00	212.1	101@4000	6.25	L
	Eight, 74, 76	8	3.00	4.50	254.4	122@4200	6.25	L
	Eight, Custom, 75, 77	8	3.00	4.50	254.4	122@4200	6.25	L
1938	Terraplane Six, 80	6	3.00	5.00	212.1	96@3900	6.25	L
	Terraplane DeLuxe, 81	6	3.00	5.00	212.1	101@4000	6.25	L
	Terraplane, Super, 82	6	3.00	5.00	212.1	101@4000	6.25	L
	Six, Standard, 112	6	3.00	4.125	175.0	83@4000	6.5	L
	Six, DeLuxe, 112	6	3.00	4.125	175.0	83@4000	6.5	L
	Six, Custom, 83	6	3.00	5.00	212.1	101@4000	6.25	L
	Eight, DeLuxe, 84	8	3.00	4.50	254.4	122@4200	6.25	L
	Eight, Custom, 85, 87	8	3.00	4.50	254.4	122@4200	6.25	L
1939	Six, 112	6	3.00	4.125	174.9	86@4000	6.7	L
	Pacemaker, 91	6	3.00	5.00	212.0	96@3900	6.7	L
	Six, 92	6	3.00	5.00	212.0	96@3900	6.2	L
	Country Club Six, 93	6	3.00	5.00	212.0	101@4000	6.25	L
	Big Boy Six, 98	6	3.00	4.125	174.9	86@4000	6.7	L
	Country Club Eight, 95	8	3.00	4.50	254.5	122@4200	6.25	L
	Country Club Eight, 97	8	3.00	4.50	254.5	122@4200	6.25	L
1940	Traveler, 40-T	6	3.00	4.125	174.9	92@4000	6.5	L
	DeLuxe, 40-P	6	3.00	4.125	174.9	92@4000	6.5	L
	Country Club Six, 43	6	3.00	5.00	212.0	102@4000	6.5	L
	Super Six, 41	6	3.00	5.00	212.0	102@4000	6.5	L
	Eight, 44	8	3.00	4.50	254.5	128@4200	6.5	L
	Country Club Eight, 47	8	3.00	4.50	254.5	128@4200	6.5	L
	Big Boy Six, 48	6	3.00	5.00	212.0	98@4000	6.5	L
1941	Traveler, 10-T	6	3.00	4.125	174.9	92@4000	7.25	L
	DeLuxe Six, 10-P	6	3.00	4.125	174.9	92@4000	7.25	L
	Big Boy Six, 18	6	3.00	5.00	212.0	98@4000		L
	Super Six, 11	6	3.00	5.00	212.0	102@4000	6.5	L
	Commodore Six, 12	6	3.00	5.00	212.0	102@4000	6.5	L
	Commodore Eight, 14	8	3.00	4.50	254.5	128@4200	6.5	L
	Commodore Eight, 15	8	3.00	4.50	254.5	128@4200	6.5	L
	Commodore Eight, 17	8	3.00	4.50	254.5	128@4200	6.5	L
1942	Traveler, 20T	6	3.00	4.125	174.9	92@4000	7.25	L
	DeLuxe Six, 20-P	6	3.00	4.125	174.9	92@4000	7.25	L
	Super Six, 21	6	3.00	5.00	212.0	102@4000	6.5	L
	Commodore Six, 22	6	3.00	5.00	212.0	102@4000	6.5	L

MFR	CARBURETOR MODEL	VEN	WHEEL-BASE	TIRES	BODY	WEIGHT	PRICE
C	310S		124	6.25 x 16	5 ps	3130	1125
C	329S	1	120	6.00 x 16	5 ps	2880	785
C	330S	1	120/127	6.25 x 16	5 ps	3045	830
C	330S	1	120/127	6.25 x 16	5 ps	3075	925
C	344S	2	122	6.00 x 16	6 ps	2990	945
C	377S	2	122/129	6.25 x 16	6 ps	3135	1010
C	377S	2	122/129	6.25 x 16	6 ps	3195	1110
C		2	124	6.00 x 16	6 ps	2695	995
C	402S	2	117	6.00 x 16	6 ps	2885	864
C	417S	2	117	6.00 x 16	6 ps	2925	915
C		1	112	5.50 x 16	6 ps	2620	755
C		1	112	5.50 x 16	6 ps	2620	765
C	417S	2	122	6.00 x 16	6 ps	3005	984
C	402S	2	122	6.50 x 16	6 ps	3155	1060
C	402S	2	122/129	6.50 x 16	6 ps	3190	1171
C	W1-438S	1	112	6.00 x 16	6 ps	2712	806
C	W1-438S	1	118	6.00 x 16	6 ps	2867	854
C	W1-438S	1	118	6.00 x 16	6 ps	2897	908
C	W1-437S	1	122	6.25 x 16	6 ps	3023	995
C	W1-438S	1	119	6.00 x 16	6 ps	2902	884
C	WDO-430S	2	122	6.50 x 16	6 ps	3193	1079
C	WDO-430S	2	129	6.50 x 16	6 ps	3268	1174
C	WDO-454S	2	113	5.50 x 16	6 ps	2940	763
C	WDO-454S	2	113	5.50 x 16	6 ps	2930	806
C	WDO-461S	2	125	6.25 x 16	6 ps	3240	952
C	WDO-461S	2	118	6.00 x 16	6 ps	3050	870
C	WDO-455S	2	118	6.00 x 16	6 ps	3185	952
C	WDO-455S	2	125	6.50 x 16	6 ps	3285	1118
C	WDO-454S	2	125	6.00 x 16	7 ps	3140	1095
C	WA1-454S	1	116	5.50 x 16	6 ps	2870	824
C	WA1-454S	1	116	6.00 x 16	6 ps	2945	925
C	WDO-501S	2	128	6.00 x 16	7 ps	3155	1223
C	WDO-501S	2	121	6.00 x 16	6 ps	3040	1007
C	WDO-501S	2	121	6.25 x 16	6 ps	3135	1087
C	WDO-502S	2	121	6.25 x 16	6 ps	3250	1132
C	WDO-502S	2	121	6.50 x 16	4 pcc	3235	1225
C	WDO-502S	2	128	6.50 x 16	6 ps	3370	1330
C	WDO-501S	2	116	5.50 x 16	6 ps	2940	904
C	WDO-501S	2	116	6.00 x 16	6 ps	2975	977
C	WDO-501S	2	121	6.00 x 16	6 ps	3080	1092
C	WDO-501S	2	121	6.25 x 16	6 ps	3145	1181

YEAR	MODEL	ENGINE						
		CYLS	BORE	STROKE	DISPL	HP@RPM	C.R.	VLV
	Commodore Eight, 24	8	3.00	4.50	254.5	128@4200	6.5	L
	Commodore Eight, 25	8	3.00	4.50	254.5	128@4200	6.5	L
	Commodore Eight, 27	8	3.00	4.50	254.5	128@4200	6.5	L
1946	Super Six, 51	6	3.00	5.00	212.0	102@4000	6.5	L
	Commodore Six, 52	6	3.00	5.00	212.0	102@4000	6.5	L
	Super Eight, 53	8	3.00	4.50	254.4	128@4200	6.5	L
	Commodore Eight, 54	8	3.00	4.50	254.4	128@4200	6.5	L
1947	Super Six, 171	6	3.00	5.00	212.0	102@4000	6.5	L
	Commodore Six, 172	6	3.00	5.00	212.0	102@4000	6.5	L
	Super Eight, 173	8	3.00	4.50	254.4	128@4200	6.5	L
	Commodore Eight, 174	8	3.00	4.50	254.4	128@4200	6.5	L
1948	Super Six, 481	6	3.562	4.375	261.7	121@4000	6.5	L
	Commodore Six, 482	6	3.562	4.375	261.7	121@4000	6.5	L
	Super Eight, 483	8	3.00	4.50	254.4	128@4200	6.5	L
	Commodore Eight, 484	8	3.00	4.50	254.4	128@4200	6.5	L
1949	Super Six, 491	6	3.562	4.375	261.7	121@4000	6.5	L
	Commodore Six, 492	6	3.562	4.375	261.7	121@4000	6.5	L
	Super Eight, 493	8	3.00	4.50	254.4	128@4200	6.5	L
	Commodore Eight, 494	8	3.00	4.50	254.4	128@4200	6.5	L
1950	Pacemaker, 500	6	3.562	3.875	231.8	112@4200	6.5	L
	Pacemaker DeLuxe, 50A	6	3.562	3.875	231.8	112@4200	6.5	L
	Super Six, 501	6	3.562	4.375	261.7	123@4000	6.5	L
	Commodore Six, 502	6	3.562	4.375	261.7	123@4000	6.5	L
	Super Eight, 503	8	3.00	4.50	254.4	128@4200	6.5	L
	Commodore Eight, 504	8	3.00	4.50	254.4	128@4200	6.5	L
1951	Pacemaker Custom, 4A	6	3.562	3.875	231.8	112@4000	6.7	L
	Super Six Custom, 5A	6	3.562	4.375	261.7	123@4000	6.7	L
	Commodore Six Custom, 6A	6	3.562	4.375	261.7	123@4000	6.7	L
	Hornet, 7A	6	3.812	4.50	308.2	145@3800	7.2	L
	Commodore Eight Custom, 8A	8	3.00	4.50	254.4	128@4200	6.7	L
1952	Pacemaker, 4B	6	3.562	3.875	231.8	112@4000	6.7	L
	Wasp, 5B	6	3.562	4.375	261.7	127@4000	6.7	L
	Commodore Six, 6B	6	3.562	4.375	261.7	127@4000	6.7	L

MFR	CARBURETOR MODEL	VEN	WHEEL-BASE	TIRES	BODY	WEIGHT	PRICE
C	WDO-502S	2	121	6.25 x 16	6 ps	3280	1223
C	WDO-502S	2	121	6.50 x 15	4 pcc	3235	1311
C	WDO-502S	2	128	6.50 x 16	6 ps	3395	1429
C	WDO-501S	2	121	6.00 x 16	6 ps	3085	1555
C	WDO-501S	2	121	6.00 x 16	6 ps	3150	1699
C	WDO-502S	2	121	6.00 x 15/	6 ps	3235	1668
				6.50 x 15			
C	WDO-502S	2	121	6.50 x 15	6 ps	3305	1774
C	WDO-501S	2	121	7.10 x 15	6 ps	3110	1749
C	WDO-501S	2	121	7.10 x 15	6 ps	3175	1896
C	WDO-502S	2	121	7.10 x 15	6 ps	3260	1862
C	WDO-502S	2	121	7.10 x 15	6 ps	3330	1972
C	WDO-647S	2	123.8	7.10 x 15	6 ps	3500	2222
C	WDO-647S	2	123.8	7.10 x 15	6 ps	3540	2399
C	WDO-648S	2	123	7.10 x 15	6 ps	3525	2343
C	WDO-648S	2	123	7.10 x 15	6 ps	3600	2514
C	WDO-647S	2	124	7.10 x 15	6 ps	3555	2207
C	WDO-647S	2	124	7.10 x 15	6 ps	3625	2383
C	WDO-648S	2	124	7.10 x 15	6 ps	3565	2296
C	WDO-648S	2	124	7.10 x 15	6 ps	3650	2472
C		1	119	7.10 x 15	6 ps	3510	1933
C		1	119	7.10 x 15	6 ps	3520	1959
C	WDO-647SA	2	124	7.10 x 15	6 ps	3590	2105
C	WDO-647SA	2	124	7.10 x 15	6 ps	3655	2282
C	WDO-648S	2	124	7.10 x 15	6 ps	3605	2189
C	WDO-648S	2	124	7.10 x 15	6 ps	3675	2366
C	WAI-749S	1	119	7.10 x 15	6 ps	3460	2145
C	WGD-776S	2	124	7.10 x 15/	6 ps	3563	2287
				7.60 x 15			
C	WGD-776S	2	124	7.10 x 15/	6 ps	3600	2480
				7.60 x 15			
C	WGD-776S	2	124	7.10 x 15/	6 ps	3600	2568
				7.60 x 15			
C	WDO-648S	2	124	7.10 x 15/	6 ps	3620	2568
				7.60 x 15			
C		1	119	7.10 x 15	6 ps	3390	2311
C	M-729-SZ	2	119	7.10 x 15/	6 ps	3485	2466
				7.60 x 15			
C	M-729-SZ	2	124	7.10 x 15/	6 ps	3595	2674
				7.60 x 15			

YEAR	MODEL	ENGINE CYLS	BORE	STROKE	DISPL	HP@RPM	C.R.	VLV
	Hornet, 7B	6	3.812	4.50	308.2	145@3800	7.2	L
	Commodore Eight, 8B	8	3.00	4.50	254.4	128@4200	6.7	L
1953	Jet, 1C	6	3.00	4.75	201.5	104@4000	7.5	L
	Super Jet, 2C	6	3.00	4.75	201.5	104@4000	7.5	L
	Wasp, 4C	6	3.562	3.875	231.8	127@4000	6.7	L
	Super Wasp, 5C	6	3.562	3.875	231.8	127@4000	6.7	L
	Hornet, 7C	6	3.812	4.50	308.2	145@3800	7.2	L
1954	Jet, 1D	6	3.00	4.75	201.5	104@4000	7.5	L
	Super Jet, 2D	6	3.00	4.75	201.5	104@4000	7.5	L
	Jet Liner, 3D	6	3.00	4.75	201.5	104@4000	7.5	L
	Wasp, 4D (1)	6	3.562	3.875	231.8	126@4400	7.0	L
	Super Wasp, 5D (2)	6	3.562	4.375	261.7	140@4000	7.0	L
	Hornet Special, 6D (3)	6	3.812	4.50	308.2	160@3800	7.5	L
	Hornet, 7D	6	3.812	4.50	308.2	160@3800	7.5	L
	Itala	6	3.00	4.75	201.5	114@4000		L
	Optional engines:							
	(1)	6	3.562	4.375	261.7	140@4000	7.0	L
	(1)	6	3.562	3.875	231.8	129	7.5	L
	(2)	6	3.562	4.375	261.7	143	7.5	L
	(2)	6	3.562	4.375	261.7	149		L
	(3)	6	3.812	4.50	308.2	170		
1955	Super Wasp, 3554-1	6	3.00	4.375	185.6	115@4000	8.0	L
	Custom Wasp, 3554-2	6	3.00	4.375	185.6	115@4000	8.0	L
	Hornet Super, 3556-1	6	3.812	4.50	308.2	160@3800	7.5	L
	Hornet Custom, 3556-2	6	3.812	4.50	308.2	160@3800	7.5	L
	Hornet Super, 3558-1	V8	3.812	3.50	319.6	208@4200	7.8	OH
	Hornet Custom, 3558-2	V8	3.812	3.50	319.6	208@4200	7.8	OH
	Itala	6	3.00	4.75	201.5	114@4000		L
	For 1955-56 Rambler was designated a Hudson Rambler. However, see Nash for these models.							
1956	Wasp Super, 3564	6	3.00	4.75	201.4	120@4000	7.5	L
	Hornet Super, 3565	6	3.812	4.50	308.2	165@3800	7.5	L
	Hornet Custom, 3566	6	3.812	4.50	308.2	165@3800	7.5	L
	Hornet Custom, 3568	V8	4.00	3.50	351.9	220@4600	9.55	OH
	Hornet Special Super	V8	3.50	3.25	250.1		8.0	OH
1957	Hornet Super, 357-1	V8	4.00	3.25	326.7	255@4700	9.0	OH
	Hornet Custom, 357-2	V8	4.00	3.25	326.7	255@4700	9.0	OH

MFR	CARBURETOR MODEL	VEN	WHEEL-BASE	TIRES	BODY	WEIGHT	PRICE
C	M-729-SZ	2	124	7.10 x 15/	6 ps	3600	2769
				7.60 x 15			
C	M-729-SZ	2	124	7.10 x 15/	6 ps	3630	2769
				7.60 x 15			
C		1	105	5.90 x 15	6 ps	2650	1858
C		1	105	6.40 x 15	6 ps	2700	1954
C	WGD-776S	2	119	7.10 x 15	6 ps	3380	2311
C	WGD-776S	2	119	7.10 x 15	6 ps	3480	2466
C	WGD-776S	2	124	7.10 x 15/	6 ps	3570	2769
				7.60 x 15			
C		1	105	5.90 x 15	6 ps	2675	1858
C		1	105	6.40 x 15	6 ps	2725	1954
C		1	105	6.40 x 15	6 ps	2760	2057
C	WA1-749S	1	119	7.10 x 15	6 ps	3440	2256
C	WGD-2115S	2	119	7.10 x 15	6 ps	3525	2466
C	WGD-2115S	2	124	7.10 x 15	6 ps	3560	2619
C	WGD-2115S	2	124	7.10 x 15	6 ps	3620	2769
C			105		2 pc	2710	4800
C	WA1-2114S						
C	WA1-2009SA	1	114.2	6.70 x 15	6 ps	3524	2290
C	WA1-2009SA	1	114.2	6.70 x 15	6 ps	3347	2460
C	WGD-2252S	2	121.2	7.10 x 15	6 ps	3495	2565
C	WGD-2252S	2	121.2	7.10 x 15	6 ps	3562	2760
C	WGD-2231S	2	121.2	7.10 x 15	6 ps	3806	2825
C	WGD-2231S	2	121.2	7.10 x 15	6 ps	3846	3015
			105		2 pc	2710	4800
C	WA1-2009SA	1	114.2	6.70 x 15	6 ps	3264	2420
C	WGD-2252S	2	121.2	7.10 x 15	6 ps	3545	2774
C	WGD-2252S	2	121.2	7.10 x 15	6 ps	3636	3023
C	WGD-2231S	2	121.2	7.60 x 15	6 ps	3862	3290
C	WGD-2352	2	114.2	6.70 x 15	6 ps	3467	2630
C	WCFB-2593SA	4	121.2	8.00 x 14	6 ps	3631	2821
C	WCFB-2593SA	4	121.2	8.00 x 14	6 ps	3678	3011

YEAR	MODEL	ENGINE						
		CYLS	BORE	STROKE	DISPL	HP@RPM	C.R.	VLV

HUMMINGBIRD — — Talmadge Judd, Kingsport, Tenn., ca 1946

YEAR	MODEL	CYLS	BORE	STROKE	DISPL	HP@RPM	C.R.	VLV
1946		4				20		

HUPMOBILE — — Hupp Motor Car Corp., Detroit, Mich., 1908-41

YEAR	MODEL	CYLS	BORE	STROKE	DISPL	HP@RPM	C.R.	VLV
1930	Standard Six, S	6	3.25	4.25	211.6	70@3200	4.8	L
	Standard Eight, C	8	3.00	4.75	268.6	100@3200	5.2	L
	Standard Eight, H	8	3.50	4.75	365.6	133@3400	5.2	L
	Standard Eight, U	8	3.50	4.75	365.6	133@3400	5.2	L
1931	Century Six, S	6	3.25	4.25	211.6	70@3200	4.8	L
	Century Eight, L	8	2.875	4.625	240.2	90@3200	5.2	L
	Standard Eight, C	8	3.00	4.75	286.6	100@3200	5.2	L
	Standard Eight, H	8	3.50	4.75	365.6	133@3400	5.2	L
	Standard Eight, U	8	3.50	4.75	365.6	133@3400	5.2	L
1932	Standard Six, S, 214	6	3.25	4.25	211.6	70@3200	5.1	L
	Standard Eight, L, 218	8	2.875	4.625	240.2	90@3200	5.2	L
	Standard Eight, C, 221	8	3.00	4.75	268.6	100@3200	5.2	L
	Standard Eight, H, 225	8	3.50	4.75	365.6	133@3400	5.2	L
	Standard Eight, U, 237	8	3.50	4.75	365.6	133@3400	5.2	L
	Second series:							
	Standard Six, B, 216	6	3.375	4.25	228.1	75@3200	5.0	L
	Standard Eight, F, 222	8	2.938	4.625	250.7	93@3600	5.4	L
	Standard Eight, I, 226	8	3.062	4.75	279.9	103@3400	5.48	L
1933	Standard Six, K, 321	6	3.375	4.25	228.1	90@3800	5.75	L
	Standard Six, KK, 321A	6	3.375	4.25	228.1	90@3400	5.75	L
	Standard Eight, F, 322	8	3.00	4.625	261.5	93@3600	5.47	L
	Standard Eight, I, 326	8	3.188	4.75	303.2	109@3500	5.34	L
	Standard Six, B, 316	6	3.375	4.25	228.1	75@3200		L
1934	Standard Six, KK, 421A	6	3.375	4.25	228.1	90@3400	5.25	L
	Standard Six, K, 421	6	3.375	4.25	228.1	90@3400	5.25	L
	Six, 417W	6	3.50	3.875	224.0	80@3400	5.32	L
	Six, 421J	6	3.50	4.25	245.3	93@3400	5.75	L
	Eight, F, 422	8	3.00	4.625	261.5	96@3600	5.47	L
	Eight, I, 426	8	3.188	4.75	303.2	109@3500	5.34	L
	Eight, 427T	8	3.188	4.75	303.2	115@3500	5.80	L
1935	Six, 517W	6	3.50	3.875	223.7	91@3500	5.75	L
	Six, 518D	6	3.50	3.875	223.7	91@3500	5.75	L
	Six, 521J	6	3.50	4.25	245.3	101@3600	5.75	L
	Eight, 521-0	8	3.188	4.75	303.2	120@3500	5.75	L
	Eight, 527T	8	3.188	4.75	303.2	120@3500	5.75	L
1936	Six, 618D	6	3.50	4.25	245.3	101@3600	5.75	L

MFR	CARBURETOR MODEL	VEN	WHEEL-BASE	TIRES	BODY	WEIGHT	PRICE
						1350	
S	U-2	1	114	5.25 x 19	5 ps	2885	1095
S	UU-2	2	121	6.00 x 19	5 ps	3640	1695
S			124	6.50 x 19	5 ps	3955	2080
S			137	6.50 x 19	7 ps	4225	2495
S	U-2	1	114	5.50 x 19	5 ps	2985	995
S	UU-2	2	118	5.50 x 19	5 ps	3275	1295
S	UU-2	2	121	6.00 x 19	5 ps	3730	1595
S			125	6.50 x 19	5 ps	4095	1895
S			137	6.50 x 19	7 ps	4360	2295
S	U-2	1	114	5.50 x 19	5 ps	2985	795
S			118	5.50 x 19	5 ps	3275	995
S			121	6.00 x 19	5 ps	3730	1195
S			125	6.50 x 19	5 ps	4095	1455
S			137	6.50 x 19	7 ps	4400	1955
S	DXR-2		116.5	5.50 x 18	5 ps	3095	895
S	UUR-2	2	122	6.00 x 17	5 ps	3550	1295
S	UUR-2	2	126	6.50 x 17	5 ps	3785	1595
C	258S	1	121	6.00 x 17	5 ps	3290	995
C	W1	1	121	5.50 x 17	5 ps	3190	895
S	UUR-2	2	122	6.00 x 17	5 ps	3650	1195
S	UUR-2	2	126	6.50 x 17	5 ps	3845	1445
S			116	5.50 x 18	5 ps	3095	895
C	W1	1	121	6.00 x 17	5 ps	3200	795
C	W1	1	121	6.00 x 17	5 ps	3290	895
S	EX32	2	117	6.00 x 16	5 ps	3075	845
S			121	6.50 x 16	6 ps	3325	1095
S	UUR-2	2	122	6.00 x 17	5 ps	3665	1045
S	UUR-2	2	126	6.50 x 17	5 ps	3845	1145
S	EE-22	2	127	7.00 x 16	6 ps	3700	1245
S	EX32	2	117	6.00 x 16	5 ps	3075	745
S	EX32	2	118	6.00 x 16	6 ps	2945	845
S	EX32	2	121	6.50 x 16	5 ps	3325	1095
C	W1-317S	1	121	6.50 x 16	6 ps	3447	1195
C	W1-317S	1	127.5	7.00 x 16	5 ps	3700	1395
C	W1-316S	1	118	6.00 x 16	6 ps	2945	845

YEAR	MODEL	ENGINE						
		CYLS	BORE	STROKE	DISPL	HP@RPM	C.R.	VLV
	Six, 618G	6	3.50	4.25	245.3	101@3600	5.75	L
	Eight, 621N	8	3.188	4.75	303.2	120@3500	5.80	L
	Eight, 621-O	8	3.188	4.75	303.2	120@3500	5.80	L
1937	Six, 718G	6	3.50	4.25	245.3	101@3600	5.75	L
	Eight, 721N	8	3.188	4.75	303.2	120@3500	5.8	L
1938	Six, 822E	6	3.50	4.25	245.3	101@3600	5.75	L
	Eight, 825H	8	3.188	4.75	303.2	120@3500	5.8	L
1939	Six, RE915	6	3.50	4.25	245.3	101@3600	5.75	L
	Six, 922E	6	3.50	4.25	245.3	101@3600	5.75	L
	Eight, 925H	8	3.188	4.75	303.2	120@3500	5.8	L
1940	Skylark, R-015	6	3.50	4.25	245.3	101@3600	5.75	L
1941	Skylark Custom, R-115	6	3.50	4.25	245.3	101@3600	5.75	L

MFR	CARBURETOR MODEL	VEN	WHEEL-BASE	TIRES	BODY	WEIGHT	PRICE
C	W1-316S	1	118	6.00 x 16	6 ps	3040	890
C	W1-333S	2	121	6.50 x 16	6 ps	3550	1075
C	W1-333S	2	121	6.50 x 16	6 ps	3447	1195
C	W1-398S	1	118	6.00 x 16	6 ps	3000	855
C		2	121	6.50 x 16	6 ps	3535	1035
C		1	122	6.00 x 16	5 ps	3370	1180
C		2	125	6.50 x 16	5 ps	3955	1325
C	W1	1	115	6.00 x 16	5 ps		895
C	W1	1	122	6.25 x 16	5 ps	3400	995
C	WDO	2	125	6.50 x 16	5 ps	4085	1145
C		1	115	6.00 x 16	5 ps	3000	1145
C		1	115	6.25 x 16	5 ps	3000	1095

YEAR	MODEL	ENGINE						
		CYLS	BORE	STROKE	DISPL	HP@RPM	C.R.	VLV
IMP — — International Motor Products, Glendale, Cal., 1949-ca 1950								
1949-50		1				7.5		
	A Gladden air-cooled engine was used in this car.							
IMPERIAL — — Chrysler Corp., Detroit, Mich., 1955-75								
1955	Imperial, C69	V8	3.812	3.625	331.1	250@4600	8.5	OH
	Crown Imperial, C70	V8	3.812	3.625	331.1	250@4600	8.5	OH
1956	Imperial, C73	V8	3.938	3.625	353.1	280@4600	9.0	OH
	Crown Imperial, C70	V8	3.938	3.625	353.1	280@4600	9.0	OH
1957	Imperial, IM1-1	V8	4.00	3.90	392.7	325@4600	9.25	OH
	Imperial Crown, IM1-2	V8	4.00	3.90	392.7	325@4600	9.25	OH
	Imperial LeBaron, IM1-4	V8	4.00	3.90	392.7	325@4600	9.25	OH
	Crown Imperial	V8	4.00	3.90	392.7	325@4600	9.25	OH
1958	Imperial, LY1-L	V8	4.00	3.90	392.7	345@4600	10.0	OH
	Imperial Crown, LY1-M	V8	4.00	3.90	392.7	345@4600	10.0	OH
	Imperial LeBaron, LY1-H	V8	4.00	3.90	392.7	345@4600	10.0	OH
	Crown Imperial	V8	4.00	3.90	392.7	345@4600	10.0	OH
1959	Imperial Custom, MY1-L	V8	4.188	3.75	413.2	350@4600	10.1	OH
	Imperial Crown, MY1-M	V8	4.188	3.75	413.2	350@4600	10.1	OH
	Imperial LeBaron, MY1-H	V8	4.188	3.75	413.2	350@4600	10.1	OH
	Crown Imperial	V8	4.188	3.75	413.2	350@4600	10.1	OH
1960	Custom Imperial, PY1-L	V8	4.188	3.75	413.2	350@4600	10.1	OH
	Imperial Crown, PY1-M	V8	4.188	3.75	413.2	350@4600	10.1	OH
	Imperial LeBaron, PY1-H	V8	4.188	3.75	413.2	350@4600	10.1	OH
	Crown Imperial	V8	4.188	3.75	413.2	350@4600	10.1	OH
1961	Custom Imperial, RY1-L	V8	4.188	3.75	413.2	350@4600	10.1	OH
	Imperial Crown, RY1-M	V8	4.188	3.75	413.2	350@4600	10.1	OH
	Imperial LeBaron, RY1-H	V8	4.188	3.75	413.2	350@4600	10.1	OH
	Crown Imperial	V8	4.188	3.75	413.2	350@4600	10.1	OH
1962	Custom Imperial, SY1-L	V8	4.188	3.75	413.2	340@4600	10.1	OH
	Imperial Crown, SY1-M	V8	4.188	3.75	413.2	340@4600	10.1	OH
	Imperial LeBaron, SY1-H	V8	4.188	3.75	413.2	340@4600	10.1	OH
1963	Custom Imperial, TY1-L	V8	4.188	3.75	413.2	340@4600	10.1	OH
	Imperial Crown, TY1-M	V8	4.188	3.75	413.2	340@4600	10.1	OH
	Imperial LeBaron, TY1-H	V8	4.188	3.75	413.2	340@4600	10.1	OH
1964	Imperial Crown, VY1-M	V8	4.188	3.75	413.2	340@4600	10.1	OH
	Imperial LeBaron, VY1-H	V8	4.188	3.75	413.2	340@4600	10.1	OH
1965	Imperial Crown, AY1-M	V8	4.188	3.75	413.2	340@4600	10.1	OH
	Imperial LeBaron, AY1-H	V8	4.188	3.75	413.2	340@4600	10.1	OH
1966	Imperial Crown, BY3-M	V8	4.312	3.75	439.7	350@4400	10.1	OH

MFR	CARBURETOR MODEL	VEN	WHEEL-BASE	TIRES	BODY	WEIGHT	PRICE
			63		2 pr		500
C	WCFB-2126S	4	130	8.20 x 15	6 ps	4565	4483
C	WCFB-2126S	4	149.5	8.90 x 15	6 ps	5180	6973
C	WCFB-2314S	4	133	8.20 x 15	6 ps	4575	4832
C	WCFB-2314S	4	149.5	8.90 x 15	6 ps	5145	7603
C	WCFB-2590S	4	129	9.50 x 14	6 ps	4640	4838
C	WCFB-2590S	4	129	9.50 x 14	6 ps	4740	5406
C	WCFB-2590S	4	129	9.50 x 14	6 ps	4765	5743
C	WCFB-2590S	4	149.5	9.50 x 14	8 pl	5960	15,000
C	AFB-2651S	4	129	9.50 x 14	6 ps	4590	4945
C	AFB-2651S	4	129	9.50 x 14	6 ps	4755	5632
C	AFB-2651S	4	129	9.50 x 14	6 ps	4780	5969
C	AFB-2651S	4	149.5	9.50 x 14	8 pl	5960	15,075
C	AFB-2797S	4	129	9.50 x 14	6 ps	4735	5016
C	AFB-2797S	4	129	9.50 x 14	6 ps	4830	5647
C	AFB-2797S	4	129	9.50 x 14	6 ps	4865	6103
C	AFB-2797S	4	149.5	9.50 x 14	8 pl	5960	16,000
C	AFB-2927S	4	129	8.20 x 15	6 ps	4700	5029
C	AFB-2927S	4	129	8.20 x 15	6 ps	4770	5647
C	AFB-2927S	4	129	8.20 x 15	6 ps	4860	6318
C	AFB-2927S	4	149.5	8.90 x 15	8 pl	5960	16,000
C	AFB-3108S	4	129	8.20 x 15	6 pht4	4740	5111
C	AFB-3108S	4	129	8.20 x 15	6 pht4	4855	5649
C	AFB-3108S	4	129	8.20 x 15	6 pht4	4875	6428
C	AFB-3108S	4	149.5	8.90 x 15	8 pl	5960	16,000
C	AFB-3251S	4	129	8.20 x 15	6 pht4	4620	5106
C	AFB-3215S	4	129	8.20 x 15	6 pht4	4680	5644
C	AFB-3215S	4	129	8.20 x 15	6 pht4	4725	6422
C	AFB-3256S	4	129	8.20 x 15	6 pht4	4690	5243
C	AFB-3256S	4	129	8.20 x 15	6 pht4	4740	5656
C	AFB-3256S	4	129	8.20 x 15	6 pht4	4830	6434
C	AFB-3644S	4	129	8.20 x 15	6 pht4	4970	5581
C	AFB-3644S	4	129	8.20 x 15	6 pht4	5005	6455
C	AFB-3871S	4	129	8.20 x 15	6 pht4	5015	5691
C	AFB-3871S	4	129	8.20 x 15	6 pht4	5080	6499
C	AFB-4131S	4	129	9.15 x 15	6 pht4	4990	5733

YEAR	MODEL	ENGINE						
		CYLS	BORE	STROKE	DISPL	HP@RPM	C.R.	VLV
	Imperial LeBaron, BY3-H	V8	4.312	3.75	439.7	350@4400	10.1	OH
1967	Imperial, CY1-M	V8	4.312	3.75	439.7	350@4400	10.1	OH
	Imperial Crown, CY1-M	V8	4.312	3.75	439.7	350@4400	10.1	OH
	Imperial LeBaron, CY1-H	V8	4.312	3.75	439.7	350@4400	10.1	OH
1968	Imperial Crown	V8	4.312	3.75	439.7	350@4400	10.1	OH
	Imperial LeBaron	V8	4.312	3.75	439.7	350@4400	10.1	OH
1969	Imperial Crown	V8	4.312	3.75	439.7	350@4400	10.1	OH
	Imperial LeBaron	V8	4.312	3.75	439.7	350@4400	10.1	OH

MFR	CARBURETOR MODEL	VEN	WHEEL-BASE	TIRES	BODY	WEIGHT	PRICE
C	AFB-4131S	4	129	9.15 x 15	6 pht4	5090	6540
H	R-3667A	4	127	9.15 x 15	6 ps	4715	5374
H	R-3667A	4	127	9.15 x 15	6 pht4	4725	5836
H	R-3667A	4	127	9.15 x 15	6 pht4	4790	6661
H	R-3918A	4	127	9.15 x 15	6 ps	4685	5654
H	R-3918A	4	127	9.15 x 15	6 pht4	4815	6940
H	R-4166A	4	127	9.15 x 15	6 ps	4741	5753
H	R-4166A	4	127	9.15 x 15	6 pht4	4775	6131

YEAR	MODEL	ENGINE						
		CYLS	BORE	STROKE	DISPL	HP@RPM	C.R.	VLV

JAEGER — — Jaeger Motor Car Co., Belleville, Mich., 1933

YEAR	MODEL	CYLS	BORE	STROKE	DISPL	HP@RPM	C.R.	VLV
1933	Six					70		
	Engine was by Continental. Only six or seven Jaegers were built.							

JOMAR — — Saidel Sports Racing Cars, Manchester, N.H., 1955

YEAR	MODEL	CYLS	BORE	STROKE	DISPL	HP@RPM	C.R.	VLV
1955		4	2.50	3.64	71.5	36@4400	7.0	L
	GT	4	2.50	3.64	71.5			L
	Climax				67.0	85		OH
	Engine in Climax was supercharged Coventry Climax. Others used Ford Anglia engine.							

JORDAN — — Jordan Motor Car Co., Cleveland, Oh., 1916-31

YEAR	MODEL	CYLS	BORE	STROKE	DISPL	HP@RPM	C.R.	VLV
1930	Standard Line 80	8	2.875	4.75	246.7	80@3000	5.16	L
	Great Line 90	8	3.00	4.75	268.6	85@3200	5.16	L
	70	8	2.875	4.75	246.7	80@3000	5.16	L
	Speedway Z	8	3.375	4.50	322.2	114@3000	5.4	L
1931	80	8	2.875	4.75	246.2	80@3000	5.16	L
	90	8	3.00	4.75	268.6	85@3200	5.16	L

MFR	CARBURETOR MODEL	VEN	WHEEL-BASE	TIRES	BODY	WEIGHT	PRICE
			113		5 ps	2800	700
			84		2 pc	1400	2995
			84		2 pc		3495
			84		2 pc		4195
S	U-2	1	120	5.50 x 18	5 ps	3590	1795
S	UU-2	2	125	6.00 x 18	5 ps	3790	2695
S	U-2	1	120	5.50 x 18	5 ps	3500	1495
S	UU-2	2	145	7.00 x 18	5 ps	4575	5550
S	U-2	1	120	5.50 x 18	5 ps	3440	1795
S	UU-2	2	120/131	6.00 x 18	5 ps	3900	2595

YEAR	MODEL	ENGINE CYLS	BORE	STROKE	DISPL	HP@RPM	C.R.	VLV

KAISER — — Kaiser-Frazer Corp., Willow Run, Mich., 1946-55

YEAR	MODEL	CYLS	BORE	STROKE	DISPL	HP@RPM	C.R.	VLV
1946	K-85*	6	3.25	3.75	187.0	85@3600	7.3	L
1947	Special, K-100	6	3.312	4.375	226.2	100@3600	7.3	L
	Custom, K-101	6	3.312	4.375	226.2	100@3600	7.3	L
1948	Special, K4815	6	3.312	4.375	226.2	100@3600	7.3	L
	Custom, K4825	6	3.312	4.375	226.2	100@3600	7.3	L
1949-50	K-49	6	3.312	4.375	226.2	112@3600	7.3	L
1951	Special, K-51	6	3.312	4.375	226.2	115@3650	7.3	L
	DeLuxe, K-51	6	3.312	4.375	226.2	115@3650	7.3	L
1952	Special, K-52†	6	3.312	4.375	226.2	115@3650	7.3	L
	DeLuxe, K-52†	6	3.312	4.375	226.2	115@3650	7.3	L
1953	Dragon, K-5301	6	3.312	4.375	226.2	118@3650	7.3	L
	DeLuxe, K-53	6	3.312	4.375	226.2	118@3650	7.3	L
	Manhattan, K-53	6	3.312	4.375	226.2	118@3650	7.3	L
	Carolina, K-53	6	3.312	4.375	226.2	118@3650	7.3	L
1954	Special, K-545	6	3.312	4.375	226.2	118@3650	7.3	L
	Manhattan, K-542‡	6	3.312	4.375	226.2	140@3800	7.3	L
1955	Manhattan‡	6	3.312	4.375	226.2	140@3800	7.3	L

* The K-85 had front-wheel drive. Six of these were built

† Early 1952 models carried 'Virginian' as model name.

‡ The last Manhattan models used a supercharged engine. All Kaiser engines were based on the Continental F-6226 engine.

KAISER-DARRIN — — Kaiser-Frazer Corp., Willow Run, Mich., 1954-57

YEAR	MODEL	CYLS	BORE	STROKE	DISPL	HP@RPM	C.R.	VLV
1954	161	6	3.125	3.50	161.1	90@4200	7.6	F

Later models were leftover 1954's. Engines were by Willys.

KELLER — — Keller Motor Corp., Huntsville, Ala., 1948-50

YEAR	MODEL	CYLS	BORE	STROKE	DISPL	HP@RPM	C.R.	VLV
1948	Chief	4	3.25	4.00	132.7	49@3600		L
	Super Chief	4	3.435	4.375	162.0	58@3600	7.0	L

See Bobbi-Car.

KING MIDGET — — Midget Motors Supply Co.; Midget Motors Corp., Athens, Oh., 1949-69

YEAR	MODEL	CYLS	BORE	STROKE	DISPL	HP@RPM	C.R.	VLV
1947-51		1				6		L
1952-57		1	3.00	3.25	23.0	7.5@3000	5.75	L
1958-68		1	3.375	3.25	29.1	12@3600		L

KISSEL — — Kissel Motor Car Co., Hartford, Wis., 1906-31

YEAR	MODEL	CYLS	BORE	STROKE	DISPL	HP@RPM	C.R.	VLV
1930	6-73	6	2.875	4.75	185.0	73@3500	5.15	L
	8-95	8	2.875	4.75	246.5	95@3400	5.35	L

MFR	CARBURETOR MODEL	VEN	WHEEL-BASE	TIRES	BODY	WEIGHT	PRICE
C		1	117	6.00 x 15	5 ps		
C		1	123.5	6.50 x 15	5 ps	3295	1967
C		1	123.5	6.50 x 15			
C	WAI	1	123.5	7.10 x 15	5 ps	3358	1868
C	WAI	1	123.5	7.10 x 15			
C	WCD/WAI	1/2	123.5	7.10 x 15	6 ps	3311	1995
C	WGD	2	118.5	6.70 x 15	6 ps	3150	1983
C	WGD	2	118.5	6.70 x 15	6 ps	3225	2088
C	WGD	2	118.5	6.70 x 15	6 ps	3126	2036
C	WGD	2	118.5	6.70 x 15	6 ps	3171	2143
C	WGD	2	118.5	6.70 x 15	6 pht4	3435	2924
C	WGD	2	118.5	6.70 x 15	6 ps	3200	2513
C	WGD	2	118.5	6.70 x 15	6 ps	3265	2650
C	WGD	2	118.5	6.70 x 15	6 ps	3185	2375
C	WGD	2	118.5	6.70 x 15	6 ps	3305	2389
C	WGD	2	118.5	7.10 x 15	6 ps	3375	2670
C	WGD	2	118.5	6.70 x 15	6 ps	3375	2670
C	YF-2094S	1	100	5.90 x 15	2 pr	2175	3668
			92	5.50 x 15	2 pcv	1800	895
C		1	92	5.50 x 15	5 psw2	2250	1245
				5.50 x 8	1 pr		356
			72	4.00 x 8/	2 pr	450	560
				5.50 x 8			
			76.5	8.50 x 8	2 pr	690	1029
Sc	SX359	1	117	6.00 x 30	5 ps	3150	1695
Sc	SX372	1	125	6.00 x 30	5 ps	3527	2095

YEAR	MODEL	CYLS	BORE	STROKE	DISPL	HP@RPM	C.R.	VLV
		ENGINE						
	8-126	8	3.25	4.50	298.6	126@3600	5.35	L
1931	6-73	6	2.875	4.75	185.0	73@3500	5.15	L
	8-95	8	2.875	4.75	246.5	95@3400	5.35	L
	8-126	8	3.25	4.50	298.6	126@3600	5.35	L

After 1928, Kissel autos were generally referred to as White Eagle, at least by the manufacturer.

KRIM-GHIA — — Krim-Ghia Import Co., Detroit, Mich., 1966-ca 1969

YEAR	MODEL	CYLS	BORE	STROKE	DISPL	HP@RPM	C.R.	VLV
1966		4	3.03	3.13	90.4	86		
		V8			245.0			OH

Must have been based on imported bodies and mechanical components, but this assumption is unverified.

KURTIS — — Kurtis-Kraft, Inc.; Kurtis Sports Car Corp., Glendale, Cal., 1949; 1953-55

YEAR	MODEL	CYLS	BORE	STROKE	DISPL	HP@RPM	C.R.	VLV
1949	500-S	V8	3.188	3.75	239.4	100@3600		L
1953	500-S	(Various engines)						
1954-55	500-M	V8	3.812	3.625	331.1	250@4600	9.1	OH

MFR	CARBURETOR MODEL	VEN	WHEEL-BASE	TIRES	BODY	WEIGHT	PRICE
Sc	SX316	1	132/139	6.75 x 30	7 ps	4680	3885
Sc		1	117	6.00 x 30	5 ps	3150	1595
Sc		1	125	6.00 x 30	5 ps	3527	1995
Sc		1	132/139	6.75 x 30	7 ps	4680	3785
					2 pr		
					2 pr		
			100	5.50 x 15	2 pcv	2300	3995
					2 pr		4985+ engine
					2 pr	2506	5900

YEAR	MODEL	ENGINE						
		CYLS	BORE	STROKE	DISPL	HP@RPM	C.R.	VLV

LA FAYETTE — — Nash Motor Co., Kenosha, Wis., 1934-36

YEAR	MODEL	CYLS	BORE	STROKE	DISPL	HP@RPM	C.R.	VLV
1934	Standard Six, 110	6	3.25	4.375	217.8	75@3200	5.3	L
	Special Six, 110	6	3.25	4.375	217.8	75@3200	5.3	L
1935	Standard Six, 3510	6	3.25	4.375	217.8	80@3000	5.54	L
	Special Six, 3510	6	3.25	4.375	217.8	80@3000	5.54	L
1936	Six, 3610	6	3.25	4.375	217.8	83@3200	5.54	L
	Six, 3610 (Second series)	6	3.25	4.375	217.8	83@3200	5.54	L
	This make was continued as Nash, Lafayette model.							

LA SALLE — — Cadillac Motor Division, General Motors Corp., Detroit, Mich., 1927-40

YEAR	MODEL	CYLS	BORE	STROKE	DISPL	HP@RPM	C.R.	VLV
1930	340	V8	3.312	4.938	340.0	90@3000	5.18	L
1931	345	V8	3.375	4.938	353.0	95@3000	5.35	L
1932	345B	V8	3.375	4.938	353.0	115@3000	5.38	L
1933	345C	V8	3.375	4.938	353.0	115@3000	5.40	L
1934	50-350	8	3.00	4.25	240.3	90@3700	6.0	L
1935	50-350	8	3.00	4.25	240.3	95@3700	6.5	L
1936	36-50	8	3.00	4.375	248.0	105@3600	6.25	L
1937	37-50	V8	3.375	4.50	322.0	125@3400	6.25	L
1938	38-50	V8	3.375	4.50	322.0	125@3400	6.25	L
1939	39-50	V8	3.375	4.50	322.0	125@3400	6.25	L
1940	40-50	V8	3.375	4.50	322.0	130@3400	6.25	L
	Special 40-52	V8	3.375	4.50	322.0	130@3400	6.25	L

LINCOLN — — Lincoln Motor Co., Division of Ford Motor Co., Detroit, Mich., 1920+

YEAR	MODEL	CYLS	BORE	STROKE	DISPL	HP@RPM	C.R.	VLV
1930	L	V8	3.50	5.00	384.8	90@2800	4.8	L
1931	K-201	V8	3.50	5.00	384.8	120@2900	5.2	L
1932	KA	V8	3.50	5.00	384.8	125@3900	5.2	L
	KB	V12	3.25	4.50	448.0	150@3400	5.2	L
1933	KA	V8	3.00	4.50	381.7	125@3400	5.2	L
	KB	V12	3.25	4.50	448.0	150@3400	5.2	L
1934	KA	V12	3.125	4.50	414.2	150@3400	5.2	L
	KB	V12	3.125	4.50	414.2	150@3400	5.2	L
1935	KA	V12	3.125	4.50	414.2	150@3400	6.4	L
	KB	V12	3.125	4.50	414.2	150@3400	6.4	L
1936	K	V12	3.125	4.50	414.2	150@3400	6.4	L
	K	V12	3.125	4.50	414.2	150@3400	6.4	L
	Zephyr	V12	2.75	3.75	267.3	110@3800	6.7	L
1937	K	V12	3.125	4.50	414.2	150@3400	6.4	L
	K	V12	3.125	4.50	414.2	150@3400	6.4	L
	Zephyr	V12	2.75	3.75	267.3	110@3900	6.7	L

CARBURETOR MFR	MODEL	VEN	WHEEL-BASE	TIRES	BODY	WEIGHT	PRICE
M	B	1	113	5.50 x 17	5 ps	3000	635
M	B	1	113	5.50 x 17	5 ps	3030	685
M	B	1	113	5.50 x 17	5 ps	3030	620
M	B	1	113	6.00 x 16	5 ps	3030	680
M	B2	1	113	6.00 x 16	5 ps	2950	675
S	AX-2	1	113	6.00 x 16	6 ps	2950	675
O			134	6.50 x 19	5 ps9	4690	2565
O			134	6.50 x 19	5 ps	4650	2295
O			130/136	7.00 x 17	5 ps	4850	2495
O			130/136	7.00 x 17	5 ps	4805	2245
S			119	7.00 x 16	5 ps	3960	1695
S	EE-15	2	119	7.00 x 16	5 ps	3780	1545
S			120	7.00 x 16	5 ps	3635	1225
S	AA25	2	124	7.00 x 16	5 ps	3810	1260
C	WDO-392S	2	120	7.00 x 16	5 ps	3830	1380
C	WDO-423S	2	120	7.00 x 16	5 ps	3470	1320
C	WDO-460S	2	123	7.00 x 16	5 ps	3790	1320
C	WDO-460S	2	123	7.00 x 16	5 ps	3900	1440
S	O3	1	136	7.00 x 20	5 ps	4790	4500
S	DD-3	2	136	7.00 x 20	5 ps	5300	4600
S	DD-3	2	136	7.00 x 18	5 ps	5300	3200
S	DD-3	2	145	7.50 x 18	5 ps	5750	4600
S	EE-22	2	136	7.00 x 18	5 ps	4989	3200
S	DD-3	2	145	7.50 x 18	5 ps	5491	4500
S	EE-22	2	136	7.00 x 18	5 ps	5044	3400
S	EE-22	2	145	7.50 x 18	7 ps	5510	4500
S	EE-22	2	136	7.50 x 17	5 ps	5375	4300
S	EE-22	2	145	7.50 x 17	7 ps	5535	4600
S	EE-22	2	136	7.50 x 17	5 ps	5476	4300
S	EE-22	2	145	7.50 x 17	7 ps	5591	4600
CG	AA1-121	2	122	7.00 x 16	6 ps	3349	1320
S	EE-22	2	136	7.50 x 17	5 ps	5700	4450
S	EE-22	2	145	7.50 x 17	7 ps	5905	4750
CG	AA1-121	2	122	7.00 x 16	6 ps	3349	1265

YEAR	MODEL	ENGINE						
		CYLS	BORE	STROKE	DISPL	HP@RPM	C.R.	VLV
1938	Zephyr, 86H	V12	2.75	3.75	267.3	110@3900	6.7	L
	K	V12	3.125	4.50	414.2	150@3400	6.4	L
	K	V12	3.125	4.50	414.2	150@3400	6.4	L
1939	Zephyr, 96H	V12	2.75	3.75	267.3	110@3900	6.7	L
	K	V12	3.125	4.50	414.2	150@3400	6.4	L
	K	V12	3.125	4.50	414.2	150@3400	6.4	L
1940	Zephyr, 06H	V12	2.875	3.75	292.0	120@3500	7.2	L
	H	V12	3.125	4.50	414.2	150@3400	6.4	L
	H	V12	3.125	4.50	414.2	150@3400	6.4	L
1941	Zephyr, 16H	V12	2.875	3.75	292.0	120@3500	7.0	L
	Continental, 16H	V12	2.875	3.75	292.0	120@3500	7.0	L
	Custom, 168H	V12	2.875	3.75	292.0	120@3500	7.0	L
1942	Zephyr, 26H	V12	2.938	3.75	305.0	130@3600	7.0	L
	Continental, 26H	V12	2.938	3.75	305.0	130@3600	7.0	L
	Custom, 268H	V12	2.938	3.75	305.0	130@3600	7.0	L
1946	Zephyr, 66H	V12	2.938	3.75	305.0	130@3600	7.2	L
	Continental	V12	2.938	3.75	305.0	130@3600	7.2	L
1947	Zephyr, 76H	V12	2.938	3.75	305.0	130@3600	7.0	L
	Continental	V12	2.938	3.75	305.0	130@3600	7.0	L
1948	876H	V12	2.875	3.75	292.0	125@3600	7.2	L
	Continental	V12	2.875	3.75	292.0	125@3600	7.2	L
1949	9EL	V8	3.50	4.375	336.7	152@3600	7.0	L
	Cosmopolitan, 9EH	V8	3.50	4.375	336.7	152@3600	7.0	L
1950	OEL	V8	3.50	4.375	336.7	152@3600	7.0	L
	Cosmopolitan, OEH	V8	3.50	4.375	336.7	152@3600	7.0	L
1951	1EL	V8	3.50	4.375	336.7	154@3600	7.0	L
	Cosmopolitan, 1EH	V8	3.50	4.375	336.7	154@3600	7.0	L
1952	Cosmopolitan	V8	3.80	3.50	317.5	160@3900	7.5	OH
	Capri	V8	3.80	3.50	317.5	160@3900	7.5	OH
1953	Cosmopolitan	V8	3.80	3.50	317.5	205@4200	8.0	OH
	Capri	V8	3.80	3.50	317.5	205@4200	8.0	OH
1954	Cosmopolitan	V8	3.80	3.50	317.5	205@4200	8.0	OH
	Capri	V8	3.80	3.50	317.5	205@4200	8.0	OH
1955	Custom, 73A	V8	3.94	3.50	340.9	225@4400	8.5	OH
	Capri, 73B	V8	3.94	3.50	340.9	225@4400	8.5	OH
1956	Capri	V8	4.00	3.667	368.6	285@4600	9.0	OH

MFR	CARBURETOR MODEL	VEN	WHEEL-BASE	TIRES	BODY	WEIGHT	PRICE
CG	AA1-121	2	125	7.00 x 16	6 ps	3444	1375
S	EE-22	2	136	7.50 x 17	5 ps	5527	4900
S	EE-22	2	145	7.50 x 17	7 ps	5672	5100
CG	AA1-121	2	125	7.00 x 16	6 ps	3620	1399
S	EE-22	2	136	7.50 x 17	5 ps	5735	4905
S	EE-22	2	145	7.50 x 17	7 ps	5880	5109
CG	AA1-121	2	125	7.00 x 16	6 ps	3660	1439
S	EE-22	2	136	7.50 x 17	5 ps	5735	4905
S	EE-22	2	145	7.50 x 17	7 ps	5880	5109
CG	AA1-121	2	125	7.00 x 16	6 ps	3660	1439
CG	AA1	2	125	7.00 x 16	5 ps2	3890	2812
CG	AA1	2	138	7.00 x 16	8 ps	4250	2704
CG	AA1	2	125	7.00 x 15	6 ps	3920	1700
CG	AA1	2	125	7.00 x 15	5 ps2	4000	3000
CG	AA1	2	138	7.00 x 15	8 ps	4380	2950
CG	AA1	2	125	7.00 x 15	6 ps		
CG	AA1	2	125	7.00 x 15	5 ps2		
CG	AA1	2	125	7.00 x 15	6 ps	4015	2185
CG	AA1	2	125	7.00 x 15	5 ps2	4125	4125
H	AA-1	2	125	7.00 x 15			
H	AA-1	2	125	7.00 x 15			
H	885-FFC	2	121	8.20 x 15	6 ps	4009	2574
H	885-FFC	2	125	8.20 x 15	6 ps	4274	3238
H	885-FFC	2	121	8.00 x 15	6 ps	4015	2574
H	885-FFC	2	125	8.20 x 15	6 ps	4330	3238
H	885-FFC	2	121	8.00 x 15	6 ps	4130	2796
H	885-FFC	2	125	8.00 x 15	6 ps	4415	3472
		2	123	8.00 x 15	6 ps	4125	3517
		2	123	8.00 x 15/	6 ps	4140	3661
				8.20 x 15			
H	2140	4	123	8.00 x 15/	6 ps	4125	3522
				8.20 x 15			
H	2140	4	123	8.20 x 15	6 ps	4140	3766
H	2140	4	123	8.00 x 15	6 ps	4135	3522
H	2140	4	123	8.00 x 15/	6 ps	4245	3711
				8.20 x 15			
		4	123	8.00 x 15	6 ps	4235	3653
		4	123	8.00 x 15/	6 ps	4275	3752
				8.20 x 15			
O		4	126	8.00 x 15	6 ps	4315	4212

YEAR	MODEL	ENGINE						
		CYLS	BORE	STROKE	DISPL	HP@RPM	C.R.	VLV
	Premiere	V8	4.00	3.667	368.6	285@4600	9.0	OH
	Continental Mark II	V8	4.00	3.667	368.6	300@4800	10.0	OH
1957	Capri	V8	4.00	3.667	368.6	300@4800	10.0	OH
	Premiere	V8	4.00	3.667	368.6	300@4800	10.0	OH
	Continental Mark II	V8	4.00	3.667	368.6	300@4800	10.0	OH
1958	Capri	V8	4.297	3.703	429.6	375@4800	10.5	OH
	Premiere	V8	4.297	3.703	429.6	375@4800	10.5	OH
	Continental Mark III	V8	4.297	3.703	429.6	375@4800	10.5	OH
1959	Capri	V8	4.297	3.703	429.6	350@4400	8.75	OH
	Premiere	V8	4.297	3.703	429.6	350@4400	8.75	OH
	Continental Mark IV	V8	4.297	3.703	429.6	350@4400	8.75	OH
1960	*	V8	4.297	3.703	429.6	315@4100	10.1	OH
	Premiere	V8	4.297	3.703	429.6	315@4100	10.1	OH
	Continental Mark V	V8	4.297	3.703	429.6	315@4100	10.1	OH
	* No separate model designation.							
1961	Continental Mark III	V8	4.297	3.703	429.6	300@4100	10.0	OH
1962	Continental	V8	4.297	3.703	429.6	300@4100	10.0	OH
1963	Continental	V8	4.297	3.703	429.6	320@4600	10.1	OH
1964	Continental	V8	4.297	3.703	429.6	320@4600	10.1	OH
1965	Continental	V8	4.297	3.703	429.6	320@4600	10.1	OH
1966	Continental	V8	4.375	3.828	462.0	340@4600	10.5	OH
1967	Continental	V8	4.375	3.828	462.0	340@4600	10.25	OH
1968	*	V8	4.375	3.828	462.0	340@4600	10.25	OH
	* No separate model designation.							
1969	Continental	V8	4.375	3.828	462.0	365@4600	10.5	OH
	Continental Mark III	V8	4.375	3.828	462.0	365@4600	10.5	OH

LITTLE DUDE — — Hawaiian Motor Co., Los Angeles, Cal., ca 1969

YEAR	MODEL	CYLS	BORE	STROKE	DISPL	HP@RPM	C.R.	VLV
ca 1969		F2			21.6	18.6		
	Engine was built by Aichi Machine Industry of Japan, and was an opposed, air-cooled type.							

LITTLEMAC — — Thompson Motor Corp., Muskatine, Ia., 1930-31

YEAR	MODEL	CYLS	BORE	STROKE	DISPL	HP@RPM	C.R.	VLV
1930-31	CF	4	3.125	4.25	130.4	18		L

MFR	CARBURETOR MODEL	VEN	WHEEL-BASE	TIRES	BODY	WEIGHT	PRICE
O		4	126	8.00 x 15/	6 ps	4347	4601
				8.20 x 15			
C		4	126	8.00 x 15	4 pht2	4825	9695
C		4	126	8.00 x 15	6 ps		4794
C		4	126	8.00 x 15/	6 ps	4527	5294
				8.20 x 15			
C		4	126	8.00 x 15	4 pht2	4800	9966
H	4150	4	131	9.00 x 14	6 ps		4951
H	4150	4	131	9.00 x 14	6 ps		5565
H	4150	4	131	9.00 x 14/	6 ps		6072
				9.50 x 14			
C	AFB-2853S	4	131	9.50 x 14	6 ps	4823	5090
C	AFB-2853S	4	131	9.50 x 14	6 ps	4887	5594
C	AFB-2853S	4	131	9.50 x 14	6 ps	5061	6845
C	ABD-2965S	2	131	9.50 x 14	6 ps	5016	5441
C	ABD-2965S	2	131	9.50 x 14	6 ps	5064	5945
C	ABD-2965S	2	131	9.50 x 14	6 ps	5143	6845
C	ABD-	2	123	9.00 x 14/	6 ps	4927	6069
				9.50 x 14			
C	ABD-	2	123	9.00 x 14/	6 ps	4966	6074
				9.50 x 14			
C	AFB-	4	123	9.00 x 14/	6 ps	4936	6270
				9.50 x 14			
C	C3VE-9510B	4	126	9.15 x 15	6 ps	5055	6292
C	C3VE-9510B	4	126	9.15 x 15	6 ps	5075	6166
C	C6VF-9510B	4	126	9.15 x 15	6 ps	5085	5750
C	4362	4	126	9.15 x 15	6 ps	5049	5795
C	C8VF-9510E	4	126	9.15 x 15	6 ps	4937	5970
A	C8VF-9510J	4	126	9.15 x 15	6 ps	5005	6063
A	C8VF-9510J	4	117.2	8.55 x 15	6 ps	4550	6910
			77.6				
			80		2 pc	1560	438

YEAR	MODEL	ENGINE						
		CYLS	BORE	STROKE	DISPL	HP@RPM	C.R.	VLV

MARKETEER — — Electric Marketeer Mfg. Co., Redlands, Cal., 1954

YEAR	MODEL	CYLS	BORE	STROKE	DISPL	HP@RPM	C.R.	VLV
1954						3		
	This was an electric car.							

MARKETTE — — Westinghouse Electric Corp., Pittsburgh, Pa., 1967

YEAR	MODEL	CYLS	BORE	STROKE	DISPL	HP@RPM	C.R.	VLV
1967						4.5		
	An electric car.							

MARMON — — Marmon Motor Car Co., Indianapolis, Ind., 1902-33

YEAR	MODEL	CYLS	BORE	STROKE	DISPL	HP@RPM	C.R.	VLV
1930	8-69	8	2.812	4.25	211.2	84@3400	5.25	L
	8-79	8	3.188	4.75	303.2	110@3400	5.50	L
	Big Eight	8	3.25	4.75	315.2	125@3400	5.50	L
1931	8-70	8	2.812	4.25	211.2	84@3400	5.50	L
	88	8	3.25	4.75	315.2	125@3400	5.50	L
	Sixteen	V16	3.125	4.00	490.8	200@3400	6.0	OH
1932	70	8	2.812	4.25	211.2	84@3400	5.50	L
	8-125	8	3.25	4.75	315.2	125@3400	5.50	L
	Sixteen	V16	3.125	4.00	490.8	200@3400	6.0	OH
1933	Sixteen	V16	3.125	4.00	490.8	200@3400	6.0	OH

MARQUETTE — — Buick Motor Co., Flint, Mich., 1930

YEAR	MODEL	CYLS	BORE	STROKE	DISPL	HP@RPM	C.R.	VLV
1930	30	6	3.125	4.625	212.8	67@3000	5.20	L

MARS ELECTRIC — — Electric Fuel Propulsion, Inc., Ferndale, Mich., 1966-

YEAR	MODEL	CYLS	BORE	STROKE	DISPL	HP@RPM	C.R.	VLV
1968						15		
	An electric car.							

MARTIN — — Commonwealth Research Corp., New York, N.Y., 1954-

YEAR	MODEL	CYLS	BORE	STROKE	DISPL	HP@RPM	C.R.	VLV
1954	Stationette	4	2.25	3.00	47.7	24		L

MAVERICK — — Maverick Motors, Mountain View, Cal., 1953-55

YEAR	MODEL	CYLS	BORE	STROKE	DISPL	HP@RPM	C.R.	VLV
1953		V8	3.812	3.625	331.1	210@4150	8.25	OH
	Engine was by Cadillac; others available on order.							

MERCER — — Mercer Motors Corp., New York, N.Y., 1931

YEAR	MODEL	CYLS	BORE	STROKE	DISPL	HP@RPM	C.R.	VLV
1931		8	3.375	4.50	322.2	140@3300	5.25	L

The two prototypes of this make were an attempt to revive the old and revered name. The only chassis made were constructed by Elcar, using mainly leftover Elcar parts.

CARBURETOR MFR	MODEL	VEN	WHEEL-BASE	TIRES	BODY	WEIGHT	PRICE
					2 pr		
					2 pc	1730	2000
Sc	T	1	118	5.50 x 19	5 ps	3103	1520
Sc	U	1	125	6.00 x 19	5 ps	3900	2020
Sc	UUR2	2	136	6.50 x 19	5 ps	4210	2720
Sc	UUR2	2	112.8	5.50 x 19	5 ps	2823	995
S	UUR2	2	130/136	6.50 x 19	5 ps	4375	2220
S	DDR3	2	145	7.00 x 19	5 ps	5360	5200
S	UUR2	2	112.8	5.50 x 19	5 ps	2823	995
S	UUR2	2	125	6.00 x 18	5 ps	3653	1395
S	DDR3	2	145	7.00 x 18	5 ps	5360	5700
S	DDR2	2	145	7.00 x 18	5 ps	5360	4825
M	VM3	1	114	5.25 x 18	5 ps	3076	1060
			89		5 ps	4160	
					3 psw2		1000
			122/128		2 pr	3100	5440
			135	7.00 x 19			

YEAR	MODEL	ENGINE						
		CYLS	BORE	STROKE	DISPL	HP@RPM	C.R.	VLV
MERCER COBRA — — Copper Development Association, Inc., New York, N.Y., 1964								
1964		V8	4.00	2.875	289.0			
	This car, apparently experimental, used a Shelby-modified Ford engine.							
MERCURY — — Ford Motor Co., Detroit, Mich., 1939+								
1939	99A	V8	3.188	3.75	239.4	95@3600	6.15	L
1940	09A	V8	3.188	3.75	239.4	95@3600	6.15	L
1941	19A	V8	3.188	3.75	239.4	95@3600	6.15	L
1942	29A	V8	3.188	3.75	239.4	95@3600	6.15	L
1946	69M	V8	3.188	3.75	239.4	100@3800	6.75	L
1947	79M	V8	3.188	3.75	239.4	100@3800	6.75	L
1948	89M	V8	3.188	3.75	239.4	100@3800	6.75	L
1949	9CM	V8	3.188	4.00	255.4	110@3600	6.8	L
1950	OCM	V8	3.188	4.00	255.4	110@3600	6.8	L
1951	51M	V8	3.188	4.00	255.4	112@3600	6.8	L
1952	Custom	V8	3.188	4.00	255.4	125@3700	7.2	L
	Monterey	V8	3.188	4.00	225.4	125@3700	7.2	L
1953	Custom	V8	3.188	4.00	255.4	125@3800	7.2	L
	Monterey	V8	3.188	4.00	255.4	125@3800	7.2	L
1954	Custom	V8	3.625	3.10	256.0	161@4400	7.5	OH
	Montery	V8	3.625	3.10	256.0	161@4400	7.5	OH
1955	Custom	V8	3.75	3.30	291.6	188@4400	7.6	OH
	Monterey	V8	3.75	3.30	291.6	188@4400	7.6	OH
	Montclair	V8	3.75	3.30	291.6	188@4400	7.6	OH
1956	Medalist	V8	3.80	3.44	312.1	210@4600	9.0	OH
	Custom	V8	3.80	3.44	312.1	210@4600	9.0	OH
	Monterey	V8	3.80	3.44	312.1	210@4600	9.0	OH
	Montclair	V8	3.80	3.44	312.1	210@4600	9.0	OH
1957	Monterey	V8	3.80	3.44	312.1	255@4600	9.75	OH
	Montclair	V8	3.80	3.44	312.1	255@4600	9.75	OH

CARBURETOR MFR	MODEL	VEN	WHEEL-BASE	TIRES	BODY	WEIGHT	PRICE
		2	108	6.50 x 16	2 pr		
S	EE1	1	116	6.00 x 16	5 ps	3013	957
S	EE1	1	116	6.00 x 16	5 ps	3103	987
S	EE1	1	118	6.50 x 16	5 ps	3221	987
S	EE1	1	118	6.50 x 16	6 ps	3263	1065
H	94	2	118	6.50 x 15	5 ps	3270	1412
			118	6.50 x 15	5 ps	3268	1752
O	59A-9510	2	118	6.50 x 15			
H	885FFC	2	118	7.10 x 15	6 ps	3386	2031
H	885FFC	2	118	7.10 x 15	6 ps	3386	2031
H	885FFC	2	118	7.10 x 15	6 ps	3550	2189
H	885FFC	2	118	7.10 x 15/	6 ps	3390	2249
				7.60 x 15			
H	885FFC	2	118	7.10 x 15/	6 ps	3375	2330
				7.60 x 15			
H	1901FFC	2	118	7.10 x 15	6 ps	3390	2251
H	1901FFC	2	118	7.10 x 15/	6 ps	3375	2333
				7.60 x 15			
H	2140	4	118	7.10 x 15	6 ps	3480	2551
H	2140	4	118	7.10 x 15/	6 ps	3515	3333
				7.60 x 15			
		4	119/118	7.10 x 15/	6 ps	3450	2277
				7.60 x 15			
		4	119/118	7.10 x 15/	6 ps	3500	2400
				7.60 x 15			
		4	119/118	7.10 x 15	6 ps		2685
		4	119	7.10 x 15	6 ps	3500	2313
		4	119	7.10 x 15/	6 ps	3520	2410
				7.60 x 15			
		4	119	7.10 x 15/	6 ps	3570	2555
				7.60 x 15			
		4	119	7.10 x 15/	6 ps	3610	2786
				7.60 x 15			
H		4	122	8.00 x 14/	6 ps	3890	2645
				8.50 x 14			
H		4	122	8.00 x 14/	6 ps	3905	3188
				8.50 x 14			

YEAR	MODEL	ENGINE						
		CYLS	BORE	STROKE	DISPL	HP@RPM	C.R.	VLV
	Turnpike Cruiser	V8	3.80	3.44	312.1	255@4600	9.75	OH
	Commuter	V8	3.80	3.44	312.1	255@4600	9.75	OH
1958	Standard	V8	3.80	3.44	312.1	235@4600	9.7	OH
	Monterey	V8	4.30	3.30	383.4	312@4600	10.5	OH
	Montclair	V8	4.30	3.30	383.4	330@4600	10.5	OH
	Park Lane	V8	4.30	3.70	429.8	360@4600	10.5	OH
	Commuter	V8	4.30	3.30	383.4	312@4600	10.5	OH
	Voyager	V8	4.30	3.30	383.4	330@4600	10.5	OH
	Colony Park	V8	4.30	3.30	383.4	330@4600	10.5	OH
1959	Monterey	V8	3.80	3.44	312.1	210@4400	8.75	OH
	Montclair	V8	4.30	3.30	383.4	322@4600	10.0	OH
	Park Lane	V8	4.30	3.70	429.8	345@4400	10.0	OH
	Commuter	V8	4.30	3.30	383.4	280@4400	10.0	OH
	Voyager	V8	4.30	3.30	383.4	322@4600	10.0	OH
	Colony Park	V8	4.30	3.30	383.4	322@4600	10.0	OH
1960	Comet	6	3.50	2.50	144.3	90@4200	8.7	OH
	Monterey (1)	V8	3.80	3.44	312.1	205@4000	8.9	OH
	Montclair	V8	4.30	3.70	429.9	310@4100	10.0	OH
	Park Lane	V8	4.30	3.70	429.9	310@4100	10.0	OH
	Colony Park	V8	4.30	3.70	429.9	310@4100	10.0	OH
	Commuter (1)	V8	3.80	3.44	312.1	205@4000	8.9	OH
	Optional engine:							
	(1)	V8	4.30	3.30	383.4	280@4200	8.5	OH
1961	Comet (1)	6	3.50	2.50	144.3	85@4200	8.7	OH
	Comet S-22 (1)	6	3.50	2.50	144.3	85@4200	8.7	OH
	Meteor 600 (2, 3, 5)	V8	3.75	3.30	291.6	175@4200	8.8	OH
	Meteor 800 (2, 3, 4)	V8	3.75	3.30	291.6	175@4200	8.8	OH
	Monterey (3, 4)	V8	3.75	3.30	291.6	175@4200	8.8	OH
	Colony Park (3, 4)	V8	3.75	3.30	291.6	175@4200	8.8	OH
	Commuter (2, 3, 4)	V8	3.75	3.30	291.6	175@4200	8.8	OH
	Optional engines:							
	(1)	6	3.50	3.94	227.3	101@4400	8.7	OH

MFR	CARBURETOR MODEL	VEN	WHEEL-BASE	TIRES	BODY	WEIGHT	PRICE
H		4	122	8.00 x 14/	6 pht4	4015	3849
				8.50 x 14			
H		4	122	8.50 x 14	6 psw4	4195	2973
H		4	122	8.00 x 14	6 ps	3875	2617
H		4	122	8.00 x 14/	6 ps	4160	2721
				8.50 x 14			
H		4	122	8.00 x 14/	6 ps	4155	3236
				8.50 x 14			
H		4	122	8.00 x 14/	6 pht4	4390	3944
				8.50 x 14			
H		4	122	8.50 x 14	6 psw4	4485	3105
H		4	122	8.50 x 14	6 psw4	4540	3635
H		4	122	8.50 x 14	6 psw4	4605	3775
H	2300	2	126	8.00 x 14	6 ps	3895	2832
O		4	126	8.50 x 14	6 ps	4205	3308
C	AFB-2853S	4	128	8.50 x 14/	6 ps	4386	4031
				9.00 x 14			
		4	126	8.50 x 14	6 psw4	4405	3215
		4	126	8.50 x 14	6 psw4	4483	3793
		4	126	8.50 x 14	6 psw4	4535	3932
H		1	114	6.00 x 13/	6 ps	2432	2053
				6.50 x 13			
H	2300	2	126	8.00 x 14/	6 ps	3981	2730
				9.00 x 14			
C	ABD-2965S	2	126	8.50 x 14	6 ps	4255	3280
C	ABD-2965S	2	126	8.50 x 14/	6 pht4	4380	3858
				9.00 x 14			
C	ABD-2965S	2	126	8.00 x 14	6 psw4	4558	3837
H	2300	2	126	8.00 x 14	6 psw4	4301	3127
H	1908	1	114/	6.00 x 13/	6 ps	2411	2055
			109.5	6.50 x 13			
H	1908	1	114	6.00 x 13	6 ps2	2441	2284
H		1	120	7.50 x 14	6 ps	3714	2589
H		1	120	7.50 x 14	6 ps	3762	2767
O		2	120	7.50 x 14	6 ps	3777	2871
O		2	120	7.50 x 14	6 psw4	4131	3120
O		2	120	7.50 x 14	6 psw4	4115	2924
H	1908	1					

YEAR	MODEL	ENGINE						
		CYLS	BORE	STROKE	DISPL	HP@RPM	C.R.	VLV
	(2)	6	3.625	3.60	222.9	135@4000	8.4	OH
	(3)	V8	4.00	3.50	351.9	220@4400	8.9	OH
	(4)	V8	4.047	3.781	389.1	300@4600	9.6	OH
	(5)	V8	4.047	3.781	389.1	330@5000	9.6	OH
1962	Comet (1)	6	3.50	2.50	144.0	85@4200	8.7	OH
	Comet Custom (1)	6	3.50	2.50	144.0	85@4200	8.7	OH
	Comet S-22 (1)	6	3.50	2.50	144.0	85@4200	8.7	OH
	Meteor	6	3.50	2.938	170.0	101@4400	8.7	OH
	Meteor Custom	6	3.50	2.938	170.0	101@4400	8.7	OH
	Meteor S-33	6	3.50	2.938	170.0	101@4400	8.7	OH
	Meteor	V8	3.50	2.875	221.0	145@4500	8.7	OH
	Meteor Custom (3)	V8	3.50	2.875	221.0	145@4500	8.7	OH
	Meteor S-33 (3)	V8	3.50	2.875	221.0	145@4500	8.7	OH
	Monterey	6	3.625	2.609	223.0	138@4200	8.4	OH
	Monterey (2)	V8	3.75	3.297	292.0	170@4200	8.8	OH
	Monterey Custom (2)	V8	3.75	3.297	292.0	170@4200	8.8	OH
	Colony Park (2)	V8	3.75	3.297	292.0	170@4200	8.8	OH
	Commuter (2)	V8	3.75	3.297	292.0	170@4200	8.8	OH
	Optional engines:							
	(1)	6	3.50	2.938	170.0	101@4400	8.7	OH
	(2)	V8	4.00	3.50	351.9	220@4300	8.9	OH
	(2)	V8	4.047	3.781	389.2	300@4600	9.6	OH
	(2)	V8	4.125	3.781	404.2	385@5800	10.9	OH
	(3)	V8	3.80	2.875	260.8	164@4400	8.7	OH
1963	Comet (1, 2)	6	3.50	2.50	144.3	85@4200	8.7	OH
	Comet Custom (1, 2)	6	3.50	2.50	144.3	85@4200	8.7	OH
	Comet S-22 (1, 2)	6	3.50	2.50	144.3	85@4200	8.7	OH
	Comet Villager (1, 2)	6	3.50	2.50	144.3	85@4200	8.7	OH
	Meteor	6	3.50	2.938	169.6	101@4400	8.7	OH
	Meteor Custom	6	3.50	2.938	169.6	101@4400	8.7	OH
	Meteor S-33	6	3.50	2.938	169.6	101@4400	8.7	OH
	Meteor Country Cruiser	6	3.50	2.938	169.6	101@4400	8.7	OH
	Meteor (2)	V8	3.50	2.875	221.0	145@4400	8.7	OH
	Meteor Custom	V8	3.80	2.875	260.8	164@4400	8.7	OH
	Meteor S-33	V8	3.80	2.875	260.8	164@4400	8.7	OH
	Meteor Country Cruiser (3)	V8	3.50	2.875	221.0	145@4400	8.7	OH
	Monterey (3, 4)	V8	4.047	3.781	389.1	250@4400	8.9	OH

MFR	CARBURETOR MODEL	VEN	WHEEL-BASE	TIRES	BODY	WEIGHT	PRICE
O		2					
O		4					
O		4					
H	1909	1	114	6.00 x 13/	5 ps	2457	2139
				6.50 x 13			
H	1909	1	114	6.00 x 13/	5 ps	2468	2226
				6.50 x 13			
H	1909	1	114	6.00 x 13	5 ps2	2458	2368
H	1909	1	116.5	6.50 x 14	6 ps	3035	2443
H	1909	1	116.5	6.50 x 14	6 ps	3043	2531
H	1909	1	116.5	6.50 x 13	5 psc2		2509
O	C20E-9510-N	2	116.5	6.50 x 14	6 ps	3035	2443
O	C20E-9510-N	2	116.5	6.50 x 14	6 ps	3043	2531
O	C20E-9510-N	2	116.5	6.50 x 14	5 psc2		2612
H		1	120	7.50 x 14	6 ps	3721	2726
O		2	120	7.50 x 14	6 ps	3823	2835
O		2	120	8.00 x 14	6 ps	3836	2965
O		2	120	8.00 x 14	6 psw4	4198	3289
O		2	120	8.00 x 14	6 psw4	4171	3029
O	C3GF-9510	1	114	6.50 x 14	6 ps	2499	2139
O	C3GF-9510	1	114	6.50 x 14	6 ps	2508	2226
O	C3GF-9510	1	114	6.50 x 14	6 ps2	2512	2368
O	C3GF-9510	1	109.5	6.50 x 14	6 psw4	2736	2756
O	C30F-9510-A	1	116.5/	6.50 x 14	6 ps	2959	2340
			115.5				
O	C30F-9510-A	1	116.5/	6.50 x 14	6 ps	2965	2428
			115.5				
O	C30F-9510-A	1	116.5	6.50 x 14	6 pht2	2964	2628
O	C30F-9510-A	1	115.5	6.50 x 14	6 psw4	3253	2886
O	C30F-9510-C	2	116.5	6.50 x 14	6 ps	3091	2443
O	C30F-9510-C	2	116.5	6.50 x 14	6 ps	3097	2531
O	C30F-9510-C	2	116.5	6.50 x 14	6 pht2	3096	2732
O	C30F-9510-C	2	115.5	6.50 x 14	6 psw4	3385	2990
O	C3MF-9510	2	120	7.50 x 14	6 ps	3935	2887

YEAR	MODEL	ENGINE						
		CYLS	BORE	STROKE	DISPL	HP@RPM	C.R.	VLV
	Monterey Custom (3, 4)	V8	4.047	3.781	389.1	250@4400	8.9	OH
	Monterey S-55 (3)	V8	4.047	3.781	389.1	250@4400	8.9	OH
	Colony Park	V8	4.047	3.781	389.1	250@4400	8.9	OH
	Optional engines:							
	(1)	6	3.50	2.938	169.6	101@4400	8.7	OH
	(2)	V8	3.80	2.875	260.4	164@4400	8.7	OH
	(3)	V8	4.047	3.781	389.1	300@4600	9.6	OH
	(3)	V8	4.047	3.781	389.1	330@5000	9.6	OH
	(4)	V8	4.125	3.781	404.2	385@5800	11.5	OH
	(4)	V8	4.125	3.781	404.2	405@5800	11.5	OH
	(4)	V8	4.23	3.781	425.1	410@5600	11.5	OH
1964	Comet 202	6	3.50	2.938	169.6	101@4400	8.7	OH
	Comet 404	6	3.50	2.938	169.6	101@4400	8.7	OH
	Comet Caliente	6	3.50	2.938	169.6	101@4400	8.7	OH
	Comet Cyclone	V8	4.00	2.875	289.0	210@4400	9.0	OH
	Monterey (1)	V8	4.047	3.781	389.1	250@4400	9.4	OH
	Montclair (1)	V8	4.047	3.781	389.1	250@4400	9.4	OH
	Park Lane	V8	4.047	3.781	389.1	250@4400	9.4	OH
	Commuter	V8	4.047	3.781	389.1	250@4400	9.4	OH
	Optional engines:							
	(1)	V8	4.234	3.797	427.7	410		OH
	(1)	V8	4.234	3.797	427.7	425@6000		OH
1965	Comet 202 (1)	6	3.688	3.185	200.2	120@4400	9.2	OH
	Comet 404 (1)	6	3.688	3.185	200.2	120@4400	9.2	OH
	Comet Caliente (1)	6	3.688	3.185	200.2	120@4400	9.2	OH
	Comet Cyclone	V8	4.00	2.875	289.0	200@4400	9.3	OH
	Monterey (3)	V8	4.047	3.781	389.1	250@4400	9.4	OH
	Montclair (2, 3)	V8	4.047	3.781	389.1	250@4400	9.4	OH
	Park Lane	V8	4.047	3.781	389.1	300@4600	10.1	OH
	Commuter	V8	4.047	3.781	389.1	250@4400	9.4	OH
	Optional engines:							
	(1)	V8	4.00	2.875	289.0	225@4800		OH
	(2)	V8	4.047	3.781	389.1	266@4400	9.4	OH
	(3)	V8	4.234	3.797	427.7	425@6000	11.1	OH
1966	Comet 202	6	3.68	3.125	199.4	120@4400	9.2	OH
	Comet Capri	6	3.68	3.125	199.4	120@4400	9.2	OH
	Comet Caliente	6	3.68	3.125	199.4	120@4400	9.2	OH
	Comet Voyager	6	3.68	3.125	199.4	120@4400	9.2	OH
	Comet Villager	6	3.68	3.125	199.4	120@4400	9.2	OH
	Comet Cyclone	V8	4.00	2.875	289.0	200@4000	9.3	OH
	Comet Cyclone GT (1)	V8	4.054	3.78	390.3	265@4400	9.5	OH

MFR	CARBURETOR MODEL	VEN	WHEEL-BASE	TIRES	BODY	WEIGHT	PRICE
O	C3MF-9510	2	120	7.50 x 14	6 ps	3950	3075
O	C3MF-9510	2	120	7.50 x 14	6 pht2	3990	3650
O	C3MF-9510	2	120	7.50 x 14	6 psw4	4306	3295
O		4					
O		4					
O		4					
O		3 x 2					
O		4					
O	C3YF-9510F	1	114	6.50 x 14	6 ps	2580	2182
O	C3YF-9510F	1	114	6.50 x 14	6 ps	2588	2269
O	C3YF-9510F	1	114	6.50 x 14	6 ps	2668	2350
O	C4GF-9510D	4	114	6.50 x 14	6 pht2	3044	2655
O	C4MF-9510D	2	120	8.00 x 14	6 ps	3985	2892
O	C4MF-9510D	2	120	8.00 x 14	6 ps	3996	3116
O	C4MF-9510D	2	120	8.00 x 14	6 ps	4035	3348
O	C4MF-9510D	2	120	8.00 x 14	6 psw4	4259	3236
O	C50F-9510E	1	114/109.5	6.95 x 14	6 ps	2624	2163
O	C50F-9510E	1	114/109.5	6.95 x 14	6 ps	2629	2248
O	C50F-9510E	1	114	6.95 x 14	6 ps	2659	2327
O	C5MF-9510A	2	114	6.95 x 14	6 pht2	2994	2625
O	C5MF-9510A	2	123	8.15 x 15	6 ps	3853	2782
O	C5MF-9510A	2	123	8.15 x 15	6 ps	3933	3073
O	C5AF-9510E	4	123	8.15 x 15	6 ps	3988	3301
O	C5MF-9510A	2	119	8.15 x 15	6 psw4	4178	3235
O	C3PF-9510-A	1	116	6.95 x 14	6 ps	2825	2263
O	C3PF-9510-A	1	116	6.95 x 14	6 ps	2844	2378
O	C3PF-9510-A	1	116	6.95 x 14	6 ps	2846	2453
O	C3PF-9510-A	1	113	7.75 x 14	6 psw4	3244	2790
O	C3PF-9510-A	1	113	7.75 x 14	6 psw4	3244	2553
O	C40F-9510-AM	2	116	6.95 x 14	5 pht2	3074	2700
O	C6AF-9510-AM	2	116	6.95 x 14	5 pht2	3315	2891

YEAR	MODEL	ENGINE						
		CYLS	BORE	STROKE	DISPL	HP@RPM	C.R.	VLV
	Comet Cyclone GTA	V8	4.054	3.78	390.3	265@4400	9.5	OH
	Monterey (1, 2, 3)	V8	4.054	3.78	390.3	265@4400	9.5	OH
	Montclair (1, 2, 3)	V8	4.054	3.78	390.3	265@4400	9.5	OH
	Park Lane (3)	V8	4.054	3.98	411.0	330@4600	10.5	OH
	Commuter	V8	4.054	3.78	390.3	265@4400	9.5	OH
	Colony Park	V8	4.054	3.78	390.3	265@4400	9.5	OH
	S-55	V8	4.125	3.98	425.5	345@4600	10.5	OH
	Optional engines:							
	(1)	V8	4.05	3.78	390.3	275@4400	9.5	OH
	(2)	V8	4.05	3.98	411.0	330@4600	10.5	OH
	(3)	V8	4.125	3.98	425.5	345@4600	10.5	OH
1967	Comet 202 (1)	6	3.68	3.125	199.4	120@4400	9.2	OH
	Comet Capri (1)	6	3.68	3.125	199.4	120@4400	9.2	OH
	Comet Caliente (1)	6	3.68	3.125	199.4	120@4400	9.2	OH
	Comet Voyager (1)	6	3.68	3.125	199.4	120@4400	9.2	OH
	Comet Villager (1)	6	3.68	3.125	199.4	120@4400	9.2	OH
	Comet Cyclone	V8	4.001	2.875	289.0	200@4400	9.3	OH
	Comet Cyclone GT	V8	4.047	3.78	389.0	320@4800	10.5	OH
	Cougar (2, 3)	V8	4.001	2.875	289.0	200@4400	9.3	OH
	Cougar XR-7	V8	4.001	2.875	289.0	200@4400	9.3	OH
	Monterey (4, 5)	V8	4.047	3.78	389.0	270@4400	9.5	OH
	Montclair (4, 5)	V8	4.047	3.78	389.0	270@4400	9.5	OH
	Park Lane (5)	V8	4.047	3.98	409.6	330@4600	10.5	OH
	Brougham (5)	V8	4.047	3.98	409.6	330@4600	10.5	OH
	Marquis (5)	V8	4.047	3.98	409.6	330@4600	10.5	OH
	S-55	V8	4.125	3.98	425.5	345@4600	10.5	OH
	Commuter (4, 5)	V8	4.047	3.78	389.0	270@4400	9.5	OH
	Colony Park (4, 5)	V8	4.047	3.78	389.0	270@4400	9.5	OH
	Optional engines:							
	(1)	V8	4.047	3.78	389.0	270@4400	9.5	OH
	(2)	V8	4.001	2.875	289.0	225@4800	9.8	OH
	(3)	V8	4.047	3.78	389.0	320@4800	10.5	OH
	(4)	V8	4.047	3.98	409.6	330@4600	10.5	OH
	(5)	V8	4.125	3.98	425.5	345@4600	10.5	OH
1968	Comet (1, 2, 3, 7, 8)	6	3.68	3.125	200.0	115@3800	8.8	OH
	Montego (1, 2, 3, 7, 8)	6	3.68	3.125	200.0	115@3800	8.8	OH
	Montego MX (1, 2, 3, 7, 8)	6	3.68	3.125	200.0	115@3800	8.8	OH
	Cyclone (2, 3, 7, 8)	V8	4.00	3.00	302.0	210@4600	9.0	OH
	Cougar * (2, 4, 6, 8)	V8	4.00	2.875	289.0	195@	9.0	OH
	Cougar XR-7 (*, 2, 4, 6, 8)	V8	4.00	2.875	289.0	195@	9.0	OH
	Monterey (4, 5, 9)	V8	4.05	3.78	389.6	265@4400	9.5	OH

MFR	CARBURETOR MODEL	VEN	WHEEL-BASE	TIRES	BODY	WEIGHT	PRICE
O	C6AF-9510-AM	2	116	6.95 x 14	5 pht2	3374	
O	C6AF-9510-AM	2	123	8.15 x 15	6 ps	3903	2854
O	C6AF-9510-AM	2	123	8.15 x 15	6 ps	3921	3087
O	C6MF-9510-E	4	123	8.15 x 15	6 ps	4051	3389
O	C6AF-9510-AM	2	119	8.45 x 15	6 psw4	4280	3240
O	C6AF-9510-AM	2	119	8.45 x 15	6 psw4	4332	3502
O	C6AF-9510-AD	4	123	8.15 x 15	5 pht2	4031	3292
O	C6MF-9510-D	2					
O	C6MF-9510-E	4					
O	C6AF-9510-AD	4					
A	C7DF-9510-Z	1	116	7.35 x 14	6 ps	2825	2336
A	C7DF-9510-Z	1	116	7.35 x 14	6 ps	2860	2436
A	C7DF-9510-Z	1	116	7.35 x 14	6 ps	2871	2535
A	C7DF-9510-Z	1	113	7.75 x 14	6 psw4	3230	2604
A	C7DF-9510-Z	1	113	7.75 x 14	6 psw4	3252	2841
A	C7DF-9510-Z	2	116	7.35 x 14	6 pht2	3075	2737
A	C7AF-9510-AE	4	116	7.75 x 14	6 pht2	3372	
A	C7DF-9510-Z	2	111	7.35 x 14	4 pht2	3005	2851
A	C7DF-9510-Z	2	111	7.35 x 14	4 pht2	3015	3081
H	C70F-9510-A	4	123	8.15 x 15	6 ps	3798	2904
	C7AF-9510-AE	4	123	8.15 x 15	6 ps	3863	3187
	C7AF-9510-AE	4	123	8.15 x 15	6 ps	4011	3736
	C7AF-9510-AE	4	123	8.15 x 15	6 ps	3980	3896
	C7AF-9510-AE	4	123	8.15 x 15	6 pht2	3995	3989
A	C7AF-9510-AE	4	123	8.15 x 15	6 pht2	3956	3511
	C7AF-9510-AE	4	119	8.45 x 15	6 psw4	4178	3289
	C7AF-9510-AE	4	119	8.45 x 15	6 psw4	4258	3657
H	C70F-9510-A	4					
A	C80F-9510-E	1	116	7.35 x 14	5 pht2	3078	2477
A	C80F-9510-E	1	116	7.75 x 14	6 ps	2982	2504
A	C80F-9510-E	1	116/113	7.75 x 14	6 ps	3007	2657
A	C8AF-9510-AF	2	116	7.75 x 14	5 pht2	3208	2768
A	C8AF-9510-AF	2	111	E70 x 14	5 pht2	3117	2933
A	C8AF-9510-AF	2	111	E70 x 14	5 pht2	3151	3232
A	C8AF-9510-M	2	123	8.15 x 15	6 ps	3895	3052

YEAR	MODEL	CYLS	BORE	STROKE	DISPL	HP@RPM	C.R.	VLV
		ENGINE						
	Montclair (4, 5, 9)	V8	4.05	3.78	389.6	265@4400	9.5	OH
	Park Lane	V8	4.05	3.78	389.6	315@4600	10.5	OH
	Marquis (9)	V8	4.05	3.78	389.6	315@4600	10.5	OH
	Commuter (4, 5, 9)	V8	4.05	3.78	389.6	265@4400	9.5	OH
	Colony Park (4, 5, 9)	V8	4.05	3.78	389.6	265@4400	9.5	OH
	Optional engines:							
	(1)	V8	4.00	3.00	302.0	210@4600	9.0	OH
	(2)	V8	4.00	3.00	302.0	230@4800	10.0	OH
	(3)	V8	4.05	3.78	389.6	265@4400	9.5	OH
	(4)	V8	4.05	3.78	389.6	280@4400	10.5	OH
	(5)	V8	4.05	3.78	389.6	315@4600	10.5	OH
	(6)	V8	4.05	3.78	389.6	325@4800	10.5	OH
	(7)	V8	4.05	3.78	389.6	335@4800	10.5	OH
	(8)	V8	4.234	3.78	425.9	390@5600	10.9	OH
	(9)	V8	4.125	3.98	425.5	340@4600	10.5	OH
	(9)	V8	4.125	3.98	425.5	360@4600	10.5	OH
	(*)							
	* Engine used earlier.	V8	4.00	3.00	301.6	210@4600		
1969	Montego Comet	6	3.68	3.91	249.5	155@4000	8.6	OH
	Montego (1, 3, 4)	6	3.68	3.91	249.5	155@4000	8.6	OH
	Montego MX (1, 3, 4)	6	3.68	3.91	249.5	155@4000	8.6	OH
	Cyclone (1, 3, 4)	V8	4.00	3.00	301.6	220@4400	9.5	OH
	Cyclone CJ	V8	4.13	3.98	426.5	335@5200	10.6	OH
	Cougar (1, 3)	V8	4.00	3.50	351.9	250@4600	9.0	OH
	Cougar XR-7 (1, 3)	V8	4.00	3.50	315.9	250@4600	9.0	OH
	Monterey (2)	V8	4.05	3.78	389.6	265@4400	9.5	OH
	Monterey Custom (2)	V8	4.05	3.78	389.6	265@4400	9.5	OH
	Marauder (2)	V8	4.05	3.78	389.6	265@4400	9.5	OH
	Marauder X-180	V8	4.36	3.59	428.8	360@4600	10.5	OH
	Marquis	V8	4.36	3.59	428.8	320@4400	10.5	OH
	Marquis Brougham	V8	4.36	3.59	428.8	320@4400	10.5	OH
	Optional engines:							
	(1)	V8	4.00	3.50	351.9	290@4800	10.7	OH
	(2)	V8	4.05	3.78	386.9	280@4400	10.5	OH
	(3)	V8	4.05	3.78	389.6	320@4800	10.5	OH
	(4)	V8	4.23	3.78	425.0	390@5600	10.9	OH

MFR	CARBURETOR MODEL	VEN	WHEEL-BASE	TIRES	BODY	WEIGHT	PRICE
A	C8AF-9510-M	2	123	8.15 x 15	6 ps	3897	3331
A	C8AF-9510-B	4	123	8.15 x 15	6 ps	4019	3552
A	C8AF-9510-B	4	123	8.15 x 15	5 pht2	3987	3685
A	C8AF-9510-M	2	119	8.15 x 15	6 psw4	4212	3441
A	C8AF-9510-M	2	119	8.15 x 15	6 psw4	4259	3760
A	C90F-9510-BD	1	116	7.35 x 14	5 pht2	3087	2532
A	C90F-9510-BD	1	116	7.75 x 14	6 ps	3060	2556
A	C90F-9510-BD	1	116/113	7.75 x 14	6 ps	3094	2718
A	C8AF-9510-BD	2	116	7.75 x 14	5 pht2	3273	2771
A	C8AF-9510-B	4	116	7.75 x 14	5 pht2	3634	3224
A	C9ZF-9510-A	2	111.1	E78 x 14	5 pht2	3219	3016
A	C9ZF-9510-A	2	111.1	E78 x 14	5 pht2	3221	3315
A	C9AF-9510-B	2	124/121	8.25 x 15/	6 ps	3948	3158
				8.55 x 15			
A	C9AF-9510-B	2	124/121	8.25 x 15/	6 ps	4013	3377
				8.55 x 15			
A	C9AF-9510-B	2	121	8.25 x 15	5 pht2	4044	3368
A	C9AF-9510-B	2	121	H70 x 15	5 pht2	4191	4091
A	C9AF-9510-J	2	124/121	8.55 x 15	6 ps	4226	3857
A	C9AF-9510-J	2	124	8.55 x 15	6 ps	4195	4129

YEAR	MODEL	ENGINE CYLS	BORE	STROKE	DISPL	HP@RPM	C.R.	VLV

MERRY OLDS – – American Air Products Corp., Fort Lauderdale, Fla., 1958-62

YEAR	MODEL	CYLS	BORE	STROKE	DISPL	HP@RPM	C.R.	VLV
1959-62		1				4		

Engine was a Clinton, air-cooled.

MERRY RUNABOUT – – Greg-San Klassic Kars, Glendale, Cal., ca 1960

YEAR	MODEL	CYLS	BORE	STROKE	DISPL	HP@RPM	C.R.	VLV
1960						2.5		

Used a Lawson engine.

METROPOLITAN – – American Motors Corp., Detroit, Mich., 1954-62

YEAR	MODEL	CYLS	BORE	STROKE	DISPL	HP@RPM	C.R.	VLV
1954	541, 542	4	2.578	3.50	73.2	42@4500	7.2	OH
1955	541, 542	4	2.578	3.50	73.2	42@4500	7.2	OH
1956	541, 542	4	2.578	3.50	73.2	42@4500	7.2	OH
1957	561, 562 (1500)	4	2.875	3.50	90.9	52@4500	7.2	OH
1958	561, 562 (1500)	4	2.875	3.50	90.9	52@4500	7.2	OH
1959	561, 562 (1500)	4	2.875	3.50	90.9	52@4500	7.2	OH
1960	561, 562 (1500)	4	2.875	3.50	90.9	52@4500	7.2	OH
1961	561, 562 (1500)	4	2.875	3.50	90.9	52@4500	7.2	OH
1962	561, 562 (1500)	4	2.875	3.50	90.9	52@4500	7.2	OH

The Metropolitan was a unique automobile, as it was an imported car, but was manufactured by Austin of England specifically for American Motors and not sold outside of the U.S.

MOHS – – Mohs Seaplane Corp., Madison, Wis., 1967+

YEAR	MODEL	CYLS	BORE	STROKE	DISPL	HP@RPM	C.R.	VLV
1968-69	68A	V8			304			OH
	68B	V8			549			
	68C	V8			392			
	68D	V12			530			
1973	Safarikar				392			

* This car had a single door opening in the rear, termed Ostentatienne Opera Sedan.

The 68D model used a Seagrave engine, based initially on a Pierce-Arrow V12.

MULTIPLEX – – Multiplex Mfg. Co., Berwick, Pa., 1952-54

YEAR	MODEL	CYLS	BORE	STROKE	DISPL	HP@RPM	C.R.	VLV
1953	186	4			121.8	87@4400		F
	186	6	3.125	3.50	161.1	124@4500		F

Used modified Willys engines. This was the second Multiplex to have been built in Berwick; the first was back in 1913.

MUNTZ – – Muntz Motor Works, Glendale, Cal.; Muntz Car Co., Evanston, Ill., 1950-54

YEAR	MODEL	CYLS	BORE	STROKE	DISPL	HP@RPM	C.R.	VLV
1950	Jet	V8	3.812	3.623	331.1	160@3800	7.5	OH
1950	Jet	V8	3.50	4.375	336.7	156@3600	7.0	L
1954	Jet	V8	3.80	3.50	317.5	205@4200	8.0	OH

CARBURETOR MFR	MODEL	VEN	WHEEL-BASE	TIRES	BODY	WEIGHT	PRICE
					2 pr	425	1500
			50		2 pr	190	
Z	30-VIG-10	1	85	5.20 x 13	3 pht2	1843	1445
Z	30-VIG-10	1	85	5.20 x 13	3 pht2	1843	1445
Z	30-VIG-10	1	85	5.20 x 13	3 pht2	1825	1445
Z	30-VIG-10	1	85	5.20 x 13	3 pht2	1825	1406
		1	85		3 pht2	1875	1626
		1	85		3 pht2	1875	1626
		1	85		3 pht2	1890	1673
		1	85		3 pht2	1890	1673
		1	85		3 pht2	1890	1673
H				7.50 x 20	6 ps1*	5740	19,600
				7.50 x 20	6 ps1*		25,600
				7.50 x 20			
				7.50 x 20			
H		4	131	8.00 x 17.5	6 pcv2	5400	14,500
			85		2 pr		
			94		2 pc	1705	
			113		4 pht2		
		2	116	7.60 x 15	4 pht2	3780	5250
			116	7.60 x 15	4 pht2		

YEAR	MODEL	ENGINE CYLS	BORE	STROKE	DISPL	HP@RPM	C.R.	VLV
	Initial run of twenty-eight chassis used Cadillac engines. Balance of production used Lincoln engines.							

MURENA — — Murena Motors Corp., Ltd., New York, N.Y., 1969-

YEAR	MODEL	CYLS	BORE	STROKE	DISPL	HP@RPM	C.R.	VLV
1969		V8	4.36	3.59		360@4600	10.5	OH

MUSTANG — — Mustang Engineering Corp., Renton, Wash., 1948

YEAR	MODEL	CYLS	BORE	STROKE	DISPL	HP@RPM	C.R.	VLV
1948		4				59		
	Used Hercules engine.							

CARBURETOR			WHEEL-	TIRES	BODY	WEIGHT	PRICE
MFR	MODEL	VEN	BASE				
		4	118		6 psw	3770	14,950
			102		5 ps2		1235

YEAR	MODEL	ENGINE						
		CYLS	BORE	STROKE	DISPL	HP@RPM	C.R.	VLV

NASH — — Nash Motor Co., Kenosha, Wis., 1917-54

YEAR	MODEL	CYLS	BORE	STROKE	DISPL	HP@RPM	C.R.	VLV
1930	Single 6	6	3.125	4.375	201.3	60@2800	5.00	OH
	Twin Ignition 6	6	3.375	4.50	242.0	74.5@2800	5.00	OH
	Twin Ignition 8	8	3.25	4.50	298.6	100@3200	5.25	OH
1931	6-60	6	3.125	4.375	201.3	65@2800	5.00	OH
	8-70	8	2.875	4.375	227.2	78@3300	5.00	OH
	8-80	8	3.00	4.25	240.0	87.5@3400	5.25	OH
	8-90	8	3.25	4.50	298.6	115@3600	5.25	OH
1932	960	6	3.125	4.375	201.3	65@2800	5.00	L
	970	8	2.875	4.375	227.2	78@3200	5.00	L
	980	8	3.00	4.25	240.0	94@3400	5.25	OH
	990	8	3.25	4.50	298.6	115@3600	5.25	OH
	6, 1060	6	3.125	4.375	201.3	70@3000	5.0	L
	8, 1070	8	3.00	4.375	247.4	85@3200	5.0	L
Second Series	Special 8, 1080	8	3.125	4.25	260.8	100@3400	5.25	OH
	Advanced 8, 1090	8	3.625	4.50	371.5	125@3600	5.25	OH
	Ambassador 8, 1090	8	3.625	4.50	371.5	125@3600	5.25	OH
1933	Big 6, 1120	6	3.25	4.375	217.7	75@3200	5.30	L
	Standard 8, 1130	8	3.00	4.375	247.4	80@3200	5.10	L
	Special 8, 1170	8	3.00	4.375	247.4	85@3200	5.10	L
	Advanced 8, 1180	8	3.125	4.25	260.8	100@3400	5.25	OH
	Ambassador 8, 1190	8	3.375	4.50	322.0	125@3600	5.25	OH
1934	Big 6, 1220	6	3.375	4.375	234.8	88@3200	5.25	OH
	Advanced 8, 1280	8	3.125	4.25	260.8	100@3400	5.25	OH
	Ambassador 8, 1290	8	3.375	4.50	322.0	125@3600	5.25	OH
1935	Advanced 6, 3520	6	3.375	4.375	234.8	88@3200	5.25	OH
	Ambassador 8, 3580	8	3.125	4.25	260.8	100@3400	5.25	OH
	Advanced 8, 3580	8	3.125	4.25	260.8	100@3400	5.25	OH
1936	Ambassador Super, 3680	8	3.125	4.25	260.8	102@3400	5.25	OH
	Ambassador	6	3.375	4.375	234.8	93@3400	5.25	OH
	400 Deluxe, 3640A	6	3.375	4.375	234.8	90@3400	5.61	L
	400 Standard, 3640	6	3.375	4.375	234.8	90@3400	5.61	L
1937	Lafayette 400	6	3.375	4.375	234.8	90@3400	5.61	L
	Ambassador, 3720	6	3.375	4.375	234.8	95@3400	5.67	OH
	Ambassador, 3780	8	3.125	4.25	260.8	105@3400	5.64	OH
1938	Lafayette Master, 3810	6	3.375	4.375	234.8	95@3400	5.83	L
	Lafayette Deluxe, 3810	6	3.375	4.375	234.8	95@3400	5.83	L
	Ambassador, 3820	6	3.375	4.375	234.8	105@3400	6.0	OH
	Ambassador, 3880	8	3.125	4.25	260.8	115@3400	6.0	OH

MFR	CARBURETOR MODEL	VEN	WHEEL-BASE	TIRES	BODY	WEIGHT	PRICE
C			114.2	5.00 x 19	5 ps	2850	1005
M			118/128.2	5.50 x 19	5 ps	3535	1415
M			124/133	6.50 x 19	5 ps	4000	1795
C	DRT-08	1	114.2	5.00 x 19	5 ps	2800	845
S	E-2	2	116.2	5.25 x 19	5 ps	3000	995
M			121	5.50 x 18	5 ps	3360	1295
S	UUR-2	2	124/133	6.50 x 19	5 ps	4000	1565
C			114.2	5.00 x 19	5 ps	2800	845
S	EE-2	2	116.2	5.25 x 19	5 ps	3000	995
S	UUR-2	2	121	6.00 x 18	5 ps	3360	1295
S	UUR-2	2	124/133	6.50 x 19	5 ps	4000	1595
S	E-2	2	116	5.25 x 18	5 ps	3200	840
S	EE-22	2	121	5.50 x 18	5 ps	3400	1015
S	UUR-2	2	128	6.50 x 17	5 ps	3870	1320
S	UUR-2	2	133	7.00 x 18	5 ps	4350	1595
S	UUR-2	2	142	7.00 x 18	5 ps	4510	1855
S	EX-2		116	5.50 x 17	5 ps	3125	745
S	EX-2		116	5.50 x 17	5 ps	3200	845
			121	5.50 x 18	5 ps	3400	975
S	UUR-2	2	128	6.50 x 17	5 ps	3870	1320
S	UUR-2	2	133/142	7.00 x 18	5 ps	4510	1595
S	EX-32	1	116	5.50 x 17	5 ps	3370	755
S	EE-22	2	121	6.50 x 16	5 ps	3540	995
S	UUR-2	2	133/142	7.00 x 17	5 ps	4330	1475
S	EX-32	1	120	6.25 x 16	5 ps	3540	875
S	EE-22	2	125	6.50 x 16	5 ps	3750	1095
S	EE-22	2	125	6.50 x 16	5 ps	3750	1220
S	EE-1		125	6.50 x 16	5 ps	3710	885
S	EX-2/AX-2	2	125	6.25 x 16	5 ps	3820	995
S	EX-22	2	117	6.00 x 16	6 ps	3020	765
S	EX-22	2	117	6.00 x 16	6 ps	2970	740
S	AX-2		117	6.00 x 16	6 ps	3240	845
S	EX-32	2	121	6.25 x 16	6 ps	3400	1025
S	EE-1		125	7.00 x 16	6 ps	3720	1165
S	AX-2	2	117	6.00 x 16	6 ps	3200	850
S	EX-22	2	117	6.00 x 16	6 ps	3300	900
S	EX-32		121	6.25 x 16	6 ps	3460	1050
S	EE-1		125	6.00 x 17	6 ps	3790	1200

YEAR	MODEL	ENGINE						
		CYLS	BORE	STROKE	DISPL	HP@RPM	C.R.	VLV
1939	Lafayette Special, 3910	6	3.375	4.375	234.8	99@3400	6.3	L
	Lafayette Deluxe, 3910	6	3.375	4.375	234.8	99@3400	6.3	L
	Ambassador, 3920	6	3.375	4.375	234.8	105@3400	6.0	OH
	Ambassador, 3980	8	3.125	4.25	260.8	115@3400	6.0	OH
1940	Lafayette, 4010	6	3.375	4.375	234.8	99@3400	6.3	L
	Ambassador, 4020	6	3.375	4.375	234.8	105@3400	6.0	OH
	Ambassador, 4080	8	3.125	4.25	260.8	115@3400	6.0	OH
1941	Ambassador 600 Special, 4140	6	3.125	3.75	172.6	75@3600	6.87	L
	Ambassador 600 Deluxe, 4140	6	3.125	3.75	172.6	75@3600	6.87	L
	Ambassador, 4160	6	3.375	4.375	234.8	105@3400	6.0	OH
	Ambassador, 4180	8	3.125	4.25	260.8	115@3400	6.0	OH
1942	Ambassador 600, 4240	6	3.125	3.75	172.6	75@3600	6.87	L
	Ambassador, 4260	6	3.375	4.375	234.8	105@3400	6.5	OH
	Ambassador, 4280	8	3.125	4.25	260.8	115@3400	6.6	OH
1946	Super 600	6	3.125	3.75	172.6	82@3800	7.0	L
	Ambassador Super	6	3.375	4.375	234.8	112@3400	6.8	OH
1947	600	6	3.125	3.75	172.6	82@3800	7.0	L
	Ambassador	6	3.375	4.375	234.8	112@3400	6.8	OH
1948	600	6	3.125	3.75	172.6	82@3800	7.0	L
	Ambassador	6	3.375	4.375	234.8	112@3400	7.02	OH
1949	Super 600	6	3.125	3.75	172.6	82@3800	7.0	L
	Super Special 600	6	3.125	3.75	172.6	82@3800	7.0	L
	Custom 600	6	3.125	3.75	172.6	82@3800	7.0	L
	Ambassador Super	6	3.375	4.375	234.8	112@3400	7.02	OH
	Ambassador Super Special	6	3.375	4.375	234.8	112@3400	7.02	OH
	Ambassador Custom	6	3.375	4.375	234.8	112@3400	7.02	OH
1950	Super	6	3.125	4.00	184.0	85@3800	7.0	L
	Super Custom	6	3.125	4.00	184.0	85@3800	7.0	L
	Ambassador	6	3.375	4.375	234.8	115@3400	7.3	OH
	Ambassador Custom	6	3.375	4.375	234.8	115@3400	7.3	OH
1951	Rambler Super	6	3.125	3.75	172.6	82@3800	7.25	L
	Rambler Custom	6	3.125	3.75	172.6	82@3800	7.25	L
	Statesman Deluxe	6	3.125	4.00	184.0	85@3800	7.0	L
	Statesman Super	6	3.125	4.00	184.0	85@3800	7.0	L
	Statesman Custom	6	3.125	4.00	184.0	85@3800	7.0	L
	Ambassador Super	6	3.375	4.375	234.8	115@3400	7.3	OH
	Ambassador Custom	6	3.375	4.375	234.8	115@3400	7.3	OH
1952	Rambler Super	6	3.125	3.75	172.6	82@3800	7.25	L
	Rambler Custom	6	3.125	3.75	172.6	82@3800	7.25	L
	Statesman Super	6	3.125	4.25	195.6	88@3800	7.10	L
	Statesman Custom	6	3.125	4.25	195.6	88@3800	7.10	L

MFR	CARBURETOR MODEL	VEN	WHEEL-BASE	TIRES	BODY	WEIGHT	PRICE
S	EE-1		117	6.00 x 16	6 ps	3285	840
S	EE-1		117	6.00 x 16	6 ps	3350	885
C	WAI-435S	1	121	6.25 x 16	6 ps	3450	985
C	WAI-436S	1	125	7.00 x 16	6 ps	3800	1235
C	WDO-4585	2	117	6.00 x 16	6 ps	3275	875
C	WAI-435S	2	121	6.25 x 16	6 ps	3380	985
C	WDO-465S	2	125	7.00 x 15	6 ps	3655	1195
C	513S		112	5.50 x 16	6 ps	2615	805
C	513S		112	5.50 x 16	6 ps	2630	837
C	435S		121	6.25 x 16	6 ps	3300	970
C	WDO-511S	2	121	6.50 x 16	6 ps	3465	1091
C	WDO-538S	2	112	5.50 x 16	5 ps	2650	893
C	WAI-464S	1	121	6.25 x 16	5 ps	3335	1044
C	WDO-538S	2	121	6.50 x 16	5 ps	3485	1094
C	WAI-611S	1	112	6.00 x 16	5 ps	2740	1342
C		1	121	6.50 x 15	5 ps	3335	1511
			112	6.00 x 16	5 ps	2786	1574
			121	6.50 x 15	5 ps	3387	1968
C	WAI-662S	1	112	6.40 x 15			
C	WAI-464S	1	121	7.10 x 15			
C	WAI-694S	1	112	6.40 x 15	5 ps		1832
C	WAI-694S	1	112	6.40 x 15	5 ps		1880
C	WAI-694S	1	112	6.40 x 15	5 ps		
C	WAI-683S	1	121	7.10 x 15	5 ps		2279
C	WAI-683S	1	121	7.10 x 15	5 ps		2348
C	WAI-683S	1	121	7.10 x 15	5 ps		2489
C	WAI-694S	1	112	6.40 x 15	6 ps	2965	1623
C	WAI-694S	1	112	6.40 x 15	6 ps	2990	1773
C	WAI-746S	1	121	7.10 x 15	6 ps	3350	1929
C	WAI-746S	1	121	7.10 x 15	6 ps	3390	2079
C	YF-757S	1	100	5.90 x 15	5 psw2	2515	1885
C	YF-757S	1	100	5.90 x 15	5 pht2	2420	1968
C	YF-824S	1	112	6.40 x 15	3 pc	2835	1841
C	YF-824S	1	112	6.40 x 15	6 ps	2970	1955
C	YF-824S	1	112	6.40 x 15	6 ps	2990	2125
C	WAI-746S	1	121	7.10 x 15	6 ps	3410	2330
C	WAI-746S	1	121	7.10 x 15	6 ps	3445	2501
C		1	100	5.90 x 15	5 psw2	2515	2003
C		1	100	5.90 x 15	5 pht2	2420	2094
C		1	114.2	6.70 x 15	6 ps	3045	2178
C		1	114.2	6.70 x 15	6 ps	3070	2332

YEAR	MODEL	ENGINE						
		CYLS	BORE	STROKE	DISPL	HP@RPM	C.R.	VLV
	Ambassador Super	6	3.50	4.375	252.6	120@3700	7.30	OH
	Ambassador Custom	6	3.50	4.375	252.6	120@3700	7.30	OH
1953	Rambler Super	6	3.125	4.00	184.1	85@3800	7.25	L
	Rambler Custom	6	3.125	4.00	184.1	85@3800	7.25	L
	Statesman Super	6	3.125	4.25	195.6	100@3800	7.45	L
	Statesman Custom	6	3.125	4.25	195.6	100@3800	7.45	L
	Ambassador Super	6	3.50	4.375	252.6	120@3700	7.30	OH
	Ambassador Custom	6	3.50	4.375	252.6	120@3700	7.30	OH
1954	Rambler Deluxe	6	3.50	4.00	230.9	85@3800	7.25	L
	Rambler Super	6	3.50	4.00	230.9	85@3800	7.25	L
	Rambler Custom	6	3.50	4.00	230.9	85@3800	7.25	L
	Statesman Super	6	3.125	4.25	195.6	110@4000	8.50	L
	Statesman Custom	6	3.125	4.25	195.6	110@4000	8.50	L
	Ambassador Super (1)	6	3.50	4.375	252.6	130@3700	7.60	OH
	Ambassador Custom (1)	6	3.50	4.375	252.6	130@3700	7.60	OH
	Optional engine:							
	(1)	6	3.50	4.375	252.6	140@4000	8.0	OH
	Became American Motors in spring 1954. Listing is continued under heading of American Motors.							

NASH-HEALEY — — Nash Motors Co., Kenosha, Wis., 1951-55

YEAR	MODEL	CYLS	BORE	STROKE	DISPL	HP@RPM	C.R.	VLV
1951	25	6	3.375	4.375	234.8	125@4000	8.1	OH
1952	25	6	3.375	4.375	234.8	125@4000	8.1	OH
1953	25	6	3.375	4.375	234.8	125@4000	8.1	OH
(Early)								
1953								
(Late)	25	6	3.50	4.375	252.6	140@4000	8.0	OH
1954	25	6	3.50	4.375	252.6	140@4000	8.0	OH
1955	25	6	3.50	4.375	252.6	140@4000	8.0	OH

NAVAJO — — Navajo Motor Car Co., New York, N.Y., 1953-54

YEAR	MODEL	CYLS	BORE	STROKE	DISPL	HP@RPM	C.R.	VLV
1954		V8	3.188	4.00	255.4	130		L

CARBURETOR MFR	MODEL	VEN	WHEEL-BASE	TIRES	BODY	WEIGHT	PRICE
C		1	121.2	7.10 x 15	6 ps	3430	2557
C		1	121.2	7.10 x 15	6 ps	3480	2716
C	YF-2014S	1	100	5.90 x 15	5 psw2	2555	2003
C	YF-2014S	1	100	6.40 x 15	5 pht2	2550	2125
C	WCD-2034S	2	114.2	6.70 x 15	6 ps	3045	2178
C	WCD-2034S	2	114.2	6.70 x 15	6 ps	3070	2332
C	YH-895S	1	121.2	7.10 x 15	6 ps	3430	2557
C	YH-895S	1	121.2	7.10 x 15	6 ps	3480	2716
C	YF-2014S	1	100	5.90 x 15	5 ps2	2425	1550
C	YF-2014S	1	100/108	6.40 x 15	6 ps	2570	1795
C	YF-2014S	1	100/108	6.40 x 15	6 ps	2630	1965
C	YF-2098S	1	114.2	6.70 x 15	6 ps	3045	2158
C	YF-2098S	1	114.2	6.70 x 15	6 ps	3095	2332
C	YH-895S	1	121.2	7.10 x 15	6 ps	3430	2417
C	YH-895S	1	121.2	7.10 x 15	6 ps	3505	2600
C		2					
			102	6.40 x 15	2 pr	2690	4063
			102	6.40 x 15	2 pr	2750	5868
			102/108	6.40 x 15	2 pr	2700	
			102/108	6.40 x 15	2 pht2	2600	
			108	6.40 x 15	2 pht2	2990	4721
			108	6.40 x 15	2 pht2	2800	5128
			116		2 pr	2300	2895

YEAR	MODEL	ENGINE						
		CYLS	BORE	STROKE	DISPL	HP@RPM	C.R.	VLV
OAKLAND — — Oakland Motor Car Co., Pontiac, Mich., 1907-31								
1930	101	V8	3.438	3.375	251.0	85@3000	5.0	H
1931	301	V8	3.438	3.375	251.0	85@3400	5.0	H
	The Oakland became the Pontiac V8 for 1932.							
OLDSMOBILE — — Oldsmobile Div., General Motors Corp., Lansing, Mich., 1896+								
1930	Standard F-30	6	3.188	4.125	197.5	62@3000	5.2	L
	Special F-30	6	3.188	4.125	197.5	62@3000	5.2	L
	Deluxe F-30	6	3.188	4.125	197.5	62@3000	5.2	L
1931	Standard F-31	6	3.188	4.125	197.5	65@3350	5.06	L
	Deluxe F-31	6	3.188	4.125	197.5	65@3350	5.06	L
1932	F-32	6	3.312	4.125	213.3	71@3200	5.30	L
	L-32	8	3.00	4.25	240.3	82@3200	5.50	L
1933	F-33	6	3.375	4.125	221.4	80@3200	5.30	L
	L-33	8	3.00	4.25	240.3	90@3350	5.50	L
1934	F-34	6	3.3125	4.125	213.3	84@3250	5.70	L
	L-34	8	3.00	4.25	240.3	90@3350	5.70	L
1935	E-35	6	3.312	4.125	213.3	90@3400	6.00	L
	L-35	8	3.00	4.25	240.3	100@3400	6.20	L
1936	F-36	6	3.312	4.125	213.3	90@3400	6.00	L
	L-36	8	3.00	4.25	240.3	100@3400	6.20	L
1937	F-37	6	3.438	4.125	229.7	95@3400	6.10	L
	L-37	8	3.25	3.875	257.1	110@3600	6.20	L
1938	F-38	6	3.438	4.125	229.7	95@3400	6.10	L
	L-38	8	3.25	3.875	257.1	110@3600	6.20	L
1939	6-60	6	3.438	3.875	216.0	90@3200	6.2	L
	6-70	6	3.438	4.125	229.7	95@3300	6.1	L
	8-80	8	3.25	3.375	257.1	110@3500	6.2	L
1940	F-40-60	6	3.438	4.125	229.7	95@3400	6.1	L
	G-40-70	6	3.438	4.125	229.7	95@3400	6.1	L
	L-40-90	8	3.25	3.875	257.1	110@3600	6.3	L
1941	Special F-41-66	6	3.50	4.125	238.1	100@3400	6.1	L
	Dynamic Cruiser G-41-76	6	3.50	4.125	238.1	100@3400	6.1	L
	Custom Cruiser H-41-96	6	3.50	4.125	238.1	100@3400	6.1	L
	E-41-68	8	3.25	3.875	257.1	110@3600	6.3	L
	J-41-78	8	3.25	3.875	257.1	110@3600	6.3	L
	L-41-98	8	3.25	3.875	257.1	100@3400	6.3	L
1942	66	6	3.50	4.125	238.1	110@3400	6.5	L
	76	6	3.50	4.125	238.1	100@3400	6.5	L

MFR	CARBURETOR MODEL	VEN	WHEEL-BASE	TIRES	BODY	WEIGHT	PRICE
M	DO	1	117	5.50 x 18	5 ps	3205	995
M	DO	1	117	5.50 x 18	5 ps	3138	995
J	A		113.5	5.25 x 18	5 ps	2940	995
J	A		113.5	5.25 x 18	5 ps	2920	970
J	A		113.5	5.25 x 18	5 ps	2990	1025
S	DRX-2		113.5	5.25 x 18	5 ps	2855	845
S	DRX-2		113.5	5.25 x 18	5 ps	3000	990
S	EC-2		116.5	6.00 x 17	5 ps	3035	875
S	EE-2		116.5	6.00 x 17	5 ps	3260	975
S	EC-22		115	5.50 x 17	5 ps	3165	855
S	EE-22		119	6.00 x 17	5 ps	3305	955
S	EX-22		114	5.50 x 17/	5 ps	3100	755
				6.50 x 16			
S	EE-1		119	7.00 x 16	5 ps	3470	965
S	EX-22		115	6.25 x 16	5 ps	3285	790
S	EE-1		121	7.00 x 16	5 ps	3530	940
C	WI-351S	1	115	6.25 x 16	5 ps	3179	795
C	WDO	2	121	7.00 x 16	5 ps	3401	910
C	3515		117	6.50 x 16	5 ps	3310	920
C	3455		124	7.00 x 16	5 ps	3510	1035
C	W1-388	1	117	6.50 x 16	5 ps	3285	970
C	WDO-389	2	124	7.00 x 16	5 ps	3490	1081
C	425S		115	6.00 x 16	5 ps	3000	889
C	425S		120	6.00 x 16	5 ps	3180	952
C	3895		120	6.50 x 16	5 ps	3340	1043
C	467S		116	6.00 x 16	5 ps	3100	899
C	467S		120	6.50 x 16	5 ps	3220	963
C	WDO-389S	2	124	7.00 x 15	5 ps	3555	1131
C	WA1-504S	1	119	6.00/650 x 16	6 ps	3230	945
C	WA1-504S	1	125	6.50 x 16	6 ps	3390	1010
C	WA1-504S	1	125	7.00 x 15	6 ps	3410	1099
C	WDO-503S	2	119	6.50 x 16	6 ps	3360	987
C	WDO-503S	2	125	6.50 x 16	6 ps	3500	1045
C	WDO-503S	2	125	7.00 x 15	6 ps	3500	1135
C	523S		119	6.00 x 16	6 ps	3315	1005
C	523S		125	6.50 x 16	6 ps	3465	1065

YEAR	MODEL	ENGINE						
		CYLS	BORE	STROKE	DISPL	HP@RPM	C.R.	VLV
	68	8	3.25	3.875	257.1	110@3600	6.5	L
	78	8	3.25	3.875	257.1	110@3600	6.5	L
	98	8	3.25	3.875	257.1	110@3600	6.5	L
1946	66	6	3.50	4.125	238.1	82@3800	7.0	L
	76	6	3.50	4.125	238.1	82@3800	7.0	L
	78	8	3.25	3.875	234.8	112@3400	6.8	L
	98	8	3.25	3.875	234.8	112@3400	6.8	L
1947	Special 66	6	3.50	4.125	238.1	94@3400		L
	Special 68	8	3.25	3.875	257.1	94@3400		L
	Dynamic Cruiser 76	6	3.50	4.125	238.1	94@3400		L
	Dynamic Cruiser 78	8	3.25	3.875	271.1	104@3600		L
	Custom Cruiser 98	8	3.25	3.875	257.1	104@3600		L
1948	Dynamic 66	6	3.50	4.125	238.1	100@3400	6.5	L
	Dynamic 76	6	3.50	4.125	238.1	100@3400	6.5	L
	Dynamic 68	8	3.25	3.875	257.1	110@3600	6.5	L
	Dynamic 78	8	3.25	3.875	257.1	110@3600	6.5	L
	Futuramic 98	8	3.25	3.875	257.1	115@3600	7.0	L
1949	Futuramic 76	6	3.531	4.375	231.5	105@3400	6.5	L
	Futuramic 76 Deluxe	6	3.531	4.375	231.5	105@3400	6.5	L
	Futuramic 88	V8	3.75	3.438	303.7	135@3600	7.25	OH
	Futuramic 88 Deluxe	V8	3.75	3.438	303.7	135@3600	7.25	OH
	Futuramic 98	V8	3.75	3.438	303.7	135@3600	7.25	OH
	Futuramic 98 Deluxe	V8	3.75	3.438	303.7	135@3600	7.25	OH
1950	76	6	3.531	4.375	231.5	105@3400	6.5	L
	76 Deluxe	6	3.531	4.375	231.5	105@3400	6.5	L
	88	V8	3.75	3.438	303.7	135@3600	7.25	OH
	88 Deluxe	V8	3.75	3.438	303.7	135@3600	7.25	OH
	98	V8	3.75	3.438	303.7	135@3600	7.25	OH
	98 Deluxe	V8	3.75	3.438	303.7	135@3600	7.25	OH
1951	88	V8	3.75	3.438	303.7	135@3600	7.5	OH
	Super 88	V8	3.75	3.438	303.7	135@3600	7.5	OH
	98	V8	3.75	3.438	303.7	135@3600	7.5	OH
	98 Deluxe	V8	3.75	3.438	303.7	135@3600	7.5	OH
1952	88 Deluxe	V8	3.75	3.438	303.7	145@3600	7.5	OH
	Super 88	V8	3.75	3.438	303.7	160@3600	7.5	OH
	98	V8	3.75	3.438	303.7	160@3600	7.5	OH

MFR	CARBURETOR MODEL	VEN	WHEEL-BASE	TIRES	BODY	WEIGHT	PRICE
C	503S		119	6.50 x 16	6 ps	3445	1045
C	503S		125	6.50 x 16	6 ps	3580	1105
C	503S		127	7.00 x 15	6 ps	3715	1275
C	WA1-504S	1	119	6.50 x 16	5 ps	3380	1369
C	WA1-504S	1	125	6.50 x 16	5 ps	3540	1450
C	WDO-503S	2	125	6.50 x 16	5 ps	3670	1512
C	WDO-503S	2	127	6.50 x 16	5 ps	3810	1690
C	WAI-504S	1	119	6.00 x 16	5 ps	3355	1450
C	WDO-504S	2	119	6.50 x 16	5 ps	3460	1505
C	WAI-504S	1	125	6.50 x 16	5 ps	3590	1655
C	WCD-665S	2	125	6.50 x 16	5 ps	3705	1710
C	WCD-665S	2	127	7.00 x 15	5 ps.	3795	1790
C	WA1-651S	1	119	6.00 x 16	5 ps	3355	1556
C	WA1-651S	1	125	6.50 x 16	5 ps	3525	1659
C	WDO-650S	2	119	6.50 x 15	5 ps	3460	1614
C	WDO-650S	2	125	6.50 x 16	5 ps	3655	1717
C	WDO-650S	2	125	7.00 x 15	5 ps	3795	1917
C	WA1-709S	1	119.5	7.10 x 15	5 ps	3340	1832
C	WA1-709S	1	119.5	7.60 x 15/	5 ps	3375	1974
				7.10 x 15			
C	WGD-714S	2	119.5	7.60 x 15	5 ps	3615	2244
C	WGD-714S	2	119.5	7.60 x 15	5 ps	3645	2375
C	WGD-714S	2	125	7.60 x 15	5 ps	3890	2500
C	WGD-714S	2	125	7.60 x 15	5 ps	3925	2594
C	WA1-764S	1	119.5	7.60 x 15/	5 ps	3320	1819
				7.10 x 14			
C	WA1-764S	1	119.5	7.10 x 15/	5 ps	3340	1887
				7.60 x 15			
C	WGD-714SA	2	119.5	8.20 x 15	5 ps	3515	1978
C	WGD-714SA	2	119.5	8.20 x 15	5 ps	3520	2056
C	WGD-714SA	2	122	7.60 x 15	5 ps	3765	2299
C	WGD-714SA	2	122	8.20 x 15	5 ps	3775	2393
R	BB	2	119.5	7.60 x 15	6 ps	3542	2111
R	BB	2	120	7.60 x 15	6 ps	3636	2328
R	BB	2	122	7.60 x 15	5 pht2	3762	2545
R	BB	2	122	7.60 x 15/	6 ps	3787	2610
				8.20 x 15			
R	BB	2	120	7.60 x 15	6 ps	3608	2327
C	WGD	4	120	7.60 x 15	6 ps	3649	2462
C	WGD	4	124	7.60 x 15/	6 ps	3765	2786
				8.10 x 15			

YEAR	MODEL	ENGINE						
		CYLS	BORE	STROKE	DISPL	HP@RPM	C.R.	VLV
1953	88 Deluxe	V8	3.75	3.438	303.7	150@3600	8.0	OH
	Super 88	V8	3.75	3.438	303.7	165@3600	8.0	OH
	98	V8	3.75	3.438	303.7	165@3600	8.0	OH
	Fiesta	V8	3.75	3.438	303.7	165@3600	8.0	OH
1954	88	V8	3.875	3.438	324.3	170@4000	8.25	OH
	Super 88	V8	3.875	3.438	324.3	185@4000	8.25	OH
	Super 88 Deluxe	V8	3.875	3.438	324.3	185@4000	8.25	OH
	98	V8	3.875	3.438	324.3	185@4000	8.25	OH
	98 Deluxe	V8	3.875	3.438	324.3	185@4000	8.25	OH
1955	88	V8	3.875	3.438	324.3	185@4000	8.5	OH
	Super 88	V8	3.875	3.438	324.3	202@4000	8.5	OH
	Super 88 Deluxe	V8	3.875	3.438	324.3	202@4000	8.5	OH
	98	V8	3.875	3.438	324.3	202@4000	8.5	OH
	98 Deluxe	V8	3.875	3.438	324.3	202@4000	8.5	OH
1956	88	V8	3.875	3.438	324.3	230@4400	9.25	OH
	Super 88	V8	3.875	3.438	324.3	240@4400	9.25	OH
	Super 88 Deluxe	V8	3.875	3.438	324.3	240@4400	9.25	OH
	98	V8	3.875	3.438	324.3	240@4400	9.25	OH
	98 Deluxe	V8	3.875	3.438	324.3	240@4400	9.25	OH
1957	Golden Rocket 88	V8	4.00	3.688	371.0	277@4400	9.5	OH
	Golden Rocket Super 88	V8	4.00	3.688	371.0	277@4400	9.5	OH
	Starfire 98	V8	4.00	3.688	371.0	277@4400	9.5	OH
1958	Dynamic 88	V8	4.00	3.688	371.0	265@4400	10.0	OH
	Super 88 (1)	V8	4.00	3.688	371.0	305@4600	10.0	OH
	98 (1)	V8	4.00	3.688	371.0	305@4600	10.0	OH
	Optional engine:							
	(1)	V8	4.00	3.688	371.0	312@4600	10.0	OH
1959	Dynamic 88 (1)	V8	4.00	3.688	371.0	270@4600	9.75	OH
	Super 88	V8	4.125	3.688	394.3	315@4600	9.75	OH
	98	V8	4.125	3.688	394.3	315@4600	9.75	OH
	Optional engine:							
	(1)	V8	4.00	3.688	371.0	300@4600	9.75	OH
1960	88 (1)	V8	4.00	3.688	371.0	240@4600	8.75	OH
	Super 88	V8	4.125	3.688	394.3	315@4600	9.75	OH
	98	V8	4.125	3.688	394.3	315@4600	9.75	OH

MFR	CARBURETOR MODEL	VEN	WHEEL-BASE	TIRES	BODY	WEIGHT	PRICE
C	WGD	2	120	7.60 x 15	6 ps	3642	2327
R	4GC	4	120	7.60 x 15	6 ps	3673	2462
R	4GC	4	124	7.60 x 15/	6 ps	3779	2786
				8.00 x 15			
R	4GC	4	124	8.00 x 15	5 pcv2	4453	5715
C	WGD	2	122	7.60 x 15	6 ps	3719	2337
R	4GC	4	122	7.60 x 15	6 ps	3780	2477
R	4GC	4	122	7.60 x 15	6 pht2	3775	2688
R	4GC	4	126	7.60 x 15	6 pht2	3851	2826
R	4GC	4	126	7.60 x 15	6 ps	3895	2806
R	2GC	2	122	7.60 x 15	6 ps	3707	2362
R	4GC	4	122	7.60 x 15	6 ps	3762	2503
R	4GC	4	122	7.60 x 15	6 pht4	3825	2788
R	4GC	4	126	7.60 x 15/	6 ps	3864	2833
				8.00 x 15			
R	4GC	4	126	7.60 x 15	6 pht4	3976	3140
R	2GC	2	122	7.10 x 15	6 ps	3748	2443
R	4GC	4	122	7.60 x 15	6 ps	3768	2595
R	4GC	4	122	7.60 x 15	6 pht4	3869	2836
R	4GC	4	126	7.60 x 15/	6 ps	4028	3253
				8.00 x 15			
R	4GC	4	126	7.60 x 15	6 pht4	4167	3506
R	4GC	4	122	8.50 x 14	6 ps	4000	2798
R	4GC	4	122	8.50 x 14/	6 ps	4044	3030
				9.00 x 14			
R	4GC	4	126	8.50 x 14/	6 ps	4322	3741
				9.00 x 14			
R	2GC	2	122.5	8.50 x 14	6 ps	3985	2837
R	4GC	4	122.5	8.50 x 14	6 ps	4008	3112
R	4GC	4	126.5	8.50 x 14/	6 ps	4316	3824
				9.00 x 14			
R	2GC	2	123	8.50 x 14	6 ps	4130	2902
R	4GC	4	123	9.00 x 14	6 ps	4135	3178
R	4GC	4	126.3	9.00 x 14	6 ps	4390	3890
R	2GC	2	123	8.50 x 14	6 ps	4091	2900
R	4GC	4	123	8.50 x 14	6 ps	4128	3176
R	4GC	4	126.3	9.00 x 14	6 ps	4360	3887

YEAR	MODEL	ENGINE						
		CYLS	BORE	STROKE	DISPL	HP@RPM	C.R.	VLV
	Optional engine:							
	(1)	V8	4.00	3.688	371.0	260@4400		OH
1961	88	V8	4.125	3.688	394.3	250@4200	8.75	OH
	Super 88	V8	4.125	3.688	394.3	325@4600	10.0	OH
	98	V8	4.125	3.688	394.3	325@4600	10.0	OH
	F-85 (1)	V8	3.50	2.797	215.3	155@4800	8.75	OH
	F-85 Deluxe (1)	V8	3.50	2.797	215.3	155@4800	8.75	OH
	Optional engine:							
	(1)	V8	3.50	2.797	215.3	185@4800	10.25	OH
1962	F-85 Standard (1)	V8	3.50	2.797	215.3	155@4800	8.75	OH
	F-85 Deluxe (1)	V8	3.50	2.797	215.3	155@4800	8.75	OH
	88 (2)	V8	4.125	3.688	394.3	330@4600	10.25	OH
	Super 88 (2)	V8	4.125	3.688	394.3	330@4600	10.25	OH
	Starfire	V8	4.125	3.688	394.3	345@4600	10.5	OH
	98	V8	4.125	3.688	394.3	330@4600	10.5	OH
	F-85 Cutlass	V8	3.50	2.797	215.3	185@4800	10.25	OH
	Optional engine:							
	(1)	V8	3.50	2.797	215.3	185@4800	10.25	OH
	(2)	V8	4.125	3.688	394.3	260@4400	8.75	OH
1963	Standard F-85 (1)	V8	3.50	2.797	215.3	155@4800	8.75	OH
	Deluxe F-85 (1)	V8	3.50	2.797	215.3	155@4800	8.75	OH
	Cutlass F-85	V8	3.50	2.797	215.3	185@4800	10.25	OH
	Jet Fire F-85	V8	3.50	2.797	215.3	215@4600	10.25	OH
	88 (2)	V8	4.125	3.688	394.3	280@4400	10.25	OH
	Super 88	V8	4.125	3.688	394.3	330@4600	10.25	OH
	Starfire	V8	4.125	3.688	394.3	345@4800	10.5	OH
	98	V8	4.125	3.688	394.3	330@4600	10.25	OH
	Custom Sports Coupe 98	V8	4.125	3.688	394.3	345@4800	10.5	OH
	Optional engines:							
	(1)	V8	3.50	2.797	215.3	185@4800	10.25	OH
	(2)	V8	4.125	3.688	394.3	330@4600	10.25	OH
	(1)	V8	3.50	2.797	215.3	195@4800	10.75	OH
	(2)	V8	4.125	3.688	394.3	260@4400	8.75	OH
1964	Standard F-85	V6	3.75	3.406	225.7	155@4400	9.0	OH
	Deluxe F-85	V6	3.75	3.406	225.7	155@4400	9.0	OH
	Standard F-85 (1)	V8	3.938	3.391	330.2	230@4400	9.0	OH
	Deluxe F-85 (1)	V8	3.938	3.391	330.2	230@4400	9.0	OH
	Cutlass F-85	V8	3.938	3.391	330.2	290@4800	10.25	OH
	Vista-Cruiser F-85	V8	3.938	3.391	330.2	230@4400	9.0	OH

CARBURETOR MFR	MODEL	VEN	WHEEL-BASE	TIRES	BODY	WEIGHT	PRICE
R	7019052	2	123	8.00 x 14	6 ps	4031	2900
R	4GC	4	123	8.00 x 14	6 ps	4065	3176
R	4GC	4	126	8.50 x 14	6 ps	4231	3887
R	2GC	2	112	6.50 x 13	6 ps	2541	2384
R	2GC	2	112	6.50 x 13	6 ps	2547	2519
R	2GC	2	112	6.50 x 13	6 ps	2599	2457
R	2GC	2	112	6.50 x 13	6 ps	2634	2592
R	2GC	2	123	8.00 x 14	6 ps	4038	2997
R	2GC	2	123	8.00 x 14/	6 ps	4069	3273
				8.50 x 14			
R	4GC	4	123	8.00 x 14	6 pht2	4213	4131
R	4GC	4	126	8.50 x 14	6 ps	4258	3984
R	4GC	4	112	6.50 x 13	5 pc	2651	2694
R	4GC	4					
R	2GC	2					
R	2GC	2	112	6.50 x 13	6 ps	2629	2457
R	2GC	2	112	6.50 x 13	6 ps	2659	2592
R			112	6.50 x 13	6 pc	2679	2694
R			112	6.50 x 13	6 pht2	2774	3048
R	7023052	2	123	8.00 x 14	6 ps	3998	2995
R	4GC	4	123	8.00 x 14	6 ps	4027	3246
R	4GC	4	123	8.00 x 14/	6 pht2	4172	4129
				8.50 x 14			
R	4GC	4	126	8.50 x 14	6 ps	4240	3982
R	4GC	4	126	8.50 x 14	5 psc2	4285	4381
R	4GC	4					
R	4GC	4					
R	4GC	4					
R	2GC	2					
R			115	6.50 x 14	6 ps	2629	2397
R			115	6.50 x 14	6 ps	2659	2505
R	2GC	2	115	7.00 x 14	6 ps		2469
R	2GC	2	115	7.00 x 14	6 ps	3140	2577
R	4GC	4	115	7.00 x 14	5 psc2	3141	2644
R	2GC	2	115	7.00 x 14	6 psw4	3729	3072

YEAR	MODEL	ENGINE						
		CYLS	BORE	STROKE	DISPL	HP@RPM	C.R.	VLV
	Jetstar 88 (1)	V8	3.938	3.391	330.2	245@4600	10.25	OH
	Jetstar I	V8	4.125	3.688	393.3	345@4800	10.5	OH
	Dynamic 88 (2)	V8	4.125	3.688	394.3	280@4400	10.25	OH
	Super 88 (3)	V8	4.125	3.688	394.3	330@4600	10.25	OH
	Starfire	V8	4.125	3.688	394.3	345@4800	10.5	OH
	98 (3)	V8	4.125	3.688	394.3	330@4600	10.25	OH
	Optional engines:							
	(1)	V8	3.938	3.375	328.8	290@4800	10.25	
	(2)	V8	4.125	3.688	394.3	260@4400	8.75	
	(2)	V8	4.125	3.688	394.3	330@4600	10.25	
	(3)	V8	4.125	3.688	394.3	345@4800	10.5	
1965	Standard F-85	V6	3.75	3.406	225.7	155@4400	9.0	OH
	Deluxe F-85	V6	3.75	3.406	225.7	155@4400	9.0	OH
	Standard F-85	V8	3.938	3.391	330.2	250@4800	9.0	OH
	Deluxe F-85	V8	3.938	3.391	330.2	250@4800	9.0	OH
	Cutlass F-85	V8	3.938	3.391	330.2	315@5200	10.25	OH
	Vista-Cruiser F-85	V8	3.938	3.391	330.2	250@4800	9.0	OH
	Custom F-85	V8	3.938	3.391	330.2	250@4800	9.0	OH
	Jetstar 88 (2)	V8	3.938	3.391	330.2	260@4800	10.25	OH
	Jetstar I (2)	V8	3.938	3.391	330.2	260@4800	10.25	OH
	Dynamic 88 (3, 4)	V8	3.938	3.391	330.2	310@4400	10.25	OH
	Delta 88 (4, 5)	V8	3.938	3.391	330.2	310@4400	10.25	OH
	Starfire	V8	3.938	3.391	330.2	310@4400	10.25	OH
	98 (1)	V8	4.125	3.969	424.3	360@4800	10.25	OH
	F-85 4-4-2	V8	4.00	3.969	399.0	345@4800	10.25	OH
	Optional engines:							
	(1)	V8	3.938	3.391	330.2	310@4400	10.25	OH
	(2)	V8	3.938	3.391	330.2	315@5200	10.25	OH
	(3)	V8	4.125	3.969	424.3	300@4400	9.0	OH
	(4)	V8	4.125	3.969	424.3	360@4800	10.25	OH
	(5)	V8	4.125	3.969	424.3	370@4800	10.25	OH
1966	Standard F-85-L	V6	3.875	3.531	249.9	155@4200	8.5	OH
	Deluxe F-85-L	V6	3.875	3.531	249.9	155@4200	8.5	OH
	Standard F-85	V8	3.938	3.391	330.2	250@4800	9.0	OH
	Deluxe F-85	V8	3.938	3.391	330.2	250@4800	9.0	OH
	Cutlass F-85 (1)	V8	3.938	3.391	330.2	315@5200	10.25	OH
	Vista-Cruiser F-85	V8	3.938	3.391	330.2	250@4800	9.0	OH
	Custom F-85	V8	3.938	3.391	330.2	250@4800	9.0	OH
	F-85 4-4-2	V8	4.00	3.969	399.0	350@5000	10.5	OH
	Jetstar 88 (1)	V8	3.938	3.391	330.2	260	10.25	OH

MFR	CARBURETOR MODEL	VEN	WHEEL-BASE	TIRES	BODY	WEIGHT	PRICE
R	2GC	2	123	7.50 x 14	6 ps	3729	2935
R	4GC	4	123	8.00 x 14	5 psc2	4019	3603
R	2GC	2	123/120	8.00 x 14/	6 ps	3966	3005
				7.50 x 14			
R	4GC	4	123	8.00 x 14	6 ps	4009	3256
R	4GC	4	123	8.00 x 14	6 pht2	4167	4138
R	4GC	4	126	8.50 x 14	6 ps	4234	3993
R	4GC	4					
R	2GC	2					
R	4GC	4					
R	4GC	4					
			115	6.95 x 14	6 ps	2991	2346
			115	7.35 x 14	6 ps	3016	2451
R	2GC	2	115	6.95 x 14	6 ps	3174	2416
R	2GC	2	115	7.35 x 14	6 ps	3218	2521
R	4GC	4	115	7.35 x 14	5 psc2	3221	2586
R	2GC	2	120	7.75 x 14	6 psw2		2874
R	2GC	2	115	7.35 x 14	6 psw4	3762	3078
R	2GC	2	123	7.75 x 14	6 ps	3762	2878
R	2GC	2	123	7.75 x 14	5 psc2	3982	3528
R	2GC	2	123	8.25 x 14	6 ps	3908	2947
R	2GC	2	123	8.25 x 14	6 ps	3940	3094
R	2GC	2	123	8.25 x 14	5 psc2	4152	4063
R	4GC	4	126	8.55 x 14	6 ps	4186	3919
R	4GC	4	115	7.75 x 14			
R	2GC	2					
R	4GC	4					
R	2GC	2					
R	4GC	4					
R	4GC	4					
R	7026027	1	115	6.95 x 14	6 ps	3001	2401
R	7026027	1	115	7.35 x 14	6 ps	3023	2497
R	2GC	2	115	6.95 x 14	6 ps	3187	2471
R	2GC	2	115	7.35 x 14	6 ps	3210	2567
R	2GC	2	115	7.35 x 14	6 ps	3240	2673
R	2GC	2	120	8.25 x 14	6 psw4	3713	2935
R	2GC	2	115	7.35 x 14	6 psw4	3765	3137
R	4MV	4	115	7.35 x 14	6 pht2	3478	3015
R	7026058	4	123	7.75 x 14	6 ps	3765	2927

YEAR	MODEL	ENGINE						
		CYLS	BORE	STROKE	DISPL	HP@RPM	C.R.	VLV
	Dynamic 88 (2)	V8	4.125	3.969	424.3	310	10.25	OH
	Delta 88 (2)	V8	4.125	3.969	424.3	310	10.25	OH
	Starfire 88	V8	4.125	3.969	424.3	375@4800	10.5	OH
	98	V8	4.125	3.969	424.3	365@4800	10.25	OH
	Toronado	V8	4.125	3.969	424.3	385@4800	10.5	OH
	Toronado Custom	V8	4.125	3.969	424.3	365@4800	10.5	OH
	Optional engines:							
	(1)	V8	3.938	3.391	330.2	320@3600	10.25	OH
	(2)	V8	4.125	3.969	424.3	300@4400	9.0	OH
1967	Standard F-85-L	V6	3.875	3.531	249.9	155@4200	8.5	OH
	Cutlass F-85-L	V6	3.875	3.531	249.9	155@4200	8.5	OH
	Standard F-85 (2, 3)	V8	3.938	3.391	330.2	250@4800	9.0	OH
	Cutlass F-85 (2, 3)	V8	3.938	3.391	330.2	250@4800	9.0	OH
	Cutlass Supreme F-85 (2, 3, 4)	V8	3.938	3.391	330.2	320@5200	10.25	OH
	Vista-Cruiser F-85 (3)	V8	3.938	3.391	330.2	250@4800	9.0	OH
	Custom Vista-Cruiser F-85 (3)	V8	3.938	3.391	330.2	250@4800	9.0	OH
	Delmont 88, 330 (1, 5, 6, 7)	V8	3.938	3.391	330.2	250@4800	9.0	OH
	Delmont 88, 425	V8	4.125	3.969	424.3	300@4000	9.0	OH
	Delta 88, (5, 6)	V8	4.125	3.969	424.3	300@4000	9.0	OH
	Delta Custom 88 (5, 6)	V8	4.125	3.969	424.3	300@4000	9.0	OH
	98 (7)	V8	4.125	3.969	424.3	365@4800	10.25	OH
	Toronado	V8	4.125	3.969	424.3	385@4800	10.5	OH
	Toronado Deluxe	V8	4.125	3.969	424.3	385@4800	10.5	OH
	F-85 4-4-2	V8	4.00	3.969	399.0	350@5000	10.5	OH
	Optional engines:							
	(1)	V8	3.938	3.391	330.2	260@4800	10.25	
	(2)	V8	3.938	3.391	330.2	310@5200	9.0	
	(3)	V8	3.938	3.391	330.2	320@5200	10.25	
	(4)	V8	4.00	3.969	399.0	300@4600	10.5	
	(5)	V8	4.125	3.969	424.3	310@4400	10.25	
	(6)	V8	4.125	3.969	424.3	365@4800	10.25	
	(7)	V8	4.125	3.969	424.3	375@4800	10.5	
1968	Standard F-85-L	V6	3.875	3.531	249.9	155@4200	8.5	OH
	Cutlass F-85-L	V6	3.875	3.351	249.9	155@4200	8.5	OH
	Standard F-85 (1)	V8	4.062	3.385	351.0	250@4400	9.0	OH
	Cutlass F-85 (1)	V8	4.062	3.385	351.0	250@4400	9.0	OH
	Cutlass Supreme F-85 (2)	V8	4.062	3.385	351.0	310@4200	10.25	OH
	Custom Vista-Cruiser F-85 (1, 2, 3)	V8	4.062	3.385	351.0	310@4200	10.25	OH
	F-85 4-4-2 (2, 3, 4)	V8	3.875	4.25	401.0	350@4800	10.5	OH
	Delmont 88 (1, 5, 6)	V8	4.057	3.385	350.1	250@4400	9.0	OH
	Delta 88 (6)	V8	4.125	4.25	454.4	310@4200	10.25	OH

MFR	CARBURETOR MODEL	VEN	WHEEL-BASE	TIRES	BODY	WEIGHT	PRICE
R	7026250	4	123	8.25 x 14	6 ps	3920	3013
R	7026250	4	123	8.25 x 14	6 ps	3969	3160
R	7026250	4	123	8.25 x 14	6 pht2	3988	3564
R		4	126	8.85 x 15	6 ps	4182	3966
R		4	119	8.85 x 15	6 psc2	4312	4617
R		4	119	8.85 x 15	6 psc2	4386	4812
R	4MV	4					
R	2GC	2					
R	7026027	1	115	7.75 x 14	6 ps	3031	2457
R	7026027	1	115	7.75 x 14	6 ps	3055	2552
R	7026027	2	115	7.75 x 14	6 ps	3208	2527
R	7026027	2	115	7.75 x 14	6 ps	3223	2622
R	4MV	4	115	7.75 x 14	6 ps	3258	2726
R	2GC	2	120	8.25 x 14	9psw4	3858	3136
R	2GC	2	115	7.75 x 14	6 psw4	3796	3228
R	2GC	2	123	8.55 x 14	6 ps	3867	3008
R	7026250	4	123	8.55 x 14	6 ps	3968	3071
R	7026250	4	123	8.55 x 14	6 ps	3986	3218
R	7026250	4	123	8.55 x 14	6 pht4	4081	3582
R	4MV	4	126	8.85 x 14	6 ps	4242	4009
R	4MV	4	119	8.85 x 14	6 pht2	4310	4674
R	4MV	4	119	8.85 x 14	6 pht2	4362	4896
R	7026250	4	115	7.75 x 14	6 pht2		
R	7026028	1	116	7.75 x 14	6 ps	3108	2560
R	7026028	1	116	7.75 x 14	6 ps	3143	2674
R	7028250	4	116	7.75 x 14	6 ps	3304	2665
R	7028250	4	116	7.75 x 14	6 ps	3325	2779
R	7028250	4	116/112	7.75 x 14	6 ps		2884
R	7028250	4	121	8.25 x 14	6 psw4	3917	3367
R	7028251	4	112	F70 x 14	6 pht2	3512	3150
R	7028250	4	123	8.55 x 14	6 ps	3873	3146
R	7029250	4	123	8.55 x 14	6 ps	3979	3357

YEAR	MODEL	ENGINE						
		CYLS	BORE	STROKE	DISPL	HP@RPM	C.R.	VLV
	Custom Delta 88 (5, 6)	V8	4.125	4.25	454.4	310@4200	10.25	OH
	98	V8	4.125	4.25	454.4	365@4600	10.25	OH
	Toronado (7)	V8	4.125	4.25	454.4	375@4600	10.25	OH
	Optional engines:							
	(1)	V8	4.062	3.385	351.0	310@4800	10.25	
	(2)	V8	3.875	4.25	401.0	290@4600	9.0	
	(3)	V8	3.875	4.25	401.0	325@4600	10.5	
	(4)	V8	3.875	4.25	401.0	360@5400	10.5	
	(5)	V8	4.125	4.25	454.4	320@4200	10.75	
	(6)	V8	4.125	4.25	454.4	365@4600		
	(7)	V8	4.125	4.25	454.4	400	10.25	
1969	F-85	V6	3.875	3.531	249.9	155@4200	8.5	OH
	Cutlass F-85 (1)	V6	3.875	3.531	249.9	155@4200	8.5	OH
	Cutlass Supreme F-85 (1)	V8	4.062	3.385	351.0	310@4800	10.25	OH
	F-85 4-4-2 (2)	V8	3.875	4.25	401.0	350@4800	10.5	OH
	Vista-Cruiser F-85	V8	4.062	3.385	351.0	310@4800	10.25	OH
	Delta 88 (5)	V8	4.062	3.385	351.0	250@4400	9.0	OH
	Delta Custom 88 (3)	V8	4.125	4.25	454.4	310@4200	9.0	OH
	Delta Royale (3)	V8	4.125	4.25	454.4	310@4200	9.0	OH
	98	V8	4.125	4.25	454.4	365@4600	10.25	OH
	Toronado (4)	V8	4.125	4.25	454.4	375@4600	10.25	OH
	Optional engines:							
	(1)	V8	4.062	3.385	351.0	325@5400	10.5	
	(2)	V8	3.875	4.25	401.0	325@4600	10.5	
	(2)	V8	3.875	4.25	401.0	360@5400	10.5	
	(3)	V8	4.125	4.25	454.4	390@5000	10.25	
	(4)	V8	4.125	4.25	454.4	400@4800	10.25	

OMEGA — — Suspensions International Corp., Manhasset, N.Y.; Omega Cars Division, Charlotte, N.C., 1966-

YEAR	MODEL	CYLS	BORE	STROKE	DISPL	HP@RPM	C.R.	VLV
1966		V8	4.00	3.00	301.6			OH
1967		V8	4.00	2.875	289.0	225@6000		OH
1968	GT-R	V8	4.00	2.875	289.0			OH

OVERLAND — — Willys-Overland Co., Toledo, Oh., 1903-30

YEAR	MODEL	CYLS	BORE	STROKE	DISPL	HP@RPM	C.R.	VLV
1930	Whippet 96A	4	3.125	4.75	145.7	40@3200	5.4	L
	Whippet 98A	6	3.125	3.875	178.3	50@3000	5.12	L
	Became Willys-Overland.							

MFR	CARBURETOR MODEL	VEN	WHEEL-BASE	TIRES	BODY	WEIGHT	PRICE
R	7029250	4	123	8.55 x 14	6 pht4	4059	3721
R	7029250	4	126	8.85 x 14	6 ps	4197	4155
R	4MV	4	119	8.85 x 15	6 pht2	4322	4750
R	1BV	1	116		6 pc2	3076	2544
R	1BV	1	116		6 ps	3151	2705
R	4MV	4	116		6 ps	3353	2921
R	4MV	4	112		6 pht2	3512	3184
R	4MV	4	121		6 psw4	3927	3440
R	2GC	2	124		6 ps	3975	3205
R	2GC	2	124		6 ps	4064	3415
R	2GC	2	124		6 pht2	4067	3819
R	4MV	4	127		6 ps	4245	4238
R	4MV	4	119		6 pht2	4295	4818
							8500
H			94.5	7.35 x 14	2 pc	2595	8250
			94.5	7.35 x 14	2 pc	2500	
T	S-40	1	103.2	4.75 x 19	5 ps	2412	535
T	S-40	1	112.5	5.00 x 19	5 ps	2693	785

YEAR	MODEL	ENGINE						
		CYLS	BORE	STROKE	DISPL	HP@RPM	C.R.	VLV

PACKARD — — Packard Motor Car Co., Detroit, Mich., 1903-55; Studebaker-Packard Corp., Detroit, Mich., 1955-58

YEAR	MODEL	CYLS	BORE	STROKE	DISPL	HP@RPM	C.R.	VLV
1930	Standard Eight, 726	8	3.188	5.00	319.2	90@3200		L
	Standard Eight, 733	8	3.188	5.00	319.2	90@3200		L
	Custom Eight, 740	8	3.50	5.00	384.8	106@3200		L
	DeLuxe Eight, 745	8	3.50	5.00	384.8	106@3200		L
	Eight Speedster, 734	8	3.50	5.00	384.8	125@3400		L
1931	Standard Eight, 826	8	3.188	5.00	319.2	100@3200		L
	Standard Eight, 833	8	3.188	5.00	319.2	100@3200		L
	DeLuxe Eight, 840	8	3.50	5.00	384.8	120@3200		L
	DeLuxe Eight, 845	8	3.50	5.00	384.8	120@3200		L
1932	Standard Eight, 901	8	3.188	5.00	319.2	110@3200	6.0	L
	Standard Eight, 902	8	3.188	5.00	319.2	110@3200	6.0	L
	DeLuxe Eight, 903	8	3.188	5.00	319.2	110@3200	6.0	L
	DeLuxe Eight, 904	8	3.188	5.00	319.2	110@3200	6.0	L
	Eight, 900	8	3.188	5.00	319.2	110@3200	6.0	L
	Twelve, 905	V12	3.438	4.00	445.5	160@3200	6.0	L
	Twelve, 906	V12	3.438	4.00	445.5	160@3200	6.0	L
1933	Eight, 1001	8	3.188	5.00	319.2	120@3200	6.0	L
	Eight, 1002	8	3.188	5.00	319.2	120@3200	6.0	L
	Super Eight, 1003	8	3.50	5.00	384.8	145@3200	6.0	L
	Super Eight, 1004	8	3.50	5.00	384.8	145@3200	6.0	L
	Twelve, 1005	V12	3.438	4.00	445.5	160@3200	6.0	L
	Twelve, 1006	V12	3.438	4.00	445.5	160@3200	6.0	L
1934	Eight, 1100	8	3.188	5.00	319.2	120@3200	6.0	L
	Eight, 1101	8	3.188	5.00	319.2	120@3200	6.0	L
	Eight, 1102	8	3.188	5.00	319.2	120@3200	6.0	L
	Super Eight, 1103	8	3.50	5.00	384.8	145@3200	6.0	L
	Super Eight, 1104	8	3.50	5.00	384.8	145@3200	6.0	L
	Super Eight, 1105	8	3.50	5.00	384.8	145@3200	6.0	L
	Twelve, 1107	V12	3.438	4.00	445.5	160@3200	6.0	L
	Twelve, 1108	V12	3.438	4.00	445.5	160@3200	6.0	L
1935	120	8	3.25	3.875	257.2	110@3850	6.5	L
	Eight, 1200	8	3.188	5.00	319.2	130@3200	6.5	L
	Eight, 1201	8	3.188	5.00	319.2	130@3200	6.5	L
	Eight, 1202	8	3.188	5.00	319.2	130@3200	6.5	L
	Super Eight, 1203	8	3.50	5.00	384.8	150@3200	6.0	L
	Super Eight, 1204	8	3.50	5.00	384.8	150@3200	6.0	L
	Super Eight, 1205	8	3.50	5.00	384.8	150@3200	6.0	L
	Twelve, 1207	V12	3.438	4.25	445.5	175@3200	6.4	L
	Twelve, 1208	V12	3.438	4.25	445.5	175@3200	6.4	L

MFR	CARBURETOR MODEL	VEN	WHEEL-BASE	TIRES	BODY	WEIGHT	PRICE
D			127.5	6.00 x 20	5 ps	4265	2085
D			134.5	6.50 x 20	5 ps	4325	2275
D			140.5	7.00 x 19	5 ps	4560	3585
D			145.5	7.00 x 19	5 ps	4805	4985
D		2	134.0	6.50 x 19	4 ps	4580	6000
D			127.5	6.50 x 19	5 ps	4479	2385
D			134.5	6.50 x 19	5 ps	4488	2675
D			140.5	7.00 x 19	5 ps	4955	3795
D			145.5	7.00 x 19	7 ps	5080	4285
O			129.5	6.50 x 19	5 ps	4570	2350
O			136.5	6.50 x 19	5 ps	4590	2885
O			142.1	7.00 x 19	5 ps	5045	3445
O			147.1	7.00 x 19	7 ps	5195	3695
O			127.8	6.50 x 17	5 ps	4115	1895
S	EE-3	2	142.1	7.50 x 18	5 ps	5635	4245
S	EE-3	2	147.8	7.50 x 18	7 ps	5765	4495
S	EE22	2	127.5	7.00 x 17	5 ps	4335	2150
S	EE22	2	136	7.00 x 17	5 ps	4590	2385
S	EE22	2	135	7.00 x 17	5 ps	4815	2750
S	EE22	2	142	7.00 x 17	7 ps	4965	3090
S	EE3	2	142	7.50 x 17	5 ps	5385	3860
S	EE3	2	147	7.50 x 17	7 ps	5600	4085
S	EE22	2	129	7.00 x 17	5 ps	4640	2350
S	EE22	2	136	7.00 x 17	5 ps	4660	2585
S	EE22	2	141	7.00 x 17	7 ps	4945	2655
S	EE22	2	135	7.00 x 17	5 ps	4890	2950
S	EE22	2	142	7.00 x 17	5 pcs	4985	3255
S	EE22	2	147	7.00 x 17	7 ps	5245	3290
S	EE3	2	142	7.50 x 17	5 ps	5530	3960
S	EE3	2	147	7.50 x 17	7 ps	5700	4185
S	EE-14	2	120	7.00 x 16	5 ps	3510	1060
S	EE23	2	127	7.00 x 17	5 ps	4780	2385
S	EE23	2	134	7.00 x 17	5 ps	4815	2585
S	EE23	2	139	7.00 x 17	5 ps	4955	2755
S	EE23	2	132	7.00 x 17	5 ps	5030	2990
S	EE23	2	139	7.00 x 17	5 pcs	5150	3170
S	EE23	2	144	7.00 x 17	5 ps	5300	3390
S	EE3	2	139	7.50 x 17	5 ps	5700	3960
S	EE3	2	144	7.50 x 17	7 ps	5790	4285

YEAR	MODEL	ENGINE						
		CYLS	BORE	STROKE	DISPL	HP@RPM	C.R.	VLV
1936	120B	8	3.25	4.25	282.1	120@3800	6.5	L
	Eight, 1400	8	3.188	5.00	319.2	130@3200	6.5	L
	Eight, 1401	8	3.188	5.00	319.2	130@3200	6.5	L
	Eight, 1402	8	3.188	5.00	319.2	130@3200	6.5	L
	Super Eight, 1403	8	3.50	5.00	384.8	150@3200	6.3	L
	Super Eight, 1404	8	3.50	5.00	384.8	150@3200	6.3	L
	Super Eight, 1405	8	3.50	5.00	384.8	150@3200	6.3	L
	Twelve, 1407	V12	3.438	4.25	473.4	175@3200	6.4	L
	Twelve, 1408	V12	3.438	4.25	473.4	175@3200	6.4	L
1937	Six, 115C	6	3.438	4.25	236.7	100@3600	6.3	L
	120	8	3.25	4.25	282.1	120@3600	6.5	L
	Super Eight, 1500	8	3.188	5.00	319.2	130@3200	6.5	L
	Super Eight, 1501	8	3.188	5.00	319.2	130@3200	6.5	L
	Super Eight, 1502	8	3.188	5.00	319.2	130@3200	6.5	L
	Twelve, 1506	V12	3.438	4.25	473.4	175@3200	6.4	L
	Twelve, 1507	V12	3.438	4.25	473.4	175@3200	6.4	L
	Twelve, 1508	V12	3.438	4.25	473.4	175@3200	6.4	L
1938	Six, 1600	6	3.50	4.25	245.3	100@3600	6.52	L
	Eight, 1601	8	3.25	4.25	282.1	120@3800	6.6	L
	Eight, 1601-D	8	3.25	4.25	282.1	120@3800	6.6	L
	Eight, 1602	8	3.25	4.25	282.1	120@3800	6.6	L
	Super Eight, 1603	8	3.188	5.00	319.2	130@3200	6.5	L
	Super Eight, 1605	8	3.188	5.00	319.2	130@3200	6.5	L
	Twelve, 1607	V12	3.438	4.25	473.4	175@3200	6.5	L
	Twelve, 1608	V12	3.438	4.25	473.4	175@3200	6.5	L
1939	Six (110), 1700	6	3.50	4.25	245.3	100@3200	6.52	L
	Eight, 1701	8	3.25	4.25	282.1	120@3600	6.41	L
	Eight, 1702	8	3.25	4.25	282.1	120@3600	6.41	L
	Super Eight, 1703	8	3.188	5.00	319.2	130@3200	6.45	L
	Super Eight, 1705	8	3.188	5.00	319.2	130@3200	6.45	L
	Twelve, 1707	V12	3.438	4.25	473.4	175@3200	6.3	L
	Twelve, 1708	V12	3.438	4.25	473.4	175@3200	6.3	L
1940	Six (110), 1800	6	3.50	4.25	245.3	100@3200	6.39	L
	Eight (120), 1801	8	3.25	4.25	282.1	120@3600	6.41	L
	Eight (120), 1801	8	3.25	4.25	282.1	120@3600	6.41	L
	Super Eight (160), 1803	8	3.50	4.625	356.0	160@3500	6.45	L
	Super Eight (160), 1804	8	3.50	4.625	356.0	160@3500	6.45	L
	Super Eight (160), 1805	8	3.50	4.625	356.0	160@3500	6.45	L
	Custom Super Eight, 1806	8	3.50	4.625	356.0	160@3500	6.45	L
	Custom Super Eight, 1807	8	3.50	4.625	356.0	160@3500	6.45	L
	Custom Super Eight, 1808	8	3.50	4.625	356.0	160@3500	6.45	L

MFR	CARBURETOR MODEL	VEN	WHEEL-BASE	TIRES	BODY	WEIGHT	PRICE
S	EE-14	2	120	7.00 x 16	5 ps	3535	1075
S	EE23	2	127	7.00 x 17	5 ps	4815	2385
S	EE23	2	134	7.00 x 17	5 ps	4975	2585
S	EE23	2	139	7.00 x 17	7 ps	4955	2755
S	EE23	2	132	7.00 x 17	5 ps	5080	2990
S	EE23	2	139	7.00 x 17	5 pcs	5100	3170
S	EE23	2	144	7.00 x 17	7 ps	5300	3390
S	EE3	2	139	7.50 x 17	5 ps	5695	3960
S	EE3	2	144	7.50 x 17	7 ps	5810	4285
CG	AOC-2	1	115	6.50 x 17	5 ps	3265	1060
S	EE-14	2	120/138	7.00 x 16	5 ps	3465	1235
S	EE23	2	127	7.50 x 16	5 ps	4530	2630
S	EE23	2	134	7.50 x 16	5 ps	4670	2835
S	EE23	2	139	7.50 x 16	5 ps	4700	3010
S	EE-3	2	132	8.25 x 16	5 ps	5395	3870
S	EE-3	2	139	8.25 x 16	5 ps	5525	3940
S	EE-3	2	144	8.25 x 16	5 ps	5600	4270
CG	AO-25	1	122	6.50 x 16	5 ps	3525	1070
S	EE-14	2	127	7.00 x 16	5 ps	3650	1325
S	EE-14	2	127	7.00 x 16	5 ps	3685	1540
S	EE-14	2	148	7.00 x 16	7 ps	4195	1955
S	EE23	2	127	7.50 x 16	5 ps	4530	2790
S	EE23	2	139	7.50 x 16	7 ps	4700	3165
S	EE-3	2	134	8.25 x 16	5 ps	5525	4155
S	EE-3	2	139	8.25 x 16	7 ps	5600	4485
CG	AOC-25	1	122	6.50 x 16	5 ps	3400	995
S	EE-16	2	127	7.00 x 16	5 ps	3605	1196
S	EE-16	2	148	7.00 x 16	7 ps	4100	1702
S	EE-23	2	127	7.00 x 16	5 ps	3930	1732
S	EE-23	2	148	7.00 x 16	7 ps	4425	2156
S	EE-3	2	134.4	8.25 x 16	5 pcs	5590	4255
S	EE-3	2	134.4	8.25 x 16	7 ps	5750	4485
S	BXOV-26	1	122	6.25 x 16	5 ps	3200	996
S	EE-16	2	127	6.50 x 16	5 ps	3520	1166
S	EE-16	2	127	6.50 x 16	5 ps	3495	1246
	AAV-16	2	127	7.00 x 16	5 ps	3855	1655
S	AAV-16	2	138	7.00 x 16	5 ps	4165	1919
S	AAV-16	2	148	7.00 x 16	7 ps	4425	2051
S	AAV-16	2	127	7.00 x 16	5 pcs	3900	2243
S	AAV-16	2	138	7.00 x 16	5 ps	4210	2422
S	AAV-16	2	148	7.00 x 16	7 ps	4510	2554

YEAR	MODEL	ENGINE						
		CYLS	BORE	STROKE	DISPL	HP@RPM	C.R.	VLV
1941	Six (110) 1900	6	3.50	4.25	245.3	100@3600	6.71	L
	DeLuxe Six (110), 1900	6	3.50	4.25	245.3	100@3600	6.71	L
	Eight (120), 1901	8	3.25	4.25	282.0	120@3600	6.85	L
	Clipper, 1951	8	3.25	4.25	282.0	125@3600	6.85	L
	Super Eight (160), 1903	8	3.50	4.625	356.0	160@3600	6.85	L
	DeLuxe Super Eight (160), 1903	8	3.50	4.625	356.0	160@3600	6.85	L
	DeLuxe Super Eight (160), 1904	8	3.50	4.625	356.0	160@3600	6.85	L
	Custom Super Eight (180), 1906	8	3.50	4.625	356.0	160@3600	6.85	L
	Custom Super Eight (180) 1907	8	3.50	4.625	356.0	160@3600	6.85	L
	Custom Super Eight (180) 1908	8	3.50	4.625	356.0	160@3600	6.85	L
1942	Clipper Special (110), 2000	6	3.50	4.25	245.3	105@3600	6.71	L
	Clipper Custom (110), 2010	6	3.50	4.25	245.3	105@3600	6.71	L
	Clipper Custom (110), 2020	6	3.50	4.25	245.3	105@3600	6.71	L
	Clipper Special (120), 2001	8	3.25	4.25	282.0	125@3600	6.85	L
	Clipper Custom (120), 2011	8	3.25	4.25	282.0	125@3600	6.85	L
	Clipper Custom (120), 2021	8	3.25	4.25	282.0	125@3600	6.85	L
	Super Eight (160), 2003	8	3.50	4.625	356.0	165@3600	6.85	L
	Super Eight (160), 2023	8	3.50	4.625	356.0	165@3600	6.85	L
	Super Eight (160), 2004	8	3.50	4.625	356.0	165@3600	6.85	L
	Super Eight (160), 2005	8	3.50	4.625	356.0	165@3600	6.85	L
	Super Eight (160), 2055	8	3.50	4.625	356.0	165@3600	6.85	L
	Custom Super 8 Clipper (180) 2006	8	3.50	4.625	356.0	165@3600	6.85	L
	Cus. Sup. 8 Clipper (180) 2006 Sp.	8	3.50	4.625	356.0	165@3600	6.85	L
	Cus. Sup. 8 Clipper (180) 2007	8	3.50	4.625	356.0	165@3600	6.85	L
	Cus. Sup. 8 Clipper (180) 2008	8	3.50	4.625	356.0	165@3600	6.85	L
1946	Six Clipper, 2100	6	3.50	4.25	245.3	105@3600	6.71	L
	Eight Clipper, 2101, 2111	8	3.25	4.25	282.0	125@3600	6.85	L
	Super Eight, 2103	8	3.50	4.625	356.0	165@3600	6.85	L
	Custom Super Eight, 2106, 2126	8	3.50	4.625	356.0	165@3600	6.85	L
1947	Six, Clipper, 2100, 2130	6	3.50	4.25	245.3	105@3600	6.71	L
	Eight Clipper, 2101, 2111	8	3.25	4.25	282.0	125@3600	6.85	L
	Super Eight, 2103	8	3.50	4.625	356.0	165@3600	6.85	L
	Custom Super Eight, 2106, 2126	8	3.50	4.625	356.0	165@3600	6.85	L
1948	Eight, 2201	8	3.50	3.75	288.6	130@3600	7.0	L
	Eight Deluxe, 2211	8	3.50	3.75	288.6	130@3600	7.0	L
	Super Eight, 2202, 2232	8	3.50	4.25	327.1	145@3600	7.0	L
	Super Eight DeLuxe, 2222	8	3.50	4.25	327.1	145@3600	7.0	L
	Custom Eight, 2206, 2226, 2233	8	3.50	4.625	356.0	160@3600	7.0	L
1949	Eight, 2201, 2211	8	3.50	3.75	288.6	135@3600	7.0	L
	Super 8 2202, 2222, 2232	8	3.50	4.25	327.1	145@3600	7.0	L
	Custom 8 2206, 2226, 2233	8	3.50	4.625	356.0	160@3600	7.0	L

MFR	CARBURETOR MODEL	VEN	WHEEL-BASE	TIRES	BODY	WEIGHT	PRICE
S	BXOV-26	1	122	6.50 x 15	5 ps	3260	1076
S	BXOV-26	1	122	6.50 x 15	5 ps	3280	1136
S	EE-16	1	127	7.00 x 15	5 ps	3535	1291
C	WDO	2	127	7.00 x 15	5 ps	3725	1420
S	AAV-26	2	127	7.00 x 16	5 ps	3995	1795
S	AAV-26	2	127	7.00 x 16	4 pcv2	3985	2112
S	AAV-26	2	138	7.00 x 16	5 ps	4305	2054
S	AAV-26	2	127	7.00 x 16	5 pcv2	4040	4595
S	AAV-26	2	138	7.00 x 16	5 ps	4350	2632
S	AAV-26	2	148	7.00 x 16	7 ps	4590	2769
C	WA1-530S	1	120	6.50 x 15	5 ps	3435	1232
C	WA1-530S	1	120	6.50 x 16	5 ps	3460	1299
C	WA1-530S	1	122	6.50 x 15	5 pcv2	3315	1375
C	WDQ-512S	2	120	6.50 x 15	5 ps	3560	1275
C	WDQ-512S	2	120	6.50 x 17	5 ps	3585	1341
C	WDQ-512S	2	127	7.00 x 15	5 pcv2	3905	1786
C	WDO-531S	2	127	7.00 x 15	6 ps	4005	1688
C	WDO-531S	2	127	7.00 x 15	5 pcv2	3905	1786
C	WDO-531S	2	138	7.00 x 16	6 ps	4090	1893
C	WDO-531S	2	148	7.00 x 16	7 ps	4325	2034
C	WDO-531S	2	148	7.00 x 16	7 ps	4315	1888
C	WDO-531S	2	127	7.00 x 15	6 ps	4030	2196
C	WDO-531S	2	127	7.00 x 15	5 pcv2	3920	4519
C	WDO-531S	2	138	7.00 x 16	6 ps	4280	2440
C	WDO-531S	2	148	7.00 x 16	7 ps	4525	2523
C	WA1-530S	1	120	6.50 x 15	6 ps	3435	1306
C	WDO-512S	2	120/127	6.50 x 15	8 ps	3520	1315
C	WDO-512S	2	127	7.00 x 15	6 ps	4005	1728
C	WDO-531S	2	127/148	7.00 x 15	6 ps	4030	2136
C	WA1-530S	1	120	6.50 x 15	6 ps	3495	1745
C	WDO-512S	2	120	6.50 x 15	6 ps	3670	1947
C	WDO-531S	2	127	7.00 x 15	6 ps	3995	2391
C	WDO-531S	2	127	7.00 x 15	6 ps	4060	3274
C	WDO-644S	2	120/148	6.50 x 16	6 ps		2150
C	WDO-644S	2	120	6.50 x 16	6 ps		2375
C	WDO-643A	2	120/141	7.00 x 15	6 ps		2690
C	WDO-643A	2	120/141	7.00 x 15	7 ps		3650
C	WDO-531S	2	127/148	7.00 x 15	6 ps		3675
C	WDO-644SA	2	120	6.50 x 16	6 ps	3815	2249
C	WDO-643A	2	120/141	7.00 x 15	6 ps		2827
C	WDO-531S	2	127/148	7.00 x 15	6 ps		3750

YEAR	MODEL	ENGINE						
		CYLS	BORE	STROKE	DISPL	HP@RPM	C.R.	VLV
	Second series:							
	Eight, 2301	8	3.50	3.75	288.6	135@3600	7.0	L
	Super Eight, 2302	8	3.50	4.25	327.1	150@3600	7.0	L
	Super Eight Deluxe, 2332	8	3.50	4.25	327.1	150@3600	7.0	L
	Custom Eight, 2306, 2333	8	3.50	4.625	356.0	160@3600	7.0	L
1950	Eight, 2301	8	3.50	3.75	288.6	135@3600	7.0	L
	Super Eight, 2302	8	3.50	4.25	327.1	150@3600	7.0	L
	Super Eight, 2322	8	3.50	4.25	327.1	150@3600	7.0	L
	Super Eight, 2332	8	3.50	4.25	327.1	150@3600	7.0	L
	Custom Eight, 2306	8	3.50	4.625	356.0	160@3600	7.0	L
	Custom Eight, 2333	8	3.50	4.625	356.0	160@3600	7.0	L
1951	200, 2401	8	3.50	3.75	288.6	135@3600	7.0	L
	200 DeLuxe, 2401	8	3.50	3.75	288.6	135@3600	7.0	L
	250, 2401	8	3.50	4.25	327.1	150@3600	7.0	L
	300, 2402	8	3.50	4.25	327.1	150@3600	7.0	L
	400. 2406	8	3.50	4.25	327.1	150@3600	7.0	L
1952	200, 2501	8	3.50	3.75	288.6	135@3600	7.0	L
	200 Deluxe, 2501	8	3.50	3.75	288.6	135@3600	7.0	L
	250, 2531	8	3.50	4.25	327.1	150@3600	7.0	L
	300, 2502	8	3.50	4.25	327.1	150@3600	7.0	L
	400, 2506	8	3.50	4.25	327.1	155@3600	7.8	L
1953	Clipper, 2601	8	3.50	3.75	288.6	150@4000	7.7	L
	Clipper DeLuxe, 2611	8	3.50	4.25	327.1	160@3600	8.0	L
	Cavalier, 2602, 2631	8	3.50	4.25	327.1	180@4000	8.0	L
	Patrician, 2606	8	3.50	4.50	346.4	180@4000	8.0	L
	Executive, 2626	8	3.50	4.50	364.4	180@4000	8.0	L
1954	Cavalier, 5402	8	3.50	4.25	327.1	185@4000	8.0	L
	Patrician, 5406	8	3.562	4.50	358.8	212@4000	8.7	L
	Pacific, 5431	8	3.562	4.50	358.8	212@4000	8.7	L
	Series 5426	8	3.562	4.50	358.8	212@4000	8.7	L
	Note: Clipper for 1954-56 is considered a separate make and is so listed for those model years.							
1955	Patrician, 5582	V8	4.00	3.50	351.9	260@4600	8.5	OH
	Caribbean, 5588	V8	4.00	3.50	351.9	275@4800	8.5	OH
1956	Patrician, 5682	V8	4.125	3.50	374.2	290@4600	10.0	OH
	Caribbean, 5697	V8	4.125	3.50	374.2	310@4600	10.0	OH
1957	Clipper, 57L (Supercharged)	V8	3.562	3.125	249.2	275@4800	7.8	OH
1958	8-58L	V8	3.562	3.625	289.1	225@4500	8.3	OH
	Hawk, 8-58LS	V8	3.562	3.625	289.1	275@4800	7.8	OH

MFR	CARBURETOR MODEL	VEN	WHEEL-BASE	TIRES	BODY	WEIGHT	PRICE
C	WDO-644SA	2	120	7.60 x 15	6 ps	3815	2249
C	WDO-643SA	2	127/141	7.60 x 15/	6 ps	3870	2633
				8.20 x 15	6 pcv2		
C	WDO-643SA	2	127	8.20 x 15	6 pcV	4260	3350
C	WDO-531SA	2	127	8.20 x 15	6 ps	4310	3975
V	WDO-644SA	2	120	7.60 x 15	6 ps	3815	2249
C	WDO-643SA	2	127	7.60 x 15	6 ps	3870	2633
C	WDO-643SA	2	141	8.20 x 15	7 ps	4600	3950
C	WDO-643SA	2	127	8.20 x 15	5pcv2	4110	3350
C	WDO-531SA	2	127	8.20 x 15	6 ps	4310	3975
C	WDO-531SA	2	127	8.20 x 15	5 pcv2	4530	4520
C	WGD-784S	2	122	7.60 x 15	6 ps	3665	2469
C	WGD-784S	2	122	7.60 x 15	6 ps	3660	2616
C	WGD-767S	2	122	8.00 x 15	6 pht2	3820	3234
C	WGD-767S	2	127	8.00 x 15	6 ps	3875	3034
C	WGD-767S	2	127	8.00 x 15	6 ps	4115	3662
C	WGD-784S	2	122	7.60 x 15	6 ps	3680	2545
C	WGD-784S	2	122	7.60 x 15	6 ps	3685	2695
C	WGD-784S	2	122	8.00 x 15	6 pht2	3805	3318
C	WGD-928S	2	127	8.00 x 15	6 ps	3880	3116
C	WGD-928S	2	127	8.00 x 15	6 ps	4100	3797
C	WGD-784S	2	122	7.60 x 15	6 ps	3730	2598
C	WGD-928S	2	122	7.60 x 15	6 ps	3760	2745
C	WCFB-985S	4	127	8.00 x 15	6 ps	3975	3244
C	WCFB-985S	4	127	8.00 x 15	6 ps	4190	3740
C	WCFB-985S	4	149	8.20 x 15	8 ps	4650	6900
C	WCFB-2103S	4	127	8.00 x 15	6 ps	3955	3344
C	WCFB-2212S	4	127	8.00 x 15	6 ps	4190	3890
C	WCFB-2212S	4	122	8.00 x 15	6 pht2	4065	3827
C	WCFB-2212S	4	149	8.20 x 15	8 ps	4650	5610
R	4GC	4	127	8.00 x 15	6 ps	4275	3890
R		4	127	8.00 x 15	6 pcv2	4755	5932
R		4	127	8.00 x 15	6 ps	4045	4160
R		2 x 4	127	8.00 x 15	6 pht2	4590	5495
S	WW6-121	2	116.5/	7.60 x 15	6 ps	3570	3212
			120.5				
C	2575S	4	116.5/	8.00 x 14	6 ps	3505	3212
			120.5				
S	WWG-122A	2	120.5	8.00 x 14	6 pht2	3470	3995

YEAR	MODEL	ENGINE CYLS	BORE	STROKE	DISPL	HP@RPM	C.R.	VLV

PANDA — — Small Cars, Inc., Kansas City, Mo., 1955-56

YEAR	MODEL	CYLS	BORE	STROKE	DISPL	HP@RPM	C.R.	VLV
1955	Deluxe	F2	3.65	3.25	68.0	27@3600	6.1	2-Cycle
	Deluxe	4	2.50	2.25	44.2	26@5100	7.1	L
	The two-cycle engine was a flat, opposed Koehler. The four-cylinder engine was by Aerojet.							

PANTHER — — Panther Automobile Co., Bedford Hills, N.Y., 1962-63

YEAR	MODEL	CYLS	BORE	STROKE	DISPL	HP@RPM	C.R.	VLV
1962	Standard	V8			157.4	145@5000		
	M	V8			157.4	190@6500		

PEERLESS — — Peerless Motor Car Co., Cleveland, Oh., 1900-32

YEAR	MODEL	CYLS	BORE	STROKE	DISPL	HP@RPM	C.R.	VLV
1930	Standard Eight	8	2.875	4.75	246.7	85@3200	5.0	L
	Master Eight	8	3.375	4.50	322.1	120@3200	5.0	L
	Custom Eight	8	3.375	4.50	322.1	120@3200	5.0	L
1931	Standard Eight	8	2.875	4.75	246.7	85@3200	5.0	L
	Master Eight	8	3.375	4.50	322.1	120@3200	5.0	L
	Custom Eight	8	3.375	4.50	322.1	120@3200	5.0	L
1932	Master Eight	8	3.375	4.50	322.1	120@3200	5.0	L
	Custom Eight	8	3.375	4.50	322.1	120@3200	5.0	L
	Peerless also built a prototype V12 and a V16, but only one of each.							

PIERCE-ARROW — — Pierce-Arrow Motor Co., Buffalo, N.Y., 1901-38

YEAR	MODEL	CYLS	BORE	STROKE	DISPL	HP@RPM	C.R.	VLV
1930	125	8	3.50	4.75	356.6	125@3000	5.07	L
	126	8	3.50	5.00	385.0	132@3000	5.07	L
	132	8	3.375	4.75	340.0	115@3000	5.07	L
	139	8	3.50	4.75	365.6	125@3000	5.07	L
1931	43	8	3.50	4.75	365.6	125@3000	5.07	L
	41	8	3.50	5.00	385.0	132@3000	5.07	L
	42	8	3.50	5.00	385.0	132@3000	5.07	L
1932	54	8	3.50	4.75	365.6	125@3800	5.05	L
	53	V12	3.25	4.00	398.0	140@3200	5.05	L
	52	V12	3.375	4.00	429.0	150@3200	5.05	L
	51*	V12	3.375	4.00	429.0	150@3200	5.05	L
	* Used bodies built by LeBaron and Brunn.							
1933	836	8	3.50	4.75	365.6	135@3400	5.50	L
	1236	V12	3.375	4.00	429.0	160@3400	6.00	L
	1242	V12	3.50	4.00	461.8	175@3400	6.00	L
	1247	V12	3.50	4.00	461.8	175@3400	6.00	L
1934	836A	8	3.50	4.75	365.6	135@3400	5.50	L
	840A	8	3.50	5.00	385.0	140@3400	5.50	L
	1240A	V12	3.50	4.00	461.8	175@3400	6.00	L

MFR	CARBURETOR MODEL	VEN	WHEEL-BASE	TIRES	BODY	WEIGHT	PRICE
			70		2 pr	900	999
			70		2 pr	900	999
		2	94	6.00 x 15	2 pr	1200	4250
		4	94	5.90 x 15	2 pr	1200	4995
Sc			118	5.50 x 19	5 ps	3515	1495
Sc			125	6.00 x 19	5 ps	4340	1995
Sc			138	6.50 x 19	5 ps	4585	2945
Sc	T		118	5.50 x 19	5 ps	3515	1495
Sc	S		125	6.00 x 19	5 ps	4340	1995
Sc	S		138	6.50 x 19	5 ps	4535	2945
Sc	S		125	6.00 x 19	5 ps	4413	2320
Sc	S		125	6.50 x 19	5 ps	4630	2985
S	UUR-2	2	134	7.00 x 18	5 ps	4350	2975
S			144	7.00 x 18	7 ps	4820	4485
S			132.4	6.50 x 19	5 ps	4525	2875
S			139	7.00 x 18	5 ps	4720	3495
S			134/137	6.50 x 19	5 ps	4638	2685
S			147	7.00 x 18	7 ps	5100	4785
S			142	7.00 x 18	5 ps	4980	3695
S			137/142	6.50 x 18	5 ps	4819	2985
S			137/142	7.00 x 18	5 ps	5080	3785
S			142/147	7.00 x 18	5 ps	5395	4295
S			147	7.00 x 18	5 ps	5428	5300
S	EE-3	2	136/139	7.00 x 17	5 ps	4660	2575
S	EX-32	2	136/139	7.00 x 17	5 ps	4892	2975
S	EX-32	2	137/142	7.50 x 17	5 ps	5288	3785
S	EX-32	2	147	7.50 x 17	5 ps	5420	4295
S	EE-3	2	136	7.00 x 17	5 ps	4923	2595
S	EE-3	2	139/144	7.00 x 17	5 ps	4964	2895
S	EX-32	2	139/144	7.50 x 17	5 ps	5227	3295

YEAR	MODEL	ENGINE						
		CYLS	BORE	STROKE	DISPL	HP@RPM	C.R.	VLV
	1248A	V12	3.50	4.00	461.8	175@3400	6.00	L
1935	836A	8	3.50	4.75	365.6	135@3400	5.50	L
	845	8	3.50	5.00	385.0	140@3400	5.50	L
	1245	V12	3.50	4.00	461.8	175@3400	6.00	L
	1255	V12	3.50	4.00	461.8	175@3400	6.00	L
1936	DeLuxe Eight, 1601	8	3.50	5.00	385.0	150@3400	6.40	L
	Salon Twelve, 1602	V12	3.50	4.00	461.8	185@3400	6.40	L
	Custom Twelve, 1603	V12	3.50	4.00	461.8	185@3400	6.40	L
1937	Eight, 1701	8	3.50	5.00	385.0	150@3400	6.4	L
	Twelve, 1702, 1703	V12	3.50	4.00	461.8	185@3400	6.4	L
1938	Eight, 1801	8	3.50	5.00	385.5	150@3400	6.4	L
	Twelve, 1802, 1803	V12	3.50	4.00	461.8	185@3400	6.4	L
	The 1938's were re-numbered 1937 production models.							

PIRANHA – – AMT Corp., Phoenix, Ariz., 1967

YEAR	MODEL	CYLS	BORE	STROKE	DISPL	HP@RPM	C.R.	VLV
1967		F6	3.438	2.937	163.6	140@3600		OH
	The flat-six Corvair engine was used.							

PLAYBOY – – Playboy Motor Car Co., N. Tonawanda, N.Y., 1947-51

YEAR	MODEL	CYLS	BORE	STROKE	DISPL	HP@RPM	C.R.	VLV
1947-48	A-48	4	2.875	3.50	90.9	40@3600	7.5	L
	B-7	4	3.25	4.00	133.0	48@3200	7.1	L

PLYMOUTH – – Chrysler Corp., Detroit, Mich., 1928+

YEAR	MODEL	CYLS	BORE	STROKE	DISPL	HP@RPM	C.R.	VLV
1930	30U	4	3.625	4.75	196.1	48@2800	4.6	L
1931	PA	4	3.625	4.75	196.1	56@2800	4.9	L
1932	New Finer, PB	4	3.625	4.75	196.1	65@3400	4.9	L
1933	Thrift, PC	6	3.125	4.125	189.8	70@3600	5.5	L
	Standard, PC	6	3.125	4.125	189.8	70@3600	5.5	L
	DeLuxe, PD	6	3.125	4.125	189.8	70@3600	5.5	L
1934	Standard, PG	6	3.125	4.375	201.3	77@3600	5.8	L
	Standard, PF	6	3.125	4.375	201.3	77@3600	5.8	L
	DeLuxe, PE	6	3.125	4.375	201.3	77@3600	5.8	L
1935	Business, PJ	6	3.125	4.375	201.3	85@3600	6.7	L
	DeLuxe, PJ	6	3.125	4.375	201.3	85@3600	6.7	L
1936	Business, P1	6	3.125	4.375	201.3	82@3600	6.7	L
	DeLuxe, P2	6	3.125	4.375	201.3	82@3600	6.7	L
1937	Business, P3	6	3.125	4.375	201.3	82@3600	6.7	L

CARBURETOR MFR	MODEL	VEN	WHEEL-BASE	TIRES	BODY	WEIGHT	PRICE
S	EX-32	2	147	7.50 x 17	7 ps		4295
S	EE-3	2	136	7.00 x 17	5 ps	4780	2395
S	EE-3	2	139/144	7.00 x 17	5 ps	4964	2895
S	EX-32	2	138/144	7.50 x 17	5 ps	5233	3295
S	EX-32	2	147	7.50 x 17	7 ps	5439	4295
S	EE-3	2	139/144/	7.00 x 17/	5 ps	5565	3195
			147	7.50 x 17			
S	EX-32	2	139/144	7.50 x 17	5 ps	5810	3695
S	EX-32	2	147	7.50 x 17	7 ps	6015	4795
S	EE-3	2	138/144	7.00 x 17	5 ps	5675	3375
S	EX-32	2	138/144/	7.50 x 17	5 ps	5920	3895
			148				
S	EE-3	2	138/144	7.00 x 17			
S	EX-32	2	138/144/	7.50 x 17			
			148				
							6000
C			90	5.00 x 12	2 pc	2035	985
C		1	90	5.90 x 12	2 pr	2083	985
C		1	109	4.75 x 19	5 ps	2595	625
C			109.4	4.75 x 19	5 ps	2730	635
C	4A2	1	112.4/121	5.25 x 18	5 ps	2875	635
C	C6A2	1	107.8	5.25 x 17	5 ps	2553	545
C	C6A2	1	107.8	5.25 x 17	5 ps	2523	510
C	C6A2	1	112	5.25 x 17	5 ps	2645	575
C	C6A4	1	107.8	5.25 x 17	5 ps2	2538	510
C	C6A4	1	107.8	5.25 x 17	5 ps	2693	600
C	C6A4	1	113.5	6.00 x 16	5 ps	2848	660
C	C6D1	1	113	5.25 x 17	5 ps	2720	570
C	C6D1	1	113/128	6.00 x 16	5 ps	2790	660
C	C6D2	1	113	5.25 x 17	5 ps	2750	590
C	C6D2	1	113/128	6.00 x 16	5 ps	2820	660
C	C6D2	1	112	5.50 x 16	5 ps	2841	665

YEAR	MODEL	ENGINE						
		CYLS	BORE	STROKE	DISPL	HP@RPM	C.R.	VLV
	DeLuxe, P4	6	3.125	4.375	201.3	82@3600	6.7	L
1938	Roadking, P5	6	3.125	4.375	201.3	82@3600	6.7	L
	DeLuxe, P6	6	3.125	4.375	201.3	82@3600	6.7	L
1939	Roadking, P7	6	3.125	4.375	201.3	87@3600	6.7	L
	DeLuxe, P8	6	3.125	4.375	201.3	87@3600	6.7	L
1940	Roadking, P9	6	3.125	4.375	201.3	84@3600	6.7	L
	DeLuxe, P10	6	3.125	4.375	201.3	84@3600	6.7	L
1941	DeLuxe, P11	6	3.125	4.375	201.3	87@3800	6.7	L
	Special DeLuxe, P12	6	3.125	4.375	201.3	87@3800	6.7	L
1942	DeLuxe, P14S	6	3.125	4.375	201.3	95@3400	6.8	L
	Special DeLuxe, P14C	6	3.125	4.375	201.3	95@3400	6.8	L
1946-48	DeLuxe, P15S	6	3.25	4.375	217.8	95@3600	6.6	L
	Special DeLuxe, P15C	6	3.25	4.375	217.8	95@3600	6.6	L
1949	DeLuxe, P17	6	3.25	4.375	217.8	97@3600	7.0	L
	DeLuxe, P18	6	3.25	4.375	217.8	97@3600	7.0	L
	Special DeLuxe, P18	6	3.25	4.375	217.8	97@3600	7.0	L
1950	DeLuxe, P19	6	3.25	4.375	217.8	97@3600	7.0	L
	DeLuxe, P20	6	3.25	4.375	217.8	97@3600	7.0	L
	Special DeLuxe, P20	6	3.25	4.375	217.8	97@3600	7.0	L
1951	Concord, P22	6	3.25	4.375	217.8	97@3600	7.0	L
	Cambridge, P23	6	3.25	4.375	217.8	97@3600	7.0	L
	Cranbrook, P23	6	3.25	4.375	217.8	97@3600	7.0	L
1952	Concord, P22	6	3.25	4.375	217.8	97@3600	7.0	L
	Cambridge, P23	6	3.25	4.375	217.8	97@3600	7.0	L
	Cranbrook, P23	6	3.25	4.375	217.8	97@3600	7.0	L
1953	Cambridge, P24-1	6	3.25	4.375	217.8	100@3600	7.1	L
	Cranbrook, P24-2	6	3.25	4.375	217.8	100@3600	7.1	L
1954	Plaza, P25-1	6	3.25	4.375	217.8	100@3600	7.1	L
	Savoy, P25-2	6	3.25	4.375	217.8	100@3600	7.1	L
	Belvedere, P25-3	6	3.25	4.375	217.8	100@3600	7.1	L
	Late series engine:							
		6	3.25	4.625	230.2	110@3600	7.25	L
1955	Plaza, P26-1	6	3.25	4.625	230.2	117@3600	7.4	L
	Savoy, P26-3	6	3.25	4.625	230.2	117@3600	7.4	L
	Belvedere, P26-2	6	3.25	4.625	230.2	117@3600	7.4	L
	Plaza, P27-1	V8	3.563	3.25	259.2	167@4400	7.6	OH

MFR	CARBURETOR MODEL	VEN	WHEEL-BASE	TIRES	BODY	WEIGHT	PRICE
C	C6D2	1	112/132	6.00 x 16/	5 ps	2914	745
				6.50 x 16			
C	B6H1	1	112	5.50 x 16	5 ps	2809	730
C	C6J1	1	112/132	6.00 x 16/	5 ps	2894	803
				6.50 x 16			
C	D6A1	1	114	5.50 x 16	5 ps	2839	726
C	D6A1	1	114/117/	6.00 x 16/	5 ps	2909	615
			134	6.50 x 16			
C	BB-D6A2	1	117.5	5.50 x 16	5 ps	2869	740
C	BB-D6A2	1	117.5/137	6.00 x 16/	5 ps	2924	805
				6.50 x 16			
C	BB-D6A2	1	117.5	6.00 x 16	5 ps	2899	809
C	BB-D6A2	1	117.5/137	6.00 x 16/	5 ps	2959	877
				6.50 x 16			
C	BB-D6G1	1	117.5	6.00 x 16	6 ps	3001	889
C	BB-D6G1	1	117.5	6.00 x 16	6 ps	3036	935
C	BB-D6G1	1	117.5	6.00 x 16	6 ps	3082	1284
C	BB-D6G1	1	117.5	6.00 x 16	6 ps	3107	1362
C	BB-D6H1	1	111	6.40 x 15	6 ps2	2951	1507
C	BB-D6H1	1	118.5	6.70 x 15	6 ps	3059	1566
C	BB-D6H1	1	118.5	6.70 x 15	6 ps	3079	1644
C	BB-D6H1	1	111	6.40 x 15	6 ps2	2946	1507
C	BB-D6H1	1	118.5	6.70 x 15	6 ps	3068	1566
C	BB-D6H1	1	118.5	6.70 x 15	6 ps	3072	1644
C	BB-D6H1	1	111	6.40 x 15	6 ps2	2969	1688
C	BB-D6H1	1	118.5	6.70 x 15	6 ps	3104	1754
C	BB-D6H1	1	118.5	6.70 x 15	6 ps	3109	1841
C	BB-D6H2	1	111	6.40 x 15	6 ps2	2959	1768
C	BB-D6H2	1	118.5	6.70 x 15	6 ps	3068	1837
C	BB-D6H2	1	118.5	6.70 x 15	6 ps	3088	1929
C	BB-D6H2	1	114	6.70 x 15	6 ps	2983	1765
C	BB-D6H2	1	114	6.70 x 15	6 ps	3023	1873
C	BB-D6H2	1	114	6.70 x 15	6 ps	3004	1765
C	BB-D6H2	1	114	6.70 x 15	6 ps	3036	1873
C	BB-D6H2	1	114	6.70 x 15	6 ps	3050	1953
C	BB-E9T1	1					
C	2063SA	1	115	6.50 x 15	6 ps	3129	1781
C	2063SA	1	115	6.70 x 15	6 ps	3154	1880
C	2063SA	1	115	6.70 x 15	6 ps	3159	1979
		2	115	6.70 x 15	6 ps	3246	1884

YEAR	MODEL	ENGINE						
		CYLS	BORE	STROKE	DISPL	HP@RPM	C.R.	VLV
	Savoy, P27-3	V8	3.563	3.25	259.2	167@4400	7.6	OH
	Belvedere, P27-2	V8	3.563	3.25	259.2	167@4400	7.6	OH
1956	Plaza, P28-1	V8	3.25	4.625	230.2	125@3600	7.6	L
	Savoy, P28-2	6	3.25	4.625	230.2	125@3600	7.6	L
	Belvedere, P28-3	6	3.25	4.625	230.2	125@3600	7.6	L
	Suburban, P28	6	3.25	4.625	230.2	125@3600	7.6	L
	Plaza, P29-1 (1)	V8	3.75	3.125	276.1	187@4400	8.0	OH
	Savoy, P29-2 (1)	V8	3.75	3.125	276.1	187@4400	8.0	OH
	Belvedere, P29-3 (1)	V8	3.75	3.125	276.1	187@4400	8.0	OH
	Suburban, P29 (1)	V8	3.75	3.125	276.1	187@4400	8.0	OH
	Fury, P29-3	V8	3.812	3.312	302.5	240@4800	9.25	OH
	Optional engine:							
	(1)	V8	3.625	3.25	268.8	180@4400	8.0	OH
1957	Plaza, P30-1	6	3.25	4.625	230.2	132@3600	8.0	L
	Savoy, P30-2	6	3.25	4.625	230.2	132@3600	8.0	L
	Belvedere, P30-3	6	3.25	4.625	230.2	132@3600	8.0	L
	Suburban, P-30	6	3.25	4.625	230.2	132@3600	8.0	L
	Plaza, P31-1 (1, 2)	V8	3.75	3.125	276.1	197@4400	8.0	OH
	Savoy, P31-2 (2)	V8	3.906	3.125	299.6	215@4400	8.5	OH
	Belvedere, P31-3 (2)	V8	3.906	3.125	299.6	215@4400	8.5	OH
	Suburban, P31 (2)	V8	3.906	3.125	299.6	215@4400	8.5	OH
	Fury, P31	V8	3.906	3.312	317.6	290@5400	9.25	OH
	Optional engines:							
	(1)	V8	3.906	3.125	299.6	215@4400	8.5	OH
	(2)	V8	3.906	3.125	299.6	235@4400		
1958	Plaza, LP1-L	6	3.25	4.625	230.2	132@3600	8.0	L
	Savoy, LP1-M	6	3.25	4.625	230.2	132@3600	8.0	L
	Belvedere, LP1-H	6	3.25	4.625	230.2	132@3600	8.0	L
	Suburban, LP1	6	3.25	4.625	230.2	132@3600	8.0	L
	Plaza, LP2-L (1)	V8	3.906	3.312	317.6	225@4400	9.0	OH
	Savoy, LP2-M (1)	V8	3.906	3.312	317.6	225@4400	9.0	OH
	Belvedere, LP2-H (1)	V8	3.906	3.312	317.6	225@4400	9.0	OH
	Suburban, LP2 (1)	V8	3.906	3.312	317.6	225@4400	9.0	OH
	Fury, LP2-H (2)	V8	3.906	3.312	317.6	290@5200	9.25	OH
	Optional engines: (1)	V8	3.906	3.312	317.6	250@4400		OH
	(2)	V8	4.062	3.375	350.0	305@5000	10.0	OH
	(2)	V8	4.062	3.375	350.0	315@4500		OH
1959	Savoy, MP1-L	6	3.25	4.625	230.2	132@3600	8.0	L
	Belvedere, MP1-M	6	3.25	4.625	230.2	132@3600	8.0	L

MFR	CARBURETOR MODEL	VEN	WHEEL-BASE	TIRES	BODY	WEIGHT	PRICE
		2	115	6.70 x 15	6 ps	3265	1983
		2	115	6.70 x 15	6 ps	3267	2082
C	BBS-2293S	2	115	6.70 x 15	6 ps	3145	1926
C	BBS-2293S	2	115	6.70 x 15	6 ps	3160	2025
C	BBS-2293S	2	115	6.70 x 15	6 ps	3170	2109
C	BBS-2293S	2	115	6.70 x 15	6 psw4	3375	2314
C	BBD-2407S	2	115	6.70 x 15	6 ps	3275	2030
C	BBD-2407S	2	115	6.70 x 15	6 ps	3295	2129
C	BBD-2407S	2	115	6.70 x 15	6 ps	3325	2213
C	BBD-2407S	2	115	6.70 x 15	6 psw4	3565	2417
C	WCFB-2442S	4	115	7.10 x 15	6 pht2	3650	2866
C	BBD-2259SB	2					
C	BBS-2567S	1	118	7.50 x 14	6 ps	3260	2055
C	BBS-2567S	1	118	7.50 x 14	6 ps	3265	2194
C	BBS-2567S	1	118	7.50 x 14	6 ps	3270	2310
C	BBS-2567S	1	122	7.50 x 14	6 psw4	3665	2494
C		2	118	7.50 x 14	6 ps	3405	2155
C	BBD-2512S	2	118	7.50 x 14	6 ps	3415	2294
C	BBD-2512S	2	118	7.50 x 14	6 ps	3475	2410
C	BBD-2512S	2	122	7.50 x 14	6 psw4	3840	2594
C	WCFB-2631S	2 x 4	118	8.00 x 14	6 pht4	3595	2925
C	BBD-2512S	2					
C		2					
C	BBS-2567S	1	118	7.50 x 14	6 ps	3255	2169
C	BBS-2567S	1	118	7.50 x 14	6 ps	3220	2305
C	BBS-2567S	1	118	7.50 x 14	6 ps	3255	2440
C	BBS-2567S	1	122	7.50 x 14/	6 psw4	3580	2486
				8.00 x 14			
C	BBS-2644S	2	118	7.50 x 14	6 ps	3415	2277
C	BBS-2644S	2	118	7.50 x 14	6 ps	3400	2413
C	BBS-2644S	2	118	7.50 x 14	6 ps	3430	2547
C	BBS-2644S	2	122	7.50 x 14/	6 psw4	3740	2593
				8.00 x 14			
C	WCFB-2631S	4	118	8.00 x 14	6 pht2	3510	3067
		F.I.					
C	BBS-2567S	1	118	7.50 x 14	6 ps	3275	2283
C	BBS-2567S	1	118	7.50 x 14	6 ps	3275	2440

YEAR	MODEL	ENGINE						
		CYLS	BORE	STROKE	DISPL	HP@RPM	C.R.	VLV
	Suburban, MP1	6	3.25	4.625	230.2	132@3600	8.0	L
	Savoy, MP2-L (1)	V8	3.906	3.312	317.6	230@4400	9.0	OH
	Belvedere, MP2-M (1)	V8	3.906	3.312	317.6	230@4400	9.0	OH
	Suburban, MP2 (1)	V8	3.906	3.312	317.6	230@4400	9.0	OH
	Fury, MP2-H (1)	V8	3.906	3.312	317.6	230@4400	9.0	OH
	Sport Fury, MP2-P (1)	V8	3.906	3.312	317.6	260@4400	9.0	OH
	Optional engine:							
	(1)	V8	4.125	3.375	360.8	305@4600	10.1	OH
1960	Fleet Special	6	3.406	4.125	225.5	145@4000	8.5	OH
	Savoy, PP1-L	6	3.406	4.125	225.5	145@4000	8.5	OH
	Belvedere, PP1-M	6	3.406	4.125	225.5	145@4000	8.5	OH
	Fury, PP1-H	6	3.406	4.125	225.5	145@4000	8.5	OH
	Suburban, PP1	6	3.406	4.125	225.5	145@4000	8.5	OH
	Fleet Special (1)	V8	3.906	3.312	317.6	230@4400	9.0	OH
	Savoy, PP2-L (1)	V8	3.906	3.312	317.6	230@4400	9.0	OH
	Belvedere, PP2-M (1)	V8	3.906	3.312	317.6	230@4400	9.0	OH
	Fury, PP2-H (1)	V8	3.906	3.312	317.6	230@4400	9.0	OH
	Suburban, PP2 (1)	V8	3.906	3.312	317.6	230@4400	9.0	OH
	Optional engine:							
	(1)	V8	4.125	3.375	360.8	305@4800	10.0	OH
1961	Fleet Special	6	3.406	4.125	225.5	145@4000	8.2	OH
	Savoy, RP1-L (2, 3)	6	3.406	4.125	225.5	145@4000	8.2	OH
	Belvedere, RP1-M (2, 3)	6	3.406	4.125	225.5	145@4000	8.2	OH
	Fury, RP1-H (2, 3)	6	3.406	4.125	225.5	145@4000	8.2	OH
	Suburban, RP1	6	3.406	4.125	225.5	145@4000	8.2	OH
	Fleet Special (1, 2)	V8	3.906	3.312	317.6	230@4400	9.0	OH
	Savoy, RP2-L (1, 2)	V8	3.906	3.312	317.6	230@4400	9.0	OH
	Belvedere, RP2-M (1, 2)	V8	3.906	3.312	317.6	230@4400	9.0	OH
	Fury, RP2-H (1, 2)	V8	3.906	3.312	317.6	230@4400	9.0	OH
	Suburban, RP2 (1, 2)	V8	3.906	3.312	317.6	230@4400	9.0	OH
	Optional engines:							
	(1)	V8	3.906	3.312	317.6	260@4400		OH
	(1)	V8	4.125	3.375	360.8	305@4800	9.0	OH
	(1)	V8	4.25	3.375	383.0	330@4800	10.0	OH
	(2)	V8	4.25	3.375	383.0	325@4800	10.0	OH
	(2)	V8	4.25	3.375	383.0	330@5200	10.0	OH
	(2)	V8	4.25	3.375	383.0	340@5000	10.0	OH
	(2)	V8	4.188	3.75	413.2	375@5000	10.0	OH
	(2)	V8	4.188	3.75	413.2	350@4600	10.0	OH

MFR	CARBURETOR MODEL	VEN	WHEEL-BASE	TIRES	BODY	WEIGHT	PRICE
C	BBS-2567S	1	122	7.50 x 14	6psw4	3625	2641
C	BBD-2824S	2	118	7.50 x 14	6 ps	3390	2402
C	BBD-2824S	2	118	7.50 x 14	6 ps	3430	2559
C	BBD-2824S	2	122	7.50 x 14	6 psw4	3725	2761
C	BBD-2824S	2	118	7.50 x 14	6 ps	3455	2691
C	AFB-2813S	4	118	7.50 x 14	6 pht2	3475	2927
C	BBS-2985S	1	118	7.50 x 14	6 ps		2277
C	BBS-2985S	1	118	7.50 x 14	6 ps	3365	2310
C	BBS-2985S	1	118	7.50 x 14	6 ps	3375	2439
C	BBS-2985S	1	118	7.50 x 14	6 ps	3400	2575
C	BBS-2985S	1	122	8.00 x 14	6 psw4	3740	2668
C	BBD-2921S	2	118	7.50 x 14	6 ps		2396
C	BBD-2921S	2	118	7.50 x 14	6 ps	3500	2429
C	BBD-2921S	2	118	7.50 x 14	6 ps	3520	2559
C	BBD-2921S	2	118	7.50 x 14	6 ps	3550	2694
C	BBD-2921S	2	122	8.00 x 14	6 psw4	3890	2787
C	BBS-3098S	1	118	7.00 x 14	6 ps	3305	2277
C	BBS-3098S	1	118	7.00 x 14	6 ps	3310	2312
C	BBS-3098S	1	118	7.00 x 14	6 ps	3315	2441
C	BBS-3098S	1	118	7.00 x 14	6 ps	3350	2577
C	BBS-3098S	1	122	7.50 x 14	6 psw4	3715	2670
C	BBD-2921S	2	118	7.50 x 14	6 ps	3460	2396
C	BBD-2921S	2	118	7.50 x 14	6 ps	3465	2432
C	BBD-2921S	2	118	7.50 x 14	6 ps	3470	2561
C	BBD-2921S	2	118	7.50 x 14	6 ps	3515	2696
C	BBD-2921S	2	122	7.50 x 14/	6 psw4	3885	2790
				8.00 x 14			
		4					
C	AFB-3105S	4					
C	AFB-2903S	2 x 4					
C	AFB-2968S	4					
C	AFB-2790S	2 x 4					
C	AFB-3084S	2 x 4					
C	AFB-3084S	2 x 4					
C	AFB-3108S	4					

YEAR	MODEL	ENGINE						
		CYLS	BORE	STROKE	DISPL	HP@RPM	C.R.	VLV
	(3)	V8	4.125	3.375	360.8	305@4800	9.0	OH
1962	Fleet Special	6	3.406	4.125	225.5	145@4000	8.2	OH
	Savoy, SP1-L	6	3.406	4.125	225.5	145@4000	8.2	OH
	Belvedere, SP1-M	6	3.406	4.125	225.5	145@4000	8.2	OH
	Fury, SP1-H	6	3.406	4.125	225.5	145@4000	8.2	OH
	Suburban, SP1	6	3.406	4.125	225.5	145@4000	8.2	OH
	Fleet Special	V8	3.906	3.312	317.6	230@4400	9.0	OH
	Savoy, SP2-L (1)	V8	3.906	3.312	317.6	230@4400	9.0	OH
	Belvedere, SP2-M (1)	V8	3.906	3.312	317.6	230@4400	9.0	OH
	Fury, SP2-H (1)	V8	3.906	3.312	317.6	230@4400	9.0	OH
	Sport Fury, SP2-P	V8	4.125	3.375	360.8	305@4800	9.0	OH
	Suburban, SP2 (1)	V8	4.125	3.375	360.8	230@4400	9.0	OH
	Optional engines:							
	(1)	V8	3.906	3.312	317.6	260@4400	9.0	OH
	(1)	V8	4.125	3.375	360.8	305@4800	9.0	OH
1963	Savoy, TP1-L	6	3.406	4.125	225.5	145@4000	8.2	OH
	Belvedere, TP1-M	6	3.406	4.125	225.5	145@4000	8.2	OH
	Fury, TP1-H		3.406	4.125	225.5	145@4000	8.2	OH
	Savoy, TP2-L (1)	V8	3.906	3.312	317.6	230@4400	9.0	OH
	Fury, TP2-H (1)	V8	3.906	3.312	317.6	230@4400	9.0	OH
	Sport Fury, TP2-P (1)	V8	3.906	3.312	317.6	230@4400	9.0	OH
	Optional engines:							
	(1)	V8	4.125	3.375	360.8	265@4400	9.0	OH
	(1)	V8	4.25	3.375	383.0	330@4600	10.0	OH
1964	Savoy, VP1-L	6	3.406	4.125	225.5	145@4000	8.4	OH
	Belvedere, VP1-M	6	3.406	4.125	225.5	145@4000	8.4	OH
	Fury, VP1-H	6	3.406	4.125	225.5	145@4000	8.4	OH
	Savoy, VP2-L (1)	V8	3.906	3.312	317.6	230@4400	9.0	OH
	Belvedere, VP2-M (1)	V8	3.906	3.312	317.6	230@4400	9.0	OH
	Fury, VP2-H (1)	V8	3.906	3.312	317.6	230@4400	9.0	OH
	Sport Fury, VP2-P (1)	V8	3.908	3.312	317.6	230@4400	9.0	OH
	Optional engines:							
	(1)	V8	4.125	3.375	360.8	265@4400	9.0	OH
	(1)	V8	4.25	3.375	383.0	330@4600	10.0	OH
	(1)	V8	4.25	3.75	425.6	365@4800	10.3	OH
1965	Barracuda, AV1-P	6	3.406	4.125	225.5	145@4000	8.4	OH
	Barracuda, AV2-P	V8	3.625	3.312	273.5	180@4200	8.8	OH

MFR	CARBURETOR MODEL	VEN	WHEEL-BASE	TIRES	BODY	WEIGHT	PRICE
C	AFB-3105S	4					
C	BBS-3231S	1	116	6.50 x 14	6 ps	2955	2193
C	BBS-3231S	1	116	6.50 x 14	6 ps	2960	2262
C	BBS-3231S	1	116	6.50 x 14	6 ps	2960	2399
C	BBS-3231S	1	116	6.50 x 14	6 ps	2990	2563
C	BBS-3231S	1	116	7.00 x 14	6 psw4	3225	2609
C	BBS-3231S	1	116	7.00 x 14	6 ps	3115	2351
C	BBS-3231S	1	116	7.00 x 14	6 ps	3115	2369
C	BBS-3231S	1	116	7.00 x 14	6 ps	3095	2507
C	BBS-3231S	1	116	7.00 x 14	6 ps	3125	2670
C	AFB-3252S	4	116	7.00 x 14	5 pht2	3195	2851
			116	7.00 x 14	6 psw4	3390	2717
C	AFB-3252S	4					
C	BBS-3466S	1	116	7.00 x 14	6 ps	3020	2262
C	BBS-3466S	1	116	7.00 x 14	6 ps	3020	2399
C	BBS-3466S	1	116	7.00 x 14	6 ps	3075	2563
C	BBD-3472S	2	116	7.00 x 14	6 ps	3235	2507
C	BBD-3472S	2	116	7.00 x 14	6 ps	3265	2670
C	BBD-3472S	2	116	7.00 x 14	6 pht2	3235	2851
C	BBD-3475S	2					
C	AFB-3437S	4					
C	BBS-3679S	1	116	7.00 x 14/	6 ps	3040	2280
				7.50 x 14			
C	BBS-3679S	1	116	7.00 x 14	6 ps	3065	2417
C	BBS-3679S	1	116	7.00 x 14	6 ps	3045	2573
C	BBD-3682S	2	116	7.00 x 14/	6 ps	3210	2388
				7.50 x 14			
C	BBD-3682S	2	116	7.00 x 14/	6 ps	3225	2525
				7.50 x 14			
C	BBD-3682S	2	116	7.00 x 14	6 ps	3230	2681
C	BBD-3682S	2	116	7.00 x 14	6 pht2	3270	2864
C	BBD-3684S	2					
C	AFB-3611S	4					
C	AFB-3704S	4					
C	BBS-3839S	1	106	6.50 x 13	5 pht2	2725	2453
C	BBD-3843S	2	106	7.00 x 13	5 pht2	2930	2535

YEAR	MODEL	ENGINE						
		CYLS	BORE	STROKE	DISPL	HP@RPM	C.R.	VLV
	Belvedere I	6	3.406	4.125	225.5	145@4000	8.4	OH
	Belvedere II	6	3.406	4.125	225.5	145@4000	8.4	OH
	Belvedere I (1, 2, 3)	V8	3.625	3.312	273.5	180@4200	8.8	OH
	Belvedere II (1, 2, 3)	V8	3.625	3.312	273.5	180@4200	8.8	OH
	Satellite, (1, 3)	V8	3.625	3.312	273.5	180@4200	8.8	OH
	Fury I	6	3.406	4.125	225.5	145@4000	8.4	OH
	Fury II	6	3.406	4.125	225.5	145@4000	8.4	OH
	Fury III	6	3.406	4.125	225.5	145@4000	8.4	OH
	Fury I (1, 2, 3)	V8	3.906	3.312	317.6	230@4400	9.0	OH
	Fury II (1, 2, 3, 4)	V8	3.906	3.312	317.6	230@4400	9.0	OH
	Sport Fury (1, 2, 3, 4)	V8	3.906	3.312	317.6	230@4400	9.0	OH
	Optional engines:							
	(1)	V8	4.25	3.625	383.0	330@4600	10.0	OH
	(2)	V8	3.906	3.312	317.6	230@4400	9.0	OH
	(3)	V8	4.25	3.75	425.6	365@4800	10.3	OH
	(4)	V8	4.25	3.375	383.0	270@4400	9.2	OH
1966	Barracuda, BV1-P	6	3.406	4.125	225.5	145@4000	8.4	OH
	Belvedere I, BR1-L	6	3.406	4.125	225.5	145@4000	8.4	OH
	Belvedere II, BR1-H	6	3.406	4.125	225.5	145@4000	8.4	OH
	Fury I, BP1-L	6	3.406	4.125	225.5	145@4000	8.4	OH
	Fury II, BP1-M	6	3.406	4.125	225.5	145@4000	8.4	OH
	Fury III, BP1-H	6	3.406	4.125	225.5	145@4000	8.4	OH
	Barracuda, BV1-P	V8	3.625	3.312	273.5	180@4200	8.8	OH
	Belvedere I, BR2-L (1)	V8	3.625	3.312	273.5	180@4200	8.8	OH
	Belvedere II, BR2-H (1)	V8	3.625	3.312	273.5	180@4200	8.8	OH

MFR	CARBURETOR MODEL	VEN	WHEEL-BASE	TIRES	BODY	WEIGHT	PRICE
C	BBS-3839S	1	116	7.35 x 14/	6 ps	3105	2236
				7.75 x 14			
C	BBS-3839S	1	116	7.35 x 14/	6 ps	3100	2321
				7.75 x 14			
C	BBD-3843S	2	116	7.35 x 14/	6 ps	3200	2330
				7.75 x 14			
C	BBD-3843S	2	116	7.35 x 14/	6 ps	3155	2415
				7.75 x 14			
C	BBD-3843S	2	116	7.35 x 14	5 pht2	3220	2612
C	BBS-3839S	1	119/121	7.35 x 14/	6 ps	3490	2401
				8.25 x 14			
C	BBS-3839S	1	119	7.35 x 14	6 ps	3485	2500
C	BBS-3839S	1	119	7.35 x 14	6 ps	3505	2649
C	BBD-3847S	2	119/121	7.75 x 14/	6 ps	3655	2505
				8.55 x 14			
C	BBD-3847S	2	119/121	7.75 x 14/	6 ps	3660	2604
				8.55 x 14			
C	BBD-3847S	2	119	7.75 x 14	6 pht2	3715	2920
C	AFB-3855S	4					
C	BBD-3847S	2					
C	AFB-3859S	4					
C	AFB-3855S	4					
H	R-3271	1	106	6.50 x 13	5 pht2	2800	2556
H	R-3271	1	116	7.75 x 14/	6 ps	3040	2315
				6.95 x 14			
H	R-3271	1	116	6.95 x 14/	6 ps	3035	2405
				7.35 x 14/			
				7.75 x 14			
H	R-3271	1	119/121	7.35 x 14/	6 ps	3485	2479
				8.55 x 14			
H	R-3271	1	119	7.35 x 14	6 ps	3480	2579
H	R-3271	1	119	7.35 x 14	6 ps	3505	2718
C	BBD-4113S	2	106	7.00 x 13	5 pht2	2930	2637
C	BBD-4113S	2	116	7.35 x 14/	6 ps	3210	2409
				7.75 x 14/			
				8.25 x 14			
C	BBD-4113S	2	116	7.35 x 14/	6 ps	3195	2499
				7.75 x 14/			
				8.25 x 14			

YEAR	MODEL	ENGINE						
		CYLS	BORE	STROKE	DISPL	HP@RPM	C.R.	VLV
	Fury I, BP2-L (2)	V8	3.906	3.312	317.6	230@4400	9.0	OH
	Fury II, BP2-M (2)	V8	3.906	3.312	317.6	230@4400	9.0	OH
	Fury III, BP2-H (2)	V8	3.906	3.312	317.6	230@4400	9.0	OH
	Sport Fury, BP2-P (2)	V8	3.906	3.312	317.6	230@4400	9.0	OH
	V.I.P., BP2-H-43 (2)	V8	3.906	3.312	317.6	230@4400	9.0	OH
	Satellite, BR2-P (1)	V8	3.625	3.312	273.5	180@4200	8.8	OH
	Optional engines:							
	(1)	V8	4.25	3.375	383.0	325@4800	10.0	OH
	(1)	V8	4.25	3.75	425.6	425@5000	10.25	OH
	(2)	V8	4.25	3.375	383.0	270@4400	9.2	OH
	(2)	V8	4.312	3.75	438.2	365@4600	10.1	OH
1967	Barracuda, CB1-H	6	3.406	4.125	225.5	145@4000	8.4	OH
	Belvedere, CR1-E	6	3.406	4.125	225.5	145@4000	8.4	OH
	Belvedere I, CR1-L	6	3.406	4.125	225.5	145@4000	8.4	OH
	Belvedere II, CR1-H	6	3.406	4.125	225.5	145@4000	8.4	OH
	Fury I, CP1-E	6	3.406	4.125	225.5	145@4000	8.4	OH
	Fury II, CP1-L	6	3.406	4.125	225.5	145@4000	8.4	OH
	Fury III, CP1-M	6	3.406	4.125	225.5	145@4000	8.4	OH
	Belvedere, CB2-H (1, 4)	V8	3.625	3.312	273.5	180@4200	8.8	OH
	Belvedere CR2-E	V8	3.625	3.312	273.5	180@4200	8.8	OH
	Belvedere I, CR2-L (2, 3)	V8	3.625	3.312	273.5	180@4200	8.8	OH
	Belvedere II, CR2-H (2, 3)	V8	3.625	3.312	273.5	180@4200	8.8	OH
	Satellite, CR2-P (2)	V8	3.625	3.312	273.5	180@4200	8.8	OH
	GTX, CR2-P (6)	V8	4.325	3.75	440.0	375@4600	10.1	OH
	Fury I, CP2-E (3, 5)	V8	3.906	3.312	317.6	230@4400	9.2	OH
	Fury II, CP2-L (3, 5)	V8	3.906	3.312	317.6	230@4400	9.2	OH
	Fury III, CP2-M (3, 5)	V8	3.906	3.312	317.6	230@4400	9.2	OH
	Sport Fury, CP2-H (3, 5)	V8	3.906	3.312	317.6	230@4400	9.2	OH
	VIP, CP2-P (3, 5)	V8	3.906	3.312	317.6	230@4400	9.2	OH
	Optional engines:							

MFR	CARBURETOR MODEL	VEN	WHEEL-BASE	TIRES	BODY	WEIGHT	PRICE
S	WW3-258	2	119/121	7.75 x 14/	6 ps	3655	2584
				8.55 x 14			
S	WW3-258	2	119/121	7.75 x 14/	6 ps	3665	2684
				8.55 x 14			
S	WW3-258	2	119/121	7.75 x 14/	6 ps	3715	2823
				8.55 x 14			
S	WW3-258	2	119	7.75 x 14	5 pht2	3730	3006
S	WW3-258	2	119	7.75 x 14	6 pht4	3780	3133
C	BBD-4113S	2	116	7.35 x 14	5 pht2	3255	2695
C	AFB-4130S	4					
C	AFB-4139S	2 x 4					
	BBD-4125S	2					
C	AFB-4130S	4					
H	R-3275-1A	1	108	6.50 x 13	5 pht2	2730	2449
H	R-3279-1A	1	117	7.75 x 14	6 psw4	3455	2579
H	R-3279-1A	1	116/117	7.35 x 14/	6 ps	3065	2356
				7.75 x 14			
H	R-3279-1A	1	116/117	7.35 x 14/	6 ps	3055	2434
				7.75 x 14/			
				8.25 x 14			
H	R-3279-1A	1	119/122	7.75 x 14/	6 ps	3490	2517
				8.55 x 14			
H	R-3279-1A	1	119	7.75 x 14	6 ps	3470	2614
H	R-3279-1A	1	119	7.75 x 14	6 ps	3515	2746
C	BBD-4113-S	2	108	7.00 x 13	5 pht2	2865	2530
C	BBD-4113-SA	2	117	7.75 x 14	6 psw4	3575	2673
C	BBD-4113SA	2	116/117	7.35 x 14/	6 ps	3220	2450
				7.75 x 14			
C	BBD-4113SA	2	116/117	8.25 x 14	6 ps	3210	2528
C	BBD-4113SA	2	116	7.35 x 14	5 pht2	3245	2747
C	AFB-4326S	4	116	7.75 x 14	5 pht2	3535	3178
S	WW3-272	2	119/122	7.75 x 14/	6 ps	3590	2622
				8.55 x 14			
S	WW3-272	2	119/122	7.75 x 14/	6 ps	3595	2719
				8.55 x 14			
S	WW3-272	2	119/122	7.75 x 14/	6 ps	3615	2851
				8.55 x 14			
S	WW3-272	2	119	7.75 x 14	5 pht2	3625	3033
S	WW3-272	2	119	7.75 x 14	6 pht4	3705	3182

YEAR	MODEL	ENGINE						
		CYLS	BORE	STROKE	DISPL	HP@RPM	C.R.	VLV
	(1)	V8	3.625	3.312	273.5	235@5200	10.5	OH
	(2)	V8	3.906	3.312	317.6	230@4400	9.2	OH
	(3)	V8	4.25	3.375	383.0	270@4400	9.2	OH
	(3)	V8	4.25	3.375	383.0	325@4800	10.0	OH
	(4)	V8	4.25	3.375	383.0	280@4200	10.0	OH
	(5)	V8	4.312	3.75	438.2	375@4600	10.1	OH
	(6)	V8	4.25	3.75	425.6	425@5000	10.25	OH
1968	Barracuda, BH	6	3.406	4.125	225.5	145@4000	8.4	OH
	Belvedere, RL	6	3.406	4.125	225.5	145@4000	8.4	OH
	Satellite, RH	6	3.406	4.125	225.5	145@4000	8.4	OH
	Fury I, PE	6	3.406	4.125	225.5	145@4000	8.4	OH
	Fury II, PL, PE	6	3.406	4.125	225.5	145@4000	8.4	OH
	Fury III, PM, PX	6	3.406	4.125	225.5	145@4000	8.4	OH
	Belvedere, RL (1, 2, 3)	V8	3.625	3.312	273.5	190@4400	9.0	OH
	Road Runner, RM (2, 3)	V8	4.25	3.375	383.0	335@5200	10.0	OH
	Satellite, RH (1, 2, 3)	V8	3.625	3.312	273.5	190@4400	9.0	OH
	Sport Satellite, RP (2, 3)	V8	3.906	3.312	317.6	230@4400	9.2	OH
	GTX, RS (3)	V8	4.325	3.75	440.7	375@4600	10.1	OH
	Fury I, PE (1, 2, 4)	V8	3.906	3.312	317.6	230@4400	9.2	OH
	Fury II, PE, PL (1, 2, 4)	V8	3.906	3.312	317.6	230@4400	9.2	OH
	Fury III (1, 2, 4)	V8	3.906	3.312	317.6	230@4400	9.2	OH
	Sport Fury (1, 2, 4)	V8	3.906	3.312	317.6	230@4400	9.2	OH
	VIP, PP, PM (1, 2, 4)	V8	3.906	3.312	317.6	230@4400	9.2	OH
	Optional engines:							
	(1)	V8	4.25	3.375	383.0	290@4400	9.2	OH
	(2)	V8	4.25	3.375	383.0	330@5000	10.0	OH
	(3)	V8	4.25	3.75	425.6	425@5000	10.25	OH
	(4)	V8	4.325	3.75	440.7	375@4600	10.1	OH
1969	Barracuda, BH	6	3.406	4.125	225.5	145@4000	8.4	OH
	Belvedere, RL	6	3.406	4.125	225.5	145@4000	8.4	OH
	Satellite, RH	6	3.406	4.125	225.5	145@4000	8.4	OH

MFR	CARBURETOR MODEL	VEN	WHEEL-BASE	TIRES	BODY	WEIGHT	PRICE
C	BBD-4113SA	2					
S	WW3-172	2					
C	AFB-4326S	4					
H	R-3919A	1	108	6.95 x 14	5 pht2	2725	2605
H	R-3921A	1	116/117	7.35 x 14/	6 ps	2995	2483
				8.25 x 14			
H	R-3921A	1	116/117	7.35 x 14/	6 ps	3000	2572
				8.25 x 14			
H	R-3921A	1	119	8.25 x 14	6 ps	3455	2660
H	R-3921A	1	119/122	8.25 x 14/	6 ps	3470	2757
				8.55 x 14			
H	R-3921A	1	119	8.25 x 14	6 ps	3485	2890
C	BBD-4416S	2	116/117	7.35 x 14/	6 ps	3165	2577
				8.25 x 14			
C	AVS-4426S	4	116	F70 x 14	6 pc	3390	2896
C	BBD-4416S	2	116/117	7.35 x 14/	6 ps	3160	2666
				8.25 x 14			
C	BBD-4420S	2	116	7.35 x 14	5 pht2	3155	2822
C	AVS-4428S	4	116	F70 x 14	5 pht2	3470	3355
C	BBD-4420S	2	119	8.25 x 14	6 ps	3580	2635
C	BBD-4420S	2	119/122	8.25 x 14/	6 ps	3595	2862
				8.55 x 14			
C	BBD-4420S	2	119/122	8.25 x 14/	6 ps	3605	2995
				8.55 x 14			
C	BBD-4420S	2	119	8.25 x 14	5 pht2	3620	3206
C	BBD-4420S	2	119/122	8.25 x 14/	6 pht4	3655	3326
				8.55 x 14			
C	AVS-4426S	4					
C	AVS-4428S	4					
H	R-4163A	1	108	6.95 x 14	5 pht2	2731	2674
H	R-4163A	1	116/117	7.35 x 14/	6 ps	2993	2548
				8.25 x 14			
H	R-4163A	1	116/117	7.35 x 14/	6 ps	2998	2635
				8.25 x 14			

YEAR	MODEL	ENGINE						
		CYLS	BORE	STROKE	DISPL	HP@RPM	C.R.	VLV
	Fury I, PE	6	3.406	4.125	225.5	145@4000	8.4	OH
	Fury II, PL	6	3.406	4.125	225.5	145@4000	8.4	OH
	Fury III, PM	6	3.406	4.125	225.5	145@4000	8.4	OH
	Barracuda, BH (1)	V8	3.906	3.312	317.6	230@4400	9.2	OH
	Belvedere, RL (2, 3)	V8	3.906	3.312	317.6	230@4400	9.2	OH
	Satellite, RH (2, 3)	V8	3.906	3.312	317.6	230@4400	9.2	OH
	Road Runner, RM (3)	V8	4.25	3.375	383.0	335@5200	10.0	OH
	Sport Satellite, RP (2, 3)	V8	3.906	3.312	317.6	230@4400	9.2	OH
	GTX, RS (3)	V8	4.312	3.75	438.2	375@4600	10.1	OH
	Fury I, PE (2)	V8	3.906	3.312	317.6	230@4400	9.2	OH
	Fury II, PL (2)	V8	3.906	3.312	317.6	230@4400	9.2	OH
	Fury III, PL, PM (2)	V8	3.906	3.312	317.5	230@4400	9.2	OH
	Sport Fury, PH (2)	V8	3.906	3.312	317.6	230@4400	9.2	OH
	VIP, PP, PM (2)	V8	3.906	3.312	317.6	230@4400	9.2	OH
	Optional engines:							
	(1)	V8	4.04	3.312	339.7	275@5000	10.5	OH
	(2)	V8	4.25	3.375	383.0	290@4400	9.2	OH
	(2)	V8	4.25	3.375	383.0	330@5000	10.0	OH
	(3)	V8	4.25	3.75	425.6	425@5000	10.25	OH

PONTIAC – – Pontiac Motor Car Co., Div. General Motors Corp., Pontiac, Mich., 1926+

YEAR	MODEL	CYLS	BORE	STROKE	DISPL	HP@RPM	C.R.	VLV
1930	6-30	6	3.312	3.875	200.0	60@3000	4.9	L
1931	401	6	3.312	3.875	200.0	60@3000	4.9	L
1932	402	6	3.312	3.875	200.0	65@3400	5.10	L
	302	V8	3.438	3.375	251.0	85@3400	5.20	H
1933	601	8	3.188	3.50	223.4	75@3600	5.70	L
1934	603	8	3.188	3.50	223.4	84@3600	6.20	L
1935	Standard 701	6	3.375	3.875	208.0	80@3600	6.20	L
	605	8	3.188	3.50	223.4	84@3800	6.20	L
	DeLuxe 701	6	3.375	3.875	208.0	80@3600	6.20	L
1936	Master Silver Streak, 6BB	6	3.375	3.875	208.0	80@3600	6.2	L
	DeLuxe Silver Streak, 6BA	6	3.375	3.875	208.0	80@3600	6.2	L
	Straight 8 Silver Streak, 8BA	8	3.25	3.50	232.3	87@3800	6.2	L
1937	DeLuxe 6, 6CA	6	3.438	4.00	222.7	85@3500	6.2	L
	DeLuxe 8, 8CA	8	3.25	3.75	248.9	99@3800	6.2	L

MFR	CARBURETOR MODEL	VEN	WHEEL-BASE	TIRES	BODY	WEIGHT	PRICE
H	R-4163A	1	120	7.75 x 15	6 ps	3513	2744
H	R-4163A	1	120/122	7.75 x 15/	6 ps	3528	2841
				8.55 x 15			
H	R-4163A	1	120	7.75 x 15	6 ps	3543	2979
C	BBD-4607S	2	108	6.95 x 14	5 pht2	2894	2780
C	BBD-4607S	2	116/117	7.35 x 14/	6 ps	3166	2638
				8.25 x 14			
C	BBD-4607S	2	116/117	7.35 x 14/	6 ps	3171	2725
				8.25 x 14			
C	AVS-4615S	4	116	7.35 x 14	5 pht2	3455	3083
C	BBD-4607S	2	116/117	7.35 x 14/	6 ps	3211	2911
				8.25 x 14			
C	AVS-4617S	4	116	F70 x 15	5 pht2	3515	3416
C	BBD-4607S	2	120	7.75 x 15	6 ps	3632	2849
C	BBD-4607S	2	120/122	7.75 x 15/	6 ps	3647	2946
				8.55 x 15			
C	BBD-4607S	2	120/122	7.75 x 15/	6 ps	3607	3084
				8.55 x 15			
C	BBD-4607S	2	120	7.75 x 15	5 pht2	3682	3283
C	BBD-4607S	2	120/122	8.25 x 15	6 pht2	3712	3433
M	AA35		110	5.00 x 29	5 ps	2745	825
M	AA35		112	5.00 x 29	5 ps	2843	745
M			114	5.25 x 18	5 ps	2960	725
M			117	6.00 x 17	5 ps	3310	945
C	W1	1	115	5.50 x 17	5 ps	3020	695
C	W1	1	117.2	6.00 x 17	5 ps	3350	765
C	306S	1	112	6.00 x 16	5 ps	3245	715
C	298S	1	116.6	6.50 x 16	5 ps	3450	830
C	306S	1	112	6.00 x 16	5 ps	3300	765
C	340S	1	112	6.00 x 16	5 ps	3235	720
C	342S	1	112	6.00 x 16	5 ps	3300	770
C	322S	1	116.6	6.50 x 16	5 ps	3415	815
C	352S		116.6	6.00 x 16	5 ps	3265	881
C	350S			6.50 x 16	5 ps	3410	939

YEAR	MODEL	ENGINE						
		CYLS	BORE	STROKE	DISPL	HP@RPM	C.R.	VLV
1938	DeLuxe 6, 6DA	6	3.438	4.00	222.7	85@3500	6.2	L
	DeLuxe 8, 8DA	8	3.25	3.75	248.9	100@3700	6.2	L
1939	Quality DeLuxe 6, 26EA	6	3.438	4.00	222.7	85@3520	6.2	L
	DeLuxe 120-6, 26EB	6	3.438	4.00	222.7	85@3520	6.2	L
	DeLuxe 8, 28EA	8	3.25	3.75	248.9	100@3700	6.2	L
1940	Special 6, 25HA	6	3.438	4.00	222.7	87@3520	7.2	L
	DeLuxe 6, 26HB	6	3.438	4.00	222.7	87@3520	7.2	L
	DeLuxe 8, 28HA	8	3.25	3.75	248.9	100@3700	7.1	L
	Torpedo 8, 29HB	8	3.25	3.75	248.9	103@3700	7.1	L
1941	DeLuxe Torpedo 6, JA25	6	3.562	4.00	239.2	90@3200	7.5	L
	Streamliner Torpedo 6, JB26	6	3.562	4.00	239.2	90@3200	7.5	L
	Custom Torpedo 6, JC24	6	3.562	4.00	239.2	90@3200	7.5	L
	DeLuxe Torpedo 8, JA27	8	3.25	3.75	248.9	103@3500	7.5	L
	Streamliner Torpedo 8, JB28	8	3.25	3.75	248.9	103@3500	7.5	L
	Custom Torpedo 8, JC29	8	3.25	3.75	248.9	103@3500	7.5	L
1942	Torpedo 6, 25KA	6	3.562	4.00	239.2	90@3200	7.5	L
	Streamliner 6, 26KB	6	3.562	4.00	239.2	90@3200	7.5	L
	Streamliner Chieftain, 26KB	6	3.562	4.00	239.2	90@3200	7.5	L
	Torpedo 8, 27KA	8	3.25	3.75	248.9	103@3500	7.5	L
	Streamliner 8, 28KB	8	3.25	3.75	248.9	103@3500	7.5	L
	Streamliner Chieftain 8, 28KB	8	3.25	3.75	248.9	103@3500	7.5	L
1946	Torpedo 6, 25, (6LA)	6	3.562	4.00	239.2	94@3400	6.5	L
	Streamliner 6, 26 (6LB)	6	3.562	4.00	239.2	94@3400	6.5	L
	Torpedo 8, 27 (8LA)	8	3.25	3.75	248.9	108@3700	6.5	L
	Streamliner 8, 28 (8LB)	8	3.25	3.75	248.9	108@3700	6.5	L
1947	Torpedo 6, 25 (6MA)	6	3.562	4.00	239.2	94@3400	6.5	L
	Streamliner 6, 26 (6MB)	6	3.562	4.00	239.2	94@3400	6.5	L
	Torpedo 8, 27 (8MA)	8	3.25	3.75	248.9	108@3700	6.5	L
	Streamliner 8, 28 (8MB)	8	3.25	3.75	248.9	108@3700	6.5	L
1948	Torpedo 6, (25PA)	6	3.562	4.00	239.2	94@3400	6.5	L
	Streamliner 6, (26PB)	6	3.562	4.00	239.2	94@3400	6.5	L
	Torpedo 8, (27PA)	8	3.25	3.75	248.9	108@3700	6.5	L
	Streamliner 8, (28PB)	8	3.25	3.75	248.9	108@3700	6.5	L
1949	Streamliner 25	6	3.438	4.00	239.2	90@3400	6.5	L
	DeLuxe 25	6	3.438	4.00	239.2	90@3400	6.5	L
	Chieftain 25	6	3.438	4.00	239.2	90@3400	6.5	L
	Chieftain DeLuxe 25	6	3.438	4.00	239.2	90@3400	6.5	L
	Streamliner 27	8	3.25	3.75	248.9	104@3600	6.5	L
	DeLuxe 27	8	3.25	3.75	248.9	104@3600	6.5	L
	Chieftain 27	8	3.25	3.75	248.9	104@3600	6.5	L
	Chieftain Deluxe 27	8	3.25	3.75	248.9	104@3600	6.5	L

MFR	CARBURETOR MODEL	VEN	WHEEL-BASE	TIRES	BODY	WEIGHT	PRICE
C	401S		117	6.00 x 16	5 ps	3295	916
C	350S		122	6.50 x 16	5 ps	3415	980
C	WA1-433S	1	115	6.00 x 16	5 ps	3000	866
C	WA1-433S	1	120	6.00 x 16	5 ps	3165	922
C	WA1-433S	1	120	6.50 x 16	5 ps	3265	970
C	WA1-463S	1	117	6.00 x 16	5 ps	3125	876
C	WA1-463S	1	120	6.00 x 16	5 ps	3210	932
C	WA1-462S	1	120	6.50 x 16	5 ps	3300	970
C	WA1-462S	1	122	6.50 x 16	5 ps	3475	1072
C	WA1-494S	1	119	6.00 x 16	5 ps	3235	921
C	WA1-494S	1	122	6.50 x 16	5 ps	3365	980
C	WA1-494S	1	122	6.50 x 16	5 ps	3355	1052
C	WDO-469S	2	119	6.00 x 16	5 ps	3285	946
C	WDO-469S	2	122	6.50 x 16	5 ps	3425	1005
C	WDO-469S	2	122	6.50 x 16	5 ps	3430	1077
C	WA1-494S	1	119	6.00 x 16	5 ps	3305	985
C	WA1-521S	1	122	6.50 x 16	5 ps	3415	1035
C	WA1-521S	1	122	6.50 x 16	5 ps	3460	1085
C	WDO-540S	2	119	6.00 x 16	5 ps	3360	1010
C	WDO-540S	2	122	6.50 x 16	5 ps	3485	1060
C	WDO-540S	2	122	6.50 x 16	5 ps	3515	1110
C	WA1-537S	1	119	6.00 x 16	5 ps	3361	1427
C	WA1-537S	1	122	6.50 x 16	5 ps	3490	1510
C	WDO-548S	2	119	6.00 x 16	5 ps	3436	1455
C	WDO-548S	2	122	6.50 x 16	5 ps	3550	1538
C	WA1-537S	1	119	6.00 x 16	5 ps	3220	1512
C	WA1-537S	1	122	6.50 x 16	5 ps	3450	1598
C	WCD-6305	2	119	6.00 x 16	5 ps	3405	1559
C	WCD-6305	2	122	6.50 x 16	5 ps	3515	1645
C	WA1-537S	1	119	6.00 x 16			
C	WA1-537S	1	122	6.50 x 16			
C	WCD-630S	2	119	6.00 x 16			
C	WCD-630S	2	122	6.50 x 16			
C	WA1-537S	1	120	7.10 x 15	5 ps	3270	1740
C	WA1-537S	1	120	7.10 x 15	5 ps	3315	1835
C	WA1-537S	1	120	7.10 x 15	6 ps	3275	1761
C	WA1-537S	1	120	7.10 x 15	6 ps	3290	1556
C	WCD-6305B	2	120	7.10 x 15	5 ps	3360	1808
C	WCD-6305B	2	120	7.10 x 15	5 ps	3380	1903
C	WCD-6305B	2	120	7.10 x 15	6 ps	3360	1829
C	WCD-6305B	2	120	7.10 x 15	6 ps	3380	1924

YEAR	MODEL	ENGINE						
		CYLS	BORE	STROKE	DISPL	HP@RPM	C.R.	VLV
1950	Streamliner 25	6	3.438	4.00	239.2	90@3400	6.5	L
	DeLuxe	6	3.438	4.00	239.2	90@3400	6.5	L
	Chieftain	6	3.438	4.00	239.2	90@3400	6.5	L
	DeLuxe	6	3.438	4.00	239.2	90@3400	6.5	L
	Super DeLuxe	6	3.438	4.00	239.2	90@3400	6.5	L
	Streamliner 27	8	3.375	3.75	268.2	108@3600	6.5	L
	DeLuxe	8	3.375	3.75	268.2	108@3600	6.5	L
	Chieftain	8	3.375	3.75	268.2	108@3600	6.5	L
	DeLuxe	8	3.375	3.75	268.2	108@3600	6.5	L
	Super DeLuxe	8	3.375	3.75	268.2	108@3600	6.5	L
1951	Streamliner 25	6	3.562	4.00	239.2	96@3400	6.5	L
	DeLuxe 27	6	3.562	4.00	239.2	96@3400	6.5	L
	Chieftain 27	6	3.562	4.00	239.2	96@3400	6.5	L
	DeLuxe 27	6	3.562	4.00	239.2	96@3400	6.5	L
	Super DeLuxe 27	6	3.562	4.00	239.2	96@3400	6.5	L
	Streamliner 27	8	3.375	3.75	268.4	116@3600	6.5	L
	DeLuxe 27	8	3.375	3.75	268.4	116@3600	6.5	L
	Chieftain 27	8	3.375	3.75	268.4	116@3600	6.5	L
	DeLuxe 27	8	3.375	3.75	268.4	116@3600	6.5	L
	Super DeLuxe 27	8	3.375	3.75	269.4	116@3600	6.5	L
1952	Chieftain 25	6	3.562	4.00	238.2	100/102	6.8/	L
						@3400	7.7	
	DeLuxe 25	6	3.562	4.00	239.2	100/102	6.8/	L
						@3400	7.7	
	Super DeLuxe 25	6	3.562	4.00	239.2	100/102	6.8/	L
						@3400	7.7	
	Chieftain 27	8	3.375	3.75	268.4	118/122	6.8/	L
						@3600	7.7	
	DeLuxe 27	8	3.375	3.75	268.4	118/122	6.8/	L
						@3600	7.7	
	Super DeLuxe 27	8	3.375	3.75	268.4	118/122	6.8/	L
						@3600	7.7	
1953	Chieftain Six 25	6	3.438	4.00	239.2	115@3800	7.0	L
	DeLuxe	6	3.438	4.00	239.2	115@3800	7.0	L
	Custom	6	3.438	4.00	239.2	115@3800	7.0	L
	Chieftain Eight 25	8	3.375	3.75	268.4	118@3600	6.8	L
	DeLuxe	8	3.375	3.75	268.4	118@3600	6.8	L
	Custom	8	3.375	3.75	268.4	118@3600	6.8	L
1954	Chieftain Six Special 25	6	3.438	4.00	239.2	115/118	7.0/	L
						@3800	7.7	

MFR	CARBURETOR MODEL	VEN	WHEEL-BASE	TIRES	BODY	WEIGHT	PRICE
C	WA1-717S	1	120	7.10 x 15	5 ps	3304	1724
C	WA1-717S	1	120	7.10 x 15	5 ps	3309	1819
C	WA1-717S	1	120	7.10 x 15	5 ps	3299	1745
C	WA1-717S	1	120	7.10 x 15	5 ps	3304	1840
C	WA1-717S	1	120	7.10 x 15	5 pht2	3359	2058
C	WCD-719S	2	120	7.10 x 15	5 ps	3389	1792
C	WCD-719S	2	120	7.10 x 15	5 ps	3399	1887
C	WCD-719S	2	120	7.10 x 15	5 ps	3384	1813
C	WCD-719S	2	120	7.10 x 15	5 ps	3389	1908
C	WCD-719S	2	120	7.10 x 15	5 pht2	3439	2127
R	7002870	1	120	7.10 x 15	5 pcs	3248	1824
R	7002870	1	120	7.10 x 15	5 pcs	3263	1927
R	7002870	1	120	7.10 x 15	5 ps	3273	1903
R	7002870	1	120	7.10 x 15	5 ps	3273	2006
R	7002870	1	120	7.10 x 15	5 pht2	3353	2244
C	WCD-179S	2	120	7.10 x 15	5 pcs	3343	1900
C	WCD-719S	2	120	7.10 x 15	5 pcs	3348	2003
C	WCD-719S	2	120	7.10 x 15	5 ps	3363	1977
C	WCD-719S	2	120	7.10 x 15	5 ps	3373	2081
C	WCD-719S	2	120	7.10 x 15	5 pht2	3433	2320
R	BC	1	120	7.10 x 15	5 ps	3278	2015
R	BC	1	120	7.10 x 15	5 ps	3278	2119
R	BC	1	120	7.10 x 15	5 pht2	3368	2370
C	WCD-715S	2	120	7.10 x 15	5 ps	3378	2090
C	WCD-715S	2	120	7.10 x 15	5 ps	3378	2194
C	WCD-715S	2	120	7.10 x 15	5 pht2	3448	2446
C	WCD-2010S	2	122	7.10 x 15	5 ps	3381	2015
C	WCD-2010S	2	122	7.10 x 15	5 ps	3396	2119
C	WCD-2010S	2	122	7.10 x 15	5 pht2	3421	2370
C	WCD-719SA	2	122	7.10 x 15	5 ps	3456	2090
C	WCD-719SA	2	122	7.10 x 15	5 ps	3471	2194
C	WCD-719SA	2	122	7.10 x 15	5 pht2	3496	2446
C	WCD-2010S	2	122	7.10 x 15	6 ps	3391	2027

YEAR	MODEL	ENGINE						
		CYLS	BORE	STROKE	DISPL	HP@RPM	C.R.	VLV
	DeLuxe 25	6	3.438	4.00	239.2	115/118	7.0/	L
						@3800	7.7	
	Custom 25	6	3.438	4.00	239.2	115/118	7.0/	L
						@3800	7.7	
	Chieftain Eight Special 27	8	3.375	3.75	268.4	127/122	7.7/	L
						@3800	6.8	
	DeLuxe 27	8	3.375	3.75	268.4	127/122	7.7/	L
						@3800	6.8	
	Custom 27	8	3.375	3.75	268.4	127/122	7.7/	L
						@3800	6.8	
	Star Chief Eight DeLuxe 28	8	3.375	3.75	268.4	127/122	7.7/	L
						@3800	6.8	
	Custom 28	8	3.375	3.75	268.4	127/122	7.7/	L
						@3800	6.8	
1955	Chieftain 27	V8	3.75	3.25	287.2	180@4600	8.0	OH
	Chieftain 27	V8	3.75	3.25	287.2	180@4600	8.0	OH
	Star Chief 28	V8	3.75	3.25	287.2	180@4600	8.0	OH
	Star Chief Custom 28	V8	3.75	3.25	287.2	180@4600	8.0	OH
1956	Chieftain 27 (860)	V8	3.938	3.25	316.6	205@4600	8.9	OH
	Chieftain 27 (870)	V8	3.938	3.25	316.6	205@4600	8.9	OH
	Chieftain Custom 27	V8	3.938	3.25	316.6	205@4600	8.9	OH
	Star Chief 28	V8	3.938	3.25	316.6	227@4800	8.9	OH
	Star Chief Custom 28	V8	3.938	3.25	316.6	227@4800	8.9	OH
1957	Chieftain 27	V8	3.938	3.562	347.0	252@4600	8.5	OH
	Super Chief 27	V8	3.938	3.562	347.0	270@4800	8.5	OH
	Star Super Chief 27	V8	3.938	3.562	347.0	270@4800	8.5	OH
	Star Chief 28	V8	3.938	3.562	347.0	270@4800	8.5	OH
	Star Chief Custom 28	V8	3.938	3.562	347.0	270@4800	8.5	OH
	Bonneville 28	V8	3.938	3.562	347.0	270@4800	8.5	OH
1958	Chieftain 25	V8	4.062	3.562	369.4	240@4500	8.6	OH
	Chieftain 27	V8	4.062	3.562	369.4	240@4500	8.6	OH
	Super Chief 28	V8	4.062	3.562	369.4	240@4500	8.6	OH
	Star Super Chief 28	V8	4.062	3.562	369.4	255@4500	8.6	OH
	Star Super Chief 27	V8	4.062	3.562	369.4	255@4500	8.6	OH

MFR	CARBURETOR MODEL	VEN	WHEEL-BASE	TIRES	BODY	WEIGHT	PRICE
C	WCD-2010S	2	122	7.10 x 15	6 ps	3406	2131
C	WCD-2010S	2	122	7.10 x 15	5 pht2	3421	2382
C	WCD-2122S	2	122	7.10 x 15	6 ps	3451	2102
C	WCD-2122S	2	122	7.10 x 15	6 ps	3466	2206
C	WCD-2122S	2	122	7.10 x 15	5 pht2	3491	2458
C	WCD-2122S	2	124	7.10 x 15	6 ps	3536	2301
C	WCD-2122S	2	124	7.10 x 15	6 ps	3536	2394
R	7006100	2	122	7.10 x 15/ 7.60 x 15	6 ps	3511	2164
R	7006100	2	122	7.10 x 15/ 7.60 x 15	6 ps	3511	2268
R	7006100	2	124	7.10 x 15	6 ps	3556	2362
R	7006100	2	124	7.10 x 15	6 ps	3556	2455
R	7008696	2	122	7.10 x 15/ 7.60 x 15	6 ps	3512	2259
R	7008696	2	122	7.10 x 15/ 7.60 x 15	6 ps	3512	2374
R	7008696	2	122	7.60 x 15	6 psw2	3642	3089
R	7007900	4	124	7.10 x 15	6 ps	3577	2488
R	7007900	4	124	7.10 x 15	6 pht2	3567	2696
R	7009832	2	122	8.00 x 14/ 8.50 x 14	6 ps	3560	2527
R	7009829	4	122	8.00 x 14/ 8.50 x 14	6 ps	3585	2664
R	7009829	4	122	8.50 x 14	6 psw2	3750	3481
R	7009829	4	124	8.00 x 14	6 ps	3630	2839
R	7009829	4	124	8.00 x 14	6 ps	3645	2896
R	7009829	4	124	8.00 x 14	6 pcv2	4285	5782
R	7011703	2	122	8.00 x 14	5 pcv2	3850	3019
R	7011703	2	122	8.00 x 14/ 8.50 x 14	6 ps	3735	2638
R	7011703	2	122	8.00 x 14	6 ps	3770	2834
C	AFB-2751S	4	124	8.00 x 14	6 ps	3825	3071
C	AFB-2751S	4	124	8.00 x 14	6 psw4	4065	3350

YEAR	MODEL	ENGINE						
		CYLS	BORE	STROKE	DISPL	HP@RPM	C.R.	VLV
	Bonneville Custom 25	V8	4.062	3.562	369.4	255@4500	8.6	OH
1959	Catalina 21	V8	4.062	3.75	388.9	245@4200	8.6	OH
	Star Chief 24	V8	4.062	3.75	388.9	245@4200	8.6	OH
	Custom 27	V8	4.062	3.75	388.9	260@4200	8.6	OH
	Bonneville 28	V8	4.062	3.75	388.9	260@4200	8.6	OH
	Opt. engine all lines:	V8	4.062	3.75	388.9	315@4600	8.6	OH
1960	Catalina 21	V8	4.062	3.75	388.9	215@3600	8.6	OH
	Ventura 23	V8	4.062	3.75	388.9	215@3600	8.6	OH
	Star Chief 24	V8	4.062	3.75	388.9	215@3600	8.6	OH
	Custom 27	V8	4.062	3.75	388.9	281@4400	8.6	OH
	Bonneville 28	V8	4.062	3.75	388.9	281@4400	8.6	OH
	Opt. engine all lines:	V8	4.062	3.75	388.9	318@4600	10.75	OH
1961	Tempest 21 (1)	4	4.062	3.75	194.5	110@3800	8.6	OH
	Catalina 23	V8	4.062	3.75	388.9	215@3600	8.6	OH
	Ventura 25	V8	4.062	3.75	388.9	215@3600	8.6	OH
	Star Chief 26	V8	4.062	3.75	388.9	215@3600	8.6	OH
	Custom 27	V8	4.062	3.75	388.9	235@3600	8.6	OH
	Bonneville 28	V8	4.062	3.75	388.9	235@3600	8.6	OH
	Optional engine:							
	(1)	V8	3.50	2.80	215.5	155@4600	8.8	OH
1962	Tempest 21 (1)	4	4.062	3.75	194.5	110@3800	8.6	OH
	Catalina 23 (2,3,4,5,7,9)	V8	4.062	3.75	388.9	215@3600	8.6	OH
	Star Chief 26 (4,6,8,9,10)	V8	4.062	3.75	388.9	215@3600	8.6	OH
	Custom 27	V8	4.062	3.75	388.9	215@3600	8.6	OH
	Bonneville 28 (6,8,9)	V8	4.062	3.75	388.9	235@3600	8.6	OH
	Grand Prix 29 (2,5,7,9)	V8	4.062	3.75	388.9	303@4600	10.25	OH
	Optional engines:							
	(1)	4	4.062	3.75	194.5	120@3800	10.25	OH
	(1)	4	4.062	3.75	194.5	140@3800	10.25	OH
	(1)	4	4.062	3.75	194.5	166@3800	10.25	OH
	(1)	4	4.062	3.75	194.5	115@4000	8.6	OH
	(1)	V8	3.50	2.80	215.5	185@4800	10.25	OH
	(2)	V8	4.062	3.75	388.9	230@4000	8.6	OH
	(3)	V8	4.062	3.75	388.9	267@4200	10.25	OH
	(4)	V8	4.062	3.75	388.9	303@4600	10.25	OH

MFR	CARBURETOR MODEL	VEN	WHEEL-BASE	TIRES	BODY	WEIGHT	PRICE
C	AFB-2751S	4	122	8.00 x 14	6 pht2	3710	3481
R	7013061	2	122	8.00 x 14	6 ps	3955	2704
R	7013061	2	124	8.00 x 14	6 ps	4005	3005
C	AFB-2820S	4	122	8.00 x 14	6 psw4	4370	3532
C	AFB-2820S	4	124/122	8.00 x 14	6 pht4	4085	3333
		3 x 2					
R	7015073	2	122	8.00 x 14/	6 ps	3935	2702
				8.50 x 14			
R	7015073	2	122	8.00 x 14	6 pht4	3990	3047
R	7015073	2	124	8.00 x 14	6 ps	3995	3003
C	AFB-2975S	4	122	8.50 x 14	6 psw4	4360	3530
C	AFB-2975S	4	124	8.00 x 14	6 pht4	4065	3331
R	7019061	1	112	6.50 x 15/	6 ps	2800	2165
				6.00 x 15			
R	7019060	2	119	8.00 x 15/	6 ps	3725	2702
				8.50 x 15			
R	7019060	2	119	8.00 x 15/	6 pht4	3795	3047
				8.50 x 15			
R	7019060	2	123	8.00 x 15/	6 ps	3840	3003
				8.50 x 15			
C	AFB-3123S	4	119	8.50 x 15	6 psw4	4185	3530
C	AFB-3123S	4	123	8.00 x 15	6 pht4	3895	3331
R	7019863	2					
R	7020061	1	112	6.00 x 15	6 ps	2815	2240
R	7020060	2	120/119	8.00 x 14/	6 ps	3765	2796
				8.50 x 14			
R	7020060	2	123	8.00 x 14	6 ps	3875	3097
R	7020060	2	119	8.00 x 15	6 psw4	4255	3624
C	AFB-3123A	4	123/119	8.00 x 14	6 pht4	4005	3425
C	AFB 3123S	4	120	8.00 x 14	5 pht2	3835	3490
R	7020061	1					
R	7020062	1					
R	7020079	4					
R	7020062	1					
R	7020078	4					
R	7020075	2					
R	7020071	2					
C	AFB-3326S	4					

YEAR	MODEL	ENGINE						
		CYLS	BORE	STROKE	DISPL	HP@RPM	C.R.	VLV
	(4)	V8	4.062	3.75	388.9	235@3600		OH
	(5, 6)	V8	4.062	3.75	388.9	318@4600	10.75	OH
	(7, 8)	V8	4.062	3.75	388.9	333@4800	10.75	OH
	(9)	V8	4.062	3.75	388.9	348@4800	10.75	OH
	(10)	V8	4.062	3.75	388.9	283@4400	10.25	OH
1963	Tempest 4-21 (1)	4	4.062	3.75	194.5	115@4000	8.6	OH
	Le Mans 22 (1)	4	4.062	3.75	194.5	115@4000	8.6	OH
	Catalina 23 (2,3,4,5,6)	V8	4.062	3.75	388.9	215@3600	8.6	OH
	Star Chief 26 (2, 3, 4)	V8	4.062	3.75	388.9	215@3600	8.6	OH
	Bonneville 28 (2, 3, 4)	V8	4.062	3.75	388.9	235@3600	8.6	OH
	Grand Prix 29 (4, 5, 7)	V8	4.062	3.75	388.9	303@4600	10.25	OH
	Optional engines:							
	(1)	V8	3.718	3.75	325.8	260@4800	10.25	OH
	(1)	4	4.062	3.75	194.5	120@3800	10.25	OH
	(1)	4	4.062	3.75	194.5	140@4400	10.25	OH
	(1)	4	4.062	3.75	194.5	166@4800	10.25	OH
	(2)	V8	4.062	3.75	388.9	235@3600	8.6	OH
	(2)	V8	4.062	3.75	388.9	303@4600	10.25	OH
	(3)	V8	4.062	3.75	388.9	230@4000	8.6	OH
	(4)	V8	4.062	3.75	388.9	313@4600	10.25	OH
	(5)	V8	4.09	4.00	420.4	353@5000	10.75	OH
	(6)	V8	4.062	3.75	388.9	267@4200	10.25	OH
	(7)	V8	4.062	3.75	388.9	283@4400	10.25	OH
1964	Tempest 20	6	3.75	3.25	215.4	140@4200	8.6	OH
	Tempest Custom 21	6	3.75	3.25	215.4	140@4200	8.6	OH
	Le Mans 22	6	3.75	3.25	215.4	140@4200	8.6	OH
	Tempest 20 (1, 4, 8)	V8	3.718	3.75	325.8	250@4600	8.6	OH
	Tempest Custom (1, 4, 8)	V8	3.718	3.75	325.8	250@4600	8.6	OH
	Le Mans 22 (1, 4, 8)	V8	3.718	3.75	325.8	250@4600	8.6	OH
	Catalina 23 (3,5,6,7,8,9)	V8	4.062	3.75	388.9	235@4000	8.6	OH
	Star Chief 26 (3, 5, 7, 9)	V8	4.062	3.75	388.9	235@4000	8.6	OH
	Bonneville 28 (2, 3, 4, 9)	V8	4.062	3.75	388.9	306@4800	10.5	OH
	Grand Prix 29 (2, 3, 4, 9)	V8	4.062	3.75	388.9	306@4800	10.5	OH
	Optional engines:							
	(1)	V8	3.718	3.75	325.8	280@4800	10.5	OH
	(2)	V8	4.094	4.00	421.2	338		OH
	(2)	V8	4.094	4.00	421.2	320@4400	10.5	OH
	(3)	V8	4.062	3.75	388.9	303@4600	10.5	OH
	(4, 5)	V8	4.062	3.75	388.9	230@4000	8.6	OH
	(6)	V8	4.062	3.75	388.9	267@4200	10.5	OH
	(7)	V8	4.062	3.75	388.9	283@4400	10.5	OH

MFR	CARBURETOR MODEL	VEN	WHEEL-BASE	TIRES	BODY	WEIGHT	PRICE
C	AFB-3123S	4					
R	7013063	3 x 2					
C	AFB-3123S	4					
R	7013063	3 x 2					
R	7020070	2					
R	7023067	1	112	6.00 x 15	6 ps	2835	2241
R	7023067	1	112	6.00 x 15	6 psc2	2865	2418
R	7023066	2	120/119	8.00 x 14	6 ps	3755	2795
R	7023066	2	123	8.00 x 14	6 ps	3885	3096
C	AFB-3479S	4	123	8.00 x 14	6 pht4	3985	3423
C	AFB-3479S	4	120	8.00 x 14	5 psc2	3915	3489
R	7023067	1					
R	7023067	1					
R	7023069	4					
R	7023063	2					
R	7013063	3 x 2					
R	7023060	2					
R	7023060	2					
R	7024164	1	116	6.50 x 14	6 ps	2970	2313
R	7024164	1	116	6.50 x 14	6 ps	2990	2399
R	7024164	1	116	6.50 x 14	5 psc2	2975	2491
R	7023071	2	116	7.00 x 14	6 ps	3225	2421
R	7023071	2	116	7.00 x 14	6 ps	3245	2507
R	7023071	2	116	7.00 x 14	5 psc2	3230	2599
R	7023066	2	120/119	8.00 x 14	6 ps	3770	2806
R	7023066	2	123	8.00 x 14	6 ps	3885	3107
C	AFB-3647S	4	123	8.00 x 14	6 pht4	3995	3433
C	AFB-3647S	4	120	8.00 x 14	5 psc2	3930	3499
C	AFB-3686S	4					
C	AFB-3650S	4					
C	AFB-3647S	4					
R	7023063	2					
R	7023066	2					
R	7023066	2					

YEAR	MODEL	ENGINE						
		CYLS	BORE	STROKE	DISPL	HP@RPM	C.R.	VLV
	(7)	V8	4.062	3.75	388.9	306@4800	10.5	OH
	(8)	V8	4.062	3.75	388.9	348@4900	10.75	OH
	(9)	V8	4.062	3.75	388.9	330@4600	10.75	OH
	(9)	V8	4.094	4.00	421.2	350@4600	10.75	OH
	(9)	V8	4.094	4.00	421.2	370@3800	10.75	OH
1965	Tempest 233	6	3.75	3.25	215.4	140@4200	8.6	OH
	Tempest 235	6	3.75	3.25	215.4	140@4200	8.6	OH
	Le Mans 237	6	3.75	3.25	215.4	140@4200	8.6	OH
	Tempest 233 (1)	V8	3.718	3.75	325.8	250@4600	9.2	OH
	Tempest 235 (1)	V8	3.718	3.75	325.8	250@4600	9.2	OH
	Le Mans 237 (1)	V8	3.718	3.75	325.8	250@4600	9.2	OH
	Catalina 252 (3, 5, 6, 7)	V8	4.062	3.75	388.9	256@4600	8.6	OH
	Star Chief 256 (3, 5, 6, 7)	V8	4.062	3.75	388.9	256@4600	8.6	OH
	Bonneville 262 (2, 3, 4, 6)	V8	4.062	3.75	388.9	333@5000	10.5	OH
	Grand Prix 266 (2, 3, 4, 6)	V8	4.062	3.75	388.9	333@5000	10.5	OH
	Optional engines:							
	(1)	V8	3.718	3.75	325.8	285@5000	10.5	OH
	(1)	V8	4.062	3.75	388.9	335@5000	10.75	OH
	(2)	V8	4.062	3.75	388.9	256@4600	8.6	OH
	(3)	V8	4.062	3.75	388.9	290@4600	10.5	OH
	(3)	V8	4.062	3.75	388.9	338@4800	10.75	OH
	(4)	V8	4.094	4.00	421.2	338@4600	10.5	OH
	(5)	V8	4.094	4.00	421.2	376@5000	10.75	OH
	(6)	V8	4.094	4.00	421.2	356@4800	10.75	OH
	(7)	V8	4.062	3.75	388.9	325@4800	10.5	OH
1966	Tempest 233 (1)	6	3.875	3.25	230.0	165@4700	9.0	OH
	Tempest Custom 235 (1)	6	3.875	3.25	230.0	165@4700	9.0	OH
	Le Mans 237 (1)	6	3.875	3.25	230.0	165@4700	9.0	OH
	Tempest '223 (2)	V8	3.718	3.746	325.8	250@4600	9.2	OH
	Tempest Custom 235 (2)	V8	3.718	3.746	325.8	250@4600	9.2	OH
	Le Mans 237 (2)	V8	3.718	3.746	325.8	250@4600	9.2	OH
	GTO 242 (3)	V8	4.062	3.746	388.9	335@5000	10.75	OH
	Catalina 252 (3, 4)	V8	4.062	3.746	388.9	256@4600	8.6	OH
	Star Chief Executive 256 (3, 4)	V8	4.062	3.746	388.9	256@4600	8.6	OH
	Bonneville 262 (5)	V8	4.062	3.746	388.9	333@5000	10.5	OH
	Grand Prix 266 (5)	V8	4.062	3.746	388.9	333@4600	10.5	OH
	Optional engines:							
	(1)	6	3.875	3.25	230.0	207@5200	10.5	OH

MFR	CARBURETOR MODEL	VEN	WHEEL-BASE	TIRES	BODY	WEIGHT	PRICE
C	AFB-3648S	4					
R	7024178	3 x 2					
R	7024178	3 x 2					
R	7023078	3 x 2					
R	7023078	3 x 2					
R	7025167	1	115	6.95 x 14	6 ps	2975	2263
R	7025167	1	115	6.95 x 14	6 ps	2980	2348
R	7025167	1	115	6.95 x 14	6 ps	3020	2496
R	7025071	2	115	7.45 x 14	6 ps	3215	2369
R	7025071	2	115	7.45 x 14	6 ps	3220	2454
R	7025071	2	115	7.45 x 14	6 ps	3260	2602
R	7025066	2	121	8.25 x 14	6 ps	3750	2748
R	7025066	2	124	8.25 x 14	6 ps	3860	3042
C	AFB-3895S	4	124	8.25 x 14	6 pht4	3990	3362
C	AFB-3895S	4	121	8.25 x 14	5 psc2	3940	3426
C	AFB-3899S	4					
C	AFB-3895S	4					
R	7025060	2					
R	7025060	2					
R	7024178	3 x 2					
C	AFB-3895S	4					
R	7024078	3 x 2					
R	7024078	3 x 2					
C	AFB-3895S	4					
R	7026167	1	116	6.95 x 14	6 ps	3075	2331
R	7026167	1	116	6.95 x 14/	6 ps	3100	2415
				7.35 x 14			
R	7026167	1	116	6.95 x 14/	6 pht4	3195	2701
				7.35 x 14			
R	7026071	2	116	7.35 x 14	6 ps	3270	2426
R	7026071	2	116	7.35 x 14	6 ps	3295	2510
R	7026071	2	116	7.35 x 14	6 pht4	3390	2796
C	AFB-4033S	4	116	8.25 x 14	5 psc2	3445	2783
R	7026066	2	121	8.25 x 14/	6 ps	3825	2866
				8.55 x 14			
R	7026066	2	124/121	8.55 x 14	6 ps	3955	3165
C	AFB-4033S	4	124/121	8.55 x 14	6 pht4	4110	3517
C	AFB-4033S	4	121	8.55 x 14	6 pht2	4005	3549
R	7026261	4					

YEAR	MODEL	ENGINE						
		CYLS	BORE	STROKE	DISPL	HP@RPM	C.R.	VLV
	(2)	V8	3.718	3.75	325.8	285@5000	10.5	OH
	(3)	V8	4.062	3.75	388.9	360@5200	10.75	OH
	(4)	V8	4.062	3.75	388.9	290@4600	10.5	OH
	(5)	V8	4.062	3.75	388.9	325@4800	10.5	OH
	(5)	V8	4.094	4.00	421.2	338@4600	10.5	OH
	(5)	V8	4.094	4.00	421.2	356@4800	10.75	OH
	(5)	V8	4.094	4.00	421.2	376@5000	10.75	OH
1967	Tempest 233 (1)	6	3.875	3.25	306.6	165@4700	9.0	OH
	Tempest Custom 235 (1)	6	3.875	3.25	306.6	165@4700	9.0	OH
	Le Mans 237 (1)	6	3.875	3.25	306.6	165@4700	9.0	OH
	Safari 239 (1)	6	3.875	3.25	306.6	165@4700	9.0	OH
	Tempest 233 (2)	V8	3.718	3.75	325.7	250@4600	9.2	OH
	Tempest Custom 235 (2)	V8	3.718	3.75	325.7	250@4600	9.2	OH
	Le Mans 237 (2)	V8	3.718	3.75	325.7	250@4600	9.2	OH
	Safari 239 (2)	V8	3.718	3.75	325.7	250@4600	9.2	OH
	GTO 242 (3)	V8	4.125	3.746	400.5	335@5000	10.75	OH
	Catalina 252 (5, 6, 7)	V8	4.125	3.746	400.5	265@4600	8.6	OH
	Executive 256 (5, 6, 7)	V8	4.125	3.746	400.5	265@4600	8.6	OH
	Bonneville 262 (5, 7, 8)	V8	4.125	3.746	400.5	333@5000	10.5	OH
	Grand Prix 266 (5, 8)	V8	4.125	3.746	400.5	350@5000	10.5	OH
	Firebird 223 (1)	6	3.875	3.25	306.6	165@4700	9.0	OH
	Firebird 223 (1, 2, 4)	V8	3.718	3.75	325.7	250@4600	9.2	OH
	Firebird 400	V8	4.125	4.00	427.6	335@5000	10.75	OH
	Optional engines:							
	(1)	6	3.875	3.25	230.0	215@5200	10.5	OH
	(2)	V8	3.718	3.746	325.8	285@5000	10.5	OH
	(3)	V8	4.125	3.746	400.5	360@5100	10.75	OH
	(3)	V8	4.125	3.746	400.5	255@4600	8.6	OH
	(4)	V8	4.125	3.746	400.5	325@4800	10.75	OH
	(5)	V8	4.125	4.00	427.6	360@4600	10.5	OH
	(5)	V8	4.125	4.00	427.6	376@5100	10.75	OH
	(6)	V8	4.125	3.746	400.5	290@4600	10.5	OH
	(6)	V8	4.125	3.746	400.5	333@5000	10.5	OH
	(7)	V8	4.125	3.746	400.5	325@4800	10.5	OH
	(8)	V8	4.125	3.746	400.5	265@4600	8.6	OH
1968	Tempest 233 (1)	6	3.875	3.531	249.9	175@4800	9.0	OH
	Tempest Custom 235 (1)	6	3.875	3.531	249.9	175@4800	9.0	OH
	Tempest Le Mans 237 (1)	6	3.875	3.531	249.9	175@4800	9.0	OH
	Tempest Safari 239	6	3.875	3.531	249.9	175@4800	9.0	OH
	Firebird 223 (1)	6	3.875	3.531	249.9	175@4800	9.0	OH
	Tempest 233 (2)	V8	3.875	3.75	353.8	265@4600	9.2	OH

MFR	CARBURETOR MODEL	VEN	WHEEL-BASE	TIRES	BODY	WEIGHT	PRICE
R	7025178	3 x 2					
R	7026066	2					
C	AFB-4033S	4					
C	AFB-4033S	4					
R	7025078	3 x 2					
R	7025078	3 x 2					
R	7027167	1	115	7.75 x 14	6 ps	3140	2388
R	7027167	1	115	7.75 x 14	6 ps	3145	2482
R	7027167	1	115	7.75 x 14	6 pht4	3265	2771
R	7027167	1	115	7.75 x 14	6 psw2	3390	2936
R	7027071	2	115	7.75 x 14	6 ps	3321	2483
R	7027071	2	115	7.75 x 14	6 ps	3326	2577
R	7027071	2	115	7.75 x 14	6 pht4	3446	2866
R	7027071	2	115	7.75 x 14	6 psw2	3571	3031
R	7027263	4	115	F70 x 14	5 psc2	3425	2871
R	7027066	2	121	8.25 x 14	6 ps	3825	2866
R	7027066	2	124/121	8.55 x 14	6 ps	3955	3165
C	AFB-4243S	4	124/121	8.55 x 14	6 pht4	4110	3517
C	AFB-4243S	4	121	8.55 x 14	6 pht2	4005	3549
R	7027167	1	108	E70 x 14	5 pht2	2955	2666
R	7027071	2	108	E70 x 14	5 pht2	3123	2761
R	7027263	4	108	E70 x 14			
		4					
		4					
R	7028065	1	116/112	7.75 x 14	6 ps	3307	2509
R	7028065	1	116/112	7.75 x 14	6 ps	3297	2602
R	7028065	1	116/112	7.75 x 14	6 pht4	3407	2916
R	7028065	1	116/112	7.75 x 14	6 psw2	3677	3107
R	7028065	1	108	E70 x 14	5 pht2	3061	2781
R	7028071	2	116/112	8.25 x 14	6 ps	3488	2615

YEAR	MODEL	ENGINE						
		CYLS	BORE	STROKE	DISPL	HP@RPM	C.R.	VLV
	Tempest Custom 235 (2)	V8	3.875	3.75	353.8	265@4600	9.2	OH
	Tempest Le Mans 237 (2)	V8	3.875	3.75	353.8	265@4600	9.2	OH
	Tempest Safari 239	V8	3.875	3.75	353.8	265@4600	9.2	OH
	Firebird 223 (2, 7)	V8	3.875	3.75	353.8	265@4600	9.2	OH
	Tempest GTO 242 (3, 4, 5)	V8	4.125	3.746	400.5	350@5000	10.75	OH
	Catalina 252 (3, 4, 5)	V8	4.125	3.746	400.5	290@4600	10.5	OH
	Executive 256 (8)	V8	4.125	3.746	400.5	290@4600	10.5	OH
	Bonneville 262 (3, 4, 5, 8)	V8	4.125	3.746	400.5	340@4800	10.5	OH
	Grand Prix 266 (3, 4, 5)	V8	4.125	3.746	400.5	350@5000	10.75	OH
	Optional engines: (1)	6	3.875	3.531	249.9	215@5200	10.5	OH
	(2)	V8	3.875	3.75	353.8	320@5100	10.5	OH
	(3)	V8	4.125	3.746	400.5	265@4600	8.6	OH
	(4)	V8	4.125	4.00	427.6	375@4800	10.5	OH
	(5)	V8	4.125	4.00	427.6	390@5200	10.75	OH
	(6)	V8	4.125	3.746	400.5	360@5100	10.75	OH
	(7)	V8	4.125	3.746	400.5	330@4800	10.75	OH
	(7)	V8	4.125	3.746	400.5	335@5000	10.75	OH
	(8)	V8	4.125	3.746	400.5	340@4800	10.5	OH
1969	Tempest 233 (1)	6	3.875	3.53	249.8	175@4800	9.0	OH
	Tempest Custom 235 (1)	6	3.875	3.53	249.8	175@4800	9.0	OH
	Le Mans 237 (1)	6	3.875	3.53	249.8	175@4800	9.0	OH
	Firebird 223 (1)	6	3.875	3.53	249.8	175@4800	9.0	OH
	Tempest 223 (2, 3)	V8	3.875	3.75	353.8	265@4600	9.2	OH
	Tempest Custom 236 (2, 3)	V8	3.875	3.75	353.8	265@4600	9.2	OH
	Le Mans 237 (2, 3)	V8	3.875	3.75	353.8	265@4600	9.2	OH
	GTO 242 (7)	V8	4.125	3.75	400.5	350@5000	10.75	OH
	Firebird 223	V8	3.875	3.75	353.8	265@4600	9.2	OH
	Firebird 400 (3, 4)	V8	4.125	3.75	400.5	330@4800	10.75	OH
	Catalina 252 (5)	V8	4.125	3.75	400.5	290@4600	10.5	OH
	Executive 256 (5)	V8	4.125	3.75	400.5	290@4600	10.5	OH
	Bonneville 262 (5)	V8	4.125	4.00	427.6	360@4600	10.5	OH
	Grand Prix 276 (5)	V8	4.125	3.75	400.5	350@5000	10.75	OH
	Optional engines:							
	(1)	6	3.875	3.531	249.8	215@5200	10.5	OH

MFR	CARBURETOR MODEL	VEN	WHEEL-BASE	TIRES	BODY	WEIGHT	PRICE
R	7028071	2	116/112	8.25 x 14	6 ps	3478	2708
R	7028071	2	116/112	8.25 x 14	6 pht4	3588	3022
R	7028071	2	116/112	8.25 x 14	6 psw2	3858	3213
R	7028071	2	108	F70 x 14	5 pht2	3224	2887
R	7028266	4	112	G77 x 14	5 pht2	3506	3101
R	7028063	2	121	8.25 x 14/	6 ps	3888	3004
				8.55 x 14/			
				8.85 x 14			
R	7028063	2	121/124	8.55 x 14/	6 ps	4002	3309
				8.85 x 14			
R	7028263	4	121/124	8.55/8.85 x14	6 ps	4122	3530
R	7028266	4	121	8.55 x 14	5 pht2	4075	3697
R							
R							
R							
R							
R							
R							
R							
R							
R							
R	7029165	1	116/112	7.75 x 14	6 ps	3250	2557
R	7029165	1	116/112	7.75 x 14	6 ps	3235	2651
R	7029165	1	116/112	7.75 x 14	6 pht2	3360	2965
R	7029165	1	108	E70 x 14	6 pht2	3080	2831
R			116/112	7.75 x 14	6 ps	3439	2668
R			116/112	7.75 x 14	6 ps	3424	2762
R			116/112	8.25 x 14	6 pht4	3549	3076
R	7029263	4	112	G78 x 14	6 pht2	3503	3156
R			108	E70 x 14	6 pht2	3248	2942
R			108	E70 x 14	6 pht2		
R	7028066	2	122	8.55 x 15/	6 ps	3945	3090
				8.85 x 15			
R	7028066	2	125/122	8.55 x 15/	6 ps	4045	3394
				8.85 x 15			
R	7029262	4	125/122	8.55 x 15/	6 ps	4180	3626
				8.85 x 15			
R	7029263	4	125	8.55 x 15	6 pht2	3715	3866

YEAR	MODEL	ENGINE CYLS	BORE	STROKE	DISPL	HP@RPM	C.R.	VLV
	(1)	6	3.875	3.531	249.8	230@5400	10.5	OH
	(2)	V8	3.875	3.75	353.8	330@5100	10.5	OH
	(3)	V8	3.875	3.75	353.8	265@4600	9.2	OH
	(4)	V8	3.875	3.75	353.8	325@5100	10.5	OH
	(4)	V8	4.125	3.75	400.5	330@4800	10.75	OH
	(5)	V8	4.125	4.00	427.6	390@5200	10.75	OH
	(6)	V8	4.125	4.00	427.6	370@4800	10.5	OH
	(7)	V8	4.125	4.00	427.6	366@5100	10.75	OH
	(7)	V8	4.125	4.00	427.6	370@5500	10.75	OH

POWELL — — Powell Sports Wagons, Compton, Cal., 1955-56

YEAR	MODEL	CYLS	BORE	STROKE	DISPL	HP@RPM	C.R.	VLV
1955-56	Sports Wagon	6	3.25	4.375	217.8	90		L
	Re-claimed Plymouth engines were used.							

PRIBIL — — Pribil Safety Aircar Co., Saginaw, Mich., 1937

YEAR	MODEL	CYLS	BORE	STROKE	DISPL	HP@RPM	C.R.	VLV
1937		4			91			

This was an experimental streamlined car with tubular frame. It is probable that only one was built. Engine was by Continental.

PUBLIX — — Publix Motorcar Co., Washington, D.C.; Buffalo, N.Y., 1947-48

YEAR	MODEL	CYLS	BORE	STROKE	DISPL	HP@RPM	C.R.	VLV
1948	Standard	1				2.5		
	Custom	2				10.1		

Various small engines were used in this small three-wheeler.

PUP — — Pup Motor Car Co., Spencer, Wis., 1948

YEAR	MODEL	CYLS	BORE	STROKE	DISPL	HP@RPM	C.R.	VLV
1948		1				7.5		
		2				10		
	Engines were from Briggs & Stratton.							

CARBURETOR MFR	MODEL	VEN	WHEEL-BASE	TIRES	BODY	WEIGHT	PRICE
			117				1095
			126		8 ps2	2400	
			50	4.00 x 8	2 pr	ca250	300
			68		2 pr	600	595
			68		2 pr	600	595

YEAR	MODEL	ENGINE						
		CYLS	BORE	STROKE	DISPL	HP@RPM	C.R.	VLV

REO — — Reo Motor Car Co., Lansing, Mich., 1904-36

YEAR	MODEL	CYLS	BORE	STROKE	DISPL	HP@RPM	C.R.	VLV
1930	Series 15	6	3.375	5.00	268.3	80@3200	5.3	L
	Flying Cloud, 20	6	3.375	5.00	268.3	80@3200	5.3	L
	Flying Cloud, 25	6	3.375	5.00	268.3	80@3200	5.3	L
1931	Flying Cloud, 25	6	3.375	5.00	268.3	85@3200	5.3	L
	Series 21	6	3.375	5.00	268.3	85@3200	5.3	L
	Series 21	8	3.00	4.75	268.6	90@3300		L
	Royale, 31	8	3.375	5.00	358.0	125@3300	5.3	L
	Royale, 35	8	3.375	5.00	358.0	125@3300	5.3	L
	Royale Elite	8	3.375	5.00	358.0	125@3300	5.3	L
1932	Flying Cloud, 21	6	3.375	5.00	268.3	85@3200	5.3	L
	Flying Cloud, 25	6	3.375	5.00	268.3	85@3200	5.3	L
	Flying Cloud, 21	8	3.00	4.75	268.6	90@3300	5.37	L
	Flying Cloud, 25	8	3.00	4.75	268.6	90@3300	5.37	L
	Royale, 31	8	3.375	5.00	357.8	125@3300	5.3	L
	Royale, 35	8	3.375	5.00	357.8	125@3300	5.3	L
	Royale, 52	8	3.375	5.00	357.8	125@3300	5.3	L
1932								
(Late)	S-6	6	3.125	5.00	230.1	80@3200		
1933	S-6	6	3.375	5.00	268.4	85@3200	5.3	
	Flying Cloud, S-2	6	3.375	5.00	268.4	85@3200		
	Royale Standard	8	3.375	5.00	357.8	125@3300	5.3	
	Royale Elite, N-1	8	3.375	5.00	357.8	125@3300	5.3	
	Royale Custom, N-2	8	3.375	5.00	357.8	125@3300	5.3	
1934	Flying Cloud, S-2	6	3.375	5.00	268.4	85@3200	5.3	
	Flying Cloud, S-3	6	3.375	5.00	268.4	85@3200	5.3	
	Royale Eight, N-1	8	3.375	5.00	357.8	125@3300	5.3	
	Royale Custom, N-2	8	3.375	5.00	357.8	125@3300	5.3	
	Flying Cloud, 4S	6	3.375	5.00	268.4	85@3200	5.3	
1935	Flying Cloud, 5S	6	3.375	5.00	268.4	85@3200	5.3	
	Flying Cloud, 6A	6	3.375	4.25	228.1	90@3400	7.0	
	Royale Six, 7S	6	3.375	5.00	268.4	95@3400	5.4	
1936	Flying Cloud, 6G	6	3.375	4.25	228.1	85@3400	7.0	

ROAMER — — Roamer Consolidated Corp., Kalamazoo, Mich., 1916-30

YEAR	MODEL	CYLS	BORE	STROKE	DISPL	HP@RPM	C.R.	VLV
1930	8-78	8	2.75	4.75	225.7	75@3400	4.94	L
	8-80	8	3.25	4.50	298.6	86@3000	5.0	L
	8-88	8	3.25	4.50	298.6	86@3000	5.0	L

CARBURETOR			WHEEL-	TIRES	BODY	WEIGHT	PRICE
MFR	MODEL	VEN	BASE				
Sc	UX-53		116	6.00 x 18	5 ps	3300	1195
Sc	UX-53		120	6.00 x 18	5 ps	3700	1595
Sc	UX-53		124	6.50 x 18	5 ps	3795	1795
Sc	T		125	6.50 x 17	5 ps	3950	1565
Sc	T		121	6.00 x 17	5 ps	3645	995
Sc			121	6.00 x 17	5 ps	3740	1195
Sc	S		131	6.50 x 18	5 ps	4375	1985
Sc	S		135	6.50 x 18	5 ps	4650	2445
Sc	S		131	6.50 x 18	5 ps	4500	2070
Sc			121	6.00 x 17	5 ps	3645	995
Sc			125	6.00 x 17	5 ps	3950	1565
Sc			121	6.00 x 17	5 ps	3740	1195
Sc			125	6.50 x 17	5 ps	3950	1595
Sc			131	6.50 x 18	5 ps	4375	1985
Sc			135	6.50 x 18	5 ps	4650	2445
Sc			152	6.50 x 18	7 ps	5010	3695
Sc			117	5.50 x 17	5 ps	3405	995
Sc			117	5.50 x 17/	5 ps	3405	995
				6.00 x 17			
Sc			118	6.00 x 17	5 ps	3540	995
S	EE-23	2	131	6.50 x 18	5 ps	4725	1745
S	EE-23	2	131	6.50 x 18	5 ps	4850	1845
S	EE-23	2	135	6.50 x 18	5 ps	4690	2445
Sc			118	6.00 x 17	5 ps	3590	845
Sc			118	6.00 x 17	5 ps	3590	795
			135	6.50 x 18	5 ps	5015	1700
			131	6.50 x 18	5 ps	4765	1500
Sc			118	6.00 x 17	5 ps	3630	895
C	304S		118	6.00 x 17	5 ps	3630	895
S	EX-32		115	6.25 x 16	5 ps	3220	845
C	304S		118	6.50 x 16	5 ps	3595	985
C	338S		115	6.25 x 16	5 ps	3300	845
Sc			120	6.00 x 20	5 ps	3440	1795
Sc			126	6.00 x 20	5 ps	3570	1985
Sc			136	6.50 x 20	5 ps	3880	2985

YEAR	MODEL	ENGINE						
		CYLS	BORE	STROKE	DISPL	HP@RPM	C.R.	VLV

ROCKEFELLER — — Rockefeller Sports Car Corp., Rockville Center, L.I., N.Y., 1949-53

YEAR	MODEL	CYLS	BORE	STROKE	DISPL	HP@RPM	C.R.	VLV
1949	Yankee	V8						L
1953	Yankee	V8						L
	The Rockefeller used Ford and possibly Mercury engines.							

ROCKET — — Hewson Pacific Corp., Los Angeles, Cal., 1948

YEAR	MODEL	CYLS	BORE	STROKE	DISPL	HP@RPM	C.R.	VLV
1948		4				65		
		6				95		

ROCKNE — — Rockne Motors Corp. (Subsidiary of Studebaker Corp.), Detroit, Mich., 1932-33

YEAR	MODEL	CYLS	BORE	STROKE	DISPL	HP@RPM	C.R.	VLV
1932	Standard 65	6	3.125	4.125	189.8	65@3200	5.25	L
	DeLuxe 65	6	3.125	4.125	189.8	65@3200	5.25	L
	Standard 75	6	3.25	4.125	205.3	72@3200	5.0	L
	De Luxe 75	6	3.25	4.125	205.3	72@3200	5.0	L
1933	10	6	3.125	4.125	189.8	70@3200	5.0	L
	DeLuxe 10	6	3.125	4.125	189.8	70@3200	5.0	L

ROLLS-ROYCE — — Rolls-Royce of America, Inc., East Springfield, Mass., 1921-31

YEAR	MODEL	CYLS	BORE	STROKE	DISPL	HP@RPM	C.R.	VLV
1930	Phantom I	6	4.25	5.50	468.1			OH
1931	Phantom I	6	4.25	5.50	468.1	*	4.5	OH
	* One reference gives 100@2250, despite the notion that Rolls-Royce did not publicize engine output.							

ROOSEVELT — — Marmon Motor Car Co., Indianapolis, Ind., 1930-31

YEAR	MODEL	CYLS	BORE	STROKE	DISPL	HP@RPM	C.R.	VLV
1930		8	2.75	4.25	201.9	72@3200	5.25	L
1931		8	2.75	4.25	201.9	77@3400	5.25	L
	For 1931, this was officially listed as Roosevelt model of Marmon.							

RUGER — — Ruger Cars Division; Sturm, Ruger & Co., Southport, Conn., 1969

YEAR	MODEL	CYLS	BORE	STROKE	DISPL	HP@RPM	C.R.	VLV
1969		V8	4.13	3.98	427.0	425@6000	11.1	OH
	Onlytwo Ruger cars were built, although production had been planned. Exterior followed very closely that of the 1930 eight-liter Bentley. Engine was by Ford.							

RUXTON — — New Era Motors, Inc., New York, N.Y., 1929-30

YEAR	MODEL	CYLS	BORE	STROKE	DISPL	HP@RPM	C.R.	VLV
1930	C	8	3.00	4.75	268.6	100@3400	5.25	L

CARBURETOR			WHEEL-	TIRES	BODY	WEIGHT	PRICE
MFR	MODEL	VEN	BASE				
					2 pr		
					4 pr	2000	2500
			106	6.40 x 15	3 pr	2000	1500
			106	6.40 x 15	3 pr		
S	UR2	1	110	5.25 x 18	5 ps	2595	635
S	UR2	1	110	5.25 x 18	5 ps	2675	680
S	UR2	1	110	5.50 x 18	5 ps	3000	735
S	UR2	1	110	5.50 x 18	5 ps	3085	780
S	UR2	1	110	5.25 x 18	5 ps	2675	615
S	UR2	1	110	5.25 x 18	5 ps	2715	660
O			143.5/	7.00 x 20	ch		13,325
			144.8				
O			144.8	7.00 x 20	ch		13,325
S				5.50 x 19	5 ps	2833	1075
S				5.50 x 19	5 ps	2833	995
H		2 x 4	131	7.00 x 18	4 pt	3480	13,000
Z		2	130	6.00 x 19	5 ps	4670	3195

YEAR	MODEL	ENGINE						
		CYLS	BORE	STROKE	DISPL	HP@RPM	C.R.	VLV

SAVAGE — — Auto Craft Co., Milwaukee, Wis., 1969

YEAR	MODEL	CYLS	BORE	STROKE	DISPL	HP@RPM	C.R.	VLV
1969	GT-340	V8	4.04	3.31	339.4	280@5000	10.5	OH
	GT-383	V8	4.25	3.375	383.0	335@5000	10.0	OH
	GT-440	V8	4.32	3.75	439.7	380@4600	10.0	OH

The Savage was a modified Plymouth Barracuda.

SAVIANO — — Saviano Vehicles, Inc., Warren, Mich., 1960

YEAR	MODEL	CYLS	BORE	STROKE	DISPL	HP@RPM	C.R.	VLV
1960	Scat					25		

SCOOTMOBILE — — Norman Anderson, Corunna, Mich., ca 1946-52

YEAR	MODEL	CYLS	BORE	STROKE	DISPL	HP@RPM	C.R.	VLV
1946								
1952		2				12		

This was a diminutive three-wheeler with single wheel at the rear and overall length of nine feet.

SEAGRAVE — — Seagrave Fire Apparatus Co., Columbus, Oh., 1960

YEAR	MODEL	CYLS	BORE	STROKE	DISPL	HP@RPM	C.R.	VLV
1960		4	3.438	4.375	162.0	65		L

A single prototype was designed and built for Seagrave by Detroit National Automobile Co. An announcement of proposed production was made but never came to pass. Engine in this prototype was a Continental F-162.

SHELBY — — Shelby-American, Inc., Santa Fe Springs, Cal., 1962; Shelby Automotive, Venice, Cal. and Ionia, Mich., 1962-68; Ford Motor Co., Detroit, Mich., 1968-70

YEAR	MODEL	CYLS	BORE	STROKE	DISPL	HP@RPM	C.R.	VLV
1965	GT350	V8	4.005	2.875	289.7	306@6000	10.5	OH
1966	GT350	V8	4.005	2.875	289.7	306@6000	10.5	OH
1967	GT350	V8	4.005	2.875	289.7	306@6000	10.5	OH
	GT500	V8	4.125	3.984	427.0	355@6000	10.5	OH
1968	GT350	V8	4.00	3.00	320.7	250@4800	10.5	OH
	GT500	V8	4.125	3.984	427.0	360@5400	10.5	OH
	GT500KR	V8	4.235	3.788	426.9	400@5600	11.6	OH
1969	GT350	V8	4.00	3.50	351.8	290@4800	10.7	OH
	GT500	V8	4.125	3.984	427.0	335@5200	10.7	OH

SKYLINE — — Skyline, Inc., Jamaica, N.Y., 1953

YEAR	MODEL	CYLS	BORE	STROKE	DISPL	HP@RPM	C.R.	VLV
1953	X50	6	3.125	3.50	161.1	85@3800	7.0	L

SQUIRE — — Auto Sport Importers, Inc., Philadelphia, Pa., 1968-

YEAR	MODEL	CYLS	BORE	STROKE	DISPL	HP@RPM	C.R.	VLV
1968	SS 100	6	3.68	3.91	249.5	170	9.0	OH

S & S — — Sayers & Scovill, Cincinnati, Oh., 1924-32

YEAR	MODEL	CYLS	BORE	STROKE	DISPL	HP@RPM	C.R.	VLV
1930-32	PL	8	3.375	4.50	322.0			L

	CARBURETOR		WHEEL-	TIRES	BODY	WEIGHT	PRICE
MFR	MODEL	VEN	BASE				
		4	108	205 x 14	2 pht2	3300	4600
			108	205 x 14	2 pht2	3500	
			108	205 x 14	2 pht2	3600	
			80			1700	1390
					2 pr		350
			93.5	5.50 x 12	2 pc	1700	3000
H		4	108	7.75 x 15/	2 pc	2800	
				6.95 x 14			
H		4	108	E70 x 15	2 pc	2800	
H	4150	4	108	E70 x 15	2 pc	2723	4311
H	2604+2605	2 x 4	108	E70 x 15	2 pc	3286	
H		4	108	E70 x 15	2 pc	3146	4116
H		4	108	E70 x 15	2 pc	3445	4317
H		4	108	E70 x 15	2 pc		4472
A		4	108	F60 x 15	2 pc	3600	
H		4	108	F60 x 15	2 pc	3850	—
			100		5 pcv2		3000
			104.5	6.00 x 16	2 pr	2200	9000
					7 pl	3750	5100

YEAR	MODEL	ENGINE						
		CYLS	BORE	STROKE	DISPL	HP@RPM	C.R.	VLV

This company specialized in ambulance and hearse production but also built limousines for passenger use. Engine size corresponds with the Continental 12K of this period which produced 114 HP at 3300 rpm.

STARLITE — — Kish Industries, Inc., Lansing, Mich., ca 1959

YEAR	MODEL	CYLS	BORE	STROKE	DISPL	HP@RPM	C.R.	VLV
1959				Electric				

STATIONETTE — — Martin Stationette Associates; Commonwealth Research Associates, New York, N.Y., 1954

YEAR	MODEL	CYLS	BORE	STROKE	DISPL	HP@RPM	C.R.	VLV
1954		4				24		

The Stationette was a three-wheeler which used a Hercules engine. At least one was built and exploited but production is questionable.

STORM — — Sports Car Development Corp., Detroit, Mich., 1954

YEAR	MODEL	CYLS	BORE	STROKE	DISPL	HP@RPM	C.R.	VLV
1954	Z-250	V8				250		

Engine was a modified Dodge.

STORY — — Tom Story, Portland, Ore., 1950

YEAR	MODEL	CYLS	BORE	STROKE	DISPL	HP@RPM	C.R.	VLV
1950		V8	2.60	3.20	135.9	113	10.5	L

Engine was a modified Ford V8-60.

STUDEBAKER — — Studebaker Corp., Studebaker-Packard Corp., South Bend, Ind., 1902-64; Studebaker Corp., of Canada, Ltd., Hamilton, Ontario, 1964-66

YEAR	MODEL	CYLS	BORE	STROKE	DISPL	HP@RPM	C.R.	VLV
1930	Dictator, GL	6	3.375	4.125	221.4	68@3200	4.8	L
	Dictator, FC	8	3.062	3.75	221.0	72@3200	5.15	L
	Commander, GJ	6	3.375	4.625	248.3	75@3000	4.8	L
	Commander, FD	8	3.062	4.25	250.4	80@3600	5.0	L
	President 125, FH	8	3.50	4.375	336.7	115@3200	5.0	L
	President 135, FE	8	3.50	4.375	336.7	115@3200	5.0	L
1931	Six, 54	6	3.25	4.125	205.3	70@3200	5.2	L
	Commander, 70	8	3.062	4.25	250.4	101@3200	5.2	L
	Dictator, 61	8	3.062	3.75	221.0	81@3200	5.15	L
	President, 80	8	3.50	4.375	336.7	122@3200		L
	President, 90	8	3.50	4.375	336.7	122@3200		L
1932	Six, 55	6	3.25	4.625	230.2	80@3200	5.0	L
	Dictator, 62	8	3.062	3.75	221.0	85@3200	5.0	L
	Commander, 71	8	3.062	4.25	250.4	101@3200	5.15	L
	President, 91	8	3.50	4.375	336.7	122@3600	5.1	L
1933	Six, 56	6	3.25	4.625	230.2	85@3200	5.5	L
	Commander, 73	8	3.062	4.00	235.7	100@3800	5.5	L
	President, 82	8	3.062	4.25	250.4	110@3600	5.0	L
	President, 92	8	3.50	4.375	336.7	132@3400	5.5	L
1934	Dictator, A	6	3.25	4.125	205.3	88@3600	6.3	L
	Special Dictator	6	3.25	4.125	205.3	88@3600	6.3	L

CARBURETOR			WHEEL-	TIRES	BODY	WEIGHT	PRICE
MFR	MODEL	VEN	BASE				
			82		2 pcv2		3000
					2 pc		1000
					2 pr		
			97			2080	3500
S			115	5.50 x 19	5 ps	3080	1195
S			115	5.50 x 19	5 ps	3095	1285
S			120	5.50 x 19	5 ps	3235	1425
S			120	6.50 x 19	5 ps	3255	1515
S			125		5 ps	4045	1795
S			135		7 ps	4235	2095
S			114	5.25 x 19	5 ps	2900	895
S	UUR-2		124	6.00 x 19	5 ps	3095	1150
S	UUR-2		114	5.25 x 19	5 ps	3525	1585
S			130	6.50 x 19	5 ps	4250	1850
S			136	6.50 x 19	7 ps	4260	2150
S			117	5.50 x 18	5 ps	3170	915
S	UUR-2		117	5.50 x 18	5 ps	3240	1050
S	UUR-2		125	6.00 x 18	5 ps	3545	1445
S	EE-22	2	135	6.50 x 18	5 ps	4260	1750
S	EX-22	1	117	5.50 x 17	5 ps	3310	915
S	EE-22	2	117	6.00 x 17	5 ps	3385	1075
S	EE-22	2	125	6.50 x 17	5 ps	3640	1385
S	EE-22	2	135	7.00 x 17	5 ps	4380	1685
S	UR21		113	5.50 x 17	5 ps	2910	790
S	UR21		113	5.50 x 17	5 ps	2895	740

YEAR	MODEL	ENGINE						
		CYLS	BORE	STROKE	DISPL	HP@RPM	C.R.	VLV
	Commander, B	8	3.062	3.75	221.0	103@3800	6.3	L
	President, C	8	3.062	4.25	250.4	110@3600	6.3	L
1935	Dictator, 1A	6	3.25	4.125	205.3	88@3600	6.3	L
	Commander	8	3.062	4.25	250.4	107@3800	6.0	L
	President	8	3.062	4.25	250.4	110@3600	6.5	L
1936	Dictator, 3A, 4A	6	3.25	4.375	217.0	90@3400	6.3	L
	President, 2C	8	3.062	4.25	250.4	115@3600	6.5	L
1937	Dictator, 5A, 6A	6	3.25	4.375	217.8	90@3400	6.0	L
	President, 3C	8	3.062	4.25	250.4	115@3600	6.5	L
1938	Commander, 7A	6	3.312	4.375	226.0	90@3400	6.0	L
	State Commander, 8A	6	3.312	4.375	226.0	90@3400	6.0	L
	State President, 4C	8	3.062	4.25	250.4	110@3600	6.0	L
1939	Champion Custom, G	6	3.00	3.875	164.3	72		L
	Champion Deluxe, G	6	3.00	3.875	164.3	72		L
	Commander, 9A	6	3.312	4.375	193.3	90@3400	6.0	L
	State President, 5C	8	3.062	4.25	250.4	110@3600	6.0	L
1940	Champion Custom, 2G	6	3.00	3.875	164.3	78@4000	6.5	L
	Champion Deluxe, 2G	6	3.00	3.875	164.3	78@4000	6.5	L
	Commander, 10A	6	3.062	4.375	193.3	90@3400	6.0	L
	President, 6C	8	3.062	4.25	250.4	110@3600	6.0	L
1941	Champion Custom, 3G	6	3.00	4.00	169.6	80@4000	6.5	L
	Champion Custom Deluxe, 3G	6	3.00	4.00	169.6	80@4000	6.5	L
	Champion Deluxe, 3G	6	3.00	4.00	169.6	80@4000	6.5	L
	Commander Custom, 11A	6	3.062	4.375	226.2	94@3600	6.5	L
	Commander Deluxe, 11A	6	3.062	4.375	193.3	94@3600	6.5	L
	Commander Skyway, 11A	6	3.062	4.375	193.3	94@3600	6.5	L
	President Custom, 7C	8	3.062	4.25	250.4	117@4000	6.5	L
	President Deluxe, 7C	8	3.062	4.25	250.4	117@4000	6.5	L
	President Skyway, 7C	8	3.062	4.25	250.4	117@4000	6.5	L
1942	Champion Custom, 4G	6	3.00	4.00	169.6	80@4000	6.5	L
	Champion Deluxe, 4G	6	3.00	4.00	169.6	80@4000	6.5	L
	Commander Custom, 12A	6	3.312	4.375	193.3	94@3600	6.5	L
	Commander Deluxe, 12A	6	3.312	4.375	193.3	94@3600	6.5	L
	Commander Skyway, 12A	6	3.312	4.375	193.3	94@3600	6.5	L
	President Custom, 8C	8	3.062	4.25	250.4	117@3800	6.5	L
	President Deluxe, 8C	8	3.062	4.25	250.4	117@3800	6.5	L
	President Skyway, 8C	8	3.062	4.25	250.4	117@3800	6.5	L
1946	Skyway Champion, 5G	6	3.00	4.00	169.6	80@4000	6.5	L
1947	Champion Deluxe, 6G	6	3.00	4.00	169.6	80@4000	6.5	L
	Champion Regal Deluxe, 6G	6	3.00	4.00	169.6	80@4000	6.5	L
	Commander Regal Deluxe, 14A	6	3.312	4.375	193.3	94@3600	6.5	L

MFR	CARBURETOR MODEL	VEN	WHEEL-BASE	TIRES	BODY	WEIGHT	PRICE
S	E-33		119	6.00 x 17	5 ps	3310	970
S	EE-22	2	123	6.50 x 17	5 ps	3490	1220
S	EX-22		114	6.00 x 16	6 ps	3030	745
S	EE-1		120	6.50 x 16	6 ps	3600	1015
S	EE-1		124	7.00 x 16	6 ps	3790	1330
S	EX-23		116	6.00 x 16	5 ps	3110	755
S	EE-22	2	125	6.50 x 16	5 ps	3600	1045
S	EX-23		116	6.00 x 16	5 ps	3130	880
S	EE-1		125	6.50 x 16	6 ps	3620	1165
S	BXO-26		116.5	6.00 x 16	6 ps	3140	965
S	BXO-26		116.5	6.00 x 16	6 ps	3215	1040
S	AAO-161		122	6.50 x 16	6 ps	3455	1205
C	WO-444S	1	110	5.50 x 16	5 ps	2360	740
C	WO-444S	1	110	5.50 x 16	5 ps	2345	800
S	BXO-26	1	116.5	6.00 x 16	6 ps	3200	965
S	AAO-161	2	122	6.50 x 16	6 ps	3440	1110
C	WO-468S	1	110	5.50 x 16	5 ps	2390	740
C	WO-468S	1	110	5.50 x 16	5 ps	2415	785
S	BXO-26	1	116.5	6.25 x 16	6 ps	3180	965
S	AAO-161	2	122	6.50 x 16	6 ps	3420	1095
C	WA1-496S	1	110	5.50 x 16	5 ps	2480	795
C	WA1-496S	1	110	5.50 x 16	5 ps	2500	825
C	WA1-496S	1	110	5.50 x 16	5 ps	2500	860
S	BXOV-26	1	119	6.25 x 16	6 ps	3210	1010
S	BXOV-26	1	119	6.25 x 16	6 ps	3225	1075
S	BXOV-26		119	6.25 x 16	6 ps	3240	1100
S	AAV-26	2	124.5	7.00 x 16	6 ps	3450	1140
S	AAV-26	2	124.5	7.00 x 16	6 ps	3475	1205
S	AAV-26	2	124.5	7.00 x 16	6 ps	3440	1210
C	WA1-496S	1	110	5.50 x 16	5 ps	2520	804
C	WA1-496S	1	110	5.50 x 16	5 ps	2545	839
C	WA1-496S	1	119	5.50 x 16	6 ps	3265	1044
S	BXOV-26	1	119	6.25 x 16	6 ps	3280	1089
S	BXOV-26	1	119	6.25 x 16	6 ps	3300	1124
S	AAV-26	2	124	7.00 x 15	6 ps	3485	1161
S	AAV-26	2	124	7.00 x 15	6 ps	3500	1206
S	AAV-26	2	124	7.00 x 15	6 ps	3540	1241
C	WE-532S	1	112	5.50 x 16	6 ps	2566	1097
C	WE-532S	1	112	5.50 x 15	6 ps	2735	1477
C	WE-532S	1	112	5.50 x 16	6 ps	2760	1551
S	BXOV-26	1	119	6.50 x 15	6 ps	3265	1760

YEAR	MODEL	ENGINE						
		CYLS	BORE	STROKE	DISPL	HP@RPM	C.R.	VLV
	Commander Deluxe 14A	6	3.312	4.375	193.3	94@3600	6.5	L
	Land Cruiser, 14A	6	3.312	4.375	193.3	94@3600	6.5	L
1948	Champion Deluxe, 7G	6	3.00	4.00	169.6	80@4000	6.5	L
	Champion Regal Deluxe, 7G	6	3.00	4.00	169.6	80@4000	6.5	L
	Commander Deluxe, 15A	6	3.312	4.375	193.3	94@3600	6.5	L
	Commander Regal Deluxe, 15A	6	3.312	4.375	193.3	94@3600	6.5	L
	Land Cruiser, 15A	6	3.312	4.375	193.3	94@3600	6.5	L
1949	Champion Deluxe, 8G	6	3.00	4.00	169.6	80@4000	6.5	L
	Champion Regal Deluxe, 8G	6	3.00	4.00	169.6	80@4000	6.5	L
	Commander Deluxe, 16A	6	3.312	4.375	193.3	94@3600	6.5	L
	Commander Regal Deluxe, 16A	6	3.312	4.375	193.3	94@3600	6.5	L
	Land Cruiser, 16A	6	3.312	4.375	193.3	94@3600	6.5	L
1950	Champion Deluxe, 9G	6	3.00	4.00	169.6	85@4000	7.0	L
	Champion Regal Deluxe, 9G	6	3.00	4.00	169.6	85@4000	7.0	L
	Commander Deluxe, 17A	6	3.312	4.375	193.3	102@3200	7.0	L
	Commander Regal Deluxe, 17A	6	3.312	4.375	193.3	102@3200	7.0	L
	Land Cruiser, 17A	6	3.312	4.375	193.3	102@3200	7.0	L
1951	Champion Custom, 10G	6	3.00	4.00	169.6	85@4000	7.0	L
	Champion Deluxe, 10G	6	3.00	4.00	169.6	85@4000	7.0	L
	Champion Regal, 10G	6	3.00	4.00	169.6	85@4000	7.0	L
	Commander Regal, H	V8	3.375	3.25	232.6	120@4000	7.0	OH
	Commander State, H	V8	3.375	3.25	232.6	120@4000	7.0	OH
	Land Cruiser, H	V8	3.375	3.25	232.6	120@4000	7.0	OH
1952	Champion Custom, 12G	6	3.00	4.00	169.6	85@4000	7.0	L
	Champion Deluxe, 12G	6	3.00	4.00	169.6	85@4000	7.0	L
	Champion Regal, 12G	6	3.00	4.00	169.6	85@4000	7.0	L
	Commander Regal, 3H	V8	3.375	3.25	232.6	120@4000	7.0	OH
	Commander State, 3H	V8	3.375	3.25	232.6	120@4000	7.0	OH
	Land Cruiser, 3H	V8	3.375	3.25	232.6	120@4000	7.0	OH
1953	Champion Custom, 14G	6	3.00	4.00	169.6	85@4000	7.0	L
	Champion Deluxe, 14G	6	3.00	4.00	169.6	85@4000	7.0	L
	Champion Regal, 14G	6	3.00	4.00	169.6	85@4000	7.0	L
	Commander Deluxe, 4H	V8	3.375	3.25	232.6	120@4000	7.0	OH
	Commander Regal, 4H	V8	3.375	3.25	232.6	120@4000	7.0	OH
	Land Cruiser, 4H	V8	3.375	3.25	232.6	120@4000	7.0	OH
1954	Champion Custom, 15G	6	3.00	4.00	169.6	85@4000	7.5	L

MFR	CARBURETOR MODEL	VEN	WHEEL-BASE	TIRES	BODY	WEIGHT	PRICE
S	BXOV-26	1	119	6.50 x 15	6 ps	3265	1761
S	BXOV-26	1	123	6.50 x 15	6 ps	3340	2043
C	WE-661S	1	112	5.50 x 15	6 ps	2720	1546
C	WE-661S	1	112	5.50 x 15	6 ps	2730	1620
S	BXOV-26	1	119	6.50 x 15	6 ps	3190	1851
S	BXOV-26	1	119	6.50 x 15	6 ps	3405	2325
S	BXOV-26	1	123	6.50 x 16	6 ps	3275	2142
C	WE-661S	1	112	6.40 x 15	6 ps	2745	1625
C	WE-661S	1	112	6.40 x 15	6 ps	2750	1762
S	BXOV-26	1	119	6.50 x 15	6 ps	3240	2019
S	BXOV-26	1	119	6.50 x 15	6 ps	3245	2140
S	BXOV-26	1	123	6.50 x 15	6 ps	3325	2328
C	WE-715S	1	113	6.40 x 15	6 ps	2750	1597
C	WE-715S	1	113	6.40 x 15	6 ps	2755	1676
S	BXOV-26	1	120	7.60 x 15	6 ps	3255	1902
S	BXOV-26	1	120	7.60 x 15	6 ps	3265	2024
S	BXOV-26	1	124	7.60 x 15	6 ps	3356	2187
C	WE-715S	1	115	6.40 x 15	6 ps	2695	1769
C	WE-715S	1	115	6.40 x 15	6 ps	2717	1749
C	WE-715S	1	115	6.40 x 15	6 ps	2720	1833
S	AAUVB-26	2	115	7.00 x 15	6 ps	3065	2023
S	AAUVB-26	2	115	7.00 x 15	6 ps	3070	2143
S	AAUVB-26	2	119	7.00 x 15	6 ps	3165	2289
C	WE-715S	1	115	6.40 x 15	6 ps	2695	1769
C	WE-715S	1	115	6.40 x 15	6 ps	2720	1862
C	WE-715S	1	115	6.40 x 15	6 ps	2725	1946
S	AAUVB-26	2	115	7.10 x 15	6 ps	3085	2121
S	AAUVB-26	2	115	7.10 x 15	6 ps	3075	2208
S	AAUVB-26	2	119	7.10 x 15	6 ps	3155	2365
C	WE-989S	1	116.5	6.40 x 15	6 ps	2710	1767
C	WE-989S	1	116.5/	6.40 x 15	6 ps	2735	1863
			120.5				
C	WE-989S	1	116.5/	6.40 x 15	6 ps	2745	1949
			120.5				
S	WWUVL-26	2	116.5/	7.10 x 15	6 ps	3075	2121
			120.5				
S	WWUVL-26	2	116.5/	7.10 x 15	6 ps	3095	2208
			120.5				
S	WWUVL-26	2	120.5	7.10 x 15	6 ps	3180	2316
C	WE-2190S	1	116.5	6.40 x 15	6 ps	2735	1801

YEAR	MODEL	ENGINE						
		CYLS	BORE	STROKE	DISPL	HP@RPM	C.R.	VLV
	Champion Deluxe, 15G	6	3.00	4.00	169.6	85@4000	7.5	L
	Champion Regal, 15G	6	3.00	4.00	169.6	85@4000	7.5	L
	Commander Deluxe, 5H	V8	3.375	3.25	232.6	120@4000	7.5	OH
	Commander Regal, 5H	V8	3.375	3.25	232.6	120@4000	7.5	OH
	Land Cruiser, 5HY	V8	3.375	3.25	232.6	120@4000	7.5	OH
1955	Champion Custom, 16G	6	3.00	4.375	185.6	101@4000	7.5	L
	Champion Deluxe, 16G	6	3.00	4.375	185.6	101@4000	7.5	L
	Champion Regal, 16G	6	3.00	4.375	185.6	101@4000	7.5	L
	Commander Custom, 16G* (1)	V8	3.562	2.81	224.3	140@4500	7.5	OH
	Commander Deluxe, 16G* (1)	V8	3.562	2.81	224.3	140@4500	7.5	OH
	Commander Regal, 16G* (1)	V8	3.562	2.81	224.3	140@4500	7.5	OH
	President Deluxe, 6H	V8	3.562	3.25	259.2	185@4500	7.5	OH
	President State, 6H	V8	3.562	3.25	259.2	185@4500	7.5	OH
	Speedster	V8	3.562	3.25	259.2	185@4500	7.5	OH
	Optional engine:							
	(1)	V8	3.562	2.81	224.3	166@4500	8.0	OH
	* Later standard engine:	V8	3.562	3.25	259.2	162@4500	7.5	OH
1956	Champion, 56G	6	3.00	4.375	185.6	101@4000	7.8	L
	Flight Hawk, 56G	6	3.00	4.375	185.6	101@4000	7.8	L
	Commander, 56B (1)	V8	3.562	3.625	259.2	170@4500	7.8	OH
	Power Hawk, 56B (1)	V8	3.562	3.625	259.2	170@4500	7.8	OH
	President, 56H (2)	V8	3.562	3.625	259.2	195@4500	7.8	OH
	Sky Hawk, 56H (2)	V8	3.562	3.625	259.2	195@4500	7.8	OH
	Golden Hawk, 56J	V8	4.00	3.50	351.8	275@4600	9.5	OH
	Optional engines:							
	(1)	V8	3.562	3.625	259.2	185@4500	8.3	OH
	(2)	V8	3.562	3.625	259.2	210@4500		OH
1957	Scotsman, 57G	6	3.00	4.375	185.6	101@4000	7.8	L
	Champion Custom, 57G	6	3.00	4.375	185.6	101@4000	7.8	L
	Champion Deluxe, 57G	6	3.00	4.375	185.6	101@4000	7.8	L
	Silver Hawk, 57G	6	3.00	4.375	185.6	101@4000	7.8	L

MFR	CARBURETOR MODEL	VEN	WHEEL-BASE	TIRES	BODY	WEIGHT	PRICE
C	WE-2108S	1	116.5/	6.40 x 15/	6 ps	2765	1918
			120.5	6.70 x 15			
C	WE-2108S	1	116.5/	6.40 x 15/	6 ps	2780	2026
			120.5	6.70 x 15			
S	WW6-112C	2	116.5/	7.10 x 15	6 ps	3105	2179
			120.5				
S	WW6-112C	2	116.5/	7.10 x 15	6 ps	3120	2287
			120.5				
S	WW6-112C	2	120.5	7.10 x 15	6 ps	3180	2438
C	WE-2108S	1	116.5	6.40 x 15	6 ps	2790	1783
C	WE-2108S	1	116.5/	6.40 x 15/	6 ps	2805	1885
			120.5	6.70 x 15			
C	WE-2108S	1	116.5/	6.40 x 15/	6 ps	2815	1993
			120.5	6.70 x 15			
S	WW6-115	2	116.5	6.40 x 15	6 ps	3065	1919
S	WW6-115	2	116.5/	6.40 x 15/	6 ps	3075	2014
			120.5	6.70 x 15			
S	WW6-115	2	116.5/	6.40 x 15/	6 ps	3080	2127
			120.5	6.70 x 15			
C	WCFB-2219S	4	120.5	7.10 x 15	6 ps	3165	2311
C	WCFB-2219S	4	120.5	7.10 x 15	6 ps	3220	2381
C	WCFB-2219S	4	120.5	7.10 x 15	4 pht2	3301	3252
C	WE-2108S	1	116.5	6.40 x 15	6 ps	2835	1993
C	WE-2108S	1	120.5	6.40 x 15	5 pc	2780	1982
S	WW6-117	2	116.5	6.70 x 15	6 ps	3140	2121
S	WW6-117	2	120.5	6.70 x 15	5 pc	3095	2097
S	WW6-117	2	116.5/	6.70 x 15/	6 ps	3295	2485
			120.5	7.10 x 15			
S	WW6-117	2	120.5	6.70 x 15	5 pht2	3215	2473
C	WCFB-2394S	4	120.5	7.10 x 15	5 pht2	3360	3057
		4					
		4					
C	WE-2417S	1	116.5	6.40 x 15/	6 ps	2725	1826
				6.70 x 15			
C	WE-2417S	1	116.5	6.40 x 15	6 ps	2785	2049
C	WE-2417S	1	116.5	6.40 x 15	6 ps	2810	2171
C	WE-2417S	1	120.5	6.40 x 15	5 pc	2790	2142

YEAR	MODEL	ENGINE						
		CYLS	BORE	STROKE	DISPL	HP@RPM	C.R.	VLV
	Commander Custom, 57B (1)	V8	3.562	3.25	259.2	180@4500	8.3	OH
	Commander Deluxe, 57B (1)	V8	3.562	3.25	259.2	180@4500	8.3	OH
	President, 57H (2)	V8	3.562	3.625	289.1	210@4500	8.3	OH
	Silver Hawk, 57H (2)	V8	3.562	3.625	289.1	210@4500	8.3	OH
	Golden Hawk, 57H	V8	3.562	3.625	289.1	275@4800	7.8	OH
	Classic, 57B	V8	3.562	3.625	289.1	225@4500	8.3	OH
1958	Scotsman, 58G	6	3.00	4.375	185.6	101@4000	7.8	L
	Champion, 58G	6	3.00	4.375	185.6	101@4000	7.8	L
	Silver Hawk, 58G (1)	V8	3.562	3.25	259.2	180@4500	8.3	OH
	Commander, 58B	V8	3.562	3.25	259.2	180@4500	8.3	OH
	President, 58H	V8	3.562	3.625	289.1	225@4500	8.3	OH
	Golden Hawk, 58H	V8	3.562	3.625	289.1	275@4800	8.3	OH
	Studebaker - Packard, 58L	V8	3.562	3.625	289.1	225@4800	8.3	OH
	Studebaker - Packard Hawk, 58L	V8	3.562	3.625	289.1	275@4800	7.8	OH
	Optional engine:							
	(1)	V8	3.562	3.625	289.1	225@4500	8.3	OH
1959	Lark Deluxe, 59S	6	3.00	4.00	169.6	90@4000	8.3	L
	Regal, 59S	6	3.00	4.00	169.6	90@4000	8.3	L
	Silver Hawk, 59S	6	3.00	4.00	169.6	90@4000	8.3	L
	Lark Regal, 59V	V8	3.562	3.25	259.2	180@4500	8.8	OH
	Silver Hawk, 59V	V8	3.562	3.25	259.2	180@4500	8.8	OH
1960	Lark Deluxe, 60S	6	3.00	4.00	169.6	90@4000	8.3	L
	Regal, 60S	6	3.00	4.00	169.6	90@4000	8.3	L
	Lark Deluxe, 60V	V8	3.562	3.25	259.2	195@4500	8.8	OH
	Regal, 60V	V8	3.562	3.25	259.2	195@4500	8.8	OH
	Hawk, 60H	V8	3.562	3.625	289.1	210@4500	8.8	OH
1961	Lark Deluxe, 61S	6	3.00	4.00	169.6	112@4500	8.5	OH
	Regal, 61S	6	3.00	4.00	169.6	112@4500	8.5	OH
	Lark Deluxe, 61V (1)	V8	3.562	3.25	259.2	180@4500	8.8	OH
	Regal, 61V (1)	V8	3.562	3.25	259.2	180@4500	8.8	OH
	Lark Cruiser, 61V (1)	V8	3.562	3.25	259.2	180@4500	8.8	OH
	Hawk	V8	3.562	3.625	289.1	210@4500	8.8	OH
	Optional engine:							
	(1)	V8	3.562	3.25	259.2	195@4500		OH

MFR	CARBURETOR MODEL	VEN	WHEEL-BASE	TIRES	BODY	WEIGHT	PRICE
S	WW6-117	2	116.5	6.70 x 15	6 ps	3105	2173
S	WW6-117	2	116.5	6.70 x 15	6 ps	3140	2295
S	WW6-117A	2	116.5	6.70 x 15	6 ps	3205	2407
C	WCFB-2574S	4	120.5	6.70 x 15	5 pc	3185	2263
S	WCFB-2574S	4	120.5	7.10 x 15	5 pht2	3400	3182
C	WCFB-2574S	4	120.5	7.10 x 15	6 ps	3270	2539
C	BBRI-2724S	1	116.5	6.40 x 15	6 ps	2740	1874
C	BBRI-2724S	1	116.5	6.40 x 15	6 ps	2835	2253
S	WW6-117B	2	120.5	6.40 x 15	6 pc	2810	2219
S	WW6-117B	2	116.5	7.50 x 14/	6 ps	3185	2378
				8.00 x 14			
C	2574S	4	120.5/	8.00 x 14/	6 ps	3365	2639
			116.5	7.50 x 14			
S	WW6-122A	4	120.5	8.00 x 14	6 pht2	3470	3282
C	2575S	4	120.5/	8.00 x 14	6 ps	3505	3212
			116.5				
S	WW6-122A	4	120.5	8.00 x 14	6 pht2	3470	3995
C	2574S	4					
C	AS-2876S	1	108.5/113	5.90 x 15	6 ps	2605	1995
C	AS-2876S	1	108.5/113	5.90 x 15	6 ps	2600	2175
C	AS-2876S	1	120.5	6.40 x 15	6 pc	2795	2360
S	WW6-123	2	108.5/113	6.40 x 15	6 ps	2924	2310
S	WW6-123	2	120.5	6.70 x 15	6 psc	3140	2495
C	AS-2934SA	1	108.5	5.90 x 15	6 ps	2592	2046
C	AS-2934SA	1	108.5	5.90 x 15/	6 ps	2619	2196
				6.40 x 15			
S	WW6-123A	2	108.5	6.40 x 15	6 ps	2941	2181
S	WW6-123A	2	108.5	6.40 x 15/	6 ps	2966	2331
				6.70 x 14			
S	WW6-123	2	120.5	6.40 x 15	6 psc	3207	2650
C	AS-3159S	1	108.5	6.00 x 15	6 ps	2665	2005
C	AS-3159S	1	108.5/113	6.00 x 15/	6 ps	2692	2155
				6.50 x 15			
S	WW6-123A	2	108.5	6.50 x 15	6 ps	2941	2140
S	WW6-123A	2	108.5/113	6.50 x 15/	6 ps	2966	2290
				6.70 x 15			
S	WW6-123A	2	113	6.70 x 15	6 ps	3001	2458
S	WW6-123A	2	120.5	6.70 x 15	5 psc	3205	2650
		4					

YEAR	MODEL	ENGINE						
		CYLS	BORE	STROKE	DISPL	HP@RPM	C.R.	VLV
1962	Lark Deluxe	6	3.00	4.00	189.6	112@4500	8.25	OH
	Regal	6	3.00	4.00	189.6	112@4500	8.25	OH
	Daytona	6	3.00	4.00	189.6	112@4500	8.25	OH
	Deluxe (1, 2)	V8	3.562	3.25	259.2	180@4500	8.5	OH
	Regal (1, 2)	V8	3.562	3.25	259.2	180@4500	8.5	OH
	Daytona (1, 2)	V8	3.562	3.25	259.2	180@4500	8.5	OH
	Cruiser (1, 2)	V8	3.562	3.25	259.2	180@4500	8.5	OH
	Gran Turismo Hawk (2, 3)	V8	3.562	3.625	289.1	210@4500	8.5	OH
	Optional engines:							
	(1)	V8	3.562	3.625	289.1	210@4500	8.5	OH
	(1)	V8	3.562	3.25	259.2	195@4500	8.5	OH
	(2)	V8	3.562	3.625	289.1	225@4500	8.5	OH
	(3)	V8	3.562	3.25	259.2	180@4500	8.5	OH
1963	Lark Regal	6	3.00	4.00	169.6	112@4500	8.25	OH
	Lark Custom	6	3.00	4.00	169.6	112@4500	8.25	OH
	Daytona	6	3.00	4.00	169.6	112@4500	8.25	OH
	Lark Regal (1, 2)	V8	3.562	3.25	259.2	180@4500	8.5	OH
	Custom (1, 2)	V8	3.562	3.25	259.2	180@4500	8.5	OH
	Daytona (1,2)	V8	3.562	3.25	259.2	180@4500	8.5	OH
	Cruiser (2)	V8	3.562	3.625	289.1	210@4500	8.5	OH
	Hawk (2)	V8	3.562	3.625	289.1	210@4500	8.5	OH
	Avanti, R-Q (3)	V8	3.562	3.625	289.1	225@4500	10.25	OH
	Optional engines:							
	(1)	V8	3.562	3.625	289.1	210@4500	8.5	OH
	(1)	V8	3.562	3.25	259.2	195@4500	8.5	OH
	(2)	V8	3.562	3.625	289.1	225@4500	8.5	OH
	(3)	V8	3.562	3.625	289.1	280@4500	9.0	OH
	(3)	V8	3.562	3.625	289.1	315	10.25	OH
	After 1963, Studebaker was built only by Studebaker-Packard Co. of Canada.							

STUDILLAC – – Bill Frick Motors, Rockville Center, L.I., N.Y., 1953-54

YEAR	MODEL	CYLS	BORE	STROKE	DISPL	HP@RPM	C.R.	VLV
1954		V8	3.688	3.625	309.8	230@4400	8.25	OH
	Cadillac engine in a Studebaker chassis and body = the Studillac.							

STUTZ – – Stutz Motor Car Co., Indianapolis, Ind., 1911-35

YEAR	MODEL	CYLS	BORE	STROKE	DISPL	HP@RPM	C.R.	VLV
1930	Eight, MA	8	3.375	4.50	322.0	113@3300	5.5	OHC
	Eight, MB	8	3.375	4.50	322.0	113@3300	5.5	OHC

	CARBURETOR		WHEEL-	TIRES	BODY	WEIGHT	PRICE
MFR	MODEL	VEN	BASE				
C	AS-3370S	1	113/109	6.00 x 15	6 ps	2760	2040
C	AS-3370S	1	113/109	6.50 x 15	6 ps	2770	2190
C	AS-3370S	1	109	6.00 x 15/ 6.50 x 15	6 pht2	2765	2308
S	WW6-127	2	113	6.50 x 15	6 ps	3015	2175
S	WW6-127	2	113/109	6.50 x 15/ 6.70 x 15	6 ps	3025	2325
S	WW6-127	2	109	6.50 x 15/ 6.70 x 15	6 pht2	3015	2443
S	WW6-127	2	113	6.50 x 15	6 ps	3030	2493
S	WW6-127	2	120.5	6.70 x 15	5 pht2	3230	
S	WW6-127						
C	RBS-3538S	1	113/109	6.00 x 15	6 ps	2790	2160
C	RBS-3538S	1	109/113	6.00 x 15	6 ps	2800	2285
C	RBS-3538S	1	109/113	6.00 x 15/ 6.50 x 15	6 pht2	2795	2308
S	WW6-130	2	113/109	6.00 x 15	6 ps	3000	2295
S	WW6-130	2	113/109	6.00 x 15	6 ps	3010	2420
S	WW6-130	2	109/113	6.00 x 15	6 pht2	3035	2443
S	WW6-130	2	113	6.00 x 15	6 ps	3065	2595
S	WW6-130	2	120.5	6.70 x 15	6 pht2	3280	3095
C	AFB-3506S	4	109	6.70 x 15	4 pht2	3140	4445
C	AFB-3540S	4					
C	AFB-3540S	4					
C	AFB-3507S	4					
C	AFB-3506S	4					
			120.5	7.10 x 15	4 pht2		4002
Z			134.5	6.50 x 20	5 ps	4918	3695
Z			145	6.50 x 20	5 ps	5045	3855

YEAR	MODEL	ENGINE						
		CYLS	BORE	STROKE	DISPL	HP@RPM	C.R.	VLV
1931	Six, LA	6	3.375	4.50	241.5	85@3100	5.5	OHC
	Eight, MA	8	3.375	4.50	322.0	113@3300	5.5	OHC
	Eight, MB	8	3.375	4.50	322.0	113@3300	5.5	OHC
1932	Six, LAA	6	3.375	4.50	241.5	85@3150	5.25	OHC
	SV-16	8	3.375	4.50	322.0	113@3300	5.5	OHC
	DV-32	8	3.375	4.50	322.0	156@3900	5.0	DOHC
1933	Six, LAA	6	3.375	4.50	241.5	85@3100	5.25	OHC
	SV-16	8	3.375	4.50	322.0	113@3300	5.5	OHC
	DV-32	8	3.375	4.50	322.0	156@3900	5.0	DOHC
1934	SV-16	8	3.375	4.50	322.0	113@3300	5.5	OHC
	DV-32	8	3.375	4.50	322.0	156@3900	5.0	DOHC
1935	SV-16	8	3.375	4.50	322.0	113@3300	5.5	OHC
	DV-32	8	3.375	4.50	322.0	156@3900	5.0	DOHC

SUPER STATION WAGON — — Henney Motor Co., Freeport, Ill., 1954

YEAR	MODEL	CYLS	BORE	STROKE	DISPL	HP@RPM	C.R.	VLV
1954		8	3.562	4.50	359.0	212@4000	8.7	OH

SURREY — — E. W. Bliss Co., Canton, Oh., 1958-60

YEAR	MODEL	CYLS	BORE	STROKE	DISPL	HP@RPM	C.R.	VLV
1958-60	'03					8		

SWIFT — — Swift Mfg. Co., El Cajon, Cal.; W. M. Mfg. Co., San Diego, Cal., 1959

YEAR	MODEL	CYLS	BORE	STROKE	DISPL	HP@RPM	C.R.	VLV
1959	T	1				3		

MFR	CARBURETOR MODEL	VEN	WHEEL-BASE	TIRES	BODY	WEIGHT	PRICE
Z			127.5	6.00 x 19	5 ps	4520	2245
Z			134.5	6.50 x 20	5 ps	4918	3195
Z			145	6.50 x 20	5 ps	5045	3865
Z			127.5	6.00 x 19	5 ps	4118	1620
Z			134/145	6.50 x 20	5 ps	4885	2995
Sc			134/145	7.00 x 20	5 ps	5185	3995
Z	105DS	2	127.5	6.00 x 19	5 ps	4520	1895
Z	105DS	2	134/145	7.00 x 18	5 ps	4845	3095
S	EE3	2	134/145	7.00 x 18	5 ps	5045	3695
			134/145	7.00 x 18	5 ps	4845	3095
			134/145	7.00 x 18	5 ps	5045	3795
Z			134.5/145	7.00 x 18	5 ps	4745	3095
S			134.5/145	7.00 x 18	5 ps	4895	3795
			156	8.20 x 15	6 psw4		
			67		2 pr	700	1095
			66		2 pr	230	795

YEAR	MODEL	CYLS	BORE	STROKE	DISPL	HP@RPM	C.R.	VLV

TERRAPLANE (ESSEX TERRAPLANE) — — Hudson Motor Car Co., Detroit, Mich., 1933-37

YEAR	MODEL	CYLS	BORE	STROKE	DISPL	HP@RPM	C.R.	VLV
	For 1930 - 32 See Essex.							
1933	Standard Six	6	2.938	4.75	193.1	70@3200	5.8	L
	Special Six	6	2.938	4.75	193.1	70@3200	5.8	L
	Eight	8	2.938	4.50	244.0	94@3200	5.8	L
1934	Challenger Six, KS	6	3.00	5.00	212.0	80@3600	5.8	L
	Major Six, KU	6	3.00	5.00	212.0	85@3600	5.8	L
	Special Six, K	6	3.00	5.00	212.0	80@3600	5.8	L
1935	Special Six, G	6	3.00	5.00	212.0	88@3800	7.0	L
	DeLuxe Six, GU	6	3.00	5.00	212.0	88@3800	7.0	L
1936	De Luxe Six, 61	6	3.00	5.00	212.0	88@3800	6.0	L
	Custom Six, 62	6	3.00	5.00	212.0	88@38C0	6.0	L
1937	De Luxe Six, 71	6	3.00	5.00	212.0	96@3900	6.25	L
	Super Six, 72	6	3.00	5.00	212.0	101@4000	6.25	L
	See Hudson for 1938.							

THRIF-T — — Tri-Wheel Motor Corp., Springfield, Mass., 1955

YEAR	MODEL	CYLS	BORE	STROKE	DISPL	HP@RPM	C.R.	VLV
1955		F2				10		
	Engine was a flat, opposed type by Onan.							

TOWNE SHOPPER — — International Motor Car Co., San Diego, Cal., 1948

YEAR	MODEL	CYLS	BORE	STROKE	DISPL	HP@RPM	C.R.	VLV
1948		2				10.6		

TRI-CAR — — The Tri-Car Co., Wheatland, Pa., 1955

YEAR	MODEL	CYLS	BORE	STROKE	DISPL	HP@RPM	C.R.	VLV
1955		2						
	This three-wheeler had a vertical engine by Lycoming.							

TUCKER — — Tucker Corp., Willow Run, Mich., 1946-48

YEAR	MODEL	CYLS	BORE	STROKE	DISPL	HP@RPM	C.R.	VLV
1946-48	Torpedo	F6	4.50	3.50	334.1	166@3000	7.1	L
	Engine used in most Tuckers was a flat six with opposed cylinders.							

CARBURETOR MFR	MODEL	VEN	WHEEL-BASE	TIRES	BODY	WEIGHT	PRICE
C			106	5.25 x 17	5 ps	2345	555
C			106	5.25 x 17	5 ps	2415	575
C			113	6.00 x 16	5 ps	2640	675
C			112	5.25 x 17	5 ps	2670	635
C			116	6.00 x 16	5 ps	2780	740
C			112	5.50 x 17	5 ps	2710	675
C	W1-309S	1	112	6.00 x 16	5 ps	2655	655
C	W1-309S	1	112	6.00 x 16	5 ps	2710	705
C	W1-331S	1	115	6.00 x 16	5 ps	2770	670
C	W1-331S	1	115	6.00 x 16	5 ps	2810	720
C	W1-348S	1	117	6.00 x 16	5 ps	2865	830
C	W1-348S	1	117	6.00 x 16	5 ps	2905	905
			85		2 pr	900	800
			63	4.00 x 8	2 pc	600	595
							995
		2 x 1	128		6 ps	4235	2485

YEAR	MODEL	ENGINE						
		CYLS	BORE	STROKE	DISPL	HP@RPM	C.R.	VLV

VALIANT – – Chrysler Corp., Detroit, Mich., 1960-69

YEAR	MODEL	CYLS	BORE	STROKE	DISPL	HP@RPM	C.R.	VLV
1960	V-100, QX1-L	6	3.406	3.125	170.9	101@4400	8.5	OH
	V-200, QX1-H	6	3.406	3.125	170.9	101@4400	8.5	OH
	Optional engine, both lines:	6	3.406	4.125	225.5	148@5200		OH
1961	V-100, RX1-L	6	3.406	3.125	170.9	101@4400	8.2	OH
	V-200, RX1-H	6	3.406	3.125	170.9	101@4400	8.2	OH
	Optional engine, both lines:	6	3.406	4.125	225.5	148@5200		
1962	V-100, SV1-L	6	3.406	3.125	170.9	101@4400	8.2	OH
	V-200, SV1-H	6	3.406	3.125	170.9	101@4400	8.2	OH
	Signet, SV1-P	6	3.406	3.125	170.9	101@4400	8.2	OH
	Optional engine, all lines:	6	3.406	4.125	225.5	145@4000	8.2	OH
1963	V-100, TV1-L	6	3.406	3.125	170.9	101@4400	8.2	OH
	V-200, TV1-H (1)	6	3.406	3.125	170.9	101@4400	8.2	OH
	Signet, 200, TV1-P (1)	6	3.406	3.125	170.9	101@4400	8.2	OH
	Optional engine:							
	(1)	6	3.406	4.125	225.5	145@4000	8.2	OH
1964	V-100, VV1-L (1)	6	3.406	3.125	170.9	101@4400	8.5	OH
	V-200, VV1-H (1)	6	3.406	3.125	170.9	101@4400	8.5	OH
	Signet 200, VV1-P (1)	6	3.406	3.125	170.9	101@4400	8.5	OH
	Optional engine:							
	(1)	V8	3.625	3.312	273.5	180@4200	8.8	OH
1965	100, AV1-L (1, 2, 3)	6	3.406	3.125	170.9	101@4400	8.5	OH
	200, AV1-H (1, 2, 3)	6	3.406	3.125	170.9	101@4400	8.5	OH
	Signet, AV1-P (1, 2, 3)	6	3.406	3.125	170.9	101@4400	8.5	OH
	Barracuda, AV1-P (1, 2, 3)	6	3.406	4.125	225.5	145@4000	8.4	OH
	Barracuda, AV2-P (3)	V8	3.625	3.312	273.5	180@4200	8.8	OH
	Optional engines:							
	(1)	V8	3.625	3.312	273.5	180@4000	8.8	OH
	(2)	6	3.406	4.125	225.5	145@4000	8.4	OH
	(3)	V8	3.625	3.312	273.5	235@5200	10.5	OH
1966	V-100, BV1-L	6	3.406	3.125	170.9	101@4400	8.5	OH
	V-200, BV1-H	6	3.406	3.125	170.9	101@4400	8.5	OH
	Signet, BV1-H	6	3.406	3.125	170.9	101@4400	8.5	OH
	Optional engines, all lines:	6	3.406	4.125	225.5	145@4000	8.4	OH
		V8	3.625	3.312	273.5	180@4200	8.8	OH
1967	100, CV1-L (1, 2)	6	3.406	3.125	170.9	115@4400	8.5	OH
	Signet, CV1-H (2)	6	3.406	4.125	225.5	145@4000	8.4	OH
	Optional engines:							
	(1)	6	3.406	4.125	225.5	145@4000	8.4	OH

MFR	CARBURETOR MODEL	VEN	WHEEL-BASE	TIRES	BODY	WEIGHT	PRICE
B	BBS-2900S	1	106.5	6.50 x 13	6 ps	2635	2053
B	BBS-2900S	1	106.5	6.50 x 13	6 ps	2655	2130
B	BBS-3093S	1	106.5	6.50 x 13	6 ps	2590	2016
B	BBS-3093S	1	106.5	6.50 x 13	6 ps	2600	2112
		4					
B	BBS-3229S	1	106.5	6.50 x 13	6 ps	2500	1991
B	BBS-3229S	1	106.5	6.50 x 13	6 ps	2510	2087
B	BBS-3229S	1	106.5	6.50 x 13	5 pht2	2515	2230
B	BBS-3237S	1					
C	BBS-3462S	1	106	6.50 x 13	6 ps	2535	1973
C	BBS-3462S	1	106	6.50 x 13	6 ps	2555	2097
C	BBS-3462S	1	106.5	6.50 x 13	6 pht2	2570	2230
C	BBS-3464S	1					
C	BBS-3675S	1	106	6.50 x 13	6 ps	2575	1992
C	BBS-3675S	1	106	6.50 x 13	6 ps	2570	2112
C	BBS-3675S	1	106	6.50 x 13	6 pht2	2600	2256
C	BBD-3767S	2					
C	BBS-3833S	1	106	6.50 x 13	6 ps	2590	2050
C	BBS-3833S	1	106	6.50 x 13	6 ps	2605	2167
C	BBS-3833S	1	106	6.50 x 13	6 pht2	2620	2309
C	BBS-3839S	1	106	6.50 x 13	5 pht2	2725	2453
C	BBD-3843S	2	106	7.00 x 13	5 pht2	2930	2535
C	BBD-3843S	2					
C	BBS-3837S	1					
C	AFB-3853S	4					
B	BBS-4099S	1	106	6.50 x 13	6 ps	2630	2095
B	BBS-4099S	1	106	6.50 x 13	6 ps	2635	2226
B	BBS-4099S	1	106	6.50 x 13	5 pht2	2635	2261
H	R-3271	1					
B	BBD-4113S	2					
B	BBS-4286S	1	108	6.50 x 13	6 ps	2675	2163
H	R-3275-1A	1	108	6.50 x 13	6 ps	2680	2308
H	R-3275-1A	1					

YEAR	MODEL	CYLS	BORE	STROKE	DISPL	HP@RPM	C.R.	VLV
		ENGINE						
	(2)	V8	3.625	3.312	273.5	235@5200	10.5	OH
1968	100, VL	6	3.406	3.125	170.9	115@4400	8.5	OH
	Signet, VH	6	3.406	3.125	170.9	115@4400	8.5	OH
	Optional engine, both lines:	V8	3.625	3.312	273.5	190@4400	9.0	OH
1969	100, VL	6	3.406	3.125	170.9	115@4400	8.5	OH
	Signet, VH	6	3.406	3.125	170.9	115@4400	8.5	OH
	Optional engine, both lines:	V8	3.625	3.312	273.5	190@4400	9.0	OH

VETTA VENTURA — — Vanguard Motors Corp., Dallas, Tex., 1964-65

YEAR	MODEL	CYLS	BORE	STROKE	DISPL	HP@RPM	C.R.	VLV
1964-65		V8	3.75	3.406	300.9	250@4800	9.0	OH
	The Vetta Ventura succeeded the Apollo. Engine was by Buick.							

VIKING — — Olds Motor Works, Lansing, Mich., 1929-30

YEAR	MODEL	CYLS	BORE	STROKE	DISPL	HP@RPM	C.R.	VLV
1930	Standard, V-30	V8	3.375	3.625	259.5	81@3200	5.1	H
	Special, V-30	V8	3.375	3.625	259.5	81@3200	5.1	H
	Deluxe, V-30	V8	3.375	3.625	259.5	81@3200	5.1	H

VOLTRA — — Voltra, Inc., New York, N.Y., ca 1962

YEAR	MODEL	CYLS	BORE	STROKE	DISPL	HP@RPM	C.R.	VLV
Ca 1962			Electric					

MFR	CARBURETOR MODEL	VEN	WHEEL-BASE	TIRES	BODY	WEIGHT	PRICE
B	BBD-4113SA	2					
B	BBS-4114S	1	108	6.50 x 13	6 ps	2675	2301
B	BBS-4114S	1	108	6.50 x 13	6 ps	2680	2447
B	BBD-4416S	2					
B	BBS-4601S	1	108	6.50 x 13	6 ps	2691	2354
B	BBS-4601S	1	108	6.50 x 13	6 ps	2691	2500
			98		2 pc	2485	
J			125	6.00 x 18	5 ps	3620	1695
J			125	6.00 x 18	5 ps	3720	1795
J			125	6.00 x 18	5 ps	3820	1855
			106			1600	

YEAR	MODEL	ENGINE						
		CYLS	BORE	STROKE	DISPL	HP@RPM	C.R.	VLV
WAGON DE VILLE — — Cadillac Wagons, Ltd., Linden, N.J., 1964								
1964		V8	4.125	4.00	427.6	340@4600		OH
	Engine was from Cadillac.							
WHIPPET — — Willys-Overland Corp., Toledo, Oh., 1927-30								
1930	Four, 96A	4	3.125	4.75	145.7	40@3200	5.4	L
	Six, 98A	6	3.125	3.875	178.3	50@3000	5.12	L
	It can be contended that the Whippet was a model of Overland, but by choice, it is listed as a separate make. Leftover 1930 models seem to have been sold as 1931's.							
WILLYS — — Willys-Overland, Inc., Toledo, Oh., 1930+								
1930	Six, 98B	6	3.25	3.875	192.9	65@3400	5.6	L
1931	Six, 97	6	3.25	3.875	192.9	65@3400	5.26	L
	Six, 98D	6	3.25	3.875	192.9	65@3400	5.26	L
	Eight, 8-80D	8	3.125	4.00	245.4	80@3200	5.4	L
1932	Six, 6-90	6	3.25	3.875	192.9	65@3400	5.26	L
	Eight, 8-88	8	3.125	4.00	245.4	80@3200	5.26	L
1933	Four, 77	4	3.125	4.375	134.2	48@3200	5.13	L
	Six, 99	6	3.312	4.125	213.3	80@3400	5.26	L
	Eight, 8-88A	8	3.312	4.00	245.4	80@3200	5.4	L
1934	77	4	3.125	4.375	134.2	48@3200	5.13	L
1935	77	4	3.125	4.375	134.2	48@3200	5.23	L
1936	77	4	3.125	4.375	134.2	48@3200	5.7	L
1937	37	4	3.125	4.375	134.2	48@3200		L
1938	38	4	3.125	4.375	134.2	48@3200		L
1939	Standard 38	4	3.125	4.375	134.2	48@3200		L
	Deluxe 38	4	3.125	4.375	134.2	48@3200		L
1940	Speedway 440	4	3.125	4.375	134.2	61@3600		L
	Deluxe 440	4	3.125	4.375	134.2	61@3600		L
1941	Americar 441	4	3.125	4.375	134.2	63@3800	6.48	L
1942	Americar 442	4	3.125	4.375	134.2	63@3800	6.48	L
1947	463	4	3.125	4.375	134.2	63@4000	6.48	L
1948	463	4	3.125	4.375	134.2	63@4000	6.48	L
	663	6	3.00	3.50	148.5	72@4000	6.42	L
1949	463	4	3.125	4.375	134.2	63@4000	6.48	L
	663	6	3.00	3.50	148.5	72@4000	6.42	L
	Jeepster VJ3	4	3.125	4.375	134.2	63@4000	6.48	L
	Jeepster VJ3	6	3.00	3.50	148.5	72@4000	6.42	L
1950	463	4	3.125	4.375	134.2	63@4000	6.48	L

MFR	CARBURETOR MODEL	VEN	WHEEL-BASE	TIRES	BODY	WEIGHT	PRICE
			129.5				14,950
T		1	103.2	4.75 x 19	5 ps	2412	585
T		1	112.5	5.00 x 19	5 ps	2693	785
T		1	110	5.50 x 19	5 ps	2641	795
T	J1A	1	110	5.00 x 19	5 ps	2670	675
T	J1A	1	113	5.00 x 19	5 ps	2706	795
T	W5	1	120	5.50 x 19	5 ps	3131	995
T		1	113	5.25 x 18	5 ps	2814	610
T		1	121	5.50 x 18	5 ps	3250	830
T	D1A	1	100	5.00 x 17	4 ps	2136	445
T	D2A	1	113	5.50 x 17	5 ps		
T		1	121	6.00 x 17	5 ps	3368	995
T		1	100	5.00 x 17	4 ps	2131	445
T		1	100	5.00 x 17	4 ps	2111	495
T		1	100	5.00 x 17	4 ps	2070	425
T		1	100	5.50 x 17	5 ps	2200	538
T		1	100	5.50 x 16	5 ps	2247	563
T		1	100	5.50 x 16	5 ps	2300	563
T		1	100	5.50 x 16	5 ps	2306	614
C	WO-450S	1	102	5.50 x 16	5 ps	2238	580
C	WO-450S	1	102	5.50 x 16	5 ps	2250	672
C	WO-507S	1	104	5.50 x 16	5 ps	2230	674
C	WO 507S	1	104	5.50 x 16	5 ps	2261	811
C	WA1-613S	1	104	6.00 x 15	5 psw2		1495
C	WA1-613S	1	104	6.00 x 15			
C	WA1-645S	1	104	6.00 x 15			
C	WA1-613S	1	104	5.90/6.00x15	5 psw2	2895	1745
C	WA1-645S	1	104	5.90 x 15/ 6.00 x 15	5 psw2	2845	1890
C	WA1-613S	1	104	5.90 x 15	4 pr	2468	1495
C	WA1-645S	1	104	5.90 x 15	4 pr	2392	1530
C	WA1-613S	1	104	6.70 x 15	5 psw2	2895	1709

YEAR	MODEL	ENGINE						
		CYLS	BORE	STROKE	DISPL	HP@RPM	C.R.	VLV
	663	6	3.00	3.50	148.4	70@4000	6.42	L
	Jeepster VJ3	4	3.125	4.375	134.2	63@4000	6.48	L
	Jeepster VJ3	6	3.00	3.50	148.4	70@4000	6.42	L
	4 x 463	4	3.125	4.375	134.2	63@4000	6.48	L
	Second series:							
	473-SW	4	3.125	4.375	134.2	72@4000	7.4	F
	673-SW	6	3.125	3.50	161.1	75@4000	6.9	L
	Jeepster 473-VJ	4	3.125	4.375	134.2	72@4000	7.4	F
	Jeepster 673-VJ	6	3.125	3.50	161.1	75@4000	6.9	L
	4 x 473-SW	4	3.125	4.375	134.2	72@4000	7.4	F
1951	473-SW	4	3.125	4.375	134.2	72@4000	7.4	F
	673-SW	6	3.125	3.50	161.1	75@4000	6.9	L
	Jeepster 473-VJ	4	3.125	4.375	134.2	72@4000	7.3	F
	Jeepster 673-VJ	6	3.125	3.50	161.1	75@4000	6.9	L
	4 x 473-SW	4	3.125	4.375	134.2	72@4000	7.4	F
1952	473-SW	4	3.125	4.375	134.2	72@4000	7.4	F
	673-SW	6	3.125	3.50	161.1	75@4000	6.9	L
	4 x 473-SW	4	3.125	4.375	134.2	72@4000	7.4	F
	Deluxe, 475-SW	4	3.125	4.375	134.2	72@4000	7.4	F
	Deluxe, 4 x 475-SW	4	3.125	4.375	134.2	72@4000	7.4	F
	Deluxe, 685	6	3.125	3.50	161.1	75@4000	6.9	L
	Aero Lark Deluxe 675	6	3.125	3.50	161.1	90@4400	7.6	F
	Aero Wing Super Deluxe 685	6	3.125	3.50	161.1	90@4400	7.6	F
	Aero Ace Custom 685	6	3.125	3.50	161.1	90@4400	7.6	F
	Aero Eagle 685	6	3.125	3.50	161.1	90@4400	7.6	F
1953	Deluxe, 475	4	3.125	4.375	134.2	72@4000	7.4	F
	Deluxe, 4 x 475	4	3.125	4.375	134.2	72@4000	7.4	F
	Deluxe, 685	6	3.125	3.50	161.1	90@4200	7.6	F
	Aero Lark Deluxe 675	6	3.125	3.50	161.1	75@4000	6.9	L
	Aero Ace Custom 685	6	3.125	3.50	161.1	90@4200	7.6	F
	Aero Eagle 685	6	3.125	3.50	161.1	90@4200	7.6	F
	Aero Falcon Super Deluxe	6	3.125	3.50	161.1	90@4200	7.6	F
	Aero Six 675	6	3.125	3.50	161.1	75@4000	6.9	L
1954	Aero Lark 654	6	3.125	3.50	161.5	90@4200	7.6	F
	Aero Ace	6	3.125	3.50	161.5	90@4200	7.6	F
	Aero Ace Deluxe	6	3.125	3.50	161.5	90@4200	7.6	F
	Aero Eagle	6	3.125	3.50	161.5	90@4200	7.6	F
	Aero Ace 226	6	3.312	4.375	226.2	115@3650	7.3	F
	Aero Eagle 226	6	3.312	4.375	226.2	115@3650	7.3	F
	Aero Eagle Custom 226	6	3.312	4.375	226.2	115@3650	7.3	F

MFR	CARBURETOR MODEL	VEN	WHEEL-BASE	TIRES	BODY	WEIGHT	PRICE
C	WA1-645S	1	104	6.70 x 15	5 psw2	2895	1814
C	WA1-613S	1	104	5.90 x 15	5 pr	2468	1603
C	WA1-645S	1	104	5.90 x 15	5 pr	2392	1639
C	WA1-613S	1	104	7.00 x 15	5 psw2	3136	2010
C	YF	1	104	6.70 x 15	6 psw2	2818	1605
C	YF	1	104	6.70 x 15	6 psw2	2831	1690
C	YF	1	104	6.40 x 15	5 pr	2459	1494
C	YF	1	104	6.40 x 15	5 pr	2485	1599
C	YF	1	104.5	7.00 x 15	6 psw2	3136	1990
C	YF-768S	1	104	6.70 x 15	6 psw2	2818	1783
Z	39	1	104	6.70 x 15	6 psw2	2831	1866
C	YF-768S	1	104	6.40 x 15	5 pr	2459	1597
Z	39	1	104	6.40 x 15	5 pr	2485	1703
C	YF-768S	1	104.5	7.00 x 15	6 psw2	3174	2204
			104	6.70 x 15	6 psw2	2818	1783
C	YS-924S	1	104	6.70 x 15	6 psw2	2831	1866
			104.5	6.70 x 15	6 psw2	3174	2235
			104	6.70 x 15	6 psw2	2818	1862
			104.5	6.70 x 15	6 psw2	3174	2304
C	YS-924S	1	104	6.70 x 15	6 psw2	2850	1949
C	YF-924S	1	108		6 ps2	2487	1731
C	YF-924S	1	108		6 ps2	2570	1989
C	YF-924S	1	108		6 ps2	2584	2074
C	YF-924S	1	108		6 pht2	2575	2155
			104	6.70 x 15	6 psw2	2818	1862
			104.5	7.00 x 15	6 psw2	3174	2304
C	YF-924S	1	104	6.70 x 15	6 psw2	2850	1949
C	YF-937S	1	108	5.90 x 15	6 ps	2509	1732
C	YF-924S	1	108	6.40 x 15	6 ps	2735	2038
C	YF-924S	1	108	6.40 x 15	6 pht2	2575	2157
C	YF-924S	1	108	6.40 x 15	6 ps	2529	1861
C	YF-937S	1	108	5.90 x 15	6 ps	2511	
C	YF-924S	1	108	6.40 x 15	5 ps	2661	1669
C	YF-924S	1	108	6.40 x 15	5 ps	2709	1805
C	YF-924S	1	108	6.40 x 15	5 ps		2023
C	YF-924S	1	108	5.90 x 15	5 pht2	2778	2167
C	WGD	2	108	6.40 x 15	5 pht2		2411
C	WGD	2	108	6.40 x 15	5 ps	2778	1990
C	WGD	2	108	6.40 x 15	5 pht2	2847	

YEAR	MODEL	ENGINE						
		CYLS	BORE	STROKE	DISPL	HP@RPM	C.R.	VLV
	Deluxe 654-AAZ	6	3.125	3.50	161.5	90@4200	7.6	F
1955	Custom	6	3.312	4.375	226.2	115@3650	7.3	F
	Series 685	6	3.125	3.50	161.1	90@4200	7.6	F
	6-226-A	6	3.312	4.375	226.2	115@3650	7.3	L
1956	475	4	3.125	4.375	134.2	72@4000	7.6	F
	6-226	6	3.312	4.375	226.2	115@3650	7.3	L
1957-58	No evidence of passenger cars being offered, other than Jeep, which is classed as a utility vehicle.							
1959	F4-134	4	3.125	4.375	134.2	72@4000	7.4	F
1960	F4-134	4	3.125	4.375	134.2	72@4200	7.4	F
	L6-226	6	3.312	4.375	226.2	105@3600	6.86	L
1961	F4-134	4	3.125	4.375	134.2	75@4000	7.4	F
	L6-226	6	3.312	4.375	226.2	105@3600	6.86	L
1962	F4-134	4	3.125	4.375	134.2	75@4000	7.4	F
	L6-226	6	3.312	4.375	226.2	105@3600	6.86	L
	After 1962, only the Jeep appears to have been offered.							
WILLYS-KNIGHT — — Willys-Overland, Inc., Toledo, Oh., 1914-32								
1930	Six, 70B	6	2.938	4.375	177.9	53@3000	5.5	S
	Great Six, 66B	6	3.375	4.75	255.0	82@3200	5.5	S
1931	Six, 87	6	2.938	4.375	177.9	55@3300	5.58	S
	Six, 66D	6	3.375	4.75	255.0	87@3200	5.5	S
1932	Six, 95	6	2.938	4.375	177.9	60@3400	5.5	S
	Six, 66D	6	3.375	4.75	255.0	87@3200	5.26	S
WINDSOR — — Moon Motor Car Co., St. Louis, Mo., 1929-30								
1930	Standard 6-69	6	2.875	4.75	185.0	47@2600	5.0	L
	DeLuxe 6-69	6	2.875	4.75	185.0	47@2600	5.0	L
	Standard 6-75	6	3.375	4.00	214.7	66@3150	4.94	L
	DeLuxe 6-75	6	3.375	4.00	214.7	66@3150	4.94	L
	8-85	8	3.00	4.75	268.8	85@3100	5.28	L
	Royal 8-92	8	3.00	4.75	268.8	85@3100	5.28	L
WOODILL — — Woodill Fiberglass Body Corp., Justin, Cal., 1952-58								
1953	Wildfire	6	3.125	3.50	161.1	90@4200		F
	While a Willys engine was standard, other types were available as options.							

MFR	CARBURETOR MODEL	VEN	WHEEL-BASE	TIRES	BODY	WEIGHT	PRICE
C	VF-924S	1	108	6.70 x 15	5 psw2	2831	
			108	6.40 x 15	5 ps	2778	1725
			104	6.70 x 15	5 psw2	2831	1997
C	WGD-2052-SA	1			6 ps	2778	1725
C		1	104.5	7.00 x 15	6 psw2	3174	
C		1	104.5	7.00 x 15	6 psw2	3278	
			104.5	7.00 x 15	6 psw2	2944	
			104.5	7.00 x 15	6 psw2	2858	1995
			104.5	7.00 x 15	6 psw2	2971	2258
			104.5	6.70 x 15	6 psw2	2858	2095
			104.5	6.70 x 15	6 psw2	2971	2344
			104.5	6.70 x 15	6 psw2	2858	2095
			104.5	6.70 x 15	6 psw2	2971	2344
T			112.5	5.50 x 19	5 ps	2973	1075
T			120	6.00 x 19	5 ps	3934	1785
T			112.5/115	5.50 x 19	5 ps	3001	1075
T	V5		120	6.00 x 18	5 ps	3400	1095
T			113	5.50 x 18	5 ps	3031	895
T			121	6.00 x 17	5 ps	3775	1395
S			120	5.25 x	5 ps	3095	1145
S			120	5.25 x	5 ps	3195	1395
S			120	5.50 x	5 ps	3040	1395
S			120	5.50 x	5 ps		1595
S			125.5	6.00 x	5 ps	3520	1695
S			125.5/140	6.50 x	5 ps	3655	1995
			101	6.40 x 15	2 pr	1620	3263

YEAR	MODEL	ENGINE						
		CYLS	BORE	STROKE	DISPL	HP@RPM	C.R.	VLV

YANK – – Custom Auto Works, San Diego, Cal., 1950

YEAR	MODEL	CYLS	BORE	STROKE	DISPL	HP@RPM	C.R.	VLV
1950		4	3.125	4.375	134.2	63@4000	6.48	L
	The Yank used a Willys engine.							

YANKEE CLIPPER – – Strassberger Motor Co., Menlo Park, Cal., 1954

YEAR	MODEL	CYLS	BORE	STROKE	DISPL	HP@RPM	C.R.	VLV
1954		V8	3.50	3.10	238.6	130@4200		OH
	Used Ford engine.							

CARBURETOR			WHEEL-	TIRES	BODY	WEIGHT	PRICE
MFR	MODEL	VEN	BASE				
			100		2 pr	1500	1000
			101			1900	

SPECIFICATIONS FOR CANADIAN CARS
1930-1969

YEAR	MODEL	ENGINE						
		CYLS	BORE	STROKE	DISPL	HP@RPM	C.R.	VLV

ACADIAN — — General Motors Products of Canada, Ltd., Oshawa, Ont., 1962+

YEAR	MODEL	CYLS	BORE	STROKE	DISPL	HP@RPM	C.R.	VLV
1962	Invader	4	3.875	3.25	153.3	90@4000	8.5	OH
	Beaumont	4	3.875	3.25	153.3	90@4000	8.5	OH
	Optional engine, both lines:	6	3.562	3.25	194.4	120@4400	8.5	OH
1963	Invader	4	3.875	3.25	153.3	90@4000	8.5	OH
	Canso	4	3.875	3.25	153.3	90@4000	8.5	OH
	Beaumont	4	3.875	3.25	153.3	90@4000	8.5	OH
	Optional engine, all lines:	6	3.562	3.25	194.4	120@4400	8.5	OH
1964	Invader (2)	4	3.875	3.25	153.3	90@4000	8.5	OH
	Canso (2)	4	3.875	3.25	153.3	90@4000	8.5	OH
	Beaumont (1)	6	3.562	3.25	194.4	120@4400	8.5	OH
	Beaumont Custom (1)	6	3.562	3.25	194.4	120@4400	8.5	OH
	Beaumont Sport DeLuxe (1)	6	3.562	3.25	194.4	120@4400	8.5	OH
	Optional engines:							
	(1)	6	3.875	3.25	230.8	140@4400	8.5	OH
	(2)	V8	3.875	3.00	283.0	195	9.25	OH
	(1)	V8	3.875	3.00	283.0	220		OH
1965	Invader (2)	4	3.875	3.25	153.3	90@4400	8.5	OH
	Canso (2)	6	3.562	3.25	194.4	120@4400	8.5	OH
	Beaumont (1)	6	3.562	3.25	194.4	120@4400	8.5	OH
	Beaumont DeLuxe (1)	6	3.562	3.25	194.4	120@4400	8.5	OH
	Beaumont Custom (1)	6	3.562	3.25	194.4	120@4400	8.5	OH
	Beaumont Sport DeLuxe (1)	6	3.562	3.25	194.4	120@4400	8.5	OH
	Optional engines:							
	(1)	6	3.875	3.25	230.0	140@4400	8.5	OH
	(1)	V8	4.00	3.25	326.7	350	11.0	
	(2)	V8	3.875	3.00	283.0	195	9.25	OH
	(2)	V8	4.00	3.25	326.7	250	10.5	OH
	(2)	V8	4.00	3.25	326.7	300	10.5	OH
1966	Invader	6	3.562	3.25	194.4	120@4400	8.5	OH
	Canso	6	3.562	3.25	194.4	120@4400	8.5	OH
	Canso Sport DeLuxe	6	3.562	3.25	194.4	120@4400	8.5	OH
	Optional engines; all lines:							
		V8	3.875	3.00	283.0	195@4800	9.25	OH
		V8	4.00	3.25	326.7	350	11.0	OH
	Beaumont model became separate marque with 1966 models.							
1967	Invader	6	3.562	3.25	194.4	120@4400	8.5	OH
	Canso	6	3.562	3.25	194.4	120@4400	8.5	OH
	Canso Sport DeLuxe	6	3.562	3.25	194.4	120@4400	8.5	OH
	Optional engines, all models:	6	3.875	3.53	250.0	155@4200	8.5	OH

CARBURETOR MFR	MODEL	VEN	WHEEL-BASE	TIRES	BODY	WEIGHT	PRICE
R	7020103	1	110	6.00 x 13	6 ps	2450	2611
R	7020103	1	110	6.00 x 13	6 ps	2470	2704
			110	6.00 x 13	6 ps	2455	2630
			110	6.00 x 13	6 ps	2470	2723
			110	6.50 x 13	6 ps	2500	2786
R	7023105	1					
			110	6.00 x 13	6 ps		
			110	6.00 x 13	6 ps		
R	7023105	1	115	6.50 x 14	6 ps		
R	7023105	1	115	6.50 x 14	6 ps		
R	7023105	1	115	6.50 x 14	6 pht2		
		1					
		2					
		4					
C	3379	1	110	6.90 x 14	6 ps		
R	7025105	1	110	6.95 x 14	6 ps	2645	2885
R	7025105	1	115	6.95 x 14	6 ps	2900	2863
R	7025105	1	115	6.95 x 14	6 ps	2910	2939
R	7025105	1	115	6.95 x 14	6 ps	2945	3053
R	7025105	1	115	6.95 x 14	6 pht2	2980	3285
R	7025000	1					
		4					
R	7024101	2					
		4					
		4					
R	7025105	1	110	6.50 x 13	6 ps	2635	2750
R	7025105	1	110	6.50 x 13	6 ps	2640	2885
R	7025105	1	110	6.50 x 13	6 pht2	2740	3107
R	7024101	2					
C	4027	4					
R	7025105	1	110	6.95 x 14	6 ps	2650	2804
R	7025105	1	110	6.95 x 14	6 ps	2660	2938
R	7025105	1	110	6.95 x 14	6 pht2	2690	3166
R	7026027	1					

YEAR	MODEL	ENGINE						
		CYLS	BORE	STROKE	DISPL	HP@RPM	C.R.	VLV
		V8	3.875	3.00	283.0	195@4600	9.25	OH
		V8	4.00	3.25	326.7	275	10.0	OH
1968		6	3.85	3.25	230.0	140@4400	8.5	OH
	Optional engines:	6	3.875	3.53	249.8	155@4200	8.5	OH
		V8	3.875	3.25	302.7	200@4600	9.0	OH
		V8	4.00	3.25	326.7	275	10.0	OH
		V8	4.00	3.48	349.8	295	10.25	OH
1969		6	3.875	3.25	230.0	140@4400	8.5	OH
	Optional engines:	6	3.875	3.53	249.8	155@4200	8.5	OH
		V8	3.875	3.25	306.7	200@4600	9.0	
		V8	4.00	3.48	349.8	300@4800	10.25	OH

CARBURETOR MFR	MODEL	VEN	WHEEL-BASE	TIRES	BODY	WEIGHT	PRICE
R	7027101	2					
R	7027202	4					
		1	111	7.35 x 14	6 ps	2890	2928
		1					
		2					
R	7028212	4					
R	7028212	4					
		1					
		1					
		2					
R	7029202	4					

YEAR	MODEL	ENGINE						
		CYLS	BORE	STROKE	DISPL	HP@RPM	C.R.	VLV

BEAUMONT — — General Motors Products of Canada, Ltd., Oshawa, Ont., 1966+

YEAR	MODEL	CYLS	BORE	STROKE	DISPL	HP@RPM	C.R.	VLV
1966		6	3.562	3.25	194.4	120@4400	8.5	OH
	Custom	6	3.562	3.25	194.4	120@4400	8.5	OH
	Optional engines, both lines:	6	3.875	3.25	230.0	140@4400	8.5	OH
		V8	3.875	3.00	283.0	195@4800	9.25	OH
		V8	4.00	3.25	326.7	275	10.0	OH
		V8	4.094	3.76	396.0	360	10.25	OH
1967		6	3.875	3.25	230.0	140@4400	8.5	OH
	Custom	6	3.875	3.25	230.0	140@4400	8.5	OH
	Optional engines, both lines:	6	3.875	3.53	249.8	155@4200	8.5	OH
		V8	3.875	3.00	283.0	195@4600	9.25	OH
		V8	4.00	3.25	326.7	275	10.0	OH
		V8	4.00	3.76	396.0	350	10.25	OH
1968		6	3.875	3.25	230.0	140@4400	8.5	OH
	DeLuxe	6	3.875	3.25	230.0	140@4400	8.5	OH
	Custom	6	3.875	3.25	230.0	140@4400	8.5	OH
	Sport DeLuxe	V8	4.00	3.76	396.0	350	10.25	OH
	Optional engines, all lines:							
	(1)	6	3.875	3.53	249.8	155@4200	8.5	OH
	(2)	V8	3.875	3.25	306.6	200@4600	9.0	OH
	(3)	V8	4.00	3.25	326.7	250	8.75	OH
	(4)	V8	4.00	3.25	326.7	275	10.0	OH
	(5)	V8	4.094	3.76	396.0	325@4800	10.25	OH
	(6)	V8	4.094	3.76	396.0	350@5200		OH
1969		6	3.875	3.25	230.0	140@4400	8.5	OH
	DeLuxe	6	3.875	3.25	230.0	140@4400	8.5	OH
	Custom	6	3.875	3.25	230.0	140@4400	8.5	OH
	Optional engines, all lines:	6	3.875	3.53	249.8	155@4400	8.5	OH
		V8	3.875	3.25	306.6	200@4600	9.0	OH
		V8	4.00	3.48	349.8	255@4800	9.0	OH
		V8	4.00	3.48	349.8	300@4800	10.25	OH
		V8	4.094	3.76	396.0	325@4800	10.25	OH
		V8	4.094	3.76	396.0	350@5200	10.25	OH

BUICK — — General Motors Products of Canada Ltd., Oshawa, Ont., 1951-53

YEAR	MODEL	CYLS	BORE	STROKE	DISPL	HP@RPM	C.R.	VLV
1951	Custom, 4300	8	3.188	4.125	263.3	120@3600	6.6	OH
	Custom DeLuxe, 4300	8	3.188	4.125	263.3	120@3600	6.6	OH
1952	Custom, 4300	8	3.188	4.125	263.3	120@3600	6.6	OH
	Custom DeLuxe, 4300	8	3.188	4.125	263.3	120@3600	6.6	OH
1953	Custom, 4300	8	3.188	4.125	263.3	125@3800	7.0	OH

MFR	CARBURETOR MODEL	VEN	WHEEL-BASE	TIRES	BODY	WEIGHT	PRICE
R	7023105	1	115	6.95 x 14	6 ps	2935	2884
R	7023105	1	115	6.95 x 14	6 ps	2960	3065
R	7023000	1					
		2					
C	4027	4					
R	7025000	1	115	7.35 x 14	6 ps	2955	2929
R	7025000	1	115	7.35 x 14	6 ps	3000	3109
R	7025000	1					
R	7027101	2					
R	7027202	4					
R	7027000	4					
		1	116/112	7.35 x 14	6 ps	3020	2966
		1	116/112	7.35 x 14	6 ps	3105	3087
		1	116/112	7.35 x 14	6 ps	3125	3221
R	7028210	4	112	7.35 x 14	6 pht2	3550	3757
R	7028212	1					
		2					
		4					
		4					
		4					
		1	116	7.75 x 14	6 psw2	3390	3310
		1	116/112	7.35 x 14	6 ps	3100	3097
		1	116/112	7.35 x 14	6 ps	3130	3215
		1					
		2					
		4					
		4					
		4					
		4					
			121.5	7.60 x 15	6 ps	3690	2922
			121.5	7.60 x 15	6 ps	3730	3088
			121.5	7.60 x 15	6 ps	3690	2819
			121.5	7.60 x 15	6 ps	3730	2981
			121.5	7.60 x 15	6 ps	3710	3029

YEAR	MODEL	ENGINE						
		CYLS	BORE	STROKE	DISPL	HP@RPM	C.R.	VLV

Buick was not built in Canada from 1942 through 1950. The above models were similar to the U. S. Buick Specials. Super and Roadmaster models were imported from the U. S.

CARBURETOR			WHEEL-	TIRES	BODY	WEIGHT	PRICE
MFR	MODEL	VEN	BASE				

YEAR	MODEL	ENGINE						
		CYLS	BORE	STROKE	DISPL	HP@RPM	C.R.	VLV

CADILLAC — — General Motors of Canada, Ltd., Oshawa, Ont., 1923-36

YEAR	MODEL	CYLS	BORE	STROKE	DISPL	HP@RPM	C.R.	VLV
1930	353	V8	3.375	4.938	353.4			L
1931	355A	V8	3.375	4.938	353.4	95@2900	5.15	L
	370A	V12	3.125	4.00	368.2	135@3400	5.43	OH
	452A	V16	3.00	4.00	452.4	185@3400	5.5	OH
1932	355B	V8	3.375	4.812	344.4	115@3000	5.38	L
	370B	V12	3.062	4.00	353.6	135@3400	5.3	OH
	452B	V16	3.00	4.00	452.4	165@3400	5.35	OH
1933	355C	V8	3.375	4.938	353.0			L
	370C	V12	3.125	4.00	368.0			OH
	452C	V16	3.00	4.00	452.4			OH
1934	355D	V8	3.375	4.938	353.0			L
	370D	V12	3.125	4.00	368.0			OH
	452D	V16	3.00	4.00	452.4			OH
1935	355E	V8	3.375	4.938	353.0			L
	370E	V12	3.125	4.00	368.2		6.0	OH
1936	36-60	V8	3.375	4.50	322.1	125@3600	6.25	L
	36-70	V8	3.50	4.50	346.4	135@3600	6.25	L
	36-75	V8	3.50	4.50	346.4	135@3600	6.25	L
	36-80	V12	3.125	4.00	368.2	150@3600		OH
	36-85	V12	3.125	4.00	368.2	150@3600		OH

CHEVROLET — — General Motors of Canada, Ltd., Oshawa, Ont., 1916+

YEAR	MODEL	CYLS	BORE	STROKE	DISPL	HP@RPM	C.R.	VLV
1930	Universal	6	3.312	3.75	193.9	50@2600	5.0	OH
1931	Independence	6	3.312	3.75	193.9	50@2600	5.0	OH
1932	Confederate	6	3.312	3.75	193.9	60@3000	5.2	OH
1933	Standard	6	3.312	3.50	181.0	60@3000		OH
	Master	6	3.312	4.00	206.8			OH
1934	Standard, 200	6	3.312	3.50	181.0	60@3000	5.35	OH
	Master, 100	6	3.312	4.00	206.8	80@3300	5.45	OH
1935	Standard	6	3.312	4.00	206.8	74@3200	5.45	OH
	Master	6	3.312	4.00	206.8	74@3200	5.45	OH
1936	Standard, 12	6	3.312	4.00	206.8	79@3200	6.0	OH
	Master, 10	6	3.312	4.00	206.8	79@3200	6.0	OH
1937	Master	6	3.50	3.75	216.5	85@3200	6.25	OH
	Master DeLuxe	6	3.50	3.75	216.5	85@3200	6.25	OH
1938	Master	6	3.50	3.75	216.5	85@3200	6.25	OH
	Master Deluxe	6	3.50	3.75	216.5	85@3200	6.25	OH
1939	Master, 12	6	3.50	3.75	216.5	85@3200	6.25	OH

CARBURETOR MFR	MODEL	VEN	WHEEL-BASE	TIRES	BODY	WEIGHT	PRICE
O			140/152	7.00 x 19	5 ps		4710
O			134	6.50 x 19	5 ps		3650
O			140/143	7.00 x 19	5 ps		5265
O			148	7.50 x 19	5 ps		7795
O			134/140	7.00 x 17	5 ps		4860
O			124/140	7.50 x 17	5 ps		6015
O			143/149	7.50 x 18	5 ps		8745
O			134/140		5 ps		5335
O			134/140		5 ps		6615
O							
			128/136/		5 ps		3600
			146				
			146		5 ps		6090
			154				
			128/136		5 ps		3300
			146		5 ps		5690
S	EE-25	2	121		5 ps		2440
S	EE-25	2	131		5 ps		3460
S	EE-25	2	138		5 ps		3975
S			131		5 ps		4510
S			138		5 ps		4900
C		1	107	4.75 x 19	5 ps		870
C		1	109	4.75 x 19	5 ps		820
C		1	109	5.25 x 18	5 ps		865
C	260S	1	107	5.25 x 17	5 ps		660
C	259S	1	110	5.50 x 17	5 ps		845
C	285S	1	107	5.25 x 17	5 ps2		773
C	284S	1	112	5.50 x 17	5 ps		965
					5 ps		842
					5 ps		1004
C	W1-319S	1	109	5.50 x 17	5 ps		760
C	W1-319S	1	109	5.50 x 17	5 ps		875
C	W1-346S	1	112.2	6.00 x 16	5 ps		805
C	W1-346S	1	112.2	6.00 x 16	5 ps		885
C	W1-391S	1	112.2	6.00 x 16	5 ps		1007
C	W1-391S	1	112.2	6.00 x 16	5 ps		1085
C	W1-420S	1	112	6.00 x 16	5 ps		962

YEAR	MODEL	ENGINE						
		CYLS	BORE	STROKE	DISPL	HP@RPM	C.R.	VLV
	Master DeLuxe, 10	6	3.50	3.75	216.5	85@3200	6.25	OH
1940	Master, 85	6	3.50	3.75	216.5	85@3200	6.25	OH
	Special DeLuxe	6	3.50	3.75	216.5	85@3200	6.25	OH
1941	Master DeLuxe	6	3.50	3.75	216.5	85@3200	6.25	OH
	Special DeLuxe	6	3.50	3.75	216.5	85@3200	6.25	OH
1942	Master DeLuxe	6	3.50	3.75	216.5	85@3200	6.25	OH
	Fleetline	6	3.50	3.75	216.5	85@3200	6.25	OH

CHRYSLER – – Chrysler Corp. of Canada, Ltd., Windsor, Ont., 1925+

1930	Six, CJ	6	3.125	4.25	195.6	62@3200	5.2	L
	66	6	3.125	4.25	195.6	65@3200		L
	70	6	3.125	4.75	218.6	75@3200	5.1	L
	77	6	3.375	5.00	268.4	93@3200	5.0	L
Late								
1930	Six, CJ	6	3.125	4.25	195.6	62@3200		L
	66	6	3.125	4.75	218.6	68@3000		L
	70	6	3.375	5.00	268.4	93@3200		L
1931	Six, CM	6	3.25	4.375	217.8	70@3400		L
	Eight, CD	8	3.00	4.25	240.3	82@3400		L
	Imperial Eight, CG	8	3.50	5.00	384.8	125@3200		L
Late								
1931	Deluxe Eight, CD	8	3.25	4.25	282.1	95@3400		L
1932	Six, C1	6	3.25	4.50	224.0	82@3400	5.35	L
	Eight, CP	8	3.25	4.50	298.6	100@3400		L
	Imperial Eight, CH	8	3.50	5.00	384.8	125@3200		L
1933	Six, CO	6	3.25	4.50	223.9	83@3400	5.35	L
	Royal Eight, CT	8	3.25	4.125	273.8	90@3400	5.4	L
	Imperial Eight, CQ	8	3.25	4.50	298.6	100@3400	5.2	L
	Imperial Custom Eight, CL*	8	2.50	5.00	384.8	135@3200	5.8	L
1934	Six, CA	6	3.375	4.50	241.5	93@3400	5.4	L
	Airflow Six, CY	6	3.375	4.50	241.5	93@3400	5.4	L
	Airflow Eight, CU	8	3.25	4.50	298.6	112@3400	5.4	L
	Imperial Airflow Eight, CV	8	3.25	4.875	323.5	128@3400		L
1935	Airflow Eight, C1	8	3.25	4.875	323.5	115@3400	6.2	L
	Imperial Airflow, C2	8	3.25	4.875	323.5	130@3400	6.5	L
	Imperial Custom Airflow, C3	8	3.25	4.875	323.5	130@3400	6.5	L
	Airstream Six, C6	6	3.375	4.50	241.5	93@3400	6.0	L
	Airstream Eight, CZ	8	3.25	4.125	273.8	105@3400	6.2	L
	Custom Imperial Airflow, CW*	8	3.50	5.00	384.8	150@3200	6.5	L
1936	Six, C7	6	3.375	4.50	241.5	93@3400	6.0	L

MFR	CARBURETOR MODEL	VEN	WHEEL-BASE	TIRES	BODY	WEIGHT	PRICE
C	W1-420S	1	112	6.00 x 16	5 ps		1036
C	W1-420S	1	113		5 ps		1012
C	W1-420S	1	113		5 ps		1086
C	W1-420S	1	116		5 ps		1255
C	W1-420S	1	116		5 ps		1348
C	W1-420S	1	116		5 ps		1288
C	W1-420S	1	116		5 ps		1336
C		1	109	5.00 x 19	5 ps	2695	1070
S		1	113	5.50 x 18	5 ps	2930	1345
S		1	117	5.50 x 18	5 ps	3590	1815
S		1	124	6.00 x 18	5 ps	3750	2190
S		1	109	5.25 x 19	5 ps	2695	1005
			113	5.50 x 18	5 ps	2935	1380
			117	5.50 x 18	5 ps		1815
S	UR-2	1	116	5.25 x 19	5 ps	2850	1150
S	UR-2	1	124	6.50 x 17	5 ps	3365	1950
S	DD-3		145	7.50 x 17	5 ps	4825	3890
S	UR-2	1	124	6.50 x 17	5 ps	3640	2005
S	EX-22	1	116.4	5.50 x 18	5 ps	3135	1240
S	UR-2		125	6.50 x 17	5 ps	3885	2075
S	EE-3		135/146	7.00 x 17/	5 ps	4645	2725
				7.50 x 17			
S	EX-32		117	5.50 x 17	5 ps	3143	1180
S	EX-32		120	6.00 x 17	5 ps	3483	1410
S	EX-32		126	6.50 x 17	5 ps	4030	2030
S			146	7.50 x 17	5 ps	5045	2895
			117	6.50 x 16	5 ps	3165	1100
S			115.5	6.50 x 16	6 ps	3740	1500
S	EE-22	2	123	7.00 x 16	6 ps	4150	1815
			128	7.50 x 16	6 ps	4210	2180
S	EE-22	2	123	7.00 x 16	6 ps	4000	2095
S	EE-22	2	128	7.50 x 16	6 ps	4120	2525
S	EE-22	2	137	7.50 x 16			
			118	6.25 x 16	5 ps	3105	1215
S	EE-22	2	121	6.50 x 16	5 ps	3280	1405
S	EE-22	2	146	7.50 x 17			
B			118	6.25 x 16	5 ps	3230	1285

YEAR	MODEL	ENGINE						
		CYLS	BORE	STROKE	DISPL	HP@RPM	C.R.	VLV
	Deluxe Eight, C8	8	3.25	4.125	273.8	105@3400	6.2	L
	Airflow Eight, C-9	8	3.25	4.875	323.5	115@3400	6.2	L
	Imperial Airflow, C-10	8	3.25	4.875	323.5	130@3400	6.5	L
1937	Royal Six, C-16	6	3.375	4.25	228.1	93@3600	6.5	L
	Airflow Eight, C-17	8	3.25	4.875	323.5	130@3400	6.5	L
	Imperial Eight, C-14	8	3.25	4.125	273.8	110@3600	6.7	L
	Custom Imperial, C-15	8	3.25	4.875	323.5	130@3400	6.5	L
1938	Royal Six, C-18	6	3.375	4.50	241.5	95@3600	6.2	L
	Imperial Eight, C-19	8	3.25	4.50	298.6	110@3400	6.2	L
	Custom Imperial, C-20	8	3.25	4.875	323.5	130@3400	6.5	L
1939	Royal Six, C-22	6	3.375	4.50	241.5	100@3600	6.5	L
	Royal Windsor, C-22	6	3.375	4.50	241.5	100@3600	6.5	L
	New Yorker, C-23	8	3.25	4.875	323.5	135@3400		L
	Saratoga, C-23	8	3.25	4.875	323.5	135@3400		L
	Imperial, C-23	8	3.25	4.875	323.5	135@3400		L
	Custom Imperial, C-24	8	3.25	4.875	323.5	130@3400	6.8	L
1940	Royal Six, C-25	6	3.375	4.50	241.5	110@3600		L
	Royal Windsor, C-25	6	3.375	4.50	241.5	110@3600		L
	Traveler, C-26	8	3.25	4.875	323.5	135@3400	6.8	L
	New Yorker, C-26	8	3.25	4.875	323.5	135@3400	6.8	L
	Saratoga, C-26	8	3.25	4.875	323.5	135@3400	6.8	L
	Crown Imperial, C-27	8	3.25	4.875	323.5	135@3400	6.8	L
1941	Royal Six, C-28	6	3.375	4.50	241.5	112@3600	6.8	L
	Royal Windsor, C-28	6	3.375	4.50	241.5	112@3600	6.8	L
	New Yorker, C-30	8	3.25	4.875	323.5	137@3400	6.8	L
	Saratoga, C-30	8	3.25	4.875	323.5	137@3400	6.8	L
	Crown Imperial, C-33	8	3.25	4.875	323.5	140@3400		L
1942	Royal, C-34S	6	3.438	4.50	250.6	115@3600		L
	Windsor, C-34W	6	3.438	4.50	250.6	115@3600		L
1946	Royal, C-38R	6	3.438	4.50	250.6	115@3600	6.6	L
	Windsor, C-38S	6	3.438	4.50	250.6	115@3600	6.6	L
1947	Royal, C-38S	6	3.438	4.50	250.6	115@3600	6.6	L
	Windsor, C-38W	6	3.438	4.50	250.6	115@3600	6.6	L
1948	Royal, C-38S	6	3.438	4.50	250.6	115@3600	6.6	L
	Windsor, C-38W	6	3.438	4.50	250.6	115@3600	6.6	L
1949	Royal, C-45-1	6	3.438	4.50	250.6	115@3600	6.6	L
	Windsor, C-45-2	6	3.438	4.50	250.6	115@3600	6.6	L

MFR	CARBURETOR MODEL	VEN	WHEEL-BASE	TIRES	BODY	WEIGHT	PRICE
S	EXV-3		121/133	6.50 x 16	5 ps	3595	1710
S	EXV-3		123	7.00 x 16	6 ps	4235	2210
S	EE-22	2	128	7.50 x 16	6 ps	4370	2390
C	BB		116/132		5 ps	3225	1217
S	EE-22	2	128		6 ps	4320	2160
S	AAOV-1		121		5 ps	3550	1509
S	AAOV-1		140		7 ps	4450	2777
C	BB		119/136		5 ps	3225	1316
S	AAV-2		125		5 ps	3580	1619
S	AAV-2		144		5 ps		3116
C	BB-E6N1	1	119/138		6 ps	3255	1316
C	BB-E6N1	1	125		6 ps	3275	1939
			125		6 ps	3695	1717
			125		6 ps	3770	1942
			125		6 ps	3690	1614
			144		6 ps	4590	3502
			122.5/		6 ps	3220	1300
			139.5				
			122.5		6 ps	3225	1344
			128.5		6 ps	3600	1730
			128.5		6 ps	3620	1835
			128.5		6 ps	3790	1935
			145.5		6 ps	4340	
			121.5/		6 ps	3350	1634
			139.5				
			121.5/		6 ps	3440	1760
			139.5				
			127.5		6 ps	3870	2302
			127.5		6 ps	3855	2153
			145.5		6 ps	4435	
			121.5		6 ps	3500	1745
			121.5		6 ps	3525	1831
			121.5	6.50 x 15	6 ps	3545	1782
			121.5	6.50 x 15	6 ps	3600	1911
			121.5	6.50 x 15	6 ps	3545	1961
			121.5	6.50 x 15	6 ps	3600	2103
			121.5		6 ps	3545	2353
			121.5		6 ps	3600	2511
			125.5/	7.60 x 15/	6 ps	3610	2607
			139.5	8.20 x 15			
			125.5	7.60 x 15	6 ps	3680	2800

YEAR	MODEL	ENGINE						
		CYLS	BORE	STROKE	DISPL	HP@RPM	C.R.	VLV
1950	Royal, C-48-1	6	3.438	4.50	250.6	115@3600	6.6	L
	Windsor, C-48-2	6	3.438	4.50	250.6	115@3600	6.6	L
1951	Windsor, C-51-1	6	3.438	4.50	250.6	116@3600	7.0	L
	Windsor Deluxe, C-51-2	6	3.438	4.50	250.6	116@3600	7.0	L
1952	Windsor, C-51-1	6	3.438	4.75	264.5	119@3600	7.0	L
	Windsor Deluxe, C-51-2	6	3.438	4.75	264.5	119@3600	7.0	L
1953	Windsor, C-60-1	6	3.438	4.75	264.5	119@3600	7.0	L
	Windsor Deluxe, C-60-2	6	3.438	4.75	264.5	119@3600	7.0	L
	New Yorker Deluxe, C-56-2	V8	3.812	3.625	331.1	180@4000	7.5	OH
1954	Windsor Deluxe, C-62	6	3.438	4.75	264.5	119@3600	7.1	L
1955	Windsor Deluxe, C-67	V8	3.625	3.625	299.3	188@4400	8.0	OH
	New Yorker Deluxe, C-68	V8	3.812	3.625	331.1	250@4600	8.5	OH
1956	Windsor, C-71	V8	3.812	3.625	331.1	225@4400	8.5	OH
	New Yorker, C-72	V8	3.938	3.625	353.1	280@4600	9.0	OH
1957	Windsor, C-75-2	V8	3.938	3.625	353.1	285@4600	9.25	OH
1958	Windsor, LC2W-M	V8	3.938	3.625	353.1	290@4600	10.0	OH
1959	Windsor, MC1-L	V8	4.031	3.75	382.9	305@4600	10.0	OH
1960	Windsor, PC1-L	V8	4.125	3.375	360.8	295@4600	10.0	OH
1961	Windsor, RC1-L	V8	4.125	3.375	360.8	265@4400	9.0	OH
	Saratoga, RC2-M	V8	4.25	3.375	382.9	305@4600	10.0	OH
1962	Windsor, SC1-L	V8	4.125	3.375	360.8	265@4400	9.0	OH
	Saratoga, SC2-M	V8	4.25	3.375	382.9	305@4600	10.0	OH
1963	Windsor, TC1-L	V8	4.125	3.375	360.8	265@4400	9.0	OH
	Saratoga, TC2-M	V8	4.25	3.375	382.9	305@4600	10.0	OH
1964	Windsor, VC1-L	V8	4.125	3.375	360.8	265@4400	9.0	OH
	Saratoga 300, VC2-M	V8	4.25	3.375	382.9	305@4600	10.0	OH
1965	Windsor, AC1-L	V8	4.125	3.375	360.8	265@4400	9.0	OH
	Saratoga 300, AC2-M	V8	4.25	3.375	382.9	270@4400	9.2	OH
1966	Windsor, BC1-L	V8	4.25	3.375	382.9	270@4400	9.2	OH
	No more Chryslers built in Canada until 1975 Cordoba.							

CARBURETOR MFR	MODEL	VEN	WHEEL-BASE	TIRES	BODY	WEIGHT	PRICE
			125.5/	7.60 x 15/	6 ps	3680	2607
			139.5	8.20 x 15			
			125.5	7.60 x 15	6 ps	3715	2800
			125.5/	7.60 x 15/	6 ps	3665	3166
			139.5	8.20 x 15			
			125.5	7.60 x 15	6 ps	3715	3408
			125.5	7.60 x 15	6 ps	3705	3309
			125.5	7.60 x 15	6 ps		
			125.5	7.60 x 15	6 ps	3700	3269
			125.5	7.60 x 15	6 ps		
			125.5	8.00 x 15	6 ps	4380	4055
			125.5	7.60 x 15	6 ps	3670	3629
			126	7.60 x 15	6 ps	3925	
			126	8.00 x 15	6 ps	4160	
			126	7.60 x 15	6 ps	3900	3772
			126	8.00 x 15	6 ps	4110	4294
			126	8.50 x 14	6 ps	4110	4235
			122	8.00 x 14	6 ps	3895	4264
			122	8.00 x 14	6 ps	3785	3824
C	2926	4	122	8.00 x 14	6 ps	3920	3870
C	3104	4	122	8.00 x 14	6 ps	3930	3907
C	3107	4	122	8.00 x 14	6 ps	3975	4070
C	3254	4	122	8.00 x 14	6 ps	3720	3731
C	3255	4	122	8.00 x 14	6 ps		4170
			122	8.00 x 14	6 ps	3730	3762
C	3486	4	122	8.00 x 14	6 ps		4039
			122	8.00 x 14	6 ps	3790	3886
C	3613	4	122	8.00 x 14	6 ps	3824	4201
			124	8.25 x 14	6 ps	4010	3955
			124	8.55 x 14	6 ps	4095	4279
			124	8.25 x 14	6 ps	3875	3939

YEAR	MODEL	ENGINE						
		CYLS	BORE	STROKE	DISPL	HP@RPM	C.R.	VLV

DE SOTO — — DeSoto Motor Corp. of Canada, Ltd.; Chrysler Corp. of Canada, Ltd., Windsor, Ont., 1930-60

YEAR	MODEL	CYLS	BORE	STROKE	DISPL	HP@RPM	C.R.	VLV
1930	Eight, CF	8	2.875	4.00	207.8	70@3400		L
	Six, CK	6	3.00	4.125	174.9	57@3400		L
1931	Eight, CF*	8	2.875	4.25	220.7	75@3400		L
	Six, SA	6	3.25	4.125	205.3	67@3200		L
1932	Six, SC	6	3.25	4.25	211.5	75@3400		L
1933	Six, SD	6	3.25	4.375	217.8	79@3400		L
1934	Airflow, SE	6	3.375	4.50	241.5	100@3400		L
1935	Airstream Six, SF	6	3.375	4.50	241.5	91@3400		L
	Airflow Six, SG	6	3.375	4.50	241.5	100@3400		L
1936	Airstream Six, S-1	6	3.375	4.50	241.5	93@3400		L
	Airflow Six, S-2	6	3.375	4.50	241.5	100@3400		L
1937	DeLuxe Six, S-3	6	3.375	4.25	228.1	93@3600		L
1938	DeLuxe, S-5	6	3.375	4.25	228.1	93@3600		L
1939	DeLuxe Six, S-6	6	3.375	4.25	228.1	100@3600		L
1940	DeLuxe Six, S-7	6	3.375	4.25	228.1	100@3600		L
1941	DeLuxe Six, S-8	6	3.375	4.25	228.1	105@3600		L
1942	Custom Six, S-10	6	3.438	4.25	236.6	110@3600		L
1946	Custom Six, S-11C	6	3.438	4.25	236.6	110@3600		L
1947	Custom Six, S-11C	6	3.438	4.25	236.6	110@3600		L
1948	Custom Six, S-11C	6	3.438	4.25	236.6	110@3600		L
1949	Custom Six, S-13C	6	3.438	4.25	236.6	110@3600		L
1950	Custom Six, S-14-2	6	3.438	4.25	236.6	110@3600		L
1951	Custom Six, S-15	6	3.438	4.50	250.6	116@3600		L
1952	Custom Six, S-15	6	3.438	4.75	264.5	119@3600	7.0	L
	Firedome, S-17	V8	3.625	3.344	276.1	160@4400		OH
1953	Powermaster, S-18	6	3.438	4.75	264.5	119@3600	7.0	L
	Firedome, S-16	V8	3.625	3.344	276.1	160@4400	7.1	OH
1954	Powermaster, S-20	6	3.438	4.75	264.5	119@3600	7.0	L
	Firedome, S-19	V8	3.625	3.344	276.1	170@4400	7.5	OH
1955	Firedome, S-22	V8	3.72	3.344	290.8	185@4400	7.5	OH
	Fireflite, S-21	V8	3.72	3.344	290.8	200@4400	7.5	OH
1956	Fireflite, S-24	V8	3.72	3.80	330.4	230@4400	8.5	OH
1957	Firedome, S-25	V8	3.78	3.80	341.2	270@4600	9.25	OH
	Fireflite, S-26	V8	3.78	3.80	341.2	295@4600	9.25	OH
1958	Firedome, LS2-M	V8	3.938	3.625	353.1	290@4600	10.0	OH
1959	Firedome, MS2-M	V8	4.25	3.375	383.0	305@4600	10.0	OH
1960	Adventurer	V8	4.25	3.375	383.0		10.0	OH

MFR	CARBURETOR MODEL	VEN	WHEEL-BASE	TIRES	BODY	WEIGHT	PRICE
			114	5.25 x 19	5 ps	2965	1275
			109	5.00 x 19	5 ps	2645	1110
			114	5.25 x 19	5 ps	3065	1275
			109	5.00 x 19	5 ps	2745	995
			112.4	5.25 x 18	5 ps	2993	1055
			112.4	5.50 x 17	5 ps	3140	1050
			115.5	6.50 x 16	6 ps	3580	1450
			116		5 ps	3040	1165
			115.5	6.50 x 16	5 ps	3465	1720
			118		5 ps	3220	1275
			115.5		5 ps	3590	1835
			116/132		5 ps	3229	1214
			119/136		5 ps	3205	1303
			119/138		6 ps	3230	1293
			122.5/		6 ps	3200	1272
			139.5				
			121.5		6 ps	3330	1584
			121.5		6 ps	3475	1785
			121.5	6.50 x 16	6 ps	3505	1862
			121.5	6.50 x 16	6 ps	3505	2049
			121.5	6.50 x 16	6 ps	3505	2412
			125.5	7.60 x 15	6 ps	3605	2703
			125.5	7.60 x 15	6 ps	3635	2703
			125.5	7.60 x 15	6 ps	3670	3281
			125.5	7.60 x 15	6 ps	3670	3190
			125.5	8.00 x 15	6 ps	3865	3757
			125.5	7.60 x 15	6 ps	3535	3190
			125.5	7.60 x 15	6 ps	3720	3757
			125.5	7.60 x 15	6 ps	3555	3570
			125.5	7.60 x 15	6 ps	3790	4072
			126	7.60 x 15	6 ps	3810	3646
			126	7.60 x 15	6 ps	3935	4107
			126	7.60 x 15	6 ps	3860	4176
C	2522	2	126	8.50 x 14	6 ps	3955	4472
		4	126	8.50 x 14	6 ps	4025	4678
C	2637	2	126	8.50 x 14	6 ps	3855	4282
C	2793	2	126	8.50 x 14	6 ps	3920	4142
S	3-188	2	122				

YEAR	MODEL	ENGINE						
		CYLS	BORE	STROKE	DISPL	HP@RPM	C.R.	VLV

DODGE — — Chrysler Corp. of Canada, Ltd., Windsor, Ont., 1922+

YEAR	MODEL	CYLS	BORE	STROKE	DISPL	HP@RPM	C.R.	VLV
1930	Six, DA	6	3.375	3.875	208.0	63@3000		L
	Eight, DC	8	2.875	4.25	220.7	75@3400		L
	Six, DD	6	3.125	4.125	189.8	60@3400		L
1931	Eight, DG	8	3.00	4.25	240.3	84@3400		L
	Six, DH	6	3.25	4.25	211.5	68@3400		L
1932	Eight, DK	8	3.25	4.25	282.1	90@3400		L
	Six, DL	6	3.25	4.375	217.8	79@3400		L
1933	Six DeLuxe, DP	6	3.125	4.375	201.3	75@3600		L
	Eight, DO	8	3.25	4.25	282.1	92@3400		L
	Standard Six, DQ	6	3.125	4.375	201.3	75@3600		L
1934	DeLuxe Six, DR, DRX	6	3.25	4.375	217.8	82@3600		L
	Standard Six, DT	6	3.125	4.375	201.3	82@3600		L
1935	Six, DV	6	3.125	4.375	201.3	82@3600		L
	DeLuxe Six, DV	6	3.125	4.375	201.3	82@3600		L
	Six, DU	6	3.25	4.375	217.8	85@3600		L
1936	Standard Six, D-3	6	3.125	4.375	201.3	82@3600		L
	DeLuxe Six, D-4	6	3.125	4.375	201.3	82@3600		L
	Six, D-2	6	3.25	4.375	217.8	87@3600		L
1937	Standard Six, D-6	6	3.125	4.375	201.3	82@3600		L
	DeLuxe Six, D-7	6	3.125	4.375	201.3	82@3600		L
	Custom Six, D-5	6	3.25	4.375	217.8	87@3600		L
1938	Custom Six, D-8	6	3.25	4.375	217.8	87@3600		L
	Standard Six, D-9	6	3.125	4.375	201.3	82@3600		L
	DeLuxe Six, D-10	6	3.125	4.375	201.3	82@3600		L
	Custom Six, 2nd series, D-8	6	3.375	4.062	218.1	87@3600		L
1939	Standard Six, D-12	6	3.375	3.75	201.3	82@3600		L
	DeLuxe Six, D-13	6	3.375	3.75	201.3	82@3600		L
	Custom Six, D-11	6	3.375	4.062	218.1	87@3600		L
1940	Custom Six, D-14	6	3.375	4.062	218.1	87@3600		L
	Kingsway, D-15	6	3.375	4.062	218.1	84@3600		L
	DeLuxe Six, D-16	6	3.375	4.062	218.1	84@3600		L
	Special DeLuxe, D-16	6	3.375	4.062	218.1	84@3600		L
1941	Luxury Liner, D-19	6	3.375	4.062	218.1	88@3800		L
	Kingsway, D-20	6	3.375	4.062	218.1	88@3800		L
	DeLuxe Six, D-21	6	3.375	4.062	218.1	88@3800		L
	Special DeLuxe Six, D-21	6	3.375	4.062	218.1	88@3800		L
1942	Custom Six, D-22C	6	3.375	4.25	228.1	105@3600		L

CARBURETOR			WHEEL-	TIRES	BODY	WEIGHT	PRICE
MFR	MODEL	VEN	BASE				
			112	5.00 x 19	5 ps	2835	1275
			114	5.50 x 18	5 ps	3045	1465
			109	5.00 x 19	5 ps	2668	1105
			118	5.50 x 18	5 ps	3175	1455
			114	5.00 x 19	5 ps	2820	1095
			122	6.00 x 18	5 ps	3525	1585
			114.2	5.50 x 18	5 ps	3095	1170
			115	6.00 x 16	5 ps	2755	950
			122	6.50 x 17	5 ps	3710	1630
			111	6.00 x 16	5 ps	2700	825
			117/125	6.25 x 16	5 ps	3030	1030
			114	6.25 x 16	5 ps	2925	885
			113		5 ps	2900	950
			113		5 ps	2875	990
			116		5 ps	2940	1080
			113		5 ps	2920	955
			113		5 ps	2980	1005
			116/128		5 ps	3055	1110
			112		5 ps	2930	934
			112		5 ps	2975	1018
			115/132		5 ps	3050	1110
			115/132		5 ps	3085	1193
			112		5 ps	2930	1023
			112		5 ps	2970	1070
			115/132				
			114		5 ps	2935	979
			114		5 ps	3000	1044
			117/134		5 ps	3140	1201
			119/139.5		6 ps	3115	1201
			117		6 ps	2980	995
			117		6 ps	3045	1061
			117		6 ps	3060	1088
			119.5/		6 ps	3280	1514
			137.5				
			117		6 ps	3030	1203
			117.5		6 ps	3100	1287
			117.5		6 ps	3135	1318
			119.5/		6 ps	3345	1645
			137.5				

YEAR	MODEL	ENGINE						
		CYLS	BORE	STROKE	DISPL	HP@RPM	C.R.	VLV
	DeLuxe Six, D-23	6	3.375	4.062	218.1	88@3800		L
	Special DeLuxe Six, D-23	6	3.375	4.062	218.1	88@3800		L
1946	Custom Six, D-24C	6	3.375	4.25	228.1	105@3600	6.0	L
	DeLuxe Six, D-25	6	3.375	4.062	218.1	95@3600		L
	Special DeLuxe Six, D-25	6	3.375	4.062	218.1	95@3600		L
1947	Custom Six, D-24C	6	3.375	4.25	228.1	105@3600	6.0	L
	DeLuxe Six, D-25	6	3.375	4.062	218.1	95@3600		L
	Special DeLuxe Six, D-25	6	3.375	4.062	218.1	95@3600		L
1948	Custom Six, D-24C	6	3.375	4.25	228.1	105@3600	6.0	L
	DeLuxe Six, D-25S	6	3.375	4.062	218.1	95@3600		L
	Special DeLuxe Six, D-25C	6	3.375	4.062	218.1	95@3600		L
1949	Custom Six, D-30	6	3.375	4.25	228.1	105@3600	6.0	L
	DeLuxe Six, D-31	6	3.375	4.062	218.1	97@3600	6.7	L
	DeLuxe Six, D-32	6	3.375	4.062	218.1	97@3600	6.7	L
	Special DeLuxe Six, D-32	6	3.375	4.062	218.1	97@3600	6.7	L
1950	Custom Six, D-34	6	3.375	4.25	228.1	105@3600	6.0	L
	DeLuxe Six, D-35	6	3.375	4.062	218.1	97@3600	6.7	L
	DeLuxe Six, D-36	6	3.375	4.062	218.1	97@3600	6.7	L
	Special DeLuxe Six, D-36	6	3.375	4.062	218.1	97@3600	6.7	L
1951	Kingsway, D-39	6	3.375	4.062	218.1	97@3600	6.7	L
	Crusader, D-40-1	6	3.375	4.062	218.1	97@3600	6.7	L
	Regent, D-40-2	6	3.375	4.062	218.1	97@3600	6.7	L
	Coronet, D-42	6	3.375	4.25	228.1	105@3600	6.0	L
1952	Coronet, D-42	6	3.375	4.25	228.1	105@3600	6.0	L
	Kingsway, D-39	6	3.375	4.062	218.1	97@3600	6.7	L
	Crusader, D-40-1	6	3.375	4.062	218.1	97@3600	6.7	L
	Regent, D-40-2	6	3.375	4.062	218.1	97@3600	6.7	L
1953	Crusader, D-42-1	6	3.375	4.062	218.1	97@3600	6.7	L
	Regent, D-43-2	6	3.375	4.062	218.1	97@3600	6.7	L
	Mayfair, D-43-3	6	3.375	4.062	218.1	97@3600	6.7	L
	Coronet, D-44	V8	3.438	3.25	241.3	140@4400	7.1	OH

CARBURETOR MFR	MODEL	VEN	WHEEL-BASE	TIRES	BODY	WEIGHT	PRICE
			117		6 ps	3115	1284
			117		6 ps	3150	1383
			119.5	6.00 x 16	6 ps	3360	1679
			117	6.00 x 16	6 ps	3155	1307
			117	6.00 x 16	6 ps	3175	1405
			119.5/	6.00 x 16	6 ps	3360	1847
			137.5				
			117	6.00 x 16	6 ps	3155	1438
			117	6.00 x 16	6 ps	3175	1546
			119.5/		6 ps	3360	2176
			137.5				
			117		6 ps	3155	1744
			117		6 ps	3175	1840
			123.5/	7.10 x 15/	6 ps	3460	2406
			137.5	8.20 x 15			
			111	6.40 x 15/	6 ps2	3005	1795
				6.70 x 15			
			118.5	6.70 x 15	6 ps	3150	1898
			118.5	6.70 x 15	6 ps	3165	1998
			123.5/	7.10 x 15/	6 ps	3450	2406
			137.5	8.20 x 15			
			111	6.40 x 15/	6 ps	3005	1795
				6.70 x 15			
			118.5	6.70 x 15	6 ps	3145	1898
			118.5	6.70 x 15	6 ps	3170	1998
			111	6.40 x 15/	6 ps2	3045	2205
				6.70 x 15			
			118.5	6.70 x 15	6 ps	3195	2324
			118.5	6.70 x 15	6 ps	3225	2445
			123.5/	7.10 x 15/	6 ps	3510	2928
			137.5	8.20 x 15			
			123.5/	7.10 x 15/	6 ps	3490	2833
			137.5	8.20 x 15			
			111	6.40 x 15/	6 ps2	3020	2154
				6.70 x 15			
			118.5	6.70 x 15	6 ps	3155	2272
			118.5	6.70 x 15	6 ps	3225	2367
C	D6S1	1	114	6.70 x 15	6 ps	3155	2246
C	D6S1	1	114	6.70 x 15	6 ps	3225	2367
C	D6S1	1	114	6.70 x 15	6 ps		2463
			119	7.10 x 15	6 ps	3510	3040

YEAR	MODEL	ENGINE						
		CYLS	BORE	STROKE	DISPL	HP@RPM	C.R.	VLV
1954	Crusader, D-49-1	6	3.375	4.25	228.1	108@3600	7.25	L
	Regent, D-49-2	6	3.375	4.25	228.1	108@3600	7.25	L
	Mayfair, D-49-3	6	3.375	4.25	228.1	108@3600	7.25	L
	Royal, D-50-3	V8	3.438	3.25	241.3	150@4400	7.5	OH
1955	Crusader, D-54-1	6	3.375	4.25	228.1	115@3600	7.4	L
	Regent, D-54-2	6	3.375	4.25	228.1	115@3600	7.4	L
	Mayfair, D-54-4	6	3.438	4.50	250.6	125@3600	7.5	L
	Mayfair, D-59-2	V8	3.438	3.25	241.3	157@4400	7.6	OH
	Royal Custom, D-59-3	V8	3.625	3.256	268.8	183@4400	7.5	OH
1956	Crusader, D-60-1	6	3.438	4.50	241.3	125@3600	7.5	L
	Regent, D-60-2	6	3.438	4.50	241.3	125@3600	7.5	L
	Crusader, D-61-1 (1)	V8	3.625	3.256	268.8	180@4400	8.0	OH
	Regent, D-61-2 (1)	V8	3.625	3.256	268.8	180@4400	8.0	OH
	Mayfair, D-61-3 (1)	V8	3.625	3.256	268.8	180@4400	8.0	OH
	Custom Royal, D-63-3	V8	3.812	3.312	302.5	200@4400	8.0	OH
	Optional engine:							
	(1)	V8	3.812	3.312	302.5	200@4400	8.0	OH
1957	Crusader, D-64-1	6	3.438	4.50	250.6	132@3600	7.0	L
	Regent, D-64-2	6	3.438	4.50	250.6	132@3600	7.0	L
	Crusader, D-65-1	V8	3.812	3.312	302.5	215@4400	8.0	OH
	Regent, D-65-2	V8	3.812	3.312	302.5	215@4400	8.0	OH
	Mayfair, D-65-3	V8	3.812	3.312	302.5	215@4400	8.0	OH
	Custom Royal, D-67-2	V8	3.875	3.312	312.5	235@4400	8.0	OH
1958	Crusader	6	3.438	4.50	250.6	132@3600	7.0	L
	Regent	6	3.438	4.50	250.6	132@3600	7.0	L
	Crusader	V8	3.875	3.312	312.5	220@4400	8.5	OH
	Regent	V8	3.875	3.312	312.5	220@4400	8.5	OH
	Mayfair	V8	3.875	3.312	312.5	220@4400	8.5	OH
	Custom Royal	V8	3.938	3.625	353.1	275@4400	10.0	OH
1959	Regent, ME1-L	6	3.438	4.50	250.6	135@3600	7.7	L
	Mayfair, ME1-M	6	3.438	4.50	250.6	135@3600	7.7	L
	Regent, ME2-L	V8	3.875	3.312	312.5	220@4400	8.5	OH
	Mayfair, ME2-M	V8	3.875	3.312	312.5	220@4400	8.5	OH
	Viscount, ME2-H	V8	3.875	3.312	312.5	220@4400	8.5	OH
	Custom Royal, MD3-H	V8	4.125	3.375	360.8	295@4400	10.0	OH
1960	Seneca, PD4-L	V8	3.875	3.312	312.5	225@4400	9.0	OH
	Pioneer, PD4-M	V8	3.875	3.312	312.5	225@4400	9.0	OH
	Phoenix, PD4-H	V8	3.875	3.312	312.5	225@4400	9.0	OH
	Polara, PD2-H	V8	4.125	3.375	360.8	295@4600	10.0	OH
1961	Seneca, RD4-L	V8	3.875	3.312	312.5	225@4400	9.0	OH
	Pioneer, RD4-M	V8	3.875	3.312	312.5	225@4400	9.0	OH

MFR	CARBURETOR MODEL	VEN	WHEEL-BASE	TIRES	BODY	WEIGHT	PRICE
C	D6S1	1	114	6.70 x 15	6 ps	3070	2305
C	D6S1	1	114	6.70 x 15	6 ps	3105	2415
C	D6S1	1	114	6.70 x 15	6 ps	3145	2511
			119	7.10 x 15	6 ps	3425	3405
C	2192	1	115	6.70 x 15	6 ps	3285	2286
C	2192	1	115	6.70 x 15	6 ps	3290	2402
C	2192	1	115	6.70 x 15	6 ps		2548
			115	6.70 x 15	6 ps	3440	2895
			120	7.10 x 15	6 ps	3480	3363
C	2296	1	115	6.70 x 15	6 ps	3245	2368
C	2296	1	115	6.70 x 15	6 ps	3290	2476
			115	6.70 x 15	6 ps	3335	2701
			115	6.70 x 15	6 ps	3375	2809
			115	6.70 x 15	6 ps	3355	2939
			120	7.10 x 15	6 ps	3545	3405
C	2299	2					
C	2515	1	118/122	7.50 x 14	6 ps	3455	2584
C	2515	1	118/122	7.50 x 14	6 ps	3460	2735
C	2299	2	118/122	7.50 x 14	6 ps	3555	2918
C	2299	2	118/122	7.50 x 14	6 ps	3580	3069
C	2299	2	118/122	7.50 x 14	6 ps	3590	3224
S	3-149	2	122	8.00 x 14	6 ps	3770	3749
C	2647	1	118/122	7.50 x 14	6 ps	3410	2631
C	2647	1	118/122	7.50 x 14	6 ps	3420	2795
C	2299	2	118	7.50 x 14	6 ps	3575	2956
C	2299	2	118/122	7.50 x 14	6 ps	3555	3191
C	2299	2	118/122	7.50 x 14	6 ps	3590	3311
			122	8.00 x 14	6 ps	3800	3758
			118/122	7.50 x 14	6 ps	3420	2791
			118	7.50 x 14	6 ps	3390	2979
C	2812	4	118/122	7.50 x 14	6 ps	3540	3138
C	2812	4	118/122	7.50 x 14	6 ps	3540	3325
C	2812	4	118/122	7.50 x 14	6 ps	3565	3516
			122	8.00 x 14	6 ps	3785	3744
C	2991	2	118	7.50 x 14	6 ps	3640	3211
C	2991	2	118	7.50 x 14	6 ps	3660	3376
C	2991	2	118	7.50 x 14	6 ps	3740	3562
C	3104	4	122	8.00 x 14	6 ps	3875	3769
C	3101	4	118	7.50 x 14	6 ps	3620	3211
C	3101	4	118	7.50 x 14	6 ps	3615	3377

YEAR	MODEL	ENGINE						
		CYLS	BORE	STROKE	DISPL	HP@RPM	C.R.	VLV
	Phoenix, RD4-H	V8	3.875	3.312	312.5	225@4400	9.0	OH
1962	Dart, SD2-L	V8	3.875	3.312	312.5	225@4400	9.0	OH
	Dart 330, SD2-M	V8	3.875	3.312	312.5	225@4400	9.0	OH
	Dart 440, SD2-H	V8	3.875	3.312	312.5	225@4400	9.0	OH
1963	220, TD2-L	V8	3.875	3.312	312.5	225@4400	9.0	OH
	330, TD2-M	V8	3.875	3.312	312.5	225@4400	9.0	OH
	440, TD2-H	V8	3.875	3.312	312.5	225@4400	9.0	OH
1964	330, VD2-L	V8	3.875	3.312	312.5	225@4400	9.0	OH
	440, VD2-M	V8	3.875	3.312	312.5	225@4400	9.0	OH
	Polara, VD2-H	V8	3.875	3.312	312.5	225@4400	9.0	OH
1965	330, AD1-L	6	3.40	4.125	224.7	145@4000	8.4	OH
	Polara 440, AD1-M	6	3.40	4.125	224.7	145@4000	8.4	OH
	Polara 880, AD1-H	6	3.40	4.125	224.7	145@4000	8.4	OH
	Monaco, AD1-P	6	3.40	4.125	224.7	145@4000	8.4	OH
	330, AD2-L	V8	3.906	3.312	317.5	230@4400	9.0	OH
	Polara 440, AD2-M	V8	3.906	3.312	317.3	230@4400	9.0	OH
	Polara 880, AD2-H	V8	3.906	3.312	317.3	230@4400	9.0	OH
	Monaco, AD2-P	V8	3.906	3.312	317.3	230@4400	9.0	OH
1966	Polara, BD1-L	6	3.40	4.125	224.7	145@4000	8.4	OH
	Polara 440, BD1-M	6	3.40	4.125	224.7	145@4000	8.4	OH
	Polara 880, BD1-H	6	3.40	4.125	224.7	145@4000	8.4	OH
	Monaco, BD1-P	6	3.40	4.125	224.7	145@4000	8.4	OH
	Polara, BD2-L	V8	3.906	3.312	317.3	230@4400	9.0	OH
	Polara 440, BD2-M	V8	3.906	3.312	317.3	230@4400	9.0	OH
	Polara 880, BD2-H	V8	3.906	3.312	317.3	230@4400	9.0	OH
	Monaco, BD2-P	V8	3.906	3.312	317.3	230@4400	9.0	OH
	Coronet DeLuxe, BW2-L	V8	3.906	3.312	317.3	230@4400	9.0	OH
	Coronet 440, BW2-H	V8	3.906	3.312	317.3	230@4400	9.0	OH
	Coronet 500, BW2-P	V8	3.906	3.312	317.3	230@4400	9.0	OH

DURANT — — Durant Motors of Canada, Leaside, Ont., 1922-30; Dominion Motors, Ltd., Leaside, Ont., 1930-32

YEAR	MODEL	CYLS	BORE	STROKE	DISPL	HP@RPM	C.R.	VLV
1930	4-07	4	3.875	4.00	200.4			L
	6-14	6	3.25	4.00	199.1			L
	6-17	6	3.375	4.625	248.3			L
1931	4-07	4	3.875	4.25	200.4	48@2800	5.10	L
	6-14	6	3.25	4.00	199.1	58@3100	5.32	L
	6-18	6	3.375	4.625	248.3	70@3000	5.30	L
1932	6-14	6	3.25	4.00	199.1	71@3300	5.32	L
	6-18	6	3.375	4.00	214.7	70@3400	5.41	L

MFR	CARBURETOR MODEL	VEN	WHEEL-BASE	TIRES	BODY	WEIGHT	PRICE
C	3101	4	118	7.50 x 14	6 ps	3635	3563
			116	7.00 x 14	6 ps	3155	3051
			116	7.00 x 14	6 ps	3170	3220
			116	7.00 x 14	6 ps	3195	3382
			119	7.00 x 14	6 ps	3253	3072
			119	7.00 x 14	6 ps	3262	3234
			119	7.00 x 14	6 ps	3305	3402
			119	7.00 x 14	6 ps	3300	3179
			119	7.00 x 14	6 ps	3310	3342
			119	7.00 x 14	6 ps	3340	3510
C	3999	1	121	7.75 x 14	6 ps	3630	3084
C	3999	1	121	7.75 x 14	6 ps	3650	3246
C	3999	1	121	7.75 x 14	6 ps	3655	3450
C	3999	1	121	7.75 x 14	6 pht2	3730	3673
C	4011	2	121	8.25 x 14	6 ps	3810	3226
C	4011	2	121	8.25 x 14	6 ps	3830	3388
C	4011	2	121	8.25 x 14	6 ps	3835	3592
C	4011	2	121	8.25 x 14	6 pht2	3910	3815
C	4111	1	121	7.75 x 14	6 ps	3630	3152
C	4111	1	121	7.75 x 14	6 ps	3650	3284
C	4111	1	121	7.75 x 14	6 ps	3655	3470
C	4111	1	121	7.75 x 14	6 pht2	3730	3660
C	4123	2	121	8.25 x 14	6 ps	3810	3294
C	4123	2	121	8.25 x 14	6 ps	3830	3426
C	4123	2	121	8.25 x 14	6 ps	3835	3613
C	4123	2	121	8.25 x 14	6 pht2	3910	3804
C	4123	2	117	7.35 x 14	6 ps	3075	3075
C	4123	2	117	7.35 x 14	6 ps	3226	3226
C	4123	2	117	7.35 x 14	6 pht2	3315	3450
S		1	111	5.00 x 19	5 ps		895
S		1	111	5.00 x 19	5 ps		1095
S		1	115	5.50 x 19	5 ps		
T		1		5.00 x 19	5 ps		855
S		1	111.5	5.00 x 19	5 ps		1045
S		1	115	5.50 x 19	5 ps		1225
T		1	112	5.00 x 19	5 ps		1045
T		1	115	5.25 x 19	5 ps		1145

YEAR	MODEL	ENGINE						
		CYLS	BORE	STROKE	DISPL	HP@RPM	C.R.	VLV

ERSKINE — — Studebaker Corp. of Canada, Walkerville, Ont., 1927-30

YEAR	MODEL	CYLS	BORE	STROKE	DISPL	HP@RPM	C.R.	VLV
1930	53	6	3.25	4.125	205.3	70@3200	5.8	L

MFR	CARBURETOR MODEL	VEN	WHEEL-BASE	TIRES	BODY	WEIGHT	PRICE
Sc		1	114	5.25 x 19	5 ps		1245

YEAR	MODEL	ENGINE						
		CYLS	BORE	STROKE	DISPL	HP@RPM	C.R.	VLV

FORD — — Ford Motor Co. of Canada, Ltd., Walkerville, Ont., 1905+

YEAR	MODEL	CYLS	BORE	STROKE	DISPL	HP@RPM	C.R.	VLV
1930	A	4	3.875	4.25	200.5	40@2200		L
1931	A	4	3.875	4.25	200.5	40@2200	4.22	L
1932	A	4	3.875	4.25	200.5	40@2200	4.22	L
	B	4	3.875	4.25	200.5	50@2800		L
1933	46-33	4	3.875	4.25	200.5	50@2800		L
	40-33	V8	3.062	3.75	221.0	75@3800		L
1934	40-34	V8	3.062	3.75	221.0	92@3900		L
1935	48	V8	3.062	3.75	221.0	92@3900		L
1936	68	V8	3.062	3.75	221.0	90@3800		L
1937	V8-60, 74	V8	2.60	3.20	135.9	60@3500		L
	V8-85, 78	V8	3.062	3.75	221.0	85@3800		L
1938	Standard 85, 81A	V8	3.062	3.75	221.0	85@3800		L
	Standard V8-60, 82A	V8	2.60	3.20	135.9	60@3500		L
	DeLuxe 85, 81A	V8	3.062	3.75	221.0	85@3800		L
1939	V8, 91A	V8	3.062	3.75	221.0	85@3800		L
1940	Standard, O1A	V8	3.062	3.75	221.0	85@3800		L
	DeLuxe, O1A	V8	3.062	3.75	221.0	85@3800		L
1941	Special, 11A	V8	3.062	3.75	221.0	85@3800		L
	DeLuxe, 11A	V8	3.062	3.75	221.0	85@3800		L
	Super DeLuxe, 11A	V8	3.062	3.75	221.0	85@3800		L
1942	21A	V8	3.062	3.75	221.0	85@3800		L
1946	DeLuxe *	V8	3.062	3.75	221.1	85@3800		L
	Super DeLuxe *	V8	3.062	3.75	221.1	90@3800		L
	DeLuxe	V8	3.188	3.75	239.5	90@3800		L
	Super DeLuxe V8	V8	3.188	3.75	239.5	90@3800		L
	*Produced to June 30, 1946.							
1947	DeLuxe	V8	3.188	3.75	239.5	95@3800		L
	Super DeLuxe	V8	3.188	3.75	239.5	95@3800		L
1948	DeLuxe	V8	3.188	3.75	239.5	97@3800		L
	Super DeLuxe	V8	3.188	3.75	239.5	97@3800		L
1949-53	Canadian Fords identical with U.S. products except for prices.							
1954	Mainline	V8	3.188	3.75	239.5	110@3800	7.2	L
	Customline	V8	3.188	4.00	255.5	120@3800	7.2	L
	Crestline	V8	3.188	4.00	255.5	120@3800	7.2	L

FRONTENAC — — Dominion Motors, Ltd., Leaside, Ont., 1931-33

YEAR	MODEL	CYLS	BORE	STROKE	DISPL	HP@RPM	C.R.	VLV
1931	E6-18	6	3.25	4.00	199.1	72		L
1932	6-70	6	3.25	4.00	199.1	71@3300	5.32	L
	6-85	6	3.375	4.00	214.7	75		L

CARBURETOR			WHEEL-	TIRES	BODY	WEIGHT	PRICE
MFR	MODEL	VEN	BASE				
Z		1	103.5	4.75 x 19	5 ps	2385	795
Z		1	103.5	4.75 x 19	5 ps	2460	705
Z		1	103.5	4.75 x 19	5 ps		705
		1	106	5.25 x 18	5 ps	2415	680
Z		1	112	5.25 x 17	5 ps	2550	685
D		1	112	5.50 x 17	5 ps	2675	745
S	EE1	2	112	5.50 x 17	5 ps	2730	780
S	EE1	2	112	6.00 x 16	5 ps	2900	750
S	EE1	2	112	6.00 x 16	5 ps	2900	735
S	EE 7/8	2	112	5.50 x 16	5 ps	2600	767
S	EE1	2	112	6.00 x 16	5 ps	2765	809
S	EE 7/8	2	112	6.00 x 16	5 ps	2825	885
S	EE 7/8	2	112	5.50 x 16	5 ps	2610	860
S	EE 7/8	2	112	6.00 x 16	5 ps	2865	950
		2	112	6.00 x 16			
S	F94	2	112	6.00 x 16	5 ps	2925	970
S	F94	2	112	6.00 x 16	5 ps	2945	1036
S	F94	2	114	6.00 x 16	6 ps	3033	1136
S	F94	2	114	6.00 x 16	6 ps	3121	1178
S	F94	2	114	6.00 x 16	6 ps	3146	1233
S	F94	2	114	6.00 x 16	6 ps	3146	1194
			114	6.00 x 16	5 ps	3220	1265
			114	6.00 x 16	5 ps	3240	1321
			114	6.00 x 16	5 ps	3220	1265
			114	6.00 x 16	5 ps	3240	1321
			114	6.00 x 16	5 ps	3220	1431
			114	6.00 x 16	5 ps	3240	1479
			114	6.00 x 16	5 ps	3220	1714
			114	6.00 x 16	5 ps	3240	1783
			115.5	6.70 x 15	6 ps	3263	2407
			115.5	6.70 x 15	6 ps	3276	2517
			115.5	7.10 x 15	6 ps	3820	2635
			109		5 ps		898
T		1	109	5.25 x 18	5 ps		898
			114		5 ps		1180

YEAR	MODEL	ENGINE						
		CYLS	BORE	STROKE	DISPL	HP@RPM	C.R.	VLV
1933	C-400	4	3.375	4.00	143.1	40		L
	C-600	6	3.00	4.00	199.1	65		L
	At least 1933 models were same as Continental.							

FRONTENAC – – Ford Motor Co. of Canada, Ltd., Oakville, Ont., 1959-60

YEAR	MODEL	CYLS	BORE	STROKE	DISPL	HP@RPM	C.R.	VLV
1960		6	3.50	2.50	144.3	90@4200	8.7	OH

CARBURETOR			WHEEL-	TIRES	BODY	WEIGHT	PRICE
MFR	MODEL	VEN	BASE				
M	AC	1	101.5		5 ps		670
M	B	1	107		5 ps		770
			109.5	6.00 x 13	6 ps		2627

YEAR	MODEL	ENGINE CYLS	BORE	STROKE	DISPL	HP@RPM	C.R.	VLV

GRAHAM — — Graham-Paige Motors (Canada), Ltd., Walkerville, Ont., 1932-39

YEAR	MODEL	CYLS	BORE	STROKE	DISPL	HP@RPM	C.R.	VLV
1932	New Standard Six	6	3.25	4.50	224.0	76@3400		L
	Six, 56	6	3.125	4.50	207.1	70@3200		L
	New Special Six	6	3.25	4.50	224.0	76@3400		L
	Blue Streak Eight	8	3.125	4.00	245.4	90@3400		L
1933	Standard Six, 65	6	3.25	4.50	224.0	80@3400		L
	Six, 58	6	3.25	4.50	224.0	80@3400		L
	Standard Eight	8	3.125	4.00	245.4	95@3400		L
	Custom Eight	8	3.125	4.00	245.4	95@3400		L
1934	Standard Six	6	3.25	4.50	224.0	85@3400		L
	Standard Eight, 67	8	3.125	4.00	245.5	95@3400		L
	Custom Eight, 69	8	3.25	4.00	265.4	135@4000		L
1935	Standard Six, 74	6	3.00	4.00	169.6	60@3500		L
	Special Six, 73	6	3.25	4.50	224.0	85@3400		L
	Eight, 72	8	3.125	4.00	245.4	95@3400		L
	Supercharged Eight, 75	8	3.25	4.00	265.4	140@4000		L
1936	Crusader, 80	6	3.00	4.00	169.6	70@3500		L
	Cavalier, 90	6	3.25	4.375	217.8	85@3300		L
	Supercharger, 110	6	3.25	4.375	217.8	112@4000		L
1937	Crusader, 85	6	3.00	4.00	169.6	70@3500		L
	Cavalier, 95	6	3.25	4.00	199.1	85@3300		L
	Supercharger, 116	6	3.25	4.00	199.1	106@4000		L
	Custom Supercharger, 120	6	3.25	4.00	199.1	116@4000		L
1938	Standard, 96	6	3.25	4.375	217.8	90@3600		L
	Special, 96	6	3.25	4.375	217.8	90@3600		L
	Supercharger, 97	6	3.25	4.375	217.8	116@4000		L
	Custom Supercharger, 97	6	3.25	4.375	217.8	116@4000		L
1939	Standard, 96	6	3.25	4.375	217.8	90@3600		L
	Supercharger, 97	6	3.25	4.375	217.8	116@4000		L

MFR	CARBURETOR MODEL	VEN	WHEEL-BASE	TIRES	BODY	WEIGHT	PRICE
			115	5.50 x 18	5 ps	3265	1445
			113	5.00 x 19	5 ps	3205	
			115	5.50 x 18	5 ps	3335	1505
			123	6.00 x 17	5 ps	3665	1565
			113	5.50 x 17	5 ps	3265	1170
			118	6.00 x 17	5 ps	3570	1330
			119	6.00 x 17	5 ps	3500	1320
			123	6.00 x 17	5 ps	3695	1595
			116	6.25 x 16	5 ps	3165	1035
			123	6.50 x 16	5 ps	3470	1315
			123/138	7.00 x 16	5 ps	3600	1845
			111	5.25 x 17	5 ps	2695	885
			116	6.00 x 16	5 ps	3265	1185
			123	6.50 x 16	5 ps	3470	1365
			123	7.00 x 16	5 ps	3640	1645
M			111	5.25 x 17	5 ps	2655	880
M			115	6.00 x 16	5 ps	2865	1095
M			115	6.25 x 16	5 ps	3070	1230
M			111	6.00 x 16	5 ps	2695	950
M			116	6.00 x 16	5 ps	2960	1090
M			120	6.25 x 16	5 ps	3125	1262
M			116/120	6.50 x 16	5 ps	3200	1406
			120	6.00 x 16	5 ps	3275	1440
			120	6.00 x 16	5 ps	3315	1560
			120	6.50 x 16	5 ps	3375	1740
			120	6.50 x 16	5 ps	3375	1860
			120	6.00 x 16	6 ps	3275	1290
			120	6.00 x 16	6 ps	3295	1465

YEAR	MODEL	ENGINE						
		CYLS	BORE	STROKE	DISPL	HP@RPM	C.R.	VLV

HUDSON — — Hudson Motors of Canada, Tilbury, Ont., 1932-42; 1950-54

YEAR	MODEL	CYLS	BORE	STROKE	DISPL	HP@RPM	C.R.	VLV
1932	Great Eight Standard	8	3.00	4.50	254.4	101@3600	5.8	L
	Sterling Eight	8	3.00	4.50	254.4	101@3600	5.8	L
	Major Eight	8	3.00	4.50	254.4	101@3600	5.8	L
1933	Super Six, E	6	2.938	4.75	193.0	73@3200		L
	Standard Eight T	8	3.00	4.50	254.4	101@3600		L
	Major Eight, L	8	3.00	4.50	254.4	101@3600		L
1934	Standard Eight, L, LT	8	3.00	4.50	254.4	108@3800		L
	Major Eight, LL	8	3.00	4.50	254.4	113@3800		L
1935	Special Six, GH	6	3.00	5.00	212.0	93@3800	6.25	L
	Special Eight, HT	8	3.00	4.50	254.4	113@3800	6.0	L
	DeLuxe Eight, HU	8	3.00	4.50	254.4	113@3800	6.0	L
	Custom Eight, HHU	8	3.00	4.50	254.4	113@3800	6.0	L
1936	Custom Six, 63	6	3.00	5.00	212.0	93@3800	6.25	L
	DeLuxe Eight, 64	8	3.00	4.50	254.4	113@3800	6.0	L
	Custom Eight, 67	8	3.00	4.50	254.4	113@3800	6.0	L
1937	Custom Six, 73	6	3.00	5.00	212.0	101@4000	6.25	L
	DeLuxe Eight, 74	8	3.00	4.50	254.4	122@4200	6.25	L
	DeLuxe Eight, 76	8	3.00	4.50	254.4	122@4200	6.25	L
	Custom Eight, 75	8	3.00	4.50	254.4	122@4200	6.25	L
	Custom Eight, 77	8	3.00	4.50	254.4	122@4200	6.25	L
1938	Six, 112	6	3.00	4.125	174.9	83@4000	6.5	L
	Custom Six, 83	6	3.00	5.00	212.0	101@4000	6.25	L
	DeLuxe Eight, 84	8	3.00	4.50	254.4	122@4200	6.25	L
	Custom Eight, 81	8	3.00	4.50	254.4	122@4200	6.25	L
1939	Six, 112, 90	6	3.00	4.125	174.9	86@4000	6.5	L
	Six, 92	6	3.00	5.00	212.0	96@3900	6.25	L
	Pacemaker, 91	6	3.00	5.00	212.0	96@3900	6.25	L
	Country Club, 93	6	3.00	5.00	212.0	101@4000	6.25	L
	Big Boy, 93	6	3.00	4.125	174.9	86@4000	6.5	L
	Country Club, 95	8	3.00	4.50	254.4	122@4200	6.25	L
	Country Club, 97	8	3.00	4.50	254.4	122@4200	6.25	L
1940	Traveler Six, 40	6	3.00	4.125	174.9	92@4000	7.1	L
	Super Six, 41	6	3.00	5.00	212.0	102@4000	6.5	L
	Country Club Six, 43, 48	6	3.00	5.00	212.0	102@4000	6.5	L
	Eight, 44, 47	8	3.00	4.50	254.4	128@4200	6.5	L
	DeLuxe Eight, 45	8	3.00	4.50	254.4	128@4200	6.5	L
1941	Six, 10	6	3.00	4.125	174.9	92@4000	7.25	L
	Six, 11	6	3.00	5.00	212.0	102@4000	6.5	L
	Six, 12	6	3.00	5.00	212.0	102@4000	6.5	L

MFR	CARBURETOR MODEL	VEN	WHEEL-BASE	TIRES	BODY	WEIGHT	PRICE
			119	6.00 x 17	5 ps		1595
			126	6.00 x 17	5 ps		1895
			132	6.00 x 17	5 ps		2095
			113	5.50 x 17	5 ps		1045
			119	6.00 x 17	5 ps		1485
			132	6.00 x 17	7 ps		1970
			116	6.25 x 16	5 ps		1173
			123	6.50 x 16	5 ps		1480
			116	6.00 x 16	5 ps		965
			117	6.25 x 16	5 ps		1238
			117	7.50 x 16	5 ps		1495
			124	7.50 x 16	5 ps		1545
C	W1-329S	1	120	6.00 x 16	5 ps		1192
C	W1-330S	1	120/128	6.25 x 16	5 ps		1285
C	W1-330S	1		6.25 x 16	5 ps		1503
C	WDO-377S	2	122	6.00 x 16	5 ps		1273
C	WDO-344S	2	122	6.25 x 16	5 ps		1391
C	WDO-344S	2	129	6.25 x 16	5 ps		1439
C	WDO-344S	2	129	6.25 x 16	5 ps		1561
C	WDO-344S	2	129	6.25 x 16	5 ps		1602
C		1	112	5.50 x 16	6 ps	2620	1009
C	WDO-402S	2	122	6.00 x 16	6 ps	3005	1311
C		2	122	6.50 x 16	6 ps	3155	1410
C		2	129	6.50 x 16	6 ps	3275	1617
C	W1-438S	1	112	6.00 x 16	6 ps	2712	1035
C	WDO-430S	2	118	6.00 x 16	6 ps		1203
C	WDO-430S	2	118	6.00 x 16	6 ps	2867	1127
C	WDO-438S	2	122	6.00 x 16	6 ps	3023	1288
C	W1-438S	1	119	6.00 x 16	5 ps	2902	1149
C	WDO-430S	2	122	6.50 x 16	6 ps	3193	1421
C	WDO-430S	2	129	6.50 x 16	6 ps	3215	1436
C	WA1-454S	1	113	5.50 x 16	6 ps	2940	1031
C	WDO-461S	2	118	6.00 x 16	6 ps	3050	1268
C	WDO-461S	2	125	6.25 x 16	6 ps	3240	1458
C	WDO-455S	2	118/125	6.50 x 16	6 ps	3185	1381
C	WDO-455S	2	118	6.00 x 16	6 ps	3215	1436
C	WA1-454S	1	116	6.00 x 16	6 ps	2900	1326
C	WDO-501S	2	121	6.00 x 16	6 ps	3050	1585
C	WDO-501S	2	121	6.25 x 16	6 ps	3100	1749

YEAR	MODEL	ENGINE						
		CYLS	BORE	STROKE	DISPL	HP@RPM	C.R.	VLV
	Six, 18	6	3.00	5.00	212.0	102@4000	6.5	L
	Eight, 14	8	3.00	4.50	254.4	125@4200	6.5	L
	Eight, 15	8	3.00	4.50	254.4	125@4200	6.5	L
	Eight, 17	8	3.00	4.50	254.4	125@4200	6.5	L
1942	Six, 20T	6	3.00	4.125	174.9	92@4000	7.25	L
	DeLuxe Six, 20P	6	3.00	5.00	212.0	102@4000	6.5	L
	Super Six, 21	6	3.00	5.00	212.0	102@4000	6.5	L
	Commodore Six, 22	6	3.00	5.00	212.0	102@4000	6.5	L
	Eight, 24	8	3.00	4.50	254.4	128@4200	6.5	L
	Eight, 25	8	3.00	4.50	254.4	128@4200	6.5	L
	Eight, 27	8	3.00	4.50	254.4	128@4200	6.5	L

HUPMOBILE — — Hupp Motor Car Corp., Windsor, Ont., 1933-36

YEAR	MODEL	CYLS	BORE	STROKE	DISPL	HP@RPM	C.R.	VLV
1933	Six, B316	6	3.375	4.25	228.1	75@3200		L
	Six, K321	6	3.375	4.25	228.1	90@3800		L
	Eight, F322	8	3.00	4.625	261.5	96@3600		L
	Eight, I326	8	3.188	4.75	303.2	109@3500		L
1934	Six, W417	6	3.50	3.875	224.0	80@3400		L
	Six, K421	6	3.375	4.25	228.1	90@3400		L
	Six, J421	6	3.50	4.25	245.3	93@3400		L
	Eight, F422	8	3.00	4.625	261.5	96@3600		L
	Eight, I426	8	3.188	4.75	303.2	109@3500		L
	Eight, T427	8	3.188	4.75	303.2	115@3500		L
1935	Six, W517	6	3.50	3.875	224.0	91@3500		L
	Six, D518	6	3.50	4.25	245.3	101@3600		L
	Six, J521	6	3.50	4.25	245.3	101@3600		L
	Eight, O-521	8	3.188	4.75	303.2	120@3500		L
	Eight, T527	8	3.188	4.75	303.2	120@3500		L
1936	Six, G618	6	3.50	4.50	245.3	101@3600		L
	Eight, N621	8	3.188	4.75	303.2	120@3500		L

MFR	CARBURETOR MODEL	VEN	WHEEL-BASE	TIRES	BODY	WEIGHT	PRICE
C	WDO-501S	2	128	6.50 x 16	7 ps	3155	1959
C	WDO-502S	2	121	6.25 x 16	6 ps	3260	1841
C	WDO-502S	2	121	6.25 x 16	6 ps	3400	2165
C	WDO-502S	2	128	6.25 x 16	7 ps	3440	2563
C	WA1-454S	1	116	6.00 x 16	6 ps	2940	1434
C	WDO-501S	2	116	6.00 x 16	6 ps	2975	1510
C	WDO-501S	2	121	6.00 x 16	6 ps	3080	1670
C	WDO-501S	2	121	6.25 x 16	6 ps	3145	1829
C	WDO-502S	2	121	6.25 x 16			
C	WDO-502S	2	121	6.50 x 16			
C	WDO-502S	2	128	6.50 x 16			
			116	5.50 x 18	5 ps	3095	1430
			121	6.00 x 17	5 ps	3290	1695
			122	6.00 x 17	5 ps	3650	2025
			126	6.50 x 17	5 ps	3845	2435
			117	6.00 x 16	5 ps	3040	1395
			121	6.00 x 17	5 ps	3290	1595
			121	6.50 x 16	6 ps	3425	1845
			122	6.00 x 17	5 ps	3650	1925
			126	6.50 x 17	5 ps	3845	2235
			127	7.00 x 16	6 ps	3805	2095
			117	6.00 x 16	5 ps	3130	1170
			118	6.00 x 16	6 ps	2930	1255
			121	6.50 x 16	6 ps	3325	1780
			121	6.50 x 16	6 ps	3535	1830
			127	7.00 x 16	6 ps	3700	2275
C	W1-333S	1	118	6.00 x 16	6 ps	3000	1270
C	WDO-317S	2	121	6.50 x 16	6 ps	3535	1525

YEAR	MODEL	ENGINE						
		CYLS	BORE	STROKE	DISPL	HP@RPM	C.R.	VLV

LA SALLE — — General Motors of Canada, Ltd., Oshawa, Ont., 1927-35

YEAR	MODEL	CYLS	BORE	STROKE	DISPL	HP@RPM	C.R.	VLV
1930	340	V8	3.312					L
1931	No Canadian LaSalles in 1931.							
1932	345B	V8	3.375	4.938	353.0	115@3000	5.38	L
1933	345C	V8	3.375	4.938	353.0	115@3000	5.38	L
1934	350	8	3.00	4.25	240.3	95@3700	6.5	L
1935	350	8	3.00	4.25	240.3	95@3700	6.5	L
	35-50	8	3.00					

CARBURETOR			WHEEL-	TIRES	BODY	WEIGHT	PRICE
MFR	MODEL	VEN	BASE				
O			134	6.50 x 19	5 ps		3370
O			130/136	7.00 x 17	5 ps		4200
O			130/136		5 ps		3715
S	EE-23		119	7.00 x 16	5 ps	3960	2405
			119	7.00 x 16	5 ps		2390
			120		5 ps		2005

YEAR	MODEL	ENGINE						
		CYLS	BORE	STROKE	DISPL	HP@RPM	C.R.	VLV

MARQUETTE — — General Motors of Canada, Ltd., Oshawa, Ont., 1930

YEAR	MODEL	CYLS	BORE	STROKE	DISPL	HP@RPM	C.R.	VLV
1930	30	6	3.125	4.625	212.8	67@3000	5.2	L

MC LAUGHLIN-BUICK — — General Motors of Canada, Ltd., Oshawa, Ont., 1923-42

YEAR	MODEL	CYLS	BORE	STROKE	DISPL	HP@RPM	C.R.	VLV
1930	40	6	3.438	4.625	257.6	80@2800		OH
	50	6	3.75	5.00	331.3	98@2800		OH
	60	6	3.75	5.00	331.3	98@2800		OH
1931	8-50	8	2.875	4.25	220.7	76@3200	4.8	OH
	8-60	8	3.062	4.625	272.5	90@3000	4.7	OH
	8-80	8	3.312	5.00	344.7	104@2800	4.5	OH
	8-90	8	3.312	5.00	344.7	104@2800	4.5	OH
1932	50	8	2.938	4.25	230.4	82@3200	5.09	OH
	60	8	3.062	4.625	272.5	96@3200	5.03	OH
	80	8	3.312	5.00	344.7	113@2800	4.8	OH
	90	8	3.312	5.00	344.7	113@2800	4.8	OH
1933	33-50	8	2.938	4.25	230.4	86/83@	5.25/	OH
						3200	4.84	
	33-60	8	3.062	4.625	272.5	97/91@	5.25/	OH
						3200	4.84	
	33-80	8	3.312	5.00	344.7	113/105	4.8/	OH
						@3200	4.4	
	33-90	8	3.312	5.00	344.7	113/105	4.8/	OH
						@3200	4.4	
1934	34-50	8	2.969	4.25	235.4	88@3200	5.25	OH
	34-60	8	3.094	4.625	278.2	100@3200	5.25	OH
	34-90	8	3.312	5.00	344.7	116@3200	4.55	OH
1935	35-44	8	3.094	3.875	233.1	93@3200	5.45	OH
	35-45	8	2.969	4.25	235.4	88@3200	5.25	OH
	35-46	8	3.094	4.625	278.2	100@3200	5.25	OH
	35-49	8	3.312	5.00	344.7	116@3200	4.95	OH
1936	36-44	8	3.188	3.875	274.4	93@3200	5.55	OH
	36-46	8	3.438	4.312	320.2	120@3200	5.45	OH
	36-48	8	3.438	4,312	320.2	120@3200	5.45	OH
	36-49	8	3.438	4.312	320.2	120@3200	5.45	OH
1937	Special, 44	8	3.188	4.125	263.3	100@3200	5.7	OH
	Century, 46	8	3.438	4.312	320.2	130@3400	5.75	OH
	Roadmaster, 48	8	3.438	4.312	320.2	130@3400	5.75	OH
	Limited, 49	8	3.438	4.312	320.2	130@3400	5.75	OH
1938	Special, 44	8	3.094	4.125	248.1	107@3400	6.15	OH
	Century, 46	8	3.438	4.312	320.2	141@3600	6.35	OH

CARBURETOR			WHEEL-	TIRES	BODY	WEIGHT	PRICE
MFR	MODEL	VEN	BASE				
M	FM	1	114	5.25 x 18	5 ps	3200	1335
M	T-3-S		118	5.50 x 19	5 ps		1740
M	T-4-S		124	6.50 x 19	5 ps		2010
M	T-4-S		132	6.50 x 19	5 ps		2485
M	T-3		114	5.25 x 18	5 ps	3215	1380
M	TD-2-S		118	5.50 x 18	5 ps	3870	1775
M	TD-3		124	6.50 x 19	5 ps	4320	2045
M	TD-3		132	6.50 x 19	7 ps	4525	2520
M	TD-1-S		114.8	5.50 x 18	5 ps	3215	1405
M	TD-2-S		118	6.00 x 18	5 ps	3870	1790
M	TD-3-S		126	7.00 x 18	5 ps	4320	2130
M	TD-3-S		134	7.00 x 18	5 ps		2625
M	ED-1-S		119	6.00 x 17	5 ps	3785	1465
M	ED-2-S		126.5	6.50 x 17	5 ps	4230	1905
M	ED-3		130	7.00 x 17	5 ps	4575	2275
M	ED-3		138	7.00 x 17	7 ps	4825	2835
M	ED-1-S		119	7.00 x 16	5 ps		1666
M	ED-2-S		128	7.50 x 16	5 ps		2187
M	ED-3		136	7.50 x 16	7 ps		3125
M			117	6.25 x 16	5 ps		1424
			119	7.00 x 16	5 ps		1651
			128	7.00 x 16	5 ps		2178
			136	7.50 x 16	5 ps		3075
S	EE-1	2	118.8	6.50 x 16	5 ps		1430
S	EE-2	2	122	7.00 x 16	5 ps		1735
S	EE-2	2	131	7.00 x 16	6 ps		2008
S	EE-2	2	138	7.50 x 16	8 ps		3002
S	AA-1	2	122	6.50 x 16	5 ps		1339
S	AA-2	2	125.5	7.00 x 16	5 ps		1400
S	AA-2	2	130.5	7.00 x 16	5 ps		1690
S	AA-2	2	137	7.50 x 16	5 ps		2460
S	AAV-1	2	120		5 ps		1434
S	AAV-2	2	125.5		5 ps		1793

YEAR	MODEL	ENGINE CYLS	BORE	STROKE	DISPL	HP@RPM	C.R.	VLV
	Roadmaster, 48	8	3.438	4.312	320.2	141@3600	6.35	OH
	Limited, 49	8	3.438	4.312	320.2	141@3600	6.35	OH
1939	Special, 44	8	3.094	4.125	248.1	107@3400	6.15	OH
	Century, 46	8	3.438	4.312	320.2	141@3600	6.25	OH
	Roadmaster, 48	8	3.438	4.312	320.2	141@3600	6.25	OH
	Limited, 49	8	3.438	4.312	320.2	141@3600	6.25	OH
1940	Special, 40	8	3.094	4.125	248.1	107@3400	6.1	OH
	Super, 50	8	3.094	4.125	248.1	107@3400	6.1	OH
	Century, 60	8	3.438	4.312	320.2	141@3600	6.25	OH
	Roadmaster, 70	8	3.438	4.312	320.2	141@3600	6.25	OH
	Limited, 80	8	3.438	4.312	320.2	141@3600	6.25	OH
	Limited, 90	8	3.438	4.312	320.2	141@3600	6.25	OH
1941	Special, 40	8	3.094	4.125	248.1	115@3500	6.5	OH
	Super, 50	8	3.094	4.125	248.1	125@3500	7.0	OH
	Century, 60	8	3.438	4.312	320.2	165@3800	7.0	OH
	Roadmaster, 70	8	3.438	4.312	320.2	165@3800	7.0	OH
1942	Special, 44	8	3.094	4.125	248.1		6.5	OH
	Century, 46	8	3.438	4.312	320.2		7.0	OH
	See Buick for models built 1951-53.							

MERCURY – – Ford Motor Co. of Canada, Ltd., Windsor, Ont., 1939-42; 1946-48

YEAR	MODEL	CYLS	BORE	STROKE	DISPL	HP@RPM	C.R.	VLV
1939	99A	V8	3.188	3.75	239.5	95@3600	6.5	L
1940	09A	V8	3.188	3.75	239.5	95@3600	6.5	L
1941	19A	V8	3.188	3.75	239.5	95@3600	6.5	L
1942	29A	V8	3.188	3.75	239.5	95@3600	6.5	L
1946	DeLuxe, 114	V8	3.188	3.75	239.5	100@3800	6.25	L
	Super Deluxe, 114X	V8	3.188	3.75	239.5	100@3800	6.25	L
1947	DeLuxe, 114	V8	3.188	3.75	239.5	100@3800	6.25	L
	Super Deluxe, 114X	V8	3.188	3.75	239.5	100@3800	6.25	L
1948	DeLuxe, 114	V8	3.188	3.75	239.5	100@3800	6.25	L
	Super DeLuxe, 114X	V8	3.188	3.75	239.5	100@3800	6.25	L
	After 1948, Mercury 114 was renamed Meteor.							

MERCURY – – Ford Motor Co., of Canada, Ltd., Oakville, Ont., 1959-65

YEAR	MODEL	CYLS	BORE	STROKE	DISPL	HP@RPM	C.R.	VLV
1959	Monterey	V8	4.30	3.30	383.4	280@4500	10.0	OH
1960	Monterey	V8	4.30	3.30	383.4	280@4500	10.0	OH
1961	Monterey	V8	4.00	3.50	351.9	220@4300	8.9	OH
1962	Monterey	V8	4.00	3.50	351.9	220@4300	8.9	OH
	Monterey Custom	V8	4.00	3.50	351.9	220@4300	8.9	OH
	S-55	V8	4.00	3.50	351.9	220@4300	8.9	OH
1963	400 (1)	6	3.625	3.60	222.9	138@4200	8.4	OH

MFR	CARBURETOR MODEL	VEN	WHEEL-BASE	TIRES	BODY	WEIGHT	PRICE
S	AAV-2	2	133		5 ps		2289
S	AAV-2	2	140		6 ps		3194
S	AAV-1	2	120		5 ps		1385
S	AAV-26	2	126		5 ps		1724
S	AAV-26	2	133		5 ps		2289
S	AAV-26	2	140		6 ps		3194
S	AAV-16	2	121		5 ps		1432
S	AAV-16	2	121		5 ps		1592
S	AAV-26	2	126		5 ps		1825
S	AAV-26	2	126		5 ps		1927
S	AAV-26	2	133		5 ps		2350
S	AAV-26	2	140		6 ps		3048
S	AAV-16	2	121		5 ps		1823
S	AAV-16	2	121		5 ps		2021
S	AAV-1	2	126		5 ps		2325
S	AAV-1	2	126		5 ps		2534
S	AAV-16	2	121		5 ps		1870
S	AAV-16	2	126		5 ps		2349
O	94	2	116	6.00 x 16	6 ps	2960	1141
O	94	2	116	6.00 x 16	6 ps		1228
O	94	2	118	6.50 x 16	6 ps2	3184	1335
O	94	2	118	6.50 x 16	6 ps	3240	1398
H	94	2	114	6.00 x 16	5 ps	3240	1291
H	94	2	114	6.00 x 16	5 ps	3250	1347
			114	6.00 x 16	5 ps	3240	1459
			114	6.00 x 16	5 ps	3250	1507
O		2	114	6.00 x 16	5 ps	3240	1758
O		2	114	6.00 x 16	5 ps	3250	1827
			126	8.00 x 14	6 ps	4095	3779
			126	8.00 x 14	6 ps	4032	3685
		2	120	7.50 x 14	6 ps	3808	3753
		2	120	7.50 x 14	6 ps	3823	3469
		2	120	7.50 x 14	6 ps	3836	3633
		2	120	7.50 x 14	6 pht2	3894	4225
		1	120	7.50 x 14	6 ps	3914	3225

YEAR	MODEL	ENGINE						
		CYLS	BORE	STROKE	DISPL	HP@RPM	C.R.	VLV
	Monterey (1)	6	3.625	3.60	222.9	138@4200	8.4	OH
	Monterey Custom	V8	4.00	3.50	351.9	220@4300	8.9	OH
	S-55	V8	4.00	3.50	351.9	220@4300	8.9	OH
	Optional engine:							
	(1)	V8	4.00	3.50	351.9	220@4300	8.9	OH
1964	Montclair	V8	4.00	3.50	351.9	220@4300	8.9	OH
	Park Lane	V8	4.00	3.50	351.9	220@4300	8.9	OH
	Optional engine, both lines:	V8	4.05	3.78	389.7	250@4400	9.0	OH
1965	Montclair	V8	4.00	3.50	351.9	220@4300	8.9	OH
	Park Lane	V8	4.00	3.50	351.9	220@4300	8.9	OH
	Optional engine, both lines:	V8	4.05	3.78	389.7	300@4600	10.0	OH

METEOR – – Ford Motor Co. of Canada, Ltd., Windsor, Ont.; Oakville, Ont., 1949+

YEAR	MODEL	CYLS	BORE	STROKE	DISPL	HP@RPM	C.R.	VLV
1949	DeLuxe	V8	3.188	3.75	239.5	100@3800	6.8	L
	Custom	V8	3.188	3.75	239.5	100@3800	6.8	L
1950	DeLuxe	V8	3.188	3.75	239.5	100@3800	6.8	L
	Custom DeLuxe	V8	3.188	3.75	239.5	100@3800	6.8	L
1951	DeLuxe	V8	3.188	3.75	239.5	100@3800	6.8	L
	Custom DeLuxe	V8	3.188	3.75	239.5	100@3800	6.8	L
1952	Mainline	V8	3.188	3.75	239.5	110@3800	7.2	L
	Customline	V8	3.188	4.00	255.5	120@3600	6.8	L
1953	Mainline	V8	3.188	3.75	239.5	110@3800	7.2	L
	Customline	V8	3.188	4.00	255.5	120@3600	6.8	L
	Crestline	V8	3.188	4.00	255.5	120@3600	6.8	L
1954		V8	3.188	3.75	239.5	110@3800	7.2	L
	Niagara	V8	3.188	4.00	255.5	125@3600	7.2	L
	Rideau	V8	3.188	4.00	255.5	125@3600	7.2	L
1955		V8	3.625	3.30	272.5	162@4500	7.6	OH
	Niagara	V8	3.625	3.30	272.5	175@4400	8.5	OH
	Rideau	V8	3.625	3.30	272.5	175@4400	8.5	OH
1956		6	3.625	3.60	222.9	137@4200	8.0	OH
	Niagara	6	3.625	3.60	222.9	137@4200	8.0	OH
	Rideau	6	3.625	3.60	222.9	137@4200	8.0	OH
	Optional engines, all lines:							
		V8	3.625	3.30	272.5	173@4400	8.0	OH
		V8	3.75	3.30	291.6	202@4600	8.4	OH
1957	Niagara (1)	6	3.625	3.60	222.9	144@4200	8.6	OH
	Niagara 300 (1)	6	3.625	3.60	222.9	144@4200	8.6	OH
	Rideau (2)	V8	3.75	3.30	291.6	212@4500	9.1	OH
	Rideau 500 (2)	V8	3.75	3.30	291.6	212@4500	9.1	OH
	Optional engines:							

CARBURETOR							
MFR	MODEL	VEN	WHEEL-BASE	TIRES	BODY	WEIGHT	PRICE
		1	120	7.50 x 14	6 ps	3914	3421
		2	120	7.50 x 14	6 ps	3956	3724
		2	120	7.50 x 14	6 pht2	3894	4316
		2					
		2	120	8.00 x 14	6 ps	3994	3807
		2	120	8.00 x 14	6 ps	4033	4047
		4					
		2	123	8.15 x 15	6 ps	3945	4205
		2	123	8.15 x 15	6 ps	4000	4502
		4					
			114	6.70 x 15	6 ps		2042
			114	6.70 x 15	6 ps	3180	2134
			114	6.70 x 15	6 ps	3045	1998
			114	6.70 x 15	6 ps	3050	2060
			114	6.70 x 15	6 ps	3080	2349
			114	6.70 x 15	6 ps	3087	2419
			115	6.70 x 15	6 ps	3180	2227
			115	6.70 x 15	6 ps	3230	2405
			115	6.70 x 15	6 ps	3195	2229
			115	6.70 x 15	6 ps	3255	2407
			115	6.70 x 15	6 pht2	3235	2713
			115	6.70 x 15	6 ps	3190	2433
			115	6.70 x 15	6 ps	3240	2611
			115	6.70 x 15	6 ps	3305	2729
		2	115.5	6.70 x 15	6 ps	3216	2431
		4	115.5	6.70 x 15	6 ps	3236	2566
		4	115.5	6.70 x 15	6 ps	3268	2720
		1	115.5	6.70 x 15			
		1	115.5	6.70 x 15			
		1	115.5	6.70 x 15			
		2					
		4					
		1	116	7.50 x 14	6 ps		2499
		1	116	7.50 x 14	6 ps	3300	2583
		2	118	7.50 x 14	6 ps	3460	3151
		2	118	7.50 x 14	6 ps	3480	3209

YEAR	MODEL	ENGINE						
		CYLS	BORE	STROKE	DISPL	HP@RPM	C.R.	VLV
	(1)	V8	3.625	3.30	272.5	190@4500	8.6	OH
	(2)	V8	3.80	3.44	311.9	245@4500	9.7	OH
1958	Niagara	6	3.625	3.60	222.9	145@4200	8.6	OH
	Niagara 300	6	3.625	3.60	222.9	145@4200	8.6	OH
	Rideau	6	3.625	3.60	222.9	145@4200	8.6	OH
	Rideau 500	6	3.625	3.60	222.9	145@4200	8.6	OH
	Niagara 300 (1, 2)	V8	3.625	3.30	272.5	190@4500	8.6	
	Rideau (1, 2)	V8	3.625	3.30	272.5	190@4500	8.6	
	Rideau 300 (2)	V8	4.00	3.30	331.8	265@4600	9.5	
	Optional engines:							
	(1)	V8	4.00	3.30	331.8	240@4600	9.5	OH
	(2)	V8	4.05	3.50	360.7	303@4600	10.5	OH
1959	Niagara 300	6	3.625	3.60	222.9	145@4200	8.4	OH
	Rideau	6	3.625	3.60	222.9	145@4200	8.4	OH
	Rideau 500	6	3.625	3.60	222.9	145@4200	8.4	OH
	Montcalm	6	3.625	3.60	222.9	145@4200	8.4	OH
	Optional engines, all lines:	V8	4.00	3.30	331.8	225@4400	8.9	OH
		V8	4.05	3.50	360.7	303@4600	10.0	OH
1960	Rideau	6	3.625	3.60	222.9	145@4200	8.4	OH
	Rideau 500	6	3.625	3.60	222.9	145@4200	8.4	OH
	Montcalm	6	3.625	3.60	222.9	145@4200	8.4	OH
	Optional engines, all lines:	V8	4.00	3.30	331.8	225@4400	8.9	OH
		V8	4.00	3.50	360.7	300@4600	9.6	OH
1961	Rideau	6	3.625	3.60	222.9	135@4000	8.4	OH
	Rideau 500	6	3.625	3.60	222.9	135@4000	8.4	OH
	Montcalm	6	3.625	3.60	222.9	135@4000	8.4	OH
1962-63	No production.							
1964		6	3.625	3.60	222.9	138@4200	8.4	OH
	Custom	6	3.625	3.60	222.9	138@4200	8.4	OH
	Optional engines, both lines:	V8	4.00	3.50	331.8	220@4300	8.9	OH
		V8	4.05	3.78	389.6	300@4600	9.6	OH
1965	Rideau	6	4.00	3.188	240.3	150@4000	9.2	OH
	Rideau 500	6	4.00	3.188	240.3	150@4000	9.2	OH
	Montcalm	6	4.00	3.188	240.3	150@4000	9.2	OH
	Optional engines, all lines:	V8	4.00	3.50	331.8	220@4300	9.3	OH
		V8	4.05	3.78	389.6	300@4600	10.1	OH
1966	Rideau (1, 2)	6	4.00	3.188	240.3	150@4200	9.2	OH
	Rideau 500 (1, 2)	6	4.00	3.188	240.3	150@4200	9.2	OH
	Montcalm (1, 2)	6	4.00	3.188	240.3	150@4200	9.2	OH
	Montcalm S-33 (2)	V8	4.00	2.875	289.0	200@4400	9.3	OH
	Optional engines:							

CARBURETOR MFR	MODEL	VEN	WHEEL-BASE	TIRES	BODY	WEIGHT	PRICE
		2					
		4					
		1	116	7.50 x 14			
		1	116	7.50 x 14	6 ps	3263	2590
		1	118	7.50 x 14	6 ps	3404	2784
		1	118	7.50 x 14	6 ps	3407	2989
		2	116	7.50 x 14	6 ps	3375	2929
		2	118	7.50 x 14	6 ps	3541	3127
		4	118	7.50 x 14	6 ps	3554	3331
O	C4MF-9510-U	2					
		4					
		1	118	7.50 x 14	6 ps	3411	2749
		1	118	7.50 x 14	6 ps	3440	2921
		1	118	7.50 x 14	6 ps	3444	3087
		1	118	7.50 x 14	6 ps	3469	3180
O	C4MF-9510-U	2					
		4					
		1	119	7.50 x 14	6 ps	3600	3052
		1	119	7.50 x 14	6 ps	3610	3170
		1	119	7.50 x 14	6 ps	3634	3433
H	R1406A	2					
H	R1806A	4					
		1	119	7.50 x 14	6 ps	3510	3032
		1	119	7.50 x 14	6 ps	3519	3188
		1	119	7.50 x 14	6 ps	3495	3407
		1	120	7.50 x 14	6 ps	3621	3068
		1	120	7.50 x 14	6 ps	3661	3285
		2					
		4					
		1	123/119	7.35 x 15	6 ps		3357
		1	123	7.35 x 15	6 ps		3499
		1	123/119	7.35 x 15	6 ps		3744
		2					
		4					
		1	123	7.35 x 15	6 ps	3433	3131
		1	123/119	7.35 x 15	6 ps	3444	3269
		1	123/119	7.35 x 15	6 ps	3456	3495
		2	123	7.35 x 15	6 pht2	3616	4142

YEAR	MODEL	ENGINE						
		CYLS	BORE	STROKE	DISPL	HP@RPM	C.R.	VLV
	(1)	V8	4.00	2.875	289.0	200@4400	9.3	OH
	(2)	V8	4.05	3.78	389.6	275@4400	9.5	OH
	(2)	V8	4.125	3.98	428.0	345@4600	10.5	OH
1967	Rideau	6	4.00	3.188	240.3	150@4200	9.2	OH
	Rideau 500	6	4.00	3.188	240.3	150@4200	9.2	OH
	Montcalm	6	4.00	3.188	240.3	150@4200	9.2	OH
	Montcalm S-33	V8	4.00	2.875	289.0	200@4400	9.3	OH
	Montego	V8	4.00	2.875	289.0	200@4400	9.3	OH
	Optional engines, all lines:	V8	4.05	3.78	389.6	270@4400	9.5	OH
		V8	4.05	3.78	389.6	315@4600	10.5	OH
		V8	4.05	3.98	410.2	330@4600	10.5	OH
		V8	4.125	3.98	428.0	345@4600	10.5	OH
1968	Rideau	6	4.00	3.188	240.3	150@4000	8.75	OH
	Rideau 500	6	4.00	3.188	240.3	150@4000	8.75	OH
	Montcalm	6	4.00	3.188	240.3	150@4000	8.75	OH
	Montcalm S-33	6	4.00	3.188	240.3	150@4000	8.75	OH
	Le Moyne	V8	4.00	3.00	301.6	210@4600	8.5	OH
	Optional engines, all lines:	V8	4.05	3.78	389.6	265@4400	9.5	OH
		V8	4.05	3.78	389.6	315@4600	10.5	OH
		V8	4.125	3.98	428.0	340@4600	10.5	OH
1969	Rideau	6	4.00	3.18	240.0	150@4000	8.75	OH
	Rideau 500	6	4.00	3.18	240.0	150@4000	8.75	OH
	Montcalm	6	4.00	3.18	240.0	150@4000	8.75	OH
	Montcalm S-33	V8	4.00	3.00	301.6	210@4600	8.5	OH
	Le Moyne	V8	4.00	3.00	301.6	210@4600	8.5	OH
	Optional engines, all lines:							
		V8	4.05	3.78	389.6	265@4400	9.5	OH
		V8	4.36	3.59	428.8	320@4400	10.5	OH
		V8	4.36	3.59	428.8	360@4600	10.5	OH

MONARCH — Ford Motor Co. of Canada, Ltd., Windsor, Ont.; Oakville, Ont., 1946-61

YEAR	MODEL	CYLS	BORE	STROKE	DISPL	HP@RPM	C.R.	VLV
1946	*	V8	3.188	3.75	239.5	95@3800		L
1947	*	V8	3.188	3.75	239.5	95@3800		L
1948	*	V8	3.188	3.75	239.5	97@3600		L
1949	*	V8	3.188	4.00	255.5	110@3600	6.8	L
1950	*	V8	3.188	4.00	255.5	110@3600	6.8	L
1951	*	V8	3.188	4.00	255.5	110@3600	6.8	L
1952	*	V8	3.188	4.00	255.5	125@3700	7.2	L
1953	Custom	V8	3.188	4.00	255.5	125@3700	7.2	L
	Monterey	V8	3.188	4.00	255.5	125@3700	7.2	L
1954	Custom	V8	3.625	3.10	256.0	161@4400	7.5	OH

CARBURETOR MFR	MODEL	VEN	WHEEL-BASE	TIRES	BODY	WEIGHT	PRICE
		2					
O	C5AF-9510-A	2					
		4					
		1	123	7.75 x 15	6 ps	3716	3196
		1	123/119	7.75 x 15	6 ps	3719	3329
		1	123/119	7.75 x 15	6 ps	3729	3525
		2	123	7.75 x 15	6 pht2	3860	4126
		2	123	7.75 x 15	6 pht2	3892	4194
		2					
		4					
		4					
		4					
C	4797	1	123	7.75 x 15	6 ps	3716	3386
		1	123/119	7.75 x 15	6 ps	3719	3519
		1	123/119	7.75 x 15	6 ps	3729	3702
		1	123	7.75 x 15	6 pht2	3822	3942
		2	123	7.75 x 15	6 pht2	3953	4190
		2					
		4					
		4					
		1	124	7.75 x 15	6 ps	3716	3439
		1	124/121	7.75 x 15	6 ps	3719	3571
		1	124/121	7.75 x 15	6 ps	3729	3754
		2	124	7.75 x 15	6 pht2	3860	4072
		2	124	7.75 x 15	6 pht2	3953	4190
		2					
		2					
		4					
			118	6.50 x 15	6 ps	3315	1526
			118	6.50 x 15	6 ps	3315	1675
			118	6.50 x 15	6 ps	3315	2073
			118	7.10 x 15	6 ps	3580	2635
			118	7.10 x 15	6 ps	3425	2521
			118	7.10 x 15	6 ps	3465	2968
			118	7.10 x 15	6 ps	3365	2834
			118	7.10 x 15	6 ps	3375	2854
			118	7.10 x 15	6 pht2	3440	3223
			118	7.10 x 15	6 ps	3440	3059

YEAR	MODEL	ENGINE						
		CYLS	BORE	STROKE	DISPL	HP@RPM	C.R.	VLV
	Lucerne	V8	3.625	3.10	256.6	161@4400	7.5	OH
	Lucerne Custom	V8	3.625	3.10	256.6	161@4400	7.5	OH
1955	Custom	V8	3.75	3.30	291.6	188@4400	7.6	OH
	Lucerne	V8	3.75	3.30	291.6	188@4400	7.6	OH
	Richelieu	V8	3.75	3.30	291.6	188@4400	7.6	OH
1956	Custom	V8	3.80	3.438	311.9	210@4600	8.0	OH
	Lucerne	V8	3.80	3.438	311.9	210@4600	8.0	OH
	Richelieu	V8	3.80	3.438	311.9	210@4600	8.0	OH
	Optional engine, all lines:	V8	3.80	3.438	311.9	225@4600	9.1	OH
1957	Lucerne	V8	3.80	3.44	312.8	226@4600	9.75	OH
	Richelieu	V8	3.80	3.44	312.8	225@4600	9.75	OH
	Turnpike Cruiser (1)	V8	3.80	3.44	312.8	225@4600	9.75	OH
	Optional engine:							
	(1)	V8	4.00	3.60	361.9	290@4600	9.75	OH
1958	(Not in production)							
1959	Lucerne	V8	4.30	3.30	383.4	280@4500	10.0	OH
	Richelieu	V8	4.30	3.30	383.4	322@4700	10.0	OH
	Sceptre	V8	4.30	3.70	429.8	345@4500	10.0	OH
1960	Lucerne	V8	4.30	3.30	383.4	280@4200	8.5	OH
	Richelieu	V8	4.30	3.70	429.8	310@4000	10.0	OH
	Sceptre	V8	4.30	3.70	429.8	310@4000	10.0	OH
1961	Richelieu	V8	4.00	3.50	351.8	220@4400	8.9	OH
	Optional engine:	V8	4.05	3.78	389.6	300@4600	9.6	OH
	* No separate model designation.							

CARBURETOR MFR	MODEL	VEN	WHEEL-BASE	TIRES	BODY	WEIGHT	PRICE
			118	7.10 x 15	6 ps	3570	3446
			118	7.10 x 15	6 ps	3650	3893
			119	7.10 x 15	6 ps	3450	3059
			119	7.10 x 15	6 ps	3500	3218
			119	7.10 x 15	6 ps	3600	3576
			119	7.10 x 15	6 ps	3470	3174
			119	7.10 x 15	6 ps	3500	3376
			119	7.10 x 15	6 ps	3540	3648
C	2441	4	122	8.00 x 14	6 ps	3695	3533
C	2441	4	122	8.00 x 14	6 ps	3680	3941
C	2441	4	122	8.00 x 14	6 pht2	4005	4423
		2	126	8.00 x 14	6 ps	4095	3824
		4	126	8.50 x 14	6 ps	4189	4390
		4	128	8.00 x 14	6 pht2	4356	4968
			126		6 ps	4032	3731
			126		6 ps	4302	4424
			126		6 pht2	4345	4845
O	C1AE-9510AC	2	120		6 ps	3808	3804
		4					

YEAR	MODEL	ENGINE						
		CYLS	BORE	STROKE	DISPL	HP@RPM	C.R.	VLV

NASH — — Nash Motors of Canada, Ltd., Toronto, Ont., 1950-55

YEAR	MODEL	CYLS	BORE	STROKE	DISPL	HP@RPM	C.R.	VLV
1950	Statesman, 15000	6	3.125	4.00	184.1	85@3800	7.0	L
1951	Statesman, 15100	6	3.125	4.00	184.1	85@3800	7.0	L
1952	Rambler, 15200	6	3.125	3.75	172.6	82@3800	7.25	L
	Rambler, 15200	6	3.125	4.25	195.6	88@3800	7.0	L
1953	Rambler, 15300	6	3.125	4.00	184.1	85@3800	7.25	L
	Statesman, 15300	6	3.125	4.25	195.6	100@3800	7.45	L
1954	Rambler	6	3.125	4.00	184.1	85@3800	7.25	L
	Statesman	6	3.125	4.25	195.6	110@4000	8.5	L
1955	Rambler	6	3.125	4.25	195.6	90@3800		L
	Statesman	6	3.125	4.25	195.6	110@4000	8.0	L

MFR	CARBURETOR MODEL	VEN	WHEEL-BASE	TIRES	BODY	WEIGHT	PRICE
			112		6 ps	3040	2396
			112		6 ps	2988	2891
			100	5.90 x 15	6 ps2	2410	2295
			114.3	6.70 x 15	6 ps	3045	2760
			100	5.90 x 15	6 ps2	2480	2460
			114.3	6.70 x 15	6 ps	3045	2795
			100	5.90 x 15	6 ps2	2425	2460
			114.3	6.70 x 15	6 ps	3045	3008
			100	6.40 x 15	6 ps2	2432	2150
			114.3	6.70 x 15	6 ps	3145	3207

YEAR	MODEL	ENGINE						
		CYLS	BORE	STROKE	DISPL	HP@RPM	C.R.	VLV

OAKLAND — — General Motors of Canada, Ltd., Oshawa, Ont., 1922-30

YEAR	MODEL	CYLS	BORE	STROKE	DISPL	HP@RPM	C.R.	VLV
1930	8-101	V8	3.438	3.375	250.6	82@3000	5.0	H

OLDSMOBILE — — General Motors of Canada, Ltd., Oshawa, Ont., 1921+

YEAR	MODEL	CYLS	BORE	STROKE	DISPL	HP@RPM	C.R.	VLV
1930	F-30	6	3.188	4.125	197.5			L
1931	F-31	6	3.188	4.125	197.5	65@3350	5.2	L
1932	F-32	6	3.312	4.125	213.3	74@3200	5.8	L
	L-32	8	3.00	4.25	240.3	87@3350	5.9	L
1933	F-33	6	3.312	4.125	213.3			L
	L-33	8	3.00	4.25	240.3			L
1934	F-34	6	3.312	4.125	213.3	84@3200		L
	L-34	8	3.00	4.25	240.3	90@3200		L
1935	F-35	6	3.312	4.125	213.3		6.0	L
	L-35	8	3.00	4.25	240.3		6.2	L
1936	F-36	6	3.312	4.125	213.3		6.0	L
	L-36	8	3.00	4.25	240.3		6.2	L
1937	F-37	6	3.438	4.125	229.7	95@3400	6.1	L
1938	F-38	6	3.438	4.125	229.7		6.1	L
1939	F-39	6	3.438	3.875	215.8	90@3400	6.2	L
	G-39	6	3.438	4.125	229.7	95@3400	6.1	L
1940	60	6	3.438	4.125	229.7	95@3300	6.1	L
	70	6	3.438	4.125	229.7	95@3300	6.1	L
1941	66	6	3.50	4.125	238.1	100@3400	6.1	L
	76	6	3.50	4.125	238.1	100@3400	6.1	L
	96	6	3.50	4.125	238.1	100@3400	6.1	L
1942	66	6	3.50	4.125	238.1	100@3400	6.1	L
	76	6	3.50	4.125	238.1	100@3400	6.1	L
	96	6	3.50	4.125	238.1	100@3400	6.1	L

MFR	CARBURETOR MODEL	VEN	WHEEL-BASE	TIRES	BODY	WEIGHT	PRICE
			117	5.50 x 18	5 ps		1700
C			113	5.25 x 18	5 ps	3050	1260
S			113.5	5.25 x 18	5 ps		1180
S			116.5	6.00 x 17	5 ps		1305
S			116.5	6.00 x 17	5 ps		1445
S	EC-22		115		5 ps		1195
S	EE-22	2	119		5 ps		1345
S	EX-22		114	5.50 x 17	5 ps	3055	990
S	EE-1	2	119	7.00 x 16	5 ps	3485	1290
S	EX-22		115	6.25 x 16	5 ps		1070
S	EE-1	2	121	7.00 x 16	5 ps		1330
C	W1-327S	1	115	6.50 x 16	5 ps		1045
C	WDO-328S	2	121	7.00 x 16	5 ps		1280
C	W1-351S	1	117	6.00 x 16	5 ps		1035
C	W1-388S	1	117		5 ps		1331
C	WA1-425S	1	115	6.00 x 16	5 ps		1221
C	WA1-426S	1	120	6.00 x 16			
C	WA1-466S	1	116	6.00 x 16	5 ps		1273
C	WA1-466S	1	120	6.50 x 16	5 ps		1371
C	WA1-504S	1	119	6.00 x 16	5 ps		1577
C	WA1-504S	1	125	6.50 x 16			
C	WA1-504S	1	125	7.00 x 15			
C	WA1-481S	1	119	6.00 x 16	5 ps		1593
C	WA1-481S	1	125	6.50 x 16			
C	WA1-481S	1	125	7.00 x 15			

YEAR	MODEL	ENGINE						
		CYLS	BORE	STROKE	DISPL	HP@RPM	C.R.	VLV

PIERCE-ARROW — — Studebaker Corp. of Canada, Walkerville, Ont., 1932-34

YEAR	MODEL	CYLS	BORE	STROKE	DISPL	HP@RPM	C.R.	VLV
1932	54	8	3.50	4.75	365.6	125@3000	5.05	L
	54	8	3.50	4.75	365.6	125@3000	5.05	L
	53	V12	3.25	4.00	398.2	140@3100	5.05	L
	53	V12	3.25	4.00	398.2	140@3100	5.05	L
	52	V12	3.375	4.00	429.4	150@3100	5.05	L
	52	V12	3.375	4.00	429.4	150@3100	5.05	L
1933	836	8	3.50	4.75	365.6	135@3400		L
	839	8	3.50	4.75	365.6	135@3400		L
	1236	V12	3.375	4.00	429.4	160@3400		L
	1242	V12	3.50	4.00	462.0	175@3400		L
	1247	V12	3.50	4.00	462.0	175@3400		L
1934	836A	8	3.50	4.75	365.6	135@3400		L
	840A	8	3.50	5.00	385.0	140@3400		L
	1240A	V12	3.50	4.00	462.0	175@3400		L
	1248A	V12	3.50	4.00	462.0	175@3400		L

PLYMOUTH — — Chrysler Corp. of Canada, Ltd., Windsor, Ont., 1929+

YEAR	MODEL	CYLS	BORE	STROKE	DISPL	HP@RPM	C.R.	VLV
1930	30U	4	3.625	4.75	195.3	48@2800		L
1931	PA	4	3.625	4.75	195.3	56@2800		L
1932	PB	4	3.625	4.75	195.3	65@2800		L
1933	Standard, PC	6	3.125	4.125	189.8	70@3600		L
	DeLuxe, PD	6	3.125	4.125	189.8	70@3600		L
1934	Standard, PF	6	3.125	4.375	201.3	77@3600		L
	DeLuxe, PE	6	3.125	4.375	201.3	77@3600		L
1935	Standard, PJ	6	3.125	4.375	201.3	82@3600		L
	DeLuxe, PJ	6	3.125	4.375	201.3	82@3600		L
1936	Standard, P1	6	3.125	4.375	201.3	82@3600		L
	DeLuxe, P2	6	3.125	4.375	201.3	82@3600		L
1937	Standard, P3	6	3.125	4.375	201.3	82@3600		L
	DeLuxe, P4	6	3.125	4.375	201.3	82@3600		L
1938	Standard, P5	6	3.125	4.375	201.3	82@3600		L
	DeLuxe, P6	6	3.125	4.375	201.3	82@3600		L
Late								
1938	Standard, P5	6	3.375	3.75	201.3	82@3600		L
	DeLuxe, P6	6	3.375	3.75	201.3	82@3600		L
1939	Roadking, P7	6	3.375	3.75	201.3	82@3600		L
	DeLuxe, P8	6	3.375	3.75	201.3	82@3600		L
	Custom, P8	6	3.375	3.75	201.3	82@3600		L
1940	Roadking, P9	6	3.375	4.062	218.1	84@3600		L

	CARBURETOR		WHEEL-	TIRES	BODY	WEIGHT	PRICE
MFR	MODEL	VEN	BASE				
S			137	6.50 x 18	5 ps	4819	4275
S			142	6.50 x 18	7 ps	5025	4520
S			137	7.00 x 18	5 ps	5080	5255
S			142	7.00 x 18	7 ps	5300	5475
S			142	7.00 x 18	5 ps	5395	6205
S			147	7.00 x 18	7 ps	5465	6470
			136	7.00 x 17	5 ps	4660	4095
			139	7.00 x 17	7 ps	4805	4760
			136/139	7.00 x 17	5 ps	4892	4620
			137/142	7.50 x 17	5 ps	5288	6095
			142/147	7.50 x 17	5 ps	5429	6710
			136	7.00 x 17	5 ps	4923	3375
			139/144	7.00 x 17	5 ps	4964	4110
			139/144	7.50 x 17	5 ps	5227	4680
			147	7.50 x 17	7 ps	5494	6100
			109.8	4.75 x 19	5 ps	2595	775
			109.5	4.75 x 19	5 ps	2730	795
			112/121	5.25 x 18	5 ps	2995	845
			107	5.25 x 17	5 ps	2585	730
			112	5.25 x 17	5 ps	2610	810
			108	5.25 x 17	5 ps	2745	790
			114/124	6.00 x 17	5 ps	2895	870
			113		5 ps	2890	935
			113		5 ps	2870	975
			113		5 ps	2890	913
			113		5 ps	2910	955
			112		5 ps	2895	923
			112/132		5 ps	2970	1007
			112		5 ps	2895	1006
			112		5 ps	2945	1053
			112		5 ps	2955	1029
			112/132		5 ps	2945	1053
			117		5 ps	2935	968
			114/134		5 ps	3000	1033
			114/134		5 ps	3005	1061
			117		5 ps	2960	933

YEAR	MODEL	ENGINE						
		CYLS	BORE	STROKE	DISPL	HP@RPM	C.R.	VLV
	DeLuxe, P10	6	3.375	4.062	218.1	84@3600		L
	Custom, P10	6	3.375	4.062	218.1	84@3600		L
1941	Roadking, Regular, P11	6	3.375	4.062	218.1	88@3800		L
	Roadking, Special, P11	6	3.375	4.062	218.1	88@3800		L
	DeLuxe, P12	6	3.375	4.062	218.1	88@3800		L
	Custom, P12	6	3.375	4.062	218.1	88@3800		L
1942	DeLuxe, P14S	6	3.375	4.062	218.1	88@3800		L
	Special DeLuxe, P14C	6	3.375	4.062	218.1	88@3800		L
1946	DeLuxe, P15S	6	3.375	4.062	218.1	88@3800		L
	Special DeLuxe, P15C	6	3.375	4.062	218.1	95@3600		L
1947	DeLuxe, P15S	6	3.375	4.062	218.1	95@3600		L
	Special DeLuxe, P15C	6	3.375	4.062	218.1	95@3600		L
1948	DeLuxe, P15S	6	3.375	4.062	218.1	95@3600		L
	Special DeLuxe, P15C	6	3.375	4.062	218.1	95@3600		L
1949	DeLuxe, P17	6	3.375	4.062	218.1	97@3600		L
	DeLuxe, P18	6	3.375	4.062	218.1	97@3600		L
	Special DeLuxe, P18	6	3.375	4.062	218.1	97@3600		L
1950	DeLuxe, P19	6	3.375	4.062	218.1	97@3600		L
	DeLuxe, P20	6	3.375	4.062	218.1	97@3600		L
	Special DeLuxe, P20	6	3.375	4.062	218.1	97@3600		L
1951	Cranbrook, P23-1	6	3.375	4.062	218.1	97@3600		L
	Cambridge, P23-2	6	3.375	4.062	218.1	97@3600		L
	Savoy, P22	6	3.375	4.062	218.1	97@3600		L
1952	Concord, P22	6	3.375	4.062	218.1	97@3600		L
	Suburban, P22	6	3.375	4.062	218.1	97@3600		L
	Savoy, P22	6	3.375	4.062	218.1	97@3600		L
	Cambridge, P23-1	6	3.375	4.062	218.1	97@3600		L
	Cranbrook, P23-2	6	3.375	4.062	218.1	97@3600		L
1953	Cambridge, P24-1	6	3.375	4.062	218.1	97@3600	7.1	L
	Cranbrook, P24-2	6	3.375	4.062	218.1	97@3600	7.1	L
	Belvedere, P24-2	6	3.375	4.062	218.1	97@3600	7.1	L
1954	Plaza, P25-1	6	3.375	4.25	228.2	108@3600	7.1	L
	Savoy, P25-2	6	3.375	4.25	228.2	108@3600	7.1	L
	Belvedere, P25-3	6	3.375	4.25	228.2	108@3600	7.1	L
1955	Plaza, P26-1	6	3.375	4.25	228.2	115@3600		L
	Savoy, P26-2	6	3.375	4.25	228.2	115@3600		L
	Belvedere, P26-4	6	3.438	4.50	250.6	125@3600	7.1	L
1956	Plaza, P28-1	6	3.438	4.50	250.6	125@3600	7.1	L
	Savoy, P28-2	6	3.438	4.50	250.6	125@3600	7.1	L
	Plaza, P29-1 (1)	V8	3.625	3.25	268.3	180@4400	8.1	OH
	Savoy, P29-2 (1)	V8	3.625	3.25	268.3	180@4400	8.1	OH

CARBURETOR			WHEEL-	TIRES	BODY	WEIGHT	PRICE
MFR	MODEL	VEN	BASE				
			117		5 ps	3030	1050
			117/137.5		5 ps	3045	1078
			117		5 ps	3020	1191
			117		5 ps	3035	1215
			117		5 ps	3075	1275
			117/137.5		5 ps	3100	1305
			117		6 ps	3115	1271
			117		6 ps	3155	1371
			117		6 ps	3120	1295
			117		6 ps	3185	1393
			117		6 ps	3120	1424
			117		6 ps	3160	1532
			117		6 ps	3120	1721
			117		6 ps	3160	1811
			111		6 ps2		1780
			118.5		6 ps	3150	1882
			118.5		6 ps	3170	1979
			111		6 ps2	3015	1780
			118.5		6 ps	3145	1882
			118.5		6 ps	3155	1979
			118.5	6.70 x 15	6 ps	3225	2425
			118.5	6.70 x 15	6 ps	3195	2306
			111	6.70 x 15	6 ps2	3045	2189
			111	6.40 x 15	6 ps2	3045	2138
			111	6.70 x 15	6 psw4	3260	2512
			111	6.70 x 15	6 psw4	3285	2653
			118.5	6.70 x 15	6 ps	3195	2254
			118.5	6.70 x 15	6 ps	3225	2349
			114	6.70 x 15	6 ps	3195	2271
			114	6.70 x 15	6 ps	3225	2376
			114	6.70 x 15	6 pht2	3225	2609
			114	6.70 x 15	6 ps	3070	2282
			114	6.70 x 15	6 ps	3090	2409
			114	6.70 x 15	6 ps	3110	2502
			115	6.70 x 15	6 ps	3129	2271
			115	6.70 x 15	6 ps	3154	2384
			115	6.70 x 15	6 ps	3159	2530
C	BBS-2293S	2	115	6.70 x 15	6 ps	3245	2353
C	BBS-2293S	2	115	6.70 x 15	6 ps	3160	2459
			115	6.70 x 15	6 ps	3275	2624
			115	6.70 x 15	6 ps	3295	2787

YEAR	MODEL	ENGINE						
		CYLS	BORE	STROKE	DISPL	HP@RPM	C.R.	VLV
	Belvedere, P29-3 (1)	V8	3.625	3.25	268.3	180@4400	8.1	OH
	Optional engine:							
	(1)	V8	3.812	3.312	302.5	200@4400	8.0	OH
1957	Plaza, P30-1	6	3.438	4.50	250.6	132@3600	7.1	L
	Savoy, P30-2	6	3.438	4.50	250.6	132@3600	7.1	L
	Plaza, P31-1	V8	3.812	3.312	302.5	215@4400	8.0	OH
	Savoy, P31-2	V8	3.812	3.312	302.5	215@4400	8.0	OH
	Belvedere, P31-3	V8	3.812	3.312	302.5	215@4400	8.0	OH
1958	Plaza, LP1-L	6	3.438	4.50	250.6	135@3600	7.7	L
	Savoy, LP1-M	6	3.438	4.50	250.6	135@3600	7.7	L
	Plaza, LP2-L	V8	3.875	3.312	312.5	225@4400	8.5	OH
	Savoy, LP2-M	V8	3.875	3.312	312.5	225@4400	8.5	OH
	Belvedere, LP2-H	V8	3.875	3.312	312.5	225@4400	8.5	OH
1959	Savoy, MP1-L	6	3.438	4.50	250.6	135@3600	7.7	L
	Belvedere, MP1-M	6	3.438	4.50	250.6	135@3600	7.7	L
	Suburban, MP1-L	6	3.438	4.50	250.6	135@3600	7.7	L
	Savoy, MP2-L	V8	3.875	3.312	312.5	225@4400	8.5	OH
	Belvedere, MP2-M	V8	3.875	3.312	312.5	225@4400	8.5	OH
	Fury, MP2-H	V8	3.875	3.312	312.5	225@4400	8.5	OH
	Suburban, MP2-L, MP2-H	V8	3.875	3.312	312.5	225@4400	8.5	OH
1960	Savoy, PP2-L	V8	3.875	3.312	312.5	225@4400	9.0	OH
	Belvedere, PP2-M	V8	3.875	3.312	312.5	225@4400	9.0	OH
	Fury, PP2-H	V8	3.875	3.312	312.5	225@4400	9.0	OH
	Suburban, PP2-L, PP2-H	V8	3.875	3.312	312.5	225@4400	9.0	OH
1961	Savoy, RP2-L	V8	3.875	3.312	312.5	225@4400	9.0	OH
	Belvedere, RP2-M	V8	3.875	3.312	312.5	225@4400	9.0	OH
	Fury, RP2-H	V8	3.875	3.312	312.5	225@4400	9.0	OH
	Suburban, RP2-L, M	V8	3.875	3.312	312.5	225@4400	9.0	OH
1962	Savoy, SP2-L	V8	3.875	3.312	312.5	225@4400	9.0	OH
	Belvedere, SP2-M	V8	3.875	3.312	312.5	225@4400	9.0	OH
	Fury, SP2-H	V8	3.875	3.312	312.5	225@4400	9.0	OH
1963	Savoy, TP2-L	V8	3.875	3.312	312.5	225@4400	9.0	OH
	Belvedere, TP2-M	V8	3.875	3.312	312.5	225@4400	9.0	OH
	Fury, TP2-H	V8	3.875	3.312	312.5	225@4400	9.0	OH
1964	Savoy, VP2-L	V8	3.875	3.312	312.5	225@4400	9.0	OH
	Belvedere, VP2-M	V8	3.875	3.312	312.5	225@4400	9.0	OH
	Fury, VP2-H	V8	3.875	3.312	312.5	225@4400	9.0	OH

PONTIAC — — General Motors of Canada, Ltd., Oshawa, Ont., 1926+

1930	6-30	6	3.312	3.875	200.4	60@3000	4.9	L
1931	401	6	3.312	3.875	200.4	60@3000	4.9	L

CARBURETOR			WHEEL-	TIRES	BODY	WEIGHT	PRICE
MFR	MODEL	VEN	BASE				
			115	6.70 x 15	6 ps	3325	2916
			118/122	7.50 x 14	6 ps	3260	2569
			118/122	7.50 x 14	6 ps	3265	2718
			118	7.50 x 14	6 ps	3405	2833
			118/122	7.50 x 14	6 ps	3415	3025
			118/122	7.50 x 14	6 ps	3475	3206
			118/122	7.50 x 14	6 ps	3255	2616
			118/122	7.50 x 14	6 ps	3220	2778
			118	7.50 x 14	6 ps	3415	2942
			118/122	7.50 x 14	6 ps	3400	3104
			118/122	7.50 x 14	6 ps	3420	3292
			118	7.50 x 14	6 ps	3340	2777
			118	7.50 x 14	6 ps	3360	2962
			122	8.00 x 14	6 psw4	3680	3212
			118	7.50 x 14	6 ps	3490	3123
			118	7.50 x 14	6 ps	3485	3308
			118	7.50 x 14	6 ps	3475	3498
			122	8.00 x 14	6 psw4	3815	3559
			118	7.50 x 14	6 ps	3710	3191
			118	7.50 x 14	6 ps	3690	3353
			118	7.50 x 14	6 ps	3670	3538
			122	8.00 x 14	6 psw4	4060	3629
			118	7.50 x 14	6 ps	3630	3191
			118	7.50 x 14	6 ps	3635	3354
			118	7.50 x 14	6 ps	3640	3638
			122	8.00 x 14	6 psw4	3940	3630
			116	7.00 x 14	6 ps	3140	3032
			116	7.00 x 14	6 ps	3150	3198
			116	7.00 x 14	6 ps	3165	3358
			116	7.00 x 14	6 ps	3218	3040
			116	7.00 x 14	6 ps	3225	3202
			116	7.00 x 14	6 ps	3258	3370
			116	7.00 x 14	6 ps	3265	3148
			116	7.00 x 14	6 ps	3275	3310
			116	7.00 x 14	6 ps	3295	3478
M			110	5.00 x 19	5 ps		1060
M			112	5.00 x 19	5 ps	2765	970

YEAR	MODEL	ENGINE						
		CYLS	BORE	STROKE	DISPL	HP@RPM	C.R.	VLV
1932	402	6	3.312	3.875	200.4	65@3200	5.1	L
1933	601	8	3.188	3.50	223.4			L
1934	603	8	3.188	3.50	223.4			L
1935	Standard Six	6	3.375	3.875	208.0		6.21	L
	DeLuxe Six	6	3.375	3.875	208.0		6.21	L
	Eight	8	3.188	3.50	223.4			
1936	Six, 26-00	6	3.375	3.875	208.0	80@3600	6.21	L
	Six, 27-00	6	3.375	3.875	208.0	80@3600	6.21	L
	Eight, 28-00	8	3.25	3.50	232.3	87@3800	6.21	L
1937	Six, 37-26	6	3.562	3.75	224.3		6.50	OH
1938	Special Six	6	3.50	3.75	216.5		6.25	OH
	DeLuxe Six	6	3.562	3.75	224.3		6.50	OH
1939	Arrow, 22	6	3.50	3.75	216.5	85@3200	6.25	OH
	Chieftain, 25	6	3.562	3.75	224.0	89@3400	6.5	OH
1940	Arrow, 22	6	3.50	3.75	216.5	85@3200	6.25	OH
	DeLuxe Arrow, 22S	6	3.50	3.75	216.5	85@3200	6.25	OH
	Special Six, 25	6	3.438	4.00	222.7	87@3500	6.5	OH
1941	Fleetleader, 2200	6	3.562	4.00	239.2	90@3200	6.5	L
	Fleetleader Special, 2000	6	3.562	4.00	239.2	90@3200	6.5	L
1942	Fleetleader Special	6	3.562	4.00	239.2	90@3200	6.5	L
	Fleetleader Torpedo	6	3.562	4.00	239.2	90@3200	6.5	L
1946	Fleetleader, 2200	6	3.562	4.00	239.2	90@3200	6.5	L
	Fleetleader Special, 2000	6	3.562	4.00	239.2	90@3200	6.5	L
1947	Fleetleader, 2200	6	3.562	4.00	239.2	90@3200	6.5	L
	Fleetleader Special, 2000	6	3.562	4.00	239.2	90@3200	6.5	L
1948	Fleetleader, 2200	6	3.562	4.00	239.2	90@3200	6.5	L
	Fleetleader Special, 2000	6	3.562	4.00	239.2	90@3200	6.5	L
1949	Fleetleader Special	6	3.562	4.00	239.2	93@3400		L
	Fleetleader DeLuxe	6	3.562	4.00	239.2	93@3400		L
1950	Fleetleader Special	6	3.562	4.00	239.2	93@3400		L
	Fleetleader DeLuxe	6	3.562	4.00	239.2	93@3400		L
1951	Fleetleader Special	6	3.562	4.00	239.2	96@3400		L
	Fleetleader DeLuxe	6	3.562	4.00	239.2	96@3400		L
1952	Fleetleader Special	6	3.562	4.00	239.2	100@3400		L
	Fleetleader DeLuxe	6	3.562	4.00	239.2	100@3400		L
1953	Pathfinder	6	3.562	4.00	239.2	115@3800		L
	Pathfinder DeLuxe	6	3.562	4.00	239.2	115@3800		L
	Laurentian	6	3.562	4.00	239.2	115@3800		L
1954	Pathfinder	6	3.562	4.00	239.2	115@3800		L
	Pathfinder DeLuxe	6	3.562	4.00	239.2	115@3800		L
	Laurentian	6	3.562	4.00	239.2	115@3800		L

CARBURETOR MFR	CARBURETOR MODEL	VEN	WHEEL-BASE	TIRES	BODY	WEIGHT	PRICE
M			114	5.25 x 18	5 ps		1064
C	255S		115		5 ps		985
C	283S		117.2		5 ps		1040
			112	6.00 x 16	5 ps		1081
			112	6.00 x 16	5 ps		1139
			117	6.50 x 16	5 ps		1160
C	W1-324S	1	112		5 ps		1005
C	W1-324S	1	112		5 ps		955
C	W1-322S	1	117		5 ps		1130
C	W1-406S	1	117		5 ps		922
C	W1-406S	1	112.3		5 ps		1087
C	W1-406S	1	117		5 ps		1160
C	W1-420S	1	112.3		5 ps	2930	987
C	W1-420S	1	115		5 ps	2990	1162
C	W1-420S	1	113		5 ps	3065	1059
C	W1-420S	1	113		5 ps	3115	1123
C	WA1-462S	1	116.5		5 ps	3085	1219
C	WA1-494S	1	116		5 ps	3200	1306
C	WA1-494S	1	116		5 ps	3180	1399
C	WA1-494S	1	116		5 ps	3190	1339
C	WA1-494S	1	116		5 ps	3240	1465
			116		5 ps		1490
			116		5 ps	3280	1589
			116		5 ps	3255	1516
			116		5 ps	3242	1615
			116		5 ps	3365	1788
			116		5 ps	3378	1892
			115		5 ps	3321	1933
			115		5 ps	3339	2043
			115		5 ps	3200	1956
			115		5 ps	3240	2083
			115		5 ps	3199	2307
			115		5 ps	3243	2452
			115		5 ps	3199	2222
			115		5 ps	3242	2365
			115	6.70 x 15	5 ps	3261	2222
			115	6.70 x 15	5 ps	3276	2365
			115	6.70 x 15	5 ps	3290	2512
			115	6.70 x 15	5 ps	3210	2253
			115	6.70 x 15	5 ps	3230	2391
			115	6.70 x 15	5 ps	3255	2538

YEAR	MODEL	ENGINE						
		CYLS	BORE	STROKE	DISPL	HP@RPM	C.R.	VLV
1955	Pathfinder	6	3.75	3.938	260.9	145@4200	7.5	OH
	Pathfinder DeLuxe	6	3.75	3.938	260.9	145@4200	7.5	OH
	Laurentian	6	3.75	3.938	260.9	145@4200	7.5	OH
	Optional engine, all lines:	V8	3.75	3.00	265.1	162@4400	8.0	OH
1956	Pathfinder	6	3.75	3.938	260.9	148@4200	8.0	OH
	Pathfinder DeLuxe	6	3.75	3.938	260.9	148@4200	8.0	OH
	Laurentian	6	3.75	3.938	260.9	148@4200	8.0	OH
	Optional engine, all lines:	V8	3.75	3.00	265.1	162@4400	8.0	OH
1957	Pathfinder	6	3.75	3.938	260.9	148@4200	8.0	OH
	Pathfinder DeLuxe	6	3.75	3.938	260.9	148@4200	8.0	OH
	Laurentian	6	3.75	3.938	260.9	148@4200	8.0	OH
	Optional engine, all lines:	V8	3.875	3.00	283.0	165@4400	8.0	OH
1958	Pathfinder	6	3.75	3.938	260.9	148@4200	8.0	OH
	Strato Chief	6	3.75	3.938	260.9	148@4200	8.0	OH
	Laurentian	6	3.75	3.938	260.9	148@4200	8.0	OH
	Optional engine, all lines:	V8	3.875	3.00	283.0	185@4600	8.5	OH
1959	Strato Chief, 7100	6	3.75	3.938	260.9	150@4000	8.5	OH
	Laurentian, 7500	6	3.75	3.938	260.9	150@4000	8.5	OH
	Parisienne, 7700	6	3.75	3.938	260.9	150@4000	8.5	OH
	Optional engines, all lines:	V8	3.875	3.00	283.0	185@4600	8.5	OH
		V8	3.875	3.00	283.0	230	9.5	OH
		V8	4.125	3.25	347.5	250	9.5	OH
		V8	4.125	3.25	347.5	280	9.5	OH
1960	Strato Chief, 7100	6	3.75	3.938	260.9	150@4000	8.5	OH
	Laurentian, 7500	6	3.75	3.938	260.9	150@4000	8.5	OH
	Parisienne, 7700	6	3.75	3.938	260.9	150@4000	8.5	OH
	Optional engines, all lines:	V8	3.875	3.00	283.0	170@4200	8.5	OH
		V8	3.875	3.00	283.0	230	9.5	OH
		V8	4.125	3.25	347.5	250	9.5	OH
		V8	4.125	3.25	347.5	280	9.5	OH
1961	Strato Chief, 7100	6	3.75	3.938	260.9	150@4000	9.5	OH
	Laurentian, 7500	6	3.75	3.938	260.9	150@4000	9.5	OH
	Parisienne, 7700	6	3.75	3.938	260.9	150@4000	9.5	OH
	Optional engines, all lines:	V8	3.875	3.00	283.0	170@4200	9.5	OH
		V8	3.875	3.00	283.0	230	9.5	OH
		V8	4.125	3.25	347.5	250	9.5	OH
		V8	4.125	3.25	347.5	280	9.5	OH
1962	Strato Chief, 7100	6	3.75	3.938	260.9	150@4000	8.5	OH
	Laurentian, 7500	6	3.75	3.938	260.9	150@4000	8.5	OH
	Parisienne, 7700	6	3.75	3.938	260.9	150@4000	8.5	OH
	Optional engines, all lines:	V8	3.875	3.00	283.0	170	8.5	OH

MFR	CARBURETOR MODEL	VEN	WHEEL-BASE	TIRES	BODY	WEIGHT	PRICE
			115	6.70 x 15	6 ps	3165	2228
			115	6.70 x 15	6 ps	3180	2343
			115	6.70 x 15	6 ps	3200	2485
			115	6.70 x 15	6 ps	3206	2364
			115	6.70 x 15	6 ps	3212	2473
			115	6.70 x 15	6 ps	3231	2614
			115	7.50 x 14	6 ps	3241	2580
			115	7.50 x 14	6 ps	3275	2738
			115	7.50 x 14	6 ps	3281	2888
			117	7.50 x 14	6 ps	3406	2686
			117	7.50 x 14	6 ps	3431	2856
			117	7.50 x 14	6 ps	3433	3058
		1	119	7.50 x 14	6 ps	3675	2872
		1	119	7.50 x 14	6 ps	3668	3040
		1	119	7.50 x 14	6 ps	3713	3222
		2					
		4					
		4					
		3 x 2					
		1	119	7.50 x 14	6 ps	3700	3107
		1	119	7.50 x 14	6 ps	3700	3262
		1	119	7.50 x 14	6 ps	3750	3445
		2					
		4					
		4					
		3 x 2					
		1	119	7.50 x 14	6 ps	3569	3105
		1	119	7.50 x 14	6 ps	3559	3261
		1	119	7.50 x 14	6 ps	3579	3443
		2					
		4					
		4					
		3 x 2					
		1	119	7.50 x 14	6 ps	3470	3058
		1	119	7.50 x 14	6 ps	3550	3221
		1	119	7.50 x 14	6 ps	3500	3414
		2					

YEAR	MODEL	ENGINE						
		CYLS	BORE	STROKE	DISPL	HP@RPM	C.R.	VLV
		V8	4.00	3.25	326.7	250	10.5	OH
1963	Strato Chief, 7100	6	3.875	3.25	230.0	140@4400	8.5	OH
	Laurentian, 7500	6	3.875	3.25	230.0	140@4400	8.5	OH
	Parisienne, 7700	6	3.875	3.25	230.0	140@4400	8.5	OH
	Optional engines, all lines:	V8	3.875	3.00	283.0	195@4800	9.25	OH
		V8	4.00	3.25	326.7	250	10.5	OH
		V8	4.00	3.25	326.7	300	10.5	OH
		V8	4.312	3.50	408.9	340	10.0	OH
		V8	4.312	3.50	408.9	400	11.0	OH
		V8	4.312	3.50	408.9	425	11.0	OH
1964	Strato Chief, 7100	6	3.875	3.25	230.0	140@4400	8.5	OH
	Laurentian, 7500	6	3.875	3.25	230.0	140@4400	8.5	OH
	Parisienne, 7700	6	3.875	3.25	230.0	140@4400	8.5	OH
	Optional engines, all lines:	V8	3.875	3.00	283.0	195@4800	9.25	OH
		V8	4.00	3.25	326.7	250	10.5	OH
		V8	4.00	3.25	326.7	300	10.5	OH
		V8	4.312	3.50	408.9	340	10.0	OH
		V8	4.312	3.50	408.9	400	11.0	OH
		V8	4.312	3.50	408.9	425	11.0	OH
1965	Strato Chief, 75300	6	3.875	3.25	230.0	140@4400	8.5	OH
	Laurentian, 75500	6	3.875	3.25	230.0	140@4400	8.5	OH
	Parisienne, 76300	6	3.875	3.25	230.0	140@4400	8.5	OH
	Parisienne Custom, 76500	6	3.875	3.25	230.0	140@4400	8.5	OH
	Optional engines, all lines:	V8	3.875	3.00	283.0	195@4800	9.25	OH
		V8	4.00	3.25	326.7	250	10.5	OH
		V8	4.00	3.25	326.7	300	10.5	OH
		V8	4.312	3.50	408.9	340	10.0	OH
		V8	4.312	3.50	408.9	400	10.0	OH
1966	Strato Chief (1)	6	3.875	3.531	249.8	155@4200	8.5	OH
	Laurentian (1)	6	3.875	3.531	249.8	155@4200	8.5	OH
	Parisienne (1)	6	3.875	3.531	249.8	155@4200	8.5	OH
	Grand Parisienne	V8	3.875	3.00	283.0	195@4800	9.25	OH
	Optional engines (1)	V8	3.875	3.00	283.0	195@4800	9.25	OH
	All lines:	V8	4.00	3.25	326.7	275	10.5	OH
		V8	4.094	3.76	396.0	325	10.25	OH
		V8	4.251	3.76	426.9	390	10.25	OH
		V8	4.251	3.76	426.9	425	11.0	OH
1967	Strato Chief (1)	6	3.875	3.531	249.9	155@4200	8.5	OH
	Laurentian (1)	6	3.875	3.531	249.9	155@4200	8.5	OH
	Parisienne (1)	6	3.875	3.531	249.9	155@4200	8.5	OH
	Parisienne 2+2 (1)	6	3.875	3.531	249.9	155@4200	8.5	OH

CARBURETOR MFR	MODEL	VEN	WHEEL-BASE	TIRES	BODY	WEIGHT	PRICE
		4					
		1	119	7.00 x 14	6 ps	3470	3077
		1	119	7.00 x 14	6 ps	3550	3240
		1	119	7.00 x 14	6 ps	3500	3436
		2					
		4					
		4					
		4					
		4					
		2 x 4					
		1	119	7.00 x 14	6 ps	3470	3341
		1	119	7.00 x 14	6 ps	3550	3473
		1	119	7.00 x 14	6 ps	3500	3668
		2					
		4					
		4					
		4					
		4					
		2 x 4					
		1	119	7.35 x 14	6 ps	3535	3137
		1	119	7.35 x 14	6 ps	3625	3269
		1	119	7.35 x 14	6 ps	3620	3464
		1	119	7.35 x 14	6 ps	3650	3663
		2					
		4					
		4					
		1	119	7.35 x 14	6 ps	3375	3147
		1	119	7.35 x 14	6 ps	3390	3279
		1	119	7.35 x 14	6 ps	3435	3667
		2	119	7.75 x 14	6 pht2	3600	4148
		2					
		4					
		4					
		4					
		4					
		1	119	8.25 x 14	6 ps	3395	3200
		1	119	8.25 x 14	6 ps	3410	3332
		1	119	8.25 x 14	6 ps	3455	3531
		1	119	8.25 x 14	6 pht2	3500	3718

YEAR	MODEL	ENGINE						
		CYLS	BORE	STROKE	DISPL	HP@RPM	C.R.	VLV
	Grand Parisienne, 766	V8	3.875	3.00	283.0	195@4600	9.25	OH
	Optional engines: (1)	V8	3.875	3.00	283.0	195@4600	9.25	OH
	All Lines:	V8	4.00	3.25	326.7	275	10.0	OH
		V8	4.094	3.76	396.0	325	10.25	OH
		V8	4.251	3.76	426.9	385	10.25	OH
1968	Strato Chief (1)	6	3.875	3.531	249.9	155@4200	8.5	OH
	Laurentian (1)	6	3.875	3.531	249.9	155@4200	8.5	OH
	Parisienne (1)	6	3.875	3.531	249.9	155@4200	8.5	OH
	Parisienne 2+2, 768	V8	4.00	3.25	326.7	210@4600	8.75	OH
	Grand Parisienne, 766	V8	4.00	3.25	326.7	210@4600	8.75	OH
	Optional engines: (1)	V8	4.00	3.25	326.7	210@4600	8.75	OH
	All Lines:	V8	4.00	3.48	349.8	325	10.25	OH
		V8	4.251	3.76	426.7	385	10.25	OH
		V8	4.00	3.25	326.7	275	10.0	OH
1969	Strato Chief	6	3.875	3.531	249.9	155@4200	8.5	OH
	Laurentian	6	3.875	3.531	249.9	155@4200	8.5	OH
	Parisienne	6	3.875	3.531	249.9	155@4200	8.5	OH
	Parisienne 2+2	V8	4.00	3.48	349.8	250@4800	9.0	OH
	Grand Parisienne	V8	4.00	3.48	349.8	250@4800	9.0	OH
	Optional engines, all lines:	V8	4.00	3.48	349.8	300@4800	10.25	OH
		V8	4.094	3.76	396.0	265@4800	9.0	OH
		V8	4.25	3.76	426.7	335@4800	10.25	OH
		V8	4.25	3.76	426.7	390@5400	10.25	OH

CARBURETOR MFR	MODEL	VEN	WHEEL-BASE	TIRES	BODY	WEIGHT	PRICE
		2	119	8.25 x 14	6 pht2	3605	3985
		2					
		4					
		4					
		4					
		1	119	8.25 x 14	6 ps	3465	3335
		1	119	8.25 x 14	6 ps	3470	3468
		1	119	8.25 x 14	6 ps	3520	3651
		2	119	8.25 x 14	6 pht2	3655	4002
		2	119	8.25 x 14	6 pht2	3660	4126
		2					
		4					
		4					
		4					
		1	119	8.25 x 14	6 ps	3590	3394
		1	119	8.25 x 14	6 ps	3590	3527
		1	119	8.25 x 14	6 ps	3640	3710
		2	119	8.25 x 14	6 pht2	3800	4060
		2	119	8.25 x 14	6 pht2	3895	4228
		4					
		2					
		4					
		2					

YEAR	MODEL	CYLS	BORE	STROKE	DISPL	HP@RPM	C.R.	VLV
		ENGINE						
REO — — Dominion Motors, Ltd., Leaside, Ont., 1932-33								
1932	Flying Cloud, S	6	3.125	5.00	230.1	80@3200		L
	Flying Cloud, 21	6	3.375	5.00	268.3	85@3200	5.3	L
	Flying Cloud, 25	6	3.375	5.00	268.3	85@3200	5.3	L
	Royale, 31	8	3.375	5.00	357.8	125@3300	5.3	L
	Royale Elite, 35	8	3.375	5.00	357.8	125@3300	5.3	L
	Royale Elite, 52	8	3.375	5.00	357.8	125@3300	5.3	L
	Flying Cloud, 21	8	3.00	4.75	268.6	90@3300	5.37	L
	Flying Cloud, 25	8	3.00	4.75	268.6	90@3300	5.37	L
ROCKNE — — Studebaker Corp. of Canada, Walkerville, Ont., 1932-33								
1932	65	6	3.125	4.125	189.9	65@3200		L
	75	6	3.25	4.125	205.3	72@3200		L
1933	6-10	6	3.125	4.125	189.9	70		L

CARBURETOR MFR	MODEL	VEN	WHEEL-BASE	TIRES	BODY	WEIGHT	PRICE
			117		5 ps	3405	1525
Sc			121	6.00 x 17	5 ps	3645	1470
Sc			125	6.50 x 18	5 ps	3950	
Sc			131	6.50 x 18	5 ps	4375	2705
Sc			135	6.50 x 18	5 ps	4650	3300
			152	6.50 x 18	7 ps	5010	5175
Sc			121	6.50 x 17	5 ps	3740	1885
Sc			125	6.50 x 17	5 ps	4050	2165
S		1	110	5.25 x 18	5 ps	2595	865
S		1	114	5.50 x 18	5 ps	3005	1045
			110	5.25 x 17	5 ps	2675	855

YEAR	MODEL	ENGINE						
		CYLS	BORE	STROKE	DISPL	HP@RPM	C.R.	VLV

STUDEBAKER — — Studebaker Corp. of Canada, 1911-55; Studebaker-Packard Co. of Canada, Ltd., Walkerville, Ont., 1955-66

YEAR	MODEL	CYLS	BORE	STROKE	DISPL	HP@RPM	C.R.	VLV
1930	Six, 53	6	3.25	4.125	205.3	70@3200		L
	Dictator, FC	8	3.062	3.75	221.0	70@3200		L
	Commander, FD	8	3.062	4.25	250.4	80@3200		L
	Commander, GJ	6	3.375	4.625	248.3	75@3000		L
	President, FH	8	3.50	4.375	336.7	115@3200		L
	President, FE	8	3.50	4.375	336.7	115@3200		L
1931	Six, 54	6	3.25	4.125	205.3	70@3200	5.2	L
	Dictator, 61	8	3.062	3.75	221.0	81@3200	5.15	L
	Commander, 70	8	3.062	4.25	250.4	101@3200	5.2	L
	President, 80	8	3.50	4.375	336.7	122@3200	5.1	L
	President, 90	8	3.50	4.375	336.7	122@3200	5.1	L
1932	Six, 55	6	3.25	4.625	230.2	80@3200	5.0	L
	Dictator, 62	8	3.062	3.75	221.0	85@3200	5.0	L
	Commander, 71	8	3.062	4.25	250.4	101@3200	5.2	L
	President, 91	8	3.50	4.375	336.7	122@3200	5.1	L
1933	Six, 56	6	3.25	4.625	230.2	85@3200		L
	Commander, 73	8	3.062	4.00	235.7	100@3800		L
	President, 82	8	3.062	4.25	250.4	110@3600		L
	President, 92	8	3.50	4.375	336.7	132@3400		L
1934	Dictator, A	6	3.25	4.125	205.3	88@3600		L
	Special Dictator	6	3.25	4.125	205.3	88@3600		L
	Commander, B	8	3.062	3.75	221.0	103@3800		L
	President, C	8	3.062	4.25	250.4	110@3600		L
1935	Dictator	6	3.25	4.125	205.3	88@3600		L
	Commander	8	3.062	4.25	250.4	107@3800		L
	President	8	3.062	4.25	250.4	110@3600		L
1936	Dictator, 3A	6	3.25	4.375	217.8	90@3400		L
	President	8	3.062	4.25	250.4	115@3600		L
1937	Dictator, 5A	6	3.25	4.375	217.8	90@3400		L
	President, 3C	8	3.062	4.25	250.4	115@3600		L
1938	Dictator, 7A	6	3.312	4.375	226.2	90@3400		L
	Commander, 8A	6	3.312	4.375	226.2	90@3400		L
	President, 4C	8	3.062	4.25	250.4	115@3600		L
1939	Champion, G	6	3.00	3.875	164.3	78@4000		L
	Commander, 9A	6	3.312	4.375	226.2	90@3400		L
	President, 5C	8	3.062	4.25	250.4	110@3600		L
1940	Champion, Custom	6	3.00	3.875	164.3	78@4000		L
	Champion, Deluxe	6	3.00	3.875	164.3	78@4000		L

CARBURETOR			WHEEL-	TIRES	BODY	WEIGHT	PRICE
MFR	MODEL	VEN	BASE				
Sc			114	5.50 x 19	5 ps	2950	1155
S			115	5.50 x 19	5 ps	3095	1710
S			120	5.50 x 19	5 ps	3310	1995
			120	5.50 x 19	5 ps	3235	
S			125	6.00 x 20	5 ps	4045	2355
S			135	6.50 x 19	7 ps	4305	2795
Sc			114	5.25 x 19	5 ps	2920	1155
S			114	5.25 x 19	5 ps	3055	1495
S			124	6.00 x 19	5 ps	3520	2095
S			130	6.50 x 19	5 ps	4230	2465
S			136	6.50 x 19	7 ps	4360	2865
S			117	5.50 x 18	5 ps	3170	1280
S			117	5.50 x 18	5 ps	3240	1475
S			125	6.00 x 18	5 ps	3545	2090
S			135	6.50 x 18	5 ps	4260	2550
			117	5.50 x 17	5 ps	3310	1280
			117	6.00 x 17	5 ps	3385	1515
			125	6.50 x 17	5 ps	3640	1995
			135	7.00 x 17	5 ps	4380	2470
			113	5.50 x 17	5 ps	2910	1095
			113	5.50 x 17	5 ps	2895	995
			119	6.00 x 17	5 ps	3310	1400
			123	6.50 x 17	5 ps	3490	1720
			114	6.00 x 16/	5 ps	3030	1030
				5.50 x 17			
			120	6.50 x 16	6 ps	3600	1440
			124	7.00 x 16	6 ps	3790	1970
S			116	6.00 x 16	6 ps	3110	1020
S			125	6.50 x 16	6 ps	3600	1460
S			116	6.00 x 16	5 ps	3100	970
S			125	6.50 x 16	5 ps	3600	1295
			116	6.00 x 16	5 ps	3190	1215
			116	6.00 x 16	5 ps	3215	1288
			122	6.50 x 16	5 ps	3455	1464
			110	5.50 x 16	5 ps	2360	975
			116.5	6.00 x 16	5 ps	3200	1318
			122	6.50 x 16	5 ps	3440	1510
			110	5.50 x 16	5 ps	2415	1029
			110	5.50 x 16	5 ps	2390	1086

YEAR	MODEL	ENGINE						
		CYLS	BORE	STROKE	DISPL	HP@RPM	C.R.	VLV
	Commander	6	3.312	4.375	226.2	90@3400		L
	President	8	3.062	4.25	250.4	110@3600		L
1941	Champion Custom	6	3.00	4.00	169.6	80@4000		L
	Champion DeLuxe	6	3.00	4.00	169.6	80@4000		L
	Commander	6	3.312	4.375	226.2	94@3600		L
	President	8	3.062	4.25	250.4	117@4000		L
1964	Challenger	6	3.00	4.00	169.6	112@4500	8.25	OH
	Commander	6	3.00	4.00	169.6	112@4500	8.25	OH
	Daytona	6	3.00	4.00	169.6	112@4500	8.25	OH
	Cruiser	V8	3.562	3.625	289.1	210@4500	8.5	OH
	Challenger (1)	V8	3.562	3.25	259.2	180@4500	8.5	OH
	Commander (1)	V8	3.562	3.25	259.2	180@4500	8.5	OH
	Daytona (1)	V8	3.562	3.25	259.2	180@4500	8.5	OH
	Gran Turismo Hawk (2)	V8	3.562	3.625	289.1	210@4500	8.5	OH
	Avanti, R-Q (2)	V8	3.562	3.625	289.1	240@4500	10.25	OH
	Optional engines:							
	(1)	V8	3.562	3.625	289.1	210@4500	8.5	OH
	(1, 2) *	V8	3.656	3.625	304.5	305@5200	12.0	OH
	* Engine Supercharged.							
1965	Commander	6	3.562	3.25	194.0	120@4400	8.5	OH
	Cruiser	6	3.562	3.25	194.0	120@4400	8.5	OH
	Commander	V8	3.875	3.00	283.0	195@4800	9.25	OH
	Daytona	V8	3.875	3.00	283.0	195@4800	9.25	OH
	Cruiser	V8	3.875	3.00	283.0	195@4800	9.25	OH
1966	Commander	6	3.562	3.25	194.0	120@4400	8.5	OH
	Daytona	6	3.562	3.25	194.0	120@4400	8.5	OH
	Cruiser	6	3.562	3.25	194.0	120@4400	8.5	OH
	Commander	V8	3.875	3.00	283.0	195@4800	9.25	OH
	Daytona	V8	3.875	3.00	283.0	195@4800	9.25	OH
	Cruiser	V8	3.875	3.00	283.0	195@4800	9.25	OH

CARBURETOR MFR	MODEL	VEN	WHEEL-BASE	TIRES	BODY	WEIGHT	PRICE
			116.5	6.25 x 16	5 ps	3180	1363
			122	6.50 x 16	5 ps	3420	1587
			110	5.50 x 16	5 ps	2416	1313
			110	5.50 x 16	5 ps	2450	1263
			119	7.00 x 16	6 ps	3125	1568
			124.5	7.00 x 16	6 ps	3385	1809
C	RBS-3653S	1	113/109	6.00 x 15/	6 ps	2780	2048
				6.70 x 15			
C	RBS-3653S	1	113/109	6.00 x 15/	6 ps	2815	2168
				6.70 x 15			
C	RBS-3653S	1	113/109	6.00 x 15/	6 ps		2318
				6.70 x 15			
S	WW6-132	2	113	6.50 x 15	6 ps	3280	2603
S	WW6-132	2	113/109	6.00 x 15/	6 ps	3010	2183
				6.70 x 15			
S	WW6-132	2	113/109	6.00 x 15/	6 ps	3045	2303
				6.70 x 15			
S	WW6-132	2	113/109	6.00 x 15/	6 ps	3055	2453
				6.70 x 15			
S	WW6-132	2	120	6.70 x 15	6 pht2	3280	2966
C	AFB-3589S	4	109	6.70 x 15	6 pht2	3195	4445
S	WW6-132	2					
C	AFB-3810S	2 x 4					
R	BV-7025087	1	113/109	7.35 x 15	6 ps	2815	2182
R	BV-7025087	1	113	7.35 x 15	6 ps	2820	2416
R	2GV-7025088	2	113	7.35 x 15	6 ps	2995	2319
R	2GV-7025088	2	109	7.35 x 15	6 pht2	2970	2507
R	2GV-7025088	2	113	7.35 x 15	6 ps	3070	2553
			113/109	7.35 x 15	6 ps	2880	2319
			109	7.35 x 15	6 pht2	2800	2444
			113	7.35 x 15	6 ps	2900	2545
			113/109	7.35 x 15	6 ps	3092	2456
			109	7.35 x 15	6 pht2	2985	2581
			113	7.35 x 15	6 ps	3105	2682

YEAR	MODEL	ENGINE						
		CYLS	BORE	STROKE	DISPL	HP@RPM	C.R.	VLV

TERRAPLANE (ESSEX TERRAPLANE) — — Hudson Motors of Canada, Tilbury, Ont., 1932-34

YEAR	MODEL	CYLS	BORE	STROKE	DISPL	HP@RPM	C.R.	VLV
1932	Pacemaker	6	2.938	4.75	193.1	70@3200	5.5	L
	Terraplane, First series	6	2.938	4.75	193.1	70@3200		L
1933	Terraplane	6	2.938	4.75	193.1	70@3200		L
1934	Terraplane, K	6	3.00	5.00	212.1	80@3600		L
	Terraplane, KU	6	3.00	5.00	212.1	80@3600		L

CARBURETOR MFR	MODEL	VEN	WHEEL-BASE	TIRES	BODY	WEIGHT	PRICE
M			113	5.25 x 18	5 ps	2980	1095
			106	5.25 x 17	5 ps	2250	750
			113	5.25 x 17			
			112	5.50 x 17	5 ps	2700	984
			116	6.00 x 16	5 ps	2850	1086

YEAR	MODEL	ENGINE						
		CYLS	BORE	STROKE	DISPL	HP@RPM	C.R.	VLV
VALIANT – – Chrysler Corp. of Canada, Ltd., Windsor, Ont., 1960-66								
1960	V-100, QX1-L	6	3.40	3.125	170.2	101@4400	8.5	OH
	V-200, QX1-H	6	3.40	3.125	170.2	101@4400	8.5	OH
1961	V-100, RV1-L	6	3.40	3.125	170.2	101@4400	8.5	OH
	V-200, RV1-H	6	3.40	3.125	170.2	101@4400	8.2	OH
1962	V-100, SV1-L	6	3.40	3.125	170.2	101@4400	8.2	OH
	V-200, SV1-H	6	3.40	3.125	170.2	101@4400	8.2	OH
	Signet, SV1-P	6	3.40	3.125	170.2	101@4400	8.2	OH
	Optional engine, all lines:	6	3.40	4.125	224.7	145@4000	8.2	
1963	V-100, TV1-L	6	3.40	3.125	170.2	101@4400	8.2	OH
	V-200, TV1-H	6	3.40	3.125	170.2	101@4400	8.2	OH
	Signet 200, TV1-P	6	3.40	3.125	170.2	101@4400	8.2	OH
	Optional engine, all lines:	6	3.40	4.125	224.7	145@4000	8.2	OH
1964	V-100, VV1-L	6	3.40	3.125	170.2	101@4400	8.5	OH
	V-200, VV1-H	6	3.40	3.125	170.2	101@4400	8.5	OH
	Signet 200, VV1-P	6	3.40	3.125	170.2	101@4400	8.5	OH
	Barracuda, VV1-P	6	3.40	3.125	170.2	101@4400	8.5	OH
	Optional engine, all lines:	6	3.40	4.125	224.7	145@4000	8.5	OH
1965	100, AV1-L	6	3.40	3.125	170.2	101@4400	8.5	OH
	Custom 100, AV1-H	6	3.40	3.125	170.2	101@4400	8.5	OH
	Barracuda, AV1-P	6	3.40	4.125	224.7	145@4000	8.4	OH
	200, AL1-H	6	3.40	3.125	170.2	101@4400	8.5	OH
	Custom 200, AL1-H	6	3.40	3.125	170.2	101@4400	8.5	OH
	Signet, AL1-P	6	3.40	3.125	170.2	101@4400	8.5	OH
	Optional engine, all but Barracuda:	6	3.40	4.125	224.7	145@4000	8.4	OH
1966	200, BL1-L	6	3.40	3.125	170.2	101@4400	8.5	OH
	Custom 200, BL1-H	6	3.40	3.125	170.2	101@4400	8.5	OH
	Signet, BL1-P	6	3.40	3.125	170.2	101@4400	8.5	OH
	Barracuda, BP1-P	6	3.40	4.125	224.7	145@4000	8.4	OH
	Optional engine, all but Barracuda:	6	3.40	4.125	224.7	145@4000	8.4	OH

CARBURETOR MFR	CARBURETOR MODEL	CARBURETOR VEN	WHEEL-BASE	TIRES	BODY	WEIGHT	PRICE
			106.5	6.50 x 13	6 ps	2700	2733
			106.5	6.50 x 13	6 ps	2700	2815
			106.5	6.50 x 13	6 ps	2650	2662
			106.5	6.50 x 13	6 ps	2670	2749
			106.5	6.50 x 13	6 ps	2500	2514
			106.5	6.50 x 13	6 ps	2520	2584
			106.5	6.50 x 13	6 pht2	2565	2779
			111/106	6.50 x 13	6 ps	2545	2556
			111/106	6.50 x 13	6 ps	2555	2651
			111	6.50 x 13	6 pht2	2559	2872
			111/106	6.50 x 13	6 ps	2550	2677
			111/106	6.50 x 13	6 ps	2560	2791
			111	6.50 x 13	6 pht2	2580	2988
			106	6.50 x 13	6 pht2	2740	3239
			106	6.50 x 13	6 ps	2575	2569
			106	6.50 x 13	6 ps	2570	2800
			106	6.50 x 13	6 pht2	2730	3250
			111	6.50 x 13	6 ps	2645	2775
			111	6.50 x 13	6 ps	2640	2887
			111	6.50 x 13	6 pht2	2690	3088
			111	6.50 x 13	6 ps	2700	2751
			111	6.50 x 13	6 ps	2705	2886
			111	6.50 x 13	6 pht2	2735	3083
			106	6.50 x 13	6 pht2	2810	3190

YEAR	MODEL	ENGINE CYLS	BORE	STROKE	DISPL	HP@RPM	C.R.	VLV

WILLYS — — Willys-Overland, Ltd., West Toronto, Ont., 1930-33

YEAR	MODEL	CYLS	BORE	STROKE	DISPL	HP@RPM	C.R.	VLV
1930	98B	6	3.25	3.875	192.9	65@3400		L
	8-80	8	3.125	4.00	254.4	80@3200		L
1931	97	6	3.25	3.875	192.9	65@3400	5.26	L
	98D	6	3.25	3.875	192.9	65@3400	5.26	L
	8-80D	8	3.125	4.00	245.4	80@3200	5.4	L
1932	6-90A	6	3.25	3.875	192.9	65@3400	5.26	L
	8-88A	8	3.125	4.00	245.4	80@3200	5.4	L
1933	77	4	3.125	4.375	134.2	48@3200		L

WILLYS-KNIGHT — — Willys-Overland, Ltd., West Toronto, Ont., 1927-33

YEAR	MODEL	CYLS	BORE	STROKE	DISPL	HP@RPM	C.R.	VLV
1930	Great Six, 66B	6	3.375	4.75	255.0	87@3200		S
	87	6	2.938	4.375	177.9	55@3000		S
	70B	6	2.938	4.375	177.9	53@3000		S
1931	66D	6	3.375	4.75	255.0	87@3200		S
	95	6	2.938	4.375	177.9	60@3400		S
1932	66D	6	3.375	4.75	255.0	87@3200		S
	95	6	2.938	4.375	177.9	60@3400	5.5	S
1933	66E	6	3.375	4.75	255.0	87@3200		S

CARBURETOR			WHEEL-	TIRES	BODY	WEIGHT	PRICE
MFR	MODEL	VEN	BASE				
			110	5.00 x 19	5 ps	2641	1020
			120	5.50 x 19	5 ps	3075	1725
T			110	5.00 x 19	5 ps	2670	895
T			113	5.00 x 19	5 ps	2706	1070
T			121	5.50 x 19	5 ps	3266	1520
T			113	5.25 x 18	5 ps	2928	1095
T			121	5.50 x 18	5 ps	3460	1460
			100	5.00 x 17	5 ps	2150	610
T			120	6.00 x 19	5 ps	3934	2550
T			115	5.50 x 19	5 ps	3075	1575
T			112.5	5.50 x 19	5 ps	3015	1425
T			121	6.00 x 18	5 ps	3775	1640
T			113	5.50 x 18	5 ps	3400	1190
			121	6.00 x 18	5 ps	3400	1325
T			113	5.50 x 18	5 ps	3035	1010
			121	6.00 x 17	5 ps	3830	1380

ABERCROMBIE — — Abercrombie, Fitch & Co., New York, N.Y., 1969.
A Glassic car, relabeled for this dealer in sporting goods.

AEROMOBILE — — Bertelsen Mfg. Co., Neponset, Ill., 1959-61.

ALBATROSS — — Albatross Motor Car Co., New York, N.Y., ca 1939.
At least one prototype, Type 137K, a four-passenger 'racing convertible,' was constructed on a Mercury chasis. The very racy body was designed by cartoonist Peter Arno.

AMERICAN STEAM CAR — — American Steam Automobile Co., West Newton, Mass., 1929-ca 1945.
Located in the same town as the famous Stanley, this company specialized in converting gasoline-engined cars to steam-powered ones. Although firm information is lacking, these conversions appear to have been on a custom basis, with no actual production of automobiles as generally understood.

ASTRA-GNOME — — Richard Arbib Co., Inc., (New York, N.Y.?) 1956.

AUTOETTE — — Autoette Electric Car Co., Long Beach, Cal., 1952-57.

B & B THREE WHEEL — — B & B Specialty Co., Rossmoyne, Oh., 1947.

BEARCAT — — American Buckboard Corp., Los Angeles, Cal., 1956.

BERGERMOBILE — — Berger Air-Turbine Car Co., Mount Vernon, N.Y., 1949.
A Chevrolet converted to run on compressed air; an Ingersoll-Rand air turbine was used.

BERTELSEN — — See Aeromobile.

BETTERIDGE — — 1933.

BFG — — B. F. Goodrich Co., Akron, Oh., 1946.

BREWSTER — — Springfield Mfg. Co., Springfield, Mass., 1934-36.
Brewster & Co., a famous designer and builder of custom bodies, designed bodies in the above years which were constructed by Springfield and mounted on Ford and Buick chassis. These bodies were quite distinctive in appearance.

BROGAN — — See B & B Three Wheel.

BUCKAROO — — (Manufacturer unknown) Cleveland, Oh., 1957.
This was a four-hundred-dollar car with an air-cooled engine.

CALIFORNIAN — — California Motor Car Co., Los Angeles, Cal., 1946.

CALIFORNIAN — — Warner Mfg. Co., Glendale, Cal., 1945-46.

CANNON — — Cannon Engineering Co., North Hollywood, Cal., 1955.

COLEMAN — — Coleman Motors Corp., Littleton, Col., ca 1933.
The name Coleman was given to a series of three experimental cars with an arched front axle. All were experimental and not intended for production.

COMET — — Comet Mfg. Co., Sacramento, Cal., 1951.

CUBSTER — — Osburn Wheel Co., Doylestown, Pa., 1949.

CUMMINS — — Cummins Diesel Engine Co., Columbus, Ind., ca 1935.
Cummins engines were installed in a number of passenger cars, notably in a 1935 Auburn for experimental and publicity purposes. So far as can be determined, there was no intention to manufacture although the name Cummins appears in several lists of passenger cars.

CURTISS-WRIGHT — — Curtiss-Wright Industries, El Monte, Cal., 1948.

CUSTER — — Custer Specialty Co., Dayton, Oh., ca 1953-.
This company has manufactured small gasoline-powered and electric vehicles. These are rumored to have been for use in amusement parks only.

D'ANDREA — — Gilbert D'Andrea, New York, N.Y., 1956.

DE-VO — — De-Vo Motor Car Corp., Hagerstown, Md., 1936.
This car was promoted by Norman DeVaux and presumably built by M. P. Moller Co. of Hagerstown. It is rumored that the prototype is extant in South Africa.

DOUGHERTY — — Frazer Dougherty, Sierra Madre, Cal., 1955-56.

DOW ELECTRIC — — Dow Testing Laboratory, Inc., Detroit, Mich., 1960.

DYNAMO, JR. — — Dynamo Electric Car Co., Los Angeles, Cal., 1958-59.

ELECTROMASTER — — Nepa Mfg. Co., Pasadena, Cal., 1962-64.
Reported to have a 2-hp electric motor, with weight total of 680 pounds.

FALCON — — 1938-

FORD 1901 REPLICA — — Horseless Carriage Corp., Ft. Lauderdale, Fla., 1968.

FORERUNNER — — 1955.

FORMACAR — — Marbon Div., Borg-Warner Corp., ca 1968.
This was merely a demonstration model to show the use of ABS plastic.

HAMLIN — — Hamlin Motor Co., Chicago, Ill., ca 1919-ca 1930.
Hamlin used front-wheel drive, and is reported to have built seventeen experimental models. All these were just modified chassis from other manufacturers. There is no evidence the Hamlin was ever built for sale.

HONEY BEE — — Swift Mfg. Co., El Cajon, Cal., 1959.

HOWARD — — Howard Motor International Corp., New York, N.Y. 1929-30.
The Howard is reported as having a six-cylinder Continental engine. Production, if any, must have been very small.

HYDRAMOTIVE — — Hydramotive Corp. (location unknown), 1961.
Claimed to have used a diesel engine, with reported price of $1200.

HYDRO-IMP — — Centerscope Products, Inc., Glendale, Cal., 1948.

INMAN — — Frank Inman, Goose Creek, Texas, 1946.

JOHNSONMOBILE — — Horton Johnson, Inc., Highland Park, Ill., 1959.
This had a 3-hp air-cooled Clinton engine, so it must have been a very small vehicle.

KEEN STEAM — — Keen Mfg. Co., Madison, Wis., 1958-61.

KNUDSEN — — Knudsen Mfg. & Design Co., Inc., Buffalo, N.Y., 1948.

KORFF — — Walter H. Korff, Burbank, Cal., 1952.

LAHER — — Laher Spring & Electric Car Corp., Oakland, Cal.; Memphis, Tenn., 1960-63.

LA POINTE — — Albert A. LaPointe, West Hartford, Conn., 1948.

LARSON — — Larson Boat Works, Little Falls, Minn., 1966-.

LA SAETTA — — Detroit, Mich., 1955-.

LAWLER — — Lawler Steamobile, South Gate, Cal., 1948-50.

L & E — — Lundelius & Eccleston, Los Angeles, Cal., ca 1931.
The L & E automobile, of which six were built between 1925 and 1931, was axle-less, with a De Dion-type rear drive. Apparently a five-passenger sedan was available for purchase in 1931, but no specifications seem to have been published nationally.

LEAR — — Lear Motor Corp., Reno, Nev., 1969.
William Lear's effort to build steam-powered cars was abortive. Experimental automobiles used a six-cylinder engine in a delta arrangement.

LOST CAUSE — — Lost Cause Motors, Louisville, Ky., 1963-64.
These cars were modified Chevrolet Corvairs, priced in the range of $20,000 to $23,000.

MAMECO — — Mameco Automotive Engineering, Newport Beach Cal., ca 1954.

MARKETOUR — — Marketour Electric Cars, Long Beach, Cal., 1964.

METEOR SPORTS — — Meteor Sports Cars, Denver, Col., 1956.

MIDGET — — Greenfield-Lippman, Buffalo, N.Y., 1947.

MINICAR — — Minicars, Inc., Goleta, Cal., 1969.
Used a six-cylinder air-cooled engine, possibly a Corvair.

MOBILETTE — — Mobilette Electric Cars, Long Beach, Cal., 1965-.

MOSS — — Moss Engineering Co., Inglewood, Cal., 1957.

MOTORETTE — — Motorette Corp., Buffalo, N.Y., 1946-48.

MUSTANG — — Mustang Engineering Co., Seattle, Washington, 1947-49.

NORVELL — — Jack Norvell, Los Angeles, Cal., 1946.

NU-KLEA — — Nu-Klea Automobile Corp., Lansing, Mich., 1959-60.
Purportedly an electric vehicle.

OFFENHAUSER — — 1934.

OLDS 1901 REPLICA — — Horseless Carriage Corp., Ft. Lauderdale, Fla., 1968.

PAXTON — — Paxton Engineering Co., Los Angeles, Cal., 1952-.

PERRYMOBILE — — Perrymobile Co., Los Angeles, Cal., 1942-45.

POWER CAR — — Mystic River Sales Co., Mystic, Conn., 1953.

RAMBLER 1902 REPLICA — — American Air Products Corp., Ft. Lauderdale, Fla.; Gaslight Motors Corp., Lathrup Village, Mich., 1959-60.

RICKMOBILE — — Rickmobile Co., San Francisco, Cal., 1948.

ROAD RUNNER — — Cyclone Sales Co., Los Angeles, Cal., 1963.

ROGUE — — (Manufacturer and location unknown) 1954.

ROLLSMOBILE — — Starts Mfg. Co.; Horseless Carriage Corp., Ft. Lauderdale, Fla., 1958-ca 1960.
Used a 3-hp Continental air-cooled engine.

ROUND-THE-TOWN — — T. P. Hall, San Diego, Cal., 1949-. See Airway.

ROWAN — — Rowan Controller Co. (Oceanport, N.Y. ?), 1967-69.

RSL — — RSL Corp., Cleveland, Oh., 1969-.

RUSSELL — — Raymond Russell, Detroit, Mich., 1946.

SALSBURY — — Salsbury Motors, Inc., Pomona, Cal., 1947-48.

SCARAB — — William B. Stout, 1934-46.
Three experimental passenger cars were designed and built by Stout, the last having an all-fiberglass body.

SCIMITAR — — Brooks Stevens Associates, Milwaukee, Wis., 1956-.

SCOOTER CAR — — 1949-.

SIR VIVAL — — Hollow Boring Co., Worcester, Mass., 1960.
An experimental safety car; apparently just one was built.

STAR DUST — — Los Angeles, Cal., 1953.

STOUT — — William B. Stout, 1946-.

STUART — — Stuart Motors, Kalamazoo, Mich., 1961.

SUPER CAR — — Louis R. Elrod, Cleveland, Oh., 1946.
This car had an air-cooled 15-hp engine.

TASKO — — The American Sports Car Co., Hartford, Conn., 1948.
Costing $7500, this car used a modified Mercury engine.

TAYLOR-DUNN — — Taylor-Dunn Mfg. Co., Anaheim, Cal., 1949-ca 1966.
Taylor-Dunn made three- and four-wheeler electric cars.

THORNE TIGER — — Thorne Engineering Co., Los Angeles, Cal., 1945.

THRIFT-T — — Tri-Wheel Motor Corp., Springfield, Mass., 1955.

U.S. MARK II — — U.S. Fiberglass Co., Norwood, N.J., 1956.

VAUGHN — — (Manufacturer and location unknown) 1953-54.
It is known this company attempted to market a V8-engined coupe weighing 1500 pounds.

VIKING — — Viking Corp., Miami, Fla., 1960.

WARRIOR — — Vanguard Products, Inc., Dallas, Tex., 1963.

WILLIAMS — — Williams Engine Co., Inc., Ambler, Pa., 1957-68.
Car used a gasoline engine which was converted to steam.

WORTHINGTON — — Worthington Motor Co., Stroudsburg, Pa., 1957.

X-RAY SPECIAL — — X-Ray Inc., Highland Park, Mich., 1955.

YENKO STINGER — — Sports-racing machines only.